SEVENTH EDITION

Contemporary Chinese Politics

An Introduction

James C.F. Wang
Emeritus Professor
University of Hawaii at Hilo

Prentice Hall

Upper Saddle River, New Jersey 07458

Library of Congress Cataloging-in-Publication Data

WANG, JAMES C. F.
  Contemporary Chinese politics: an introduction / James C. F. Wang—7th ed.
    p. cm.
  Includes bibliographical references and index.
  ISBN 0-13-090782-0
  1. China—Politics and government—1976– I. Title.
DS779.26 .W365 2002
951.05—dc21   2001021245

VP, Editorial Director: *Laura Pearson*
Senior Acquisitions Editor: *Heather Shelstad*
Assistant Editor: *Brian Prybella*
Editorial Assistant: *Jessica Drew*
Editorial/Production Supervision: *Joanne Riker*
Prepress and Manufacturing Buyer: *Benjamin D. Smith*
Director of Marketing: *Beth Gillett Mejia*
Cover Art Director: *Jayne Conte*
Cover Designer: *Bruce Kenselaar*
Cover Photo: *Jeremy Woodhouse/PhotoDisc, Inc.*

This book was set in 10/11 Times Roman by East End Publishing Services, Inc.,
and was printed and bound by Courier Companies, Inc. The cover was
printed by Phoenix Color Corp.

© 2002, 1999, 1995, 1992, 1989, 1985, 1980 by Pearson Education, Inc.
Upper Saddle River, New Jersey 07458

Printed in the United States of America

10 9 8 7 6 5 4 3

ISBN 0-13-090782-0

Prentice-Hall International (UK) Limited, *London*
Prentice-Hall of Australia Pty. Limited, *Sydney*
Prentice-Hall Canada Inc., *Toronto*
Prentice-Hall Hispanoamericana, S.A., *Mexico*
Prentice-Hall of India Private Limited, *New Delhi*
Prentice-Hall of Japan, Inc., *Tokyo*
Pearson Education Asia Pte. Ltd., *Singapore*
Editora Prentice-Hall do Brasil, Ltda., *Rio de Janeiro*

To Sally, my wife,
and to my children, Sarah and Eric,
for their tolerance, patience, and assistance

Contents

CHAPTER SIX
Reform for a Creditable Socialist Legal System, 139

CHAPTER SEVEN
Provincial and Local Politics: Centralism versus Regionalism, National Minorities, and the Case of Tibet, 161

CHAPTER EIGHT
Greater China: Reversion of Hong Kong and Macao, the Pearl River Delta Regional Development, and the Taiwan Question, 196

CHAPTER NINE
The Military's Role in Chinese Politics,   238

CHAPTER TEN
Democracy, Dissent, and the Tiananmen Mass Movement,   269

APPENDIX B

APPENDIX B-1

APPENDIX B-2

Preface

The seventh edition of *Contemporary Chinese Politics: An Introduction*, originally published in 1980 and revised in 1985, 1989, 1992, 1995, and 1999, is designed for both undergraduate and graduate students. The publisher and author have striven to make the text as current and as comprehensive as possible by revising and updating its content periodically. The events unfolding in China necessitate such revision and updating.

This edition contains some major revisions and additions in a number of areas. In Chapter 3 a new section is added containing an examination of recent developments in promoting "Jiang Zemin Thought" to the level of Mao and Deng, but which is designed to unify the various contending factions within the leadership. Discussion here is intended to explore the meaning of Jiang's recent ideological pronouncement of the "Three Representations" and the "Three Stresses or Talks."

In Chapter 4 an added section addresses recent amendments to the state constitution, such as recognition of private businesses as an important component to the socialist market economy (Article 6); recognition of the various rural cooperatives as belonging to the socialist market economy (Article 8); and also deletion of the term "counterrevolutionary" from Article 28.

In Chapter 5 a new section is added on corruption in China's officialdom, a sort of "malignant tumor" in Chinese body-politics. This new section considers corruption in terms of its scope, forms, causes, and remedial actions taken in recent years.

In Chapter 7, there is discussion about the introduction of primary elections on the direct village level—elections whereby villagers could write the names of their favored candidates on blank ballots. There is discussion of the extension of popular elections to townships and counties, and the possible impact of this approach on the party's control and prestige.

Also added to Chapter 7 is a review dealing with the Muslim unrest in China's vast western region, particularly in the Xinjiang Autonomous Region, and a discussion on China's environmental problems and questions that were raised in response to the building of the gigantic Three Gorges Dam.

Three new sections are added to Chapter 10. One deals with the problem of Hong Kong's judicial independence that was raised as a result of cases on the court's residency ruling and defacing of the Chinese flag. The second new section deals with the historical background of Taiwan unification, the origin of the "one China" formula, and a possible solution to the Taiwan problem within the framework of "one China."

Third, a new section is added that deals with the reasons for suppressing the quasi-religious meditation sect, the Falun Gong (Wheels of Law). The examination focuses not only on the reason for the ban, but also provides a historic perspective in terms of "over-reacting" to a religious movement, thereby "politicizing" it.

In Chapter 11 there is a section added that discusses the target set for year 2002 on reform in the troubled state-owned enterprises: including reduction of the size and the number of these establishments, as well as the gradual introduction of other forms of ownership along with public or state ownership.

Finally, in Chapter 12, a brief discussion is made on problems associated with implementation of the new nine-year compulsory education program in China.

A new feature has been added to this edition: a suggested bibliography at the end of each chapter intended as a reference for students and teachers alike. Most of these entries represent recent publications in the Chinese study field. These bibliographies augment the footnote citations for each chapter.

The preparation of the seventh edition of this book on contemporary Chinese politics would not have been possible without the help of a number of persons. Many colleagues from a large number of universities and colleges have made useful comments and suggestions. To all of them I owe a debt of gratitude. Once again I must acknowledge my great indebtedness to those China scholars whose work is cited in the text. I would also like to thank political science editors at Prentice Hall, particularly Brian Prybella and Joanne Riker, for rendering invaluable assistance in reading of the manuscript for style. And many thanks to Edith Worsencroft for typing and some editing of the revised manuscript.

Romanization of Chinese Names of Persons and Places*

CHINESE PHONETIC ALPHABET, OR THE PINYIN SYSTEM

How to Pronounce

Following is a Chinese phonetic alphabet table showing alphabet pronunciation, with approximate English equivalents. Spelling in the Wade system is in parentheses for reference.

"a" (a), a vowel, as in *far*
"b" (p), a consonant, as in *be*
"c" (ts), a consonant, as "ts" in *its*; and
"ch" (ch), a consonant, as "ch" in *church*, strongly aspirated
"d" (t), a consonant, as in *do*
"e" (e), a vowel, as "er" in *her*, the "r" being silent; but "ie," a diphthong, as in *yes* and "ei," a diphthong, as in *way*
"f" (f), a consonant, as in *foot*
"g" (k), a consonant, as in *go*
"h" (h), a consonant, as in *her*, strongly aspirated

---

*Based on official version published in Beijing Review, 1 (January 5, 1979), 18–20. A specific rule requires that the traditional spelling of historical places and persons such as Confucius and Sun Yatsen need not be changed.

"i"   (i), a vowel, two pronunciations:
        1) as in *eat*
        2) as in *sir* in syllables beginning with the consonants, *c, ch, r, s, sh, z,*
        and *zh*
"j"   (ch), a consonant, as in *jeep*
"k"   (k), a consonant, as in *kind*, strongly aspirated
"l"   (l), a consonant, as in *land*
"m"   (m), a consonant, as in *me*
"n"   (n), a consonant, as in *no*
"o"   (o), a vowel, as "aw" in *law*
"p"   (p), a consonant, as in *par*, strongly aspirated
"q"   (ch), a consonant, as "ch" in *cheek*
"r"   (j), a consonant, pronounced as "r" but not rolled, or like "z" in *azure*
"s"   (s, ss, sz), a consonant, as in *sister*; and
"sh"   (sh), a consonant, as "sh" in *shore*
"t"   (t), a consonant, as in *top*, strongly aspirated
"u"   (u), a vowel, as in *too*, also as in the French "u" in *tu* or the German
        umlauted "ü" in *Müenchen*
"v"   (v), is used only to produce foreign and national minority words, and
        local dialects
"w"   (w), used as a semivowel in syllables beginning with "u" when not pre-
        ceded by consonants, pronounced as in *want*
"x"   (hs), a consonant, as "sh" in *she*
"y"   used as a semivowel in syllables beginning with "i" or "u" when not
        preceded by consonants, pronounced as in *yet*
"z"   (ts, tz), a consonant, as in *zero*; and
"zh"   (ch), a consonant, as "j" in *jump*"

Spelling of Chinese Names of Persons

In accordance with the Chinese phonetic alphabet, the late Chairman Mao Tsetung's name will be spelled "Mao Zedong"; the late Premier Chou Enlai's name will be "Zhou Enlai"; and the late Chairman of the Standing Committee of the National People's Congress, Chu Teh, will be "Zhu De."

Following are names of party leaders of China, romanized according to the Chinese phonetic alphabet. The old spelling is in parentheses for reference.

Chairman of the Central Committee of the Chinese Communist Party:
    Hua Guofeng (Hua Kuo-feng)
Vice-Chairmen of the Party Central Committee:
    Ye Jianying (Yeh Chien-ying)
    Deng Xiaoping (Teng Hsiao-ping)
    Li Xiannian (Li Hsien-nien)
    Chen Yun (Chen Yun)
    Wang Dongxing (Wang Tung-hsing)
Members of the Political Bureau of the Party Central Committee:
    Hua Guofeng (Hua Kuo-feng)

(The following are listed in the order of the number of strokes in their surnames.)

Wang Zhen (Wang Chen)
Wei Guoqing (Wei Kuo-ching)
Ulanhu (Ulanfu)
Fang Yi (Fang Yi)
Deng Xiaoping (Teng Hsiao-ping)
Deng Yingchao (Teng Ying-chao)
Ye Jianying (Yeh Chien-ying)
Liu Bocheng (Liu Po-cheng)
Xu Shiyou (Hsu Shih-yu)
Ji Dengkui (Chi Teng-kuei)
Su Zhenhua (Su Chen-hua)
Li Xiannian (Li Hsien-nien)
Li Desheng (Li Teh-sheng)
Wu De (Wu Teh)
Yu Qiuli (Yu Chiu-li)
Wang Dongxing (Wang Tung-hsing)
Zhang Tingfa (Chang Ting-fa)
Chen Yun (Chen Yun)
Chen Yonggui (Chen Yung-Kuei)
Chen Xilian (Chen Hsi-lien)
Hu Yaobang (Hu Yao-pang)
Geng Biao (Keng Piao)
Nie Rongzhen (Nieh Jung-chen)
Ni Zhifu (Ni Chih-fu)
Xu Xianqian (Hsu Hsiang-chien)
Peng Chong (Pen Chung)

(The following are listed in the order of the number of strokes in their surnames.)

Alternate Members of the Political Bureau of the Party Central Committee:
Chen Muhua (Chen Mu-hua)
Zhao Ziyang (Chao Tsu-yang)
Seypidin (Saifudin)

Spelling of Chinese Place Names

Names of well-known places in China are listed as follows. The old spelling is in parentheses for reference.

Municipalities directly under the central authorities:
Beijing (Peking)
Shanghai (Shanghai)
Tianjin (Tientsin)

Ningxia Hui (Ningsia Hui) Autonomous Region
Yinchuan (Yinchuan)

Qinghai (Chinghai) Province
  Xining (Sining)

Shaanxi (Shensi) Province
  Xian (Sian)
  Yanan (Yenan)

Shandong (Shantung) Province
  Jinan (Tsinan)
  Qingdao (Tsingtao)
  Yantai (Yentai)

Shanxi (Shansi) Province
  Taiyuan (Taiyuan)
  Dazhai (Tachai)

Sichuan (Szechuan) Province
  Chengdu (Chengtu)
  Chongqing (Chungking)

Taiwan (Taiwan) Province
  Taibei (Taipei)

Xinjiang Uygur (Singkiang Uighur) Autonomous Region
  Urumqi (Urumchi)

Xizang (Tibet) Autonomous Region
  Lhasa (Lhasa)

Yunnan (Yunnan) Province
  Kunming (Kunming)
  Dali (Tali)

Zhejiang (Chekiang) Province
  Hangzhou (Hangchow)

ABBREVIATIONS

CP	Chinese Communist Party
Comintern	Communist Third International
CPPCC	Chinese People's Political Consultative Conference
CYL	Communist Youth League
MAC	Military Affairs Committee
NCNA	New China News Agency
NPC	National People's Congress
PLA	People's Liberation Army

Contemporary Chinese Politics

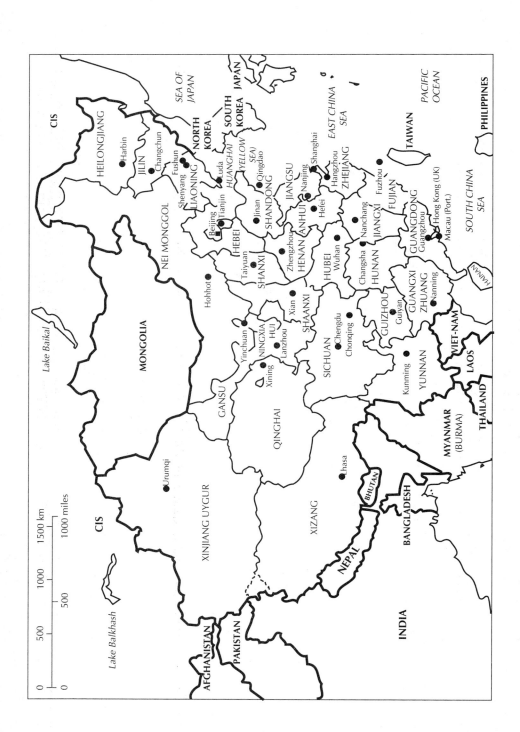

Chapter One

Introduction

Historical and Cultural Perspectives

China has one of the most ancient and continuous civilizations in the world. Its recorded history is about 3,000 years old. For instance, the beginning date of the Shang dynasty was probably around 1700 B.C. Obviously, it is not possible for us even to summarize China's long history as part of the introduction to an understanding of the Chinese political system. Particularly for those who have not been exposed to a study of Chinese civilization and history, what is proposed here instead is to provide a broad historical background by focusing on some important stages in China's historical development.

Before sketching a broad outline of Chinese history, it is necessary to point out the crucial importance of the relationship between the land and the people.

THE LAND AND THE PEOPLE*

A fundamental prerequisite for understanding China is understanding the relationship between the land and its people. China's total land area is about 3.7 million square miles, slightly greater than that of the United States. However, about 85 to 90 percent of China's more than one billion people live and work on only one-sixth of this area. The remaining land is mostly hilly and mountainous. Unlike the United States, only 15 to 20 percent of China's land area is cultivable, and much of this land has been used intensively for centuries.

*Grateful acknowledgment is hereby given for permission to use material from James C. F. Wang, *Contemporary Chinese Politics: An Introduction,* 4th ed. (Upper Saddle River, N.J.: Prentice Hall, Inc., 1991); and James C. F. Wang, "Section 5: The People's Republic of China," in Rolf H. W. Theen and Frank L. Wilson, *Comparative Politics: An Introduction to Six Countries* (Upper Saddle River, N.J.: Prentice Hall, Inc., 1986).

In addition to the limited land area available for cultivation, the climatic conditions compound the problem of food production for a vast population. The uneven rate of precipitation is one example. Rainfall comes to most parts of China in the spring and summer, usually in torrential downpours. It decreases from south to north. Average annual rainfall is about 60 to 80 inches for south China and less than 10 inches for the northwest. The fertile Yangtze River valley receives about 40 to 60 inches, while most of northern China receives about 25 inches annually.

If the torrential downpours during the rainy season are not channeled into reservoirs, a serious water shortage may result that can ultimately affect the livelihood of millions of people. The successive downpours during the rainy season can cause flooding in China's two major river systems, the Changjiang (Yangtze) (3,900 miles) and the Huanghe (Yellow) (3,600 miles) and their tributaries. The Yellow River, known as "China's Sorrow" for centuries, has caused devastating floods. It has flooded fifteen hundred times in a period of two thousand years. Its silt-laden waters have changed course at least twenty-six times. The Yellow River normally carries 57 pounds of mud per cubic yard, but when it rises after a torrential downpour, its mud-carrying capacity can reach as much as 900 pounds per cubic yard.[1] In one flood, the Yellow River overflowed its banks in a northern province, inundating towns and cities, with a loss of life estimated at close to one million. In 1981, heavy rains in late July and August caused the Yangtze River to flood over 65 percent of the counties in the southwestern province of Sichuan, leaving 1,500,000 people homeless. Chinese scientists estimate that each year 250 million tons of earth are washed into the Yangtze's three main tributaries.[2] One study showed that during the period between 206 B.C. and 1911 A.D. there were a total of 1,621 floods and 1,392 droughts, bringing endless sorrow to the Chinese people.[3]

With the factor of limited land for cultivation and the frequency of flood and drought added to the enormous population—over one billion by the official census—one can readily understand that China's primary problem is to mobilize its productive forces to feed its burgeoning population. This basic problem of population pressure on the limited land available for cultivation has plagued China throughout its history. The functions of government, and in many respects the very performance of government, have involved what John Fairbank described as the control of "the land, the manpower, and the water supply" for this agrarian society.[4]

A GLIMPSE OF CHINA'S EARLY HISTORY[5]

Inscriptions on oracle bones and tortoise shells discovered in northern China in the past century provide a well-established list of rulers for the Shang dynasty; the dates for the rulers of the feudal principality are established at about 1766–1122 B.C. The feudal agrarian society, basically growing millet or rice in the Yellow River valley, was rather advanced: In addition to writing inscriptions on oracle bones, people used cowry shells in exchange for goods, and there is evidence of the presence of domestic animals. The society was organized on a patriarchal basis but was controlled by a ruling aristocracy, which had a standing army of cavalry and chariots. Religion took the form of ancestor worship. Rulers performed both civil and religious duties.

The Kingdom of Shang was overthrown by the ruler of Zhou (Chou), a principality located in the Wei River valley, then China's western frontier. Subsequent rulers of Zhou extended the domain into the northwest. The Zhou kingdom then endured a state of decline, so that from the eighth century B.C. to the middle of the third century B.C. China was fragmented into unstable but separate principalities or fiefdoms resembling those of Europe in the Middle Ages. It was during this period that Chinese civilization grew and expanded, aided by the development of written characters, the original ideographs. Using these characters, scribes wrote books with ink on tablets of wood or bamboo. Soon anthologies of ancient verse, the classics of poetry called *Shih Ching*, and the classics of history called *Shu Ching*, were compiled by the scribes, forming the basis of early Chinese literature.

In many respects the Zhou period represented a period of intellectual growth, particularly in the area of philosophy, which concerned itself with explanations of spirits, including those of ancestors, of earth, and of heaven. During the latter reign of the Zhou Kingdom, these interpretations eventually developed into schools of philosophy. Common threads woven through these deliberations concerned the creation of an ideal society and the question of society's preservation. Among the schools of thought that flourished during this time was that of Confucianism; the sage Confucius (*c.* 551–*c.* 479 B.C.) was primarily interested in the creation of a government of goodness administered by virtuous rulers.

As the Zhou Kingdom disintegrated there arose a ruthless revolutionary ruler who built a united Chinese empire known in history as the Qin Shihuangdi (221–210 B.C.). In addition to being a ruthless ruler, the "Founder of the Empire," Qin Shihuangdi, built the Great Wall, burned books, issued death sentences for some scholars, and organized an effective, efficient administrative state, introducing an elaborate bureaucracy system with grades and honorific titles under the ultimate central direction of an emperor. He built a national capital at Sian and created an imperial force for suppressing domestic discontent and for keeping the barbarians, or those outside the Great Wall, at bay. He promulgated harsh laws and demanded absolute obedience to the emperor—the autocrat—in accordance with the precepts of the Legalists, a short-lived school of philosophy competing with Confucianism. Whereas Confucianism placed emphasis on the goodness and virtuosity of people, the Legalists denied the validity of such an assumption by insisting that there was no way to be sure that the ruler would be virtuous and morally good at all times. Therefore, the Legalists argued, there must be laws that would be fixed but impartial in their administration. Humans, as imperfect beings, must be restrained and guided by law, which in turn had been formulated by study and rectification in order to meet changing conditions.

It is perhaps interesting to note that the anti-Confucius campaign launched by Cultural Revolution radicals in 1973–74 not only criticized Confucius as a conservative reactionary for advocating the rule of a slave-owning society, but also praised the Legalist teachings. Thus, Chairman Mao was identified, by implication, with Qin Shihuangdi, the ruthless autocrat.

It was this rudimentary form of centralized civil administration, as fashioned originally by Qin Shihuangdi, that was adapted and perfected by subsequent rulers, including the alien conquerors known as Mongols (1279–1368 A.D.) and the Manchus (1644–1911 A.D.). As the people of central Asia began to have contact with the Chinese under Qin's empire, the name for the country in the east was designated as "China" by the non-Chinese.

The unified Qin Empire was one of the shortest-lived dynasties. It was succeeded by the Han Dynasty in 206 B.C., concurrent with the rise of the Roman Empire in the Mediterranean region. The Han Empire extended the boundaries of China to the Tarim basin, the Ili valley in the northwest, Manchuria and Korea in the northeast, and Annam in the south. It further refined the centralized bureaucracy by introducing a competitive system of examination as a basis for recruitment to the civil service. It was under Han-Wu-Di (140 B.C.–87 B.C.) that Confucianism (to be discussed in a separate section) became the official ideology of the state. Han deliberately selected those who were proficient in the classics to be members of the civil administration—a tradition that prevailed until the 1911 revolution. Under the Han, as Chinese territory expanded, commerce and trade beyond the border also flourished, for by then commercial and cultural contacts had been established with India and extended as far as the Indian Ocean. Silk from China reached central Asia and Rome by the first century A.D. As early as 190 A.D., Buddhism, which stressed the inevitability of suffering in life and escape from it only by eliminating desire and the need for material well-being, came to China under Han by way of India.

The collapse of the Han Dynasty was followed by a dynamic empire, the Tang (618–907 A.D.). Instead of centralized rule, the Tang rulers opted for decentralization by granting more autonomy to the provinces. Some of the Tang rulers engaged in court extravagances that brought widespread discontent to the country. Soon rebellions arose, which the Tang military force suppressed only with great difficulty. Gradually the dynasty collapsed. However, Tang was noted for the cultural enrichment it brought to Chinese civilization. Under Tang rule there was a golden age of poetry and painting amidst a life of economic prosperity and order. With cross-cultural influences from the Greco-Roman and Indo-European civilizations, sculpture reached its height during Tang rule in the seventh and eighth centuries A.D. The printing of Buddhist sutra using wooden blocks as an art form originally appeared in 868 A.D., along with large quantities of block-printed books produced under Tang.

Under the Sung Dynasty (960–1279 A.D.) the empire extended its jurisdiction to the west (Sichuan) and south China. (Gunpowder probably originated during this period, in about 1000 A.D.) But the rulers had difficulty enforcing effective control over the north, which was in effect ruled by rivals from Manchuria. By 1211–15, the Mongols had invaded the north, and their mighty cavalry, led by Genghis Khan and Kublai Khan, had swept across China, Korea, parts of central Asia, and into Austria and Hungary in Europe. China under the Sung Dynasty was noted for a number of cultural developments. From a modern political science viewpoint, there were the political reforms introduced by Wang An-Shih, who advocated appointment of a commission of experts to draft a state budget, a state monopoly of commerce, loans by the state to farmers, the abolition of state conscription of labor, and demobilization of the military—all in all a program of paternalism and state responsibility in many aspects of civil life. These reform programs generated heated debate and were eventually abandoned. The Sung Dynasty's most enduring contribution to Chinese civilization was in the development of neo-Confucianism, a blending or synthesis of Buddhism, Taoism, and Confucianism. Briefly, the synthesis represents a school of thought that implies that the essence of humanity, the *Li*, is always good and never changes. Thus, the goodness of humanity must be nurtured or cultivated through "formal education" and "self-enlightenment."[6] A government of goodness is possible only if the ruler is enlightened and virtuous.

The Mongols, who ruled China from 1279–1368, kept the system of government intact, even though its rulers, such as Kublai Khan, embarked on military conquests of Asia and parts of Europe. In China, the Mongols pursued a policy of conciliation and tolerance toward the Chinese. Kublai Khan saw to it that food was plentiful in public granaries and took care of scholars, on whom he relied to continue the governmental administration developed by previous dynasties, even though few Chinese were entrusted with the highest levels of office. He encouraged and promoted trade and contact with Europeans, notably through the Venetian explorer Marco Polo. The less-than-ninety-year Mongol rule was overthrown by a successful peasant rebellion that established the Ming Dynasty from 1368–1643.

Under Ming rule, China established extensive commercial contacts with the southern and southeastern Asian nations of India, Ceylon, Siam, Java, and Sumatra. There was trade with Japan. The Portuguese were the first Europeans to arrive in the southern ports of China, in 1514 A.D. The Dutch followed in 1622, forcibly occupying the enclave of Macao, and later the islands of Formosa (Taiwan) and Pescadores. In the late sixteenth century, through the Europeans, the Chinese under the Ming regime imported tobacco, sweet potatoes, and corn, which have constituted major agricultural products for China ever since. Printing, both with wooden blocks and with movable type, enriched the literary life. There were government presses as well as flourishing private (family) presses. The Ming period was not noted for its brilliance in either political thought or art, but it was a regime that maintained economic prosperity.

THE MANCHUS: THE LAST IMPERIAL RULERS OF CHINA

For a second time China was overrun by "barbarians" from outside the Great Wall: The Manchus invaded from the northeast and established an empire known as the Qing Dynasty, which ruled China for over 268 years, from 1644 to 1911 A.D. At the height of Manchu rule, China had extended its boundaries not only to Manchuria, but also to Mongolia, Xingjiang, Xizang (Tibet), and the far eastern portion of Russia. The Manchu court in Beijing established China's suzerainty—claiming sovereign rights, but not direct administration—over Nepal, Siam, Annam, and Korea. As alien rulers the Manchu Dynasty maintained intact the traditional Chinese political system, continuing recruitment by examination for the services of Confucian scholars as civil administrators for a vast empire. One Manchu ruler, Qian Lung, reigned for over six decades, from 1736 until 1796 A.D., at which time he was 86 years old. For its first 150 years the Qing Dynasty provided internal order and prosperity amidst a rapidly rising population. China's population stood at 60 million in 1650, but it multiplied to over 143 million in 1740 and to 265 million in 1775.

China, the "Middle Kingdom," the center of the universe, had long been admired by the Europeans for its silk products, its tea, and its art treasures. The Europeans' eagerness for trade with China, coupled with their zeal for missionary work in "heathen" China, produced a substantial amount of cultural misunderstanding. This was compounded by the demand for an "open door" trade and commerce policy, leading to the granting of territorial concessions to Europeans on Chinese soil. These pressures from abroad, plus gradual internal decay in the dynastic cycle, served as contributing factors to the decline of the Manchu empire in modern times. It is to the topic of Western impact that we must now turn in our continued discussion of Chinese history.

The first major clash between the West and China was over the importation of opium by the British for Chinese consumption. Prior to the British discovery of opium as a lucrative trade item, the Europeans, particularly the British, had an unfavorable balance of trade with China; the Chinese acquired little from the "inferior" West, but exported large quantities of Chinese tea, art objects, and porcelain to the West. As a result, the British had a trade deficit with China—until they discovered opium as an addictive drug desired by the Chinese for analgesic purposes. The importation of opium from British India turned around the Sino–British trade balance in favor of the British. Worse still, not only were the Chinese now in a terrible trade deficit situation, but opium addiction had become a serious national health problem. The imperial order to ban and confiscate opium importation was the spark that ignited the confrontation.

Complicating Sino–British relations, and Sino–European relations in general, was the Chinese practice of confining or restricting foreigners with trade and missionary objectives to one designated place in a southern port. The first Jesuits came to China in 1552 A.D.; they were followed by Mathew Ricci, who began successful missionary work in China in 1582. British envoys were subjected to the Chinese custom of bowing to the emperor whenever an imperial audience was granted. It was a humiliation and an insult to the British, who subscribed to the recognized principle of equality of status between nations. The twin pressures of trade and sovereign equality status between nations became underlying causes for the war with Great Britain that resulted in the signing of the unequal treaty of Nanking on August 24, 1842—the first severe blow dealt to an already weakening Qing empire. China was forced to open up five coastal ports where the British could reside and trade under European laws and customs, in addition to ceding Hong Kong and agreeing to treat the British on an equal basis. The treaty of Nanking was followed by a succession of treaties imposed on the Chinese by other European powers. By the time Japan defeated China in 1895, the prestige of the Qing Dynasty had reached its lowest ebb.

Let us now pause for a moment prior to our discussion of the Revolution of 1911, which brought down the imperial dynasty of Qing. It is perhaps appropriate to take a closer look now at the traditional Chinese political system that prevailed on the eve of the revolution.

THE TRADITIONAL CHINESE POLITICAL SYSTEM

To understand contemporary China, we must first look at the historical background and at the traditional political system that existed prior to the Revolution of 1911. The traditional Chinese political system was based upon a predominantly agrarian society. It was administered by an officialdom of scholars and was controlled, theoretically, by an authoritarian emperor. Although the Chinese empire was centralized, there was a great deal of regional and local autonomy. In the following pages we will examine some of the major characteristics of the traditional Chinese political system: the emperor, Confucian ideology, the gentry-officialdom, and the nature of local autonomy.

The Emperor: Mandate of Heaven and Dynastic Cycle

The Chinese emperor ruled with unlimited power over his subjects. His legitimacy and power to rule the vast empire derived from the belief that he was the "Son of Heaven" with a mandate to rule on earth. The mandate of heaven was legitimate as long as the emperor ruled in a righteous way and maintained harmony within the Chinese society and between the society and nature. A corollary to the mandate-of-heaven theory was the right to rebel if the emperor failed to maintain harmony. It was, therefore, an ancient tradition providing for rebellion as a means of deposing an intolerable imperial ruler—but rebellion was legitimate only if it succeeded.

Rebellions in Chinese history fall into two general patterns: peasant uprisings with religious overtones, and military insurrections. The peasant uprisings, such as the Taiping Rebellion of 1850, while at times widespread, only once led directly to the founding of a new imperial dynasty. The Ming Dynasty, which succeeded that of the Mongols in the fourteenth century, was founded by a laborer.[7] Peasant unrest and rebellions did, however, contribute indirectly to new dynasties by further weakening declining reigns and providing evidence of the loss of the mandate of heaven. These new dynasties, with the exception of the Ming, were founded either through a takeover by a powerful Chinese military figure, who had exploited peasant discontent and obtained the support of the scholars, or by foreign invasion.

While dynastic changes were effected through rebellion or invasion, the form and substance of government remained essentially unchanged. Each new emperor accepted the Confucian ideology, claiming the mandate of heaven for himself by virtue of success. He governed the empire through an established bureaucratic machinery administered by career officials. Each ruler was dependent upon these officials to administer the vast, populous empire. Dynasties rose and fell, but officialdom remained intact. Each of the twenty-four historic dynasties followed a common pattern of development, the dynastic cycle. At the beginning of a new dynasty, a period of national unity under virtuous and benevolent rule flourished and usually was accompanied by intellectual excitement and ferment; then, midway in the cycle, there emerged a period of mediocre rule, accompanied by signs of corruption and unrest. Finally, natural disasters occurred for which the ruler was unable to provide workable remedies, and a successful rebellion or invasion was mounted. A new dynasty was born, and the cycle repeated itself.[8]

Confucian Ideology

Confucianism, which permeated traditional Chinese society, was basically conservative and establishment-oriented. The central concepts stressed the need to achieve harmony in society through moral conduct in all relationships. The mandate of heaven implied explicit adherence to the Confucian theory of "government by goodness."[9] This code of proper behavior for the emperor and all government officials was prescribed in detail in the writings of Confucius and his disciples. Officials were recruited on the basis of competitive examinations designed to test mastery of the Confucian classics. It was assumed that once the Confucian ethic was mastered and internalized by the scholar-officials, a just and benevolent government would result. Since the government was administered by those who possessed the required ethics and code of conduct, there was really little need for either the promulgation of laws or the formal structuring of government institutions.

As the officially sanctioned political ideology, Confucianism conditioned and controlled the minds of rulers and subjects alike; it became the undisputed "orthodox doctrine of the imperial state."[10] It was perpetuated by the scholars as the basic foundation for the education of young men of means. Traditional Confucian ideology made its greatest impact on the wealthy elite. Confucianism as a humanistic philosophy served for thousands of years as a set of moral and ethical codes for correct behavior for the leaders or rulers. It left an ideological vacuum among the peasantry—the bulk of the population then, as now—who were more concerned with the burden of taxes and the hardships of life than with theories of government.[11] In later chapters we will discuss in detail how the Chinese Communist Party purposefully molded the minds of the Chinese people to conform to a different, but equally orthodox, political ideology. It is sufficient to note here the central role of political ideology in both the imperial and communist Chinese systems.

It must also be pointed out that Confucianism contained some elements of religious rites and beliefs—ancient rituals observed by the imperial officialdom. In fact,

Confucianism promulgated the concept that the emperor was the "Son of Heaven" and that he not only had the mandate to rule on earth, but as political head of the state must perform certain prescribed ceremonies necessary for order and harmony among men and in the universe. The circular marble structure of the Altar of Heaven in the Forbidden City in Beijing was one of the places where the "Son of Heaven" conducted the ceremonies. The Confucian classics also contained references to ceremonies in honor of ancestors, though some of the ceremonial practices were influenced by Buddhism and Taoism.

The Gentry-Officialdom

Under the imperial system, the government officials—the mandarins—dominated the political and economic life of China. The mandarins were those individuals who held office by virtue of imperial degrees obtained by passing the civil service examinations. They came almost solely from the wealthy landholding class with resources to provide extended education for their sons. Because of the status and the power of the office, the mandarin officials were able to acquire fortunes in landholdings for themselves and their families. They constituted the small, privileged upper class of the Chinese agrarian society. Under the imperial civil service for the Manchu Dynasty—the last dynasty before the Revolution of 1911—these officials were estimated to total not more than 40,000, or one one-hundredth of 1 percent of the population.[12] The officials of the imperial civil service wielded complete and arbitrary power over their subjects, the vast majority of whom were peasants living in the countryside. A typical magistrate for a Chinese county, according to one study, was responsible for the lives and well-being of about a quarter of a million subjects.[13] The magistrate, therefore, had to seek the cooperation and support of the large landholders to administer the county on behalf of the emperor and the central administration in Beijing. This administrative setup illustrates the gulf that existed between the educated elite and the illiterate peasants, and indicates the hierarchical structure of Chinese imperial rule.

The Chinese bureaucracy was classified into ranks and grades, each with a special set of privileges and a compensation scale. A voluminous flow of official documents and memoranda moved up and down the hierarchical ladder. At each level of the hierarchy, a certain prescribed form and literary style had to be observed—a multiplication of bureaucratic jargon. To control the huge bureaucracy, the emperor designated special censors at the various levels of government to report on the conduct of public officials. The provincial governor or the top man in a branch of the central bureaucracy in Beijing could become a bottleneck in the policy initiation and implementation process. At the lowest level of administration—the Chinese county—all important decisions affecting the community were made by the elites with the blessings of the magistrate. These decisions often disregarded, or were contrary to, the wishes of the earthbound peasants, who constituted the majority. Arbitrary decision making, unresponsive to the uneducated masses in the villages, remains to this day a basic problem in the relationship between the leaders and the led in China. In traditional Chinese politics, as in modern China, the elites or officials exercised control over the mass of peasants.

Local Autonomy

While the Chinese imperial government was centralized at the court in Beijing and was hierarchical in structure, the system did permit some degree of autonomy at the local level, provided that this did not interfere with the absolute authority of the emperor. A magistrate for a county, the lowest administrative unit in traditional China, could not possibly carry out his duties without working with and through the "local power structure."[14] While this power structure was headed by the large landowners, it also included merchants, artisans, and other persons of wealth and power in the community. As a convenient administrative arrangement, these groups were permitted by the magistrate to manage their own affairs within their own established confines. The magistrate naturally reserved the right to intervene if he deemed it necessary. Under this pragmatic arrangement, spokesmen for special interest groups in the community, such as the clans, the merchants' guilds, and the secret societies, often articulated their views and positions before the magistrate by informal and unofficial means, but never by overt pressure. It was considered an unforgivable sin for officials to organize themselves into factions that advocated competing interests of groups in the community. But articulation of group interests was often carried out by officials within the bureaucratic framework.[15] Thus, there was keen competition and maneuvering by officials within the bureaucratic setup to gain favorable decisions on a particular matter. In all instances, politics of this sort was conducted in secrecy and was influenced by the personal ties that competing officials might have with the local power structure, by their own rank within the bureaucratic hierarchy, and by their finesse in these maneuverings.

ATTEMPTS AT REFORM AND MODERNIZATION

One must keep in mind that long before the upheavals of the twentieth century—the Revolution of 1911, the Nationalist era that followed, and the rise of Chinese communism in the 1930s and 1940s—Chinese scholars, as reformers, had begun the search for a modernized China by exploring Western political, economic, and social ideas and institutions. Long before the Manchu Dynasty reached its lowest ebb, reform efforts were made to prevent further decay. Reformers basically sought remedial measures to abolish an inefficient and corrupt bureaucracy. They attempted to strengthen the imperial government's ability to meet unrest and rebellion in the countryside—the source of China's manpower, food supply, and government revenues. Unrest and rebellion were triggered by the demands of an increased population on the limited supplies the land could produce, and by the perennial recurrence of drought, flood, and famine. Reformers then sought to strengthen the old Chinese empire by making changes in such traditional institutions as the examination system and the military establishment. For instance, in the 1860s a group of provincial leaders came out openly for the need to acquire Western scientific and technological knowledge, particularly in areas related to the development of military science (arsenal manufacturing and shipbuilding for a navy). The leading advocates of these limited reforms of learning from the West were Zeng Guofan and Li Hongzhang. However, these attempts at modernization did not take root, as they were basically experimental projects undertaken on a personal level with limited resources. Led by a number of prominent scholars, a wave of reforms surfaced again in the decade of the 1890s. One reformer, Zhang Zhidong, a viceroy, advocated the adoption of Western methods in order to preserve the dynasty. Another group of scholar-reformers, led by Kang Youwei and his student Liang Qichao, proposed reform measures such as popular election of officials, public care of the aged and children, and abolition of the family. Kang Youwei and Liang Qichao even opened a school in southern China that taught students mathematics and military drills, in addition to the classics. As justification for his reform efforts, Kang advocated the theory that Confucius encouraged political and social reform.

In 1895 Kang and Liang organized a reform movement known as the Society for the Study of National Self-Strengthening. Kang Youwei and his supporters were able to enlist the endorsement of Emperor Guangxu for the reform. Guangxu issued imperial edicts calling for changes in the archaic examination system, which had by now degenerated into pure memorization of the classics and clever juxtaposition of words and phrases. Having evidently read Kang's works, the emperor called for modern schools, including an imperial university for the study of Western ideas and methods; railroad building; and military reform. These efforts were collectively known as the One-Hundred-Day Reform. Nevertheless, in September 1898 they were crushed by the empress dowager, who imprisoned the emperor in his own palace chambers. (Guides now show tourists the prison grounds at the Forbidden City in Beijing.) Reformers were either arrested or exiled, and the empress dowager declared the reform edicts null and void.

A direct reaction to the reform movement of 1898 was the outbreak of the Boxer Rebellion of 1900, blessed and encouraged by the empress dowager and the conservative elements in power. This was a last desperate effort to "protect the nation, destroy foreigners" (the slogan and battle cry for the campaign against all foreigners). The upheaval was quelled by the dispatch to Beijing of a joint military force from eleven nations, including the United States and Japan. This action resulted in China's signing another humiliating treaty in 1901 under which China was to pay an indemnity of over $300 million U.S., plus 4 percent interest, for missionary lives lost and properties damaged.

The Boxer Rebellion and the defeat by Japan in 1895 convinced some that reform alone could not possibly save the empire; this gave rise to the idea that a radical revolution might be necessary to overthrow the traditional imperial system. More importantly, some felt that a revolution must also advocate abandonment of traditional thinking and ideology.

THE CHINESE NATIONALIST REVOLUTION, 1911–1937

The Revolution of 1911

One leader who advocated revolutionary change was Dr. Sun Yatsen. In 1894 he founded a small secret society among overseas Chinese for the purpose of overthrowing the decaying Manchu Dynasty. As a revolutionary with a price on his head, much of the time Dr. Sun was forced to operate and organize abroad. After many years of hard work in southeast Asia, Japan, and Hawaii, Dr. Sun's movement took hold among educated young Chinese abroad. In 1905, 400 of Dr. Sun's followers gathered in Japan to form the first viable revolutionary movement, the Tung Meng Hui.[16] Its members took a solemn oath to bring down the alien Manchu empire and to replace it with a Chinese republic. Ten different attempts were organized and financed by the group, headquartered variously in Tokyo and Hanoi, to strike down the vulnerable Manchu rule by assassinating imperial officials. As these revolutionary attempts failed one by one, and more revolutionaries lost their lives, the movement became demoralized and ran low on funds. On October 10, 1911, an eleventh attempt was made. It resulted in a successful uprising by discontented and dissatisfied provincial officials, merchants, and imperial army commanders. The Manchu emperor abdicated, and shortly thereafter the Chinese imperial dynastic system was ended.

While Dr. Sun's revolutionary movement, comprised largely of students, youths, and overseas Chinese, gave impetus and momentum to the revolution, it was not the force that brought down the empire. It was the new imperial army, headed by Yuan Shihkai, that forced the abdication of the emperor. Under an agreement with Dr. Sun, who had little bargaining power, Yuan Shihkai assumed the powers of government immediately after the abdication and stayed on to become the first president of the Chinese republic. The new republic floundered from the start. Very few Chinese had any real understanding of Western democracy. All Chinese political traditions and institutions were designed for imperial rule and, therefore, were ill-suited for constitutional democracy. Yuan Shihkai increasingly disregarded the constitution and finally attempted to establish himself as emperor. The Chinese nation disintegrated as the new government proved incapable of commanding allegiance from the people in the midst of mounting domestic problems and the constant meddling in Chinese internal affairs by European powers and Japan. Yuan's death in 1916 marked the final collapse of the central government's effective authority.[17]

Warlordism, the May Fourth Movement, and the Nationalist Revolution

The disintegration of the Chinese nation led to the emergence of a warlord period, which prevailed for two decades, from 1916 to 1936. At Yuan's death some of his officers—and others with sufficient power—seized control of various regions. These territories were controlled by the warlords, who maintained private armies manned with conscripted peasants, to protect and extend their provincial domains. Even Sun Yatsen and his followers had to seek refuge under the protection of the warlord in Canton. Dr. Sun's revolutionary program now called for the eventual establishment of constitutional government in three stages: (1) unification of the nation through elimination of warlordism by military force and termination of foreign intervention in China; (2) a period of political tutelage to prepare the people for democratic government; and (3) the enactment of a constitution by the people. Neither the European powers nor the warlords paid any attention to the disillusioned Dr. Sun, who was now desperate for a way to save China from further disintegration.

The immediate aftermath of the Revolution of 1911 was a period of utter chaos for China. Having brought down the pillars and support system for imperial rule, the revolution provided only an unworkable paper constitution, unfamiliar to and untried by the Chinese. In the midst of chaos and disintegration, there was a revival of the call by the early reformers, such as Kang Youwei and Liang Qichao, for the study of Western ideas for the purpose of building a new nation and "a new society." This was the underlying reason for the intellectual enlightenment movement called the May Fourth era, 1919–29. The movement began as a Beijing student protest against the humiliation China had suffered at the hands of the victorious Allied powers in the Versailles Treaty negotiations, the demands and pressure by the Japanese over Chinese territorial integrity, and the spread of warlords in the provinces in China. Thousands of students marched in protest on May 4, 1919, carrying banners and shouting slogans calling for national awakening and survival. The intellectuals were joined and supported by merchants and workers, not only in Beijing, but in many major cities throughout China. The themes for this intellectual enlightenment movement were nationalism, anti-imperialism, anti-warlordism, and the call for a "new society" that could embrace "democracy and science." While thousands of students were jailed, the movement nevertheless forged on to create a lasting national ferment that formed the genesis of the subsequent Nationalist and communist revolutions in China. From then on, Chinese intellectuals served as the harbingers of change. The

May Fourth Movement led to reform in the written Chinese language, from the archaic classical style to use of the vernacular, or everyday spoken form. It also introduced the study of Western science, technology, and political ideologies, including Marxism. The movement was closely tied in with demonstrations by university students against foreign intervention in Chinese affairs and against warlordism. These activities gave impetus to a new nationalist and patriotic feeling emerging among the general population.

It was in this atmosphere—one of anger, humiliation, and disillusionment—that the Nationalist revolution took place. In 1922, Dr. Sun was forced to flee Canton for Shanghai in order to escape from the southern warlords. While in Shanghai, he was contacted by an agent of the Communist Third International (Comintern), who offered to assist the Chinese revolutionary movement by providing Soviet personnel. Dr. Sun accepted the offer and signed an agreement that reorganized his hitherto ineffective political party into a Chinese counterpart of the Soviet Union's Communist Party. Dr. Sun's party became the Nationalist Party (the Nationalists), the Guomindang, and formed an alliance with the newly formed Chinese Communist Party. Another agreement provided limited support in terms of arms and military training in the Soviet Union for members of Dr. Sun's revolutionary army. Although Dr. Sun died in 1925, a military expedition was launched in 1926 to unify China by defeating the warlords. News of the expedition both inspired the people with nationalist feelings and aroused the populace against foreign imperialism.

The expedition was launched under an uneasy alliance between Dr. Sun's followers, who were receiving financial backing from merchants in coastal cities and from large landowners in the countryside, and the members of the Chinese Communist Party, controlled by the Comintern. By March 1927 the new Nationalist government was dominated by the left-wing elements of the Guomindang and the communists with headquarters in Wuhan in central China. When the expedition gained control of eastern China on its push north, Chiang Kaishek, commander of the revolutionary armies and successor to Sun Yatsen, decided to end the internal schism between the left and the right by first eliminating members of the Chinese Communist Party within the revolutionary movement. In April 1927 a lightning strike massacred communists in the cities under Chiang's control. The surprise blow, known as the "Shanghai Massacre," was so effective that it practically decimated the communist ranks. Chiang also expelled Soviet advisers from China. He then established the Nationalist government in Nanjing, and this was recognized by most nations as the legitimate government of China in the 1940s. The remaining Chinese communists sought refuge in the mountainous regions in central China after 1930.

China under the Nationalists, 1927–1937

During the decade of Guomindang rule, from 1927 to 1937, modest progress was made in many areas of modernization, initiated by the Nationalists under the leadership of Chiang Kaishek and his Western-trained advisers and administrators. For the first time, China had a modern governmental structure. As soon as major provincial warlords were eliminated or co-opted into the system, the transportation and industrial facilities were improved and expanded in the area. Earnest attempts were made to expand elementary school education and to provide political indoctrination for the young. Most important from Chiang's point of view was the building of a more efficient and dedicated modern army for a host of purposes—including the eventual elimination of warlords and communist guerrillas in mountainous areas of central China, as well as protection of China's borders from foreign attack.

There were glaring negative features in the Nationalist balance sheet. First, no real efforts were made to provide progressive economic and social programs to improve the lot of the people. Land reform measures were few. Second, the regime alienated the intellectuals by its repressive measures against them in the guise of purging any elements of communist influence from their ranks. Third, enormous expenditures from the national treasury were devoted to the "extermination" of the Chinese communists operating in remote mountain regions. The Nationalists steadfastly refused to seek a nonmilitary solution to the problem of insurrection by the communists. Nor were they willing to seek consultation with other political groups, let alone share political power with other elements of society. The Guomindang's modest accomplishments in nation building were soon obliterated by its obsession with eliminating all opposition.

The Chinese Nationalist Revolution (1927–37), or the Nanjing Decade, has been analyzed by various China scholars. In one early work the revolution was labeled a tragedy.[18] Another scholar characterized it as an abortive revolution, implying that the successors to Dr. Sun's revolution had lost their "revolutionary momentum" and that the Nationalist regime had deteriorated into a "military dictatorship."[19] One China scholar has called the Nationalist Revolution "the misconceived revolution" because of its belief that by terminating warlord rule and foreign imperialism Chinese society would be united, instead of divided in accordance with "sectorial self-interests."[20]

Time was not on the side of the Nationalists. In 1931, when they had achieved some measure of national unification and modernization while waging encirclement campaigns against the communist guerilla forces, Japanese militarists annexed resource-rich Manchuria and made advances into northern China, inside the Great Wall. The Nationalist regime faced a hard choice in allocating its limited resources between the Japanese aggressors and the communist insurgents. In the early 1930s, Chiang's strategy was to rapidly annihilate the communist guerilla forces and then turn to face the Japanese. However, rising public sentiment, expressed in frequent demonstrations, demanded that the regime prevent further territorial losses to the Japanese. In December 1936 Chiang was forced to join in a united front with the Chinese communists to fight the Japanese. By 1937 Japan was waging full-scale war against China.

NOTES

1. *Hawaii Tribune-Herald*, October 4, 1981, p. 9.
2. *Beijing Review*, 31 (August 3, 1981), 4–5.
3. Shan-yu Yao, "The Chronological and Seasonal Distribution of Flood and Droughts in Chinese History, 206 B.C.–A.D. 1911," *Harvard Journal of Asiatic Studies*, 7 (1942), 275.
4. John King Fairbank, *The United States and China*, rev. ed. (New York: Viking Press, 1962), p. 48.
5. For early Chinese history the following are recommended readings: Kenneth Scott Latourette, *The Chinese: Their History and Culture*, 3d ed. rev. (New York: Macmillan, 1946); John K. Fairbank and Edwin O. Reischauer, eds., *The Cambridge History of China*, vol. X (Cambridge: Cambridge University Press, 1978); Bai Shouyi, ed., *An Outline History of China* (Beijing: Foreign Language Press, 1982); and Ranbir Vohra, *China's Path to Modernization: A Historical Review From 1800 to the Present* (Upper Saddle River, N.J.: Prentice Hall, 1987).
6. Lawrence Ziring and C. I. Eugene Kim, *The Asian Political Dictionary* (Santa Barbara, Calif.: ABC-CLIO, 1985), p. 105.
7. Charles P. Fitzgerald, *Revolution in China* (New York: Holt, Rinehart & Winston, 1952), pp. 12–16.
8. John King Fairbank, *United States and China*, 3d ed. (Cambridge, Mass.: Harvard University Press, 1971), pp. 90–95.
9. Ibid., p. 55.
10. Fitzgerald, *Revolution in China*, p. 23.

11. Kung-chuan Hsiao, *Rural China: Imperial Control in the Nineteenth Century* (Seattle, Wash.: University of Washington Press, 1960), pp. 253–54.
12. Fairbank, *United States and China*, pp. 20–34.
13. Ibid., p. 103.
14. Ibid., and James Townsend, *Politics in China* (Boston: Little, Brown, 1974), pp. 35–36.
15. Townsend, *Politics in China*, p. 37.
16. Fairbank, *United States and China*, p. 191. Also see Sterling Seagrave, *The Soong Dynasty* (New York: Harper & Row, 1985), pp. 76–79 and 92–94.
17. Fitzgerald, *Revolution in China*, p. 38; and Fairbank, *United States and China*, pp. 197–98.
18. Harold Robert Isaac, *Tragedy of the Chinese Revolution* (Stanford, Calif.: Stanford University Press, 1951).
19. See Lloyd E. Eastman, *The Abortive Revolution: China under Nationalist Rule, 1927–1937* (Cambridge, Mass.: Council on East Asian Studies, Harvard University Press, 1990).
20. See John Fitzgerald, ed., *The Nationalists and Chinese Society, 1923–1937: A Symposium* (Melbourne, Australia: University of Melbourne History Monographs No. 4, 1989).

SUGGESTED READINGS

Eastman, Lloyd I. *The Abortive Revolution: China under Nationalist Rule, 1927-1937* (Cambridge, Mass.: Council on East Asian Studies, Harvard University Press, 1970).
Fairbank, John King, and Merle Goldman. *China: A New History* (enl. ed.) (Cambridge, Mass.: The Belknap Press of Harvard University Press, 1998).
Fitzgerald, Charles P. *Revolution in China* (New York: Holt, Rinehart & Winston, 1952).
Isaac, Harold Robert. *Tragedy of the Chinese Revolution* (Stanford, Calif.: Stanford University Press, 1951).
Spence, Jonathan D. *The Search for Modern China,* (2d ed.) (London and New York: W. W. Norton & Company, Inc., 1999).

Chapter Two

The Origin and Rise of the Chinese Communist Movement

From Military Communism to Deng's Reforms

THE EARLY YEARS

Although Marxism was introduced in China about the time of World War I, this ideology, which called for revolution by an urban proletariat under mature capitalism, elicited little attention. Fabian socialism—progressive and social change through gradual constitutional means, developed in England in 1884—became the most popular liberal ideology imported from the West. For example, Dr. Sun's program incorporated socialist planks, including nationalization of land, a welfare state, and a planned economy. Interest in Marxism suddenly flowered among Chinese intellectuals after the 1917 Bolshevik Revolution in Russia. They saw in Lenin's revolution a relevant solution to China's political and economic problems. The keen interest in Bolshevism also reflected disillusionment with Western democracy as a model for Chinese development. In addition, it expressed Chinese bitterness over the imperialist activities of the Western democracies in China.

The early Chinese Marxists and the founders of the Chinese Communist Party were leading intellectuals in the Beijing National University (Beida). In 1918 Li Dazhao, the university's head librarian, formed a Marxist study group to which many young students, including a library assistant named Mao Zedong, were attracted. These young students were more interested in learning how to make a revolution than in theorizing about Marxism. With some urging from Comintern agents, the Chinese Communist Party (CCP) was formed on July 1, 1921. The group of thirteen intellectuals and revolutionaries, representing a total of fifty-seven members, were called together by Chen Duxiu, who became the first secretary general. Meetings for the first two party congresses were held secretly in the French concession in Shanghai to prevent harassment by the police. This was the very modest beginning of the party, and of the movement that took root in later years.

The CCP, the Comintern, and the First United Front (1922–1927)

For the first six years of the CCP's existence, 1921–27, the movement was under the control and direction of the Third International, or the Comintern. The Comintern was formed in 1919 at the insistence of Lenin, who wanted a new international organization, controlled by Moscow, to provide direction for all proletariat parties and to promote anti-imperialist revolutions throughout the world. Moscow directed and controlled the CCP and its leadership through Soviet Comintern agents who came to China with financial aid and military materiel. The leadership of the CCP before 1934, with few exceptions, was in the hands of the "returned Chinese Bolsheviks," trained for party work in Moscow under the sponsorship of the Comintern.

The Comintern's doctrine insisted that revolutions in colonial areas be based on industrial workers. Its strategy called for the participation of nonproletariat elements, such as the bourgeoisie, in a united front alliance to lead national revolutions. The manifestos adopted by four consecutive CCP congresses, from 1922 to 1925, echoed the Comintern line, calling for a revolutionary alliance with the landlord-merchant-based Guomindang, Dr. Sun's Nationalist Party. This Comintern strategy, which limited the communist base to urban industrial workers and called for individual communists to join the Guomindang under a united front, enhanced the CCP's growth as a viable political party during its early years.

The first alliance or honeymoon between the Nationalists and members of the Chinese Communist Party occurred in May 1922 at the latter's Second Party Congress in the lake region of Hangchow. Realizing the growing strength and support for the Nationalists, the party congress delegates were encouraged to ally with them by Comintern agent Maring (alias Sneevliet), a Dutch communist with organizational experience in the Dutch East Indies (now Indonesia). Maring's persuasive argument was that the weak Chinese Communist Party would be able to grow if its members joined the Guomindang (the Nationalists) as individuals and then infiltrated the latter's organizational apparatus as the instrument for a socialist revolution.

The resulting First United Front, pressured by Comintern agents, created tension within the Chinese Communist organization in its relations with Stalinist Moscow. The tension was further aggravated by the rift between Stalin and Trotsky. The Chinese communists who went to Moscow for training under the auspices of the Comintern returned to China and increasingly assumed leadership of the party. They came into conflict with those Chinese communists who all along had been questioning continued alliance with the Nationalists as a possible reversal of the proletarian nature of the socialist revolutionary movement; Comintern agents assigned to China had demanded this maneuver. In fact, there were two distinct factions that surfaced at the CCP's Fifth Party Congress in April 1927. One faction, mostly Moscow-trained returnees, supported the Comintern's continued policy of cooperating with the leftist elements of the Nationalists in Wuhan in central China, with the goal of eventually seizing control of the entire Nationalist movement. The other faction, led by Mao, gradually expressed the need to introduce land reform by working with the peasants in the countryside as a basis for revolution. Confusing and contradictory instructions from the Moscow Comintern only sharpened the schism within the party. Parenthetically, it was this rift that served as the original basis for subsequent inner party struggles, purges, and rectification campaigns.

By 1927 the united front alliance had become unworkable. Chiang Kaishek's power as commander in chief and head of the Guomindang was threatened by leftist elements in control of the revolutionary government, which was supported by the communists. As pointed out earlier, Chiang decided to purge the communists from his organization and to set up a rival government in Nanjing. Not long after, the leftist-dominated Wuhan government also turned on the communists when it became known that the Comintern, acting under direct orders from Stalin, had instructed the CCP to eliminate the landlord elements and militarists in order to transform the alliance into a new revolutionary force. The result was a bloody mass execution of the communists who were caught.

Instead of admitting the mistake in his China policy, Stalin blamed the CCP leaders for their failure to prepare the workers in Wuhan for action.[1] Partly as a rebuttal to criticism raised by Leon Trotsky, Stalin ordered the Comintern agents in China to plan a series of armed insurrections. He hoped that quick victories would silence critics of his unsuccessful united front policy.[2] On August 1, 1927, now celebrated as the founding day of the People's Liberation Army, Zhou Enlai and Zhu De led a mutiny of communist troops within the Guomindang forces in Nanchang in central China. After occupying the city briefly, the communists were forced to seek refuge as guerrillas in the hills of eastern Guangdong province. The CCP also authorized a number of "Autumn Harvest Uprisings" in the fall of 1927 in central and southern China. One of these was led by Mao Zedong in his home province of Hunan. These uprisings were ill-fated misadventures that ended in defeat and brought heavy losses to the already-decimated CCP ranks. When Mao and his group sought refuge in the mountain stronghold of Jinggangshan on the Hunan–Jiangxi border in central China, he repudiated the Comintern-inspired strategy. As a reprimand, Mao briefly lost his membership on the Politburo, the executive and policy-making body of the party.

After the rupture of the united front between the CCP and the Guomindang, the Chinese communist movement fragmented into two areas of operation: one in the cities, as an underground movement, with close links to the Comintern; the other in rural areas, as experimental soviets, operating almost autonomously and feuding constantly with the Comintern advisers. By the end of 1930, the party had been driven out of the cities, and only pockets of guerrilla bands operated in remote mountain regions of central and southern China and northern Shaanxi. The plight of the CCP was evidenced by the fact that its Central Committee had to operate underground in Shanghai's foreign concessions, and the Sixth Party Congress had to meet in Moscow in 1928. The leadership of the party was still in the hands of the returned Bolsheviks, who adhered to the Comintern policies. In a last attempt to recapture an urban base for a proletarian revolution in the summer of 1930, the CCP leadership, under Li Lisan, launched an attack from rural bases with the objective of capturing a number of cities on the Changjiang (Yangtse) River. Like previous Comintern-instigated misadventures, this one also ended in failure, with the small bases in rural mountain regions under blockage by Chiang Kaishek's forces. The Chinese communists' future at this juncture seemed bleak.

The Rise of Mao Zedong, the Second United Front, and Military Communism (1936–1946)

The future of the Chinese communist movement hinged on the survival of the small pockets of experimental soviets in the remote rural areas, mostly in central and southern China. The CCP's decision, in the fall of 1931, to establish a Chinese Soviet Republic—which would unite the scattered bases—was both a political necessity and an admission that a revolution based on an urban proletariat was no longer possible in China. Thus, by 1931, when the CCP's Central Committee moved from urban Shanghai to the rural Jiangxi soviet, a decade-long quarrel within the Chinese communist movement—

regarding the theoretical correctness of a revolutionary strategy based on the peasants—officially ended. The foremost proponent of a peasant base was the leader of the Jiangxi soviet, Mao Zedong. Mao had developed a strategy for victory during the six years he operated the Jiangxi guerrilla base. Besides the need for a highly disciplined united party, Mao's strategy contained three indispensable ingredients: (1) the development of a strong and mobile peasant-based Red Army for a protracted armed struggle; (2) the selection of a strategic terrain for military operations; and (3) the establishment of a self-sufficient economic base in the Red Army-controlled soviet areas to provide personnel and supplies for the armed struggle.[3] Mao believed that a highly disciplined party could only be built by a recruitment policy that would draw in the tough and dedicated guerrilla soldiers of the Red Army, who were predominantly poor peasants. The party became "militarized" as Mao began to build a new base for revolution.[4]

The Guomindang intensified its attack against the guerilla base in its fifth and most extensive military campaign, which included an effective blockade that deprived the guerrilla base of outside supplies, particularly salt. By 1934 the guerrilla base had to be abandoned. The communists broke out of the Guomindang encirclement and moved the surviving forces, numbering not more than 150,000, westward and then north to the Great Wall. This was the legendary Long March of more than 6,000 miles over treacherous terrain of high mountains and rivers, amidst ambushes from warlords, Guomindang troops, and hostile minorities.[5] In October 1935, after almost a year's march, the greatly reduced forces of about 20,000 survivors arrived in Yanan in the northwestern province of Shaanxi and established a new base for guerrilla operations. By this time, the stormy Politburo meeting—held at Zunyi in southwest Guizhou Province in January 1935—had selected Mao as the undisputed leader of the CCP, including the cells operating mainly in industrial centers such as Shanghai and Wuhan. This marked the end of Comintern dominance and the beginning of Mao's supremacy as the CCP's political and military leader. This supremacy lasted until his death in 1976, forty years later.

Expansion of Communism under Mao and Final Victory

When Chiang Kaishek learned that the communists had established a base in Yanan, he sent his crack troops to Shaanxi. The Guomindang force included soldiers who had been driven from Manchuria by the Japanese army in 1931. The Manchurian troops showed signs of low morale and a reluctance to fight the communists. This was largely due to effective political propaganda by the communists, which stressed the urgent need for a united front against Japan. In an effort to step up the offensive, Chiang Kaishek went to Xian in Shaanxi to direct the campaign personally. The mutinous Manchurian troops seized Chiang as a hostage in order to force him to agree to a united front policy. The Chinese communists by then had established contact with the Manchurian troops. Both Mao Zedong and Zhou Enlai served as mediators for the release of Chiang Kaishek under an agreement for a united front to fight the Japanese. This was the Xian Agreement, which temporarily terminated the civil war and marked the beginning of a second alliance between the CCP and the Guomindang.

The 1936 Xian Agreement between the CCP and the Guomindang (Nationalists) was not finally implemented until July 1937. Under the terms of the agreement, the CCP was to terminate its policy of armed insurrection against the Guomindang government in Nanking; this in effect terminated, officially at least, the state of civil war. The Chinese communist forces were to be "integrated" into the Nationalist military setup—although in practice they never adhered to the Guomindang jurisdiction, except that the official designation of the Red Army became the Eighth Route Army. And, Mao promised not to continue his land confiscation policy in rural areas. In effect, both sides were very distrustful of each other's motives and intentions.

When Japan attacked northern China in the summer of 1937, the Red Army was slowly brought into action under the united front agreement. The cessation of the civil war gave the CCP the needed respite to expand its base of operations and to strengthen its military forces for the eventual showdown with the Guomindang.[6] As China suffered repeated military defeats by the Japanese, the CCP-controlled Red Army expanded its guerilla operations behind enemy lines. Party membership grew rapidly, from a little over 20,000 at the end of the Long March in 1935, to over 800,000 in 1939, and to about 1.2 million at the end of the war in 1945. Of this enlarged party membership, perhaps a million were party members of the "military supply system," peasants and patriotic students who served the Red Army without salary but under strict military discipline.[7] They were the backbone of the leadership, not only for the communist guerrilla forces but also for the militarized border-region governments established in the areas under Red Army control. In each of these border regions, experiments in mild land reform and self-government by popular election were introduced. It was during this period that many of the practices and experiences became revolutionary traditions that persist today under the overall label "Yanan spirit."

When the Japanese surrendered in 1945, open clashes occurred between the Guomindang and the communist forces in many parts of China. China was once again engulfed in civil war, but this time the communists were in a much stronger position in terms of discipline, numerical strength, and the will to combat—not to mention having the support of the intellectuals and a large segment of the rural population. The policy of President Truman of the United States was to bring the parties together for a political settlement. A series of cease-fire agreements were reached under American supervision. The mediation efforts by General Marshall for the United States soon deteriorated. Neither side had any intention of observing the truce and settling the future of China by political means. As the strength and morale of the Guomindang forces ebbed, the People's Liberation Army won victories over the Nationalist troops equipped and supplied by the United States. By the summer and fall of 1948, the People's Liberation Army had overrun Manchuria and most of northern China. Guomindang forces were surrendering in divisional strength. With captured American military hardware, a large-scale military offensive was launched by the communists in the spring of 1949 against the remaining Guomindang forces in central and southern China. Although the Nationalists did not flee to the island of Taiwan until December 1949, the communists convened the People's Political Consultative Conference on October 1, to establish a new People's Republic of China in Beijing. At last the Chinese communist movement, which had begun as a Marxist study group, had seized power in China. A new search now began to find a suitable model to follow in building an industrially powerful China.

CHINA'S SEARCH FOR A DEVELOPMENT MODEL

After almost eight years of war with Japan and four years of civil war, the initial years of the new republic were preoccupied with the immediate problems of consolidation and reconstruction. In the beginning, the CCP formed a coalition government, applying the tenets first formulated by Mao Zedong in his "New Democracy" (1940) and "On Coalition Government" (1945).[8] In this pragmatic way, twenty-three other political groups were permitted a partial share of political authority. The central government in Beijing proliferated with ministries on economic affairs. More than 55 percent of the top national administrative posts were reserved for leaders of the CCP; the remainder were distributed among experienced and talented liberal noncommunist intellectuals. During these early years, the new regime also relied heavily on the regional pattern of government to superintend the provinces. The regional government was, in turn, bolstered by the military field armies that had conquered and had remained in these regions after the civil war.

The enormous task of reconstruction called first of all for a solution to the problem of mounting inflation. During the last few months of the Nationalist regime, prices had risen 85,000 percent.[9] Inflation abated somewhat when the new regime came to power, but with huge budget deficits from increased governmental expenditures, it still remained a serious problem. By a variety of fiscal and monetary devices, including the central control of local taxes, and the measuring of prices and wages in terms of commodity units, prices were finally stabilized by the summer of 1950.

Private industry and commerce, while restricted, were rehabilitated and developed along with the socialistic national economy. National ministries of economic production saw to it that the privately owned industries obtained needed raw materials to make their products, and that they received orders from private or state-owned enterprises for these goods and services. Rapid economic recovery was made, and by 1952 production had reached China's peak pre-1949 levels. This rapid recovery was attributable to the policy of gradualism in nationalization, with no outright confiscation of private industry. Privately owned industries were eventually transformed into joint state and private enterprises and finally into completely state-owned operations through the "buying-off" policy, under which former owners of private enterprises were paid interest on their shares at a rate fixed by the state.[10]

Land Reform: Transformation of the Countryside

The most important program enacted by the new regime from 1950 to 1953 was agrarian reform. Land redistribution, a basic plank in the CCP program, had been carried out in the early soviet phase in the Jiangxi border areas, and later in the northwest, with varying degrees of intensity. In 1949, when the CCP took over the country, some 500 million people were living in the rural villages. The land tenure system was such that "half the cultivated land was owned by less than one-tenth of the farm population, while two-thirds of the population owned less than one-fifth."[11] This serious problem of uneven land distribution was further aggravated by the large number of landless tenants who had to pay exorbitant annual rents, as high as 60 percent of their production. The 1950 Agrarian Reform Law was basically a mild reform measure that permitted rich peasants to retain their land and property (Article 6), and landlords to retain the land for their own use (Article 10). The later harsh treatment of landlords, which accompanied the implementation of land redistribution through the "struggle meetings" and the "people's tribunals" to settle accounts by the peasants, was attributable to the speedy implementation needed to prevent "foot dragging" by cadres and activists assigned to do the job and by the peasants themselves.[12] The Korean War also generated some fear on the part of the peasants of the possible return of the Nationalists.[13] Land redistribution was completed in 1952, when 113 million acres—plus draft animals and farm implements—were distributed to over 300 million landless peasants.[14]

It soon became obvious that land redistribution was only a step toward collectivizing the countryside. The millions of new landowning peasants realized very quickly that their small plots of land were too small to produce enough even to feed their own families. The individual peasants simply did not have the means to acquire modern tools, much less to build irrigation projects. Having committed themselves to the party's cause by participating in land redistribution, the peasants had to accept the party's new appeal for mutual aid teams and for the pooling together of draft animals, implements, and shared labor. In 1953–54, the mutual aid teams gave way to larger and more complicated cooperative ventures—the mandatory Agricultural Producers' Cooperatives (APCs). An agricultural producers' cooperative was, in essence, a unified management system of farm production. The individual peasants pooled their land, draft animals, implements, and houses in return for shares in the enterprise. Detailed accounting was kept, and after deductions were made for expenses incurred and taxes to be paid, income was distributed to the members on the basis of their contributions, stated in terms of shares. While the movement was voluntary, the party conducted massive campaigns to persuade and sometimes to coerce peasants to join the APCs. Although an overwhelming majority of the peasants had joined the cooperatives by 1957, official accounts showed resistance to the program. In some parts of the country, peasants deliberately consumed what they produced to avoid forced delivery to government purchasing agencies.[15]

The APCs enabled the peasants to better utilize resources and labor. During the slack seasons, surplus labor could be mobilized easily to carry on small-scale irrigation works, such as making ditches, ponds, and dams. Combined surplus labor could reclaim land through irrigation and reforestation. The APCs certainly allowed the peasants to realize greater savings and investment. Even more important was the sharing of the risks of crop failure. Individual peasants no longer had to face the possibility of bankruptcy if crops failed. But there were also many problems inherent in the APCs: Many peasants were too poor to contribute funds to the cooperatives; there was a lack of qualified technical personnel such as accountants among the illiterate peasantry to provide efficient management; and peasants were frequently unhappy when centralized purchasing and marketing operations were imposed on the cooperatives by the state, leading to intensified animosity toward the party, and a reluctance to cooperate.[16]

The First Five-Year Plan (1953–1957) and the Soviet Model

By 1953 the regime had completed the immediate tasks of rehabilitating the wartorn economy and consolidating its control over the nation. With the end of the Korean War, the regime was confident enough to embark on a rapid industrialization program. The approach selected was the Stalinist strategy of long-term centralized planning, a proven socialistic model that had enabled the Soviet Union to emerge from World War II as the second most powerful nation in the world. For ideological reasons it was the only logical strategy comprehensible to the Chinese communists at the time, particularly in view of the emerging bipolarization of the world into Soviet and Western orbits. The pragmatic Chinese were aware of the benefits of Soviet aid, in terms of both financial credit and technical assistance, which would be forthcoming to promote this model.[17]

Fundamental to the Stalinist model was the rapid buildup in the heavy industry sector through the concentrated allocation of investment into capital goods industries. The model also called for highly centralized decision making at the top to determine targets and quotas to be fulfilled by the various economic sectors.[18] In many ways, this strategy required basic structural change in the agricultural sector, from which the bulk of savings for investment must come. The introduction of agricultural producers' cooperatives was needed in order to accumulate savings through increased agricultural production and controlled consumption. The First Five-Year Plan allocated 58 percent of the 20-billion-dollar investment fund to capital goods for heavy industries.[19] The bulk of these investment funds was financed by the Chinese themselves. The Soviet Union made considerable contributions in the form of technical assistance, construction, and equipment for 154 modern industrial plants that were paid for by the Chinese, and the training of Chinese technicians. In June 1960, when Soviet-trained Chinese technicians numbered about 10,000, Soviet aid was suddenly withdrawn. By 1957, when the First Five-Year Plan was completed, an annual growth rate of 8 percent had been added to China's economic growth,[20] an impressive achievement by any standard. In addition, the First Five-Year Plan made a lasting investment in education (130,000 engineers graduated) and public health (control of such communicable diseases as cholera and typhus, which formerly had plagued the Chinese people).[21]

The First Five-Year Plan had a number of drawbacks, however. First, the plan was rather costly when one considers that the bulk of the $20 billion in investments came from the Chinese. Second, the plan required large forced savings from the agricultural sector. Third, the Stalinist model placed undue concentration of investment in such heavy industries as steel, at the expense, not only of agriculture, but also of light and consumer goods industries. Fourth, the model required a high degree of centralization and the development of an elaborate bureaucratic structure to implement, control, and monitor the plan according to fixed targets and quotas. Fifth, since planning and implementation of the model emphasized the roles of technocrats, engineers, and plant managers, it thus neglected the need to involve politically the millions of uneducated and tradition-oriented peasants in the rapid construction of an industrial socialistic state. After an agonizing reappraisal of the First Five-Year Plan, Mao and his followers launched the Great Leap Forward in an attempt to obtain a faster rate of growth and to develop a socialist economic model more suited to China's conditions and needs.

The Great Leap Forward and Communization Program, 1958–1959

Under the Great Leap Forward, the regime mobilized the creative enthusiasm of the Chinese masses for economic growth and industrialization in the same way it had mobilized them for the communist revolution.[22] The Great Leap would substitute China's most plentiful resource, manpower, for capital goods, in the same way it had successfully substituted committed men for modern weapons during the guerrilla and civil war days. The unemployed were to be put to work, and the employed were to work much harder, under military discipline, so that China could make the gigantic leap required to become an industrial power through the widespread use of labor-intensive, small-scale production. The emphasis was placed on the techniques of mass mobilization.

The program called for use of "dual technology." The Chinese economy at the end of the First Five-Year Plan consisted of a mixture of modern sectors (capital-intensive and large-scale) and traditional sectors (labor-intensive and small-scale). These two types of economic sectors in a typical developing country (like China) are more or less independent of each other. In the modern sectors, goods produced are mostly exported to earn foreign exchange to pay for the imported machines. In the traditional sectors, small-scale industries in villages are self-sufficient, providing virtually all their own consumption and production needs. Under the Great Leap strategy, the modern sector would not need to supply capital goods for the traditional sector, but the traditional sector would increase its flow of food and raw materials to build up the industrial sector. This was the meaning of the Chinese slogans so familiar during the Great Leap period: "walking on two legs" and "self-reliance in the simultaneous development of industry and agriculture." Land was to be reclaimed, and irrigation systems were to be built by the peasants, using simple tools at their disposal. Rural communities were to build "backyard furnaces" to produce enough pig iron to allow China to surpass Great Britain in steel production. Other popular small-scale projects were electric power generators and chemical fertilizer plants.

Conceptually, the Great Leap model was not only rational but also had some economic validity.[23] However, there were unrealistic expectations and an overzealous implementation of the program. In an effort to fulfill the required quotas, workers often sacrificed quality for quantity. Quality also suffered from the lack of technical knowledge among the peasants. Some statistics on increased production were based on exaggeration and fabrication. Millions of tons of pig iron, much substandard and all a long way from being steel, were produced by backyard furnaces. Pig iron accumulated along railways, which could not possibly handle its movement, causing a serious bottleneck in the entire transport system.[24]

The merging of cooperatives into people's communes was an integral part of the Great Leap program. The communes were, in essence, devices to collectivize agricultural production on a scale much larger than that of the cooperatives. Unlike the APC, the commune became a local government, performing a multiplicity of functions in agriculture, industry, education, social welfare, public health, public works, and military defense. The peasants turned over to the collective entity their ownership in land, tools, draft animals, houses, and shares in the cooperatives. They then became members of a commune, of which they claimed collective ownership. In return, they were to receive five guarantees: food, clothing, housing, medical care, and education. During the early stage of commune development (1958), communal kitchens were installed to free more women for production. In some extreme cases, men and women lived in segregated communal dormitories, with their children in communal nurseries. The people's communes were hailed with great fanfare as the ideal collective life described by classical Marxism: "From each according to his abilities, to each according to his needs."

By the spring of 1959, there were 26,000 communes. Although there was no uniform size, an average commune consisted of about 2,000 households, or about 10,000 peasants. Within each commune, peasants were organized into production brigades and production teams, the basic units of the commune. This radical experiment encountered a host of problems. For instance, the peasants could not adjust to communal kitchens and dormitories. The demands imposed by the cadres—those selected for leadership positions—for long hours of work at a feverish pace, sapped the peasants' energy and enthusiasm. Without their tiny private plots to grow vegetables to supplement their meager diet, the peasants' general health declined. Initially, the peasants were neither willing nor able to make decisions under the commune setup, which required their participation. Their inexperience in the management of complex production activities also made them reluctant to assume responsibilities. In 1959 some corrective measures were implemented: Private garden plots were permitted, forced communal living was halted, and commune members were given adequate time for rest and recreation.

The numerous problems implicit in the Great Leap and communization, accompanied by the natural disasters of flood and drought, should have doomed the program. In 1958, when the Great Leap and commune programs were launched, there was a good harvest. In 1959 heavy floods and drought laid waste almost half the cultivable land. Then, in 1960, floods, drought, and pests ravaged millions of acres. To make matters worse, the Soviets withdrew all their technicians and advisers from China in June 1960 because of a disagreement over development strategy. The drastic reduction in agricultural production stalled the drive for rapid development of industry. Famine occurred and rationing was imposed in the communes. There were large purchases of grain from abroad. China's experience was typical of an agricultural setback in developing nations: Scarce foreign exchange had to be diverted from capital goods to food imports. A new policy had to be adopted to give first priority to a minimally sufficient food supply rather than to industrialization.

Post-Great Leap: Leadership Dissension and Economic Recovery

The failure of the Great Leap brought to a head growing division within the Chinese leadership, not only over development strategy but also over the ideological implications of the strategy. This division is frequently referred to as the "red" (politics) versus "expert" (technology) controversy. Mao later made a self-criticism for the errors committed in the Great Leap. Mao's most outspoken critic was Marshal Peng Dehuai, the defense minister and a Politburo member.[25] Peng's criticism focused on three effects of the Great Leap: (1) the damage to the long-term economic development of China, which must rely on technical proficiency rather than on sheer mobilization of the masses; (2) rejection of the Soviet development model, which caused a deterioration in Sino–Soviet relations; and (3) the obvious decline in morale and efficiency he had observed in his inspection of the armed forces. Marshal Peng's central concern seemed to be that China needed a modern army, which must rest on the development of heavy industries and technical skills to produce and operate advanced weapons, including nuclear weapons. Peng delivered his criticisms at an enlarged meeting at the Politburo in Lushan in July and August of 1959. Red Guard pamphlets, circulated later during the Cultural Revolution, revealed that Mao admitted some mistakes in the implementation of the Great Leap, but in the main, he vigorously defended his role and the policies associated with the program. He demanded a showdown at a subsequent enlarged meeting of the Central Committee and won. After these Lushan meetings, Marshal Peng was purged. Mao later was criticized for the purge of Peng. As planned before the Lushan meetings, Mao stepped down as the president of the People's Republic and handed the powerful position over to Liu Shaoqi, a leading party theoretician and an able administrator.[26]

The policies initiated by Liu Shaoqi reversed and corrected the Great Leap programs. It should be noted that before Liu assumed office, the Central Committee and its Politburo, in close consultation with the party's provincial secretaries, had already made a number of recommendations to correct the mistakes of the Great Leap. Some of these measures are given here as background to the policy dissension that came into full bloom during the Cultural Revolution. First, Liu called for a reintroduction of material incentives, such as private plots and free markets, to spur agricultural production. Second, he issued directives to those who managed state enterprises to pay strict attention to profits and losses: All enterprises must be managed and evaluated in terms of efficiency. Third, Liu insisted that technical "expertise" must command ideological "redness": Managers must have more authority in their plants than the ideologues. Fourth, he declared a relaxation of centralized planning by giving local units more freedom in setting their production quotas and targets. Fifth, he demanded that basic-level cadres observe strict discipline and report accurate statistics. Sixth, Liu introduced measures to reorganize the party by placing more emphasis on party discipline and institutional control mechanisms; these measures helped him consolidate his power and place his supporters in key positions.

The economic recovery soon took shape under Liu Shaoqi's direction.[27] Agricultural development was now the top economic priority. With the introduction of material incentives and a good harvest in 1962, economic conditions improved in the countryside. With hard work and an end to constant ideological and political interference, many of the industrial projects were completed and new ones were initiated, despite the withdrawal of Soviet technical assistance. The new economic policy continued to encourage the development of medium- and small-sized industries in the countryside, such as farm equipment factories and rural electrification plants. In order to reduce China's dependence on Soviet imports, self-reliance was stressed by encouraging technological innovation and exploration for such new resources as petroleum, found in Daqing. By 1964 Premier Zhou Enlai announced that the recovery was complete, and a Third Five-Year Plan was ready for implementation in 1966. The Chinese had learned that with some realistic adjustment to suit Chinese conditions, a centralized, planned economy, based on the Stalinist model, worked for China.

The Socialist Education Campaign, 1962–1965

The Socialist Education Campaign was the prelude to the Cultural Revolution.[28] It was a campaign of ideological education and of rectification of cadre behavior (which requires honest, hard-working leadership qualities). The main theme of the campaign was class struggle, a theme for which Mao fought hard when he resumed an active political role in the party at the tenth session of the Eighth Central Committee in 1962. Mao and other top leaders had become alarmed at reports of widespread corruption among the rural cadres. They feared that the free markets and private vegetable plots were fostering the growth of economic individualism, which posed a serious threat to the collective economy. The Socialist Education Movement consisted of three interrelated mass campaigns: (1) an educational campaign to assist the formation of poor and lower-middle-class peasant associations in order to prevent the rise of a class of well-to-do middle-class peasants; (2) a rectification campaign aimed at eliminating the corrupt practices of rural cadres, such as embezzlement, large wedding parties, and misuse of public property; and (3) a purification movement for the nation—with the People's Liberation Army (PLA) heroes as models—which stressed the virtues of self-sacrifice, the collective good, and endurance of hardship.

There was a great deal of controversy with respect to the directives and guidelines issued by the Central Committee. Mao's original instructions, the "earlier ten points," were altered by the Central Secretariat on instructions from Liu Shaoqi and Deng Xiaoping, who were then responsible for the day-to-day operation of the party. There were debates and quarrels among the top leaders, primarily between Mao and Liu, on methods of investigating corrupt cadres in rural communes.[29] Mao advocated open investigation in the communes by work teams of top cadres from the center; Liu wanted in-depth investigation by covert infiltration among the peasants, both to gather true information and to ferret out the corrupt cadres.[30] There was also divergence between Mao and Liu in terms of the role of the party and its leaders in the Socialist Education Movement. Mao intended it to be a mass education movement. Liu wanted a party-controlled rectification operation, with emphasis on corrective and remedial measures, in accordance with established norms within the party organization.

The entire Socialist Education Movement was carried out under a cloud of uncertainty and contradictory instructions. The local cadres, most of them recruited after land reform in the early 1950s, had developed strategies for survival; they knew how to play the game and how to protect themselves against outside investigations by work teams dispatched from far-away Beijing or from provincial capitals. If necessary, these bureaucratized cadres would withhold information or intimidate poor peasants. By 1965 most of the Socialist Education Movement had ended in failure, mainly because of disagreements over its implementation.

Only the campaign to emulate PLA heroes was a success. It began in the military, where the soldiers were required to form small groups to systematically study Mao's writings, particularly three essays on self-sacrifice and self-negation, written for the cadres during the Yanan days. Exemplary PLA companies were formed to demonstrate their living application of the thought of Mao. This ideological education campaign within the PLA was personally supervised by the new defense minister, Lin Biao. With the campaign's success in the military, a nationwide movement to emulate the PLA was launched.

The battle lines for the Cultural Revolution were now clearly drawn. Although the party apparatus under Liu Shaoqi and Deng Xiaoping had shown its disdain for Mao's mass mobilization approach (seeing it as disruptive to the routine operation of the party and government), the PLA, under Lin Biao, had not only embraced Mao's style but also applied Mao's teachings to their activities. Mao now saw that the cadres who monopolized the party apparatus, and the career-oriented status seekers, had become resistant to change and were reluctant to accept the new socialist values. The party could no longer be considered an effective instrument for the revolutionary change Mao so desired.

THE CULTURAL REVOLUTION

Before describing the events of the Cultural Revolution, let us look briefly at some of the issues underlying this great upheaval. If we survey the voluminous literature about the Cultural Revolution, we find several basic themes that serve to explain the causes of the upheaval.[31] One popular view depicted the Cultural Revolution as an "ideological crusade" aimed at preventing gradual erosion of the revolutionary spirit fostered by the early guerrilla experience of reliance on the masses and egalitarianism. Closely related to this was the idea that a thorough rectification campaign had to be waged in order to halt further growth of bureaucratic tendencies within the party and government. Another approach contended that as the regime moved toward further development, its leaders inevitably would reach a point where resolution of policy differences regarding strategy and priority would become more difficult. Prolonged dissension among the top leadership generally resulted in a power struggle between contending groups, with each jockeying for position and eventual vindication of its views. Thus, policy differences and power struggles among a divided leadership became intertwined. In addition, the contest for power among the top leadership in China probably was intensified by the question of who would succeed Mao as leader of the party.

There is some evidence that the launching of the Cultural Revolution coincided with the deterioration of Sino–Soviet relations and the escalation of the Vietnam War by the United States. Some scholars contend that the Soviet Union's offer to China in 1965 of a joint action to counteract the United States' escalation in Vietnam served as the catalyst that triggered the policy debate among China's top leaders.[32]

Events of the Cultural Revolution

The Cultural Revolution was officially launched on August 8, 1966, when the eleventh session of the Eighth Central Committee approved a sixteen-point guideline for conducting a thorough revolution. The revolution was to be concerned not only with the economic base (the socialist collectivized economy) but also with the superstructures (education, the arts, literature, and institutional arrangements).

Some nine or ten months before the Central Committee approved the guidelines, the battle had actually begun with a controversy over the political implications of a play by a historian and playwright, Wu Han. Wu Han, who was also deputy mayor of Beijing, and his superior, Peng Zhen, mayor of Beijing and a member of the Politburo, were politically allied with Liu Shaoqi. The play *Hai Rui's Dismissal from Office*, was a historical allegory about a Ming official's final vindication after dismissal from office. Mao and his supporters charged that the purpose of the play was to vindicate Marshal Peng Dehuai, who had been purged for his 1959 criticism of Mao and the Great Leap program. When a lengthy critique of the play by Yao Wenyuan, a radical writer from Shanghai and a supporter of Mao, was refused publication in the party press, Lin Biao had it published in the PLA paper, the *Liberation Army Daily*. This action forced publication in the leading party paper, the *People's Daily*, for nationwide circulation. At first the party leaders refused to admit the political implications of the play, saying it was a purely academic matter. After Mao's supporters intensified their attack, Liu Shaoqi and Peng Zhen appointed a team to investigate the matter. The team's final report, known as the "February Outline Report," written under the direct supervision of Peng Zhen and subsequently approved by the Politburo under the acting leadership of Liu Shaoqi, called for toleration of ideas within the party, less stress on the class struggle in academic and literary fields, and a rectification campaign against the radical left. Mao rebuked the "February Report" and asked for mass criticism of art and literature.

The literary debate was followed by mass criticism, which led to purges of top party and military leaders. The purged party leaders included Beijing municipal party committee members Peng Zhen and Wu Han. General Lo Ruiqing, the chief of staff for the PLA, was also purged because of his advocacy of military professionalism and his reluctance to implement the Socialist Education Movement in the army. The attack then spread to the party committees in China's two leading universities, Beida and Qinghua. The university students organized themselves as Red Guards, Mao's "revolutionary successors."[33]

Some high school and university students throughout China formed their own Red Guard groups to investigate cadres' behavior and attitudes.[34] This gave the students an opportunity not only to air their grievances against school officials and teachers but also to vent their frustrations with the system's inability to absorb the large number of graduating youths into appropriate jobs and to provide advancement opportunities.[35] By the autumn of 1966, the Red Guard movement had grown to such proportions that normal schooling had to be abandoned. Mass criticism, led by Red Guards against the party leaders and their apparatus, became an everyday occurrence. Party leaders were dragged out into the street for failing to provide the answers the students wanted to hear. To counter the roaming Red Guards organized by university students, party leaders in many localities formed their own Red Guards. This was a period of chaos and violence as factional Red Guard groups feuded endlessly with each other. All functions of the party and some activities of government came to a standstill. The only organization that was intact was the military. The Red Guard movement was supported by the radical leaders loyal to Mao and was fueled by access to confidential information about the leaders and their policy differences. From this movement the tabloid Red Guard wall posters became a major source of insight for the outside world into the policy debates. The Central Committee and its secretariat had by now ceased to function. In its place a Central Cultural Revolution Group—dominated by the radicals, with shifting membership—now served as the party's most authoritative spokespersons, with direct lines of communication to Mao.[36]

To outside observers, China in January and February 1967 was a gigantic spectacle of big-character posters, slogans, and endless processions and meetings in a sea of banners and portraits of Mao. Factionalized Red Guard groups openly employed physical force in their frequent skirmishes against each other all over China after the party machinery had been effectively paralyzed. The established party authorities, in some cases with the active support of the local PLA commands, mounted a counterattack against the radical Red Guards, which resulted in more bloodshed. The chaos and violence reached such alarming proportions that the only remaining alternative was to call in the military to restore order and to prevent any more violence. The PLA was ordered by Mao to intervene in this domestic turmoil in January 1967. The main tasks of the military were to fill the power vacuum created by the dismantled party and government organizations in the provinces, to supervise economic production, and to prevent violence by the rampaging Red Guards. The PLA was also to provide ideological training in universities and schools and thereby to exercise control over the students after their return to campus. Military control commissions, a device that had been employed for control and consolidation of the country in the early 1950s, reappeared in order to provide supervision and control in industries and many other institutions of the party and government. By the end of 1967, the military effectively controlled China and began rather uneasily to govern.[37]

Once in control, the military intervened in provincial politics to establish provincial revolutionary committees—a new power structure to temporarily replace the provincial party committees. The provincial revolutionary committees were made up of representatives of the PLA commands, the Red Guards as a mass organization, and the repentant veteran cadres—the "three-way alliance." With the inception of the revolutionary committees, the military became the real power. The success of the revolutionary committees was dependent upon the PLA's active intervention on behalf of Mao's supporters in Beijing. Order was gradually restored in the provinces as new revolutionary committees were formed to operate as party committees, purged and cleansed of "revisionist" tendencies, at least for the moment.

The Ninth Party Congress in Beijing in April 1969 declared the end of the Cultural Revolution and the reestablishment of the party structure. The party congress, dominated by Lin Biao and his military supporters, sanctioned "a revolutionary seizure of power," as described by Edgar Snow.[38] Unity, proclaimed by Lin Biao, was the major, but short-lived, theme of the Ninth Party Congress.

Effects of the Cultural Revolution

Although the effects of the Cultural Revolution on the Chinese political system will be discussed in later chapters, it may be helpful to outline here some of the long-term effects the upheaval had on the Chinese political scene.

One direct and far-reaching effect of the Cultural Revolution was the change it brought about in the relationship between the power center in Beijing and the provinces. Beginning in 1969 there was a steady increase in the representation of the provinces at the central decision-making level, as evidenced by the number of provincial party secretaries elected to the party's Central Committee (see Table 9.1 in Chapter 9). Second, the political prominence of the military at both the central and provincial levels was more apparent during and immediately after the Cultural Revolution. The increased involvement of provincial and military authorities in decision making, both at the center and in the provinces, benefited the more pragmatic veteran administrators (who had been allies of the regional and provincial military powers) in their conflict with the more radicalized party ideologues. This rise in political influence by the provincial leaders, many of whom had their power base in the military establishment, certainly must be attributed to the military intervention in the Cultural Revolution.[39] Third, the greatest impact of the Cultural Revolution was on education.[40] As we shall see in later chapters, not only were curriculum content and teaching methods reorganized, but educational opportunities were opened up for those of rural, nonelite background. However, abolition of the examination system for university entrance and for measuring competence at the higher educational levels contributed to low academic quality in students and, in the long run, impeded the country's advanced scientific and technological development and research. Fourth, the Cultural Revolution's stress on decentralization in decision making and on mass participation in economic development programs called attention to the evils of bureaucratization, so common in all planned economic systems. To some analysts, participation in economic decision making contributed both to more institutional responsiveness and to more institutional accountability to the masses.[41]

What final assessment can one make regarding the Cultural Revolution? In its official evaluation in 1981, the Chinese Communist Party admitted that the launching of the upheaval[42] by Mao was a serious mistake, in that it was responsible for "the most severe setback" and "the heaviest losses suffered by the party."[43] Party general secretary Hu Yaobang called the decade between 1966 and 1976 an economic, cultural, and educational "catastrophe" for China.[44] Perhaps the gravest indictment that can be leveled against the Cultural Revolution is that great human suffering was caused by the radicals' witch-hunting escapades and the breakdown of regular party authority.[45] Prior to the trial of the "Gang of Four," the Chinese media published reports of one episode after another of the maltreatment and persecution of cadres and intellectuals.

No one knows exactly how many party members and intellectuals were persecuted and tortured by the Red Guards and radicals. In many cases it was sufficient merely for the accused to be labeled "rightist" or "counterrevolutionary." The denounced and their relatives were subjected to beatings, imprisonment, loss of jobs, and banishment to rural areas to do menial labor. During the 1981 trial of the Gang of Four, it was revealed that 729,511 people had been persecuted, including a number of high-ranking party and state officials. Of that group, about 34,000 died.[46] Other official figures indicated that political persecution was even more widespread. In 1978 more than 300,000 victims of false accusations and persecution were rehabilitated and exonerated.[47] In 1980 some 13,000 overseas Chinese were found to have been wrongly accused of "crimes against the state."[48] At the same time, Deng Xiaoping was personally convinced that as many as 2.9 million people had been victims of persecution during the decade of the Cultural Revolution.[49]

There seems to be no question that the Cultural Revolution was not only a gross policy error in the name of ideological purity but was also a dark page in the CCP's history. In his interview with Oriana Fallaci, Deng Xiaoping emphasized that it actually had been a civil war that decimated the ranks of the experienced veteran cadres.[50] Further, a large percentage of China's intellectuals—educators, scholars, teachers, and scientists—were uprooted from their institutions, with their talents wasted in menial work in the countryside. Finally, the Cultural Revolution failed to produce any long-term fundamental institutional changes. Most of the institutional changes actually accomplished were either abandoned or have undergone drastic alterations.

THE "GANG OF FOUR" AND THE TRIAL[51]

The top radical leaders, later known as the "Gang of Four," included Jiang Qing, Zhang Chunqiao, Yao Wenyuan, and Wang Hongwen. Jiang Qing, Mao's wife, had been a member of the Central Committee's Cultural Revolution Group, which directed the Red Guards and the upheaval, and a vice-chairperson of the Cultural Revolution Committee in the PLA under Lin Biao. Zhang Chunqiao and Yao Wenyuan were active in the Shanghai Municipal Party Committee and had used Shanghai as a base for Mao's counterattacks against Liu Shaoqi's forces during the Cultural Revolution. It was Yao who wrote the first critique of the play *Hai Rui's Dismissal from Office*, which served as the first salvo against Liu Shaoqi at the beginning of the Cultural Revolution. Both Yao and Zhang, along with Jiang Qing, subsequently became key members of the Central Committee's Cultural Revolution Group. Wang Hongwen was a young leader of the Shanghai Congress of Revolutionary Workers Rebels, a workers' group that supported the radical activities in Shanghai during the Cultural Revolution.

The radicals were a minority group within the party and advocated continuous class struggle under the dictatorship of the proletariat. Their greatest strength came from activists and young university students. As a group, the radicals had little institutional support within the society. Their survival after the Cultural Revolution was dependent upon two factors: personal support from Chairman Mao, and their fragile alliances, first with Lin Biao and then with Zhou Enlai's forces. The fact that they served as Mao's spokespersons on ideological matters during and after the Cultural Revolution gave the radicals an aura of strength. While Mao remained mentally alert, few dared to oppose his views openly for fear of incurring his wrath. The radicals' control over the mass media and over the fields of art, literature, and drama added to their strength. Hua Guofeng later charged that they had "spread a host of revisionist fallacies" and that "metaphysics" ran wild and "idealism went rampant." The radicals' base of operation was limited to a few urban centers, primarily the municipalities under the direct administration of the central government: Beijing, Shanghai, and Tianjin. Their activities were mainly concentrated in the trade union federations in these cities.

Realizing their weakness in case of a showdown, the radicals helped build an urban militia in an attempt to secure a countervailing force to the PLA. The urban militia, which was organized and controlled by the various trade union federations and municipal party committees allied with the radicals, appeared to be a potentially powerful political instrument for the radical elements within the party.[52]

During and after the Cultural Revolution, the top radical leaders acquired influence and position in the party. The Ninth Party Congress in 1969 elected all four radical leaders members of the Central Committee. Zhang Chunqiao, as first secretary of the party's Shanghai Municipal Committee, was also elected to the Politburo. With the demise of Lin Biao, the four leaders were elected to the Politburo of the Tenth Central Committee in August 1973. In addition, Wang was said to have been Mao's personal choice for vice-chairman of the party, the post previously held by Lin Biao.

When the much-delayed Fourth National People's Congress, China's equivalent to parliament, convened in January 1975, it presented an appearance of surface unity. However, behind the scenes, the radicals, led by Jiang Qing, jockeyed for power against the moderates, who supported Premier Zhou Enlai. At first Zhou made some compromises with the radicals. Zhang Chunqiao was made a vice-premier and a director of the PLA's General Political Department, responsible for the political and ideological education of the troops. But at Zhou's insistence, Deng Xiaoping was brought back and rehabilitated as a vice-premier and as the chief of staff for the PLA. Deng, considered a chief villain by the radicals, had been purged along with Liu Shaoqi during the Cultural Revolution. Zhou, in failing health, wanted Deng, who was a capable and trusted colleague, to provide the needed leadership and experience in the central government.

The Fourth National People's Congress was dominated by Zhou and his party and government veterans. Zhou made it clear at the session that in order to speed up development and modernization of the economy, it was necessary to make changes, including implementing wage differentials to spur production, placing decision making in factories in the hands of plant managers and experts, and emphasizing scientific research through the upgrading of university education. Zhou even invoked one of Mao's statements on the need for a technical revolution and for borrowing scientific and technical know-how from abroad.[53] These changes were viewed by the radicals as reversing the gains of the Cultural Revolution.

The radicals' offensives soon converged on the individual whom they considered most vulnerable in the Zhou Enlai group, the rehabilitated Deng Xiaoping, who had been designated by Zhou to implement the economic acceleration and modernization. As Zhou became increasingly incapacitated by cancer (and was hospitalized most of the time in 1975), the attacks against him and Deng intensified in the radical-controlled media. The radicals were very much concerned about who would take over the premiership in the event of Zhou's death. Wang Hongwen was said to have been dispatched on several occasions to see Chairman Mao, to persuade him to designate either Zhang Chunqiao or Jiang Qing to succeed Zhou.[54] Their aim was to at least prevent Deng Xiaoping from assuming the premiership in case Zhou should die in office. In the radicals' eyes, Deng was the "capitalist roader" who had long advocated that hard work, not politics in command, was what really mattered: "Never mind about the color of the cat as long as it catches mice." In January 1976 Zhou Enlai died. There was a genuine outpouring of affection and respect by the masses for Zhou, but as soon as the nation had paid final tribute to the leader, the battle for succession began in earnest. Wall posters in the streets of Beijing demanded that Deng Xiaoping be purged again for his efforts to restore "bourgeois rights." The campaign of vilification against Deng culminated in the April 1976 Tiananmen incident.

The entire incident at Tiananmen Square was a large, spontaneous demonstration during the traditional festival in honor of the dead. The crowd, reportedly more than 100,000 at its height, was angered by the removal of flower wreaths placed in the square to honor the late Premier Zhou. The demonstrators created disturbances and damaged property belonging to the public security units stationed at public buildings on the square. The incident was a spontaneous show of support for the late premier's policies on material development and incentives. It could also be considered a show of support for Deng Xiaoping, who was a major target for attack by the radical leaders. Toward the end of the demonstration, the radicals entered this round-of-power contest by dispatching some units of the urban militia, presumably to quell the riots. By all accounts, this show of strength by the urban militia was rather feeble and unimpressive.[55]

While the urban militia did not prevent the mass riot at Tiananmen in April 1976, an estimated 3,000 to 4,000 demonstrators were arrested by the public security forces with the assistance of the urban militia.[56] Among those arrested were workers, cadres, and intellectuals.[57] The CCP subsequently declared the demonstration "a revolutionary mass action against the radicals."[58]

The radicals used the incident for their own purposes. They labeled the disorderly conduct of the demonstrators in support of Zhou and Deng as "counterrevolutionary" and blamed Deng for instigating the incident. The radicals at this time had the support of Mao and enough Politburo members to have Deng dismissed from all positions of power and, thereby, to remove him as a candidate to succeed Zhou Enlai for the premiership. The spontaneous outburst of the huge crowd in the Tiananmen Square incident demonstrated the radicals' alienation from the masses. The radicals, nevertheless, won the first round of the succession struggle by removing Deng Xiaoping from the seat of power for the second time. The compromise choice of Hua Guofeng as first vice-chairman of the CCP, a newly designated position, and as acting premier may have been made personally by Mao, who surely by then had realized the danger of a split within the top echelons of the party. While Mao lived, he somehow kept the factions in balance—even, at times, tipping the balance slightly in favor of his radical disciples.

The campaign to criticize Deng Xiaoping sputtered forward, without arousing any genuine mass support or enthusiasm, from April through July, ending in August when a series of major earthquakes shook the Beijing area. The ancient Chinese saying that unusual natural phenomena generally precede some earth-shaking event seemed prophetic: Chairman Mao died on September 9, 1976, at the age of eighty-two. While the nation again mourned the loss of a great leader, political maneuvering for the succession contest reached its peak. At first the open dispute revolved around Mao's will. The radicals claimed that the will called for the gains and values of the Cultural Revolution to be upheld by Mao's successors. The moderates, now a close alliance of party, government, and veteran military cadres, claimed that Mao had designated in writing that Hua Guofeng be named his successor: "With you in charge, I am at ease."[59] These were merely skirmishes of the pen. The real combat took place from the end of September to the first week of October at Politburo meetings, which included some heated debates. Reportedly, the radical leaders proposed that Jiang Qing be named the new party chairperson, and Zhang Chunqiao the new premier. It has also since been reported that the radical leaders mapped out a military coup to be staged in Shanghai as a last resort in the contest for power.[60]

The final decision of the Central Committee on October 7 was firm and direct: Hua Guofeng was to succeed Mao as chairman of the party, and all opposition to this decision had to be silenced. Almost simultaneously, the four radical leaders were placed under arrest by the special security force No. 8341, directly under the supervision of the Central Committee and the Politburo and under the personal command of Politburo member Wang Dongxing. Swiftly, regular PLA units, all under the command of Politburo members, moved into Beijing, Shanghai, and other cities to disarm the urban militia. The PLA placed these cities under temporary military control to prevent any disturbances. By October 24 Hua's successful move against the radicals was complete, and an estimated one million Chinese gathered in Tiananmen Square to cheer a new leader and to celebrate the dawn of a new era for China.

The Gang of Four, along with twelve other principal defendants (all former ranking military officers closely associated with Lin Biao), were tried during November and December 1980 under the recently enacted criminal code. The trial was open to selected observers and was televised in order to demonstrate the need for a return to law and order. The pragmatic leaders hoped that by using the legal process, rather than summary execution, public confidence and respect for socialist legality would be restored. Nonetheless, the staging of the trial by the pragmatic leaders served to vindicate the position they took during the Cultural Revolution.

The new leadership also wanted to tie the Gang of Four to Lin Biao's attempted assassination of Mao and the abortive coup d'état, even though each faction had its own goals. This linkage was designed to achieve two objectives. First, it attempted to protect Mao's reputation and to downplay his close relationship with the radicals on trial. Second, the strategy was also intended to shield Hua Guofeng. An agreement reportedly was worked out to delete any reference to Hua's association with the radicals—particularly his role in suppressing the 1976 Tiananmen demonstration.[61]

The radical leaders and the former top military brass under Lin Biao were convicted of persecuting veteran party leaders, of plotting to assassinate Mao, and of organizing a secret armed rebellion. All but two of the defendants received sentences ranging from sixteen to twenty years in prison. Jiang Qing and Zhang Chunqiao were sentenced to death, with a two-year stay of execution.[62] In January 1983 the Supreme People's Court ruled that since both Jiang and Zhang had shown "sufficient repentance" and "had not resisted reform in a flagrant way" during the two-year reprieve period, the execution would not be carried out in 1983. (Jiang Qing died in May 1991 by committing suicide while under house arrest.)

The trial of the radical leaders seems to have been successful not only in repudiating the Cultural Revolution but also in meting out punishment through the judicial process. The trial represented a victory for the pragmatic leaders who were themselves victims of the Cultural Revolution. However, for cynics inside and outside of China, the trial was just another episode in the grand tradition of the Beijing opera.

The arrest of the radicals in 1976 paved the way for the twice-purged Deng Xiaoping to return to power. Gradually, Deng was able to outmaneuver the conservative hard-liners within the party. By the beginning months of 1979 he was finally able to pack the party congress with his supporters, who in turn elected Deng's handpicked leaders to control the party's Central Committee and its Politburo. The stage was now set for launching Deng's reform program, which had been dominating Chinese politics for the past decades. Deng's pragmatic reform has been called "China's Second Revolution."[63]

NOTES

1. For a detailed account of the events in 1927, see Franklin Houn, *A Short History of Chinese Communism* (Upper Saddle River, N.J.: Prentice Hall, 1967), pp. 21–33.
2. Ibid., pp. 35–38. Also see Sterling Seagrave, *The Soong Dynasty* (New York: Harper & Row, 1985), pp. 239–46.
3. James Chiuh Hsiung, *Ideology and Practice: The Evolution of Chinese Communism* (New York: Praeger, 1970), pp. 61–62. Also see Edgar Snow, *Red Star Over China* (New York: Grove Press, 1961).
4. John M. H. Lindbeck, "Transformation in the Chinese Communist Party," in *Soviet and Chinese Communist: Similarities and Differences*, ed. Donald Treadgold (Seattle: University of Washington Press, 1967), p. 76; and Stuart Schram, "Mao Tse-tung and the Chinese Political Equilibrium," *Government and Opposition*, 4, no. 1 (Winter 1969), 141–42.
5. Hsiung, *Ideology and Practice*, pp. 45–46; and Dick Wilson, *The Long March 1935: The Epic of Chinese Communism's Survival* (New York: Avon Books, First Discus Printing, 1973). Also see Edward E. Rice, *Mao's Way* (Berkeley: University of California Press, 1972), pp. 83–88. Also see Harrison E. Salisbury, *The Long March: The Untold Story* (New York: Harper & Row, Basic, 1985) and Zhou Zheng, "Long March 50th Anniversary: General Looks Back," *Beijing Review*, 40 (October 6, 1986), 19–25.
6. Hsiung, *Ideology and Practice*, pp. 52–53; and John King Fairbank, *The United States and China*, pp. 269–70.
7. Lindbeck, "Transformation in the Chinese Communist Party," p. 76.
8. See *The Selected Works of Mao Tse-tung* (Peking: Foreign Language Press, 1967), II, 339–84; III, 205–70.
9. Fairbank, *United States and China*, p. 313.
10. Houn, *Short History of Chinese Communism*, pp. 173–77.
11. E. Stuart Kirby, "Agrarian Problems and Peasantry," in *Communist China, 1949–1969: A Twenty Year Appraisal*, ed. Frank N. Trager and William Henderson (New York: New York University Press, 1970), p. 160.
12. Ezra Vogel, "Land Reform in Kwangtung 1951–1953: Central Control and Localism," *China Quarterly*, 38 (April–June 1969), 27–62.
13. Ibid., 27–62.
14. Houn, *Short History of Chinese Communism*, p. 159.
15. Ibid., p. 164; and Kirby, "Agrarian Problems and Peasantry," p. 162.

16. See the official documents dealing with the debate over the cooperatives. The texts of these documents are in Robert R. Bowie and John K. Fairbank, *Communist China, 1955–1959: Policy Documents with Analysis* (Cambridge, Mass.: Harvard University Press, 1965), pp. 92–126.

17. Discussion on the First Five-Year Plan was based on the following sources: Alexander Eckstein, *China's Economic Revolution* (London and New York: Cambridge University Press, 1977), pp. 31–66; E. L. Wheelwright and Bruce McFarlane, *The Chinese Road to Socialism: Economics of the Cultural Revolution* (New York: Monthly Review Press, 1970), pp. 31–65; and Houn, *Short History of Chinese Communism*, pp. 177–85.

18. Houn, *Short History of Chinese Communism*, pp. 178–79; Wheelwright and McFarlane, *Chinese Road to Socialism*, p. 35.

19. Houn, *Short History of Chinese Communism*, pp. 178–79.

20. Ibid., pp. 178–79.

21. Wheelwright and McFarlane, *Chinese Road to Socialism*, p. 36.

22. Discussion in this section on the Great Leap program is based on these sources: Houn, *Short History of Chinese Communism*, pp. 181–82; Fairbank, *United States and China*, pp. 369–75; Eckstein, *China's Economic Revolution*, pp. 54–65; Roderick MacFarquhar, *The Origin of the Cultural Revolution: The Contradictions among the People, 1956–1957* (New York: Columbia University Press, 1974), pp. 57–74; Hsiung, *Ideology and Practice*, pp. 185–99.

23. Eckstein, *China's Economic Revolution*, p. 59.

24. Byung-joon Ahn, *Chinese Politics and the Cultural Revolution: Dynamics of Policy Processes* (Seattle, Wash. and London: University of Washington Press, 1976), pp. 31–47.

25. *The Case of Peng Teh-huai* (Hong Kong: Union Research Institute; 1968); and J. D. Simmons, "Peng Teh-huai: A Chronological Re-examination," *The China Quarterly*, 37 (January–March 1968), 120–38. Also see Jurgen Domes, *Peng Te-Huai: The Man and the Image* (Palo Alto, Calif.: Stanford University Press, 1986).

26. There are many accounts of the Lushan decision. The latest is in Ahn, *Chinese Politics and the Cultural Revolution*, pp. 38–44.

27. The brief survey here is based on Eckstein, *China's Economic Revolution*, pp. 202–5, and on Houn, *Short History of Chinese Communism*, pp. 182–85. Also see Ahn, *Chinese Politics and the Cultural Revolution*, pp. 48–86, for a more detailed account of the recovery for the period 1962–65.

28. Discussion of the Socialist Education Campaign is drawn from these sources: Hsiung, *Ideology and Practice*, pp. 200–16; Richard Baum and Frederick C. Teiwes, *Ssu-Ch'ing: The Socialist Educational Movement of 1962–1966* (Berkeley: Center for Chinese Studies, University of California, 1968); Ahn, *Chinese Politics and the Cultural Revolution*, pp. 89–122; Philip Bridgham, "Mao's 'Cultural Revolution': Origin and Development," *China Quarterly*, 29 (January–March 1967), 1–35; Richard Baum and Frederick Teiwes, "Liu Shao-chi and the Cadres Question," *Asian Survey*, 8, no. 4 (April 1968), 323–45; and Richard Baum, *Prelude to Revolution: Mao, the Party and the Peasant Question, 1962–1966* (New York: Columbia University Press, 1975).

29. C. S. Chen, ed., *Rural People's Communes in Lien-chiang*, trans. Charles P. Ridley (Stanford, Calif.: Hoover Institution, 1969); Baum and Teiwes, "Liu Shao-chi and the Cadres Question"; and Ahn, *Chinese Politics and the Cultural Revolution*, pp. 99–108. Also see Hsiung, *Ideology and Practice*, pp. 206–8.

30. Ahn, *Chinese Politics and the Cultural Revolution*, p. 103; and for an insight into the interpersonal behavior of the cadres, see Michel Oksenberg, "The Institutionalization of the Chinese Communist Revolution: The Ladder of Success on the Eve of the Cultural Revolution," *The China Quarterly*, 36 (October–December 1968), 61–92.

31. For a bibliography on the subject, see James C. F. Wang, *The Cultural Revolution in China: An Annotated Bibliography* (New York and London: Garland Publishing, Inc., 1976). Also see the following books on the Cultural Revolution: Goo Yuan, *Born Red: A Chronicle of the Cultural Revolution* (Stanford, Calif.: Stanford University Press, 1987); Yang Jiang, *Six Chapters from My Life "Down Under,"* trans. Howard Goldblat (Hong Kong: The Chinese University Press, 1983); and Judith Shapiro and Liang Heng, *Cold Winds, Warm Winds: Intellectual Life in China Today* (Middletown, Conn.: Wesleyan University Press, 1986).

32. See Donald Zagoria, *Vietnam Triangle: Moscow, Peking, Hanoi* (New York: Pegasus, 1967); Uri Ra'amam, "Peking's Foreign Policy 'Debate,' 1965–1966," in *China's Policies in Asia and America's Alternatives*, ed. Tang Tsou (Chicago: University of Chicago Press, 1968), pp. 23–71; Robert Scalapino, "The Cultural Revolution and Chinese Foreign Policy," in *The Cultural Revolution: 1967 in Review* (Ann Arbor: Michigan Papers in Michigan Studies No. 2, Center for Chinese Studies, University of Michigan, 1968), pp. 1–15.

33. For an account of the struggle at these two universities during the Cultural Revolution, see Victor Nee, *The Cultural Revolution at Peking University* (New York: Monthly Review Press, 1969); and William Hinton,

Hundred Day War: The Cultural Revolution at Tsinghua (New York and London: Monthly Review Press, 1972).

34. See Gordon Bennett and Ronald N. Montaperto, *Red Guard: The Political Bibliography of Dai Hsiao-ai* (New York: Anchor Books, Doubleday, 1972).

35. See Michel Oksenberg, "China: Forcing the Revolution to a New Stage," *Asian Survey* 7, no. 1 (January 1967), 1–15; and John Israel, "The Red Guards in Historical Perspective: Continuity and Change in Chinese Youth Movement," *China Quarterly*, 30 (April–June 1967), 1–32.

36. See Lowell Dittmer, "The Cultural Revolution and the Fall of Liu Shao-chi," *Current Scene* 11, no. 1 (January 1973), 1–13; also his *Liu Shaoqui and the Chinese Cultural Revolution,* revised ed. (Armonk, N.Y., 1997); Israel, "Red Guards in Historical Perspective," 1–32.

37. Philip Bridgham, "Mao's Cultural Revolution in 1967: The Struggle to Seize Power," *China Quarterly*, 34 (April–June 1968), 6–36; Ellis Joffe, "The Chinese Army in the Cultural Revolution: The Politics of Intervention," *The Current Scene* 2, no. 18 (December 7, 1970), 1–25; William Whitson, *The Chinese Communist High Command: A History of Military Politics, 1927–69* (New York: Holt, Rinehart & Winston, 1971); Jean Esmein, *The Chinese Cultural Revolution* (Garden City, N.Y.: Anchor Books, Doubleday, 1973); Stanley Karnow, *Mao and China: From Revolution to Revolution* (New York: Viking, 1972), pp. 276–316.

38. Edgar Snow, "Mao and the New Mandate," *The World Today*, 25, no. 7 (July 1969), 290.

39. Parris H. Chang, "Regional Military Power: The Aftermath of the Cultural Revolution," *Asian Survey*, 12, no. 12 (December 1972), 999–1013, and "The Revolutionary Committee and the Party in the Aftermath of the Cultural Revolution," *Current Scene* 8, no. 8 (April 15, 1970), 1–10.

40. "Recent Development in Chinese Education," *Current Scene* 10, no. 1 (July 1972), 1–6.

41. See Richard M. Pfeffer, "Serving the People and Continuing the Revolution," *China Quarterly*, 52 (October–December 1972), 620–53.

42. "On Questions of Party History—Resolution on Certain Questions in the History of Our Party Since the Founding of the People's Republic of China" (adopted by the Sixth Plenary Session of the Eleventh Central Committee of the CPC on June 27, 1981), *Beijing Review*, 27 (July 6, 1981), 20.

43. Ibid.

44. Summary of an interview with the visiting editor of the Greek communist party newspaper, reported in *Ta Kung Pao Weekly Supplement* (Hong Kong), December 8, 1980, p. 3.

45. For a series of articles assessing the impact of the Cultural Revolution, see *Asian Survey*, 12, no. 12 (December 1972). Also see Maurice Meisner, *Mao's China: A History of the People's Republic* (New York: The Free Press, 1977), pp. 340–59; and David Bonavia, "The Fate of the 'New-Born Things' of China's Cultural Revolution," *Pacific Affairs*, 51, no. 2 (Summer 1981), 177–94. Also see William Hinton, *Shenfan: The Cultural Revolution in a Chinese Village* (New York: Random House, 1983).

46. *A Great Trial in Chinese History* (New York: Pergamon Press, 1981), pp. 20–21.

47. Jiang Hua, president of the Supreme People's Court, reported that 326,000 people framed or falsely imprisoned had been exonerated after investigation by the court. See Michael Weisskopf, "China Reports End of Trials," Washington Post Service, as reprinted in *Honolulu Advertiser,* January 28, 1983, p. A-18.

48. *People's Daily,* July 16, 1980, p. 1. Also see Nien Cheng, *Life and Death in Shanghai* (New York: Grove Press, 1987). The personal account was excerpted in *Time* June 8, 1987, pp. 42–56.

49. Fox Butterfield, *China: Alive in the Bitter Sea* (New York: Times Books, 1982), p. 349.

50. "Cleaning Up Mao's Feudal Mistakes," *The Guardian,* September 21, 1980, p. 16.

51. Suggested readings about the downfall of the Gang of Four include Jurgen Domes, "China in 1976: Tremors of Transition," *Asian Survey*, 13, no. 1 (January 1977), 1–17; Peter R. Moody, Jr., "The Fall of the Gang of Four: Background Notes on the Chinese Counterrevolution," *Asian Survey*, 17, no. 8 (August 1977), 711–23; Jurgen Domes, "The 'Gang of Four' and Hua Kuo-feng: Analysis of Political Events in 1976–76," *China Quarterly*, 71 (September 1977), 473–97; James C. F. Wang, "The Urban Militia as a Political Instrument in the Power Contest in China in 1976," *Asian Survey*, 18, no. 6 (June 1978), 541–59; and Andres D. Onate, "Hua Kuo-feng and the Arrest of 'Gang of Four,'" *China Quarterly*, 75 (September 1978), 540–65. For coverage at the trial by the Chinese press, see "Written Judgment of the Special Court Under the Supreme People's Court of the PRC," *Beijing Review*, 5 (February 2, 1981), 13–28; "Trial of Lin Biao and Jiang Qing Cliques—Major Points of the Indictment," *Beijing Review*, 47 (November 24, 1980), 12–17; "Trial of Lin-Jiang Cliques: Indictment of the Special Procuratorate," *Beijing Review*, 48 (December 1, 1980), 9–28. For Chinese public reaction to the trial, see Butterfield, *China: Alive in the Bitter Sea*, pp. 357–61; Richard Bernstein, *From the Center of the Earth: The Search for the Truth About China* (Boston and Toronto: Little, Brown, 1982), pp. 107–8; Frank Ching, "Mao's Widow Finally Finds Her Place in the Spotlight," *Asian Wall Street Journal Weekly,* December 22, 1980, p. 6.

52. Wang, "Urban Militia in China," p. 550.

53. Chou En-lai, "Report on the Work of the Government," *Peking Review*, 4 (January 24, 1975), 24.

54. "The Crux of 'Gang of Four's' Crimes to Usurp Party and State Power," *Peking Review*, 2 (January 7, 1977), 30.
55. Wang, "Urban Militia in China," pp. 552–53.
56. For an eyewitness account, see Roger Garside, *Coming Alive: China After Mao* (New York: McGraw-Hill, 1981), pp. 114–41. For the current status of those who were still under detention, see *Ming Pao* (Hong Kong), April 9, 1981, p. 1.
57. *Beijing Review*, 46 (November 17, 1978), 13.
58. "Communiqué of the Third Plenary Session of the Eleventh Central Committee," *Beijing Review*, 52 (December 29, 1978) 14. Also see "Carry Forward the Revolutionary Tiananmen Spirit," editorial of *Renmin Ribao*, reprinted in *Beijing Review*, 15 (April 13, 1979), 9–13; *Ming Pao* (Hong Kong), April 8 and 9, 1981, p. 1; Garside, *Coming Alive: China After Mao*, pp. 114–41; *Beijing Review*, 46 to 48 (November 17–December 1, 1978).
59. See "Chairman Mao Will Live For Ever in Our Hearts," *Peking Review*, 39 (September 24, 1976), 35; and "Comrade Wu Teh's Speech at the Celebration Rally in the Capitol," *Peking Review*, 44 (October 29, 1976), 12.
60. Wang, "Urban Militia in China," pp. 555–58.
61. See Lowell Dittmer, "China in 1981: Reform, Readjustment, Rectification," *Asian Survey*, 22, 5 (January 1982), 33–34. Also see Ching, "Mao's Widow Finally Finds Her Place in the Spotlight," *The Asian Wall Street Journal Weekly,* December 22, 1980, p. 6; and David Bonavia, "Exit Jiang left With Hua Not Far Behind," *Far Eastern Economic Review* (January 2, 1981), 12.
62. For analyses of Hua Guofeng's problems, see Parris Chang, "Chinese Politics: Deng's Turbulent Quest," *Problems of Communism*, 30 (January–February 1981), 1–21, and "The Last Stand of Deng's Revolution," 3–19; Lowell Dittmer, "China in 1980: Modernization and Its Discontents," *Asian Survey*, 21, no. 1 (January 1981), 36–42, and "China in 1981: Reform, Readjustment, Rectification," 33–35, 42–43; Xu Sangu, "Starting with Hua Guofeng's Resignation of Premiership," *Perspective* (Hong Kong), 557 (September 16, 1980), 4–6; Frank Ching, "Central Committee Said to Plan Consideration of Hua's Resignation Soon," *Asian Wall Street Journal Weekly*, December 29, 1980, p. 2; Yen Qing, "What Happened to Hua Guofeng," *Ming Pao* (Hong Kong), January 22, 23, and 24, 1981; Dorothy Grouse Fontana, "Background to the Fall of Hua Guofeng," *Asian Survey*, 22, no. 3, (March 1983), 237–60; "Hua Guofeng's Political Fate," *Issues and Studies*, 18, no. 2 (February 1981), 4–6; "The Two Whatevers and Discussions on Criteria for Truth," *Beijing Review*, 44 (November 2, 1981), 24–25, 28; "Document of the CCP's Central Committee, Chung-fa, 1981, No. 23," *Issues and Studies*, 92, no. 12 (December 1981), 71–78.
63. Harry Harding, *China's Second Revolution: Reform after Mao* (Washington, D.C.: The Brookings Institution, 1987).

SUGGESTED READINGS

Baum, Richard. *Burying Mao: Chinese Politics in the Age of Deng Xiaoping* (Princeton, NJ: Princeton University Press, 1974).

Goodman, David S. G. *Deng Xiaoping and the Chinese Revolution* (London and New York: Routledge, 1994).

Goodman, David S. G., and Beverly Hopper (eds.). *China's Quiet Revolution* (Melbourne, Australia: Longman Cheshire, 1994).

Harding, Harry. *China's Second Revolution: Reform under Mao* (Washington, D.C.: Brookings Institution, 1988).

Houn, Franklin. *A Short History of Chinese Communism* (Upper Saddle River: Prentice Hall, 1967).

Karnow, Stanley. *Mao and China: From Revolution to Revolution* (New York: Viking, 1972).

Rice, Edward. *Mao's Way* (Berkeley: University of California Press, 1972).

Salisbury, Harrison E. *The Long March: The Untold Story* (New York: Harper & Row, Basic, 1985).

Schoenhals, Michael (ed.). *China's Cultural Revolution, 1966–1969: Not a Dinner Party* (Armonk, N.Y.: M. E. Sharpe, 1996).

White, Lynn T., III. *Politics of Chop: The Organizational Causes of Violence in China's Cultural Revolution* (Princeton, N.J.: Princeton University Press, 1991).

Wilson, Dick. *The Long March 1935: The Epic of Chinese Communism's Survival* (New York: Avon Books, 1973).

Chapter Three

The Erosion of Chinese Communist Ideology

Marxism-Leninism, Mao's Thought, Dengism, and the Thinking of Jiang Zemin

Let us begin by defining the term *ideology*. It may be defined as the manner in which an individual or a group thinks. Ideology is a set of political values, feelings, and ideas that guides individuals to act or behave in a certain manner for the purpose of achieving a particular goal. It has been said that the success of the Chinese communist movement rests on two basic elements: an effective set of organizations, guided by a set of clearly stated principles.[1] Schurmann differentiates among ideologies in terms of the consequences the ideas may generate. If an idea leads to the formulation of a policy or an action, it is a "practical" ideology; but if an idea is employed for the sole purpose of molding the thinking of the individual, it is a "pure" ideology.[2] Pure ideology is a set of theories; practical ideology is based on experiences and practices. The Chinese make a clear distinction between these two sets of ideologies in their political communication. To the Chinese, the ideas of Karl Marx and of Lenin are pure ideology that have universal application. In the Chinese language, pure ideology is called *lilun* or *zhuyi*, and practical ideology is *sixiang*.

The Chinese communist ideology consists of three basic elements: (1) the influence of the Chinese Revolution, particularly the intellectual ferment of the May Fourth Movement; (2) the ideas of Marxism-Leninism; and (3) the thought of Mao Zedong. Let us keep in mind that while the thought of Mao constitutes a major portion of the Chinese communist ideology, it is by no means the only element. In the sections that follow, we shall briefly discuss the origin and the nature of the main elements of Chinese communist ideology today, including Deng Xiaoping Theory or Dengism and Jiang Zemin's theoretical thinking.

However, it is important to note that some Chinese intellectuals, including Mao, were influenced by the ideas of anarchism that were a part of modern Chinese thought.

As explained by Peter Zattow, Chinese anarchists drew their inspiration from the belief in human goodness associated with Confucianism, the egalitarianism of Daoism, and the selflessness of Buddhism;[3] and beginning with the May Fourth Movement they merged these traditional thoughts with Western ideas such as Marxism.

MARXISM-LENINISM

The theoretical foundation of the Chinese communist ideology is Marxism-Leninism. It is the guiding principle for both the party and the state. It is pure theory with universal applications. Let us examine briefly the essential features of Marxism.

The first key Marxist concept is *historical materialism.* Karl Marx began with the assertion that the character of any society is determined by the manner or the mode of production by which people make their living. The mode of production determines social structure and political order; it also determines social ideas and customs. Therefore, to change the minds of people, it is necessary to change the mode of production or the economic system. This, Marx said, is the universal truth and the "evolutionary law of human history." Every human society has at its foundation an economic base, the mode of production that produces goods and services to support human life. This economic basis, in turn, is supported by superstructures of culture, law, courts, and governmental instututions.

Having asserted that materialism determines the nature of society, Marx described how human history evolves in a predictable pattern. This is *dialectical materialism.* For this, Marx borrowed the theory of the dialectical development of history from the German philosopher Hegel. Hegel proposed that every idea or thesis, once started, goes too far and becomes exaggerated or false. When this inevitably happens, the thesis is met with an opposing idea, the *antithesis.* These two opposing ideas clash, and out of the conflict comes the *synthesis,* an entirely new idea that contains the essential truths of both opposing ideas. Soon this synthesis becomes a thesis, and the process of change continues, ad infinitum. Marx used Hegelian dialectics to predict that a communist society would inevitably result from this historical process after society had passed through certain stages: first, the primitive communal society, with no class differentiation; then the slave society, with the concept of ownership and with caste status separating the slaves and the masters; next, feudal society, with pronounced class distinctions between the lord and his serfs; and the fourth stage of development, the capitalistic society, with the owners of the means of production pitted against the impoverished workers, who lead a meager existence, suffering exploitation by the capitalists. Marx predicted that this struggle between the capitalists and the working class would result in a communist society where there would be no class distinctions. The economy would be operated under Marx's dictum: "From each according to his abilities, to each according to his needs." Finally, the state, with its coercive instruments, would no longer be needed and would wither away.

Marx believed that the course of human history must pass through these stages, but before the arrival of the communist stage, there must be intense class struggle. In fact, Marx maintained that human history is a history of class warfare. As long as property or the means of production is owned by private individuals for the purpose of exploiting the work of others, there will always be a struggle between the two classes. It is an unfair struggle, since all the superstructures of society—laws, police, courts, and other political institutions—support the property-owning class. The property-owning class has all the privileges, sanctioned by social customs and mores. Marx argued that this situation cannot endure long; the working class has no alternative except to forcefully overthrow the existing social order. He concludes the *Communist Manifesto* with a call for revolution: "Workers of the world, unite! You have nothing to lose but your chains."

It is not the purpose of this section to engage in a critique of Marxism. However, we need to keep in mind that two basic responses to this doctrine have developed under different sets of circumstances, in answer to the appalling conditions of the early industrialization Marx criticized. One was the evolution of social democracy in the West, which brought changes through constitutional reform and progressive social legislation. The other was the Russian Bolshevik Revolution, which brought change through violent revolution.

Lenin made two basic modifications to Marxism. One was his treatise on imperialism, published in 1916. Marx had predicted that a forceful but spontaneous workers' revolution would descend upon the capitalistic European societies, such as England, France, and Germany. But for over seventy years, no revolution by the working class occurred in continental Europe. When the revolution came, it came to Russia, an industrially backward country. Even more significant was the fact that the lot of workers in the advanced capitalist countries had improved through progressive social legislation. How could the disciples of Marx explain this phenomenon? Lenin answered this question in his treatise *Imperialism*. Lenin argued that capitalism had broken away from the cycle of contradiction as prescribed by Marx in his dialectical materialism theory. Capitalism had expanded and grown by seeking new sources of raw materials abroad, in undeveloped parts of the world, and by setting up factories with cheap labor in colonies, which in turn became the ready markets for the manufactured goods. Lenin rationalized the situation by claiming that the capitalist nations had developed a monopoly that accumulated enormous profits from the backward areas of the world and then rewarded labor at home with better wages and working conditions from those profits. By making concessions to labor at home, the capitalists were able to maintain the status quo, preventing a workers' revolution. Therefore, the imperialists' exploitation of the backward areas of the world had sustained capitalism. Capitalism would not collapse as long as colonial power and monopolistic capitalism could successfully exploit the backward areas of Russia, China, India, and Africa. From this analysis Lenin concluded that the first blow of the revolution must be dealt to the weakest part in the system, the colonial complex in Asia and Africa. The Bolshevik Revolution and Lenin's treatise on imperialism made sense to the Chinese intellectuals, who were frustrated by their previous efforts in revolution making. Now there was a meaningful and emotional link between nationalism on one hand and anti-imperialism on the other.

Lenin's second major modification of Marxism was in regard to organization for the revolution, which Marx had not discussed beyond saying that it would be spontaneous. In *What's To Be Done?* Lenin outlined his strategy for the working class to achieve and to maintain political power. His first key principle was that a revolutionary party was needed, led by a highly disciplined and dedicated corps of professional revolutionaries, to serve as the vanguard of the proletariat. Lenin insisted on professionalism and self-discipline in this vanguard. Another key organizational principle was the doctrine of "democratic centralism." This called for centralized decision making, with free discussion at the policy formulation level. Once a decision was made at the top, however, all must abide by it without dissent. Lenin insisted on strict discipline within a "single, unified party." The Leninist organizational model was hierarchical and pyramidal, with the supreme power vested in the hands of a few at the apex. At the base of the pyramid was the level of primary organizations—units or cells. Between the base and the apex were a myriad of intermediary organizations (see Chapter 4).

A few remarks on the state of Marxism-Leninism in China after Mao may be in order. First, there continues to be rising doubt about the validity of Marxism-Leninism among the young. American journalists stationed in China have reported an increasing lack of interest among China's youth in the compulsory study of Marxism.[4] Reportedly, a survey taken at Fudan University in Shanghai revealed that only 30 percent of the students polled believed in communism; but figures for 1997–98 showed that about 10 to 20 percent of undergraduates in some universities in Beijing have become party members as a way to ensure success in life.[5] Disillusionment about communism and the dissidents' campaign for democracy and human rights prompted Deng Xiaoping in 1979 to insist that the party adopt some basic guidelines within which criticism about the communist system could be tolerated. These guidelines directed that no one should speak against the socialist road, the dictatorship of the proletariat, the leadership of the party, Marxism-Leninism, and Mao's thought.[6] Presumably, these guidelines were intended to put a stop to the rising tide of dissent against communism.

In 1979, propaganda efforts were mounted to reiterate the applicability of Marxism-Leninism and to reinterpret its meaning in the light of the aberration of the Cultural Revolution and the liberal reforms introduced in the economic system. In July 1981, in his maiden speech as the new party chief, Hu Yaobang called Marxism the "crystallization of scientific thinking" and theory verified in practice. Hu then cautioned that Marxism was only a guide to action; as a theory it should neither be looked upon as a "rigid dogma to be followed unthinkingly" nor viewed as comprising "all the truth in the unending course of human history."[7] In answer to those who advocated the abandonment of socialism in China, numerous theoretical studies were published in the media to justify the socialist nature of Chinese society. For instance, in a theoretical essay, the vice president of the CCP's party school stated that socialism is basically public ownership of the means of production and the principle of "to each according to his work."[8] These two fundamental principles are the only way to judge the socialist nature of a society, and China—the theoreticians now argued—had completed the transfer of agriculture, handicrafts, industry, and commerce to public ownership.[9] The Chinese leaders seemed to argue that the concepts of Marxism-Leninism must go through stages of modification as dictated by new concrete conditions.[10] Now that China is a socialist society in accordance with Marxism, Hu Yaobang stressed, all Marxists must make sure that "it does not become divorced from social life and does not stagnate, wither or ossify; they must enrich it with fresh revolutionary experiences so that it will remain full of vitality."[11] The new party chief urged that the application of Marxism-Leninism be integrated with the "concrete practice of China's realities."[12]

We must now turn to a discussion of the thought of Mao Zedong.

THE THOUGHT OF MAO ZEDONG

Mao Zedong, The Man

Wind and thunder are stirring.
Flags and banners are flying
Wherever men live.
Thirty-eight years are fled
With a mere snap of the fingers
We can clasp the moon in the Ninth Heaven

And seize turtles deep down in the Five Seas;
We'll return amid triumphant song and laughter.
Nothing is hard in this world.
If you dare to scale the heights.[13]

This is the second stanza of a poem written by Mao in May 1965 when he revisited Jinggangshan, the mountain retreat where he had gathered the remnants of the defeated and disillusioned urban revolutionaries in 1927 before reorganizing them into a fighting guerrilla force. This poem shows a familiar image of Mao: a man with infinite faith in the ability of human beings to accomplish any task, no matter how difficult. Mao Zedong was a much more complex person than has commonly been portrayed. In this section we will look at Mao, the man, by focusing on his background.

Mao was born in 1893 to a middle-class, not poor, peasant family in the village of Shaoshan, Hunan Province, in central China. He was brought up in a traditional Chinese family environment, where the father exercised almost dictatorial power over the family. As a boy he learned the value of hard labor by helping his father on the farm. His primary school curriculum centered on recitation of the Confucian classics, but he enjoyed reading popular romantic literature depicting heroic adventures, peasant rebellions, and the contests of empires. At the time of the 1911 revolution, Mao was 18, a fledgling youth, not too sure of what was happening to China. His social awakening did not begin until he went to the provincial capital of Changsha for his secondary education in 1912. In Changsha he learned from the newspapers about the various revolutionary activities of Sun Yatsen and others. Excited by these events, Mao wrote his first wall poster—already a popular medium for expressing political opinions. Following local uprisings in Changsha and Wuhan, he joined the revolutionary army. Military life with its regimentation and authoritarianism did not suit young Mao, who was alert and impatient with the world around him. For some months after his short sojourn in the army, Mao toyed with the idea of becoming a lawyer. Finally, in 1918, at the age of 25, he settled for a teaching career and obtained a degree from a teacher training school. Stuart Schram, an authoritative biographer of Mao, views the five years in teacher training school as an important landmark in the shaping of Mao's future.[14] The greatest and perhaps most successful role that Mao played was as a teacher to his people: he showed them how to learn by themselves and how to learn together.[15] In later years schoolmates described the Mao of this period as a loner, but a well-behaved person.[16]

The most important change that occurred in Mao's life was the move from his native province of Hunan to Beijing, the center of political and intellectual ferment. Toward the end of World War I, Mao went to Beijing with some thirty fellow-Hunanese as members of a society to study new ideas. Through his former teacher in Changsha, Mao obtained a menial job as a librarian's assistant at Beijing National University to support himself. Although he shared a room with seven other students from Hunan, Mao was lonely. As a means of meeting people, he joined the Marxist Study Group, organized by Li Dazhao, founder of the Chinese communist movement. As Mao later admitted to Edgar Snow, at that time he was rather confused by the new ideas proliferating like mushrooms at Beijing National University, and he leaned toward anarchism while "looking for a road."[17] Before becoming a Marxist in the summer of 1920, Mao had read only three Chinese translations of major works on Marxism: *The Communist Manifesto*, by Marx; *Class Struggle,* by Kautsky; and *History of Socialism,* by Kirkupp. A year later Mao was a delegate to the founding of the Chinese Communist Party in Shanghai. From 1921 until 1927, he was an obedient Chinese communist, following the orders of the

Comintern. From 1927 to 1935, he began to shape a different movement, with reliance on the peasantry as a base. Mao's rise to leadership of the Chinese Communist Party, and his maintenance of that position until his death in 1976, are discussed in Chapter 2 and in other parts of this book.

As Lucian Pye has pointed out, Mao must be seen at various times and under various conditions.[18] In his youth he was a loner and exhibited signs of "aloofness and solitariness."[19] When he went into the field as an organizer among the workers and peasants, Mao not only dressed but also acted like them. As Mao gained power and grew as a leader, he was distinguished as a "man of decisive action, great energy, and increasing aloofness."[20] He developed his maturity as a student of Marxism-Leninism and as a theoretician of guerrilla warfare during the Yanan years of 1935 to 1940, when he wrote and lectured to the soldiers and cadres. He was then looked upon by his followers as a scholar, a teacher, and a man of wisdom—an image that remained with him long after the establishment of the People's Republic in 1949. This image of a scholar and of a man with answers to problems became veiled in an aura of mysticism and magic—the image of a charismatic leader. But the private Mao remained a Chinese scholar, reading books and reports or writing poetry in the traditional style. As many foreigners who interviewed him testified, he was a good conversationalist and was remarkably well-informed. Interestingly, he engaged in philosophic conversations about the existence of a god or gods with the late Edgar Snow.[21] Mao personally seemed to have detested the campaigns to build an image of him as a god or an emperor, to be worshipped by the people. The epithet that Mao preferred was that of a "great teacher."[22] There is really no appropriate epithet to describe so complex a man as Mao. The recent attempt to measure Mao in the scale of history has produced a number of themes on major areas of Mao's public life: philosopher, Marxist, theorist, political leader, soldier, teacher, economist, patriot, statesman, and innovator.[23] Mao's contribution to the development of the Chinese communist ideology is truly enormous. The following discussion represents only some of the salient aspects of his thought.

Before examining Mao's thought, the importance of the Yanan years in the development of Mao's thinking must be stressed. About half the articles in the first four volumes of the *Selected Works of Mao Tse-tung* were written during this period. Mao, as leader of the communist movement, was under great pressure in 1939 and 1940 to develop ideas and to provide leadership not only for the communists but also for all Chinese who would listen.[24] The fifth volume of Mao's collected works, covering the period 1949–57, was published in April 1977. It was edited mainly under the direction of Hua Guofeng and Wang Dongxing, leaders of the "Whatever" faction. Apparently, the new pragmatic leaders felt that it was sufficiently radical to merit reediting.

Peasantry as the Base for Revolution

In 1927 Mao reported on his investigation of the peasant movement in Hunan province. In the report Mao made a strong appeal to the party, then dominated by the Comintern, to exploit discontent in the countryside and to organize peasant associations as a vanguard for the revolution.[25] Mao noted that poor peasants had been fighting the landlords and feudal rule, and that the countryside was on the verge of an agrarian revolution. Mao urged that "a revolutionary tidal wave" must be generated in the countryside to mobilize the masses and to "weld them into this great force" for revolution.

The thrust of Mao's guerrilla efforts in the 1930s and 1940s was the mobilization and welding of the peasants into a formidable revolutionary force for the CCP in its quest for eventual control of the nation. This concept and practice of mobilizing the peasantry as a revolutionary base has created some controversy among scholars as to whether Mao was a heretic or an original thinker and contributor to communist theory.[26] We may attribute the origin of the idea not to Mao but to Lenin, who recognized the potential of the Russian peasants as a revolutionary force in 1905. We may also say that Mao probably was influenced by Li Dazhao, who saw the peasantry as a possible base for the revolution. The importance of Mao's contribution, as some scholars have noted, was the timing. Mao was the first orthodox Marxist-Leninist to advocate using the peasantry as a major rather than a secondary force, and he made his appeal at the time when the CCP leadership had committed the party to relying on the urban proletariat.[27] With the benefit of hindsight, we might argue that reliance on the peasants was not a conceptual contribution but rather the only practical revolutionary strategy that could be effective. Practical ideas based on experience were the keynote of Mao's practical ideology.

Mass Line and Populism

At the heart of Mao's political philosophy was the concept of "from the masses, to the masses," commonly known as the *mass line.* Briefly stated, the concept of the mass line specifies that a party policy is good only if the ideas of that policy come originally from the masses—the peasants and the workers—and only if the interests and wishes of the people are taken into account and incorporated into the policy. The implementation of a policy, no matter how good it is, must have the wholehearted support of the masses. The mass line concept is applied in several stages to achieve the enthusiastic support of the masses for its implementation. These stages have been described by John W. Lewis as "perception, summarization, authorization, and implementation."[28] First, the party cadres list the "scattered and unsystematic" views of the masses. Second, the cadres study these ideas and put them into systematic and summary form in their reports to higher authorities. Third, the higher authorities make comments or give instructions based on these systematic ideas and return them to the masses. During this stage, political education or propaganda is carried on by the cadres among the masses, not only to explain the ideas but also to test their correctness. Finally, when the masses have embraced the ideas as their own, the ideas are translated into concrete action.[29] According to Mao, this is not the end; the proper application of the mass line must repeat the process several times "so that each time these ideas emerge with greater correctness and become more vital and meaningful."[30]

The mass line concept, formulated during the Jiangxi soviet days of the 1930s, was an effective method for securing the support of the masses. The application of the mass line required that both the leaders and the masses go through an educational process, learning from and supporting each other. It provided for a continuous dialogue between the leaders and the led. In going through the various stages of the mass line process, the masses were given ample opportunity to participate in the decision-making process, and the leaders were able to obtain popular commitment for policies and programs.

While Mao had immense respect for the virtues of the masses, this did not mean that there were not limits to what the masses could do. The Red Guards' demonstrations and big-character posters during the Cultural Revolution were applications of the mass line.[31] As we saw in Chapter 2, however, when the fighting between the various factions of Red Guards reached a state of anarchy, Mao did not hesitate to call in the army to restore order in the tradition of Lenin's democratic centralism. Stuart Schram writes that Mao, who clearly opposed unrestricted mass rule, prevented the Shanghai radicals from organizing leaderless people's committees.[32] Within limits, the concept of mass line does provide a monitoring device on the bureaucratic elite and their tendency to rule the inarticulate masses by party and governmental sanction.[33]

Mass line is considered Mao's theoretical contribution to populism.[34] At the root of this concept is the assertion that simple people—peasants and workers—possess virtue and wisdom. Mao again seems to agree with Li Dazhao, who once said that one becomes more humanistic as one gets closer to the soil. The methods of mass campaigns and small study groups, developed for applying the mass line, have been what Townsend terms "the primary institutions of Mao's populism."[35]

Closely associated with the mass line is Mao's belief in the intellectual tradition of voluntarism: Human will and determination will, in the end, remove all obstacles to making a better world. To Mao, it is this human will—diligence, hard work, and self-reliance—that must be inculcated into the minds of China's impoverished masses, whose potential had been inhibited by centuries of ignorance and superstition. Before and particularly during the Cultural Revolution, repeated references were made to Mao's favorite folk tale about a foolish old man who was able to move mountains through faith and perseverance. The tale, or parable, conveys the idea that it is necessary to rely on one's strength and to have faith in one's own ability to accomplish revolutionary tasks in building a new society.[36]

Theory and Practice

"We should not study the words of Marxism-Leninism, but study their standpoint and approach in viewing problems and solving them," Mao wrote in a theoretical essay in 1943.[37] He warned that too much reliance on purely abstract ideas or theory yields nothing but dogmatism, for theory is of no value if it does not involve practice. For Mao, the process of cognition involved more than merely what one observes and conceptualizes from observations. There was a third element—action or practice for the purpose of making changes in the material world. Knowledge cannot be separated from practice, since it begins with our experience. For example, Mao wrote that Marxism as a theory did not experience imperialism, and therefore, it was good only up to a point. When Lenin, who had perceived and experienced imperialism, added imperialism to the body of Marxist theory, it became meaningful to the Chinese situation. Theory must be subject to modification as changes occur and as new experiences enter into the situation. Marxism, according to Mao, must take into account both the historic experience and the characteristics of China in order to discover solutions to that country's problems. If one compares Mao's essay to practice with the writings of American pragmatists, such as John Dewey and William James, one finds many interesting parallels. As John Bryan Starr has noted, the philosophy of American pragmatists suggested not only that we discover the world around us but that we also "know how to remake it."[38]

An example of the application of theory and practice can be seen in Chinese education during the 1950s and the Cultural Revolution, when students split their time between study and work in rural areas. Another example was revealed in Mao's attitude toward student participation in the Cultural Revolution. He would fondly tell the millions of students that they were the "revolutionary successors" and that the only way they could learn about revolution was to dare to make revolution in the streets. Perhaps the most important point to remember about Mao's treatise on practice is that Mao thought that one can discover knowledge and truth only through practice, which must become an integral part of theory, or conceptual knowledge. This conceptual knowledge will be changed by additional experiences and practices. If knowledge comes from practice, as Mao argued, then practice means action, or at the very least, an orientation toward action.

Contradiction

Mao's theory of contraction, which may have been formulated in collaboration with others, begins with the assertion that society has always been full of contradictions: life–death, sun–moon, darkness–lightness, black–white, individual–collective, and red (meaning politically correct)–expert. It is from the juxtaposition of these contradictions that changes can take place in society. Change takes place because there is a tendency for one aspect of the contradiction "to transfer itself to the position of its opposite" through some type of struggle between the two opposites. Adhering to Marxist theory, Mao said that all conflicts are class conflicts between social groups: prior to socialism, peasants versus landlords; now, proletariat versus bourgeoisie. The origin of this theory, sometimes known as the "law of unity of opposites," can be traced to Hegelian dialectics and Marxian dialectical materialism. As others have noted, Mao probably was also influenced by the traditional concept of opposites, yin and yang.[39] The idea that conflict and change are normal was certainly revolutionary. As was said in Chapter 1, the traditional Chinese society, under Confucianism, had been told to strive for harmony and to maintain the status quo. The theory of contradictions is considered by many to be the core of the thought of Mao Zedong.

Mao felt that the interplay of contradictions would continue even though society had advanced into the higher level of socialism. In 1957 Mao said that none of the socialist countries, including China and the Soviet Union, could transcend the contradictions of social classes by forgetting the class struggle. In an essay entitled "On the Correct Handling of Contradictions Among the People,"[40] Mao advanced the idea that class struggle would continue for an indefinite period of time. It would no longer be in regard to the contradictions between "friends" and "enemies" but rather would apply to those between proletarian and bourgeois thinking and behavior. In 1957 Mao explained that there are two types of contradictions: "antagonistic contradiction" between ourselves and the enemy; and "nonantagonistic contradiction" among working people, between peasants and workers, or between cadres and the masses. The nonantagonistic contradictions are essentially matters of ideological and political right and wrong. Since there are two different types of contradictions, Mao proposed two different methods of resolving these conflicts. For antagonistic contradictions, the proletariat dictatorship must suppress the reactionary elements in society; but for the nonantagonistic contradictions among the people, a continuous process of struggle and criticism must be employed to "raise the level of consciousness" and to correct erroneous thinking and behavior of the people. It is through this continuous process of struggle and criticism that unity can be achieved. The key objective of struggle and criticism is to proletarianize the behavior and thinking of the individual, no matter what economic background he or she may possess. It is the "proletarian consciousness" that is important in the final determination of one's class status.[41] Mao defined several major nonantagonistic contradictions or problems that the Chinese must resolve: (1) those between heavy industry and agriculture; (2) those between central and local authorities; (3) those between urban and rural; (4) those between national minorities and the Han Chinese over pluralism or radical assimilation.[42]

Mao made it clear that there were bound to be conflicts and struggles to resolve issues within the party:

> Opposition and struggle between different ideas constantly occur within the Party, reflecting contradictions between the classes and between the old and new in society. If in the Party there were no contradictions and no ideological struggles to solve them, the life of the Party would come to an end.[43]

The intraparty disputes, which have beset the party since the 1930s, usually are to be resolved by rectification campaigns; but when the contradictions within the party are so severe that they cause a serious "cleavage of opinion" among the members of the Politburo, the contradictions must be resolved by some type of mass campaign.

The Cultural Revolution has been viewed both as a rectification campaign and as a mass campaign for class struggle to resolve the contradictions between the proletariat and the bourgeoisie. It was called a "Cultural Revolution" because, according to both Marx and Mao, the construction of a socialist society demands transformation in the superstructure of culture, customs, and habits to eliminate the contradictions between proletariat collectivism and bourgeois individualism.[44]

Most Americans tend to be very skeptical about the utility of Mao's theory on contradiction, treating it as a piece of incomprehensible diatribe. It is very difficult for our highly technological and analytical minds to understand why, for instance, the workers and staff in a blast furnace attribute their higher output to simply studying the dialectics on contradiction. Still, the theory of contradiction was said to have helped the peasants and workers develop "a habit of analysis." Take, for instance, the case of the blast furnace. The workers and staff sat down and analyzed why the conventional way of increasing the temperature of the furnace brought about an increase in output only up to a certain level. By altering the structure of the layers of the furnace through analysis, they were able to control the flow of coal gas and to realize a greater yield after the standard level of pressure had been applied.[45] Another example is of peasants who have just been thrust into a position of leadership in their village and are daily confronted by a host of conflict-of-interest situations for which they must provide resolution. By studying the theory of contradiction, they are able to carry on some analyses of their own and to feel more confident in providing resolution to the conflicts.[46] In addition, the theory of contradiction is useful, as pointed out by Schurmann, in a struggle-and-criticism session, where the deviant individual's erroneous thinking is brought into sharp focus to facilitate correction through thought reform.[47] Finally, the theory of contradiction, by focusing on the law of unity of opposites, compels those involved in a conflict situation to agree on the proper means for resolving the conflict. Schurmann describes how discussion of a controversial issue at the Politburo level first produces two opposite sets of opinions and then results in the adoption of one set of opinions as a majority view and the other set as a minority view. Before a decision is reached, however, there must be what Schurmann calls the "juxtaposition" or polarization of opinion as a logical consequence of the application of the theory of contradiction.[48]

Permanent Revolution[49]

The ideas about change and struggle contained in Mao's essays on practice and contradictions logically lead to his concept of a permanent, or continuous, revolution: If society is rampant with contradictions, then "ceaseless change and upheaval" must be the normal condition to enable the society to reach a higher level of proletarian consciousness. The continuous class struggle is therefore necessary to create the "new socialist man."

Mao emphasized that his concept of the permanent revolution was different from Leon Trotsky's, a point that Khrushchev seemed to have missed. In 1959 Khrushchev compared two concepts, labeling Mao's concept of a permanent revolution a mixture of anarchism, Trotskyism, and adventurism. One essential difference was that Trotsky was merely concerned about "the transition from the democratic to the socialistic stage of the revolution," while Mao was concerned about "a separate stage of social transformation" during which the revolutionary environment must be maintained to eliminate all bourgeois influences and tendencies and to rebuild the superstructures.[50] Another difference was that Trotsky and Stalin would permit a new class of technocrats to emerge in order to establish a new economic base. Mao, on the other hand, argued that a new economic base does not necessarily bring about a new superstructure; class struggle must continue from the beginning to the end and while the society is undergoing transformation. Mao believed that "politics must take command so that the elites understand the correct ideological line." The contradictions must be solved by continuous struggle or revolution. Mao would insist: "We must destroy the old basis for unity, pass through a struggle, and unite on a new basis." Viewed from this perspective, both the Socialist Education Movement and the Cultural Revolution were important examples of the theory of permanent revolution. At the heart of Mao's theory of permanent revolution is the thesis that even after the establishment of a new economic base, both individuals and institutions can acquire bourgeois tendencies and thus change the color of the revolution.

In light of the events since Mao's death and the pragmatic leaders' quest for political and economic reform, how have the basic tenets of Mao's thought come to be viewed in China? To what extent has there been modification of Mao's thought?

First, efforts were made by pragmatic leaders to demolish the myth that Mao was the only contributor to the thought of Mao. The party's assessment of its history clearly stated that Mao's thought was "a summary of the experiences that have been confirmed in the practice of the Chinese revolution." In other words, it was the product of "collective wisdom," since "many outstanding leaders of our party made important contributions to the formulation and development of Mao Zedong Thought."[51] The new leaders took the position that Mao's thought had been contaminated by the erroneous "ultra-Left" ideas of the radicals. The 1981 party assessment maintained that Mao's thought must continue to play the guiding role in China's revolution; it should not be discarded "just because Comrade Mao Zedong made mistakes in his later years."[52] The party document went on to point out that "it is likewise entirely wrong to adopt a dogmatic attitude toward the sayings of Mao Zedong, to regard whatever he said as the immutable truth which must be mechanically applied everywhere, and to be unwilling to admit honestly that he made mistakes in his later years."[53]

Second, major modifications have been made with regard to Mao's concepts and ideas of class struggle, continued revolution, and contradiction.[54] The Cultural Revolution, the party now said, conformed neither to Marxism-Leninism nor to Chinese reality: "They represent an entirely erroneous appraisal of the prevailing class relations."[55] The actual targets of the upheaval were neither "revisionist" nor "capitalist" but instead were Marxist and socialist principles.[56] The 1981 party document declared that "class struggle no longer constitutes the principal contradiction after the exploiters have been eliminated as classes in socialist society."[57] While there would be class struggles in the future, they would differ in terms of scale, targets, and methods. Large-scale class struggle, such as that of the Cultural Revolution, which stressed the overthrow of one class by another, was no longer to be tolerated.[58] The targets for future class struggle would be counterrevolutionaries; enemy agents; criminals who engage in economic crimes such as bribery, embezzlement, and profiteering; and the remnants of the Gang of Four.[59] Since class struggle was no longer the principal contradiction in Chinese society, "tempestuous mass movement" was no longer the appropriate method to be employed. Instead, legal procedures embodied in the state constitution and party rules ought to be prescribed as the proper way for handling different types of contradictions in society.[60] Thus, the theory of contradiction must be discarded because it is not only wrong but "runs counter to Marxism-Leninism and Chinese conditions."[61]

The party's assessment went on to say that labeling party leaders as "capitalist roaders" failed to distinguish the people from the enemy.[62] The reinterpretation then invoked Mao by saying that class struggle between antagonistic classes was eliminated when landlords and rich peasants were eliminated in the 1950s. Moreover, to differentiate among classes according to people's political attitudes, as the radicals had done in the Cultural Revolution, was fallacious because "it is impossible to make scientific judgment of class by using people's thinking as a yardstick."[63] The principal contradiction, it argued, was no longer between the proletariat and the bourgeoisie but between the need of the people for more and better material well-being and the present low level of economic development.[64] Since the downfall of the radicals, certain "social contradictions" had surfaced—for example, the craving for Western-type individual freedom and decadent lifestyle versus the socialist system and the people's interest.[65] The method for resolving these new "social contradictions" should be that of criticism, not of physical struggle.

MAO'S LEGACY AND DE-MAOIZATION

The thinking of Mao was very complex, as we have pointed out. His ideas had their roots in the Chinese intellectual tradition, particularly in the May Fourth Movement, in the Marxist-Leninist tradition, and in the revolutionary experiences of the Chinese Communist Party. Yet Mao's populist approach, contained in the concept of the mass line, was distinct and went beyond Marx, Lenin, and the Chinese tradition. The vision that the semiliterate peasants and workers—collectively, the masses—could be the source of ideas and inspiration for the leaders was truly revolutionary. The application of this core concept enabled the CCP to secure popular support from the period of guerrilla operations in the 1930s and 1940s through the land reform and communization movements in the 1950s and 1960s. The failure of the Great Leap, and the questions raised about the results of the Cultural Revolution, make it appear doubtful that Mao's concept has been realized. Yet in spite of the dampening effect of the Great Leap and the Cultural Revolution, Mao's prescription for a proper relationship between the leaders and the led in the mass line formula remains a fundamental work style for the Chinese leaders. The state constitution of 1982 and the party charter of 1982 enshrine this Maoist vision of relying on the masses for inspiration, support, and implementation of policies and programs. It is the mass line as an ideological concept that has given the Chinese their national identity.[66]

Mao's practical ideology also has functioned as a guide, if not as a basis, on which individuals in Chinese society shape their attitudes and regulate their behavior. These ideas serve as a set of preferred societal values against which actions and thoughts are judged. Mao's philosophical ideas and teachings, such as human will and determination, self-sacrifice, and service to the people, have become an integral part of today's value system, governing behavior. To many Americans, and to some of Mao's own colleagues, the idea of a permanent revolution and of ceaseless change may be too unsettling, bordering on anarchy, but in Mao's vision, the revolution is like a pair of straw sandals that have no definite pattern but rather "shape themselves in the making." Stuart Schram's tribute to Mao is worth quoting: "Mao has left the sandal of the Chinese revolution unfinished, but it has already begun to take shape, and for a long time to come it can scarcely fail to bear his stamp."[67]

Ideology alone could not have had such a great impact on China. In the final analysis, it took a man like Mao, with exceptional skill and acumen as a political leader, to translate ideas into concrete actions and to make people do over a long period of time what the leader wanted. No other Chinese leader in modern times was involved directly in so many important issues over such a long period of time as was Mao Zedong.[68]

Mao, however, has been subjected to intensive criticism since 1978. One of the first such criticisms appeared in the publication of a speech made by Zhou Enlai to the First All-China Youth Congress in 1949, in which Zhou warned young people not to look upon Mao as a demigod.[69] Zhou related a story about how unhappy Mao was when he learned that a school textbook had said that he had been opposed to superstition when he was a boy of ten. On the contrary, Zhou explained, Mao believed in gods when he was a little boy and "prayed to Buddha for help" at one time when his mother became ill.[70] Zhou's message to youth in 1949 was twofold: They should not regard Mao as an infallible leader, and they should seek truth from facts. It is this blind worship of Mao that has been deemphasized. Truth, including Mao's thought, as the leaders now insist, must eventually be tested by practice—this is the major theme in China's policy of moderation.

After a lengthy debate at the Third Plenary Session of the Eleventh Central Committee meeting (December 18–22, 1978), China's new leadership agreed that the time had come for the people to "emancipate their thinking, dedicate themselves to the study of new circumstances, things, and questions, and uphold the principle of seeking truth from facts."[71] While paying tribute to Mao's "outstanding leadership," the party's Central Committee nevertheless found that Mao had made mistakes: "It would not be Marxist to demand that a revolutionary leader be free of all shortcomings and errors."[72] This was the beginning of the drive to deemphasize Mao and to dispel the myth of his infallibility, which had been built up over the years by the radicals. Anti-Mao posters appeared in Beijing in late 1978 and early 1979, along with the party's admission of "erroneous" action in the Tiananmen Square incident in April 1976 and its reexamination of the events of the Cultural Revolution. In December 1978 the Central Committee exonerated and rehabilitated a host of top leaders purged in 1959 and during the Cultural Revolution for opposing Mao or his policies, including Pen Dehuai, Peng Zhen, Bo Yibo, and Tao Zhu. Deng Xiaoping, who repeatedly endured Mao's wrath, has been quoted as saying that Mao was perhaps "seventy percent correct and thirty percent wrong."[73]

The Central Committee's final assessment of Mao came at its June 1981 session when it approved the report on the party history.[74] The document represented a culmination of intensive discussion and debate about Mao's role in the party. The report was initiated by the pragmatic leaders under Deng Xiaoping. It may be instructive for us to find out how these leaders evaluated Mao and what they considered to be Mao's mistakes.

First, an agonizing attempt had been made by the pragmatic leaders to distinguish between Mao as leader and the body of ideas collectively known as the thought of Mao Zedong. Deng Xiaoping repeatedly emphasized that Mao's contribution to the Chinese communist revolution could not possibly be "obliterated" and that "the Chinese people will always cherish his memory."[75] In the party document, Mao's thought was considered "a correct theory" and "a body of correct principles and a summary of practical experience."[76] It went on to point out that it would be wrong to deny its guiding role in the Chinese revolution "just because Comrade Mao Zedong made mistakes in his later years."[77]

One may ask why they insisted on such a distinction. One possible reason may be that this was a necessary political compromise to placate opposition within the party and the army. The army in particular still found it difficult to denounce Mao's leadership after years of religious adherence to his ideology.[78] Chinese leaders now argued that Mao made a "tremendous contribution" in the formation of his thought. But that did not imply that "every word Mao uttered and every article he wrote, much less his personal mistakes, belong to the Mao Zedong Thought."[79] It was obvious that the party was not prepared to completely denounce Mao, as Khrushchev had denounced Stalin in 1956. Chinese theoreticians and propagandists adhered to the line that "under no circumstance should one confuse a leader's mistakes with the scientific ideological system named after him or describe the mistakes as a component part of the scientific system."[80] To either abandon Mao's thought[81] or reject Mao's correct ideas would "lead China along a dangerous path, bring a great loss to us and court disaster."[82] During the top leaders' debate in 1978, the venerable Marshal Ye emphasized that "we cannot negate entirely Mao Zedong Thought." He expressed the fear that if the party lost its theoretical and ideological base, China would regress to its position prior to 1949.[83]

What mistakes had Mao committed in his later years? The party's official assessment identified five major political errors that were largely attributed to Mao.

First, the 1957 "rightist" rectification campaign launched after the "Hundred Flowers Bloom" movement was misdirected. Instead of criticizing "a handful of bourgeois rightists," the class struggle was extended in scope and intensity so that it eventually engulfed a substantial segment of the population. The intellectuals particularly were branded unfairly as "rightists," and were purged. Some leaders now in power admitted that Mao was not the only one responsible for the large-scale purge of the intellectuals in 1957; other senior party officials had supported the ill-considered policy at the time.[84]

Second, Mao was responsible for mistakes committed in the 1958 Great Leap Forward and the commune programs. He was blamed for the "Leftist" errors in promoting "excessive targets" and issuing "arbitrary decisions." The party assessment charged that Mao violated his own principles by initiating the Great Leap and the commune programs without thorough investigation, study, and experimentation. He was criticized for "smugness" and "arrogance" and charged with being impatient—looking for "quick results" and ignoring economic realities. One senior party leader extended the blame to the entire Central Committee that had endorsed the Great Leap decision in 1958.[85] While the party assessment noted that Mao had made self-criticism in 1962 for his mistakes in the 1958 Great Leap, this did not exonerate him from the error.

Third, Mao erred in forcing the Eighth Central Committee in 1959 to launch a vicious campaign to discredit and vilify a number of senior party leaders, including Marshal Peng Dehuai, the defense minister at the time, for disagreeing with Mao over the Great Leap policies. Mao was condemned for launching a struggle within the top party leadership that "gravely undermined inner-party democracy" at all levels.[86]

Fourth, Mao was blamed for widening the erroneous policy of class struggle and mistakenly applying the theory of contradiction in another mass campaign, the Socialist Education Campaign, in 1963. Here Mao was blamed for insisting that the contradiction between the proletariat and the bourgeoisie was the main contradiction and for proclaiming that the bourgeoisie class continued to exist under socialism. The 1963

Socialist Education Campaign focused on party leaders who had taken "the capitalist road." Mao, the party assessment in 1981 pointed out, had contradicted himself—treating contradiction among the people as contradiction with the enemy. The 1963 mass campaign unjustly purged a large number of party cadres and plunged China once again into confusion and chaos.

Finally, according to the party assessment, the greatest mistake Mao made was the Great Proletarian Cultural Revolution in 1966. The new pragmatic leaders viewed this upheaval as an extreme expansion of Mao's "ultra-Left" ideas of class struggle and continued revolution.[87] The party declared that the theses of the Cultural Revolution were not only erroneous but also inconsistent with Mao's thought, for these ideas misinterpreted the class relations that existed in China at that time. The very things the Cultural Revolution denounced were, in fact, Marxist and socialist principles. To insist on continued revolution, Deng now pointed out, was to make a "wrong judgment of the Chinese reality." The gravest of all Mao's mistakes, in Deng's view, was the attack launched during the Cultural Revolution on veteran party leaders with years of dedicated revolutionary service and administrative experience.[88] Deng revealed that Mao himself admitted a year or two before his death that the Cultural Revolution had been wrong because it had resulted in the "decimation" of experienced cadres through purge and physical abuse and, in effect, had constituted a nationwide "civil war."[89]

The party's assessment charged that in the Cultural Revolution—where "one class overthrows the other"—Mao had violated his own mass line principles. The upheaval was "divorced both from the party organization and from the masses."[90] It involved masses but was "devoid of mass support" because, the new leaders now argued, it was launched by Mao personally with the knowledge that "the majority of the people were opposed to the 'ultra-Left' ideas."[91] The party assessment concluded that the Cultural Revolution was initiated by one leader, Mao, who labored under "misapprehension" and was taken advantage of by the radicals. The final result of the Cultural Revolution was "catastrophe to the party, the state, and the whole people."[92]

The new leaders also made remarks about Mao as a leader and about his personal character. Deng found Mao's "patriarchal behavior" to be a major shortcoming, an "unhealthy style of work": "He acted as a patriarch. He never wanted to know the ideas of others, no matter how right they could be; he never wanted to hear opinions different from his."[93] Associated with this behavior was Mao's "smugness" about his early success, which led to his "overindulgence" of ultra-Left ideas in his later years. He became "overconfident" and "arrogant."[94] He also was accused of "feudal practice," a disparaging remark used by Deng to describe Mao as a leader and as a person. To Deng, the manner in which Mao chose Lin Biao as his successor in 1969 clearly illustrated Mao's feudal practice—he behaved as though he were the emperor who could pass on the reign to his chosen successor.

Perhaps the most damaging condemnation of Mao was for his promotion of the "personality cult" that viewed him as a demigod and treated his thought as "infinite and boundless."[95] The party assessment concluded that Mao had gradually isolated himself from the masses and the party, he had "acted more and more arbitrarily and subjectively, and increasingly put himself above the Central Committee of the party." Thus, he had become less "democratic."[96] With Mao's image reduced to that of a Marxist mortal, Hu Yaobang, the party's new general secretary, declared at the 1982 party congress that "personality cult" must henceforth be forbidden.[97] Further, the new leaders abolished the practice of lifelong tenure for leaders.[98]

In effect, what the Chinese said in their reevaluation was that there were really two Mao Zedongs: a good Mao and a bad Mao. The serious mistakes of his later years must be renounced, but his thought, ideas, and practice—as reinterpreted and modified by the pragmatists now in power—must be preserved and enshrined. Was this a true and accurate assessment of Mao, or was it some sort of "convoluted logic"?[99] Can we really separate the man from his ideas? Was the Mao of the Great Leap and the Cultural Revolution really different from the Mao that existed before 1957? Was Mao more innovative and less arrogant before 1957? Can we really say in the same breath that Mao violated his own principles and practices but was also "the spiritual asset of the party"? It may also be argued that Mao had always been an innovator who preferred an "alternative model of development for China."[100] Perhaps the Great Leap and the Cultural Revolution were actually symbols of Mao's constant search for a new lifestyle.[101]

Certainly, the process of assessing Mao is by no means complete. We have not exhausted our study of Mao the man nor of his role in Chinese history.[102] Nevertheless, the reevaluation of Mao has yielded and will continue to yield important facts—as well as varied perspectives—on his role in the Chinese revolution and his legacy to the people. Meantime, Mao, who has been dead for twenty-five years, has not been rejected by the Chinese people altogether. Judging by the hundreds of books on Mao that have appeared in bookstores in China in the past few years, his image has made a comeback—not as a feared, ruthless, godless dead leader, but as a folk god. His laminated portrait has been displayed on trucks, taxicabs, and walls of rural homes as an omen or good luck charm to fend off evils and misfortunes. The new deification of Mao may have begun in Guangzhou in South China as a fad; it spread nationwide by 1992. The cult of Mao worship may simply be the manifestation of a recurring need for the Chinese to look for a folk deity in hard as well as good times under economic reform. From that perspective, the appearance of Mao portraits may be to some Chinese another way of criticizing the current leadership by showing nostalgia for more stable times when there was no inflation and there was guaranteed job security—the "iron rice bowl." According to a survey conducted in 1992 by a research group at the People's University in Beijing, four in ten out of a sample of over 3,000 said they were not entirely satisfied with political and economic conditions, but six in ten gave their approval. Nevertheless, on the 100th anniversary of Mao's birth on December 26, 1993, party chief Jiang Zemin claimed that Deng's reform ideas are rooted in Mao's thought despite their inherent contradictions.

The most revealing recent biography about Mao and Deng Xiaoping has been the book written by an old China hand, the late Harrison E. Salisbury.[103] Mao is portrayed in this book as a decadent, traditional emperor surrounded by young dancing girls. According to Salisbury he embarked on ruinous adventures during his rule, in addition to pursuing the destruction of his colleagues with demonic zeal.

Even more revealing was the publication of a book about Mao's private life by his personal physician, Li Zhisui, covering the twenty-two year period from 1955 to 1976.[104] Leaving aside the fact that Dr. Li seemed to have relied on whatever information Mao had passed on to him, as well as some of the internal documents, conversations with others with whom Li came into contact, and his personal observations, the memoir does reveal that Mao behaved as the latter-day emperor of China; Mao's private quarters were in reality the "imperial court." Mao was depicted as being obsessed with his personal power and fearful of perceived or factual disloyalty by his colleagues within the party hierarchy. Mao demonstrated disregard for morality as he engaged frequently in sexual escapades with younger women who served him in his inner sanctum.

IDEOLOGY IN FLUX: RESURGENCE
AND REDEFINITION

How to Prevent the Corrosive Influence
of Bourgeois Tendencies and the 1986 Policy on Culture
and Ideology

For reasons of party unity and political stability, pragmatic reformers reached a compromise with the orthodox hard-liners by adopting the party's resolution on culture and ideology at the Sixth Plenum of the Twelfth Central Committee on September 28, 1986.[105] Deng Liquan, the former propaganda chief who lost his position for pushing the "Spiritual Pollution" campaign in 1983, revealed that the 1986 party resolution on culture and ideology produced intense debate within the party hierarchy, so much so that the original text went through eight or nine different drafts.[106] Let us now summarize briefly the key points in the 1986 party document on culture and ideology.

First, the party resolution admitted that the economic reforms had produced changes in people's outlook and orientation toward ideology. It asked the key question: "Will we be able to resist the decadent bourgeois and feudal ideologies and avoid the danger of deviating from the right direction?"[107] Evidently as a concession to the reformers, the resolution then stated that China must keep its door open and continue the reforms, so long as the "Four Basic Principles" (socialist road, people's dictatorship, party leadership, and Marxism-Leninism-Mao's thought) were to be upheld.

Second, the resolution condemned the "capitalist ideology and social system ... and the ugly and decadent aspects of capitalism" but, on the other hand, encouraged learning from "developing capitalist countries the advanced science, technology, and applicable expertise and economic management."[108] In other words, the party resolution, as a compromise between two contending factions, wanted to have the best of both worlds. In case there was any doubt or confusion as to which direction China was headed, the document stated that "the ultimate ideal of our party is to build a communist society that applies the principle, 'from each according to his needs.'"[109] Third, as a concession to the orthodox hard-liners, who had criticized the reformers and those intellectuals who openly questioned the validity of Marxism, the 1986 party resolution on culture and ideology reiterated that "Marxism is the theoretical basis of socialism" and that "we have to depend on Marxism as our guiding theory." But, as a rebuke to Hu Yaobang and perhaps Deng Xiaoping to some extent, the orthodox hard-liners had their last word on Marxism's validity: "It is wrong to regard Marxism as a rigid dogma. It is also wrong to negate its basic tenets, view it as an outdated theory and blindly worship bourgeois philosophies and social doctrines."[110] Although it condemned bourgeois liberalization as "negating the socialist system in favor of capitalism," the 1986 party document tiptoed cautiously about academic freedom, of "creative writing," and freedom of discussion— all these could be permitted if "Marxism is to serve as a guide in academic work and the arts."[111] Fourth, perhaps in deference to Chen Yun and other orthodox hard-liners for their concern about the need to combat "the corrosive ethics" brought on by the open door policy, the 1986 party document spoke of "socialist ethics" and "socialist morality." Socialist ethics must reject "both the idea and the practice of pursuing personal interests at the expense of others ... putting money above all else, abusing power for personal gains, cheating and extortion."[112]

The compromise on culture and ideology reached between the orthodox hard-liners and the pragmatic reformers, as reflected in the party document, was short-lived. The promise of academic freedom, freedom for creative writing, and freedom of discussion by the intellectuals under the slogan of "let a hundred flowers bloom" (a revival of the 1957 slogan) was discarded instantly when university students' demonstrations erupted in December 1986. Once again the pendulum seemed to have swung slightly to the left and the party intensified the campaign against "bourgeois liberalization." Within a week the *People's Daily* issued two front-page editorials urging the eradication of bourgeois liberalization that "poisons our youth, is harmful to socialist stability, disrupts our reform and open door policy."[113] Bourgeois liberalization was now defined as "an idea negating the socialist system in favor of capitalism."[114] Newspaper editorials charged that there were a few people who advocated "the capitalist road" and "capitalist practices." Then on January 12, a *People's Daily* commentator lashed out against those who advocated "complete Westernization"—meaning "learning from Western science, technology, culture, politics, ideology, and ethics"—and against those who held that socialism had failed in the last thirty years.[115] Obviously these comments were aimed at intellectuals like Fang Lizhi and Liu Binghua who had already been expelled from the party. The commentator made a convoluted argument that the open door policy and "complete Westernization" were two different things: It was possible to master advanced science and technology from capitalist countries but to discard at the same time "the capitalist ideology and social system which safeguard exploitation and oppression, as well as its evil and corrupt aspects."[116] Du Yun, vice minister of the State Education Commission, charged that the December 1986 student demonstrations reflected the influence of bourgeois liberalization that had appeared in the last few years.[117]

Thus China is now facing an ideological dilemma: how to adhere to the ideological rigidity of Marxism-Leninism and Mao's Thought without stifling the desire of the intellectuals for thinking anew in the process of modernization. Is it possible for China's leaders to make a clear distinction between capitalistic techniques on the one hand, and the capitalistic values that associate closely with these advanced scientific developments, on the other? Is it not inevitable, one may ask, for people to demand more freedom and free choices once capitalistic techniques are introduced into the economic system? China scholar and economist Jan Prybyla argues that in essence "capitalist techniques cannot be completely separated from the pluralistic system from which they have evolved."[118] There is no doubt that economic reforms will most likely warn these orthodox ideologues that, with more liberties and prosperity, there is a corresponding rise in people's expectation of more freedom and more free choices, which may in turn raise doubts about the validity of socialism and Marxism.[119] Deng Xiaoping, a man who tried to bridge the gap between the two contending factions, argued that there was a need to modernize, but not to "derevolutionize," to make the socialist system work, but not to "negate" it in favor of capitalism. But the ultimate question remains: How is this to be done?

An answer to which the party leaders agreed in the aftermath of the December 1986 student demonstrations was to reiterate and reinstitute the Four Basic Principles laid down by Deng in 1978–79 when the "Democracy Wall" movement was crushed. Zhao Ziyang, then the new party chief, ruled out a political campaign against the intellectuals but reaffirmed that the party leadership must adhere to these basic principles.[120] In a lengthy talk on January 20, 1987 in the Great Hall of the People in Beijing, Zhao proposed that if party members follow the Four Basic Principles, it would be possible to keep bourgeois liberalization in check. Zhao insisted that the battle against bourgeois liberalization must be limited to remaining within the party as "an inner party issue."[121] Zhao then indicated that to build socialism with Chinese characters required "the integration of the universal truth of Marxism-Leninism with the practice of China's development and reform."[122] On the importance of adherence to the Four Basic Principles, the pragmatic reformers now had the support of the orthodox hard-liners. Peng Zhen told the NPC standing committee on January 21, 1987 that these principles were the result of China's socialist revolution and an integral part of its constitutional makeup.[123] Peng said that it was the historic conclusion that "if there were no CCP, there would be no new China; only socialism can save China."[124] In other words, the "bird" of economic reform must be caged—to use the late Chen Yun's famous metaphor—by Deng's Four Basic Principles, in which the party leadership was paramount. Zhao made it clear that "anyone who departs from Marxism on so serious a question will be censured by the party and the masses."[125] A number of dissenters within the party who raised questions about the party's continued dominance and control had been asked to resign from the party or face expulsion.[126] But in the end, Zhao was sacked during the 1989 Tiananmen protest on the charge that he was not too keen on the anti-bourgeois-liberalization campaign. (See Chapter 10.)

Since the June 1989 Tiananmen crackdown, not only have Deng's Four Basic Principles been reemphasized, but old slogans laden with heavy ideological content have been revived. In Li Peng's report on the work of the government to the NPC on March 20, 1990, he declared that adherence to the Four Basic Principles must be combined with the policies of reform and opening to the outside world. He cautioned that

> We oppose the political propositions in contravention of the Constitution put forward by people trying to negate the socialist system in China and leadership by the Chinese Communist Party under the banners of freedom, democracy, and human rights.[127]

He then proposed in one breath that

> We should conduct intensive education in the need to uphold the Four Cardinal Principles and oppose bourgeois liberalization and in patriotism, collectivism, socialism, communism, self-reliance, hard work, revolutionary traditions and professional ethics.[128]

DENGISM: CHINA AS AN ECONOMIC GIANT IN THE TWENTY-FIRST CENTURY

Deng Xiaoping's ideas and policies on economic reform over the past twenty years (since 1978) have been collectively named the "Theory of Deng" or "Dengism." Basically, this is a collection of Deng's remarks concerning the building of socialism with Chinese characteristics that include market-style reforms and an open door to foreign investment. At the Fourteenth Party Congress, held in October 1992, Deng's ideas and policies on reform were elevated to the status of a theory: "Comrade Deng Xiaoping is the chief architect of our socialist reform, of the open door policy and of the modernization program."[129] Deng's theory is now regarded as "the product of the integration of the universal principle of Marxism-Leninism with the practice of the Chinese Second Revolution—

economic construction, reform and opening to the outside world."[130] Reminiscent of the adulation for Mao, Deng was cited no fewer than thirteen times in Jiang Zemin's report to the party congress in 1992; an annotated dictionary, the *Thought of Deng Xiaoping*, has been published containing some 2,000 of Deng's speeches.

Finally, Deng's theory was enshrined by the Eighth National People's Congress, held March 15–31, 1993, which amended Article 15 of the 1982 state constitution by deleting the requirement for state enterprises to fulfill their obligations under the state plan. Words in the constitution that referred to a planned economy have been replaced by the words "socialist market economy." In short, Deng's market reform for China's economy has won the final battle over the hard-liners. Thus, as Deng Xiaoping approached his final years, he saw to it that market reform was firmly established as China's road to modernization.

China in 1992–93 was in the midst of a booming economy. In 1992 its domestic growth product (minus foreign investment) was over 12 percent. By 1993 it had become evident that China must once again apply the brakes to its fast-growing economy as banks began to face shortages of cash and inflation soared to more than 20–30 percent in most urban areas. Drastic measures had to be taken such as raising interest rates, reducing government operations by 20 percent, curbing bank lending for speculative investments, cutting down infrastructure spending, and calling a temporary halt to price decontrol. Some of these measures were recommended by the World Bank in its August 1993 report on China. The International Monetary Fund reported in the spring of 1993 that the Chinese economy had become the third largest in the world, next only to the United States and Japan, based on a new method of comparing a country's goods and services in terms of purchasing power instead of as compared with some other nation's currency.[131]

At the Fifteenth Party Congress, Deng's ideas of "socialism with Chinese characteristics" also has been elevated to that of an ideological theory as the newly approved amendment to the 1982 party constitution now reads: that "the Chinese Communist Party takes Marxism-Leninism, Mao Zedong Thought, and Deng Xiaoping Theory as its guide to action."[132]

PROMOTION OF "JIANG ZEMIN'S THOUGHT": A UNIFYING IDEOLOGY FOR THE NEW ERA

With both Mao Zedong's Thought and Deng Xiaoping's Theory now enshrined in the party's constitution [approved in September 1997 (see Appendix B-2)] as its guide to action, it may not be surprising that there would soon be wide discussion, if not decision, by the party to add Jiang Zemin Thought to the ideological pantheon.

A deliberate move has been undertaken recently by those close to Jiang Zemin in the party's upper echelon to promote the so-called "Thought of Jiang Zemin"—a move reminiscent of Mao's own promotion for the "Thought of Mao Zedong" while he was still alive. The move to elevate Jiang's status and image to those of Deng or Mao may be influenced most likely by Jiang's reelection as the party chief as the Sixteenthth Party Congress approaches—scheduled to be convened in the fall of 2002. By then, Jiang will have been the party's helmsman for more than thirteen years.

Deng's economic reform for the past twenty years has brought material well-being for the people, as well as problems. China's Gross Domestic Product (GDP) grew at a rate of about 10 percent in 1996, the same as in 1995. There has been a prosperous consumer goods supply and a growing demand for products. Per capita income for urban residents increased about fourfold from 1978 to 1991, and the rural peasants enjoyed over a 4 percent gain in the same period.[133] These figures still place China in the lower third of the world's population in terms of per capita income and consumption.[134] Despite this comparison, it has been estimated that China is soon expected to export well over $100 billion worth of electronic machinery, color TV sets, and auto parts, making it a formidable world exporter.[135]

Deng's economic reform has generated a host of problems. First, there surfaced in China, as well as in other parts of Asia, the so-called "new rich," a term used by some Western analysts to describe the new wealthy group of entrepreneurs who were the real beneficiaries of the economic reform.[136] The "new rich" are not yet "a new capitalist class," as described by David Goodman, but they do have a close relationship with the party and government through which they have been allowed to prosper. In China under economic reform, the new entrepreneur elites have embraced a different set of moral values: do anything to get rich by themselves as individuals. They are obsessed with moneymaking which becomes their only objective in life. It should also be noted that corruption has run rampant in officialdom and in the most capitalistic sectors of the economy.[137] Finally, there is continuing worry about the dangers of decadent influences from the West. In 1995 Chinese Communist Party chief Jiang Zemin told the delegates attending the NPC session to promote traditional culture and guard against corrupt ideas from the West. In short, there is a need for some sort of spiritual or moral and ethical revival in China.

Jiang Zemin, now the undisputed heir to Deng Xiaoping, named at the September 1997 Party Congress, must search for a "new way of thinking" as he leads China in the early twenty-first century. Even before Deng's death in February 1997, Jiang Zemin began to advance his own thoughts, not only with the hope of solving China's moral deterioration but also as a way of ideologically justifying or legitimatizing "socialism with Chinese characteristics" or a "socialist market economy" in accelerating economic reform or liberalization by privatization of state-owned enterprises.

The following represents a brief summary of the "new thinking" espoused by Jiang Zemin.

"Spiritual Civilization"

Jiang Zemin's push for "spiritual civilization" is perhaps one of the most important aspects of his "new ideological campaign" against moral and ethical deterioration and social disorder that has swept China under economic reform. To what extent "spiritual civilization" represents Jiang Zemin's own thinking is debatable. The formulation of the ideological campaign was said to have been drafted initially by Jiang's inner circle of close advisers from Shanghai with an invaluable assist from a corps of remnant "leftists" under the leadership of Deng Liquan, once a vocal critic of economic reform.[138] The ideological campaign was adopted at the party's sixth plenum of the Fourteenth Central Committee on October 14, 1996. Whereas on the one hand the party resolution promoting socialist ethical and cultural progress praised Deng Xiaoping's "theory of building socialism with Chinese characteristics," it also pointedly identified the existing problems in social, ethical, and cultural life under Deng's reform:

> The standard of moral conduct has been lowered in some spheres, and the practice of worshipping money, seeking pleasure and individualism has grown; feudal superstitions and

such social vices as pornography, gambling and drug abuse have resurfaced; production of shoddy and fake goods and fraud have become a social scourge . . . the phenomenon of corruption has been spreading in some places, seriously damaging the work style of the party and the government; and a number of people have a weak concept of the state, and waver and doubt the future of socialism. In assessing the situation confronting the promotion of ethical and cultural moralism, on no account should we neglect the existence of these problems.[139]

To solve these problems, Jiang Zemin's "spiritual civilization" calls for education in patriotism, collectivism, and socialism and vigorous advancement of "social morality, professional ethics and family virtues." It (the party resolution) wanted to foster "a hard-working and pioneering spirit of the whole nation." (This sounds like the familiar Protestant work ethic.) Then it also revived the old Maoist slogan of "service to the people" and "loving the collective" as a part of the new socialist ethics.[140] For urban residents, said the party resolution, efforts must be made by all units to foster "a beautiful environment" and "good social order" by working out blueprints for model cities.[141] In the rural township and villages there must be plans for "civilized" villages and townships to strengthen the party's grassroots collective organizations and to break away from "outmoded customs" and "illegal religious activities."[142] Finally, the party resolution concerning spiritual civilization called for renewed theoretical awareness about distinction between "Marxism versus anti-Marxism," "dialectical materialism versus idealism," "socialist public ownership as the mainstay versus privatization," and "socialist versus feudalistic and corrupt capitalist ideology and culture."[143] (As for the invasion of corrupting Western ideas, China recently restricted access to the Internet in many cities.)[144] Criminals have been executed en masse, six or seven thousand each year, for even minor offenses such as gambling and drug dealing.[145] In cities and towns, ideological classes have been reinstituted with the mass campaign practices of the 1960s and 1970s, such as emulating new model families who put garbage in plastic bags and keep sidewalks clean.[146] Calls were also issued by the party for introducing new moral values, in place of the selfish moneymaking obsession.

To the ordinary Chinese, the most serious moral problem has been rampant corruption by party and government officials at high, as well as low, levels. Many Chinese have always been rather skeptical about official efforts made in apprehending higher officials who engaged in corrupt practices. On the eve of convening the Fifteenth Party Congress, September 1997, the central party discipline inspection commission found that former Beijing city mayor, Chen Xitong, a former member of the Politburo, had engaged in embezzlement of large sums of public funds. On August 25, the commission ruled that he be expelled from party membership and that he be criminally prosecuted for wrongdoing. Of course, expulsion of a Politburo member and former mayor of the capitol city has served as an example of the party's vigilance in apprehending corrupt officials. Corruption in China has become so systemic that it requires more than an ideological campaign such as "spiritual civilization" to ever straighten up the party-state apparatus and the people who staff these offices. It will take enactment of a rule of law under which there would be rigorous enforcement and speedy just prosecution.

Neo-Conservatism and Nationalism.[147] Jiang's "spiritual civilization" is also part and parcel of the rising tide of "neo-conservatism" and nationalism in China. Supporters of neo-conservatism and nationalism are rich entrepreneurs, as well as poorly paid academics, who were not only disgusted by rampant corruption, but who were also concerned about the society's decline in moral rectitude. The neo-conservative answers to spiritual decline represent revival of good old nationalism, pride in the country, and Confucian values, including respect for authority—meaning the party under Jiang Zemin's core leadership. There is also agitation for a ban on decadent foreign influences.

Hong Kong has now reverted back to China; Taiwan must soon be united with the motherland; if necessary, by force, comes the cry throughout China. As another way of exhibiting nationalism, *The People's Daily* intoned in its headline that China must also establish its maritime claim over the disputed Spratly Islands in the South China Sea.

Market Economy as "Primary Stage of Socialism"

Readers will recall from the beginning of this chapter that Karl Marx had asserted that historical materialism determines the nature of society and that a communist society would inevitably go through several stages of development, the last of which, before the arrival of communism, is a mature, or fully developed, capitalist society. In other words, classless communism would have to evolve from an advanced capitalistic industrial society.

There has been some debate as to what exactly is Deng Xiaoping's rather vague "socialism with Chinese characteristics"? Is it "socialist market economy"? But isn't market economy a form of capitalism or capitalistic practice? In November 1993, the Fourteenth Central Committee stated, nevertheless, China's modernization had entered "a new stage" that is "linked with the basic system of socialism."[148] With the introduction of stock companies with listed shares and liability, the system of responsibility of factory manager, and now the use of blasphemous capitalistic phrases such as "merger," "acquisition," "downsizing," and selling-off state-owned enterprises that were once the mainstay of socialism, it becomes increasingly necessary from the ideological viewpoint to justify China's persistent claim as a socialist state. Or, more appropriately, the Jiang Zemin-led leadership core in the post-Deng transition must fend off the criticism of the remnant "left-thinkers;" or simply co-opt them within the party so that there is the inner-party stability, tranquility, and ideological correctness to support the economic reform that has been going on for the last two decades and that will continue.

On May 29, 1997, Jiang Zemin spoke at the graduation ceremony for provincial and ministerial level cadres in an advanced study course at the Central Party School. In that address he pronounced that "China is still in the primary stage of socialism."[149] Jiang Zemin paid tribute to Deng Xiaoping for advancing his "theory of building socialism with Chinese characteristics." He also reiterated that Deng's theory serves as a foundation for formulating "our line, principles and policies." Then he went on to explain why it is necessary to reemphasize Deng's "building socialism with Chinese characteristics":

> The reason we re-emphasize this question today is that in front of unprecedented opportunities and challenges and the arduous tasks to tackle difficult problems of reform and create a new situation, the key for us to resolve various contradictions, clarify different doubts and understand why we must carry out the existing line and policies, but not other lines and policies, lies in a unified understanding and correct mastering of the basic national conditions that China is still in the primary stage of socialism.[150]

There is, Jiang pointed out, the basic contradiction in society in the primary stage of socialism between, on the one hand, "people's ever-growing material and cultural demands" and, on the other hand, "backward social productive forces." The basic task for China, Jiang Zemin intoned, "is to concentrate efforts to develop social productive forces."[151] One of these "concrete efforts" is to "perfect the ownership structure with public ownership serving as the main body and joint development of the economy of diversified owner-ships" to form "a modern enterprise system"[152] The primary stage of socialism may last as long as 100 years, predicted Li Junru, director of the theory bureau of the party's pro-paganda department.[153]

Jiang Zemin is not the originator of the concept of "primary stage of socialism" for justifying economic reforms from the 1982 second landform, to the contract respon-sibility system (See Chapter 11), to the 1987 "socialist market economy," to the 1992 "socialism with Chinese characteristics," and to the 1997 phasing out of state-owned enterprises. In fact, according to Yan Qiaqi, an exiled former Zhao Ziyang advisor, Jiang borrowed the concept from the ousted former party chief Zhao Ziyang, who, under the lead-ership of Bao Tong (jailed briefly after the 1989 Tiananmen crackdown, and who headed the research unit for political structural reform), instructed some of his close advisors to come up with some ideological justification for market economy.[154]

Ten years ago Zhao Ziyang reported to the Thirteenth Party Congress propounding the concept of "primary stage of socialism" as the basic line of the party.[155] Zhao argued then that China was in the primary stage of socialism and that "the Chinese people can-not take the socialist road without going through the stage of fully developed capital-ism," nor could they "jump over" the stage of highly developed productive forces.[156] Zhao went on to explain that building socialism in a backward country such as China "is something new in the history of the development of Marxism": a stage through which an essentially agriculture-based society would gradually be transformed into a modern industrial country.[157] Zhao then formulated a set of principles as long-term guidelines during this primary stage of socialism: expand productive forces under modernization, per-sist in the reform process, adhere to an open policy of economic and technological exchange and cooperation, and endeavor "to build a higher degree of democracy on the basis of stability and unity."[158] According to one scholar, this "offers the market econ-omy a theoretical legitimacy."[159] As explained by a theorist in the Central Party School in 1988, China under the primary stage of socialism "is still immature, retaining many tra-ditions and traces of the old society, including some elements of private ownership."[160] And in this stage of socialism "it is necessary to develop an economy with different types of ownership, with public ownership remaining predominant."[161]

One theorist in the party, Gong Shiqi, argued that "socialism cannot be built on a natural economy," which has been the situation for China's countryside and which has now "given way to a commodity economy." Under the primary stage of socialism, China must develop "the commercial, financial, technological and labor markets" and promote "com-mon prosperity."[162] In addition, as interpreted by another theorist in the party, under the primary stage of socialism, China must build "socialist culture and ethics" and oppose "the influence of decadent feudalist and capitalist ideas."[163] Finally, in 1987 the basic pur-pose of Zhao Ziyang and the party theorists for advancing the theory or concept of the pri-mary stage of socialism was twofold: to justify continuation of reform policies and to silence "leftist" thinking, such as the long essay by Deng Liquan in 1976, that China under the reform was abandoning socialism, and those on the "right" for their "interfer-ence" in implementing the party's correct line and policy.[164]

Jiang Zemin's Reinterpretation of the Primary Stage of Socialism at the Fifteenth Party Congress

A portion of Jiang's report to the 1997 Party Congress contained further expla-nation about the primary stage of socialism. In his long speech he reiterated the thesis he presented at the Central Party School that "Socialism is the primary stage of communism, and China is in the primary stage of socialism; that is, the stage of underdevelopment."[165] He pointed out that the primary stage of socialism would be a long one which is "a historical stage we cannot jump over"; it is during this long stage that "we shall accomplish industrialization and the socialization, market orientation and modernization of the economy."[166] Jiang argued in the speech, obviously as a way of justifying the need for continuing economic reform, that "it is necessary to deepen the reform and resolve the deep-rooted contradictions and crucial problems which may arise during structural transformation." [167] Then he cautioned that "we should maintain vigilance against the 'Right' tendencies, but primarily against the 'Left.'"[168] Thus, he pleaded that market economy must be developed and China must also "take an active part in international economic cooperation and competition."[169]

It seems obvious that Jiang Zemin, as China's new leader after Deng Xiaoping, must justify ideologically why economic reforms must continue and that these reform measures have not really deviated from the basic tenets of Marxism.

Education in Patriotism. In his closing remarks to the Sixth plenary session of the Fourteenth Party Central Committee in late October 1996, Party Chairman Jiang Zemin delivered his idea on the need to strengthen education in patriotism, particularly among the youth. He made the point that it was not about "narrow nationalism," even though priority was to be given to China's sovereignty and security. He argued that the content of patriotism includes "the efforts to persist in opening up, conscientiously learning the strong points of various nations around the world, and actively introducing advanced science and technology and managerial expertise to enhance self-reliance capability and accelerate the development of the motherland."[170] He then urged the young to learn China's long history and splendid culture in China's endeavor for socialist modernization and the push forward for reform in order to revitalize the Chinese nation.[171] Education in patriotism was then incorporated as a part of the party's resolution at the 6th Plenary Session of the Fourteenth Central Committee on October 10, 1996: "In modern China, patriotism and socialism have been integrated with the great practice of building socialism with Chinese characteristics."[172] Jiang's call for "national revitalization" or patriotism certainly contained some undesirable elements of extremely hostile, if not poisonous, strains of "parochial nationalism" when the Chinese media mounted a campaign with patriotic messages nationwide.

Jiang's Contrasting Thought for Unifying Contending Forces. On the surface it appears that Jiang Zemin prefers to express his thoughts in clusters of three separate ideas. But when one closely examines these ideas, it is obvious that they really serve an important political purpose: That is, he must placate the contending forces so as to secure his continued helmsmanship into the twenty-first century, or at least at the Sixteenth Party Congress in 2002.

Let us take a brief look at some of Jiang Zemin's recent ideological pronouncements.

"The Three Representations" In his report delivered at the 1997 Fifteenth Party Congress he included at least three major policy areas: Promotion of advanced productive development with the establishment of a socialist market economy as the goal, promotion of cultural and ethical progress embodied in his push for "spiritual civilization" (discussed in a previous section), and dedication to broaden basic welfare and benefits for the people.[173]

In mid-March 2000, the party's propaganda and organization departments began to circulate the "Three Representations" as Jiang's latest contribution to a unifying ideology, followed by endorsement by a number of top party leaders who extolled the thought as a new contribution to the development of Marxism.[174] This is really an expression by the current third-generation leadership, led by Jiang Zemin, to impress upon, or provide ideological direction for the forthcoming fourth-generation leadership that it is necessary to continue adherence to market reform programs under which there would be benefits for both the masses (aimed as an appeal to the left) and those who have accumulated wealth since the party embarked on reform of the socialist system.[175] For Jiang and his successors it would be a win-win situation for adherence to the "Three Representations" would ultimately produce guaranteed reform, continued economic development, and political stability.

The "Three Talks or Stresses."   In December 1995, under the mounting pressure for curbing widespread fraudulent practices engaged in by high party officials, Jiang Zemin was compelled to make a pitch for mobilizing the party and the general populace to wage a battle to combat corruption in the officialdom. (See Chapter 4 on the topic of corruption exposures.) The so-called "Three Talks or Stresses" were really slogans reminiscent of bygone days in the form of mass ratification campaigns when Mao's radicalism was on the ascendancy. These "Three Talks" refer to (1) talk about or study (jiang xuexi)—an appeal to party officials to not only intensively study Marxism, Leninism, and Mao's and Deng's Thought, but also to learn from the exposure and expulsion of high party officials, such as the former mayor of Beijing, for their misdeeds or corruption; (2) talk about or stress politics (jiang zhengzhi)—strict adherence to the party's directives or resolutions and leadership to condemn the evil corruptive practices by officials (see Chapter 5 on corruption); (3) talk about correct work style and practice (jiang zhengfeng)—requirement that the masses strictly follow orders and not tolerate unauthorized protests and demonstrations.

Jiang's plank for "talk politics" signifies most clearly his "turn to the Left," [176] as pointed out by one analyst—a turn designed to arrest the continued deterioration of the usefulness of politics or in thinking and practice inside and outside the party. It has been said that Jiang's revival of talk about politics was influenced by a letter written by some 125 veteran party cadres, including a number of known Maoist leftists,[177] urging him to do more talking about politics or discussing Marxism-Leninism and Mao's Thought. Party cadres, including some retired high-level ones, have "lost their revolutionary fervor, committing unlawful activities," which contributed to public anger and consequently caused damage to the party's image.[178] Some cadres seemed to have lost faith in socialism and forgotten about or dared not talk about the socialist virtues or benefits; they were afraid of speaking about their duties and responsibilities as members of the party and as public servants.[179] Thus, Jiang not only ordered more discussion about politics but also stepped up political work and ideological stress among party ranks.

The rush for the promotion of Jiang Zemin Thought by some of his key supporters in the party hierarchy is by no means without criticism. For instance, Qiao Shi, a retired Political Bureau member, has offered some caution on the rush for promoting Jiang Zemin Thought by pointing out that a thought or theory must first be proven or experienced by practice.[180] Even Jiang Zemin himself had commented on another occasion that it was through practice that there would be "a new stage in the development of Marxism in China."[181] Thus, some leaders inside or outside the Politburo complained that the move to elevate Jiang Zemin Thought to the level of Deng's Theory and Marxism per se was not really appropriate.[182]

Is Jiang Zemin eager to promote himself to the level of Deng Xiaoping, or even Mao? One China scholar has described Jiang as a "pragmatist" and even conservative.[183] However, another China scholar, in his biographical study, depicts Jiang as patriotic and generally conservative, certainly not a Maoist zealot.[184] In some ways Jiang is closer to Deng Xiaoping for achieving economic reform objectives. Jiang is attempting to strive for a consensus within the ideologically factionalized leadership. What most likely influenced Jiang to seek seemingly contrasting ideas from education in patriotism and stress on politics (study the need to seek advanced technological expertise from abroad under the open door policy) is perhaps his wish to develop a synthesis so that not only would there be continued economic improvement for the masses, but also a rejuvenated party.

NOTES

1. Franz Schurmann, *Ideology and Organization in Communist China* (Berkeley: University of California Press, 1966).
2. Ibid., pp. 21–22.
3. Peter Zattow, *Anarchism and Chinese Political Culture* (New York: Columbia University Press, 1990).
4. Richard Bernstein, *From the Center of the Earth: The Search for the Truth About China*, (Boston and Toronto: Little, Brown, 1982), pp. 104–105.
5. Bernstein, *From the Center of the Earth*, p. 104; and Erik Eckholm, "At China's Colleges, a Rush Party, as in Communist," *The New York Times*, January 31, 1998, pp. A1 and A5.
6. "Recognize Correctly the Situation and Policy by Upholding the Four Guidelines," *Hongqi*, 5 (March 1, 1981), 2–11; "Overcoming Two Erroneous Trends of Thought," *Beijing Review*, 24 (June 8, 1979), 3.
7. "Hu Yaobang's Speech," *Beijing Review*, 28 (July 13, 1981), 20.
8. Feng Wenbin, "Following the Party Line Laid Down by the Third Plenum, Resolutely March Forward on the Socialist Road," *Hongqi*, 10 (May 16, 1981), 2–12. Also see *Beijing Review*, 23, 25, and 26 (June 8, 22, and 29, 1981).
9. "Nature of Chinese Society," *Beijing Review*, 23 (June 8, 1981), 22.
10. Ibid., pp. 7–8.
11. "Hu Yaobang's Speech," 20.
12. Ibid., 20.
13. Mao-Tse-tung, "Ching Kanshan Revisited," *Peking Review*, 1 (January 2, 1976), 5.
14. Stuart Schram, *Mao Tse-tung* (London: Penguin, 1970), p. 36.
15. See Enrica Collotti Pischel, "The Teacher," in *Mao Tse-tung in the Scale of History*, ed. Dick Wilson (London: Cambridge University Press, 1977), pp. 144–73.
16. Lucian Pye, *Mao-Tse-tung, the Man in the Leader* (New York: Basic Books, 1976), pp. 20–21.
17. Edgar Snow, *Red Star Over China* (New York: Grove Press, 1961), p. 151.
18. Pye, *Mao Tse-tung, the Man in the Leader*, pp. 17–38.
19. Ibid., pp. 17–38.
20. Ibid., p. 23.
21. Edgar Snow, *The Long Revolution* (New York: Vintage Books, 1973), pp. 170–71.
22. Ibid., p. 169.
23. Wilson, ed., *Mao Tse-tung in the Scale of History*.
24. Hsiung, *Ideology and Practice: The Evolution of Chinese Communism*, p. 67.
25. Mao Tse-tung, "Report on an Investigation of the Peasant Movement in Hunan," in *Selected Works of Mao Tse-tung* (Peking: Foreign Language Press, 1967), vol. i, pp. 23–59.
26. Benjamin I. Schwartz, *Communism and China: Ideology in Flux* (Cambridge, Mass.: Harvard University Press, 1968), p. 41; Hsiung, *Ideology and Practice*, pp. 61–62; and Chester C. Tan, *Chinese Political Thought in the Twentieth Century* (Garden City, N.Y.: Doubleday, 1971), pp. 345–46.
27. Hsiung, *Ideology and Practice*, p. 67; and Conrad Brandt, Benjamin Schwartz, and John Fairbank, *A Documentary History of Chinese Communism* (New York: Atheneum, 1966), pp. 80–93.
28. John W. Lewis, *Leadership in Communist China* (Ithaca, N.Y.: Cornell University Press, 1963), p. 72.

29. Mao Tse-tung, "Some Questions Concerning Methods of Leadership," in *Selected Works of Mao Tse-tung* (Peking: Foreign Language Press, 1967), vol. iii, pp. 117–22.
30. Ibid., p. 113.
31. See Lowell Dittmer, "Mass Line and Mass Criticism in China: An Analysis of the Fall of Liu Shao-chi," *Asian Survey*, 13, no. 8 (August 1973), 772–92.
32. Stuart Schram, "The Marxist," in *Mao Tse-tung in the Scale of History*, p. 48. Also in Lewis, *Leadership in Communist China*, p. 79.
33. Lewis, *Leadership in Communist China*, pp. 84–86.
34. James R. Townsend, "Chinese Populism and the Legacy of Mao Tse-tung," *Asian Survey*, 18, no. 11 (November 1977), 1006–11.
35. Ibid., p. 1009.
36. See James C. F. Wang, "Values of the Cultural Revolution," in the *Journal of Communication*, 27, no. 3 (Summer 1977), 41–46. Also see Maurice Meisner, "Utopian Goals and Ascetic Values in Chinese Communist Ideology," *Journal of Asian Studies*, 28, no. 1 (November 1968), 101–10.
37. Mao Tse-tung, "On Practice," *Selected Works of Mao Tse-tung* (Peking: Foreign Language Press, 1967), vol. i, pp. 295–309.
38. John Bryan Starr, *Ideology and Culture: An Introduction to the Dialectic of Contemporary Chinese Politics* (New York: Harper and Row, 1973), p. 30.
39. Hsiung, *Ideology and Practice*, pp. 102–3; Pye, *Mao Tse-tung: The Man in the Leader*, p. 45; Schram, "The Marxist," p. 60.
40. *Selected Works of Mao Tse-tung* (Peking: Foreign Language Press, 1977), vol. v, pp. 384–421.
41. Starr, *Ideology and Culture*, p. 128.
42. Mao Tse-tung, "On the Ten Major Relationships, April 25, 1956," *Peking Review*, 1 (January 1, 1977), 10–25.
43. Mao Tse-tung, "On Contradiction," in *Selected Works of Mao Tse-tung* (Peking: Foreign Language Press 1967), vol. i, p. 517.
44. William Hinton, *Turning Point in China: An Essay on the Cultural Revolution* (New York: Monthly Review Press, 1972).
45. Shih Kang, "Dialectics in Blast Furnaces," *Peking Review*, 41 (October 12, 1973), 19–20.
46. The illustration is given by Gray and Cavendish, *Chinese Communism in Crisis* (New York and London: Holt, Rinehart & Winston, 1968), pp. 59–60.
47. Schurmann, *Ideology and Organization*, p. 54.
48. Ibid., p. 55.
49. "Talks at the Chengtu Conference, March 1958" in Stuart Schram, ed., *Chairman Mao Talks to the People, Talks and Letters, 1956–1971* (New York: The Pantheon Asia Library, 1974), p. 108. For further insights into the concept, see Schram's two articles, "Mao Tse-tung and the Theory of Permanent Revolution," *China Quarterly*, 46 (April–June 1971), 221–44, and "The Marxist," pp. 56–62. Also, see John Bryan Starr, "Conceptual Foundations of Mao Tse-tung's Theory of Continuing Revolution," *Asian Survey*, 11, no. 6 (June 1971), 610–28.
50. Starr, "Conceptual Foundations of Mao Tse-tung's Theory," p. 612.
51. Mao Tse-tung, "On Question of Party History," *Selected Works of Mao Tse-tung*, 29.
52. "How to Define Mao Zedong Thought," *Beijing Review*, 1 (January 7, 1980), 5–6. Also see Deng Xiaoping's interview with Oriana Fallaci, *Guardian Weekly* (September 21, 1980), p. 17.
53. Mao Tse-Tung, 35.
54. Ibid. On the matter of class struggle, see the following issues of *Beijing Review*: 7 (February 18, 1980), 6; 20 (May 19, 1980), 24; 22 (June 2, 1980), 24; 34 (August 24, 1981), 3; 44 (November 2, 1981), 20; 17 (April 26, 1982), 3; 33 (August 16, 1982), 17; 49 (December 6, 1982), 16.
55. Mao Tse-tung, 21.
56. Ibid.
57. Ibid., p. 37.
58. See editorial in the *People's Daily*, November 6, 1982, p. 1; and Xi Xuan, "Why Should a Theory be Discarded?" *Beijing Review*, 44 (November 2, 1981), 20.
59. *People's Daily* (November 6, 1982), p. 1.
60. "Communiqué of the Third Plenary Session of the Eleventh Central Committee, Adopted on December 22, 1978," *Peking Review*, 52 (December 29, 1978), 19.
61. Ibid., p. 11; and *Beijing Review*, 7 (December 18, 1980), 6.
62. Xuan "Why Should a Theory be Discarded?" p. 20.
63. Ibid., pp. 21–22.
64. "Current Class Struggle," *Beijing Review*, 17 (April 26, 1982), 3.
65. Ibid.

66. Townsend, "Chinese Populism and the Legacy of Mao Tse-tung," p. 1011.

67. Schram, "The Marxist," p. 69.

68. Mike Oksenberg, "Mao's Policy Commitments, 1921–1976," *Problems of Communism*, 25, no. 6 (November–December 1976), 19–26. Also see his article "The Political Leader," in *Mao Tse-tung in the Scale of History*, pp. 88–98.

69. Chou En-lai, "Learn from Mao Tse-tung," *Peking Review*, 43 (October 27, 1978), 7.

70. Ibid., p. 8.

71. Communiqué of the Third Plenary Session of the Eleventh Central Committee of the Communist Party of China, pp. 14–15.

72. Ibid., p. 15.

73. *Ming Pao* (Hong Kong) November 30, 1978, p. 1.

74. Mao Tse-tung pp. 8–39.

75. Deng Xiaoping's interview with Oriana Fallaci in "Deng: Cleaning Up Mao's Feudal Mistakes," p. 16.

76. Mao Tse-tung, 29.

77. Ibid., p. 35.

78. See Dittmer, "China in 1981: Reform, Readjustment, and Rectification," pp. 34, 42.

79. "Differentiations Are Necessary," *Beijing Review*, 38 (September 21, 1982), 17.

80. Mao Tse-tung, 35; and "Differentiations Are Necessary," p. 17.

81. Huang Kecheng, "How to Assess Chairman Mao and Mao Zedong Thought," *Beijing Review*, 17 (April 17, 1981), 22.

82. Ibid.

83. See text of document entitled "Senior Cadres' Appraisal of Mao Zedong," in *Issues and Studies*, 16, no. 5 (May 1980), 77.

84. Kecheng, "How to Assess Chairman Mao and Mao Zedong Thought." Also see "Deng: Cleaning Up Mao's Feudal Mistakes," 17.

85. Kecheng, "How to Assess Chairman Mao and Mao Zedong Thought."

86. Mao Tse-tung, 19.

87. Kecheng, "How to Assess Chairman Mao and Mao Zedong Thought," 21; and "Deng: Cleaning Up Mao's Feudal Mistakes," 16.

88. "Deng: Cleaning Up Mao's Feudal Mistakes," 16.

89. Ibid.

90. "Had 'Cultural Revolution' Mass Support?" *Beijing Review*, 47 (November 23, 1981), 20–21.

91. Mao Tse-tung, 22.

92. Ibid.

93. "Deng: Cleaning up Mao's Feudal Mistakes," 7, 18.

94. Mao Tse-tung, 19, 25. Also see "Hu Yaobang's Speech," 12.

95. "The Correct Concept of Individual Role in History," *People's Daily*, July 4, 1980, p. 1. Also see Mao Tse-tung, 25.

96. Mao Tse-tung, 25.

97. Ibid.

98. *People's Daily,* August 14, 1981, p. 1.

99. Krishna P. Gupta, "Mao's Uncertain Legacy," *Problems of Communism*, 31 (January–February 1982), 45. One China scholar felt the Mao assessment in the early 1980s was not really "de-Maoism," but a Dengist effort to "use Mao's charism." See Jean C. Robinson, "Mao after Death: Charisma and Political Legitimacy," *Asian Survey*, 28, no. 3 (March 1988), 353–68.

100. Gupta, "Mao's Uncertain Legacy," 50.

101. Ibid.

102. For scholarship on Mao, see Ross Terrill, *Mao: A Biography* (New York: Harper and Row, 1980); Dick Wilson, *The People's Emperor Mao: A Biography of Mao Tse-tung* (New York: Doubleday, 1980); Maurice Meisner, "Most of Maoism's Gone, But Mao's Shadow Isn't," *Sunday New York Times,* July 5, 1981, p. E-15; Raymond F. Wylie, *The Emergence of Maoism* (Stanford, Calif.: Stanford University Press, 1980).

103. Harrison E. Salisbury, *The New Emperors: China in the Era of Mao and Deng* (Boston: Little, Brown, 1992).

104. See Li Zhisui, *The Private Life of Chairman Mao* (New York: Random House, 1994).

105. See *Beijing Review*, 40 (October 6, 1986), i–viii.

106. *Zhengming*, 109 (November 1986), 30.

107. *Beijing Review*, 40 (October 6, 1986), ii.

108. Ibid., iii.
109. Ibid.
110. Ibid., vii.
111. Ibid.
112. Ibid., iv.
113. See *Beijing Review*, 3 (January 19, 1987), 15.
114. Ibid.
115. *People's Daily*, January 12, 1987, p. 1.
116. *Beijing Review*, 3 (January 19, 1987), 16.
117. *Beijing Review*, 8 (February 23, 1987), 14; and *New York Times,* January 19, 1987, p. 1.
118. Jan S. Prybyla, "China's Economic Experiment: From Mao to Market," *Problems of Communism* (January–February, 1986), 23.
119. *Wall Street Journal,* February 2, 1987, p. 19.
120. *Beijing Review*, 5 and 6 (February 9, 1987), 26–29.
121. Ibid., p. 28.
122. Ibid., p. 30.
123. *People's Daily,* January 22, 1987, p. 1.
124. Ibid.
125. *Beijing Review*, 5 and 6 (February 9, 1987), 29–36. Also see these issues in *People's Daily*: (January 15, 1987), 1 and 4; (January 29, 1987), 1; (January 30, 1987), 1; (February 2, 1987), 1; and (February 22, 1987), 1.
126. See *Zhengming*, 119 (September 1987), 13–14.
127. *Beijing Review* (April 4–22, 1990), 11.
128. Ibid., xviii.
129. Jiang Zenin, "Accelerating Reform and Opening Up," *Beijing Review* (26 October–1 November 1992), 16.
130. Li Haibo, "The Man Who Makes History," *Beijing Review* (12–18 October 1992), 17.
131. The New York Times Service as reprinted in the *Honolulu Star-Bulletin,* 20 May 1993, p. A-12.
132. See *China Daily,* September 19, 1997, p. 2.
133. Robert A. Scalapino, "Deng's China: What Lies Ahead," in Shao Chuan Leng, ed., *Reform and Development in Deng's China.* (Lanham, Md.: University Press of America, 1994), p. 172.
134. Yoichi Funabashi, Michael Oksenberg, and Heinrich Weiss, *An Emerging China in a World of Interdependence: A Report to the Trilateral Commission.* (New York, Paris, and Tokyo, May 1994), p. 1.
135. "Rethinking China," *Business Week*, March 4, 1996, p. 59.
136. See David G. Goodman, "China: The State and Capitalist Revolution," *Pacific Review*, 5, no. 4 (1992), 350–59. Also see Richard Robinson and David Goodman, *The New Rich in Asia: Mobile Phones, McDonalds and Middle-Class Revolution* (London: Routledge, 1993), p. 350. Also see Jonathan Spence and Annping Chin, "Deng's Heirs," *New Yorker*, March 10, 1996, pp. 68–77.
137. See Hilton Root, "Corruption in China: Has It Become Systemic?" *Asian Survey*, 36 no. 8 (August 1996), pp. 741– 757; and Melanie Manion, "Corruption by Design: Bribery in Chinese Enterprise Licensing," unpublished manuscript, Faculty of Social Sciences, Lingnan College (Hong Kong), 1994.
138. Que Tao, "*Jingshen wenming weihui zuo jiang yunjie*" (Spiritual Civilization Committee: A Gathering of the Left), *Zhengming* (Hong Kong), (November 1996), 26–29.
139. "Resolutions in the CCP Central Committee Regarding Important Questions on Promoting Socialist Ethical and Cultural Progress," adopted at the Sixth Plenum of the Fourteenth CCP Central Committee, October 10, 1996, *Beijing Review* (November 4-10, 1996), 22.
140. Ibid., p. 25. For discussion on the debates by Chinese intellectuals in the 1980s, see the book by Jing Wang, *High Culture Fever: Politics, Aesthetics, and Ideology in Deng's China* (Berkeley: University of California Press, 1997).
141. Ibid., p. 28.
142. Ibid., p. 29.
143. Ibid., p. 30.
144. Kathy Chen, "China Intensifies Ideological Campaign," *Wall Street Journal*, September 13, 1996, p. A-6.
145. "China Embarks on Crusade for a Moral Reformation," *Los Angeles Times*, as reprinted in *Honolulu Advertiser*, September 15, 1996, p. A-2.
146. Ibid.
147. Discussion on the section is culled from "The New Nationalism," in *China Transition: Towards the New Millennium* (Hong Kong: Review Publishing Company, 1997), pp. 17–19; Matt Forney, "Patriot Games," *Far Eastern Economic Review*, (October 3, 1996), 22–26; Yongnian Zheng, "Nationalism,

Neo-Authoritarianism, and Political Liberalism: Are They Shaping Political Agenda in China?" *Asian Affairs: An American Review*, 19, no. 4 (Winter 1993), 207–223 ; and Jean Philippe Béja, "The Rise of National Confucianism," in *China Perspectives* (Hong Kong), no. 2 (November–December 1995), 6–13.

148. See "Decision of the CCP Central Committee on Some Issues Concerning the Establishment of a Socialist Market Economic Structure—Adopted on November 14, 1993 by the Third Plenary Session of the Fourteenth Central Committee of the CCP," *Beijing Review* (November 22–28, 1993), 12–31.
149. "Upholding the Banner of Deng's Theory," *Beijing Review* (August 25–31, 1997), 10-13.
150. Ibid., 12.
151. Ibid.
152. Ibid.
153. "How to Understand Jiang's Important Speech," *Beijing Review* (August 25–31, 1997), 16.
154. Yan Qiaqi, "*Chuji jieduanlun di qiyuan*" (The Origin of the Primary Stage Thesis), *The Trend* (Hong Kong) (September 1997), 36–37.
155. Zhao Ziyang, "Advance Along the Road of Socialism with Chinese Characteristics: Report Delivered at the Thirteenth National Congress of the CCP on October 25, 1987," *Beijing Review* (November 9–15, 1987), 25–28.
156. Ibid., 25–26.
157. Ibid., 27.
158. Ibid.
159. See Zheng, "Nationalism, Neo-Authoritarianism, and Political Liberalism" p. 216.
160. See Gong Shiqi, "Economic Features of Primary Stage of Socialism," *Beijing Review* (February 15–28, 1988), 18.
161. Ibid., 19.
162. Ibid., 20.
163. Dai Yannian, "An Important Thesis on Building Socialism," *Beijing Review* (November 9–15, 1987), 7.
164. Ibid., 9.
165. Jiang Zemin, "Hold High the Great Banner of Deng Xiaoping Theory for an All-Round Advancement of the Cause of Building Socialism with Chinese Characteristics into the 21st Century," report delivered at the Fifteenth National Congress of the CCP on September 12, 1997, *Beijing Review* (October 6–12, 1997), 16.
166. Ibid.
167. Ibid., 17.
168. Ibid.
169. Ibid., 18.
170. See "Jiang Zemin's Speech on Education in Patriotism," *Beijing Review* (June 2–8, 1997), 20.
171. Ibid.
172. See "Resolution of the CPC Central Committee Regarding Important Questions on Promoting Socialist Ethical and Cultural Progress," *Beijing Review* (November 4–10, 1996), 25.
173. See "Hold High the Great Banner of Deng Xiaoping Theory in All-Round Advancement of the Cause of Building Socialism with Chinese Characteristics into the 21st Century," *Beijing Review* (October 6-12, 1997), 12–13.
174. Lo Bin, "Jiang Zemin's Self-Promotion of Jiang Zemin Thought," *Zhengming* (Hong Kong), no. 271 (May 2000), 12–14.
175. Xin Yong, "Inside Account; The Reason for Proposing Jiang Zemin's 'Three Representations,'" *The Mirror* (Hong Kong), no. 275 (June 2000), 20–22.
176. Lo Bin, "The Background of Jiang Zemin's 'Talk about Politics,'" *Zhengming* (Hong Kong) (February 1996) 6–7.
177. Ibid.
178. Ibid.
179. Ibid., 7.
180. See Lo Bin, "Jiang Zemin's Self-Promotion of 'Jiang Zemin Thought,'" *Zhengming* (Hong Kong), no. 271 (May 2000), 12–14.
181. See Jiang Zemin speech on May 29, 1997 in a graduating ceremony for provincial cadres at the Central Party School, "Upholding the Banner of Deng's Theory," *Beijing Review* (August 25-31, 1997), 10–11.
182. Bin, "Jiang Zemin's Self-Promotion of 'Jiang Zemin Thought,'" 13.
183. Wally Wo Lap Lam, *The Era of Jiang Zemin* (New York and Singapore: Prentice Hall, 1999).
184. Bruce Gilley, *Tiger on the Brink: Jiang Zemin and China's New Elite* (Berkeley: University of California Press, 1998).

SUGGESTED READINGS

Gilley, Bruce, *Tiger on the Brink: Jiang Zemin and China's New Elite* (Berkeley: University of California Press, 1998).

Hsiung, James. *Ideology and Practice: The Evolution of Chinese Communism* (New York: Praeger, 1970).

Kalpana, Misra. *From Post-Maoism to Post Marxism: The Erosion of Official Ideology in Deng's China* (New York and London: Routledge, 1998).

Lam, Wally Wo Lap. *The Era of Jiang Zemin* (New York and Singapore: Prentice Hall, 1999).

Leys, Simon. *Chinese Shadow* (Middlesex, England: Penguin, 1978).

Pye, Lucian. *Mao Tse-tung, the Man in the Leader* (New York: Basic Books, 1976).

Salisbury, Harrison E. *The New Emperors: China in the Era of Mao and Deng* (Boston: Little, Brown, 1992).

Schram, Stuart. *Mao Tse-tung* (London: Penguin, 1970).

Schurmann, Franz. *Ideology and Organization in Communist China* (Berkeley: University of California Press, 1966).

Schwartz, Benjamin I. *Communism and China: Ideology in Flux* (Cambridge, Mass: Harvard University Press, 1968).

Snow, Edgar. *Red Star over China* (New York: Grove Press, 1961).

Terrill, Ross. *Mao: A Biography* (New York: Harper & Row, 1980).

Wang, Ting. *High Culture Fever: Athletics and Ideology in Deng's China* (Berkeley: University of California Press, 1996).

Chapter Four

Political Institutions of the Party-State

*Structural Issues
and the Policy Process*

Most of us who are familiar with democratic political systems tend to think of political institutions in terms of the different functions they must perform: executive (administrative), legislative, and judicial. In democratic societies these functions or powers are generally defined by state constitutions. Constitutions in democratic societies do not undergo drastic changes due to periodic upheavals. For China, because of its revolutionary nature as a state, there have been changes and upheavals, as discussed in Chapter 2, particularly during the Cultural Revolution decade (1966–76), when the goal of the upheaval, as instigated by Mao, was to "revolutionize" the established institutions. However, taking contemporary political developments in the People's Republic of China as a whole, we see that the basic structure of political institutions remains the same as that existing prior to the Cultural Revolution in terms of (1) continued party control or monopoly, (2) the hierarchical pattern, (3) methods by which party control is exercised, and (4) the highly bureaucratic nature of the political system.

In this chapter we will look more closely at two areas: first, the party as a basic political institution; second, the central government as an entrenched, cumbersome, bureaucratic machine in need of structural reform.

The Chinese Communist Party (CCP) is the source of all political power and has the exclusive right to legitimize and control all other political organizations. The CCP alone determines the social, economic, and political goals for society. The attainment of these goals is pursued through careful recruitment of members and their placement in party organs that supervise and control all other institutions and groups in society. All other institutions in China are controlled by the elites, who are themselves leaders of the party hierarchy.

THE HIERARCHICAL STRUCTURE OF THE PARTY

The salient characteristics of the party as an organization are that it is hierarchical, pyramidal, and centralist in nature. A simplified representation of the structure of the CCP is shown in Figure 4.1. The pyramidal structure of the CCP has four main levels of organizations: (1) the central organizations; (2) the provincial organizations; (3) the xian (county) or district organizations; and (4) the basic and primary organizations—party branches in schools, factories, and villages.

CENTRAL-LEVEL PARTY ORGANS AND FUNCTIONS

In this section the central level of the party structure will be discussed in some detail. As we study the highest level of the party's organizations, we need to bear in mind that it is this network of overcentralized organizations that initiates, at the Politburo and Central Committee levels, or at the apex, policy decisions that are perfunctorily approved by the Central Committee. As we look at the overall organizational chart for the party in Figure 4.1, we see that the emphasis is on the flow of authority from top to bottom in accordance with the Leninist organizational concept of centralism. China, North Korea, and Vietnam have the only Leninist parties remaining after the collapse of the Soviet Union bloc in 1990–91.

FIGURE 4.1   Simplified Model of CCP Organizational Pyramid. *Source:* Modified version of Joseph L. LaPalombara, *Politics within Nations* (Upper Saddle River, N.J.: Prentice Hall, 1974), p. 527. By permission of publisher.

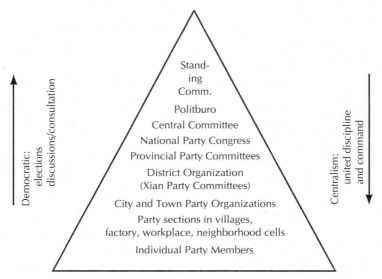

The National Party Congress

In conformity with the tradition of a Leninist party, the CCP vests its supreme authority, at least nominally, in the National Party Congress (NPC). During its seventy-six year history, fifteen National Party Congresses have convened. The 1969, 1973, 1977, and 1982 party constitutions all stipulated that a congress must meet every five years. The two longest intervals between congresses were eleven years and thirteen years, between the Seventh Congress in 1945 and the Eighth Congress in 1956, and between the Eighth Congress and the Ninth Congress in 1969. The party constitutions of 1956, 1969, 1973, 1977, and 1982 contain a proviso, an escape clause, which states that "under special circumstances, it [the National Party Congress] may be convened before its due date or postponed" by the Central Committee. The 1982 party constitution also stipulated that the party congress may be convened if more than one-third of the provincial party organizations so request. Since the party congress generally meets in a perfunctory manner to approve policy changes recommended by the Central Committee, generally its sessions have been short, a week or two in duration.

We do not know how the delegates are chosen. The procedures for selection are generally determined by the Central Committee. Presumably, delegates are selected at the provincial and district levels to reflect the "constellation of power" at the central level. It is also possible for the power at the center to engage in slate making. The process of packing the congress at various levels of the party organization to represent factionalized leaders also may be in operation. Wang Hongwen, a radical leader from Shanghai, had been accused of pressuring his close supporters to run for the position of delegate for the Tenth Party Congress.[1] However, it was revealed in 1968 by Xie Fuzhi, the minister for public security, that delegates to the Second through the Seventh Party Congresses had been appointed.[2] The Central Committee instructed that delegates to the 1982 party congress be elected "by secret ballot after full consultation at party congresses" at every level of the party structure. For the first time, the instructions stipulated that "the number of candidates shall be greater than the number of delegates to be elected."[3] This was an attempt to democratize the party's election process. In addition, the Central Committee urged election to the party congress of experts in economics, science, and technology, and of women and minorities.

The sheer size of the party congress—2,074 delegates for the Fifteenth Congress (1997)—makes it too unwieldy a body to be truly deliberative. However, the party congress does have certain basic functions to perform. Generally speaking, each session of the party congress has three standard items that constitute the entire agenda: a political report by the party chairperson or the chairperson's designee, a report on the revision of the party constitution, and the election of the Central Committee and its Standing Committee.

In 1982 some modification was made to the party congress agenda. The Central Committee in its February 1982 resolution set five agenda items:[4] report of the Central Committee, report by the party's discipline inspection commission, revision of the party constitution, outline of the long-term economic development plan, and election of a new Central Committee and Politburo.

A major task of the National Party Congress is to select the new Central Committee. Perhaps selection is not the proper term to describe the actual process involved: A preliminary list of those to become members of the Central Committee is usually drawn up by the key leaders in the hierarchy, and then the list is presented to the party congress for formal ratification. For instance, the draft list for members of the Eighth Central Committee (1956) was prepared by Liu Shaoqi supporters—Peng Zhen and An Ziwens.[5] At the Twelfth Party Congress (1982), delegates were given colored computer cards listing the names of all nominees for the Central Committee and for Central Advisory Commission membership. It was reported that during the balloting, delegates were permitted to delete any names on the list, as was the practice of the Seventh Party Congress (1945). Another feature introduced at the 1982 party congress, presumably a measure designed to democratize the party, gave delegates the right to "write up" names not on the nominations list.[6]

The party constitution adopted by the 1982 party congress was said to have been initiated by Deng Xiaoping, Hu Yaobang, and Hu Qiaomu, a key member of the Central Secretariat before he was elevated to the Politburo, and a former president of the Chinese Academy of Sciences. Hu Qiaomu and Peng Zhen presided over the drafting of the 1982 party constitution. The draft was circulated for discussion and comment at the Fifth Plenum of the Eleventh Central Committee in February.[7] After further revision by the Politburo and the Central Secretariat, it was sent to all levels of the party apparatus for discussion. While the 1977 party constitution was influenced by the remnants of the Left led by Hua Guofeng and Wang Dongxing, the 1982 party constitution represented the influence and power of Deng Xiaoping. The preparation of the 1982 party constitution was actually carried out in the winter of 1979 by the leaders associated with Deng. It went through four drafts before being introduced at the last session of the Eleventh Central Committee for adoption. The 1982 party constitution was as lengthy and detailed as the 1956 party constitution.

Some students of Chinese politics have pointed out that in addition to the important tasks of ratification of the party constitution and election of the Central Committee, the party congress accepts and reviews political reports from party leaders.[8] Reports presented at the National Party Congress have been published, and one can infer policy shifts and program emphasis from them. Since the Central Committee debates are never published except for occasional communiqués summarizing policy formulations and personnel changes, reports of the National Party Congress provide a unique source of information about the issues and programs of concern to the party. For example, at the party's Fourteenth Congress, held in October 1992, 2,000 delegates approved the party line for the next five years, or until 1997. It was outlined in the general secretary's lengthy speech that China must embrace the reform known as "socialist market economy," which was initiated by the 89-year-old paramount leader, Deng Xiaoping.[9] As it will be pointed out in later paragraphs, the September 1997 Party Congress not only reaffirmed Deng's party line about continued economic reform but also other key matters such as age limit for top leaders.

Finally, there has always been a great deal of fanfare and publicity focused on the party congress. This is more than mere public relations work by the party. The convocation of the congress serves as a rallying point for the party members and for the populace in general. It creates a feeling of participation in the important decisions of the party among the delegates themselves, many of whom come from very humble backgrounds and remote regions of China. It instills in them the "sense of commitment" to and unity with their leaders and the party.[10] In 1982, for the first time, television programs focused on the proceedings of the 1982 party congress. Provincial and local stations broadcast many features about the party, including new songs composed for the occasion.

In view of the limited duration and agenda of the party congress, the question arises as to how preparations for it are made. Technically, the outgoing Central Committee is responsible for preparing the forthcoming congress. In practice, however, the Politburo or the Standing Committee of the Politburo prepares the agenda and designates members to draft the political reports and work on the new party constitution under its supervision. We probably can assume that political reports from the Seventh Party Congress (1945) through the Tenth Party Congress (1973) received personal approval from Mao. There have been admissions of hasty preparation for the proceedings of the party congress. Mrs. Liu Shaoqi (Wang Guangmei) admitted, under Red Guard interrogation during the Cultural Revolution, that "everything was done in a hurry" in preparation for the Eighth Party Congress (1956).[11]

Evidently, this was not the case when preparations for the 1982 party congress were initiated in the winter of 1979. The agenda for the 1982 party congress was not approved until February 1980 at the Central Committee's sixth plenary session.[12] The date for convening the party congress was not set by the Politburo until the spring of 1982, a delay of more than two years—yet within the five-year interval prescribed by the previous 1977 constitution. There were several reasons for the long delay in convening the party congress: (1) Deng Xiaoping needed time to consolidate his power by first installing Hu Yaobang and Zhao Ziyang in key party and governmental positions; (2) the vestiges of the "Whatever" faction had to be removed from the center of power; and (3) the issue of how to assess Mao needed to be decided before delegate selection to the new party congress could take place. Thus, disunity and disagreement had to be minimized or eliminated. In short, Deng needed time to arrange matters so that his control over delegate selection would be assured.

The Fourteenth Party Congress, convened in October 1992, represented the final triumph of Deng Xiaoping when it endorsed wholeheartedly his "socialist market economy," or "building socialism under Chinese characteristics"—the official party acceptance of capitalist tools as "magic weapons" for a prosperous China (see the section on Dengism in Chapter 3).

The Fifteenth Party Congress, convened in September 1997, was the one in which Jiang Zemin took personal control as Deng Xiaoping had passed away seven months prior to the convocation. Some 2,074 delegates attended the gathering, which, in accordance with the 1982 CCP constitution, must be held in five-year intervals. Based on past practice, major decisions, such as the composition of the Politburo, were predetermined at an enlarged Politburo meeting at Beidaihe, the summer resort, in early September.[13] Specifically, according to one account, four key matters were decided at those meetings which the full Fifteenth Party Congress would have to approve perfunctorily: the age limit for leading cadres to serve at top slots in the party; elimination of the military's representation at the Politburo; approval of the list for membership in the Politburo, its Standing Committee, and the central secretariat; and invitation to retired leading cadres to serve as advisors on major decision-making matters.[14] In essence, the national party congress merely "rubber stamps" the decisions made by top leaders in exclusive meetings prior to convening the convocation—the standard operating procedure in the party's history.

The Central Committee

The party constitution vests in the Central Committee the supreme power to govern party affairs and to enact party policies when the party congress is not in session. The large size of the Central Committee makes it an unwieldy body for policy making. Although the Central Committee as a collective body rarely initiates party policy, it must approve or endorse policies, programs, and major changes in membership of leading central organs. Thus, with a few exceptions, the Central Committee usually holds annual plenary sessions, either with its own full membership and alternate membership in attendance, or with non-Central Committee members as well in enlarged sessions. The few deviations from the norm occurred during the Korean War (1950–53), during the turbulent period prior to the Cultural Revolution (1962–66), and during the Lin Biao affair (1971–73). These regularized plenums of the Central Committee are the forums through which party and state policies and programs are discussed and ratified. On at least two occasions— the October 1955 plenum (enlarged), and the August 1959 plenum (enlarged)—the Central Committee became the "ultimate" body in deciding which agricultural policies were to be implemented. This occurred as a result of dissension among top leaders of the party.[15]

There has been a steady increase in the size of the Central Committee. The first session of the Eighth Party Congress (1956) expanded the full membership of the Central Committee from 44 to 97. The Fifteenth Central Committee, elected in September 1997, has a total membership of 344 (193 full and 151 alternate members).

There are several reasons why the membership of the Central Committee has increased its size. First, increased membership in the Central Committee reflects the phenomenal growth of the party membership as a whole since the Cultural Revolution, from approximately 17 million in 1961, to over 28 million at the time of the Tenth Party Congress in August 1973, to 53 million when the Fourteenth Party Congress convened in 1992; and to 58 million when the Fifteenth Party Congress convened in September 1997. Second, as in the former Soviet Union, membership in the Central Committee has been used as a reward for loyal service to the party and to the government. Preeminent scholars and scientists have been elevated to Central Committee membership. Third, the Ninth and Tenth Party Congresses expanded Central Committee membership in order to make it reflect post-Cultural Revolution party leadership recruitment policy—increased representation by workers and peasants who have rendered significant political service to the party.

The Fourteenth Party Congress elected a total of 319 (189 full and 130 alternate) members for the Central Committee. Approximately 57 percent of the total were newly elected and 42 percent were holdovers from the Thirteenth Central Committee.[16] Xiaowei Zang has characterized the Fourteenth Central Committee as a "political technocratic" leadership in that they were younger in age—(approximately 81 percent were between 50 and 64); better educated, with 84 percent having a college education; and with technical or bureaucratic experience (65 percent worked in engineering, finance, industrial bureaus, and other government party offices).[17]

Approximately 42 percent of the 193 full members of the Fifteenth Central Committee represented central party and government administrative cadres, or the technical-bureaucratic elites; military representation on the Fifteenth Central Committee full membership was about 22 percent, approximately the same as for the Fourteenth Central Committee in 1992. The provincial party government elites totaled 32 percent of the full membership, and the remaining 4 percent was composed of mass organizations, intellectuals, and model workers (those selected by party cells in factories for their loyalty and hard work).

The Politburo and Its Standing Committee: The Apex of Power

The principle of Lenin's democratic centralism calls for decision-making power within the party to be vested in a small number of key leaders who occupy positions at the apex of the power structure, the Political Bureau (Politburo). The formal language in the party constitution does not reveal the actual power of this top command of the CCP. The party constitutions of 1969, 1973, 1977, and 1982 simply stipulate that the Politburo shall be elected by the Central Committee in full session and shall act on its behalf when the Central Committee is not in session. The day-to-day work of the Politburo is carried out by its Standing Committee, the apex of the pyramidal structure of the party.[18] In essence, it is the Politburo and its Standing Committee that possess "boundless" power over the general policies of the party and all important matters of the regime that affect the government organs.[19] It is the Politburo that selects top personnel to direct the vast apparatus of the party, the government, and the military.

The Politburo holds frequent meetings; discussion is said to be frank and unrestrained. It has been compared to a corporate board of directors.[20] Decisions of the Politburo are generally reached by consensus after thorough discussion of the available alternatives.

According to the party constitution, the Central Committee elects members to the Politburo and its Standing Committee, but between 1935 and 1975 the actual selection rested in the hands of Chairman Mao. In fact, the determination of which Central Committee members were to sit on the powerful Politburo had been termed Mao's "personal prerogative."[21] Franklin Houn points out that Mao followed a general set of guidelines in his selection of candidates to Politburo membership: seniority in the party, contributions made to Mao's own rise to power, and loyalty and usefulness to Mao and to the party.[22]

At the Fifteenth Party Congress held in September 1997, about six months after Deng Xiaoping's death, a new seven-member Standing Commitee of the Politburo, the "apex of the apex" in the party, was elected by secret ballot. Of the seven members, five are holdovers: Jiang Zemin, the party's general secretary; Li Peng, the designated head of the National People's Congress (the Chinese legislative body); Zhu Rongji, economic czar and the incoming premier of the State Council; Li Ruihuan; and Hu Jintao. One of the two new members of the Standing Committee is Wei Jianxing; he was appointed as the party's discipline inspection chief in 1992 and became concurrently the temporary mayor of Beijing in 1995 after his party inspection unit indicted the former mayor for corruption. The other is Li Lanqing; he was formerly with the First Auto Works in the northeast and served as foreign trade minister in the 1990s. He has been a vice-premier.

The average age of the 1997 elected Politburo's Standing Committee, similar to an executive committee of a board of directors, is about 65, slightly higher than the previous Standing Committee's average of 63; five have had formal education up to the university level and/or have studied abroad. The others had their training in party organization work and as carpenters or auto workers in supervisory positions. Of the other fifteen members of the Politburo, eight (more than 50 percent) are holdovers from the previous Politburo elected in 1992, and the remaining seven are new members.

A more detailed biographic review of the Politburo's Standing Committee members is to be found in the next chapter on the leadership core under Jiang Zemin.

Other Principal Organs of the Central Committee

The Central Committee and its Politburo are serviced by a host of centralized organs, responsible for executing party policies and managing party affairs. Some of this machinery deals with the routine matters of party organization, propaganda, and united front work. However, four principal central party organs need to be briefly mentioned here: the Central Secretariat, the Military Affairs Committee, the Central Commission for Discipline Inspection, and the Central Advisory Commission (abolished in 1992).

The Central Secretariat. The Central Secretariat, as it existed from 1956–66, was the administrative and staff agency that supervised the party's numerous functional departments, paralleling the functional ministries of the central government. The total number of these central party functional departments may once have reached more than eighteen. Membership of the Central Secretariat was not fixed: It ranged from six or seven to ten or eleven top-ranking Central Committee members. For over a decade, the Central Secretariat was under the control of Deng Xiaoping, who served as its general secretary. Deng and the members of the Central Secretariat used the machinery to make or influence many important party decisions without even consulting Mao, the chairman of the party.[23]

The reinstitution of a general secretariat and the abolition of the post of party chairperson must be viewed as an obvious rejection of Mao's practice of "overconcentration of personal power" in the party. The daily work of the party or of the Central Committee was to be supervised by the Central Secretariat headed by Hu Yaobang, who in turn was assisted by eleven other members (one died in January 1983), four of whom were concurrently members of the Politburo. The 1982 party constitution makes it clear that the daily work of the Central Committee is to be carried out by the Central Secretariat under the overall direction of the Politburo and its Standing Committee. Article 21 of the 1982 party constitution stipulates that the general secretary must be a member of the Standing Committee of the Politburo and that it is his or her responsibility to convene its meetings.

The Central Secretariat now consists of seven major departments:[24] organization, propaganda, united front work, liaison office with the fraternal parties abroad, publication office of the *People's Daily*, a policy research office, and an office of party schools.

We now know that the Central Secretariat meets twice a week behind the red walls of Zhongnanhai, a part of the former imperial palace and now both party headquarters and the seat of the central government, the State Council. Members of the Central Secretariat, elected by the National Party Congress, can initiate and formulate policies on anything they wish. The Central Secretariat has invited leaders in industry, commerce, agriculture, science, and education to Zhongnanhai to brief its members on current developments or problems. In addition, it processes a large volume of mail received from party cells and branches, as well as from the public.

Significant changes had been made by the Thirteenth Party Congress on membership election to and the role of the Central Secretariat. The Central Committee no longer elects the Central Secretariat members under the revision of the party charter (see second paragraph under Section 4 in Appendix B-1). Members of the Central Secretariat are now appointed by the Politburo, subject to approval or endorsement of the Central Committee; and it is now the working body of the Standing Committee and the Politburo.

The Military Affairs Committee. Although the Military Affairs Committee (MAC) is a subunit of the Central Committee of the CCP, it reports directly to the Politburo and its Standing Committee. The MAC supervises the administration of the armed forces and makes policies in national defense. The MAC directly controls the General Political Department (GPD), the party's political agent within the PLA, which is in theory a branch of the Ministry of Defense but in practice operates independently of it. The GPD is responsible for the political education of the troops and publishes the *Liberation Army Daily*, the military's own daily newspaper.

The basic function of the MAC has been its exclusive responsibility in directing the party's military activities, including the power to appoint and remove military personnel. As a subunit of the Central Committee, with responsibility for strategy and tactics of the Chinese army, it can be traced back to the guerrilla days of the early 1930s.[25] After the 1935 Zunyi Conference, Mao assumed the chair of the Revolutionary Military Committee, the predecessor of the present MAC. By that time the committee had assumed the responsibilities of educating the troops in political matters and of approving the party's political commissars assigned to the various armies. The MAC operates through a standing committee; the members of that committee regularly conduct inspection trips to the seven regional military commands and submit reports directly to the Politburo. Throughout the years the MAC has held periodic special work conferences for military leaders from all regions and provinces on military and political–ideological topics. New policies and directives are explained at these conferences to ensure proper implementation. From around 1954 on, the MAC has also been responsible for conducting numerous political training schools for army officers. Ralph Powell points out that MAC supervision of the PLA is extensive and direct, covering even the most routine matters.[26]

A longstanding practice, instituted by Mao, was to have the party chairperson automatically serve as the chairperson of the MAC. That practice was abandoned by the 1982 party constitution, which stipulates only that the chairperson of the MAC must be a member of the Standing Committee of the Politburo (see Article 21 in Appendix B). In 1978 Deng Xiaoping assumed the chairmanship of the MAC, assisted by a permanent vice-chairman, Yang Shangkun, a trusted Deng associate. The three military marshals—Ye Jiangying, Xu Xiangqian, and Nie Rongzhen—served as nominal vice-chairmen of the commission by tradition.

Since his ascension to power in the 1980s, Deng had been the top party cadre whom the military could trust as the chairman of the MAC. At one time Deng was trying unsuccessfully to persuade the military to accept the late Hu Yaobang, then the party chief, as his successor to the chairmanship of the MAC.[27]

Deng submitted his resignation as the MAC chairman to the CCP Politburo on September 4, 1989, thus ending his reign of more than a decade over the military. After endorsing Deng's resignation, the CCP Central Committee elected as the new MAC chairman Jiang Zemin, the new party chief in the aftermath of the Tiananmen crackdown. Now the Maoist tradition had been restored—that the party chairman concurrently holds the MAC chairmanship.

Although no official list of MAC members has been published, two general guidelines seem to determine its composition: (1) members include most of the senior military figures, particularly the PLA marshals; and (2) members usually reflect the composition of the Politburo. The size of the MAC ranges from at least ten members to perhaps nineteen or twenty. Traditionally, the first vice chair of the MAC concurrently serves as the minister of defense. By 1982 that tradition, too, was abandoned. One recent defense minister, Zhang Aiping, then age 72, was elevated from the position of deputy chief of staff in the military's senior command. Zhang was not, at the time of his appointment as defense chief, a vice chairman of the MAC. The chief of staff for the PLA is usually a member of the Standing Committee of the MAC. There is also an interlocking membership situation existing among the MAC, the Politburo, and in Central Committee. The high degree of interlocking membership between the MAC and the Politburo was such that at least nine members of the Politburo elected by the Eleventh Central Committee (1977) had been members of the MAC. Similarly, at least ten members of the Politburo elected in 1982 had been members of the MAC, including Deng and Yang Shangkun.

Officially the Fourteenth Central Committee in October 1992 listed Jiang Zemin, Liu Huaqing, Zhang Zhen, Chi Haotian, Zhang Wannian, Yu Yongbo, and Fu Quanyou as members of the MAC. In order to accommodate Deng, who was no longer a member of the Central Committee or the Politburo in 1987, the party charter had to be amended. Article 21 now reads that "The members of the Military Affairs Committee of the Central Committee are decided on by the Central Committee" (see Section 4 in Appendix B-1), instead of the requirement that the MAC chairman must be a member of the Politburo's Standing Committee.

The Fifteenth Party Congress (1997) elected two senior generals to the Politburo: General Chi Haotian and General Zhang Wannian. In accordance with a prior decision by the top party leaders at Beidaihe, no military leader was to be elected to the Politburo's Standing Committee (as mentioned earlier). Both General Chi and General Zhang, allied with Jiang Zemin, also have been elected to the party's Military Affairs Committee and appointed as the commission's vice chairmen.

Of the seven Military Affairs Committee members elected in September 1997, two (Wang Ke and Wang Ruilin, the long-time personal secretary to Deng Xiaoping) are now replacing aging Generals Liu Huaqing and Zhang Zhen. The remaining five are holdovers (Jiang Zemin, the chairman, Zhang Wannian, Chi Haotian, Fu Quanyou, and Yu Yongbo).

The Central Commission for Discipline Inspection. The true functions of the original party discipline control commission had not been spelled out anywhere, not even in the informative party constitution of 1956, which gave the hierarchical structure of the original Control Commission. However, based on recent revelations, the reestablished party control mechanism seems to have the following main functions: (1) maintenance of party morale and discipline; (2) control over the performance of party organizations; and (3) investigation of breaches of party discipline.[28]

The party constitution of 1977 created a new control device—the Central Commission for Discipline Inspection—to strengthen party discipline and internal party democracy in the aftermath of the abusive practices instituted during the Cultural Revolution by the radical leaders. The new commission for party discipline is charged with the task of enforcing party rules and regulations, as well as with the development of sound party style, including the inculcation of all the requisite party virtues. In 1978 the third plenary session of the Eleventh Central Committee elected the first hundred-member Central Commission for Discipline Inspection, headed by veteran party administrator Chen Yun.[29] Prior to the Cultural Revolution, the sixty-member Control Commission operated through a standing committee of nine or ten members.[30] The standing committee for the newly formed Central Commission for Discipline Inspection consisted of twenty-four party veterans, all purged or mistreated during the Cultural Revolution. In its first report, published in March 1979, the party's inspection commission urged that any false charges, wrong punishments, and frame-ups leveled against any party member be corrected and the victims rehabilitated. Thus, a first step was taken to tighten the slackened party discipline and to restore internal party democracy.

The Central Commission for Discipline Inspection was given considerable power and jurisdiction by the 1982 party constitution to monitor party rules and regulations; it reports directly to the Central Committee on violations of party discipline and on the implementation of party policies and decisions. An elaborate system of local commissions for inspecting party discipline was also established at the various party levels. The commission and its subsidiary bodies were also made responsible for providing education among party members about party discipline and work style.

If correct party style is a matter of life and death for the central party, to use the words of Chen Yun (the first secretary for the Commission for Discipline Inspection), then some serious efforts must be made to rebuild the party on the basis of discipline and rules that will regulate and govern the behavior of party members. From this perspective, the guidelines for inner party political life must be considered a major accomplishment of the commission. Upon recommendation of the commission, the Central Committee in March 1980 adopted a set of twelve guidelines, or guiding principles, for inner party political life.[31] These general guidelines correct the abuses, anarchy, and laxity in party discipline that prevailed during the Cultural Revolution. Collectively, these guidelines tell us clearly what happened to the party when Mao permitted radical ideologues to seize the party machinery and disrupt inner party life. These rules may be read as a catalog of indictments against Mao's personal arbitrary rule and the ills of the party. For instance, one of the guidelines is to uphold the collective leadership of the party, not individual, arbitrary decision making. On important issues the guidelines now provide for collective discussion by the rank and file of the party and for decision making by the party committee. The fostering of a "personality cult" is now strictly prohibited: There may be no celebration of leaders' birthdays, no gifts, and no congratulatory messages. Henceforth, no memorial hall shall be erected for any living person, nor shall a street, place, or school be named after a party leader.

The new inner party political life guidelines demand tolerance for dissenting views at the discussion stage of policy making. No punishment is to be given for erroneous statements by a party member—as long as these dissenting opinions do not advocate factional activities or divulge party and state secrets. It is a criminal act to organize secret groups within the party. Party members are to speak the truth and to be honest in words and deeds. There shall be no abridgment of a party member's right to participate in meetings or to criticize any party organization or individual at party meetings. All party committees are to hold regular meetings and elections. Erroneous tendencies and evil deeds such as graft, embezzlement, factionalism, anarchism, extreme individualism, bureaucraticism, and special privileges are to be opposed at all times. In inner party struggles, a correct attitude must be adopted toward those who make mistakes, but "it is prohibited to wage ruthless struggle against those erring party members." Everyone is equal within the party and before party rules and regulations. No party member is permitted to show favoritism toward family or relatives. Finally, all party members must be reviewed and rewarded in accordance with their ability and competence. Hu Yaobang, formerly the party general secretary, argued that lifelong tenure in a leadership position should be abolished, and that emphasis should be placed on promoting those capable party cadres who are in their prime.

The commission may have been given another role when it was assigned the task of drafting the document on guidelines for inner party political life and shepherding its passage through the Central Committee: that of serving as a central organ for supervising the implementation of the guidelines. The commission has encountered difficulties and resistance among party members and cadres as regards this new role. A proper attitude toward good work style and party life, notwithstanding the promulgation of the guidelines, is still lacking.

In recent years an important area of the commission's task has been its investigation of violations of party discipline committed by party members. The crackdown on party cadres who engaged in corrupt practices became urgent as the number of cases mounted nationwide. Some party cadres took advantage of their position and power by engaging in bribery, smuggling, and embezzlement as economic reform took shape and as the open door policy to the outside world widened. In its first nationwide conference, held in 1983, the Discipline Inspection Commission revealed that the number of cases investigated for discipline violations committed by party cadres was a staggering 380,000.[32] In the southern province of Guangdon alone, over 500 party members were expelled in one year as a result of the commission's investigation into various "economic crimes" such as smuggling and embezzlement of public funds.[33]

The commission identified three main problems in its work: party cadres' refusal to reveal their wrongdoing; party leaders' reluctance to report their subordinates, friends, and family members for wrongdoing; and party leaders' habit of providing cover for their shady operations.[34] Further, there were reports that the commission itself had developed a lenient attitude toward some offending party cadres.[35]

There is widespread violation of party discipline. During the Fourteenth Party Congress, which convened in October 1992, it was revealed that there were over 870,000 party discipline violation investigations of corruption, and that 154,000 members had been expelled during the period from 1987 to 1992.

In its 1996 annual organization summary report, the Central Commission for Discipline Inspection revealed that 89 percent of the expelled 170,000 party members, out of a grand total of 850,000, had committed "economic crimes," which consisted mostly of corruption, bribery, and falsification of accounts in the use of public funds. The expulsion from party membership and trial of some eighteen high party and government officials—including Chen Xitong, former Politburo member and party chief for Beijing—charged with embezzlement of perhaps over $2 billion of public funds, have been made public to demonstrate how vigilant the party has been in instituting investigations of higher cadres for their wrongdoings. Thus, party officials hope to restore some public confidence in the party.

The Central Advisory Commission. Another new central-level body established by the 1982 party constitution was the Central Advisory Commission, designed to serve as "political assistance and consultant to the Central Committee" (see Article 22 of the 1982 constitution in Appendix B). Membership on the commission was limited to party elders with at least forty years of party service. This was mainly a device to permit party elders to vacate their long-held positions so as to provide some upward mobility for younger members. Also, the Central Advisory Commission was intended to do away with the tradition of providing life tenure for top leaders in the party. As consultants, commission members could attend plenary meetings of the Central Committee without a vote. The Advisory Commission's vice-chairperson was also permitted to attend Politburo meetings exofficio, if necessary. The Advisory Commission could make recommendations to the Central Committee, at least on paper, on party policy formulation or on tasks assigned by the Central Committee.

The original purpose of the Central Advisory Commission was twofold: to provide a means by which the aged party veterans, the Long March generation, or simply the "Gang of Elders," could retire from active service; and to enable the younger leaders to tap the experience and wisdom of the veterans. The original intention was certainly not to endow the commission with any real political power to influence the inner party decision-making process. The "Gang of Elders," presumably retired from active politics, demonstrated considerable residual power, however, particularly in the inner party debate that forced Hu Yaobang to resign. The Central Advisory Commission members attended and perhaps voted to accept Hu's resignation as party chief at an enlarged session of the Politburo in mid-January 1987. If, in fact, they did take part in the voting at the enlarged Politburo meeting, then they violated the party constitution, which granted no such power (Article 22 of the 1982 party constitution stated that members of the Central Advisory Commission could attend Politburo meetings as nonvoting participants). As it turned out, there were as many Central Advisory Commission members as there were members of the Politburo at that crucial meeting when Hu Yaobang resigned and Zhao Ziyang was made the acting party chief. Even before that fateful enlarged Politburo meeting, a number of the Central Advisory Commission members had played a key role in speaking out on party matters.[36] The unexpected role of members of the Central Advisory Commission caused some party members to question whether the retired veterans were fronting for some members of the Central Committee who chose to remain silent and invisible on so important an issue as the resignation of the party's general secretary.[37] The events surrounding Hu's forced resignation seemed to indicate that the Central Advisory Commission had gradually evolved into a political force representing the views of the orthodox hard-liners in the never-ending contest for political succession. The Central Advisory Commission was finally abolished by the Fourteenth Party Congress in October 1992.

PROVINCIAL PARTY ORGANS AND FUNCTIONS

Theoretically speaking, provincial party committees derive their power from the party congresses at the provincial level. The 1982 party constitution (Article 24, see Appendix B) mandates that party congresses at the provincial level and in autonomous regions, in municipalities under the central government, and in cities with districts be held at least once every three years. Each provincial party committee is generally run by a standing committee consisting of the first secretary and a number of subordinate secretaries within the hierarchy of the provincial party structure.

The provincial party committee is responsible for supervision and provides direction over five basic areas: organization and control of the party; economic activities in agriculture, industry, finance, and trade; capital construction; mobilization of women and youth; and research for policy development. Initially, the provincial party committees played a subordinate role in supervising provincial economic development. This was more pronounced during the period of high centralization of the First Five-Year Plan (1953–56), when the national functional ministries had a great deal of authority and control over the provincial party activities. During and after the Great Leap Forward (1957–59), there was a period of decentralization; the provincial party committees were given greater responsibility and more power in managing economic activities in the provinces. In many respects the provincial party committees behaved as though they were "underdeveloped nations" in bidding for resources to develop economic and productive activities.[38]

Since the provincial party committees and their subordinate primary party organs within the provinces are responsible for implementing party policies, they hold a unique position within the party structure. The first secretary of the provincial party committee wields an enormous amount of power. Provincial party secretaries, as pointed out by one study, on occasion have deliberately refused to carry out directives from the center.[39]

This power is reflected in and enhanced by the provincial party secretaries' participation in central party affairs (see Chapter 7).

PRIMARY PARTY ORGANS AND FUNCTIONS

Below the provincial party committees are the primary units at the county level and below. They are the "fighting bastions" (to use the phraseology in the 1982 party constitution) for carrying out the party policies and line. It is here that the party makes its immediate contact with the rest of the society. Like the provincial party structure, all basic units of the party are headed by a party secretary, who in turn is guided by a party committee. Party units at the primary level never contest policies and programs imposed from above. However, honest and vigorous discussion often prevails at these lower-level party meetings.

The lowest level of party organization, the so-called primary party units or cells, are party branches formed in "factories, shops, schools, city neighborhoods, co-operatives, farms, townships, towns, villages, companies of the People's Liberation Army and other basic units, where there are three or more full party members," in accordance with Article 30 of the 1982 party constitution, as amended in 1987. The 1997 official figure on the total number of party branches at the lowest level is 3.4 million grassroots units.[40] It is at this level that the organizational functions of the party are carried out. Membership recruitment, political and ideological education about the party line, exercise of party discipline, and maintenance of "close ties with the masses." It is generally the party branch in a given enterprise, or office that provides leadership, supervision, and guidance in party affairs. Like the first secretaries in the higher party organizations, the party branch secretary exercises overall leadership. In addition, a party branch secretary also serves as a "friend, counselor, and guardian of all the people under his [or her] jurisdiction."[41] Popular literature and drama often depict the party branch secretary as one who is always fearless, fair, firm, and devoted to the welfare of his or her people in the unit.

The party committee is the leading organizational unit, providing leadership, supervision, and management of all political and economic activities in the countryside. But as party discipline slackened, and as opportunities arose for persons with special privileges to use their office for personal gain, it was not uncommon to find the corrupt practices of party secretaries exposed. There were also a number of cases of commandism (communist work style characterized by dictating or ordering) and incompetence found within the ranks of party secretaries.[42] The party committee at the basic level directs party organizational work and is responsible for general policy. It also controls the assignment of personnel at the local level.

We can summarize by saying that the party was highly institutionalized from the 1950s to the early 1960s. This was interrupted during the turbulent years 1966 to 1976 by the Cultural Revolution. The process of reinstitutionalization now appears to be accelerating. The process of reinstitution began soon after Deng Xiaoping came back to power in the late 1970s and early 1980s, but after two decades of economic reform, the party as an institution has lost much of its luster and is beset with corruption. The party's 3.4 million organizational cells at the grassroots level are no longer bastions for collectivism, or even socialism. The party is concerned about the rising tide of individualism and the influence of bourgeois Western thinking and culture. More serious is the central party's gradual loss of control over the provincial party organizations (see Chapter 7).

THE GOVERNMENT AND THE PARTY: INTERLOCKING STRUCTURE AND DECISION MAKING

In this section we shall examine the structure of the Chinese central government by focusing on the central government complex. Subjects to be discussed include constitutions, the National People's Congress (NPC), and the State Council and its multifarious agencies. Before we take up these topics, two general comments must be made about the Chinese national government. First, as discussed in the previous section, the Chinese Communist Party controls and directs the complex system of government machinery. It is through the agencies of the government that the policies and programs approved by the party are implemented. The CCP closely monitors how the government executes its directives. Second, the People's Republic of China is a unitary state. In a federated system, such as that of the United States or the former Soviet Union, certain governmental powers and responsibilities are reserved for local governments. Under a unitary system, all powers theoretically are vested in the central government and must be specifically delegated to local governments by the central authority. This centralization of power in the national government has led to perennial debate in China over the degree and nature of power to be allocated to local governments. The governments in the provinces and local units generate constant pressure for decentralization by seeking to increase their discretional power over such local affairs as finances and allocation of resources. The topics of provincial and local politics and government will be discussed in detail in Chapter 7.

The 1982 Constitution[43]

The 1982 constitution is China's fourth state constitution (see Appendix A). The 1978 constitution was said to have become obsolete, in that it "no longer conforms to present realities or needs of the life of the state."[44]

We are told that the 1982 constitution was the product of more than two years of work by the Committee for Revision of the Constitution, which was established in September 1980 by the Fifth NPC. The revised draft of this constitution was circulated within party and government circles for debate and discussion. Reportedly, 7.3 million speakers commented on the draft constitution at millions of meetings held across the nation. The review produced over a million suggestions for revision.[45] The final version of the draft was adopted by the Fifth NPC at its session on December 4, 1982. The Sixth NPC, which met in June 1983, was elected, organized, and conducted under the provisions of the 1982 constitution.

One major change in the 1982 constitution was deletion of lavish praise for Mao and of reference to the Cultural Revolution in the preamble. In its place the new constitution affirms adherence to the four fundamental principles of socialism: the socialist road, the people's dictatorship, the leadership of the CCP, and Marxism-Leninism and Mao Zedong Thought.

Articles 79–81 provide for the election of a president of the republic—a position the 1975 and 1978 constitutions failed to provide for, presumably in deference to Mao's long opposition to Liu Shaoqi, the president under the 1954 constitution who subsequently was purged in 1966 and died while under house arrest. Another new feature was the establishment of the State Military Council to provide direction for the armed forces (see Articles 93–94 in Appendix A). As will be discussed in Chapter 7, the 1982 constitution restricts the role of rural people's communes to economic management in rural areas; they no longer have responsibilities in local government and administration.

A provision in the 1982 constitution that aroused a flurry of speculation was Article 31, which authorizes the NPC to establish "special administrative regions." To many, this provision opened the way for the return of Hong Kong, Macao, or even Taiwan to China as "special administrative regions." Thus, two recent agreements[46]—the 1984 Sino–British Joint Agreement on Hong Kong's reversion to China in 1997 and the 1987 Sino–Portuguese Declaration on Macao's return in 1999—invoked Article 31 for establishing the two territories as "special administrative regions" that would enjoy "a higher degree of autonomy."

The area of ambiguous change concerns the control of China's armed forces. While the 1978 constitution, in Article 19, stated specifically that the chairman of the party's Central Committee commands the nation's armed forces, the 1982 constitution, in Articles 93 and 94, places the armed forces under the command of the chairman of the Central Military Commission—which is theoretically responsible to the National People's Congress. However, there is some confusion as to whether the party's powerful committee on military affairs supersedes the constitutional provision stated here. There is really no clear delineation of the two organs in terms of their respective power, except the vague explanation that

> The draft of the revised Constitution not only confirms the leading role of the Chinese Communist Party in state political life but also stipulates that the Party must carry out activities within the extent of the Constitution and the Law.... Therefore, the Party's leadership over the armed forces could not be taken to mean that the armed forces do not belong to the state.[47]

The 1982 constitution contains twenty-two articles dealing with fundamental rights and duties of citizens, such as the equality of all citizens before the law, inviolability of the dignity of the person, and prohibition of extralegal detention of citizens. Article 35 briefly states that "Citizens of the People's Republic of China enjoy freedom of speech, of the press, of assembly, of association, of procession and of demonstration." This new article was a revised version of Article 45 of the 1978 constitution, which provided citizens the right to "speak out freely, air their views fully, hold great debates, and write big-character posters." After a short flurry of wall posters put up by the young dissidents during the "democracy wall" movement in 1978–79 under the guarantees of the 1978 constitution, China's pragmatic reformers led by Deng Xiaoping saw these rights being used as weapons by ultra-leftists to advance their aims. The wall posters are viewed by the present leaders as instruments that may be used by dissenters to incite "anarchism" and "factionalism." Thus, the rights to "speak out freely, air their views fully, hold great debates, and write big-character posters" were deleted from the 1982 constitution.

Theoretically, Article 35 of the 1982 constitution guarantees citizens the right "to enjoy freedom of speech, of the press, of assembly, of association, of procession and of demonstration." The extent to which these rights can be exercised is, in fact, limited by Article 54. That provision lays down a set of conditions under which citizens have the duty and responsibility "to safeguard the security, honor and interest of the motherland; they must not commit acts detrimental to the security, honor and interests of the motherland." Moreover, Article 51 states that the rights guaranteed by Article 35 "may not infringe upon the interests of the state, of society and of the collective, or upon the lawful freedoms and rights of other citizens." This means that stern and repressive measures may be taken by the state to suppress any dissident engaging in "counterrevolutionary activities."

RECENT CONSTITUTIONAL AMENDMENTS, 1999

At the second session of the Ninth National People's Congress on March 15, 1999, several changes were approved as amendments to the 1982 state constitution. The following is a brief summary discussion on five of these recent constitutional amendments.[48]

Section 7 to the Preamble. Parallel to the change in the party constitution preamble (see Appendix B-2), Section 7 to the preamble of the 1982 state constitution has also been revised to read that the party's guidance to action must be by Marxism-Leninism, Mao Zedong Thought, and Deng Xiaoping Theory. Thus, Deng's Theory has been included as the guide to action in both the party and the 1982 state constitutions.

Article 5 on Rule of Law. A new phrase has been added as the opening section to Article 5, to read as follows:

> The People's Republic of China practices ruling the country in accordance with the law and building a socialist country of law."[49]

The president of China's Supreme People's Court is quoted as saying that the amendment is an integral part of "Deng Xiaoping's thinking about democracy and a complete legal system."[50] The change represents a strategy for governing China regardless of leadership change or "changes in the views and focus of leaders." And this makes the state constitution a stable one.[51] From this viewpoint, it is a milestone for rule of law in China.

Article 6 on diverse ownership and different mode of distribution in the economy. What has been amended is the significant addition of a third sentence which reads

> During the primary stage of socialism, the State adheres to the basic economic system with the public ownership remaining dominant and diverse sectors of the economy developing side by side, and to the distribution system with the distribution according to work remaining dominant and the co-existence of a variety of modes of distribution.

The significance of the change is recognition of the economic reform that has taken place in that, while public ownership of major means of production is still dominant, there are also developments in private business supplementary to the economy and important components to the socialist market economy. Rural farmers do not own land, but their contract for the use of land is for thirty years since 1993, and this remains unchanged.

Article 8 on the rural double-tier management system. The revision reads that

> rural collective economic organizations practice the double-tier management system that combines unified and separate operations on the basis of the household-based output related contract responsibility system

to replace the first sentence of the original Article 8. Then the original second sentence has been revised to read

Various forms of the cooperative economy in rural areas such as producers, supply and marketing, credit and consumers' cooperatives belong to the sector of the socialist economy under collective ownership by the working people.

And the last paragraph in the original Article 8 has been revised to read

Working people who are members of rural economic collectives have the right, within the time prescribed by law, to farm plots of crop land and hilly land allotted for private use, engage in household sideline production and raise privately owned livestock.

The recent constitutional changes reflect what has taken place for the past twenty years in the rural economy. Under rural reform that began in the 1980s, essentially led by the state and local rural townships and villages, the emphasis was on publicly owned firms for economic development. Then in the 1990s a state-sponsored privatization program was initiated at township and village levels which enables these local governments to sell their rural enterprises for private operation instead of state-sponsored privatization by way of shareholding arrangements. Jean C. Oi's study of rural reform in the past two decades shows that by 1997 about one-third of 520,000 of the collectively owned enterprises had gone through some form of rural reform, and of these about 21.3 percent had become shareholding operations.[52] (This was the origin of the double-tier management system for both unified and separate operations.) According to Jean Oi, by 1996 China had more than 22 million rural enterprises employing more than 135 million rural workers.[53]

The other part of the revised Article 8 grants members of rural collectives the right to farm plots of hilly and crop land for private use, as well as the right to engage in household sideline production and/or raise privately owned livestock.

Article 11 on protection for individual economy. The beginning sentence to Article 11 now reads

Individual, private and other non-public economies that exist within the limits prescribed by law are major components of the socialist market economy.

The revision now specifically refers to individual, private, and other nonpublic economies rather than as originally, "the individual economy of urban and rural working people," by placing emphasis on the wording, "non-public economies" as an important component of the socialist market economy instead of "socialist public economy"—a response written into the state constitution to reflect the growing develop-ment of private businesses nationwide. In the past private businesses had a "low social status" and often were "discriminated against in business operations," wrote one reporter.[54] More important, as revealed by the general manager of Beijing Santi Service Corporation, from now on the nonpublic or private economy will have legal protection to enable it to grow further.[55] It is hoped the amendment will ease many people's minds so far as legal guarantees are concerned for these private enterprises.[56]

Article 28 on deletion of "counter-revolutionary activities." For many both inside and outside of China the amendment to Article 28 by deletion of the term "counter-revolutionary" from the original text has been a riddle. Article 28 now reads as follows:

The state maintains public order and suppresses treasonable and other criminal activities that endanger state security.

The old term "counter revolutionary" had been a catchall offense against the state—for example, the student demonstration on Tiananmen in June 1989 was officially labeled counterrevolutionary. The removal of the term in Article 28 does not mean that these activities on the square would have been tolerated, but the term, as sanctioned in the original version of Article 28 of the 1982 state constitution, has been a politically loaded term and has carried with it the notion of overthrow by a revolution or revolt. The old term "counter-revolution" conjures up all the reckless goings-on of Mao's Cultural Revolution during the late 1960s. How this new amendment to Article 28 of the 1982 constitution has affected the provisions in the criminal code on the so-called "counter-revolutionary" offenses is, at the time of this writing, unclear or uncertain.

NATIONAL PEOPLE'S CONGRESS AND ITS LAWMAKING ROLE

The NPC is the highest government organ and has constitutional duties similar to those of many parliamentary bodies in other nations. It is empowered to amend the constitution, to make laws, and to supervise their enforcement. Upon recommendation of the president of the People's Republic, the NPC designates, and may remove, the premier and other members of the State Council and can elect the president of the Supreme People's Court and the Chief Procurator of the Supreme People's Procuratorate. These structural relationships are reflected in Figure 4.2.

TABLE 4.1   The National People's Congress, 1954–1998

NPC	Year Convened	Number of Delegates	Chief of State	Constitution Promulgated
1st	1954	1,226	Mao Zedong	Constitution of 1954
2nd	1959	1,226	Liu Shaoqi	
3rd	1964 (Dec.)			
	1965 (Jan.)	3,040	Liu Shaoqi	
4th	1975	2,885	—	Revised, 1975
5th	1978	3,459	—	Revised, 1978
6th	1983	2,978	Li Xiannian[a]	Revised, 1982
7th	1988 (March)	2,978	Yang Sangkun[b]	Revised, 1987
8th	1993 (March)	2,903	Jiang Zemin[c]	Revised, 1987
9th	1998 (March)	2,877	Jiang Zemin	Revised, 1998

[a]Elected by the Sixth NPC on June 18, 1993.
[b]Elected by the Seventh NPC on April 8, 1988.
[c]Elected by the Eighth NPC March 1993.
Source: Delegate number is based on "Brief Notes about the People's Congresses," in *Renmin Ribao* (February 27, 1978), 2. For delegates to the Sixth NPC, see "Sixth NPC Meets in Beijing," *Beijing Review*, 24 (June 13, 1983), 5. For the Seventh NPC, see the *New York Times*, March 26, 1988, p. 3. For delegates to the Eighth NPC, see *Beijing Review* (April 12–18, 1993), 5.

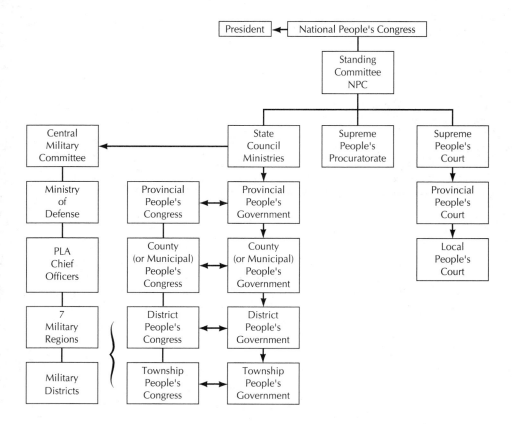

FIGURE 4.2   Governmental Structure of People's Republic of China (1982 Constitution). *Source:* A modified version based on Kim and Ziring, *An Introduction to Asian Politics* (Upper Saddle River, N.J.: Prentice Hall, 1977), p. 74. By permission of the publisher.

Since 1954, nine National People's Congresses have been convened, as shown in Table 4.1. The Sixth NPC, convened in June 1983, had a ratio of one deputy, or delegate, for every 1.04 million people in rural areas, and one for every 130,000 people in the urban areas. Sparsely populated provinces and autonomous regions, however, were entitled to no less than fifteen delegates each. The Sixth NPC, dominated by Deng Xiaoping and his reform-minded supporters, seemed to have achieved some degree of stability under a moderate and pragmatic program. Deng and his reformers were able to control the Seventh NPC, held in 1988, and the Eighth NPC, which convened in March 1993.

Working Sessions of the NPC

A session of the NPC generally meets for a period of about two weeks. During that period only a handful of full plenary meetings are convened to discuss and approve reports of the central government. Delegates or deputies are divided into groups, according to regions, which meet constantly throughout the two-week period when the NPC is in session. It is at these group meetings that one can find occasional spirited discussions on matters of national concern. It is there that the delegates can exercise their oversight functions by submitting motions or inquiries on the performance of the various administrative bodies in the central government. At these sessions vice-ministers representing the central government usually are present on the floor either to answer questions or to provide information about governmental affairs. It has been revealed that during the Sixth NPC (1983–88), deputies raised 830 motions and 14,215 suggestions, criticisms, and opinions to the congress on a variety of subjects. The ad hoc committee served as a clearinghouse, referring these motions to the various governmental agencies concerned for comment.[57]

It was reported that at the end of the Third Plenum, Sixth NPC, delegates made a total of 2,832 recommendations, criticisms, and suggestions.[58] About 744, or 26.3 percent of the total, were resolved or had action taken on them by the governmental units concerned. A large majority, about 73 percent, were either being processed or were shelved for further study.[59]

Recently there has been criticism about the caliber of delegates selected to the NPC. Qian Jiaju, a noted economist, pointed out that the practice of selecting NPC delegates from model workers in industries and trades did not provide the NPC with the qualified delegates it needed for policy making.[60] He revealed with some candor that most members on the NPC finance committee could neither follow the discussion at the sessions nor comprehend the process of budget making. This view was contradicted by a Chinese TV reporter, who followed the NPC debate on the proposed bankruptcy law by pointing out that there was heated debate and that the NPC was no longer a "rubber stamp."[61] Delegates to the NPC in its 1997 session presented to the legislative body 603 motions; some were suggestions and/or criticisms of the government's work—some 124 motions dealt with various draft laws to be considered by the NPC.[62]

Standing Committee of the NPC

When the NPC is not in session, its Standing Committee serves as the executive body to act on behalf of the congress. While the Standing Committee is elected by the NPC, it is this committee that has the power to conduct elections of the deputies of the NPC and to convene the NPC sessions. Since the NPC meets once a year at most, the Standing Committee controls a great deal of that body's powers.

The 1982 constitution gives the Standing Committee the power to enforce martial law in the event of domestic disturbance. Article 67(20) (see Appendix A) states that the NPC's Standing Committee can declare martial law either for the country as a whole or for a particular province, autonomous region, or municipality directly under the central government. Hypothetically, measures for suppression of domestic disturbance can now be constitutionally instituted and enforced. Presumably the NPC, through its Standing Committee, could suppress upheavals similar to the Cultural Revolution, if it wants to exert its constitutional prerogatives in the event of a national crisis situation. On the other hand, this provision may provide an avenue through which factional groups within the party and government leadership could very well seize power by suppressing the opposition forces in a power contest.

On May 20, 1989, at the height of the student demonstration in Tiananmen Square, the promulgation of martial law in the capital city of Beijing by the republic's president and premier raised a constitutional controversy, for there was no formal involvement by the Standing Committee in the issuance of the martial law order. (Wan Li, then chairman of the Standing Committee, was traveling in the United States.)

Also, the 1982 constitution gives the Standing Committee the powers and functions normally possessed by the NPC itself, to serve as an interim national congress when the NPC is not in session. The Standing Committee now supervises a new system of parliamentary committees on nationalities, law, finance and economics, public health, education, foreign affairs, overseas Chinese, and any other areas deemed necessary (Article 70, Appendix A). As an interim NPC, the Standing Committee can enact and amend decrees and laws in civil and criminal affairs, including those affecting the structure of the central government. It can annul any administrative regulations and decisions of the central government, and it has the power to interpret the constitution. In order that the Standing Committee be an independent body, its members are not permitted to hold posts in any branch of the central government concurrently.

NPC's Potential as a Creditable Legislative Institution

As seen in Table 4.1, the Eighth National People's Congress convened in March 1993. Since 1983 the NPC has consisted of about 3,000 delegates—a rather cumbersome body for deliberative purposes. Apparently the size of the NPC has been expanded to broaden representation and to allow greater participation in national government.

In drafting the 1982 constitution, the question was raised as to whether the size of the NPC should be reduced to a more manageable level. The suggestion evidently was rejected on the grounds that it was necessary to have "every class, every social strata, every nationality, every locality, and every field of work" represented. The size of the 1993 NPC—2,903 deputies—remained cumbersome.

The enormous size of the NPC raises the question of whether this institution was ever intended to be a genuinely deliberative body. The argument can be made that if the NPC was intended to be a "rubber stamp" for the CCP, then it might as well be very large and representative.

One piece of evidence indicating that the NPC behaved contrary to popular expectations that it would be the "rubber stamp" for the party was the approval in the 1992 session of the controversial Three Gorges Dam Project on the Yangtzee River.[63] The huge 2,000-meter-long hydroelectric dam would cost $12 billion, with two dozen hydroelectric generators producing 17,680 megawatts of electricity per year. The construction of the gigantic project would force as many as one million residents to move their farms and houses to make room for the 370-mile reservoir. In defiance of the party leadership, a number of deputies of the 1992 NPC session raised objections to the project. When the final vote was called there were 1,767 for, 77 against, and 664 abstentions. The debate on the Three Gorges Project contained criticism of Premier Li Peng. At the Eighth NPC in March 1993 as many as 11 percent of the 2,960 deputies either cast negative votes against Li Peng's reelection for the premiership or abstained.

Law-Making and the NPC. Qiao Shi, as chairman of the Standing Committee of the Eighth NPC (1993–1998), strove to strengthen the NPC lawmaking ability. In fact, Qiao Shi has been known for legal reform and for fashioning the NPC to be more like a parliament with lawmaking authorities. He was reportedly credited with recruitment of legal experts from abroad to reorganize the NPC's Legislative Commissions,[64] which drafted many of China's economic laws (to be discussed in Chapter 6). In his view, the NPC must embrace "socialist market economy" laws and regulations needed for opening up opportunities and making use of capitalistic tools. For some time since 1993 while he was head of the NPC, Qiao Shi was said to have used it as a base for contests of power.[65]

The volume of laws enacted by the NPC and its Standing Committee, from 1978 on to 1997, has totaled 300, in addition to over 4,000 local laws and regulations enacted for the same period affecting many aspects of China's "political, economic and public activities."[66] (For a more detailed discussion about some of these laws enacted by the NPC, see Chapter 6.) It is this aspect of Qiao Shi's push for legal reform and law-making through the NPC that has led to speculation that Qiao Shi was a possible contender or challenger to Jiang Zemin at the Fifteenth Party Congress.[67] Qiao Shi has evidently followed the late Peng Zhen in the latter's efforts to formulate legal reform and policies in the 1980s by using the NPC and its Standing Committee as the appropriate mechanism. During the four years (1992–1996) under his leadership of the NPC, Qiao Shi, as chairman of its Standing Committee, steered the enactment of some ninety-four laws, thirty-eight of which would serve what Qiao Shi termed "the legal framework of the socialist market economy."[68] (See also Chapter 6.)

The NPC, through its Standing Committee under Qiao Shi, has developed several other functions besides lawmaking. One such function has been supervising judicial and administrative organs in law enforcement. Qiao Shi pointed out that since 1992 NPC has enacted laws and regulations pertaining to administrative and criminal procedures. In addition, it has established administrative penalties for misconduct on the part of officers and workers in administrative and judicial organizations while at the same time safeguarding the rights and interests of citizens.[69]

Another NPC lawmaking function is the investigatory power in law enforcement. Qiao Shi revealed that from 1994 to 1996, the Standing Committee had organized forty-six inspection groups for the purpose of supervising enforcement of some thirteen laws:

> After inspection, the NPC Standing Committee will hear and discuss the reports submitted by law enforcement inspection groups, notify the relevant organs of its conclusions and suggestions and ask these organs to solve the problems that have been discovered. The organs will also report to the NPC on their handling of the problems.[70]

In reviewing these functions of the NPC and its Standing Committee and the law-making role undertaken by Qiao Shi, now retired or "ousted" from his position of power at the Fifteenth Party Congress (1997), one would have to agree with Kevin J. O'Brien that the NPC is merely "an arena" through which "minority opinions" are expressed and "procedural regularity" can be observed.[71] The NPC, as China's parliament, has not dared to initiate crucial policies not sanctioned by the party. But in recent years NPC deputies have learned to use the confirmation power for top central government positions, such as premiership and vice premierships, as "parliamentary" checks against party leadership nominations for these positions. In the March 1998 session of the NPC, Li Peng, slated to be the head of the NPC, and Zhu Rongji, the incoming premier, overcame the confirmation hurdles in terms of respectful majority ballots cast by the NPC deputies. Zhu Rongji, the new premier, received 98 percent of a total of 2,877 delegates who voted.

In the March 1995 session of the NPC, the delegates showed their independence by registering their opposition to the CCP leadership's nomination of its two Politburo members for the State Council's vice-premiership. Normally, the delegates would unanimously approve the top party leadership's nomination. But on this occasion there were dissenting votes for the nomination of two Politburo members for the vice-premier-ship. Wu Bangguo's approved nomination contained 196 no votes. When it came to acceptance votes for Jiang Chunyun, the other Politburo member selected by the party for a vice-premiership, there was a significant expression among the NPC delegates showing their disapproval of the party's choice: There were 605 votes against Jiang, 391 abstentions, and 10 simply refused to vote for him.[72] Reasons for the opposition to Jiang Chunyun were perhaps based on his age—64—and his tendency to condone corruption while a party leader in Shandong province. Opposition to Wu Bangguo, a Shanghai tech-nocrat who had worked with Jiang Zemin, now CCP general secretary, and Zhu Rongji, China's economic "czar," might be attributed to Wu's designation as the new man in charge of dismantling the state-owned enterprises.[73] The overall significance of the whole affair is the fact that here is more evidence that the NPC is not necessarily a "rubber stamp" for the party.

In his book on China's parliament, Kevin O'Brien points out that the National People's Congress since Deng Xiaoping's reform period had become "a barometer of the political climate,"[74] rather than merely a "forum for policy review," as it had been during the late 1950s and 1960s.[75] However, O'Brien feels it is the Chinese Communist Party that leads in policy formulation of the National People's Congress sessions.

THE STATE COUNCIL

The State Council, the nation's highest executive organ, administers the government through functional ministries and commissions, as indicated in Table 4.3. The constitu-tion stipulates that the State Council be composed of a premier, vice-premiers, and heads of national ministries and commissions. The State Council may also include others, such as vice-ministers. The membership of the State Council has ranged from a low of thirty to over one hundred members. As the government expanded over the years, the number of ministries and commissions expanded to a peak of forty-nine just prior to the Cultural Revolution.

To streamline the ministerial structure within the State Council, the total number of ministries and commissions was reduced in 1981–82, from ninety-eight to forty-one, mainly through the merging of functions and staff. As of May 1998 there was a total of

TABLE 4.2   Composition of the State Council, 1993 and 1998

	State Council Ministers Appointed by	
	8th NPC (1993)	*9th NPC (1998)*
Premier	1	1
Vice-premiers	4	4
Ministers	59	36
Secretary-General	1	1
	65	42

Source: For 1993, see *Beijing Review,* (29 March–4 April 1993), 8. For 1998, see *Beijing Review,* (27 April–3 May 1998), 20.

thirty-six ministries and commissions. The composition of the State Council is shown in Table 4.2.

Since the full State Council is too large for effective decision making, in practice this role has been assumed by an inner cabinet of the premier and his vice-premiers.[76] In 1982–83 the inner cabinet consisted of a premier, four vice-premiers, ten State Council senior counselors, and a secretary-general for the Office of the State Council. The personnel of the State Council has remained relatively stable over the years. During the Cultural Revolution this body suffered much less than the party apparatus, largely due to the leadership of Zhou Enlai, who was premier from 1949 until his death in 1976. Zhou stayed away from the debates during the initial stage of the revolution but joined Mao and Lin Biao when he realized their faction would emerge dominant. For Zhou's support, concessions were made for the State Council, including exemption from participation in the upheaval by scientists and technicians. As Thomas Robinson points out, Zhou was Mao and Lin's "chief problem solver, troubleshooter, negotiator, organizer, administrator, guide-advisor to revolutionary groups, and local enforcer of Central Committee policy."[77] It has been estimated that between one-half and two-thirds of the 366 ministers, vice-ministers, commissioners, and vice-commissioners kept their posts during the turbulent period from 1966 to 1968.[78] Another reason for the stability of the State Council, whose members represented a concentration of administrative and technical expertise, was the need for production to continue unimpeded. The ability of the State Council to issue directives, often jointly with the party's leading committees, is evidence that the central civil bureaucracy was quite institutionalized and functionally effective in spite of the turmoil during the Cultural Revolution.

Doak Barnett has described the State Council aptly as the "command headquarters" for a network of bureaus and agencies staffed by cadres who administer and coordinate the government's programs at the provincial and local levels.[79] The degree of centralization of authority has fluctuated over the regime's history. During the First Five-Year Plan, from 1953 to 1957, the ministries had enormous power over the provincial authorities in terms of quota fulfillment, allocation of resources, and management of such enterprises as factories and mines. The increasing complexity of coordinating the economy and the gravitation of power to the individual ministries, the "ministerial autarky," led to numerous problems and a continuing debate over centralization versus decentralization.[80] In 1957, during the Great Leap, decentralization was instituted by giving the provinces authority to administer and coordinate consumer-goods-oriented industries. The decentralization of the Great Leap hampered central planning and resulted in inefficiency. Following the failure of the Great Leap, a modified version of centralization was adopted until the Cultural Revolution ushered in another period of decentralization.[81] With the reestablishment of planning operations and the emphasis on research and development under the Sixth Five-Year Plan (1981–85), approved by the Fifth NPC in December 1982, the pendulum once again has swung back to more centralization. In his report to the Fifth NPC, Premier Zhao Ziyang indicated that to execute the Sixth Five-Year Plan, it was necessary for the State Planning Commission to exercise strict control over the volume of total investment in fixed assets. Investments in capital construction were to be placed under the control of the Bank of Construction of China.[82] Most ministries under the State Council are concerned with economic affairs; a minority deal with matters such as defense, foreign relations, public security, civil and minority affairs, education, and public health. The ministries on economic matters in early 1998 can be grouped into the categories shown in Table 4.3.

Several new features were added to the State Council by the 1982 constitution. First, a group of ten senior administrators were designated as advisors to the State Council. These senior advisors were retired veteran administrators such as Bo Yibo, age 75, who had been a vice-premier and minister for machine building, and Geng Biao, age 74, former Politburo member and defense minister. Second, tenure for the premiership was now limited to two consecutive five-year terms. Finally, the 1982 constitution mandated the establishment within the State Council of an independent audit agency, under the supervision of the premier, for the purpose of auditing the revenues and expenditures of the various ministries both at the central and provincial levels. The power of audit may eventually become an effective instrument in monitoring and checking the vast Chinese bureaucracy.[83] A majority of the twenty-three new ministers and vice ministers appointed in 1998–99 were in their fifties and early sixties, slightly younger than their predecessors.

In March 1998 the NPC reduced the central government's ministry-level units from forty to twenty-nine (See Table 4.3) in addition to a 50 percent cut of personnel in the State Council within three years, as mentioned earlier.

In the spring of 1998 the State Council General Office, the nerve center for the central government which oversees some twenty-nine departments and commissions (Table 4.3), was restructured as a reform measure. The restructuring represents a reduction from forty such state agencies prior to the reform to twenty-nine departments, a significant 72.5 percent cutback. There was a concurrent reduction in staff for the General Office from a total of 435 to 217, almost a 50 percent decrease in leadership personnel.[84]

Another aspect of reform for the General Office of the State Council which took place in April 1998 was the introduction of appointments of bureau department-level leaders by democratic recommendation and an election system, instead of the old practice of appointment by higher levels.[85] Thus, the system of selection and appointment to

TABLE 4.3   Departments under the State Council since April 1998

Ministries (Commissions)	
1. Foreign Affairs	13. Justice
2 National Defense	14. Finance
3. Development Planning Commission	15. Personnel, Labor
	16. Labor & Social Security
4. Economic and Trade Association	17. Land & Resources
	18. Construction
5. Education	19. Railways
6. Science & Technology	20. Communications
7. Assn. of Science, Technology for National Defense	21. Information Industry
	22. Water Resources
	23. Agriculture
8. Ethnic Affairs Assn.	24. Foreign Trade
9. Public Security	25. Culture
10. State Security	26. Public Health
11. Supervision	27. Family Planning
12. Civil Affairs	28. People's Bank
	29. National Audit

Source: "Departments under the State Council," *Beijing Review, April 6-12, 1998, p. 35.*

staff positions in the central government nerve center, the General Office of the State Council, has become more open.[86] Under the reform the age level of staff members was reduced to 37.5 years and some 92 percent possessed college level or above education.[87]

PROBLEMS IN CHINA'S POLITICAL INSTITUTIONS

Three key problems can be identified in the Chinese political institutions that have been discussed so far. One is the issue of party–government separation. Solving this interlocking problem at one time as an institutional reform goal, but interlocking now is lessened at the top echelon. The second problem is the need for streamlining the state bureaucracy by eliminating or merging the multitude of administrative departments. It was announced before the convening of the Ninth NPC in March 1998 that some 15 ministries would be either eliminated or merged, in addition to four new ones created. The third issue is the perennial problem of political structural reform focusing on the interlocking of government and party.

Interlocking Structure of the Government and Party

To students who are familiar with Western constitutions, it is often a surprise to read in the Chinese constitution the stipulation that the party is "the core of leadership of the whole Chinese people," and that "the working class exercises leadership over the state through its vanguard, the Communist Party of China." This, of course, means that the governmental institutions in China exist to serve the party.

The Chinese Communist Party controls and directs the machinery of state through an interlocking system of party personnel and a structure parallel to that of the state government. Fewer high party leaders held high government positions concurrently in 1982–83 than at any previous time. The 1977–78 period represented a heightened state of interlocking between the party and government hierarchy. The best example was Hua Guofeng, who was chairman of the CCP, premier of the central government, and chairman of the party's Military Affairs Commission. Of the thirteen vice-premiers of the State Council elected by the Fifth NPC in 1978, nine were members of the powerful CCP Politburo, and all were members of the CCP Central Committee elected in 1977. Of the thirty-six ministers in charge of various governmental agencies, twenty-nine, or 81 percent, were members of the Central Committee. All major economic ministries, including economic planning, capital construction, research and development, foreign trade, and heavy and light industries, were in the hands of ministers who were members of either the Politburo or the Central Committee. In fact, the party's highest policy-making body, the Politburo, is functionally organized to parallel the government ministries, with members specializing in the various governmental activities. In each state bureaucracy, there is always the presence of the party cell of leading CCP members who provide direction for the state organ. The party has always been able to exercise its control in a state bureaucracy by supervising its personnel. Thus, the state structure and the party are not truly parallel entities, since they interlock from top to bottom.

The party control over the state bureaucracy has been the subject of much discussion among scholars. Too often students of Chinese politics look at the bureaucracy under the State Council as if it were an independent power base competing with the party. The fact that all the forty-five ministers approved by the Eighth NPC were members of the CCP's Central Committee demonstrates that the State Council is not only interlocked with the party but is also controlled by it. Conflicts that do occur are not primarily between the government and the party but rather are intraparty conflicts between high-ranking party members.

Interlocking Relationships of Politburo Members. The interlocking relationships of the members of the Politburo, the highest decision-making body of the party, not only demonstrate how the party exercises its control over the central government but also give an indication of possible areas of speciality and of power bases for the top elites who are members of the Politburo. Several questions need to be posed here about the State Council, an enormous national administration comprised of more than forty bureaucratic departments and commissions, which in turn are staffed by more than forty thousand bureaucrats. First, what is the premier's "span of control" over the multitude of administrative units? As mentioned earlier, there was an inner cabinet within the State Council for policy formulation and problem solving. This inner cabinet was formally established in 1982–83 to constitute a standing committee, consisting of the premier, the five vice-premiers, the secretary-general for the State Council or the premier's office, plus ten senior advisors or counselors. Second, how often does the premier hold his cabinet meetings? According to a study by Michel Oksenberg, the inner cabinet meets regularly each week to discuss policy issues.[88] There is obviously elaborate staff work involved in the management of the State Council office: the setting of agenda for meetings, and the preparation of documents and background analysis, which is often generated by the research institutes associated with the Chinese Academy of Social Sciences.[89] Since the State Council is generally preoccupied with the implementation and the monitoring of the multifarious economic programs, research (or think tank) institutes became increasingly influential in policy formulation. For instance, the Economic Reform Research Center (affiliated with the Chinese Academy of Social Sciences) has made heavy inputs to reform policies and strategies for the reform-oriented leaders in the State Council. It is probably accurate to say that the "control span" for Premier Li Peng was manageable and that he was able to devote time to policy development. It is likely that no more than fifteen key officers in the inner cabinet make daily or weekly reports to him. No doubt he delegates responsibilities for supervising a number of ministries to his five vice-premiers and the ten counselors. We know, for instance, that vice-premier Zhu Rongji, an economist, is mainly responsible for matters concerning economic reforms. Li Peng, at one time a vice-premier, was in charge of scientific, educational, and energy development. A study by Professor Oksenberg points out that the inner cabinet has been overburdened by "interagency and interprovincial disputes" and that the vice-premiers must spend an inordinate amount of time and energy in solving the disputes.[90]

The interlocking system that existed in 1987 after the Thirteenth Party Congress and before the convening of the Seventh National People's Congress, scheduled for March 1988, was still very visible. Four of the vice-premiers of the State Council were elected to the new Politburo, and Li Peng, the premier, was also a member of the Politburo's Standing Committee along with two other vice-premiers (Hu Qili and Yao Yilin). Zhao admitted in his report to the Thirteenth Party Congress that the lack of distinction between the function of the party and of the government continued to be one of the outstanding problems to be resolved. He outlined four specific steps to be taken in this area of separation of party and government functions: No full-time party secretary at a given level should hold a government post or take charge of government work; no more overlap of party departments with counterpart governmental departments; leading party groups in a government department must be held accountable at the same level for which it was established; and party discipline inspections must not deal with law violation or infractions of administrative regulations. Zhao wanted the party to handle party affairs.

Since the political demise of Zhao in May 1989, not only has there been no implementation of Zhao's reform measures for breaking up the interlocking and parallel nature of the party and government discussed above; on the contrary, the degree of interlocking has also intensified at the hierarchical level. For instance, Jiang Zemin, the reelected general secretary of the party, member of the Standing Committee of the powerful Politburo, and chairman of the Military Affairs Commission of the party's Central Committee, was elected in March 1993 as president of the People's Republic of China. Jiang is in effect the head of the party, the government, and the military. Li Peng, the premier since 1988 for the State Council, was reelected as a member of the Politburo in April 1993. Qiao Shi, a long-time member of the Politburo, was elected in March 1993 as chairman of the Standing Committee of the Eighth National People's Congress.

The Overstaffing Problem

The overstaffing problem in the Chinese government is nothing new; overstaffing has been going on since the early 1950s. During the Eighth NPC session, held in March 1993, a proposal for reducing the number of employees by 20 percent was approved. Loa Gan, secretary-general for the NPC, revealed that seven existing ministries would be phased out and six small ones instituted.[91] This was said to be contrary to what vice-premier and Politburo member Zhu Rongji (Deng's choice responsible for economic reforms) preferred: a two-thirds across-the-board reduction.[92] What can't be ascertained is whether the 20 percent or two-thirds across-the-board cut applied to the 40,000 employees referred to by the 1988 NPC, or to all 4.2 million central government employees. There were 55,000 more central government units in 1990 than in 1984, and the number of "superfluous" personnel in government departments has reached over 500,000.[93] Premier Li Peng reported to the Eighth NPC delegates that he would like to devote the next three years to streamlining the national government functions by reducing the pre-1993 total of eighty-six ministries to fifty-nine, and then to forty-one.[94]

Political Structure Reform

We shall discuss the issue of political reform by examining these questions: Why must there be political reform? What does it mean? What specific problems are the advocates of reform trying to solve? Who opposes political reform? And, finally, how soon can one expect political reform?

It was known that a number of pragmatic reformers from Deng Xiaoping on down had at one time or another advocated the need for reform in the political system. They and several scholars in the Chinese Academy of Social Sciences had been issuing warnings to the country that it would not be possible to carry out economic reforms successfully without political reform. Discussion and debate about political reform reached a peak in the summer of 1986 when the Central Party School held a seminar to address the issue. As late as November 1986, Deng had told the visiting Italian Prime Minister Bettino Craxi that the purpose of political reform in China was to "stamp out red tape, and bring the initiative of the grassroots and the people into full play."[95]

In August 1980, long before the reforms launched the ambitious urban reform in 1984 (see Chapter 11), Deng Xiaoping broached the topic of reforming the party and government leadership system at an enlarged meeting of the Politburo. Deng bemoaned the fact that the party and government institutions were plagued by problems that seriously hindered the final realization of "a superior socialism."[96] Deng itemized the bureaucratic evils in much the same way as Mao had done some fourteen years earlier at the beginning of the Cultural Revolution. Deng charged that cadres were

> . . . indulging in empty talk; sticking to rigid ways of thinking; being hidebound by convention; overstaffing administrative organs . . . circulating documents endlessly without solving problems; shifting responsibility to others . . . being arbitrary and despotic; practicing favoritism; participating in corrupt practices in violation of the law and so on.[97]

Deng also pointed out that there was a close relationship between bureaucratism and the "highly centralized management in economic, political, cultural and social fields." He observed that when the entire decision-making process is highly individualized in the hands of a few, the results are inefficiency and inability to make decisions.[98]

As discussion on political reform expanded and was encouraged by the party leaders favoring reform, the term political reform implied more than just personnel management changes. In surveying the speeches and documents for 1985 and 1986, one finds that the term political reform referred to concepts in policy science, democratization of the NPC, the separation of power between the party and government, and the strengthening of the legal system. One case in point involved reform in the policy-making process. Wan Li, a vice-premier and Politburo member, favored the system approach in policy making. Wan Li seemed to advocate policy making based on "computerized quantitative input–output analysis, rather than on an individual leader's subjective judgment."[99] He deplored the fact that China had not yet established a policy-making procedure that included research support, consultation with experts, evaluation, and feedback before a policy was adopted. Instead, Wan pointed out, China had a system of policy making by intuition or osmosis. As a first step, Wan proposed the creation of "a political climate of democracy, equality and consultation."[100] He argued that policy issues must go through three stages or processes: research, decision, and implementation.[101] He seemed to stress the need at the research stage to permit free airing of views "within certain limits." He also carefully pointed out that these free discussions could not be permitted to deviate from the ideological guidance of Marxism.[102]

The movement for studies on political reform gained increased recognition in July 1986 when Zhu Houze, then the party's propaganda chief, organized a conference of scholars and political thinkers in Beijing to establish a distinct political science in "Chinese characters" to conduct research on reform measures in the political system.[103] (Zhu Houze was fired soon after the January 1987 student demonstrations were put down and Hu Yaobang resigned.)

Another specific issue in the debate on political reform was the question of the plant manager's autonomy in decision making in the factory. As discussed earlier, there was strong opposition on these issues from party branch secretaries, who feared the loss of party power and who had the backing of the orthodox hard-liners at the top leadership level[104] (see Chapter 11). The orthodox hard-liners won a temporary victory in the aftermath of Hu Yaobang's ouster and obtained a concession from the reformers to restore the veto power to the local party secretary in some 28,000 state-owned factories.[105]

Deng Xiaoping revealed his thoughts on the meaning of political reform when Stefan Korosec, a presidium member of the League of Communists of Yugoslavia, visited China in June 1987. Deng seemed to have ruled out abandoning centralized decision making in favor of "a system of multi-party elections and a balance of the three powers"—referring to the American system of government.[106] He argued that the present system of centralized decision making was more efficient than the proposals: "The efficiency I am talking about is not efficiency of administration or economic management, but overall efficiency. We have superiority in this respect, and we should keep it."[107] Deng listed three basic areas that required "political restructuring"[108]: (1) the revitalization of the party—the problem of replacing aging leaders by younger cadres (he described the old leaders as "conservative" and as having the common tendency of looking at problems "in the light of their personal experience"); (2) the elimination of bureaucratism by instituting administrative efficiency; and (3) decentralization in decision making, or "delegating power to lower levels."

When the Thirteenth Party Congress met in late October 1987, political reform was said to be an important item for discussion. One of the major items covered in Zhao Ziyang's report to this congress on October 25, 1987, was entitled "Reforming the political structure."[109] What Zhao reported at the opening session of the congress must be viewed as representing the party consensus. (Zhao's report had gone through seven revisions, the last in mid-October 1987, and was approved by the outgoing Central Committee.)[110] In the report Zhao pointed out briefly the defects of the political system as being overconcentration of power, rampant bureaucratism, and feudal influences. He then offered seven measures as keys to political reform.[111] One, as discussed earlier, is the separation of party and government functions. Two, the delegation of powers must be pushed down to lower levels. Local matters must be handled by local authorities. Three, Zhao asked for efficiency by merging departments and their functions; he also wanted the Seventh NPC to make more laws and regulations that would govern administrative organs. Four, he wanted to establish "a system of public service" to replace the cadre system so that "public servants" are to be classified into political affairs and professional categories.[112] Five, Zhao embraced the Wan Li appeal, discussed earlier, for consultation and dialogue in decision making. In August 1993 the Politburo finally embraced Wan Li's idea for the establishment of a new "central policy consultation group" under its control for making advisory input on major policy issues. Six, improvement in the work of the NPC with younger delegates and more working rules, as well as more elections with more candidates than posts. And, finally, Zhao asked for improved legislation by the NPC on legal procedures, law enforcement procedures, and the development "of judicial organs to exercise independent authority" as prescribed by law.[113] These measures do pinpoint some of the basic problems in Chinese bureaucracy.

One of the basic weaknesses of the party–government bureaucratic machine has been the party's control and "intervention" in matters of government policy. But also there is lack of discipline in the party itself. It has become increasingly more corrupt, and its members too often subvert party directives.[114] In a case study of China's energy policy, Kenneth Lieberthal and Michel Oksenberg detailed the massive and fragmented party–state bureaucratic structure that relies on "consensus decision making" through bargaining and negotiation between competing bureaucracies.[115] Parris H. Chang points out that the Chinese policy-making process at times involves "honest disagreement" among party leaders, but at other times reflects the results of power struggles.[116] Once the leaders agree on a policy it is the party–state bureaucracies that must thrash out the concrete details.[117] Parris Chang paints a picture of many participants in the policy-making process, each with political resources at his or her command.[118]

A "Multiparty" System for China? From 1986 to 1988 there was some discussion by Chinese intellectuals of the possibility of instituting a multiparty system as an integral part of political reform. In the aftermath of the Tiananmen crackdown a symbolic gesture has been made in the area of political structure reform: the guidelines proposed by the CCP Central Committee on December 30, 1989, for improving the system of multiparty cooperation and political consultation.[119] There are at present eight so-called "democratic parties" in China that exist under the leadership of the CCP. The proposed guidelines call for an invitation by the CCP Central Committee to the principal leaders of the "democratic parties" to meet for consultation on major policies, as well as meetings for the purpose of briefing or informing these leaders on specific policy matters. The proposed guidelines also call for "an appropriate proportion" of NPC deputies to be elected and represented at the NPC Standing Committee level and other special committees. The guidelines suggest that members of the "democratic parties" be selected for government positions in the State Council, as well as selected for leading positions in the judicial organs as supervisors, procurators, auditors, and educational inspectors. Thus, it would not be surprising to see ministerial appointments in the foreseeable future given to those leaders who are not CCP members. Press reports indicated that leaders of the "democratic parties" in China expressed their readiness to participate in the proposed system of multiparty consultation and cooperation.[120]

Some leaders of the "democratic parties" are well-known Chinese intellectuals and academicians—men such as Professor Fei Xiatong, China's famed anthropologist and chairman of the China Democratic League, and the late Zhou Peiyuan, former president of Beijing University and a well-known scientist, chairman of the Jiusan Society of Scientists, Technocrats and Educators.

NOTES

1. *Renmin Ribao,* March 1, 1977; and *Ming Pao* (Hong Kong), March 3, 1977, p. 3.
2. *Survey of Chinese Mainland Press*, 4097 (January 11, 1968), 1–4.
3. "Resolution of the Convening of the Twelfth Party Congress," *Beijing Review*, 10 (March 10, 1980), 11.
4. Ibid.
5. Roderick MacFarquhar, *The Origins of the Cultural Revolution*, Vol. 1: *Contradictions among the People, 1957–1967* (New York: Columbia University Press, 1974), p. 144.
6. Lo Bin, "Inside View of the Elections at the Twelfth Party Congress," *Zhengming* (Hong Kong), 60 (October 1982), 7.
7. "Communiqué on the Fifth Plenary Session of the Eleventh Central Committee of the CCP," p. 8. Also see Lowell Dittmer, "The Twelfth Congress of the Communist Party of China," *China Quarterly*, 93 (March 1983), 112–13.
8. William Brugger, "The Ninth National Congress of the CCP," *The World Today*, 25, no. 7 (July 1969), 297–305; Roderick MacFarquhar, "China After the 10th Congress," *The World Today*, 29, no. 12 (December 1973), 514–26; Richard Wich, "The Tenth Party Congress: The Power Structure and the Succession Question," *China Quarterly*, 58 (April–May 1974), 231–48.
9. Jiang Zemin, "Accelerating Reform and Opening Up," *Beijing Review* (October 26–November 1, 1992), 16.
10. Franklin W. Houn, *A Short History of Chinese Communism*, (Upper Saddle River, NJ: Prentice Hall, 1967), p. 87.
11. MacFarquhar, *Origins of the Cultural Revolution*, p. 101.
12. "Resolution on the Convening of the Twelfth Party Congress," 11.

13. See Lo Bin, "*Qiao Shi chu-chü Yu Shiwu da xuanju neimu*" (Inside story of Qiao Shi's Ouster and the Fifteenth Party Congress Election), *Zhengming* (Hong Kong) (October 1997), 8.
14. Ibid.
15. Parris Chang, *Power and Policy in China* (University Park, Pa. and London: The Pennsylvania State University Press, 1974), p. 184.
16. Xiaowei Zang, "The Fourteenth Central Committee of the CCP: Technocracy or Political Technocracy," *Asian Survey*, 32, no. 8 (August 1993), 793.
17. Ibid.; see Zang's statistical study of the Fourteenth Central Committee, 794–800.
18. "Constitution of the Communist Party of China, Adopted by the Eleventh National Congress on August 18, 1977," *Peking Review*, 36 (September 2, 1977) 21–22.
19. Houn, *Short History of Chinese Communism*, p. 87.
20. "Board of Directors, China, Inc.," *Far Eastern Economic Review* (September 2, 1977), 9.
21. Houn, *Short History of Chinese Communism*, pp. 91–92.
22. Ibid., p. 89.
23. "Talk at the Report Meeting, 24 October 1966," in *Chairman Mao Talks to the People*, pp. 266–67.
35. "The Central Committee's Secretariat and Its Work," *Beijing Review* 19 (May 11, 1981), 21.
24. Gittings' notes on the formation of this organ in 1931 by the First All-China Soviet Congress; see John Gittings, *The Role of the Chinese Red Army* (London: Oxford University Press, 1967), pp. 263–65.
26. Ralph Powell, "Politico-Military Relationships in Communist China," External Research Staff, Bureau of Intelligence and Research, Department of State, October 1963.
27. *Far Eastern Economic Review* (February 5, 1987), 34.
28. Yeh Chien-ying, "Report on the Revision of the Party Constitution," *Peking Review*, 36 (September 2, 1977), 32. For a detailed discussion of the party's control organ prior to 1982, see Graham Young, "Control and Style: Discipline Inspection Commission since the 11th Congress," *China Quarterly* 97 (March 1984), 24–30. Also, for a more detailed study of the new party control organ see Lawrence R. Sullivan, "The Role of the Control Organs in the CCP, 1977–83," *Asian Survey*, 24, 6 (June 1984), 597–615.
29. Yeh Chien-ying, "Report on the Revision of the Party Constitution" and "Communiqué of the Third Plenary Session of the Eleventh Central Committee," *Peking Review*, 52 (December 29, 1978), 6, 16.
30. John W. Lewis, *Leadership in Communist China*, (Ithaca, N.Y.: Cornell University Press, 1963), p. 134.
31. English translation of the text can be found in "Guiding Principles for Inner Party Political Life," *Beijing Review*, 15 (April 14, 1980), 11–19. For the original text see *Hongqi*, 6 (March 16, 1980), 2–11.
32. Xinhua New Agency release as reprinted in *Ming Pao Daily* (Hong Kong) August 14, 1983, p. 1.
33. *Ming Pao Daily* (Hong Kong), August 8, 1983, p. 3.
34. *Ming Pao Daily* (Hong Kong), July 5, 1983, p. 1.
35. *Ming Pao Daily* (Hong Kong), March 19, 1983, p. 1.
36. *Zhengming*, 114 (April 1987), 15.
37. Ibid., 15.
38. Franz Schurmann, *Ideology and Organizations*, (Berkeley: University of California Press, 1956), p. 210.
39. Chang, "Provincial Party Leaders' Strategies for Survival During the Cultural Revolution," in *Elites in the People's Republic of China*, ed. Robert A. Scalapino (Seattle, Wash. and London: University of Washington Press, 1972), pp. 501–39.
40. See Jiang Zemin's report to the Fifteenth Party Congress, *Beijing Review*, 40, no. 40 (October 6–12, 1997), 31.
41. Houn, *Short History of Chinese Communism*, p. 106.
42. *People's Daily,* June 27, 1982, p. 1.
43. See Appendix A for the text of the 1982 constitution. See also Byron Weng, "Some Key Aspects of the 1982 Draft Constitution of the People's Republic of China," *China Quarterly*, 91 (September 1982), 492–506.
44. "Report on the Draft of the Revised Constitution of the People's Republic of China," *Beijing Review*, 50 (December 13, 1982), 9.
45. *Ta Kung Pao Weekly Supplement,* June 3, 1982, p. 10.
46. *Beijing Review*, 40 (October 1, 1984), i–xx and *Beijing Review*, 14 (April 6, 1987), iii–iv.
47. *Beijing Review*, 18 (May 3, 1982), 16.
48. Discussion on these amendments is culled from Xu Yan, "Discussion on the Amendment of China's Constitution," *Beijing Review* (March 8–14, 1999), 13–15; and Li Rongxia, "Constitutional Amendments: A Milestone in the Rule of Law," *Beijing Review* (May 3–9, 1999), 9–13.
49. See "Amendments to the Constitution of the People's Republic of China—Adopted on March 15, 1999," *Beijing Review* (May 3–9, 1999), 14.
50. Rongxia, "Constitutional Amendments: A Milestone," 12.

51. Ibid.
52. "Two Decades of Rural Reform in China: An Overview and Assessment," *China Quarterly*, no. 159 (September 1999), 624
53. Ibid., 620.
54. Yan, "Discussion on the Amendments of China's Constitution," 13.
55. Ibid., 14.
56. Rongxia, "Constitutional Amendments: A Milestone in the Rule of Law," op. cit., p. 11.
57. Ibid., 3; and *China Trade Report* (June 1982), p. 12. Also see Dorothy J. Sollinger, "The Fifth NPC and the Process of Policy-Making: Reform, Readjustment, and the Opposition," *Asian Survey*, 22, no. 12 (December 1982), 1239–76.
58. *People's Daily* (Overseas Edition), January 28, 1986, p. 1.
59. Ibid.
60. *Ta Kung Pao Weekly Supplement* (Hong Kong), September 4, 1986, p. 15.
61. See Ji Sanmeng, "A Functioning Legislature?" *Xexus: China in Focus* (Spring 1987), 2–6.
62. "NPC and CPPCC: Democratic Trends," *China News Analysis,* June 15, 1997, pp. 3–4.
63. See *Asian Wall Street Journal* (6 April 1992), p. 1; and *Christian Science Monitor,* 3 April 1992.
64. See *Asian Wall Street Journal,* 30 March 1993, p. 6.
65. See James A. R. Miller, *The Legacy of Tiananmen: China in Disarray* (Ann Arbor: University of Michigan Press, 1996), p. 288; and "Qiao Shi's Radical Ideas," editorial in the *Wall Street Journal*, 18 March 1997, p. A-22.
66. See Guo Xin, "Qiao Shi Discussed Questions with American Journalists," *Beijing Review* (3–9 February 1997), 25.
67. See Matt Forney, "Rule by Law," *Far Eastern Economic Review* (13 March 1997), 14–15.
68. See "NPC and CPPCC: Democratic Trends," p. 3. Also see *Remin Ribao* (*People's Daily*), 28 February 1997, p. 3.
69. "Qiao Shi Discussed Questions with American Journalists," p. 25.
70. Ibid.
71. O'Brien, "Is China's National People's Congress a 'Conservative' Legislature?" 782–794.
72. "China Elects Two Vice Premiers Amid Discord," Kyoto News Service as reprinted in the *Honolulu Star-Bulletin*, 17 March 1995, A8.
73. Ibid.
74. See Kevin J. O'Brien, *Reform without Liberalization: China's National People's Congress and the Politics of Institutional Change* (New York and Cambridge: Cambridge University Press, 1990), pp. 91-92.
75. Ibid., p. 37.
76. Donald Klein, "The State Council and the Cultural Revolution," *China Quarterly*, 35 (July–September 1968), 78–95.
77. "Chou En-lai and the Cultural Revolution in China," in James W. Robinson, ed. *The Cultural Revolution in China* (Berkeley: University of California Press, 1971), p. 279.
78. Klein, "State Council," 81.
79. See Doak Barnett, *Cadres, Bureaucracy, and Political Power in Communist China* (New York: Columbia University Press, 1967), pp. 3–17.
80. Chang, *Power and Policy in China*, p. 50.
81. Ibid., pp. 63–64, 106–108; also see Barnett, *Uncertain Passage*, pp. 136–43.
82. "Report on the Sixth Five-Year Plan," p. 24.
83. Weng, "Some Key Aspects of the 1982 Draft Constitution of the PRC."
84. These figures came from the Party Secretariat for the State Council, in Liu Jinghai and Hai Xia, "Restructuring of the State Council General Office," *Beijing Review* (September 4-20, 1998) 12.
85. Ibid.
86. Ibid.
87. Ibid.
88. See Michael Oksenberg, "China's Economic Bureaucracy," *China Business Review* (May–June 1982), 23–24. Also see John P. Burns, "Reforming China's Bureaucracy, 1979–82," *Asian Survey*, 17, 6 (June 1983), 707–714.
89. Oksenberg, "China's Economic Bureaucracy," 23–24.
90. Ibid., 24.
91. See *Beijing Review* (29 March–4 April 1993), 8.
92. James W. Robinson, See *Far Eastern Economic Review* (April 1, 1993), 13.
93. *Beijing Review* (May 25–31, 1993), 21.

94. "Report on the Work of the Government," *Beijing Review* (April 12–18, 1993), xi.
95. Xinhua News Agency release reprinted in *Ta Kung Pao Weekly Supplement* (Hong Kong), November 6, 1986, p. 3.
96. *Beijing Review*, 32 (August 11, 1986), 15. Also see *Selected Works of Deng Xiaoping* (Chinese language edition), People's Publishing House, 1983, pp. 280–302 and the English translation in *Beijing Review*, 41 (October 10, 1983), 18–22.
97. *Beijing Review*, 32 (August 11, 1986), 15.
98. Ibid.
99. See *People's Daily*, August 15, 1986, pp. 1–2. Also see *Beijing Review*, 32 (August 11, 1986), 5–6, and *China Daily*, August 23, 1986, p. 1. Also see an editorial in *China Daily*, August 9, 1986, p. 4.
100. *China Daily*, August 23, 1986, p. 1.
101. Ibid.
102. Ibid.
103. *People's Daily* (Overseas Edition), August 16, 1986, p. 3; and *China Daily*, July 22, 1986, p. 1.
104. See *Far Eastern Economic Review* (February 5, 1987), 12. Also see *Zhengming*, 112 (February 1987), 7, and the *Wall Street Journal*, February 2, 1987, p. 19.
105. See *Far Eastern Economic Review* (February 5, 1987), 13, and *Ta Kung Pao Weekly Supplement* (Hong Kong), November 6, 1986, p. 2.
106. See "Deng Calls for Speedup in Reform," *Beijing Review*, 34 (August 24, 1987), 15.
107. Ibid.
108. Ibid., 15–16.
109. "Advance Along the Road to Socialism with Chinese Characteristics," *Beijing Review*, 45 (November 9–15, 1987), 37–42.
110. *Ming Pao Daily* (Hong Kong), November 6, 1987, p. 1. Also see Joseph Fewsmith, "China's 13th Party Congress: Explicating the Theoretical Bases of Reform," *Journal of Northeast Asian Studies*, 7, no. 2 (Summer 1988), 56.
111. "Advance Along the Road to Socialism," 37–43.
112. Ibid., 40–41. For a background study on a proposal to reform the cadre system by making changes in the nomenklatura system in China, see John P. Burns, "China's Nomenklatura System," *Problems of Communism* (September–October, 1987), 36–51.
113. "Advance Along the Road to Socialism," 43.
114. See Kenneth Lieberthal, "China's Political System in the 1990s," *Journal of Northeast Asian Studies*, 10, no. 1 (Spring 1991), 73–74. Also see *China News Analysis*, 1407 (April 1, 1990), 1–9.
115. See Kenneth Lieberthal and Michel Oksenberg, *Policy-Making in China: Leaders, Structures and Process* (Princeton, N.J.: Princeton University Press, 1988).
116. See Parris Chang, *Power and Policy in China*, 2d and enlarged ed. (University Park, Pa. and London: Pennsylvania State University Press, 1978), pp. 178–81.
117. Ibid., p. 180.
118. Ibid., p. 181.
119. For the proposal, see *Beijing Review* (March 5–11, 1990), 18–22.
120. See *Beijing Review* (February 26–March 4, 1990), 18–22.

SUGGESTED READINGS

Barnett, Doak. *Cadres, Bureaucracy and Political Power in Communist China* (New York: Columbia University Press, 1967).

Chang, Parris. *Power and Policy in China* (University Park, Penn. and London: Pennsylvania State University Press, 1974).

Ch'i, Hsi-sheng. *Politics of Disillusionment: The Chinese Communist Party under Deng Xiaoping* (Armonk, N.Y. and London: M. E. Sharpe, 1991).

Fewsmith, Joseph. *Dilemmas of Reform in China: Political Conflict and Economic Debate* (Armonk, N.Y.: M. E. Sharpe, 1994).

Lam, Wally Wo-Lap. *The Era of Jiang Zemin* (Singapore, New York, and London: Prentice Hall, 1999).

Lewis, John W. *Leadership in Communist China* (Ithaca, N.Y.: Cornell University Press, 1961).

Nathan, Andres J., Zhaohui Hong, and Steven R. Smith (eds.). *Dilemmas of Reform in Jiang Zemin's China* (Boulder, Colo. and London: Lyne Rienner Publishers, 1999).

O'Brien, Kevin J. *Reform without Liberalization: China's National People's Congress and the Politics of Institutional Change* (New York and Cambridge: Cambridge University Press, 1990).

Chapter Five

Elites and the Cadre System

*Leadership Style, Factionalism,
Succession, and Recruitment*

This chapter is concerned with China's elites—the political leaders who make policies and the organizational–institutional cadres at the various levels of the party and government who implement, and sometimes attempt to influence, policy making. An examination of China's elites and cadres logically follows our study of China's political institutions in the previous chapter.

The conceptual framework for elite study and recruitment is that the selection of political and administrative–managerial leaders in any political structure is an essential system function. Gabriel A. Almond and G. Bingham Powell refer to the selection of political elites as "recruitment structure—the way by which the political system selects policy makers and executives."[1] In the case of China, the "recruitment structure" includes, first and foremost, those leaders in the top echelon of the party's hierarchy, as well as some 4.2 million cadres who manage the government units.[2]

CHARACTERISTICS OF THE RULING ELITE

As pointed out earlier, the Leninist organizational structure is hierarchical and pyramidal in that decisions are made at the top by a few party leaders: in this case the members of the Standing Committee of the Politburo—the apex of the apex in decision making. However, for decades the top leadership has been dominated first by a charismatic leader, Mao Zedong (1935–76), and then by a paramount leader, Deng Xiaoping. According to Max Weber, the classical social organization theorist, a charismatic leader is one who possesses the exceptional ability or charisma to command the devotion and loyalty of the people and whose views are considered infallible.[3] Charismatic leadership such as that exercised by Mao is also very much a personal leadership. Both Mao and Deng have been portrayed by the late Harrison E. Salisbury as China's "New Emperors."

The Fourteenth Party Congress, which convened in October 1992, abolished the Central Advisory Committee. Until then, the Chinese top elite had been dominated by what is known as a gerontocracy. The Central Advisory Committee had been made up of aged party veterans who were permitted to provide input into policy making at the top. By the early 1990s several aged leaders, mostly 80 and over, gradually passed away. The average age of the current Politburo Standing Committee is about 65. Half of the Fourteenth Central Committee members elected in 1992 were young and middle-aged technocrats—their average age was 56.3 years.

The Fifteenth Party Congress, which met in September 1997, elected a new Central Committee, which, in turn, elected a new Politburo and its Standing Committee of seven members. The average age of the 1997 elected Standing Committee of the Politburo, the "apex of the apex" in the party's hierarchy, is about 65, with five of the seven members born in the 1930s.

As more aged veteran leaders at the top, including Deng Xiaoping, pass away from the scene, the problem of gerontocratic rule will tend to fade. However, one serious problem will continue to trouble the top elites in China: elite cleavage or strife, which, in turn, produces a related succession problem.

ELITE STRIFE, FACTIONALISM, AND CHINESE INFORMAL POLITICS

Lowell Dittmer points out that "elite strife is the Achilles heel of the Chinese political system."[4] Dittmer argues that major past crises of the regime can be attributed to "severe elite conflict" at the top.[5] Mao's Cultural Revolution represented a violent pattern of elite strife or power struggle, while elite conflicts under Deng's reform measures have been "institutionalized" and have been "less disruptive."[6] Through his analysis of the four major recent power struggles—the "Gang of Four" (1976), the removal of Hua Guofeng from power (1980), the dismissal of Hu Yaobang (1987), and the removal of Zhao Ziyang (1989)—Dittmer formulated the concept of the elite conflict cycle: from "open and legitimate disagreement," to "impersonal discussion of problems," to "destruction of the target's political base," and, finally, to "formal disposition of the case" by an official party meeting convened to legitimatize the disposal.[7]

Factionalism Defined

Political maneuvers among the top leaders in Chinese politics were factionalized and did not necessarily follow ideological lines. The factions were based on personal relationships and associations. Several China scholars have often identified factions in Chinese politics as examples of this type of political behavior.[8] For instance, Parris Chang comments on the emergence of two major coalitions, or groupings, among top leaders since the arrest of the Gang of Four in 1976.[9] One coalition, the "Whatever" group, consisted of Politburo members who were Mao loyalists and who collaborated with the Gang of Four during the Cultural Revolution. Included in the "Whatever" coalition was the so-called "petroleum" or "oil" faction, a group of veteran economists and technocrats who directed the economy. Hua Guofeng became the "Whatever" coalition's symbolic leader. The pragmatists of the second coalition, led by Deng Xiaoping, consisted mainly of Politburo members who were veteran party leaders and northern military leaders.

Most of the Deng group had been victims of purges during the Cultural Revolution. Allied with the Deng pragmatists were (1) the Chen Yun economic planners, (2) elder statesmen (Ye Jianying), and (3) so-called "independents."

Another commentator, Dorothy Fontana, has constructed a factional model utilizing the familiar radical-left, left-of-center, and political-right spectrum.[10] She believes that the radical left was made up of the Gang of Four and the "Whatever" group, joined earlier by the Lin Biao supporters. The left-of-center faction included the Long March military leaders and the "oil" or "petroleum" group of central economic administrators. The political-right faction included the late Zhou Enlai, the purged party victims of the Cultural Revolution, such as Deng, and the southern military leaders who later split with the Deng group.

In 1978 Deng began taking steps to consolidate his power and control over the party. A campaign was first launched against party officials who had collaborated with the Gang of Four and were now supporters of the "Whatever" faction. The campaign soon focused on the Politburo members who were led by Hua Guofeng and Wang Dongxing and who opposed Deng's reform policies. Hua's group appealed for reconciliation with those who had made serious mistakes during and after the Cultural Revolution. Marshal Ye, Hua's mentor on the Politburo, intervened by calling for "stability and unity" in order to mitigate the leadership purge that was about to begin and perhaps save something for those Politburo members who were known to have collaborated with the Gang of Four in the past.

At the Third Plenum of the Eleventh Central Committee (December 1978), Deng made some important gains as well as some concessions. The most important gain was the designation of Deng's protégé, Hu Yaobang, as the CCP general secretary to supervise the daily administration of the party affairs in an effort to dilute Chairman Hua's power. Deng gained another victory when the Central Committee agreed to elect four of his supporters as additional members of the Politburo. Those named were Chen Yun, Deng Yingchao (widow of Zhou Enlai), Hu Yaobang, and Wang Zhen. Chen Yun's elevation to Politburo membership was owed primarily to his reputation as a realistic economic planner. Chen was also made a vice-chairman of the Politburo's Standing Committee as a way of obtaining the support of the "independents," of whom he was a leading spokesperson. In addition, nine veteran party officials purged during the Cultural Revolution were elected as additional Central Committee members. Thus, Parris Chang developed a Chinese leadership factional scheme to show the dominance of the Deng group in coalition with the groups associated with the "Elder Statesmen" group of septuagenarians.[11] As pointed out in Chapter 2, by 1982 Deng was in control of official Chinese politics.

In 1978 Deng, as a leader of what has become the "grand coalition" of pragmatic reformers, orthodox hard-liners (conservatives, or ideological left), and the professional military, began taking steps to consolidate his power and control over the party. The "grand coalition" that Deng forged has many power centers revolving around personal ties within the party hierarchy. It is dependent on power sharing, not only with the young reformers but also with the military and many aged veteran leaders, whose party experience dates as far back as the Long March in the 1930s. Deng served as a power broker for a variety of viewpoints coming from the many power centers. Because Deng shared the early communist experience of the Long March and the purges of the Cultural Revolution, as well as personal friendship with the veteran cadres, he had been able to serve as a "bridge" between the aged orthodox hard-liners (conservatives) and the younger pragmatic reformers.[12] Parris Chang has portrayed Deng as a leader who, lacking Mao's charismatic power, has had to "rely on a skillful mix of cajolery, compromise, and threat to keep the coalition together."[13] Like Mao, Deng was considered a master in the game of politics—he was frequently able to balance power by playing one group against another to remain in power as the paramount leader of the "grand coalition."[14] The forced resignation of Hu Yaobang in January 1987 is evidence of continuing differences within the "grand coalition." The orthodox hard-liners tried to create the impression that Deng was in their camp when it was shown that Deng had criticized Hu for his indecisiveness in carrying out the party directives.[15] On the other hand, Deng's decision to let Hu go might be interpreted as a move "to placate the conservatives" in order to protect the reforms introduced after 1978.[16] Or, we may view Deng's action to remove Hu as a tactical move to "preempt his adversaries' attack" by upstaging them.[17] Parris Chang thinks that the firing of Hu, Deng's closest protégé and carefully groomed successor, "reflected Deng's poor political judgment and exposed his political weakness."[18] Another China watcher thought that Deng was simply a master tactician: Having realized that it was not possible to yield to the students' demand for real democracy, Deng merely took "two steps forward and one step backward," rather than sacrificing or scrapping the reform measures altogether.[19]

The factional model, described above, has been supplemented by a bureaucratic politics model developed by Susan Shirk in her analysis of conflicts in Chinese society that were brought on by economic reform. In Shirk's analysis the vast and powerful central and regional bureaucracies in China constitute a "communist coalition," dominated by the planning agencies, heavy industries, and the vertically organized state-owned enterprises. This bureaucratic politics model postulates that known personalities within the party's hierarchy, because of their past long association with the bureaucratic entities, became the "high-level patrons" for the complex of powerful but entrenched bureaucracies and the vested interests they represent.[20] (Interest group theory and bureaucratic politics as an approach to the study of the communist system only recently gained recognition in the literature for comparative study of communism.)

The top party leadership lineup that emerged from the Thirteenth Party Congress reflected and retained the essential features of Deng's "grand coalition": a mixture of pragmatic reformers (in dominance), orthodox hard-liners' views (represented by Yao Yilin and Li Peng or Qiao Shi, whose views came closer to those of Peng Zhen), the PLA representation (reduced significantly), and the regional or provincial/municipal representation that seems to be on the rise. In addition, the powerful party provincial secretary from Sichuan in the southwest (Yang Rudai), mayors of the three municipalities of Shanghai (Jiang Zemin), Beijing (Li Ximing), and Tianjin (Li Ruihuan) were also elected to the new Politburo.

The top party leadership lineup that emerged after the 1976 Tiananmen repression was on the surface in favor of the hard-line conservatives. However, on close examination, the lineup still reflected and retained the essential features of Deng's "grand coalition": a mixture of orthodox hard-liners, represented by Li Peng, Yao Yilin and Qiao Shi (who followed generally the views of Chen Yun), the moderate reform-oriented Jiang Zemin (the new party chief), Li Ruihuan (former mayor of Tianjin), and possibly Song Ping (the party's head for organization).

While the military leadership is divided (see Chapter 9), it has strong influence in the inner party struggle. Until the aged leaders, who constituted a powerful clique, pass from the scene and there emerged a new leadership lineup, three factions in early 1990 were locked in a power struggle.[21] One faction of younger leaders, more reform- and open-door-oriented, is led by Jiang Zemin and Zhu Rongji with support from a provincial and regional power base.[22] Li Ruihuan had been more critical of the policies of the hard-liners.[23] The second faction was represented by Li Peng and Yao Yilin, whose mentor had been the 86-year-old Chen Yun, China's leading advocate of centralized planning and a critic of Deng Xiaoping's economic reform measures.[24] The Li Peng faction also had the support of the aged conservative party leaders and some segments of the central bureaucracy. This faction had basic differences with the moderate reform-oriented group led by Jiang and Zhu Rongji over the unsettled question of economic reform, converging on the extent of return to more centralized control over the economy, as well as the question of the long-run status of socialism impacted by changes in Eastern Europe and the former Soviet Union under Gorbachev. The third faction consisted of the so-called "leftist" or "Whatever" group led by Deng Liqun and a few like-minded party elders who were opposed to Deng Xiaoping's reforms and proclaimed "undying support" for whatever policy or program Mao had endorsed in the past.

The Fifteenth Party Congress, which convened in mid-September 1997, produced a rather mild inner party struggle, as discussed in the previous chapter. Jiang Zemin has been in complete control in seeing his loyal supporters elected to key positions for directing the future course of the party for at least the next five years until the Sixteenth Party Congress meets in 2002. Jiang Zemin seems to have adroitly co-opted the "conservative" elements, led by Deng Liqun, at one time the party's propaganda chief, who opposed or were critical of economic reform and the gradual emergence of "liberal thinking." Now, under Jiang Zemin, China may experience a period of transition after the death of Deng Xiaoping, who was the paramount leader for about two decades. As a way of preserving stability, the factions have made efforts to maintain surface unity with Jiang Zemin as the core leader.

How to Explain Chinese Informal and Personal Politics

Recently China scholars in the West have attempted to develop some sort of social science theoretical schema to explain the factionalism and the informal or personal politics that is ever-present in Chinese politics.[25] At the risk of being over simplistic regarding the complex schemas and arguments presented in these learned articles, an attempt is made here, probably not doing justice at all, to summarize what is being said about Chinese informal politics.

Dittmer defined Chinese informal politics as "implicit and covert," but "limited to small, closed groups," usually occurring cyclically when the structure is about to break down, as when leadership succession occurs.[26] On the other hand, Lucian Pye sees limitations in the construction of any theoretical schema for informal Chinese politics because of the "rules of personal relationships in Chinese politics" and the "workings of *guanxi* (connections)," consisting of "subtle nuances."[27] Pye makes the argument that as ideology becomes less useful in the era of economic reform, it would be the "power of personal bonding" of party leaders, as well as cadres as the elite ruling class, which would provide stability.[28]

To Frederick Teiwes, party unity for the successor generation under economic reform is "managerial" in nature rather than that of "restraining" party members; that the need for unity "is desirable" in order to "maximize the strength of the organization." Unity in this sense "is permanent in any particular leadership arrangement."[29] Tang Tsou, one of the pioneers in the conceptual studies of Chinese factionalism, argues that Chinese informal politics are merely a means to achieve certain goals; but not as "an end in themselves."[30] Thus, Deng, used informal roles or ties to prevail over Zhao Ziyang, who had the formal role as party chief, or was linked by formal institution ties (the party).[31]

Andrew Nathan, another pioneer in conceptualization and theory building on Chinese factionalism, proceeds from the premise that we must be able to distinguish between "cultural" and "institutional" variables in explaining political behavior.[32] He asks the question: Why did Chinese politicians behave and function not as factions, but "in one man's court," when Mao dominated the politics? Nathan reexamines the cultural origin in relation to institutions as a way of explaining Chinese factionalism: "Since culture and structure are mutually constituted, institutions can be said to have culture."[33] Factions exist for reasons such as their importance in the political process. But there are also other factors that induce factionalism: economic change or international events.

After more or less downplaying the use of "bureaucratic" or "bargaining" models in explaining more familiar American or other Western politics, Joseph Fewsmith presents the thesis that any explanation of Chinese politics, past or current, must consider the elements of "informal politics, formal structure and political issues."[34] Fewsmith uses the 1980s rural reform as an example of interplay between formal structure and informal or personal politics: A small group formed on the basis of personal relationship and group members' relationships or association with senior political leaders paved the way for the party's secretariat to attach the group and its ideas on rural reform to the Economic Reform Institute of the Chinese Academy of Social Science.[35] Fewsmith also argues that issues may be more crucial in the interplay of formal structure (politics) and informal (personal) politics.[36]

China scholars will continue to construct theoretical models or schema with which to explain Chinese informal and personal politics. There are bound to be disagreements as to which model or theoretical construct would best explain Chinese leadership factionalism and informal politics. However, in the final analysis, the political future of China is unpredictable and uncertain, largely because of the omnipresence of factionalism, division, and informal, or personal, power play in political leadership. In addition, this leadership is too often complicated by the uncertain role of the military, the final arbiter, which inevitably engulfs major policy formulation in Chinese politics. It is also difficult to predict simply because factions are fluid, with shifting positions on issues and changing associations in group membership.[37]

On the surface, from 1980 to the end of 1986, China was under the collective leadership of three key leaders: Deng Xiaoping, Hu Yaobang, and Zhao Ziyang. This triumvirate controlled three main pillars of the Chinese political system: the military, the party, and the central government. However, some analysts held the view that the triumvirate was merely a facade to disguise Deng Xiaoping's role as the paramount leader. Former premier Zhao Ziyang confided to visiting former Soviet premier Gorbachev in 1989 that on major issues the top leaders must seek guidance and instructions from Deng Xiaoping.

The student demonstrations of 1986–87 and 1989, to be discussed in Chapter 10, had shaken the reform-oriented triumvirate that paramount leader Deng had installed. Within two and one-half years, Deng and his fellow octogenarians were twice required to remove their choice to head the party. Since Deng Xiaoping had dominated the Chinese politics until his death in February 1997, our discussion on the leadership must begin with a look at Deng.

Deng Xiaoping: Architect of the Power Transition after Mao's Death and the Succession, 1978–1992

In 1979 Americans had a chance to observe at first hand China's new strongman, Deng Xiaoping, when he visited the United States at the invitation of President Jimmy

Carter. For eight days Deng traveled from Washington to Atlanta, Houston, and Seattle, accompanied by members of Congress and the Carter cabinet. He was interviewed by the press at each stop; he mingled with the crowd in Atlanta; and he donned a ten-gallon hat at a Texas rodeo. His tour included visits to the space technology complex and oil-drilling-machine plants in Houston, and to the Boeing plant in Seattle.

What type of person was China's paramount leader, and what were his views? Although a dedicated communist and Leninist, Deng had never been dogmatic. When China was experiencing economic recovery during the early 1960s following the disastrous Great Leap, Deng said, "It makes no difference if a cat is black or white—so long as it catches the mice." In 1975 he expressed his disdain for a requirement that everyone spend long hours after work studying correct political thought. He called the practice "social oppression." A pragmatist, Deng has advocated the line of profit-in-command, rather than Mao's dictum of politics-in-command.

Deng was born in Sichuan province in 1904. He was an early organizer for the Chinese communist movement when both he and the late Zhou Enlai were students in France under a work-study program.[38] Before returning to China in 1927 to work in an underground party cell in Shanghai, Deng studied briefly in Moscow. He joined Mao's guerilla movement during the early 1930s and took part in the Long March. His rise in the party hierarchy was rapid, and by 1955 Deng was elected to the powerful Politburo and held the position of general secretary to the party. He remained the party's general secretary until 1966, when he was purged by the radicals during the Cultural Revolution.[39] In 1974 he returned to power at the request of the then ailing Zhou Enlai and Mao to introduce reforms that would enable China to modernize its industry, agriculture, sciences, and military defense. When the Tiananmen riot erupted in 1976, Deng was again purged. Following the arrest of the Gang of Four, Deng was once more returned to power to oversee China's modernization program as a deputy premier and vice chairman of the party.[40] The twice-purged Deng realized that to fulfill his task as chief architect of modernization, he must consolidate his power by replacing the remnants of Mao's followers with his own people.[41]

The party's declaration at the Third Plenum that the 1976 Tiananmen demonstration was an "entirely revolutionary mass movement" must be viewed as a personal vindication for Deng.[42] It was also a blow to those Politburo members who, sooner or later, would have to criticize themselves about their role in support of the Gang of Four in that riot which caused Deng's second purge. Finally, after some heated discussion, the party adopted Deng's view that practice was to be the sole criterion for testing truth, and that things did not have to be done according to books or to "ossified thinking." This was a direct refutation of the "Whatever" faction's stand. Deng was not yet strong enough to demand the immediate ouster of his opponents still sitting on the Politburo. Actually, Deng had to agree to shelve for the time being any further discussion on the sensitive, divisive issue of assessing Mao's role in the Cultural Revolution.

During 1979 Deng made little headway in instituting organizational reforms because of resistance from his adversaries. However, he prevailed upon the party at its Fourth Plenum in September 1979 to add twelve new members to the Central Committee. These new members included veteran leaders Peng Zhen, Bo Yibo, and Yang Shangkun. Deng was able to install Peng Zhen and Zhao Ziyang as alternate members of the Politburo and thus further improve his numerical strength on that body.

In February 1980 Deng's final move came at the party's Fifth Plenum. Key Deng supporters Hu Yaobang and Zhao Ziyang were elevated to membership on the Politburo's Standing Committee, the apex of the apex in decision making in the party hierarchy.[43] Their elevation was preceded by the removal of four Politburo members (Wang Dongxing, Ji Dengkui, Wu De, and Chen Xilian) who were held to be collaborators of the Gang of Four and critics of Deng's policies. While Hua Guofeng remained as the nominal party chairman, his power and influence by this time were those of a mere figurehead, for it was at the Fifth Plenum that the Central Secretariat was reestablished to manage and oversee the day-to-day work of the party, presided over by Hu Yaobang, the general secretary. By September 1980 Hua also had been replaced as premier of the State Council by Zhao Ziyang at a session of the NPC. Having removed his critics from the Politburo, Deng now was in a firmer position to issue a party communiqué calling for the implementation of the modernization program. By the end of 1980, he controlled the party, government, and military. But the new era in Chinese politics was not ushered in until some time later in September 1982, when the Twelfth Party Congress was convened under the complete control and domination of China's paramount leader, Deng Xiaoping, and his supporters.

Deng Xiaoping had said that he did not want to be honored for his accomplishments,[44] and had accepted responsibility for any mistakes made under his leadership in the thirty years prior to the 1966 Cultural Revolution. However, Deng Xiaoping most likely will be accorded a unique place in history as the man who engineered the "Second Revolution" in China during the decade after Mao's death, a period that ushered China into the era of economic and political reforms. Deng was the chief architect for change and the one who dared to make significant modification in China's experiment with socialism. He opened China's door to foreign investment and transfer of technology—thus ending its long isolation from the rest of the world, an isolation imposed mainly by Mao's ideological rigidity. (Detailed discussion on these topics is included in Chapters 3 and 11). Deng and his pragmatic reformers also introduced agricultural reform in the countryside: a profit-incentive or responsibility system that replaced the egalitarian commune system. While the final verdict is not yet in, Deng's image has been damaged considerably as a result of his order and support for the military crackdown on the students in Tiananmen on June 4, 1989 (see Chapter 10). While he resigned from the only official post he held after his semiretirement at the end of 1987—that of the chairmanship of the powerful Military Affairs Committee—in the aftermath of the Tiananmen massacre, Deng still made important decisions as China's paramount leader in the years following his resignation.

Deng Xiaoping died in February 1997 at the age of 92. The transition after Deng has been rather smooth as the Jiang Zemin-led leadership core continued to rule the regime. However, the leaders have been operating under the shadow of Deng Xiaoping and will continue to do so for some time to come. This can be seen by the adoption of Deng Theory as the party's ideological guide in both the party and state constitutions (see Chapter 3). In the meantime, China scholars and China watchers will provide us with a varied assessment of Deng as the pragmatic communist and statesman in the twentieth century.[45]

JIANG ZEMIN: HEAD OF THE NEW LEADERSHIP CORE AS DENG-DESIGNATED SUCCESSOR

Jiang Zemin was 63 years old in June 1989 when he was selected to replace Zhao Ziyang as the third party chief since Mao's death in 1976. His earlier work with the party was mostly in Shanghai factories manufacturing foodstuffs, soap, and electrical machinery. In

1955 he went to Moscow as a trainee at the Stalin Automobile Factory, where he studied Russian. He returned after one year and was placed as deputy engineer at an auto plant in the northeast; in 1970 he rose to become the director of foreign affairs for the machine building ministry. In 1982 he was a vice-minister for the Ministry of Electronics Industry. In 1985 he became the Mayor of Shanghai and its party chief; two years later he was elevated to membership in the Politburo, the apex of the party's decision-making hierarchy. By then he had established wide contacts with diplomats and was able to speak several languages, including English, French, and Russian.

Jiang was obviously the personal choice of Deng Xiaoping, who selected the former to succeed the deposed Zhao as an acceptable compromise to the octogenarians in order to avoid a factional fight among the divided top leadership. Other plausible reasons for Deng's backing of Jiang might be Jiang's handling of student protests in 1986–87 when he skillfully, but peacefully, terminated an otherwise dangerous situation. Deng also might have been impressed by Jiang's plans for developing Shanghai as the premier industrial giant—the two had a secret meeting in the spring of 1989 in Shanghai. During the Tiananmen demonstration, Jiang acted decisively in support of the Center's desire to curb intellectual dissent and criticism by firing the chief editor of an outspoken Shanghai liberal economic journal. However, to some, Jiang's record in Shanghai was not by any means a distinguished one.

Nevertheless, Deng chose to designate Jiang in 1989–90 as the "core of the third generation of leaders."[46] At that time Jiang lacked some essential factors to survive and ultimately win the inner party struggles.[47] First, he did not, at the time of designation as the new leader, have any previous military association or connection to inspire the military's support. He had been recently appointed chairman of the powerful Military Affairs Committee after Deng stepped down in September 1990. China's military establishment had been under the control of Yang Shangkun and his brother Yang Baibing until they were purged in 1992. Jiang patiently built up support among the military officers by making promotions as a way of counteracting the influence of the Yang brothers.[48] In the end, with Deng's active consent, the Yang brothers were purged from their positions of power. Second, Jiang manipulated skillfully the octogenarians within the party power structure so as to moderate their criticisms.

On the eve of convening the much-delayed Seventh Plenary Session of the Thirteenth Party Congress, originally scheduled for October or November 1990, there seemed to be clear evidence that there was already some opposition building up against Jiang.[49] However, at the Fourteenth Party Congress (1992) and the Eighth National People's Congress (1992), Deng promoted the party chief, Jiang Zemin, to be his successor. By the spring of 1993 Jiang had become not only the party chief and the chairman of the party's powerful Military Affairs Committee, but also the president of the Republic—the first leader since Mao to control the party, the government, and the military.

Liu Binyan, a dissident leader now in exile at Princeton University, writes that Deng's choice of Jiang as his successor may be another one of Deng's power-balancing acts among other contending members of the Politburo's Standing Committee.[50]

Jiang was born in 1926 in Yangzhou in east China into a family of scholars. He had some exposure to missionaries during his childhood days and thus learned to speak a few words of English, of which he has a good command today. He received an electrical engineering degree from the prestigious Jiaotong University in Shanghai. It was in his college days that he developed a fondness for music; he sings well and, on occasion, displays his singing skills in public. He also plays the piano and the traditional Chinese two-string instrument known as the *erhu*. He is said to love reading, including the works of Mark Twain and Leo Tolstoy. He can recite by memory Lincoln's *Gettysburg Address*.

Jiang Zemin's trip to the United States from October 26 to November 2, 1997 was mostly symbolic rather than substantive. His White House meeting with President Bill Clinton produced no significant break through in the American-Chinese stalemate in the areas of human rights, Chinese missile sales abroad, or trade. But Jiang's presence in America did provide the status and recognition he needed as the undisputed leader of China after Deng's death. Everywhere he visited he was met with protests and demonstrations over the issues of human rights violations, the jailing of dissidents, and Tibet. Despite the protests during his visit to the United States, his meeting with President Clinton and the twenty-one-gun salute gave Jiang the honor and respect that he needed to bolster up his leadership in China. It most likely brought Jiang and his top leaders added prestige when President Clinton paid a reciprocal state visit to Beijing in June 1998, the first such visit by an American president since the 1989 Tiananmen crackdown on student protests.

THE NEW LEADERSHIP CORE

Li Peng: The Survivor and New Head of NPC

Li Peng is one of the many symbolically adopted children of the late Premier Zhou Enlai and his wife. An electrical engineer trained in the Soviet Union, Li speaks fluent Russian and some English. Before he became prominent, Li, at the age of 54, was in charge of China's hydroelectric and nuclear energy development. In 1983, Li was elevated to be one of the five vice-premiers under Zhao Ziyang. Long before he was appointed as acting premier at the end of the Thirteenth Party Congress in November 1987, Li was considered by many as the likely successor to Zhao because of his training, education, and executive experience, in addition to his good connections with the old veterans by virtue of being an adopted son of Zhou Enlai.

Li's father, an upper-middle-level party cadre, was captured and put to death by the Nationalists in 1931. Li went to Hong Kong as a youngster to live with his mother, who was then a party member working underground. In 1939 Li returned to wartime Sichuan, his native province. He became a party member in 1945 and was one of the privileged few to go to the Soviet Union for further training. Li attended the Moscow Power Institute from 1948 to 1954 and graduated with an electrical engineering degree. Until recently most of Li's work was concerned with the technical aspects of electrical power and hydroelectric development projects in Beijing. He became concurrently the minister for the State Education Commission before he was promoted to the post of vice-premier in the State Council in 1983. In the 1985 reshuffle of top echelon leaders, Li was elected to the Politburo.

When Li was designated in late November 1987 as the acting premier, several questions were raised about his elevation to succeed Zhao at the State Council.[51] These questions or concerns seem to fall into two major areas. One is his Soviet connection. His training as an engineer from the Moscow Power Institute in the 1950s placed him in the "pro-Soviet" camp. At an unusual press conference of China's vice-premiers in April 1987, Li defended his position by saying that "The second question seems to ask whether I favor a pro-Soviet policy. Here I formally declare that I am a member of the Chinese government, and also a new young member of the Communist party's Central Committee. I'll faithfully carry out the policies of the Central Committee and the government."[52] Thus it may not be fair to have labeled Li as "pro-Soviet" on the ground that he received technical training in the Soviet Union. A number of Soviet-trained technocrats, now members of the new Politburo, have supported Deng Xiaoping and Zhao Ziyang and the reform programs; they have been given important positions in the party and government.

A second question raised about Li concerns the degree of his support for economic reforms, particularly urban reform and the open door policy. Li is said to be under the influence of Chen Yun, who championed centralized planning and issued cautions on current economic reforms. Li's selection to succeed Zhao as premier was one of the compromises struck just prior to the Thirteenth Party Congress between Deng and the conservative hard-liners at Beidaihe in the summer of 1987. Apparently Zhao's opposition to Li was based on two main considerations: their disagreements on some reform measures, and Zhao's fear that Li's elevation to the premiership in time could lead to a takeover by the conservative hard-liners. There is little evidence to document Li's open opposition to any of the economic reforms. On the day when he was designated the acting premier, Li pledged to carry on both the economic reform and the open-door policies. However, at a general staff meeting of the State Council, he stated that the speed of economic reform might be "too fast."[53] For the foreseeable future Li seems to be committed to the reform policies.[54]

Li disagreed with Zhao over the issue of how to handle the Tiananmen student demonstrations. By allying himself with the hard-liners on the Politburo and Yang Shangkun, the People's Republic of China president and the then-permanent secretary for the Military Affairs Committee, Li proclaimed martial law on May 20, 1989. Since then, Li has emerged as one of the spokesmen for the hard-liners and as a target of attack and criticism by students, intellectuals, and those who have been sympathetic toward political and economic reforms. Li Peng suffered humiliation at the 1993 NPC session when more than 11 percent of the deputies voted against or abstained from his reelection as premier. Li Peng's power has been weakened considerably since 1993, and there had been signs suggesting his gradual political decline.

However, in September 1997 the departure of Qiao Shi from the Politburo made Li Peng the second-highest-ranking member on the Politburo's Standing Committee. The arrangement agreed to by the top leaders in their informal meetings in the summer at Beidaihe resort was to "promote" Li Peng to be the incoming chairman of the NPC at its next session, convened in the spring of 1998. Thus, Li Peng had survived in spite of his health and his past unpopularity among NPC delegates. By moving Li Peng to the NPC slot, Jiang Zemin and his leadership core had been freed to designate Zhu Rongji as the new premier of the State Council, a position that had been occupied by Li Peng since November 1987. (In the March 1995 session of the NPC, delegates from several provinces registered their criticism of Li Peng for his unwillingness to assume responsibility for inflation and rampant corruption in the officialdom.)

Zhu Rongji: The Economic Czar in the "Jiang–Zhu System" of Power Control

Li Peng's illness and unpopularity provided the opportunity for Jiang Zemin—with the consent and support of Deng and perhaps of the late Chen Yun, then the powerful octogenarian—to elevate Zhu Rongji, the vice-premier, to acting premier. Then, in July 1993, Zhu was concurrently named the governor for the central bank, replacing Li Peng's appointee, who was deemed unable to provide effective leadership in curbing the overheated economy. Zhu Rongji's star has been on the rise and he replaced Li Peng as premier.

Zhu Rongji is 73 years old and a graduate of China's prestigious Qinghua University, where he majored in electrical engineering. Zhu has been associated closely with the State Planning Commission. In addition, he was appointed vice-minister in charge of the State Economic Commission in 1983, before he succeeded Jiang as mayor and party chief for Shanghai in 1985. Whereas Jiang lacks a working knowledge of the intricacies of economics and trade, Zhu is very well versed in these matters. It is this combined "Jiang–Zhu *tixi* (system)" that would be the center of attention and power for China.

Zhu Rongji became the new premier at the Ninth NPC, which convened in March 1998. He is now the most powerful top leader next to Jiang Zemin. Zhu and Jiang had worked together closely in Shanghai for many years before they both came to Beijing to work for the central government. In fact, Jiang Zemin relies quite heavily on Zhu for managing the economic reform programs. From the early part of 1992 until the present, Zhu has served as chief banker for the central banking system in China, and he has been the inflation fighter. In these capacities Zhu has utilized both his practical skills in managing the economy and his academic knowledge—he concurrently holds the positions of professor and dean for the School of Economic Management at the distinguished Qinghua University (China's MIT).[55] The decision, approved by the Fifteenth Party Congress, to privatize the debt-ridden state-owned enterprises, was one of Zhu's recommendations.

Li Ruihuan: The Possible Wild Card in Future Succession Contests

Deng Xiaoping elevated Li Ruihuan to the Politburo in August 1987, not only because he was at age 53 a relatively young leader, but also because of the reforms he had introduced while serving as mayor of Tianjin, an industrial city. Li was born of a peasant background and trained as an expert carpenter at a construction company in Beijing in the early 1950s. In 1958 he had the opportunity to study at Beijing Civil Engineering Institute. He joined the party in 1959, and by the 1960s was serving as a party secretary in the building material trade. He was purged during the early part of the Cultural Revolution. In 1971 he came to Beijing and engaged in party organizational work in the lumber and building material industries. He was also active in the trade union federation in Beijing, having served as a member of the executive committee for the All China Federation of Trade Unions, a mass organization.

In 1981 Li Ruihuan became the mayor of Tianjin. As mayor he introduced significant reform work in urban housing; he insisted on work efficiency. He is reform-minded and a key supporter of Deng's reforms. He is a crowd pleaser, speaking in a plain and clear manner with humor.

He is a wild card in the serious game of power struggle and succession if there were a deadlock among Jiang Zemin, Zhu Rongji, and Li Peng. Li Ruihuan can use his new state responsibility as the long-time chairman of the National Committee of the Chinese People's Political Consultative Conference (CPPCC) as a base for his succession contest. He has many friends in China's minor political parties and is acceptable to many intellectuals and industrial units without party affiliation. Also, he has wide support from overseas Chinese, particularly in Hong Kong and Macao, the economically booming areas crucial to economic development and investment in China.

Hu Jintao:[56] May Be Jiang's Successor in 2002

Hu Jintao is the youngest member on the Politburo's Standing Committee. He is the president of the Party School for the Central Committee. Hu is also a graduate of Qinghua University, with a degree in hydroelectric engineering. He was born in 1942 in Anhui Province and is only 58 years old. His major assignment was in 1974 serving as the secretary in charge of the Gansu provincial construction committee; Gansu is known for its aridity. From that position Hu moved on to become the secretary for the province's Chinese Communist Youth League. In 1984 Hu was elevated to become the first secretary for the Central Committee's All China Youth Federation, then China's largest youth organization. Four years later, Hu was transferred to become the secretary for the party's Tibet Autonomous Regional Committee. Then, in 1992, he was elected to the Politburo's Standing Committee. His elevation to the party's highest decision-making body may be attributed to his work among the youth.

There have been reports that at the Fourth Plenary Session of the Fifteenth Party Congress some decisions were made with regard to the fourth-generation leadership succession. Party chairmanship would most likely be passed on to Hu Jintao to succeed Jiang Zemin when he steps down. Hu Jintao has been made a vice-chairman for the powerful Military Affairs Committee, the supreme party organ which directs the People's Liberation Army. This is considered a crucial step in the leadership succession move at the sixteenth Party Congress, to be convened in September 2002, and thereafter.

Wei Jianxing:[57] Enforcer for Party Discipline and Anti-Corruption

Wei Jianxing has been considered a protégé of the retired or "ousted" Politburo member Qiao Shi. This may be Jiang Zemin's way of making concessions to those who were supportive of Qiao Shi as the person in charge of the party's Central Commission for Discipline Inspection before Qiao Shi became the chairman of the NPC's Standing Committee in 1992. Wei has been credited with the exposure for corruption of Chen Xitong, former mayor of Beijing and a former member of the Politburo. Wei is 66 years old and a certified engineer from the Dalian Engineering Institute in northeast China. In the early 1950s Wei was sent to the former Soviet Union to learn business management. When he returned to China he fell victim to the Cultural Revolution. Wei lost his managerial position with a large alloy processing factory and was forced to work as a laborer in the plant. In the mid-1980s Wei served as deputy head for the central Committee's organization department. Wei has also been active with the All China Federation of Trade Unions. He took over the party discipline inspection commission from Qiao Shi and instituted grassroots inspection of corruption. By that time Wei had already been elected to the Politburo in 1992.

Li Lanqing:[58] Foreign Trade Expert and Negotiator

Li Lanqing established his reputation as a foreign trade expert, having worked as director of the Foreign Investment Administration in the central government's Ministry for Foreign Trade and Economic Relations. He was born in 1933 in east China's Jiangsu province. He graduated from a leading university in Shanghai, Fudan, in 1952.

Then he went to Moscow to work in the Gorky Automotive Works; he returned to China to work in an automobile factory in the northeast. In the 1960s he worked in the State Economic Commission and rose to the position of secretary to the commission. He worked in the various sectors of auto works before joining the administrative commission of foreign investment and the State Council's Economic and Trade Office in 1992. He then rose to the position of vice-minister for foreign trade.

Li Lanqing participated in many government trade negotiations and helped to restructure China's foreign trade system as China's open door policy expanded under Deng's reform. In addition, Li Lanqing is known for his keen interest in educational reform, particularly in providing a decent salary for teachers. He speaks both English and Russian.

FOR THE TWENTY FIRST-CENTURY:
THE FOURTH GENERATION OF LEADERS

Preparation has been underway to form a new corps of leaders to succeed the present generation of leaders led by Jiang Zemin. This new crop of leaders has been named the "fourth-generation" elites to succeed the current third generation of leaders.[59] Several in the group discussed earlier are considered members of the fourth generation group, or as the new elites. For instance, Hu Jintao, as mentioned earlier, now the vice-chair for the party, will most likely take over the top leadership position once Jiang Zemin steps down. When the new generation of successors takes over, their ascendancy will mark the end of dominance for over four decades by the revolutionary and Soviet-trained party veterans. Most of the new generation elites are university graduates, or the equivalent, and are on the whole younger in age.

Their occupational background ranges from lawyers to economists to financial experts—the category of highly trained technocrats. Included in the new generation of leaders are several who have established their names in the provinces—thus, they clearly possess regional experience and orientation.

RECRUITMENT OF PARTY MEMBERS

When the Eleventh Party Congress convened in August 1977, almost a year after the downfall of the Gang of Four, it was announced that the party had a membership of more than 35 million. In his speech, Ye Jianying pointed out that 7 million of the 35 million party members had been recruited since the last party congress in 1973, and about one-half of the total party membership had been recruited since the Cultural Revolution.[60] He admitted that there was a serious problem in party organization and discipline, which resulted from the rapid recruitment of so many party members by the Gang of Four. The old soldier, then a vice-chairperson of the party, bluntly indicated that the radicals had recruited a large number of new party members in accordance with their own standards. What Ye was demanding were tighter requirements for party membership. What he failed to mention was that the Chinese Communist Party (see Table 5.1) membership had been steadily increasing since the party came to power in 1949, and that the party had not always insisted on ideological purity and correctness as the most important criteria for membership. Party membership in 1997 reached an all-time high of 58 million members from some 3.4 million grassroots cells, the basic or primary unit of party organizations. [61] This

TABLE 5.1   CCP Membership Growth Pattern

Party Congress	Year	Number of Members
1st Congress	1921	57
2nd Congress	1922	123
3rd Congress	1923	432
4th Congress	1925	950
5th Congress	1927	57,967
6th Congress	1928	40,000
7th Congress	1945	1,211,128
8th Congress	1956	10,734,384
	1961	17,000,000
9th Congress	1969	20,000,000
10th Congress	1973	28,000,000
11th Congress	1977	35,000,000
12th Congress	1982	39,650,000
13th Congress	1987	46,000,000
14th Congress	1992	52,000,000
15th Congress	1997	58,000,000
— — —	1999–2000	61,000,000

Sources: Figures from 1921 to 1961 are based on John W. Lewis, *Leadership in Communist China* (Ithaca, N.Y.: Cornell University Press, 1963), pp. 108–20. The 1969 party membership figure is an estimate calculated on the basis of about 40 percent increase in 1973 over 1969 given by Jurgen Domes, "A Rift in the New Course," *Far Eastern Economic Review* (October 1, 1973), 3. The 1973 total and membership figure is taken from Zhou Enlai's "Report to the Tenth National Congress of the CCP," *Beijing Review*, 35–26 (September 7, 1973), 18.

The 1977 party membership figure is based on Ye Jianying, "Report on the Revision of the Party Constitution to the Eleventh Party Congress, August 13–18, 1977," *Beijing Review*, 36 (September 2, 1977), 36. The 1982 figure was based on *Beijing Review*, 36 (September 6, 1982), 6. Also see New China News Agency release of August 18, 1982, as printed in *Ming Pao* (Hong Kong), August 21, 1982, p. 1, and the *New York Times*, September 6, 1982, A-2. The 1987 party membership figure is based on *Renmin Ribao* (Overseas Edition), September 30, 1987, p. 1. Party membership for 1992 is based on *Renmin Ribao*, October 21, 1992, p. 4. Party membership for 1997 is based on Jiang Zemin's speech to the Fifteenth Party Congress, *Beijing Review*, 40, no. 40 (Oct. 6–12, 1997), 31. For party membership for year 1999–2000, see Associated Press release reprinted in the Hawai'i Tribune-Herald (Hilo), May 6, 2000, p. 4.

represents an almost 10 percent increase since 1992. Let us now discuss the factors that contributed to the expansion of party membership. As of May 2000, total party membership has been recorded at over 61 million.

Factors in Party Membership Expansion

Several general remarks may be made with respect to the growth of the CCP membership. First, for the period from 1920 to 1927, from the party's First Congress to its Fifth Congress, members of the party were primarily urban intellectuals, intermixed with some members of the proletariat from coastal cities and from mines in the inland provinces. When the Sixth Party Congress convened in 1928, most of its members had been driven underground by the Nationalists. There was a significant reduction in membership, by as much as 17,900, between the Fifth Party Congress in 1927 and the Sixth Party Congress in 1928. This reduction can be attributed to the slaughter by the Nationalists in the 1927 coup and to the subsequent defections.

Second, from the Sixth Congress in 1928 to the Seventh Congress in 1945, the primary membership recruitment shifted from intellectuals to peasants, who became the mainstay of the guerilla armies. In fact, beginning in 1939, the CCP, under the firm leadership of Mao, undertook to militarize the party membership. The 1.2 million members reached by the Seventh Congress in 1945, at the termination of the war with Japan, largely operated under the appropriate description "military communism." Party members essentially were recruited from the famed Eighth Route and from the New Fourth Armies. The late John Lindbeck noted the profound impact of the recruitment pattern in the character-building of the party membership:

> The result of the militarization policy was that dedication, fighting spirit, and responsiveness to discipline and orders became the hallmark of Communist Party members, as well as the harsher virtues of a soldier—ruthlessness, toughness, and a will to override and subdue other people. They held the guns out of which Mao's political power and everything else grew. By the time the party had conquered China, the bulk of its membership was made up of triumphant warriors.[62]

Lindbeck also pointed out that the militarization of the party membership created many problems that have continued to beset Chinese party politics. These problems—concerning the army as a special political power and as an independent interest group—will be discussed in later chapters. What we need to point out here is that the army has always been the model emulated by the CCP in organizational disciplinary matters.

Third, the period from 1945 to 1956, or from the Seventh to the Eighth Party Congress, represented the most rapid growth period in the party's history: from a little over 1.2 million members to just under 11 million members, or approximately an 886 percent increase. The years 1955–56 saw another sudden rise in membership recruitment, followed by a temporary lull and then a gigantic rise in 1956–57, when party organizational work was intensified in all rural areas of China. This was the period preceding the Great Leap Forward, launched in 1958. Although party recruitment took some great strides quantitatively—by 1961, some 90 percent of the 17 million party members had been recruited after 1949—the ideological purity of the new party recruits was questionable.

Fourth, during the period from the Eighth Party Congress in 1956 to 1961, recruitment of party members became institutionalized to ensure that party members possessed both ideological redness and technical expertise. Membership expansion during 1954 and in 1956–57 was designed to recruit personnel needed to direct and manage the nation's extensive political and economic activities. The rapid recruitment of those who possessed the needed technical skill resulted in a shift in the recruitment pattern of new party members in terms of social background.

Following this changed pattern of recruitment, the party cadre system was institutionalized to make it more attractive to intellectuals who were being co-opted into the party. By 1955 a rank system for cadres' work assignments had been instituted, based on the acquisition of technical skills. In addition, a salary scale system was promulgated along with the rank system for cadres. Recruitment and promotion rules were also instituted in the late 1950s. Recent studies point out the bureaucratization of the party. One study concludes that by 1965 China was no longer a revolutionary society because, by initial contact with the political system and a careful selection of education and occupation, a careerist could very well predict the outcome of his or her life.[63] Another study points out that one inevitable result of the institutionalization of the party in the late 1950s and the 1960s was bureaucratization, which stressed order, discipline, and routine as organizational virtues.[64] While no detailed official statistics on party membership have been released since 1961 when membership stood at 17 million, the general level of party membership has been indicated, as shown in Table 5.1. During the Cultural Revolution, aggregate membership remained at around 17 million, virtually unchanged from 1961. Membership for 1969 was approximately 20 million, a net increase of only 3 million from 1961. However, after 1969 party membership resumed its rapid rise, with the addition of 8 million members from 1969 to 1973, when the total stood at 28 million, and the addition of 7 million from 1973 to 1977, when the total stood at 35 million. This means, as Marshal Ye has indicated, that over half the 35 million party members in 1977 were recruited after the Cultural Revolution.[65] For the four-year period from 1978 to 1982, another 4 million new members were added, for a grand total of 39 million. The rate of increase has been 6 million party members from 1982 to 1987 and another 6 million from 1987 to 1992.

Without detailed data, we cannot be sure of the backgrounds of the new members recruited since the Cultural Revolution. However, fragmentary official figures showing the characteristics and social composition of new party members have been reported.[66] The party membership for the Beijing municipality may be used here as an illustration. From the Cultural Revolution to 1973, some 60,000 new members were added to the party membership roster for Beijing. Of these, about 75 percent were "workers, former poor and lower-middle peasants or children of such families," and just under 5 percent were "revolutionary intellectuals working in the fields of culture, health, science and education." The overwhelming majority of these new Beijing municipality party members were under 35 years of age, and women constituted 25 percent of the total.

Another important element in the recruitment pattern following the Cultural Revolution was the effort made to recruit members of the minority groups in the autonomous regions. Apparently, 143,000 new members from minority nationalities were admitted to party membership from 1969 to 1973. Although we do not have comprehensive official statistics for the entire CCP membership from 1961 to 1976, we may surmise, based on fragmentary data, that the new membership recruitment pattern placed greater emphasis on (1) industrial workers of urban areas, (2) women, (3) minority nationalities, and (4) youths. Since 1978 there has been a sharp increase in recruitment of party members from among intellectuals, particularly scientists and persons with technical knowledge, who in the past have been discriminated against either for being politically unreliable or for having complex social backgrounds. If the above conclusion is correct, and I believe it is not too far off target, then the CCP has greatly broadened its base, regardless of the shifting recruitment requirements.

Membership Requirements: Changing Emphasis

There is a marked difference between the party constitutions of the Eighth Congress (1956), and those of the subsequent congresses (1969, 1973, 1977, and 1982) with regard to eligibility for party membership. The 1956 constitution stipulated no class basis or origin for party membership: It was open to "all Chinese citizens" who qualified. The party constitution approved in 1969 by the Ninth Party Congress, at the end of the Cultural Revolution, and the ones adopted by the Tenth and Eleventh Party Congresses in 1973 and 1977, required that only those who are "workers, poor peasants, or lower-middle peasants" were eligible to become members of the CCP. In addition, PLA soldiers and "other revolutionary elements" might also be eligible for membership. The 1982 party constitution is less restrictive, providing that any worker, peasant, member of the armed forces, and—more significantly—intellectual may be eligible for party membership (see Article 1 in Appendix B). All recent party constitutions—1973, 1977, and 1982—prescribed four sequential requirements that an applicant for party membership must satisfy: (1) recommendation by two party members, after filing the application individually; (2) examination of the application by a party branch that solicits opinions about the applicant from both inside and outside the party; (3) acceptance of the application by the party branch at its general membership meeting; and (4) approval of the party branch's acceptance of membership by the next higher party committee. It has been a frequent practice, dating back to the late 1940s, for an applicant to be admitted to party membership solely upon the recommendation of top party leaders.[67]

All party members were obligated by both the 1969 and 1973 party constitutions to live up to the five requirements that Chairman Mao advanced for worthy revolutionary successors: to conscientiously study the works of Marx, Lenin, and Mao; to always serve the collective interests of the people and never work for private gain; to strive for united front work; to consult the masses; and to be willing to engage in criticism and self-criticism. The 1977 party constitution added three more requirements: never to engage in factional activities to split the party; to observe party discipline; and always to perform well tasks assigned by the party and to set examples as a vanguard. The added demands were designed to strengthen the standards for recruitment of party members and to tighten admission policy, in order to avoid the "crash admittance" program allegedly practiced by the purged radical leaders. In his report on the need to tighten requirements for party members, Marshal Ye said in 1977: "In recent years the Gang of Four set their own standards for party membership and practiced 'crash admittance' and as a result some political speculators and bad types have sneaked into the party."[68] The fact that the provisions for "purification of the ranks" and strict party discipline, as well as for tightening admission standards, were written into the 1977 and 1982 party constitutions illustrates the importance of the recruitment process to the party leaders and their awareness that the pattern of recruitment has great influence on the character of the party.

The 1982 constitutional requirements for party membership are almost identical to the provisions of the 1977 party constitution. However, the 1982 version stresses in Article 3 the responsibilities of party members to work "selflessly" and "absolutely never to use public office for personal gain or benefits." This provision certainly expresses the party's concern for the outbreak of widespread corruption among party members in recent years.

Party recruitment in the 1980s was still beset with problems, despite the crack-down on "crash admittance," widely practiced during the Cultural Revolution and immediately afterwards. Two of these problems were how to weed out unfit or unqualified party members, and how to upgrade party members' professionalism and competence as China moved toward modernization. In a speech to a conference of party cadres in January 1980, Deng Xiaoping stressed the fact that too many party members were simply unqualified.[69] He deplored their preoccupation with acquiring special privileges instead of serving the people.

Although no attempts have been made to implicate all those party members admitted during the Cultural Revolution, 17 million (about 40 percent of the 1982 total membership of 39 million) had been targeted for the first phase of the party rectification campaign.[70] Hu Yaobang told the 1982 party congress that beginning in mid-1983, for a period of three years until 1986, concerted efforts would be made to weed out undesirable and unqualified party members. The method used for the second stage of the housecleaning was the reregistration of all party members by national-, provincial-, and basic-level party organizations. The specific steps involved in the internal housecleaning campaign were comprehensive study of party documents, particularly those decisions endorsed by the party's Third Plenum in 1978 (including *Selected Works of Deng Xiaoping*); careful examination of party members' records; and reregistration on the new party membership roll. Special teams of investigators were dispatched by the party organizations at the central and provincial levels to lower levels—the investigations were to be supervised by a "Central Party Rectification Working Leadership Commission" under the joint leadership of Qiao Shi, a young Politburo and Central Secretariat member, and Bo Yibo, a retired old guard serving as the vice chairman for the Central Advisory Commission.[71] The requirements for membership stated in the new party constitution would be applied against party members who had been "rabble-rousers" during the Cultural Revolution or who had practiced factionalism or instigated armed violence. Hu Yaobang indicated that "those who failed to meet the requirements for membership after education shall be expelled from the party or asked to withdraw from it."[72] Also targeted for expulsion from party membership were those who had committed economic crimes, such as bribery, embezzlement, or smuggling. Originally the number targeted for expulsion by 1986 was estimated at as high as two million.[73] In 1987, at the end of the party purge, it was reported that some six million rural party members had been either transferred or simply expelled for being exposed to the "ultra-leftists" and for committing "economic crimes," but the latest official word was that only 150,000 were expelled because of the resistance.[74]

Upgrading the competence and professionalism of party members is a much harder task to accomplish. Since a majority of government leaders are party members, the problem centers on the educational level of the party cadres. The 1982 party constitution contains a special chapter on party cadres. Article 34 states that party cadres (leaders) must possess both political integrity and professional competence. But the fact remains that perhaps as many as 50 percent of the 20 million state cadres have a minimal education, equivalent to an American junior high school level. One Western source estimated that in 1985, 10 percent of the 40 million party members were illiterate and perhaps only 4 percent had any college level education.[75] A Chinese source was quoted as stating that in 1985 as many as 15 million of the 40 million party members were illiterate or poorly educated peasants.[76] An article in the *China Daily* attributed the high level of illiteracy within the party membership to Mao's dictum that the poor and uneducated peasants were the most reliable party members.[77] This is probably true among cadres at the party's basic organizational level in the countryside. Even at the party's central and provincial organizational levels, there is a dire need for trained and skilled administrators and managers. Some efforts have been made to upgrade party cadres' professional competence. Cadres younger than 40 with only a junior middle school education (the equivalent of an American eighth-grade education) have been sent to specialized party schools for three years on a rotation basis.[78] The ultimate goal in upgrading party cadres is to provide leaders at every level of the party who are "revolutionized, youthful, intellectualized, and expert."[79]

The task is enormous, considering the sheer number of party cadres who are undereducated and in need of professional training.

Party membership is still a coveted endeavor for some university students, particularly those who want to go into business and professions in order to establish themselves in society. There is wide media coverage on July 1 each year, the founding anniversary of the party, for the new party recruits. In fact, recruitment of undergraduates at China's leading university, Beida, has been increasing, from 4 percent in 1990 to about 13 percent in 1998.[80]

As of 1998, the latest year for which there is any figure available, there were a total of thirty-three million "administrative staff on the state payroll."[81] Of these, about 25 percent, or eight million, were cadre assigned to the state party and government organs at all levels. The vast majority, or twenty-five million (about 75 percent), worked in institutions including educational and medical departments.[82]

THE DEVELOPMENT OF THE CHINESE BUREAUCRACY: THE CADRE SYSTEM

A government's policies and programs are generally carried out by the functionaries who staff the administrative agencies. In the noncommunist world, we call these people bureaucrats, the "vast impenetrable and well-paid" corps of paper-shufflers.[83] The Chinese call these bureaucrats "cadres" or *ganbu*, denoting leadership skill and capability in an organizational setup. Thus, we may refer to Zhou Enlai, Hu Yaobang, or Deng Xiaoping as the party and central government's leading cadres. The intermediate layer of bureaucrats is the middle-level cadres, and those on the bottom layer, who must deal directly with the masses, are the basic-level cadres.

It should be kept in mind that not every cadre is a party member, nor is every party member a cadre. In short, *cadres* are the functionaries who staff the various party and government bureaucracies and who have authority to conduct party or government business. When we use the term *elite* in discussing Chinese politics, we are generally referring to the cadres at various levels.

On the basis of their employment, the cadres are divided into three general broad categories: state, local, and military. Each group has its own salary classification system with ranks and grades, similar to civil service systems in noncommunist countries. Urban state cadres have a system with twenty-four grades, while local cadres have twenty-six grades. Local cadres at the county level or below are paid directly by the organizations they work for. This ranking system is also associated with status, privileges, and the degree of upward mobility in the career ladder. A cadre's rank, particularly at the state level, is determined not necessarily by length of service or seniority but frequently by educational background, expertise, or technical competence. Those cadres who have served the party since the days of the Long March and the war against Japan naturally command more prestige than those who joined after the liberation in 1949. During the Cultural Revolution, the term *veteran cadres* was widely used to denote cadres who had acquired administrative experience in managing party and government affairs prior to the Cultural Revolution.

It is difficult to obtain precise figures for the total number of state, local, and military cadres in China today. We know that in 1958 there were about 8 million state cadres, or one state leader for every eighty persons in China. If we use the ratio of 1:80 as a basis for a rough estimate, the total number of state cadres in 1982 was over 27 million.[84] This figure does not include the millions of cadres at the local level and in the military, and it includes only some of the 39 million party members, many of whom are cadres. The leadership nucleus in China, as of the year 2000, most likely may reach more than 50-60 million cadres. This is the Chinese elite that must provide leadership for the masses.

Development of the Cadre System

In the early days, when the Chinese communist movement was engaged in guerrilla activities, the vast majority of the cadres were basic level. They were the link between the party and the masses, the go-betweens in the execution of party directives. They were expected, then as now, to conscientiously apply the principle "from the masses, to the masses" and to always be attentive and responsive to the wishes of the masses. Most of these basic-level cadres were peasants with experience mainly in managing governmental affairs of a rural nature. Because of the guerrilla operations, it was necessary to require all cadres to be dedicated party members and to adhere strictly to the party principle of democratic centralism. In implementing policies, these cadres supervised the tasks called for by the policies. They were required, from time to time, to conduct investigations into the results of programs and to make reports to the party. The ideal cadre during the guerrilla days was also a combat leader who lived among the masses and exemplified the traits of modesty and prudence.

After the communist takeover in 1949, a new type of cadre was needed to manage the complex social and economic affairs of the vast nation. This required persons with administrative skills and experience not possessed by the cadres who came from the rural environment and guerrilla background. A massive infusion of both party members and government cadres took place from 1949 into the early 1950s. As a stopgap measure, party membership and loyalty were no longer required for the government cadres. Instead, education, technical skill, and experience became the prerequisites for cadre rank. The cadres from the guerrilla experience were placed in special training programs to prepare them for work in complex governmental agencies. By 1953 about 59 percent of the 2.7 million cadre force were graduates of either regular or people's universities; the remaining 41 percent had attended special training courses to prepare for their work in various government agencies.[85]

The transformation of cadres from revolutionary leaders, engaged in guerrilla warfare, to government bureaucrats, concerned largely with paperwork, became formally institutionalized in 1955, when the State Council promulgated a rank classification system for the cadres.[86] Rank within the system was based on acquisition of technical skills and on when the cadre had joined the revolution. As the need for manpower in government service grew, a salary system with a promotional ladder was also established to attract career-oriented young people.[87] It has been said that by this time a cadre could predict with some accuracy future promotions and status.[88] These developments in the bureaucracy presented a host of problems for a society dedicated both to egalitarian principles and to modernization, with its concomitant requirement for specialization and expertise, which could only be administered in a complex hierarchical structure. In an effort to maintain the egalitarian society and to correct various abuses, the regime developed three major strategies, aside from the use of persuasion through education and the dispatch of special work teams, to correct specific local abuses. These strategies were rectification campaigns, the *xiafang* movement, and May Seventh cadre schools.

Rectification Campaigns

Rectification campaigns have been used to correct deviant behavior of both party and government cadres. The campaigns generally have involved education, reform, and purge. These campaigns have been undertaken periodically to strengthen the cadres' discipline, to raise their political and ideological awareness, and to combat corruption and inefficient work performance.[89]

The first rectification campaign, conducted by Mao from 1942 to 1944, following his selection as party chairperson, was designed to remove lingering opposition to his strategy for revolution. This was followed by the 1950 rectification campaign, aimed at correcting deviant attitudes among party cadres at all levels. The party cadres were criticized for "commandism," or issuing orders without proper consultation with the masses; tendencies of bureaucraticism, including excessive paper shuffling; distrusting the masses; and lack of direction and coordination in their work. The campaign was also an attempt to resolve differences between cadres from the guerrilla days and those recruited after 1949, which had created friction and tensions within the party. The 1950 campaign required the cadres to study, in a systematic way, selected key party documents, to analyze China's situation, and to participate in self-criticism during small-group discussions. These two campaigns were followed by at least six more rectification campaigns, including the Socialist Education Campaign in 1963, prior to the Cultural Revolution. As Frederick C. Teiwes has pointed out, the measures used in these successive rectification campaigns ranged from educational persuasion, to reduction of rank and pay, to punishment by purge or even death.[90]

Despite these rectification campaigns, on the eve of the Cultural Revolution, problems still existed with the cadres—as bureaucrats and administrators—because they were committed more to efficiency and orderly completion of tasks than to revolutionary enthusiasm and vision.[91] As careerists, the cadres as a whole had established political power, comfortable income, and security as life goals.[92] There were particular problems that included difficulties in actual implementation of the mass line principle, deviant behavior, acquisition of special privileges, declining morale, and increased tensions.[93] The Cultural Revolution can be considered both a gigantic rectification campaign and a mass campaign aimed to a large extent at these bureaucratic problems. The numerous rectification campaigns have created fear and uncertainty among the cadres and have led to administrative chaos and waste in the management of government activities.

Trends in the Cadre System: Reforms and Problems

Over the past two decades, life for a cadre as an intermediary has not been easy. The cadre was not able to please either those at the top of the party or the masses at the bottom. Since all decisions were subject to criticism from many directions, frequently the wisest choice was to make no decision at all. The cadres who came from the intellectual class but who possessed technical expertise were subject to special abuse as China's privileged "new class."[94] To redeem themselves, cadres opted for physical labor in the countryside, putting aside their professional development, at least temporarily.

The pendulum has now swung back to the moderation of the mid-1950s, when China's economic development demanded the rapid recruitment of capable, skilled persons as cadres to manage the nation's complex economic activities. The attacks against the new "bourgeois right" of elites and intellectuals were silenced with the downfall of the radical Gang of Four. Recently, deliberate attempts have been made to reform the cadre system. One key reform measure has been to place leadership positions in the hands of cadres who are "staunch revolutionaries, younger in age, better educated, and technically competent."[95] Hu Yaobang called for greater emphasis on cadre utilization and promotion according to education and skills: "We must work strenuously to strengthen the education and training of cadres in order to prepare personnel needed for socialist modernization."[96] To implement this directive, a rotation system for further education and training has been instituted for government cadres whose educational attainment is below the secondary level. But the task of upgrading cadres' competence seems formidable indeed when one considers the fact that a large number of cadres, both at the center and in the provinces, have only the equivalent of a primary school education.[97]

Introduction of Nomenclature. As a part of the cadre management reform, the party's organizational department published a detailed organizational management handbook setting forth guidelines, policies, and regulations for cadre management.[98] The 1983 handbook also established a Soviet-type *nomenklatura*, a comprehensive list of offices for party and state leaders in state enterprises and institutions, including scientists, professors, and even athletes. However, a study by Melanie Manion reveals that the 1983 handbook led to very little progress since 1983 to improve the cadre management system because the party leadership lacks "an emancipated outlook and boldness in innovation."[99] In 1986, however, a set of rigid rules for cadre promotion were issued.[100] To curb the widespread abuse of nepotism, the rules called for a system of secret ballots to nominate capable cadres for promotion in work units, the *danwei*.[101] One rule stated that no candidate who received less than a majority vote was to be nominated for promotion. The rules also prohibited senior officials from attending meetings at which promotion decisions were to be made. The criteria for promotion evaluation were to be on the basis of candidates' "political awareness," ability, diligence, and merits—particularly their recent achievements.[102]

Aged Cadres. Closely related to the upgrading of cadres' competence is the problem of upward mobility for the middle-aged cadres. Prior to 1986, about 2 million of the 27 million cadres working for the Central Committee and the State Council were considered veteran cadres, having been recruited before 1949.[103] These veteran cadres, advanced in age, had clung to their posts in the party and government. A retirement system was instituted to provide turnover in personnel. During 1981 and 1982, there were massive resignations of older cadres. In one machine-building industry ministry, the 13 vice ministers and 269 cadres resigned or retired at the bureau level.[104] In 1981 some 20,000 aged cadres retired in one province.[105] By early 1986 more than half of the then 2.1 million aged cadres had been retired.[106]

Bureaucratism. There are two other problems in the Chinese cadre system. One is bureaucratism, and the other is special privileges. Since 1980, bureaucratic practices have been under constant attack in China. One manifestation of bureaucratism is inertia and the resultant inability to make decisions. This foot-dragging is more evident at the middle and lower levels of the party organization and government structure. Deng Yingchao, a member of the Commission for Discipline Inspection, made a lengthy speech at one of the commission's forums charging that a few cadres have adopted a bureaucratic work style and have created a bad image for the party.[107] She characterized the bureaucratic work style as follows: "When there is a problem, they suppress it; when it is not possible to suppress it, they push the problem aside; when it cannot be pushed aside, they then procrastinate."[108] Foreign businessmen stationed in China have given vivid pictures of the cadres' bureaucratic work style.[109] Deng Xiaoping charged that cadres seemed to be devoted to rules and regulations and to exhibit obstinacy, timidity, and an air of infallibility; they spent an enormous amount of time reading the interminable flow of documents and directives.[110]

Special Privileges. Cadres are a special class in Chinese society. Like their counterparts in the former Soviet Union, they enjoy special privileges. The acquisition of these special privileges sets them apart from the masses. The problem of special privileges and material comfort for party and government cadres can best be seen by Chen Yun's talk at a high-level work conference:

> For transportation, we travel by car and do not have to walk; for housing, we have luxurious Western-style buildings....Who among you comrades present here does not have an air conditioner, a washing machine, and a refrigerator in your house? Take the TV set for example, please raise your hand if the one in your house is not imported from some foreign country.[111]

High cadres and members of their families not only have access to goods and services not available to ordinary citizens but also have access to foreign magazines and movies. Chen Yun also indicated that the children of higher cadres were the first ones to go abroad to study once the door was opened to the West in 1977. As a special privileged class, party and government cadres have been reluctant to give up any of these prerogatives.

At first the campaign against official corruption and the extravagant lifestyle of high party and government cadres seemed to coincide with Deng's attempt to oust the "Whatever" faction within the Politburo. However, subsequent campaign efforts indicated a genuine desire on the part of the leaders to make the party more creditable.[112] The general public has maintained its usual skepticism about the party and the government's ability to eventually correct such undesirable bureaucratic behavior.

From the foregoing discussion, it seems obvious that one key to Chinese bureaucratic reform lies in personnel management. During the Cultural Revolution, Mao included incompetence, corruption, favoritism, and nepotism in his often-quoted indictment of the "evils of bureaucratism." Harry Harding provides the following "organizational pathologies" of personnel management in the Chinese bureaucracy: "lack of commitment to goals and values," "lack of zeal and enthusiasm attributable to low pay," "low morale brought on by erratic changes," and "lack of skills and training."[113] Programs to retire aged bureaucrats and replace them with younger, better-educated cadres certainly represented a positive step forward. John Burns notes that the problem is further complicated by the party's long-held view that any attempt to reform the personnel system challenges or interferes with party prerogatives.[114] As long as "political considerations" are the key criteria in cadres' recruitment and there are not more applications than positions, the personnel system is subject to corruption in the form of "back-door" favoritism and rampant nepotism. The undesirable characteristics of the Chinese bureaucracy are intimately tied to "the pervasiveness of informal organization, networks of personal relations (*guanxi*), and factions within the bureaucracy."[115] In the final analysis, as was admitted in an inner party document in 1984, the entire political system's overconcentration of power in the upper hierarchy helps to produce incompetence and the inability, or unwillingness, to make decisions by the middle and lower levels of cadres in the vast bureaucracy.[116] Therefore, long-range and fundamental solutions to the endemic bureaucratic problems must be viewed from the perspective of China's overconcentrated planning and management system, as well as the insistence that the party must always exercise control and supervision over economic planning and management.[117] This realization in recent years prompted the pragmatic reformers to institute reforms, not only in the economic system (structure), but in the political system as well. However, the Tiananmen crackdown on student demonstration and the ouster of party chief Zhao Ziyang had, in reality, placed the political structural reform in the deep freezer, figuratively speaking.

CORRUPTION: A "MALIGNANT TUMOR" IN CHINESE BODY-POLITICS

Zhu Rongji, the Chinese prime minister, told the National People's Congress in 1999 that there is a "need to build a clean and honest government and punish corruption."[118] He repeated rather emotionally the same message in the spring of 2000 to the same gathering of the People's Congress. In fact, corruption is a hot topic in daily conversation by everyone in China. Since there are no reliable (only fragmentary) nationwide statistics available on how serious the epidemic in the Chinese body-politics is, one can say only that it is serious enough to ultimately affect the Chinese Communist Party's legitimacy to rule if the problem is not placed under effective control.

Scope of Corruption. Since there are no statistics nationwide for the corruption cases, the widespread scale of official corruption may be seen from the scattered statistics. Here are a few samples entries, culled from some sources:

From 1982–1987 some 16,000 cases of corruption or "economic crime" cases were placed for investigation.[119] Then, for the first six months of 1986, a total of 27,000 cases of economic crimes were investigated, an increase of 130 percent over the same period for 1985.[120] In August 1988, the party expelled or asked 109,000 corrupt members to resign—but of these only thirty were cadres holding positions above the county level.[121]

And, for the past ten years, 1989–1999, a total of 174,000 cases were reported to the prosecutors by the general public.[122] In September 1997, China launched a new round of anti-corruption campaigns by prosecuting party and government officials above the county level who committed "economic crimes" in any form whatsoever.

Another form of official corruption places official positions for sale with price tags. As reported recently, there has been rampant selling and buying of official positions.[123] A party boss and his cronies in the southwestern province of Guangxi sold sixty government positions for a large sum of money with which they then built townhouses just outside of the town.[124] The case was exposed, but the culprits received only a light sentence.

Forms of Corruption. The use of bribery or favoritism to get scarce goods or to get things done by way of "back-door" dealings have been common practices. The offspring of higher party and anti-government cadres in Hong Kong have often served as "connections" for foreign merchants who desire to establish contacts for trade with China.[125] Also widespread is the practice of gift giving and wining and dining by cadres who do business with each other—Beijing municipal authorities have imposed a new prohibition against such practices.[126] In April 1982 the party Central Committee, the State Council, and the NPC Standing Committee enacted an order that demanded life sentences or death by execution for those cadres who were involved in graft or similar corrupt practices.[127] The party's theoretical journal, the *Red Flag*, called economic crimes such as embezzlement of public funds and smuggling new elements in the class struggle.[128] The number of economic crimes committed by the offspring of senior cadres also has been on the rise; one senior army officer agreed that his son should be punished for graft in an illegal timber sale scheme.[129] For the first six months of 1986, a total of 27,000 cases of economic crimes were investigated, an increase of 130 percent over the same period for 1985. Well over 31 percent of the total were considered "serious economic crimes, cases involving more than 10,000 yuan (about U.S.$2,700)."[130]

A third form of widespread corruption, particularly along the southern coast, is the incessant occurrence of smuggling. In Xiamen in southern Fujian Province, opposite Taiwan, the wife of the party chief in Beijing was reported to have been linked with a $10 billion smuggling ring.[131] Smuggling by boats through jetties and harbors in South China ports is a common occurrence involving customs officials and party officials. It is considered a significant part of a "vast hidden economy."[132.] The Guangdon provincial source reported that its disciplinary inspection committee in 1999 "penalized" 4,505 officials for smuggling and other related corruptive activities in some 4,199 cases.[133] Many of these exposed cases have involved senior and middle-level party officials.

Organizational Corruption.[134] A particular form of official corruption that has emerged in contemporary China has been termed in studies about China under reform as "state corporation,"[135] or "entrepreneurial state."[136] "Entrepreneurial state" corruption is engaged in not only by individuals, but also by party or government units for the explicit purpose of using their power to make monetary gains.[137] Such corruptive practices are conducted covertly within the official unit and for the benefit of the unit members.[138] Often the illicit practices by official party/government agencies involve the following forms[139]: exacting fines or fees which are not authorized legally; using new regulatory agencies established under market reform, particularly at the local level, to collect arbitrary fines or charges such as road tolls by setting up illegal checkpoints on county or provincial highways; deliberately concealing records of receipts or income, underreporting funds, or retaining cash income; forming illicit "consulting" units as subsidiaries for the purpose of collecting fees from customers who do business with the parent firm; and using publicly raised funds for extra bonuses for government unit members or as supplements during times of budget shortage. It has recently been revealed in a report from the Central Disciplinary Commission to the party's Political Bureau that diplomatic officials assigned to embassies overseas have frequently engaged in illegal foreign exchange operations, commercial transactions, or even smuggling.[140]

Causes and Remedial Actions. A main cause underlying the widespread official corruption in China has been the decline and irrelevance of the Maoist communist ideology, which served as a moral compass to guide party members' thinking and actions. As discussed in Chapter 3, Mao's practical ideology functioned as a guide by which individuals in Chinese society shaped their attitudes and regulated their behavior. It is worthwhile to repeat here that these ideas served as a set of preferred societal values against which actions and thoughts were judged. Before the economic reform era, the very ideas of self-sacrifice and service to the people had constituted an essential part of the value system.

For some time in Mao's revolution the concept of egalitarianism prevailed in that everybody in society possessed the same material goods. The values and the system then made everyone poverty-stricken; it was to be a classless society with "blanket poverty."

In the 1980s Deng's economic reform changed the essence of that egalitarian, poverty-stricken puritanism by emphasizing that "to be rich" is not a social evil. Deng's "socialist market economy" encouraged and promoted the very idea of "making money" as a right. Currently, there seems to be an obsession in Chinese society for everyone to want to make money and to engage in conspicuous consumption.

Of course, corruption is an old problem in China, as well as in many other Asian societies. But in China the cultural tradition of *guanxi*, or connections, has contributed enormously to the rampant official corruption—one has to have some "connection," or know someone who does, to get anything done or to go through the "back door" to get it accomplished. This cultural trait contributes to the practice of bribery and many of the illegal transactions engaged in by officialdom in particular.

Finally, by Western standards the Chinese legal system (see Chapter 6 for detailed discussion) is still in the developmental stage. The amended Penal Code of 1997 makes illegal practices or "economic crimes" by public officials criminal offenses, but there is too often a lack of monitoring procedures for enforcement, even though the party's disciplinary commissions at all levels have been instructed to be vigilant to expose these wrongdoings by officials (see Chapter 6 on enforcement of law). There are no "institutional checks" on party and government officials such as local party chiefs or heads of various government units. It seems ironic that a reporting system on anti-corruption relies on "tip-offs" from the general public.[141] It has been disclosed that during the past ten years some 174,000 cases of official corruption have been discovered based on information from the general public.[142] In one province, 110,504 cases were reported by the public, of which about 75 percent involved embezzlement or bribery.[143]

Recently there has been wide publicity about several cases of corruption by high party/government officials. One deputy governor for Jiangxi Province in East China, the highest official ever prosecuted so far, was convicted by the People's Supreme Court on charges of bribery; he was executed as punishment. That conviction was one of the year's 132,000 cases of exposed official graft.[144] (Another case which involved a former mayor and party chief in Beijing on charges of embezzlement of public funds was also prosecuted.)[145] Also, a vice-chairman of the powerful Executive Committee for the National People's Congress and a member of the party's powerful Central Committee was investigated,[146] and sentenced to death.

Another study of local high officials who were prosecuted from 1980–1993 showed a total of twenty such officials receiving jail sentences ranging from two to twelve years and the death sentence for five of those convicted for corruption in that period.[147]

Whether these exposures of corruption by high officials will retard the spread of official corruption is not really certain. However, one action taken recently by the Personnel Ministry of the central government may provide some needed reform to combat official corruption. A set of new rules in civil service has been implemented which would launch a personnel rotation system for higher-level tenured officials in the civil service from sectional to divisional chiefs to departmental directors. These officials would be reassigned every five years to new positions at the same level in central government and provincial administrations. Other officials whose main duties involve personnel, financial management, certificate issuance, and law enforcement would also be rotated every five years. Those who refuse will be disciplined by demotion or reassignment.[148] The rotation system may involve assignment to another system or a different geographic location.[149]

Another action instituted recently was for high or top party/government officials, including their relatives, to make public disclosure of their finances. However, a report from the central party Disciplinary Investigation Commission showed there has been some foot-dragging or noncooperation regarding personal financial disclosure by high officials. Of the 22 Politburo members, the apex in power, only 11 of them complied.[150] Of a total of 832 central and provincial top-level cadres, only 75 made public disclosure of their finances.[151] An interesting figure revealed in this report is that, for the two-year period from 1998–99, some 7,300 party members were expelled or asked to resign from the party because of illegal or corruptive activities.[152]

Corruption in society as a whole and corruption in officialdom have become a cancer or tumor in the Chinese body-politic. This malignancy needs urgent attention and action by those who wield the power. It must have been excruciatingly painful for the party to adopt a resolution in 1996 in which it stated that the deterioration of moral conduct was something quite serious:

> . . . the practice of worshipping money, seeking pleasure and individualism has grown . . . the phenomenon of corruption has been spreading in some places, seriously damaging the work style of the Party and the government; and a number of people have a weak concept of the state, and waiver and doubt the future of socialism.[153]

THE NEW CIVIL SERVICE SYSTEM

Civil service revision had been a dominant reform item for the Thirteenth Party Congress in 1987. The improvement focused on an emphasis on recruitment of technical specialists or experts and reduction of the party's role in personnel management.[154] Civil service reform was interrupted by the June 1989 Tiananmen protests. However, a China scholar takes the view that with stepped-up emphasis on economic reform, cadre management efficiency will have to be improved to meet the new demands and changes.[155] On October 1, 1993, China promulgated temporary national civil service regulations that included among other reforms the requirement that open competitive examinations be held to recruit the best and most able cadres for government service.[156]

The 1987 proposal for cadre or civil service reform was intended to separate the party-government interlocking relationship, a plank endorsed by Deng Xiaoping in 1987 just prior to the Tiananmen crackdown on the student demonstrators.[157] (See Chapter 10.) As pointed out earlier, separation of party and government was advocated and supported by Zhao Ziyang, former party chief ousted in the midst of the Tiananmen crisis. It was an integral part of the 1986–87 political structural reform; and, it was a controversial reform item even though it had Deng Xiaoping's support at the party's Thirteenth Party Congress in October 1987. By August 1989, three months after Tiananmen, the movement for party-government separation was more or less terminated as Zhao Ziyang's leadership was discredited and criticized.[158] Cadre management became the focus of reform rather than changes in the civil service system as originally contemplated in 1987 by the Thirteenth Party Congress—changes that would ultimately alter the party-government relationship by separating the party's over-concentrated role on cadre recruitment and appointment.

A key provision in the 1987 proposal was to create two types of cadres under two separate management systems: political civil servants appointed for a fixed term of service, and administrative civil servants with tenure, but managed through state civil service laws. In other words, the system would resemble the familiar American system, which has two distinct classes of appointees: political ones, who serve at the pleasure of the president, governor, or mayor; and civil service appointees, who have tenure and protection under civil service laws. As pointed out in a study made by Lam Tao-Chiu and Hon S. Chan, two management experts at the Hong Kong Polytechnic University, the present Provisional Regulations on China's civil service placed more significance on "liveliness" and "vitality" in state bureaucracy rather than pre-Tiananmen emphasis on "stability." Li Peng, then the premier, was credited in 1993 with devising a system that "would allow the government to dismiss unwanted bureaucrats."[159] The Provisional Regulations now require open and competitive examinations for cadre recruitment (applicable only to nonleading positions), and transfer (applied to senior positions). Recruitment of cadres for nonleading positions now prefers those from worker or peasant backgrounds rather than college graduates who have little working experience to speak of.

As a part of civil service reform there has been public recruitment for government positions by open public examination. Thus, in 1996 some sixty-one party and government departments recruited a total of 737 positions by open examination of some 10,000 people who entered into the open contest.[160]

On the matter of evaluation of cadre performance, it is now accomplished by a three-member evaluation committee: the department head, a representative from the personnel office, and an employee representative. However, in practice, as pointed out by Lam and Chan, the final assessment has been delegated to the department head.[161]

Genuine civil service reform in managing government-party affairs is rather important to the development of legal institutions and the deepening of economic reform, the subject matters to be discussed in the chapters to follow.

NOTES

1. Gabriel A. Almond and G. Bingham Powell, *Comparative Politics Today: A World View* (Boston and Toronto: Little, Brown, 1980), p. 62.
2. The figure comes from John P. Burns, "Chinese Civil Service Reform: The 13th Party Congress Proposals," *China Quarterly*, 120 (December 1989), 740.
3. Max Weber, *The Theory of Social and Economic Organizations* (New York: Free Press, 1947), pp. 324–26.
4. Lowell Dittmer, "Pattern of Elite Strife and Succession in Chinese Politics," *China Quarterly*, 123 (September 1990), 405.
5. Ibid.
6. Ibid.
7. Ibid, 414–19.
8. For a more detailed study of factionalism in China, see Lucian Pye, *The Dynamics of Factions and Consensus in Chinese Politics: A Model and Some Propositions* (Santa Monica, Calif.: The Rand Corporation, July 1980). Also see Dorothy Fontana, "Background to the Fall of Hua Guofeng," pp. 237–60, and Richard D. Nethercut, "Leadership in China: Rivalry, Reform, and Renewal," in *Problems of Communism*, 33 (March–April 1983), 30–32. Also see a more recent study by Lowell Dittmer, "Patterns of Elite Strife and Succession in Chinese Politics," *China Quarterly*, 123 (September 1990), 405–30.
9. Parris Chang, "The Last Stand of Deng's Revolution," Journal of Northeast Asian Studies, 1, no. 2, (June 1982), 3–19.
10. Fontana, "Background to the Fall of Hua Guofeng."
11. Parris Chang, "Chinese Politics: Deng's Turbulent Quest," *Problems of Communism*, vol. 30 (January–February, 1981), 8.
12. See "How the Power Structure Works," *Far Eastern Economic Review* (March 19, 1987), 60–61.
13. *Far Eastern Economic Review* (February 5, 1987), 12.

14. See "How the Power Structure Works," 60, and *Los Angeles Times,* February 9, 1987, p. 10. Also see David M. Lampton, "Chinese Politics: The Bargaining Treadmill," *Issues and Studies*, 23, 3 (March 1987), 11–45.

15. *Asian Wall Street Journal,* March 17, 1987, p. 1, and *Far Eastern Economic Review* (February 26, 1987), 9.

16. *New York Times,* January 30, 1987, p. 22.

17. *Far Eastern Economic Review* (January 29, 1987), 12.

18. *Far Eastern Economic Review* (February 5, 1987), 35.

19. *New York Times,* January 30, 1987, p. 22.

20. "The Politics of Industrial Reform" in Elizabeth J. Perry and Christian Wong, eds., *The Political Economy of Reform in Post-Mao China* (Cambridge, Mass.: Harvard Contemporary China Series 2, 1985), pp. 197–98. Also see a recent article by a Chinese scholar studying in the United States on interest groups in China, Li Fan, "The Question of Interests in the Chinese Policy-Making Process," *China Quarterly*, 109 (March 1987), 64–71. Also see Shaochuan Leng, ed. *Changes in China: Party, State, and Society* (Lanham, Md.: University Press of America, 1989); and Andrew G. Walder, "Beyond the Deng Era: China's Political Dilemma," *Asian Affairs: An American Review*, 16, no. 2 (Summer 1989). Also see Ian Wilson and You Ji, "Leadership by 'Lines': China's Unresolved Succession," *Problems of Communism*, 34, no. 1 (January–February 1990), 28–44.

21. See *Zhengming* (Hong Kong), 157 (November 1990), 16–17 and 20–21; *Far Eastern Economic Review* (August 23, 1990), 29–31; (May 10, 1990), 8–9; (November 8, 1990), 19–20; David Bachman, "Retrogression in Chinese Politics," *Current History* (September 1990), 249–52 and 273–74; *New York Times,* July 17, 1990, p. A-2; and L. La Dang, "China's Hodgepodge of Leadership," *Wall Street Journal,* July 5, 1989, p. A-13. Also see *Christian Science Monitor,* July 18, 1990, p. 3.

22. *Far Eastern Economic Review* (August 23, 1990), 34 and 38.

23. See *Far Eastern Economic Review* (August 23, 1990), 34.

24. See *Zhengming* (Hong Kong), 156 (October 1990), 6–7; and *Far Eastern Economic Review* (May 10, 1990), 8–9.

25. There are six such articles in the *China Journal*, 34 (July 1995): Lowell Dittmer, "Chinese Informal Politics," 1–34; Lucian W. Pye, "Factions and Politics of *Guanxi*: Paradoxes in Chinese Administrative and Political Behavior," 35–54; Frederick C. Teiwes, "The Paradoxical Post-Mao Transition: From Obeying the Leader to 'Normal Politics,'" 55–94; Tang Tsou, "Chinese Politics at the Top: Factionalism or Informal Politics? Balance-of-Power Politics or a Game to Win All?" 95–156; Andrew J. Vethan and Kellee S. Tsai, "Factionalism: A New Institutionalist Restatement," 157–92; and Lowell Dittmer, "Informal Politics Reconsidered," 193–234.

    Less than a year after the publication of the six articles in the *China Journal*, two more articles on Chinese informal politics appeared in a special issue of *Asian Survey* on informal politics in East Asia, introduced by Robert A. Scalapino: Joseph Fewsmith, "Institutions, Informal Politics and Political Transition in China," *Asian Survey* vol. 36, no. 3 (March 1996), 230–45; and Lowell Dittmer and Lu Xiaobo, "Personal Politics in the Chinese Danwei under Reform," 246–67.

26. Dittmer, "Chinese Informal Politics," 33.

27. Pye, "Factions and Politics of *Guanxi*," 35.

28. Ibid., 52–53.

29. Tsou, "Paradoxical Post-Mao Transition," 93–94.

30. Teiwes, "Chinese Politics at the Top," 104.

31. Ibid., 105.

32. Vethan and Tsai, "Factionalism: A New Institutional Restatement," 158.

33. Ibid., 189.

34. Fewsmith, "Institutions, Informed Politics and Political Transition in China," 232.

35. Ibid., 234–36.

36. Ibid., 245.

37. See Richard Baum, *Burying Mao: Chinese Politics in the Age of Deng Xiaoping* (Princeton, N.J.: Princeton University Press, 1994), pp. 7–8.

38. See Nora Wang, "Deng Xiaoping: The Years in France," *China Quarterly*, 92 (December 1982), 698–705. Also see the unauthorized biography by Uli Franz, *Deng Xiaoping* (Boston and New York: Harcourt Brace Jovanovich, 1988).

39. Deng once told Oriana Fallaci that he was purged for the first time in 1932 for lending his support to Mao in the inner party struggle against the Moscow-trained returned Chinese group led at that time by Wang Ming. See Oriana Fallaci, "Deng: Cleaning Up Mao's Feudal Mistakes," the *Guardian*, September 21, 1980, p. 16.

40. Chang, "Last Stand of Deng's Revolution," 5–6. Also see Michael Ng-Quinn, "Deng Xiaoping's Political Reform and Political Order," *Asian Survey*, 22, no. 12 (December 1982), 1187–1205. Also see "Man of the Year: the Comeback Comrade," *Time* (January 6, 1986), pp. 42–45; and Harrison E. Salisbury, "The Little Man Who Could Never Be Put Down," *Time,* September 30, 1985, pp. 54–57.

41. See Chang, "Chinese Politics: Deng's Turbulent Quest," and "Last Stand of Deng's Revolution"; "A Speech at the Enlarged Meeting of the Politburo of the Central Committee" in *Issues and Studies*, 17, no. 3 (March 1981), 81–103; "Important Speech by Deng Xiaoping to the 1980 December 25 Central Work Conference" printed in *Ming Pao* (Hong Kong), May 3–8, 1981; and "Text of Deng Xiaoping's Speech at the Great Hall of People on January 16, 1980," *Ming Pao* (Hong Kong), March 2–4, 1980. Also see Suzanne Pepper, "Can the House that Deng Built Endure?" *Asian Wall Street Journal Weekly*, August 10, 1981, p. 10; Fox Butterfield, "The Pragmatists Take China's Helm," *New York Times Magazine,* December 28, 1980, pp. 22–31; and Lowell Dittmer, "China in 1980: Modernization and Its Discontents," 31–42, and "China in 1981," 33–45.

42. "Communiqué of the Third Plenary Session of the Eleventh Central Committee of the CCP."

43. Christopher Wren, "Deng Opens Drive on His Leftist Foes," *New York Times,* October 3, 1982, p. 3. Also see Frank Ching, "The Chinese Party Shuffle Bolsters Deng As Pragmatists Gain Over Ideologues," *Asian Wall Street Journal Weekly,* July 13, 1981, p. 7.

44. "An Interview with Deng Xiaoping," *Time,* November 4, 1985, p. 40.

45. See "Deng Xiaoping: An Assessment," a special issue published by *China Quarterly,* no. 135 (September 1993), which contains no less than eight articles by China scholars: David Shambaugh, "Introduction: Assessing Deng Xiaoping's Legacy," 409–11; Lucian W. Pye, "An Introductory Profile: Deng Xiaoping and China's Political Culture," 412–43; Benjamin Yang, "The Making of a Pragmatic Communist: The Early Life of Deng Xiaoping, 1904–49," 444–56; David Shambaugh, "Deng Xiaoping: The Politician,"457–90; Barry Naughton, "Deng Xiaoping: The Economist," 491–514; Martin King Whyte, "Deng Xioping: The Social Reformer," 515–35; June Teufel Dreyer, "Deng Xiaoping: The Soldier," 536–50; and Michael Yahuda, "Deng Xiaoping: The Statesman," 551–72.

46. *Zhengming* (Hong Kong) (June 28, 1989), 1.

47. Ibid.

48. Ibid.

49. *Zhengming* (Hong Kong), 155 (September 1990), 8–9.

50. See Liu Binyan, "After Deng Xiaoping: How Long Can Jiang Zemin Remain on Top?" *China Focus*, 1, no. 3 (30 April 1993), 3.

51. Information on criticism about Li Peng is culled from the following: *Zhengming* (Hong Kong), 105 (July 1986), 9–10, and 123 (January 1988), 6–10; *Christian Science Monitor,* November 25, 1987, pp. 7–8; *Asian Wall Street Journal,* November 25, 1987, pp. 1 and 13; *Ming Pao Daily* (Hong Kong), November 16, 1987, p. 1 and November 7, 1987, p. 12; and *Far Eastern Economic Review* (September 10, 1987), 46–47.

52. See *Beijing Review,* 14 (April 6, 1987), 14.

53. See *Ming Pao Daily* (Hong Kong), January 2, 1988, p. 1.

54. See *Renmin Ribao* (Overseas Edition), November 25, 1987, p. 1.

55. See Cheng Li, "University Networks and the Rise of Qinghua Graduates in China's Leadership," *Australian Journal of Chinese Affairs*, no. 32, (July 1994), 21–22.

56. See "Profile of the seven top party leaders," *China Daily,* September 20, 1997, p. 3.

57. Ibid., p. 3.

58. Ibid., p. 3.

59. See Li Cheng, "Jiang Zemin's Successors: The Rise of the 4th Generation of Leaders in the People's Republic of China," *China Quarterly,* p. 161 (March 2000), 1–40.

60. Ye Jianyin, "Report on the Revision of the Party Constitution," *Beijing Review,* vol. 36 (September 2, 1977), 36.

61. See Jiang Zemin's speech to the Fifteenth Party Congress, *Beijing Review,* 40, no. 40, (October 6–12, 1997), 31.

62. John M. L. Lindbeck, "Transformation in the Chinese Communist Party," *Soviet and Chinese Communism: Similarities and Differences*, Donald Tread, ed. (Seattle: University of Washington Press, 1967), p. 76.

63. Ezra Vogel, "From Revolutionary to Semi-Bureaucrat: The 'Regularization' of Cadres," *China Quarterly*, 29 (January–March 1967), 36–40; Michel Oksenberg, "Institutionalization of the Chinese Communist Revolution: The Ladder of Success on the Eve of the Cultural Revolution," *China Quarterly*, 36 (October–December 1968), 61–92.

64. Charles Neuhauser, "The Chinese Communist Party in the 1960s: Prelude to the Cultural Revolution," *China Quarterly*, 32 (October–December 1967), 3–36.

65. See Jianyin, "Report on the Revision of the Party Constitution," 36.

66. "New Party Members—A Dynamic Force," *Peking Review*, 27 (July 6, 1973), 6–7; "Millions of New Cadres Maturing," *Peking Review*, 52 (December 1973), 3; "Commemorating the 10th Anniversary of the CPC Central Committee's May 16 'Circular,'" *Peking Review*, 21 (May 21, 1976), 3.

67. Red Guard interrogation of Wang Guangmei, wife of Liu Shaoqi, revealed the practice of admission to party membership by recommendation by top party leaders. See Chao Tsung, *An Account of the Great Proletarian Cultural Revolution*, vol. ii (Hong Kong: Union Research Institute, 1974), pp. 836–39.

68. Jianyin, "Report on the Revision of the Party Constitution," 36.

69. "Important Talk by Deng Xiaoping," *Ming Pao* (Hong Kong), March 5, 1980, p. 1.

70. Song Renqiong, "Use the New Party Constitution to Educate New Members," *Hongqi (Red Flag)*, 24 (December 16, 1982), 15. For current status, see *Ming Pao Daily* (Hong Kong), July 9, 1984, p. 2; and *Far Eastern Economic Review* (November 3, 1983), 43–44.

71. *People's Daily* (Overseas Edition), February 7, 1986, p. 1. Also see *China Daily,* January 21, 1986, p. 1. For a discussion of the recent party rectification campaign, see Bruce J. Dickson, "Conflict and Non-Compliance in Chinese Politics: Party Rectification, 1983–87," *Pacific Affairs*, 63, no. 2 (Summer 1990), 170–190.

72. "Create a New Situation in All Fields of Socialist Modernization," *Beijing Review*, 27 (July 6, 1973), 38.

73. *Ming Pao* (Hong Kong), October 7, 1982, p. 1. Also see Lowell Dittmer, "The Twelfth Congress of the CCP," *Asian Survey* 22, no. 12, (Dec 1992), 120.

74. See *Honolulu Advertiser's* section on Asian/Pacific column, November 5, 1987, D-1.

75. *Asian Wall Street Journal,* September 15, 1985, p. 1.

76. *People's Daily,* September 25, 1981, p. 1.

77. *China Daily,* December 3, 1985, p. 1.

78. *Ming Pao* (Hong Kong), October 16, 19, and 20, 1982. Also see Song Renqiong, "Building the Revolutionized, Youthful, Intellectualized and Specialized Cadre Forces," *Hongqi (Red Flag)*, 19 (October 1, 1982), 14.

79. Renqiong, "Building the Revolutionized, Youthful, Intellectualized and Specialized Cadre Forces," 14. For a related analysis see Stanley Rosen, "The Chinese Communist Party and Chinese Society: Popular Attitudes Toward Party Membership and the Party's Image," *Australian Journal of Chinese Affairs*, 24 (July 1990), 51–92.

80. See Associated Press release as reprinted in *Honolulu Advertiser*, September 17, 1998, p. A-6.

81. Li Ning, "Government Restructuring: A Revolution in New Period", *Beijing Review* (April 27-May 3, 1998), 16.

82. Ibid.

83. Robert Sherrill, *Governing America: An Introduction* (New York: Harcourt Brace Jovanovich, 1978), p. 412.

84. See Hong-Yung Lee, "Deng Xiaoping's Reform of the Chinese Bureaucracy," *Journal of Northeast Asian Studies*, 1, no. 2 (June 1982), 21–35. The ratio for the number of people per cadre has been estimated by Lee as 1:50 for a total of 18 million state cadres.

85. See Vogel, "From Revolutionary to Semi-Bureaucrat," 45.

86. Ibid.

87. Oksenberg, "Institutionalization of the Chinese Communist Revolution," 61–92.

88. Ibid.

89. For a fuller discussion of the rectification campaigns, see Frederick C. Teiwes, "Rectification Campaigns and Purges in Communist China, 1950–61," unpublished doctoral dissertation, Columbia University, 1971, in University Microfilms, Ann Arbor, Michigan. Also see S.J. Noumoff, "China's Cultural Revolution as a Rectification Movement," *Pacific Affairs*, 11, nos. 3 and 4 (Fall and Winter 1967–68), 221–33.

90. Teiwes, "Rectification Campaigns and Purges in Communist China," 150–61.

91. Vogel, "From Revolutionary to Semi-Bureaucrat."

92. Oksenberg, "Institutionalization of the Chinese Communist Revolution."

93. See Richard Baum, *Prelude to Revolution: Mao, the Party, and the Peasant Question, 1962–66* (New York and London: Columbia University Press, 1975); and Richard Baum and Frederick Teiwes, "Liu Shao-chi and the Cadres Question," *Asian Survey*, 8, no. 4 (April 1968), 323–45.

94. *Ming Pao Daily* (Hong Kong), July 7, 1981, p. 1.

95. "Create a New Situation in All Fields of Socialist Modernization," 36.

96. Ibid.

97. Peng Zhen, "Report on Work of NPC Standing Committee," *Beijing Review*, 39 (September 29, 1980), 24–25.

98. See Melanie Manion, "The Cadres Management System, Post-Mao: The Appointment, Promotion, Transfer and Removal of Party and State Leaders," *China Quarterly*, 102 (January 1985), 203–33.

99. Ibid., 233.
100. *People's Daily* (Overseas Edition), February 3, 1986, p. 1.
101. Ibid.
102. Ibid.
103. "Reforming the Cadres System," *Beijing Review*, 9 (March 1, 1982), 3.
104. "Veteran Cadres Retire," *Beijing Review*, 7 (February 15, 1982), 5.
105. Ibid.
106. *People's Daily* (Overseas Edition), February 19, 1986, p. 1.
107. *Ming Pao Daily* (Hong Kong), April 6, 1980, p. 3.
108. Ibid. Translation is by this author.
109. Fox Butterfield, *China: Alive in the Bitter Sea*, (New York: Time Books, 1982), pp. 217, 288; and Richard Bernstein, *From the Center of the Earth*, (Boston and Toronto: Little, Brown and Co., 1982), pp. 104, 131, 134, 136–137, and 140 for anecdotes to illustrate how Chinese bureaucracy works.
110. "A Speech at the Enlarged Meeting of the Politburo, August 18, 1980," in *Issues and Studies*, 23, no. 3 (March 1981), 88; also see *Ming Pao Daily* (Hong Kong), February 14, 1982, p. 3.
111. For text of Chen Yun's speech at the CCP Central Committee Work Conference, see *Issues and Studies*, 16, no. 4 (April 1980), 82.
112. Deng Xiaoping, "A Speech at the Enlarged Meeting of the Politburo of the Central Committee, August 31, 1980," *Issues and Studies*, 17, no. 3 (March 1981), 88. Also see *Ming Pao Daily* (Hong Kong) February 14, 1982, p. 3.
113. See Harry Harding, *Organizing China: The Problems of Bureaucracy, 1949–1976* (Stanford, Calif.: Stanford University Press, 1981), pp. 3, 281.
114. John P. Burns "Reforming China's Bureaucracy 1979–82," *Asian Survey*, 17, 6 (June 1983), 715.
115. Ibid.
116. See *Ming Pao Daily* (Hong Kong), July 7, 1984, p. 8. Also see Huang Chi, "Why Deng Stresses Political Restructuring," *Beijing Review*, 38 (September 21, 1987), 14–16, and *People's Daily*, June 19, 1987, p. 1.
117. Harding, *Organizing China*, p. 353.
118. "Report on the Work of the Government," *Beijing Review* (April 5–11), 1999, 32.
119. See Liao Xin, "Corruption—Tip-offs from the General Public," *Beijing Review* (February 28, 2000), 21.
120. See Ann S. Tyson, "Beijing Takes Aim at Rampant Corruption at Higher Places," *Christian Science Monitor*, August 23, 1988, p. 1. For 1986 figures see *China Daily*, July 31, 1986, p. 1 and July 10, 1986, p. 2.
121. Ibid.
122. *New York Times*, March 11, 1999, p. A-3.
123. Ibid.
124. Ibid.
125. *Ming Pao Daily* (Hong Kong), August 14, 1981, p. 3.
126. *Ming Pao Daily* (Hong Kong), August 18, 1981, p. 1.
127. "Economic Criminals Surrender," *Beijing Review*, 17 (April 19, 1982), 7–8.
128. "Decision on Combating Economic Crimes," *Beijing Review*, 17 (April 26, 1982), 7; and *Hongqi*, 4 (February 16, 1982), 8.
129. "Senior Cadres Support Sentences on Their Criminal Sons," *Beijing Review*, 20 (May 17, 1982), 5.
130. See *China Daily*, July 31, 1986, p. 1. Also see an earlier report from *China Daily*, July 10, 1986, p. 2.
131. *New York Times*, March 6, 1999, pp. A-1 and A-10.
132. Ibid.
133. Ibid.
134. The term was coined by Xiaobo Lu in his article "Booty Socialism; Bureau-preneurs and the State in Transition," *Comparative Politics*, 3, no. 3 (April 2000), 273–293.
135. See Jean Oi, "Fiscal Reform and the Economic Foundation of Local State Corporation," *World Politics*, 45 (October 1991), 99–126.
136. See Marc Blecher, "Developmental State, Entrepreneurial State, the Political Economy of Socialist Reform in Xinji Municipality and Guanghan County," in Gordon White, *The Chinese State in the Era of Economic Reform: The Road to Crisis* (London: Macmillan, 1991).
137. Lu, "Booty Socialism, Bureau-Preneurs and the State in Transition," 274.
138. Ibid., 275.
139. Ibid., 277–282.
140. See Ni Zhijing, "Foreign Ministry's Involvement in Smuggling Exposed," in *Zhengming*, no. 267 (January 2000), 15–17.
141. See Xin, "Corruption—Tip-offs from the General Public," 21–22.
142. Ibid., 22.

143. Ibid.
144. See *Hawaii Tribune-Herald* (Hilo) reprint of Associated Press release, March 9, 2000, p. 4.
145. See *Beijing Review* (April 5, 1998), 4.
146. *New York Times,* March 5, 2000, p. A-10.
147. See *Ming Pao* (Hong Kong), October 25, 1993, p. A-8.
148. See "Rotation System to Avert Corruption," *Beijing Review* (August 26–September 1, 1999), 5.
149. See Wally Wo-Lap Lam, *The Era of Jiang Zemin* (Singapore and New York: Prentice Hall, 1999) p. 99.
150. Lo Bing, "Jiang Places His Responsibility for Official Corruption," *Zhengming* (Hong Kong), no. 270 (April 2000), 10–12.
151. Ibid.
152. Ibid., 12.
153. See "Resolutions of the CPC Central Committee Regarding   Important Questions on Promoting Socialist Ethical and Cultural Progress—Adopted at the 6th Plenum of the 14th CPC Central Committee on October 10, 1996," *Beijing Review* (November 4–10, 1996), 20.
154. See Lam Tao-Chiu and Hon S. Chan, "Reforming China's Cadre Management System," *Asian Survey*, 36, no. 8 (August 1996, 772), 86.
155. See Lam, *The Era of Jiang Zemin*, p. 99
156. Chiu and Chan, "Reforming China's Cadre System," pp. 779 and 783.
157. Discussion on this section is culled from Lam Tao-Chiu and Hon S. Chan, "Reforming China's Cadre Management System," *Asian Survey*, 36, no. 8, August 1996, 772–86.
158. Ibid., 773 and 775–77
159. Ibid; and also see *Selected Works of Deng Xiaoping*, vol. 3 (Beijing: Renmin Chubanshe, 1993), pp. 295–96.
160. See *Beijing Review*, November 4–10, 1996, p.20.
161. "Reforming China's Cadre Management System," pp. 779 and 783.

SUGGESTED READINGS

Chen, An. *Restructuring Political Power in China: Alliances and Oppositions, 1978–1998* (Boulder, Colo.: Lynne Reinner Publishers, 1999).

Evans, Richard. *Deng Xiaoping and the Making of Modern China* (Ringwood, N.Y.: Penguin Books, 1995).

Gilley, Bruce. *Tiger on the Brink: Jiang Zemin and China's New Elite* (Berkeley: University of California Press, 1998).

Goldman, David S. G. *Deng Xiaoping and the Chinese Revolution: A Political Biography* (New York and London: Routledge, 1994).

Gong, Ting. *The Politics of Corruption in Contemporary China: An Analysis of Policy Outcomes* (Westport, Conn.: Praeger Publishers, 1994).

Ruf, Gregory. *Cadres and Kin: Making a Socialist Village in West China, 1921–1991* (Stanford, Calif.: Stanford University Press, 1998).

Shambaugh, David (ed.). *Deng Xiaoping: Portrait of a Chinese Statesman* (Oxford: Oxford University Press, 1995).

Yang, Benjamin. *Deng: A Political Biography* (Armonk, N.Y.: M. E. Sharpe, 1998).

Chapter Six

Reform for a Creditable Socialist Legal System

THE CHINESE LEGAL SYSTEM

We begin this chapter on the Chinese legal system with two case studies: one, a criminal case of deviance; the other, a civil case of divorce. The purpose of these case illustrations is to enable those who are not familiar with the Chinese concept of law to have some understanding of how it works and why. Outsiders looking in at Chinese legal institutions and proceedings may get the impression that either the Chinese legal system today is nonexistent or there is no need for law at all, since there are few—if any—criminals in their society. Both of these impressions are, of course, misconceptions. The Chinese legal system is quite different from that in the West, and the manner in which deviance and disputes are handled has been shaped to a large extent by China's own revolutionary experiences of past decades, as well as by the communist political ideology.

In the criminal case,[1] a worker had stolen about $250 worth of material and equipment from his factory. A colleague and neighbor reported his deviant behavior to the factory revolutionary committee, which referred the matter to the public security unit. An investigation was made by a procurator, who—in accordance with Chinese legal practice—served as both prosecuting attorney and public defender. The procurator then presented a dossier of the case to an intermediate court. The court ordered an open trial to be held in the factory so that other factory workers could participate in the proceedings. At the trial the judge, with the help of two community-elected lay assessors, examined the charges and the evidence as presented by the procurator. A trade union leader who personally knew the defendant testified about the defendant's good character and appealed for leniency. After the defendant made a confession about his crime, the judge solicited the opinion of the masses, the workers in the factory. The consensus of the masses in attendance at the trial was that the defendant was a good worker but that his crime must be punished. Upon the suggestion of the masses, the judge sentenced the defendant to two years of labor with pay in the factory under the supervision of his fellow workers.

The civil case[2] is a divorce case. While divorce cases have been on the rise, they represent 60 percent of all civil cases in China. The case came to trial in a lower court after reconciliation attempts had been made, first by the committee that handles misdemeanors, then by the procurator, and finally by the judge's department. The hearings were held in a storefront and included a judge, two lay assessors, and a procurator. The judge heard arguments from both the husband and the wife, and then retired for an hour with the two assessors to reach a decision. The verdict was that a final reconciliation attempt was to be made over forty-eight hours, and that a divorce would be granted if this last effort failed.

The Chinese legal system utilizes two basic approaches: one, the formal set of structures and procedures seen in the two cases summarized above; the other, a set of what Professor Jerome Cohen calls "extrajudicial" structures and practices, which generally emphasize continuous education on acceptable social norms, peer pressure dynamics, and persuasion to correct deviant behavior. These two approaches, or "models," interact and coexist within the Chinese legal system.[3] From 1954 to 1956, the formalized legal structures and procedures were dominant. From the Great Leap in 1958 through the Cultural Revolution, the extrajudicial structures and practices increased in importance. Following the convocation of the Fifth NPC and the promulgation of the 1978 constitution, there has been a reversion to more formalized structures and procedures, including the revising of civil and criminal codes by a group of experts headed by Peng Zhen, a former Politburo member purged during the Cultural Revolution but then rehabilitated.[4] That modest beginning at modernization of the legal code has now come to be a "growth industry" dictated by economic reform and the rise of contracts with foreign investors and joint ventures.

The Courts: Formal Structure and Functions

The 1982 constitution provides that judicial authority for the state be exercised by three judicial organs: the people's courts, the people's procuratorates, and the public security bureaus. The Supreme People's Court is responsible and accountable to the NPC and its Standing Committee. It supervises the administration of justice of the local people's courts. The local people's courts operate at the provincial, county, and district levels. The local people's courts at the higher levels supervise the administration of justice of the people's courts at lower levels. The local people's courts are responsible and accountable to the local people's congresses at the various levels of local government. Article 125 of the 1982 constitution stipulates that all cases handled by the people's courts must be open and that the accused has the right to a defense.

When legal reforms were introduced in 1978, local people's courts were established at four levels: basic people's courts at the district and county level, intermediate people's courts at the municipal level, higher people's courts at the provincial and autonomous region level, and the Supreme People's Court at the national level. Each of the basic people's courts has a civil and criminal division presided over by a judge. An economic division has been added at the intermediate and higher levels to help process cases that involve economics and finance.

Basic People's Courts. In terms of sheer numbers, the Basic People's Courts constitute the bulk of the court system. Some 3,000 Basic People's Courts have been established at the local governmental levels, such as in the counties and cities. Generally, these courts at the basic level conduct minor civil and criminal cases involving disputes of money, infractions of a personal nature, or simply quarrels. Operating under the basic level courts are the numerous (as many as eighteen thousand in total) people's tribunals, which deal with minor civil disputes or criminal offenses. The people's tribunals usually employ either reconciliation or mediation procedures for dispute settlement (to be discussed later in this chapter). The Basic People's Court enters into a case only when these informal attempts have failed to resolve the dispute, as seen in the divorce case described at the beginning of this chapter. These Basic People's Courts do not have appellate functions and thus must be tried at the beginning or anew.[5]

Intermediate People's Courts. There are some 380 Intermediate People's Courts in the provinces, municipalities, and autonomous regions. These are courts of original jurisdiction, as well as courts of appeals or review. It is at this level that a life imprisonment or death penalty can be handed down to the convicted.[6] It is also at this level of the Chinese court system that requests for appeal of the lower court decisions can be made for review or even for a retrial by the Intermediate Courts. In a sense, these are comparable to district courts that one finds in other legal systems outside China.

Higher People's Courts and Special People's Courts. These courts, currently about thirty of them, generally handle some of the most important cases at the provincial and municipal or autonomous region levels. These courts have appellate jurisdiction over the Intermediate People's Courts, as in case of a death sentence. There are also the maritime courts, operating in coastal cities, which deal with maritime activities and disputes arising from foreign investment and enterprises (to be discussed later in this chapter).

Article 124 of the 1982 People's Republic of China constitution also created a category of special courts dealing with matters which involve the military, railways, or other state administrative agencies. For instance, the Military Court has exclusive jurisdiction over disciplinary cases for members of the People's Liberation Army (PLA). Thousands of so-called Economic Courts have been established since the economic reform that began in the early 1980s. These render decisions on contract disputes over foreign investment, liabilities, product injuries, and other tort issues.

The Supreme People's Court. This is the highest judicial organ that sits in the capital city of Beijing. In addition to its supervision and administration of the nation's court system, the highest court does have the limited function of "judicial review," as in Western jurisprudence. It does have the power to say or explain what a law is, or is not. However, it does not have the power to declare whether an enacted law or a governmental decree is constitutional. Under civil procedures, a defendant has the right to appeal, permissible on a one-time-only basis, to the court at the next highest level.[7] There have been many instances of appeals filed by defendants (estimated at about 22 percent of the cases in the 1980s)[8] that contested findings of fact and the sentence imposed.

Under Article 67 (1) and (7) of the 1982 constitution, only the Standing Committee of the National People's Congress (NPC) can interpret the constitution. The Supreme People's Court must approve any decisions on the execution of an immediate death penalty. It also has the power to retry cases in which, in the opinion of the Supreme People's Court, a judicial error has been committed. Under Article 128 of the 1982 constitution, the Supreme People's Court is responsible to the Standing Committee of the NPC. And, under Article 70, through the power delegated to it by the NPC, the Supreme People's Court can participate in legislation and even initiate bills through the law committee of the NPC.

The Procuratorate (Procurator)

Alongside the court system is a parallel system of people's procuratorates, headed by the Supreme People's Procuratorate, which is responsible to the NPC and supervises the local procuratorates at the various levels. The system of procuracy is rooted both in Chinese imperial practices and in the Napoleonic civil code, which was used in part by the Soviets and many other continental European nations in their legal systems.[9] As was mentioned earlier, the procurator serves as both prosecuting attorney and public defender during a trial. The procurator is also responsible for monitoring and reviewing the government organs, including the courts, to provide a legal check on the civil bureaucracy.[10] Further, the procuratorate is responsible for authorizing the arrests of criminals and counterrevolutionaries. In other words, the procuratorate examines charges brought by the public security bureau (the police) and decides whether to bring the case before a court for trial.

When a case is brought by the procurator for trial, it is generally considered a foregone conclusion that a guilty verdict would be rendered. According to one study in the 1980s, the success rate was almost 100 percent.[11] Article 129 of the 1982 constitution stipulates that the people's procuratorates have the responsibility to legally supervise all state organs, meaning that all state organs must conduct themselves in accordance with the law. The revised Organic Law of the People's Procuratorate can now conduct criminal investigations of wrongdoings by the cadres, institutions, or agencies of government at all levels. The procuratorate's responsibilities have also been extended to cases involving charges of treason, anti-state and anti-party activities, as well as matters of corruption, economic crimes, and supervision of detention camps and prisons.

It has been pointed out that one of the main problems in the work of the procurators has been a lack of legal qualification and training in their daily work, leaving aside the serious problem of maintaining their independence from party and political pressure.[12]

The 1954 constitution provided for independence, under the law, of the courts and procuratorates. These provisions were eliminated by both the 1975 and 1978 constitutions. The period between 1954 and 1957 witnessed the strong development of judicial independence. Judges frequently made their own decisions, disregarding the views and wishes of the party in important cases. This independence elicited much criticism from the party and resulted in increased tension between the courts and the party.[13] Coupled with the development of judicial independence was a movement to develop legal professionalism and expertise. Law schools were established, and offices of "people's lawyers" were formed in cities to provide legal aid to citizens. In 1957 the party countered judicial independence with a two-pronged attack: First, it purged or transferred to other branches of government those court cadres who advocated strengthening judicial independence and professionalism; and second, it introduced many of the extrajudicial institutions and practices for handling cases, in order to bypass the formal court system. In addition, in 1959 the functions of the local procuratorates were merged into the party's political and legal departments at the local level. Thus, for all practical purposes, local procuratorates disappeared during the Cultural Revolution, and the Supreme People's Procuratorate existed in name only.[14] As mentioned earlier, the 1982 constitution restored the 1954 constitutional provision concerning judicial integrity. Article 126 declares that all China's courts shall exercise judicial power independently without interference from "administrative organs, public organizations or individuals."

At its fourth session in April 1985, the Sixth NPC enacted the new Civil Law's General Rules, a set of general principles to serve temporarily as a civil code; it became effective in 1987.[15] Because of the rapid development in rural and urban reforms (see Chapter 11), it became necessary to replace the inadequate ad hoc administrative rules and regulations with some general principles for regulating civil disputes. The temporary civil code contains 156 articles in nine chapters that define legal principles regarding citizenship, legal entities with the rights of a person, civil rights, civil responsibilities, and legal practices in relation to foreign firms doing business in China.[16] It is important to realize that while the legal concept of a business corporation as an "artificial person" endowed with the rights of a person to sue or be sued is commonly recognized in the Western democracies, the concept is difficult for a socialist nation like China to accept. This is because under socialism the interests of a business concern and the interests of the people traditionally have been considered one and the same. The practice in China, as determined by political and administrative fiat,[17] was to hold the individual leader, not the social organization, solely responsible for any wrongdoing. However, as it will be discussed later in this chapter, Article 36 of the Civil Code now defines an organization to possess rights and liabilities as a "legal person."

THE CRIMINAL CODE AND HUMAN RIGHTS VIOLATIONS

To restore law and order after the Cultural Revolution, a set of criminal and civil procedures was drafted in 1978. The astonishing fact was that since its founding in 1949, the People's Republic had had no criminal code. At its second session in July 1979, the Fifth NPC adopted the first criminal code and procedure, which came into effect in January 1980. The code contained some 192 articles in eight major areas. These covered offenses concerning counterrevolutionary activity, public security, socialist economic order, rights of citizens, property, public order, marriage and the family, and malfeasance. Principal penalties for offenses included public surveillance, detention, fixed term of imprisonment, and death. The death sentence was reserved for adults who committed the most heinous crimes, and an exception was made for pregnant women. Productive labor and reeducation were to be stressed for detainees and prisoners.[18]

The criminal law is applicable to any offense committed by anyone within the Chinese territory regardless of citizenship but exempts those who hold diplomatic immunity status. The law is also relevant to any Chinese citizen abroad who commits offenses such as counterrevolutionary, counterfeiting of national currency or valuable securities, state secrets, embezzlement, bribes, and acts of swindling and deceit. It also applies to any foreigner who has committed any of these offenses against the state of China or any of its citizens outside its territory. While the criminal code exempts anyone who is mentally deranged, it is applicable to any person who has committed an offense in a state of drunkenness.

As described by Donald C. Clark and James V. Feinerman, the Chinese criminal code, which became effective in 1980, is basically a "Western style penal code on the

German model."[19] Chinese criminal code provides principal and supplementary (special) penalties for those who committed offenses. Principal penalties include public surveillance, detention, fixed-term and/or life imprisonment, and death by execution. Supplementary penalties include fines, deprivation of rights and confiscation of property. For foreigners, deportation is a form of supplementary penalty. The mildest form of penalty is surveillance (*guanzhi*), which involves a term of from three months to as long as two years, during which the offender must report periodically to the local public security unit after the People's Court has imposed the sentence. Under the term of surveillance, the offender continues to receive wages from his/her *danwei*, or place of employment. Detention ranges from fifteen days of "administrative punishment" to six months to as long as fifteen years.[20]

The special provisions of Chinese criminal law deal with a host of political crimes against the state: Any act or behavior that constitutes "the overthrowing of political power of the dictatorship of the proletariat and the socialist system, is a counterrevolutionary offence."[21] These provisions also deal with offenses which endanger public security or economic order, such as acts of smuggling, tax evasion, forgery of currency or securities, misappropriation of state funds, or other corruptive practices.

The criminal procedure does provide that trials must be open to the public. But, in the case of dissident Wang Dan's trial and sentencing in the fall of 1996, the police formed a cordon outside the courthouse to keep out the public; several Western reporters were warned to stay away and were asked to hand over their videotape.[22] The criminal procedure does not require an open hearing for a trial if it involves a juvenile or woman in a rape case, or in cases in which state secrets are the concern.

Punishment for minor crimes is generally governed by what is known as Security Administrative Punishment Regulations (SAPR), promulgated in 1957 and subsequently revised in 1986 and 1994. These empowered the public security (police), not the courts, to provide punishment for minor offenses. Typically, public security bureaus and their substations may issue a warning or levy fines up to 200 *renminbi* against offenders. These organs can also impose detention of up to fifteen days; often they exceed the limit many times over. Clark and Feinerman pointed out that public security bureaus handled as many as three million administrative security cases in 1992.[23] Appeal is permitted in the People's Court, a rather difficult procedure to be implemented, as these two organs "are the same two arms of the same 'political-legal' apparatus."[24]

The Chinese claim that detention has been an effective corrective measure. Public security (police) has the power to place suspected offenders in detention or labor camps without a court order. This is known as "reeducation through labor," or *lao jiao*, in which an individual may perform physical labor for a duration as long as four years. An example of court-sentenced punishment is reform through *laogai*. *Laogai* labor camps are notorious for harsh physical labor and/or torture; they are Chinese *gulags*, in the true sense of the word. One estimate is of twelve to sixteen million people languishing in *laogai* labor camps.[25]

Wang Dan, the student leader at the 1989 Tiananmen demonstration, who was released in 1993 after having served four years in prison, was placed in detention for seventeen months before he was given a trial in October 1996. At the end of this trial he was sentenced again to eleven years in prison on charges of counterrevolutionary activity—he had had printed name cards indicating that he was now a "free man," and for contacting friends. There was evidently some disagreement between the Beijing municipal procuratorate, which conducted the investigation on Wang Dan's activities, and the central political-legal commission at the highest party level. The local procuratorate found that there was no evidence Wang Dan had contacted groups abroad for dissident activities. This decision was overruled by central party authorities on instructions from party chief Jiang Zemin and Qiao Shi, chairman of the Standing Committee for the National People's Congress. They then ordered the trial, followed by sentencing of another imprisonment for Wang Dan in 1996.[26] (Wang Dan was released and put on a plane for exile to the United States in April 1998—two months before President Clinton's official visit to China.)

The death sentence is usually the penalty for the most heinous crimes. This must be approved and imposed by the Supreme People's Court after examination and review. The Criminal Law of 1979 provides categories of ordinary and counterrevolutionary offenses for which the death penalty may be imposed. From time to time new legislation, such as that enacted in 1988 and 1990, has added additional categories of crime for which the death penalty may be applied: economic crime, such as smuggling, and the sale or smuggling of pornography and drugs. The number of death sentences has been increasing since the recent Anti-Crime Campaign and the 1990 Law and Order Campaign: Amnesty International recorded 1,050 executions in 1991, 1,079 in 1992, and 4,367 in 1996.[27] Even more startling is the "unofficial" and most likely reliable figure that in 1991 as many as 20,000 people were executed.[28] Under the intensified anti-crime campaign now being waged in China, there seems to be some pressure exerted by the party to force public security (police) and the procurators to apprehend as many offenders as they can possibly produce so as to be able to claim success.[29]

Although the new criminal code represented China's effort to develop "a more predictable and equitable" criminal justice system,[30] the inclusion of "counterrevolutionary" activity as a criminal offense was reminiscent of the Cultural Revolution. The code defined the term *counterrevolutionary* so that an "overt act"—not merely a thought a person might have at a given moment against the socialist system—must be involved. It must be pointed out that a large number of those placed under detention during the Cultural Revolution were accused of committing "counterrevolutionary" offenses under a law enacted in 1951,[31] but the term has been deleted by constitutional amendment to the 1982 constitution (see Chapter 4).

In summary, Chinese criminal procedure now calls for presentment of charges by the public security bureau after an investigation has been made. The procuratorate must then examine the charges and evidence submitted by the police; and if it determines that a criminal offense has indeed been committed, it approves the arrest. Before a trial is held, the procuratorate must file an indictment against the accused. All trials must be open to the public, except when a case deals with state secrets, private lives of persons, or a minor below the age of 18.[32] A trial must be presided over by a judge, assisted by two assessors. Together they must render a decision on the accused, who now can be defended by a court-appointed lawyer.

China's criminal law and procedure, first enacted on January 1, 1980, contained general and specific provisions regarding offenses, penalties, and guidelines for application. The criminal law was amended in 1997 by redrafting it so as to make its provisions more specific and concrete when applied to criminal offenses, such as smuggling and trafficking in narcotics.[33] In other words, the revision to the criminal law was designed to meet the needs which arose from development under reforms for a "socialist market economy," as well as for combatting corruption, such as bribery and squandering public funds for lavish public entertainment.[34]

CIVIL CODE AND ECONOMIC REFORM

In April 1986 the National People's Congress adopted an important legislation known as the General Principles of Civil Law. These were modeled on the classical civil codes of continental Europe, defining rules on matters of contracts, torts, damages, property rights, and the concept of "legal personality." The civil law contains some 156 articles, [35] many of which use similar texts to those contained in the Nationalist Civil Code, which had been formulated some eighty years ago. The enactment of the 1986 civil code, which became effective in January 1987, was dictated by changing conditions brought about by economic reform introduced by Deng Xiaoping in 1978–79 when he came to power.[36] By then, the socialist planned collectivized economy had begun to undergo changes and readjustment toward what is known as market socialism. Even more compelling had been implementation of the open door policy under which foreign investment has been encouraged as an important part of reform. This meant, first of all, there must be recognition of private property rights as individual entrepreneurship had come into the economic scene. As stated in Article 1 of the civil code, there must be protection for the citizen's civil rights and the "legal person," "adapted to the needs of the development of socialist construction work and in accord with the constitution and the country's concrete circumstances." There are seventeen articles in Chapter 3 of the civil code that deal with the concept of "legal person." Under Article 36, a "legal person" refers to an organization which has rights as well as responsibilities, including civil liabilities for damages to be determined by the law. Article 75 states that individual property must be protected from seizure or destruction or encroachment or from any illegal confiscation. Thus, as stated in Article 117, any violator of property rights of individuals, state or collective, must either replace it or provide compensation at market value. Article 106 establishes civil liability for fault and compensation to the injured parties for damages. More interesting or remarkable is Article 121 of the civil code which states that both the "state organ" and "its personnel" can be held responsible for violating a citizen's rights, thus causing injury to the individual. One American legal expert felt that the principle of holding the government and its personnel responsible for "civil wrongs," even though as a general principle, "is a salutary one."[37]

Since 1987 the adoption and implementation of the civil code have resulted in an increase in court cases dealing with contract disputes, ownership of properties, and the purchase and sale of products. And, there have been an increased number of court cases, rather novel for China, regarding intellectual property, authorship and copyright disputes, use of personal portraits for advertisement of products without consent, and reputation rights.[38] Then there have been violations of intellectual property rights of American imports, a matter of intense friction and negotiation between the United States and Chinese trade authorities.

The change from a planned economy to Deng Xiaoping's socialist market economy requires not only a redefinition of the functions of China's enterprises and economic organizations but also a host of legal frameworks and bases for legal meanings of ownership and management, or simply "the establishment of the legal person system" as a standard practice commonly accepted in most capitalistic market economies. This had been clearly pointed out by one expert from China at the Sino-American Economic and Civil Law Conference held in Honolulu in June 1989. Legislatively, the state must sponsor new laws to regulate enterprise registration and verification of enterprise assets, and to establish a limited liability system, procedures for repayment of loans to state banks, contract responsibilities, requirements and rules for the merger of enterprises, rules on joint partnership operations, a set of investment laws, and a taxation scheme.

There have been as many as seven business laws enacted by the NPC since 1979. For instance, in 1981 the Fourth Session of the Fifth NPC enacted a set of regulations involving economic contracts that covered sales and purchases, industrial projects, processing plants, shipping, loans, and leasing of properties. However, the economic contract law was intended mainly to meet the increasing demands brought on by reform by providing rules with respect to banks and other financial institutions governing loans to individuals and enterprises.[39] In 1986, at the Fourth Session of the Sixth NPC another economic law was enacted to deal with enterprise investment using foreign capital exclusively.[40] Article 6 of that law states that the State Council and its appropriate unit must give approval to applications for the establishment of an enterprise financed exclusively with foreign capital; applications must be accompanied by documents indicating the qualifications of the foreign investor and the credit source. The foreign investment law also stipulates that an essential qualification for the foreign investor is that he must meet the definition of "legal person" as defined in Article 37 of the civil law. This means that there must be the necessary possession of property or finance, a managerial organization, and the capacity to assume liability.[41] The State Council must decide the types of business and the location for the proposed enterprise with wholly owned foreign capital upon examination and recommendation by the Ministry of Foreign Economic Relations and Trade. All such foreign-owned enterprises must be engaging in economic activities which would be considered "conducive" to the development of China's national economy. Wholly owned foreign enterprise is subject to special tax law in accordance with Article 17 of the said law. Interestingly enough, there is a provision in Article 13 regarding trade unions:

> Workers and administrative staff in the employment of the wholly owned foreign enterprise may set up trade unions in accordance with the law, and such unions may conduct activities to protect the lawful rights and interests of the employees.[42]

Article 5 of the law also provides two basic guarantees against nationalization or "expropriation" without "reasonable compensation" to wholly owned foreign enterprises—such as McDonald's and Kentucky Fried Chicken—should it ever occur. Under Articles 4 and 19 profits and earnings of the foreign investor shall be protected by the law, including the right of remittance by foreign employees to their earnings after taxes.

There are two other types of foreign investments present in China besides the wholly owned foreign enterprises: joint ventures and countertrade (to be discussed in Chapter 11). As pointed out by Pitman B. Potter, the various laws and regulations concerning foreign investment in China are in essence designed to provide state supervision and control.[43] Despite the state's close supervision and "managerial control," total foreign investment in terms of actual amount used had been estimated in 1993 to be $36.7 billion.[44]

Enforcement As a Problem. On the whole, in civil cases Chinese courts continuously face the problem of enforcement and execution of court decisions. It has become a regular feature in the Supreme People's Court's annual reports to the NPC that judgments on economic cases are often too difficult to enforce. Donald C. Clark writes about the general reluctance of the courts to enforce decisions in economic cases dictated to a large extent by Mao's ideology of nonantagonistic contradictions between people—which means, generally, to require no coercion. Then, as pointed out by Donald Clark, too often there is interference by local leaders and/or party officials under the accepted practice of "local protectionism."[45] Local protectionism, or preferential treatment, in civil judgments by local courts has been an entrenched traditional practice simply because of institutional dependency of the local courts on the support of the local political power base (the party and government organs) for the court's budget, personnel, and housing facilities.[46] Laws and regulations enacted by the central government are often simply ignored by local authorities, including the local courts.

In the final analysis, economic reform should require Chinese leaders to discard altogether the Marxist-Leninist theory, which does not place much importance on the role of law in social and economic development; in the Chinese view, law serves merely "as a means to promote economic change," but "not as something that develops as a result of change elsewhere."[47] However, one cannot expect laws in today's China to be developed independent of the party. For the Chinese, as pointed out by James Feinerman, laws and legal procedures are only instruments for implementing party policies.[48] As the Chinese would say, "Policy is the soul of law." This is a basic point that foreign investors must understand in dealing with the Chinese. Or as a Chinese lawyer said recently, laws in China are like software in a computer and "if the party wants, it can pull the plug any time."[49]

Growth of Lawyers and Law Firms

In both the criminal and civil procedures, provisions are made for the services of lawyers. For instance, Article 26 of the criminal code states that the accused not only has the right to defend himself or herself but also can obtain legal counsel from a lawyer or from citizens recommended by a people's organization in which the accused works or has close relatives. The court must assign a lawyer for the accused if he or she has none (Article 27).

Until very recently a lawyer's position in China was very different from that in the West. In the first place, lawyers in China were organized to practice law collectively; to some extent they still are today. They used to work for state-supported legal advisory offices, which would assign them cases; they could not engage in private practice. In fact, they then were "state legal workers," semiprofessional at best. The roles of these legal advisors were rather limited; they were not advocates or adversaries in the Western sense. When requested, they acted as legal advisors to governmental units, economic enterprises, citizens on property rights, and disputes or contract disagreements in joint ventures with foreign investors. They also dispensed legal information to the public. In the mid-1980s in the streets of major cities, such as Guangzhou (Canton), lawyers could be seen setting up street corner stands to answer questions about rent disputes, property inheritance and domestic quarrels.[50] Their role was not to protect their clients, but merely to advise them about the law. In fact, in those early days of reform, their first duty was "to safeguard the interests of the state."[51]

Lawyers' organizations known as "legal advisors' offices" existed prior to 1957 in many cities. These legal service organizations—which then numbered approximately 800, with about 2,500 full-time lawyers—disappeared in 1957 and were not revived until 1979, when the Fifth NPC enacted regulations for lawyers' services.[52] In 1979 there were 5,500 full-time and 1,300 part-time paid lawyers in some 1,500 law advisory offices in twenty-five provinces.[53] In 1983 there were about 8,000 lawyers in China, about one lawyer for every 300,000 people. This compares with 350,000 lawyers in the much less populous United States. By 1984 Beijing, the capital city, had 400 lawyers, or one for every 10,000 residents.[54] The total number of lawyers in China in 1987 has been estimated at 20,000 for a total population of over one billion.[55] As of August 1993 there were over 40,000 attorneys' offices staffed by 50,000 licensed lawyers. The shortage of legal services has become more acute as the role of lawyers has expanded with the new criminal and civil codes and as economic activities have proliferated. The Ministry of Justice had plans to augment the number of legal service personnel to include one lawyer for every 10,000 persons in the cities and one for every 50,000 peasants in the rural areas by 1985.[56] Thus, China must train as many as 200,000 qualified legal personnel by the next decade. The rate at which universities turn out law graduates certainly has not been adequate. Beida, the Beijing National University, produced only between 80 to 100 law graduates per year in the early 1980s.[57] Some provinces have resorted to short-term professional training on legal affairs to provide the needed personnel.[58] Many industrial cities experienced a critical shortage of lawyers as economic activities boomed and disputes mushroomed under urban reform. For example, in 1983 only 275 professional lawyers were practicing in Shanghai, a city with a population of 12 million, and 70 percent of them were nearing retirement age.[59] According to reports of a survey conducted by Shanghai Lawyers' Association, some 6,200 additional lawyers would be needed if all 20,000 enterprises in that city were to retain their own legal advisors.[60]

The urgent need for trained legal professionals may be seen by the steadily rising rate of contract disputes that have been brought to the courts for settlement as the result of decentralization and rural specialized household diversification. A typical local government unit, such as a county government, might sign as many as 400,000 contracts per year.[61] For a three-year period, from 1980 to 1983, the Chinese courts handled more than 89,000 contract disputes, involving millions of yuan.[62] Because of the shortage of trained professional lawyers, the common practice for a group of enterprises, usually not more than one hundred, was to retain one lawyer.[63] These lawyers carried a heavy caseload—several hundred cases per year. Chinese lawyers, as state employees, were not well paid. In fact, in the 1980s, most of them were paid at the scale of a junior bureaucrat, about 60–80 yuan or the equivalent of U.S.$20–30 per month. In addition, numerous cases of harassment and persecution against lawyers by government and party cadres have been revealed by the Chinese media.[64] In one case a judge ordered a lawyer handcuffed to a tree for more than an hour for making persistent demands that the judge take up a case.[65] These incidents of mistreatment of the lawyers prompted Qiao Shi, Politburo member and vice-premier, to demand that all party personnel respect the rights of lawyers in his talk to the 1986 conference of lawyers. The conference established, for the first time, a new professional organization, the All-China Lawyers' Association.[66]

By 1996, the total number of lawyers had reached over 90,000. Since 1992 the Ministry of Justice has required a license examination for those individuals who want to qualify for legal practice as a lawyer; the state had licensed some 40,000 lawyers in the early 1990s. In 1995 there were as many as 117,000 candidates sitting for the qualifying examination.[67] Consequently, the total number of law firms staffed by licensed lawyers reached to about 7,200.[68] However, only less than 10 percent of the law firms were financially independent of the government. The state is now putting in place enough lawyers to total 150,000.[69]

The role of Chinese lawyers has undergone major change as the demand for their services has increased; this, in turn, has been made possible by economic reform and increased foreign investment. The total number of economic dispute cases in courts rose to 650,000 in 1992. By the late 1980s and 1990s Chinese lawyers were no longer solely in service to the state, but in service to the people, by virtue of the fact that they now charge fees for these legal services. As a consequence, cooperative law firms (*hezoulüshi shiwusuo*) have flourished by the thousands since 1996.

On May 15, 1996, after more than ten revisions, the Ministry of Justice was finally able to present its draft of China's first law for the lawyers for endorsement by the Standing Committee of the National People's Congress. The new law encourages the formation of law partnership firms to represent citizens and enterprises in civil and criminal law suits or to act as agents in mediation and arbitration sessions. The new law for lawyers authorizes the Ministry of Justice as the sole power to administer nationwide tests to qualify for a license to practice and to issue the lawyer's certificate. Quoting from Justice Minister Xiao Yang's speech given in October 1993, William P. Alford has pointed out that only about 20 percent of the licensed Chinese lawyers had attained a law degree from a major university.[70] Many seemed to have some legal training and education from part-time universities run by state agencies or "adult universities" and through correspondence courses.[71]

Then there is the question of professional ethics. While Chinese lawyer training and education has been a problem for the development of a creditable legal system in China, there also has been the serious problem of professional responsibility. In his study, William Alford illustrates the practices of bribery of judges and state officials by lawyers, and *ex parte* contacts between judges and attorneys.[72] In addition, there is pressure or coercion exerted on businessmen to use only certain particular firms for legal services.[73]

There has been a setback for foreign firms and lawyers operating in China: The December 1996 Ministry of Justice rule, which became effective in January 1997, forbids foreign law firms from employing Chinese lawyers and legal assistants. A previous regulation also demanded that foreign law firms provide the government with their client list, a violation of the practice of confidential client relationship—a sacred principle in Western practice. The purpose of the new regulation forbidding foreign firms from hiring Chinese lawyers seemed to be designed "to protect Chinese firms."[74] At this writing there were some 70 foreign law firms operating in China. This rule may have some impact on foreign investment in China, as these companies tend to prefer to retain foreign law firms.

Life for a Chinese lawyer—in 1996 there were a total of more than 90,000 of them licensed to practice—has not been a smooth or respected one. While there have been new legal procedures in both civil and criminal cases, as discussed in this chapter, lawyers have been receiving frequent slights and indignities, particularly in rural areas where the number of family lawyers has been increasing steadily. Judges or police have often refused to allow them to see their clients in prison or denied meetings with witnesses for a trial. In some cases the lawyers themselves have become the victims or have been prosecuted for defending their clients.[75]

Family Law: Marriage and Divorce

Alongside of the rapid development in civil, criminal, and economic laws and regulations during the Deng reform era, there has been a multiplication of laws and regulations on family law. Notable is the 1980 Marriage Law and the 1980 Marriage Registration Regulation, which was subsequently revised or replaced by the 1986 and 1994 laws on marriage registration regulations. In addition, there were the 1985 Inheritance Law and the 1992 Protection of Women's Rights and Interests. Also, there are various provisions in the 1982 People's Republic of China (PRC) constitution (Articles 45–56), the 1986

General Civil Law Principles (Articles 68–76), the 1991 Civil Procedure Law (Articles 134–151), and the 1979 Criminal Law (Articles 142–151), which all touch on the matter of marriage and divorce. The main focus of this section will be on those aspects of family law covering marriage and divorce. Once again the family has occupied "the central position," or has become a "basic unit" in Chinese social life.[76]

There may be two basic reasons why family has again become the focal point in Chinese social life: One is the need to maintain stability after decades of turmoil and upheaval, and the second is the abandonment of collectivized production methods, now replaced by a market economy under economic reform and decentralization. Nowadays, family lawyers tend to attract professional persons and businessmen as clients to protect their rights and interests.

Article 49 of the 1982 PRC constitution provides protection for marriage and family, among many other things. This general provision has been reinforced by the 1980 Marriage Law. However, the most important element in these guarantees of marriage is the requirement for mandatory registration, as defined in Articles 9 and 19 of the 1994 Marriage Registration and Regulation Act. The purpose of marriage registration is to receive the required certificate for marriage, even though "feudal practice" places more importance on traditional ceremonies. The other aspect of the required registration for marriage is to enforce family planning or birth control. However, as pointed out in a study by Michael Palmer, as many as 80 percent of rural marriages are not registered.[77]

The divorce case introduced at the beginning of the chapter illustrates to some extent how the legal process works in China. Article 25 of the 1980 Marriage Law provides for freedom to divorce, not necessarily by "mutual consent" as provided in the 1950 Marriage Law, but it does provide that it can be granted on the basis of "breakdown of mutual affection."[78] In our example, the divorce case advanced to court, which resorted to mediation or reconciliation. In the 1980s there was some "excessive use of judicial mediation" aimed at the prevention of broken marriages. As more women initiated divorce proceedings in the late 1980s, the courts were not in favor of using mediation or reconciliation in contested divorce cases. The result was the provision in the 1991 Civil Procedure Law, which placed less emphasis on mediation. Now, as urged by the state Supreme Court's opinion, if mediation proves to be "ineffective," then considerations about "the state of affection" between the parties to the contested divorce cases may be grounds for granting divorces, in addition to mental illness, deception, or failure to fulfill a spouse's obligations.[79]

The divorce rate in China has been on the rise; it has more than doubled since the 1980s. It has been reported that 10 of every 1,000 marriages in Beijing has ended in divorce and the expectation is that 1 in every 5 marriages would end in divorce.[80] There were 655,000 divorces in 1988, up from 319,000 in 1979. About 70 percent of all divorces have been initiated by women. Economic prosperity has ushered in more independence in lifestyle in most urban areas; it is now easy to get a divorce, as the courts have relaxed their approach on grounds for divorce. If there is no contest, the parties simply go to the district court, fill out the necessary form, and pay the fee. In 1997 about 13 percent of the marriages ended in divorce.

Another recent development that has resulted from the enactment of the family laws and regulations described above has been that, increasingly, individual families retain lawyers as their legal advisors. In Shanghai more than eight hundred lawyers have been retained by families; and, in Shenzhen, the booming city near Hong Kong, more than one hundred lawyers have individual families as clients.[81] An individual family's fees for a lawyer's service range from 120 to 200 *yuan* annually.

In addition, under the State Compensation Law, which became effective in January 1995, individuals or families can now sue the government for compensation for wrongful action against an individual. The compensation law requires government units not only to compensate individuals but also to apologize to the individual victims for bureaucratic mistakes or wrongdoing.[82]

INFORMAL PRACTICES AND COMMUNITY MEDIATION

The party cadres who came from a guerrilla background acquired a set of legal experiences that relied heavily on the use of reeducation, persuasion, and social group pressure. As Victor Li has pointed out, the informal handling of deviance by guerrillas had its roots in traditional China[83] Except for very serious cases, the traditional settlement of a dispute was one of informality, compromise, and facesaving for everyone involved. Disputes were settled largely through mediation by elders in a family, clan, or village, with consultation all around. In China today we see similar mediation roles assigned to organizations, such as street or neighborhood committees, in settlement of disputes or in cases concerning deviant behavior. For instance, if a person steals a bicycle, the family is notified, and the family elders impose minor disciplinary action. If the person refuses to admit his or her wrongdoing or refuses to accept the sanction from the family, the neighborhood committee becomes involved. The leaders of the neighborhood committee then guide a group of neighbors in attempts to reeducate the offender. If the person is a first-time offender and confesses to the wrongdoing, the action is usually forgiven, and the individual is given a chance to amend his or her behavior under the supervision of the group. If the person repeats the deviant act, the public security unit is called in. The public security, or police, do not jail the individual but instead attempt reeducation. Only the incorrigibles are incarcerated in labor reform camps.[84] In a more serious criminal case, such as the one illustrated at the beginning of this chapter, the judicial proceedings are informal and emphasize mass participation in reaching a verdict. In fact, the illustration points out that the judge's sentence was handed out after the view of the masses—the fellow workers in the factory of the defendant—had been solicited.

A large percentage of both civil and criminal cases are settled in China by this type of informal method, without going through a court trial. In 1980 China institutionalized the informal method of mediation for settlement of disputes as an important feature in the new civil code and procedure. Mediation as a method for dispute settlement can now be conducted by a people's court or by people's mediation committees. As of 1982 there were about one million people's mediation committees, which are basically grassroots mass organizations. The primary role of the committees is "to mediate between the two parties by persuasion and education on a voluntary basis."[85] The process operates on the premise that conflicts or disputes are usually quarrels in a family or between neighbors, and that such conflicts can be settled most speedily and equitably by those who live within the community and act as mediators. These grassroots mass organizations exist within production brigades in communes, within neighborhoods in cities, and even in some workshops and units of industrial enterprises. As of 1982 close to six million mediators had been elected at the various basic levels with the responsibility of settling civil and minor criminal cases on the spot.[86] It has been reported that in 1980 alone the mediators handled over six million cases.[87] In Beijing 81 percent of the civil cases reportedly ended in court mediation.[88] One Western source estimated that up to 90 percent of all civil and minor criminal cases have been handled by the mediation committees.[89]

A study of mediation for the five-year period from 1980 to 1985 (see Table 6.1) shows that the total number of cases mediated has declined slightly since 1982, but the total number of mediation committees has increased steadily throughout the period, to just below one million.[90] It is safe to say that China is firmly committed to the mediation process for dispute settlement.

THE PUBLIC SECURITY BUREAU: LAW ENFORCEMENT

The public security bureau performs all the police tasks in China (national, provincial, and local) and is responsible for maintaining law and order. The operation of public security is headed by a national Ministry of State Security Affairs and has local branches in cities, towns, and villages. Its responsibilities include surveillance of the movements of citizens and foreigners and the investigation of all criminal cases. Since 1957 it has been empowered to pronounce sentence in criminal cases, including internment in labor reform camps under its control. The power of the public security bureau to sentence is another major type of extrajudicial practice, instituted in 1957, to bypass the courts. Local public security personnel are usually all members of the party or of the Communist Youth League.[91] At times public security offices have even been operated as organizations of the local party apparatus. Because of close ties with the party, the public security bureaus usually reflect the view of the party leaders in control.

Just prior to the Cultural Revolution, the procuratorate functions were carried out by the public security units. During the upheaval the attacks by Red Guards on the party frequently focused on the public security bureaus, disrupting—if not paralyzing—their functions. When the People's Liberation Army intervened in January 1967, the functions

TABLE 6.1 People's Mediation, 1980–1985

	Mediation Committees	Mediators (Million)	Cases (Million)
1980[a]	810,000	5.7	6.1
1981	n.a.	—	—
1982[b]	860,000	5.3	8.17
1983[b]	930,000	5.56	6.98
1984[b]	940,000	4.38	6.75
1985[c]	977,499	4.7	6.3

[a]*China Facts and Figures Annual* (1982).
[b]*China Statistical Annual* (1985).
[c]*People's Mediation* (1986), vol. 2.

Sources: These figures were originally prepared by Edward J. Epstein, Hong Kong, 1987, and then organized in table form by Andy Tang as printed in *Far Eastern Economic Review*, "China '87: The Door Shuts?" (March 19, 1987), 107. By permission of the publisher.

of the public security bureaus were placed under military control. During this period it became a common practice for the PLA to perform police work: arresting criminals, stopping riots, supervising prisons and labor reform camps, and even directing traffic.[92] In January 1982 the PLA's internal security units were transferred back to the Ministry of Public Security to serve as their own armed police units. This was done in an attempt to strengthen provincial and local public security power and to safeguard people's life and property.[93] The various provincial and local headquarters of the armed police were made subject to the command and direction of the party units within the Ministry of Public Security. The 1975 constitution again placed the procuratorate functions and powers in the local public security units. That constitution also prescribed that citizens could be arrested either by a decision of the courts or "by sanction of the public security organ." The constitution of 1978 restored to the people's procuratorate the sanction of arrest of criminal offenders, but assigned the duty of arrest to the public security unit. This fine distinction may not mean very much, since at the local levels, both the public security units and the procuratorate operate from the same administrative office of the party. In June 1979 the second session of the Fifth NPC enacted the new organic laws for the courts as well as a criminal procedure that delineated the relationship between public security organs and the courts as follows: The public security organ is responsible for investigation of crimes and detention of criminals; the procuratorate has the power of approving arrests and prosecuting criminal cases; the people's court is to try cases.

The restoration of the procuratorate and the enunciation of citizens' fundamental rights and duties in the 1978 constitution seemed to have provided a new framework of law and justice in post-Mao China. A campaign for human rights and equal justice for all was launched soon after the promulgation of the 1978 constitution; it reached its height in the winter of 1978, just prior to the convening of the third plenary session of the Eleventh Central Committee. Meanwhile, the Central Committee reevaluated the events of the Cultural Revolution and corrected erroneous decisions with respect to the purge of a number of top leaders. Special articles in the mass media, and wall posters in Beijing, focused on human rights and injustices to those who had been arbitrarily arrested and mistreated from the days of the Cultural Revolution to the time of the arrest of the Gang of Four. A special group of legal specialists was formed to undertake the major task of codifying and revising some thirty codes and regulations, including criminal and civil justice procedures, as mentioned earlier. The release and rehabilitation of over 100,000 "right deviationists" (a convenient label used by the radicals for those who were tagged as such in the antirightist campaign of 1957, for having attacked the party during the Hundred Flowers Bloom movement) demonstrated the new leadership's intention to observe and enforce "socialist legality and democracy." The many exposés appearing in the mass media in 1978 and 1979 pointed out clearly how widespread were the abuses sanctioned and practiced by the radicals in arbitrarily arresting and detaining cadres and masses alike. From this campaign for law and justice came the approval of regulations governing the arrest and detention of persons. The specific prohibitions contained in the new law on arrest and detention, promulgated by the second session of the Fifth NPC in June 1979, give us some idea of the state of lawlessness that had existed in China for some time. The new law provides that no person shall be arrested without a specific decision of a people's court or the approval of the procuratorate. Within three days of detention or arrest, the police (public security bureau) must submit the evidence to the procuratorate or make formal charges for the detention. The new law requires that interrogation of the detainee must commence within twenty-four hours of the arrest and that persons detained must be released immediately if there is no evidence against them. Notification must be made within twenty-four hours to the kin of the person under arrest, but this rule has not been observed during the recent massive arrests of those devotees of the religious meditation sect known as Falun Gong (see Chapter 10).

The public security bureau maintains correctional labor camps for those who have committed serious crimes, including political ones. Irrespective of the 1988 government report entitled "Criminal Reform in China," which whitewashed the brutal conditions inside the prisons, there is considerable secrecy surrounding the prison labor system—the Chinese *gulag*—where torture and slave labor have been common occurrences.[94] Under U.S. pressure, China signed an agreement in August 1992 on goods made by prison labor, in order to gain U.S. congressional approval for most-favored-nation trade status. This agreement allows reimportation inspection by the United States of exportable Chinese goods that are suspected of being made by prison slave labor.[95] The public security units are also involved in criminal reform through education and hard labor for the incarcerated. For instance, minor criminals in the city of Beijing are sent to reformatories by decision of the Beijing municipal government's reformatory committee, headed by a deputy mayor, who is assisted by a deputy director of the city's public security bureau.[96] Public security bureaus are also actively involved in the campaign to apprehend persons who engage in the "economic crimes" of smuggling, profiteering, and bribery.

The public security bureau has not been immune from corruption, a persistent ongoing practice that has besieged the party and government under economic reform. In November 1993 several dozen prominent members of the NPC made a request to Qiao Shi, then chairman of the NPC's Standing Committee, asking for institution of rectification of the public security bureaus for widespread corruptive practices discovered in these bureaus nationwide. A total of thirty-five working groups had been dispatched to the various provinces for the purpose of investigating units of the public security bureaus. In a number of provinces the investigating teams had encountered opposition from local units.[97] While hundreds of public security bureau personnel had been found guilty and dismissed in many provinces, these investigations revealed that one of the problems had been the low level of law enforcement training and education of the bureau's personnel. Many of them had attained the equivalent of an intermediate-school-level education, at best.

THE NATIONAL SECURITY AGENCY AND STATE SECURITY

In June 1983 the Sixth NPC approved a new Ministry of State Security, modeled on the former Soviet Union's Committee on National Security, commonly known as the KGB. This national security agency was established because of the expressed need to protect the state security and to strengthen China's counterespionage work. Premier Zhao reported to the NPC that the new ministry was to combine the work of the public security units, the people's armed police force, border guards, and counterintelligence organs. Apparently, China wanted to intensify its domestic surveillance to prevent "leaks" of "state secrets," particularly to foreigners. In a number of cases, party cadres with overseas connections were sentenced to prison for writing articles for Hong Kong journals under pseudonyms. In at least one case, an American scholar conducting research in China was expelled for allegedly obtaining "state secrets." (The Chinese classify information on routine matters as confidential, or secret.) The establishment of the new national security ministry led, in addition to the vast social control mechanisms already present in Chinese society, to the growth of a monstrous security bureaucracy staffed by secret agents who spy on both Chinese and foreigners.

There was a marked increase in surveillance of foreigners in China following the student demonstrations during the winter of 1986–87. Guards were augmented at the compounds where foreign diplomats and reporters lived to monitor movements of foreigners, and, most importantly, to control contact between foreigners and students. A number of foreign reporters were expelled on the grounds that they acquired so-called "illicit" internal party information on debates about the removal of Hu Yaobang. Then in April 1987 the minister for public security, Yuan Chongwu, was removed from office, ostensibly for his more liberal attitude toward the student demonstrations, and/or for his close relationship with the ousted Hu.[98] The ministry of public security took a much harsher stand against disturbances that affected public order in the aftermath of the student demonstrations. The new minister for public security, Wang Fang, who has since been removed, was considered an "insider"; he had worked within the public security ministry for years. This contrasts to the background and training of Yuan Chongwu, the ousted minister for public security. Yuan, trained in the Soviet Union as an urban planner, had a reputation for wanting to curb the police abuses and for making himself accessible to the press. At a press conference when he assumed his post in September 1985, Yuan answered a wide range of questions on student demonstrations, police behavior, and crime.[99] Under Yuan's leadership, China's national police became a member of the Interpol.

In September 1988, the NPC approved a new secrecy law to safeguard national security. The law obligates all state units, the PLA, economic enterprises, and citizens "to keep state secrets" by not disclosing to any publications any information considered confidential or secret.

By tightening the registration process, a renewed emphasis has been placed on close surveillance of visitors and resident foreigners in China. There are also more restrictions on information access from party and government units, in addition to strict prohibition for travel by foreigners to and near military installations.

IS CHINA MOVING TOWARD RULE OF LAW?

There are three compelling reasons for what the Chinese term "new beginnings" in restoring and strengthening the legal system, particularly in providing some protection for the cadres and the masses against arbitrary arrest and detention. One is the new regime's desire to create some order out of the anarchical conditions created and fostered by the radicals. Hu Yaobang told the 1982 party congress that there must be a close link between socialist democracy and the legal system "so that socialist democracy is institutionalized and codified into laws."[100] In addition to order and stability, which are necessary conditions for China's modernization, an atmosphere free from fear of arbitrary arrest and detention must be created so that China's intellectuals can dare to think, explore, and make innovations. Finally, if it is to be successful in efforts to encourage foreign trade and investment, China must demonstrate that it has a creditable legal system and that Chinese justice is workable and predictable.

One of the most interesting, if not most important, speeches made at the Fifth Session of the Eighth NPC was delivered as concluding remarks by Qiao Shi, then chairman of the NPC Standing Committee and a senior Politburo member. Qiao Shi has been pushing for legal reform toward a system of law ever since he became a key figure in the Eighth NPC. His concluding remarks on March 14, 1997, urged that the legal system be strengthened:

> We must respect and safeguard the political rights of the people, activate their initiative and creativity, and promote their participation in democratic elections, administration, supervision and policy making.[101]

Does this mean that China is moving toward a "rule of law?" As noted by Ronald C. Keith, there is a conceptual distinction between the terms *rule by law* and *rule of law*.[102] *Rule by law* refers to the use of existing law by the state, whereas *rule of law* implies fairness and predictability against leftist extremism and rule by persons.[103] Lawmaking in China in recent years does not follow the Western sense of protecting personal rights against the state or party, or of ensuring judicial independence and integrity in the administration of justice. Law making in China may be seen simply as "a process of protecting voluntary economic arrangements" under socialist market reform.[104] There has been a marked increase in the volume of laws enacted by the NPC in recent years. For instance, in 1993 it enacted nineteen laws and some seventy-two administrative statutes dealing with maintenance of market and economic order, macroeconomic control mechanisms, opening to the outside world, and improvement in administrative efficiency and integrity under the socialist market economy.[105]

On March 5, 2000 the Ninth NPC amended the Criminal Law to punish those who engage in manipulation of China's stock exchange or securities operations. The new amended version imposes heavy penalties for the following offenses in securities-and futures-related crimes: leaking inside information on securities or futures deadlines before official publication, or spreading false information which would disrupt securities markets. Punishment may be imprisonment for up to ten years, plus fines.[106]

From 1978 to 1998, there was a steady increase in the number of laws or regulations enacted at the national and local levels: three hundred twenty-seven laws and decrees by the NPC, 750 administrative laws by the State Council, and more than 5,300 local decrees.[107] While recognizing that these years of "unremitting effort" in lawmaking have undoubtedly established a significant framework for a "socialist legal system," one must also bear in mind that China's lawmaking in recent years is, in the main, intended as "legal accommodation" to the ever-evolving socialist market or "in the serve of economic growth."[108] In the final analysis, despite China's recent efforts in promoting legal reform, one needs to bear in mind that legal reform is to continue so long as it does not threaten the party's authority and political stability.

NOTES

1. Franklin P. Lam, "An Interview with Chinese Legal Officials," *China Quarterly*, 66 (June 1976), 323-37.
2. Frank Pestana, "Law in the People's Republic of China," *Asian Studies Occasional Report*, no. 1 (Arizona State University, June 1975).
3. J. Cohen, "The Party and the Courts: 1949-1959," *China Quarterly*, 38 (April-June 1969), 131–40. Discussion of "models" in the Chinese approach to the legal system is based on Victor Li's article "The Role of Law in Communist China," *China Quarterly*, 44 (October–December 1970), 7–110.
4. See "Socialist Legal System Must Not Be Played Around With," *Peking Review*, 24 (June 16, 1978), 28; and "Discussion on Strengthening China's Legal System," *Peking Review*, 45 (November 10, 1978), 5–6. Also see "Speeding the Work of Law-making," *Peking Review*, 9 (March 2, 1979), 2.
5. See James V. Feinerman, "Economic and Legal Reform in China, 1978–91," *Problems of Communism*, 40, no. 5, (September–October 1991), 70.

6. Thomas Chiu, Ian Dobinson and Mark Findlay, *Legal System of the PRC* (Hong Kong: Longman Group [Far East], Ltd., 1991), p. 72.

7. See Donald C. Clarke and James V. Feinerman, "Antagonistic Contradictions: Criminal Law and Human Rights in China," *China Quarterly*, 141 (March 1995), 139.

8. See Suzanne Ogden, *China's Unresolved Issues: Politics, Development, and Culture*, 3d ed. (Upper Saddle River, N.J.: Prentice Hall, 1995), p. 181.

9. Pestana, "Law in the PRC," p. 2. Also see Li, "Role of Law," 78; and George Ginsburgs and Arthur Stahnake, "The People's Procuratorate in Communist China: The Institution Ascendant, 1954–1957," *China Quarterly*, 34 (April-June 1968), 82–132.

10. Ginsburgs and Stahnake, "People's Procuratorate in Communist China," 90–91.

11. The source is taken from Leng Shao-Chuan and Chiu Hungdah, *Criminal Justice in Post-Mao China* (Albany, N.Y.: State University of New York Press, 1985), p. 70.

12. See Chiu, Dobinson, and Findlay, *Legal System of the PRC*, p. 80; and Ibid. p. 71.

13. For an account of these tensions and criticisms, see Cohen, "Party and the Courts: 1949–1959," 131–40.

14. Gerd Ruge, "An Interview with Chinese Legal Officials," *Chinese Quarterly*, 61 (March 1975), 118–26. Also see Lamb, "Interview with Chinese Legal Officials," 324–25.

15. See "The Civil Law's General Rules," *China News Analysis*, no. 1312 (June 15, 1986), 1–8.

16. Ibid., 5.

17. Ibid., 6.

18. For more information about China's criminal code and procedure, see *Beijing Review*, 33 (August 17, 1979), 16–27; *Beijing Review*, 23 (June 9, 1980), 17–26; *Beijing Review*, 44 (November 3, 1980), 17–28; Hungdah Chiu, "China's New Legal System," *Current History*, 459 (September 1980), 29–32; Fox Butterfield, "China's New Criminal Code," New York Times Service, as reprinted in *Honolulu Star-Bulletin,* July 20, 1979, A-19; Takashi Oka, "China's Penchant for a Penal Code," *Christian Science Monitor,* September 3, 1980, p. 3; and Stanley B. Lubman, "Emerging Functions of Normal Legal Institutions in China's Modernization," *China Under the Four Modernizations*, Part 2: *Selected Papers*, Joint Economic Committee, Congress of the United States (Washington, D.C.: Government Printing Office, December 30, 1982), pp. 235–85.

19. "Antagonistic Contradictions: Criminal Law and Human Rights in China," *China Quarterly*, 141 (March 1995), 137.

20. See Henry Hongda Wu, *Laogai—The Chinese Gulag* (Boulder, Colo.: Westview Press, 1992).

21. "The Criminal Law and the Law of Criminal Procedure," *Beijing Review*, 33 (August 17, 1979), 18.

22. Patrick E. Tyler, "Chinese Verdict Points to an Era of Harsh Rule," *New York Times,* October 31, 1996, p. A-7.

23. "Antagonistic Contradictions: Criminal Law and Human Rights in China," 141.

24. Ibid., 142.

25. See Philip Baker, "Chinese Human Rights and the Law," *Pacific Review*, 6, no. 3 (1993), 240.

26. Lo Bing, "The Inside Story of How Jiang Zemin Ordered Wang Dan's Trial," *Zhengming* (Hong Kong) November 1996, 7–9.

27. Baker, "China: Human Rights and the Law," 240. Also see the 1996 report by Amnesty International.

28. Bruce Gilley, "Rough Justice," *Far Eastern Economic Review* (July 4, 1996), 22.

29. Baker, "China: Human Rights and The Law," 242.

30. Chiu, "China's New Legal System," 32.

31. Ibid., 31.

32. Ronald C. Keith, "Transcript of Discussion with Wu Daying and Zhang Zhonglin Concerning Legal Change and Civil Rights," *China Quarterly*, 81 (March 1981), 115.

33. See Wu Naitao, "Amended Criminal Law Contains 260 More Articles," *Beijing Review* (April 28-May 4, 1997), 17–19.

34. Ibid., 18.

35. See Cheng Yanling, "China's Law of Civil Procedure," *Beijing Review* (August 16, 1982), 20–23.

36. Anthony Clark, "The Chinese Legal System: Reforms in the Balance," *China Quarterly*, 119 (September 1989), 560.

37. Marshall S. Shapo, "Comments on the Civil Responsibility Provision of the Chinese Civil Code," in *Sino-American Economic and Civil Law Conference*, 3 (May 29–June 2, 1989) East-West Center, Honolulu, Hawaii, 3.

38. See Zhao Zhongfu, "The Promulgation and Implementation of the General Principles of the Civil Law," in *Sino-American Economic and Civil Law Conference*, in ibid., 38–41.

39. See Cui Jianyuan, "Implementation of the Economic Contract Law of the People's Republic of China," *Sino-American Economic and Civil Law Conference*, 2 (May 29–June 2, 1989) East-West Center, Honolulu, Hawaii, 35–37.

40. Yuan Zhenmin, "China Adopts Law on Foreign Enterprises," *Beijing Review*, 18 (May 5, 1986), 14–15. Also see the text on wholly owned foreign enterprise law in the same issue 16–17.
41. See Ibid., 14–15.
42. "Law on Enterprises Operated Exclusively with Foreign Capital," *Beijing Review*, 18 (May 5, 1986), 17.
43. Pitman B. Potter, "Foreign Investment Law in the People's Republic of China: Dilemmas of State Control," *China Quarterly*, 141 (March 1995), 167–68.
44. Ibid., 162.
45. Donald C. Clark, "The Execution of Civil Judgment in China," *China Quarterly*, no. 141 (March 1995), 71.
46. Ibid.
47. James V. Feinerman, "Economic and Legal Reform in China, 1978-1991," *Problem of Communism*, 11, no. 5 (September–October, 1991), p. 66.
48. Ibid.
49. See Matt Forney, "Don't Hold Your Breath," *Far Eastern Economic Review* (March 7, 1996), 24.
50. *Ming Pao Daily* (Hong Kong), January 6, 1983, p. 3.
51. See HeBian, "China's Laywers," *Beijing Review*, 23 (June 7, 1982), 14.
52. Li Yun Chang, "The Role of Chinese Lawyers," *Beijing Review*, 46 (November 17, 1980), 24. Also see Lubman, "Emerging Functions of Formal Legal Institutions in China's Modernization," 251–54.
53. Chang "Role of Chinese Lawyers," 24.
54. *China Trade Report* (March 1981), 6, and *Christian Science Monitor*, July 11, 1984, p. 1.
55. See *Wall Street Journal*, April 14, 1987, p. 31.
56. "The Need for More Lawyers," *Beijing Review*, 49 (December 8, 1980), 3.
57. *Christian Science Monitor*, February 10, 1983, p. 11. Also see *New York Times*, December 5, 1982, p. 22.
58. *Ming Pao Daily* (Hong Kong), February 7, 1983, p. 3.
59. *China Daily*, February 14, 1983, p. 3.
60. Ibid.
61. *Ta Kung Pao Weekly Supplement* (Hong Kong), April 12, 1984, p. 10.
62. Ibid.
63. *China Trade Report* (April 1986), 6.
64. *Wall Street Journal*, April 14, 1987, p. 31.
65. Ibid. Also see *People's Daily*, July 6, 1987, p. 1.
66. *People's Daily* (Overseas Edition), July 6, 1986, p. 1.
67. "Law Grants Lawyers Independent Power," *Beijing Review*, (June 3–9, 1996), 6.
68. Ibid.
69. Ibid.
70. See William P. Alford, "Tasselled Loafers for Barefoot Lawyers: Transformation and Tension in the World of Chinese Legal Workers," *China Quarterly*, 141 (March 1995), 22–38. Also see Stanley Lubman, "Introduction: The Future of Chinese Law," *China Quarterly*, 141 (March 1995), 7.
71. Ibid., Alford, "Tasselled Loafers for Barefoot Lawyers," *China Quarterly*, 31. And also see William Alford and Fang Liufan, "Legal Training and Education in the 1990s: An Overview and Assessment of China's Needs," *World Bank Report*, 1994.
72. Ibid., Alford "Tasselled Loafers for Barefoot Lawyers," *China Quarterly*, 33–34.
73. Ibid.
74. See Matt Forney, "Outside the Law: Reform Reversals Hit Foreign Firms in China," *Far Eastern Economic Review* (December 26, 1992 and January 2, 1997), 18–19. Also see *Wall Street Journal*, December 13, 1996, p. A-6.
75. See Elisabeth Rosenthal, "China's Legal Evolution, the Lawyers Are Handcuffed," *New York Times*, January 6, 2000, pp. A-1 and A-11.
76. See Michael Palmer, "The Re-emergence of Family Law in Post-Mao China: Marriage, Divorce and Reproduction," *China Quarterly*, 141 (March 1995), 110 and 117.
77. Ibid., 119.
78. Ibid., 123.
79. Ibid., 124.
80. See "China's Rise in Divorce Reflects Changing Ethics," *Washington Post* article as reprinted in the *Honolulu Advertiser*, December 15, 1996, p. D–5.
81. "Lawyers Begin to Serve Families," *Beijing Review* (July 10–16, 1995), 7.
82. See Jiang Wandi, "Yes, You May Now Sue the Government," *Beijing Review* (December 4–10, 1995), 20.
83. Victor Li, "The Role of Law," *China Quarterly*, 44 (October–December 1970), 72–110.
84. Martin King Whyte, "Corrective Labor Camps in China, *Asian Survey*, 13, no. 3 (March 11, 1973), 253–69.

85. Yanling, "China's Law of Civil Procedure," 21.
86. "The Xiebeijiao Neighborhood Mediation Committee," *Beijing Review*, 47 (November 23, 1981), 24–28.
87. "Mediation Committees," *Beijing Review*, 41 (October 12, 1981), 8–9; and "China's System of Community Mediation," *Beijing Review*. Also see Lubman, "Emerging Functions of Formal Legal Institutions," 257–59.
88. Yanling, "China's Law of Civil Procedure," 21.
89. *New York Times,* December 5, 1982, p. 22.
90. *Far Eastern Economic Review* (March 10, 1987), 107.
91. Doak Barnett, *Cadres, Bureaucracy, and Political Power in Communist China* (New York: Columbia University Press, 1967), p. 227; and Ralph Powell and Chong-kun Yoon, "Public Security and the PLA," in *Asian Survey*, 12, no. 12 (December 1972), 1082–1100.
92. Barnett, *Cadres, Bureaucracy and Political Power in Communist China*, p. 227; and Powell and Yoon, "Public Security and PLA," 1082–1100.
93. *Ming Pao Daily* (Hong Kong), July 31, 1981, p. 1.
94. See *New York Times*, August 12, 1992, p. A-5; *Asian Wall Street Journal,* January 31–February 1, 1992, p. 6; *Asian Wall Street Journal,* September 3, 1992, p. 6; and *Christian Science Monitor,* April 8, 1992, p. 19.
95. *New York Times,* August 8, 1992, p. 3.
96. "Reforming Criminals: Interviewing Deputy Director of Public Security Bureau," *Beijing Review*, 8 (February 23, 1981), 24.
97. See Sheng Zeng, "Appeal to Party Central for Rectification of Public Security Bureau," *Zhengming* (Hong Kong), 195 (January 1995), 26–27.
98. See Daniel Southerland, "Chinese Hike Surveillance of Foreigners," Washington Post Service, reprinted in *Honolulu Advertiser,* April 9, 1987, p. A-14. Also see *New York Times,* April 12, 1987, p. 3.
99. *Beijing Review,* 52 (December 30, 1985), 15–18.
100. "Creating a New Situation in all Fields of Socialist Modernization," *Beijing Review,* 23 (June 6, 1980), p. 27.
101. "Rule of Law Urged as Session Closed," *Beijing Review* (March 31–April 6, 1997), 4.
102. See his paper, "Post-Deng Jurisprudence: Justice and Efficiency in a 'Rule of Law' Economy," given at the 1996 annual meeting of the Associations for Asian Studies held in April in Honolulu. Also see his book *China's Struggle for the Rule of Law* (Basingstoke, England: Macmillan, 1994)
103. Ibid., "Post-Deng Jurisprudence" pp. 9 and 35–36.
104. See Stanley Lubman, "Introduction: The Future of Chinese Law," 12–13.
105. See Li Peng, "Report on Work of Government," *Beijing Review*, 36 (April 12–18, 1992), p. xiii.
106. *Beijing Review*, January 3, 2000, 6.
107. See Li Rongxia, "Outstanding Results in Building a Legal System," *Beijing Review*, (August 16, 1999), 16.
108. "The Chinese Legal System: Continuing Commitment to the Primacy of the State," *China Quarterly*, no. 159 (September 1999), 678.

SUGGESTED READINGS

Davis, Michael D. (ed.). *Human Rights and Chinese Values: Legal, Philosophical and Political Perspectives* (Hong Kong: Oxford University Press, 1995).
Keith, Ronald C. *China's Struggle for the Rule of Law* (Basinstoke, England: Macmillan, 1994).
Murphy, J. David. *Plunder and Preservation: Cultural Property Law and Practice in People's Republic of China* (Hong Kong: Oxford University Press, 1995).
Oi, Jean C., and Andrew G. Walder (eds.). *Property Rights and Economic Reform in China* (Stanford, Calif.: Stanford University Press, 1999).
Seidman, Ann, Robert B. Seidman and Janice Payne. *Legislative Drafting for Market Reform: Some Lessons from China* (London: Macmillan, 1997).
Tanner, Murray Scot. *The Politics of Lawmaking: In Post-Mao China: Institutions, Process and Democratic Aspects* (Oxford: Oxford University Press, 1998).

Chapter Seven

Provincial
and Local Politics

Centralism versus Regionalism,
National Minorities,
and the Case of Tibet

OVERVIEW OF PROVINCIAL AND LOCAL GOVERNMENT

The government of China is administered through twenty-two provinces, five autonomous regions, and four municipalities—Beijing, Shanghai, Tianjin, and Chongqing. The five autonomous regions of Inner Mongolia, Ningxia, Xinjiang, Guangxi, and Xizang (Tibet) are located on China's borders with neighboring countries and are inhabited by minority groups. (Hainan Island was made the twenty-second province at the August 1987 meeting of the Sixth NPC's Standing Committee—it was then ratified by the Seventh NPC.)

The Constitution of 1982 specifies three layers of local political power: provinces and autonomous regions, cities and counties, and townships. The source of constitutional power at these levels is the people's congress. We must keep in mind that deputies to the provincial people's congresses are elected indirectly. The 1982 constitution states that the deputies to these congresses are to be elected by the people's congresses at the next lower level. Eligible voters at the lower level of government (in this case, the counties and townships) directly elect deputies to their own people's congresses. The electoral law now provides that election for the county people's congress is carried out by dividing the county into electoral districts, each of which elects delegates to the county people's congress. A simple chart of the provincial and local government is shown in Figure 7.1. Deputies to the provincial congress are elected for five-year terms; deputies to the township and county congresses are elected for three-year terms.

It would be wrong to assume that the people's congresses at the various local levels are legislative bodies. However, Article 99 of the 1982 constitution authorizes the local people's congresses to "adopt and issue resolutions." These bodies have six main

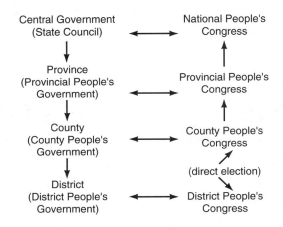

FIGURE 7.1 Provincial and Local Government Structure. *Source: Constitution of the People's Republic of China,* adopted by the Fifth NPC on December 4, 1982. See Appendix A

responsibilities: (1) to enact local statutes according to local conditions (authorized by the Organic Law of Local People's Congresses and Local Government in July 1979); (2) to ensure the observance and implementation of the state constitution, the statutes, and administrative rules; (3) to approve plans for economic development and budgets at the county level and above; (4) to elect or recall governors, mayors, and chiefs for the counties and townships; (5) to elect and recall judges and procurators; and (6) to maintain public order.

Theoretically, the deputies are not subject to the influence of local party committees—a political reform imposed under the 1982 constitution. In 1982 Peng Zhen reported that the organs at the grassroots level must be strengthened in order to serve as the basic organization of state power: "These organs must really be in the hands of the people, elected, supervised, and removed by them."[1] The party, the pragmatic leaders now maintained, neither replaces the government nor gives orders to organs of government.[2] (We need to keep in mind that these statements were based on assumptions at the time when the 1982 constitution was enacted.)

In June 1979 the Fifth NPC at its second session abolished the revolutionary committees as administrative organs of local government. They were replaced by the people's governments at all levels.[3] This action removed one of the last vestiges of the Cultural Revolution. The rationale for abolishing the revolutionary committees was that they could no longer meet the needs of socialist modernization and that their elimination would "strengthen democracy and the legal system."[4] With the abolition of the revolutionary committees, the positions and titles of governor (for the provinces), mayor (for the cities and counties), and chief (for the townships) were restored.[5] These changes regarding local people's congresses and governments were incorporated into the 1982 constitution (see Section V, Articles 95–110, in Appendix A).

ISSUES IN PROVINCIAL POLITICS

Chinese provincial politics is a complex subject. Three interrelated issues that have dominated provincial politics in China are discussed in this section.

Regionalism, Provincialism, Localism

We have noted that China is a unitary state with political power concentrated at the central government level, and that throughout China's long history there were many incidents in which centrifugal forces pulled away from the center because of geographical and sectional interests. The warlord period from 1916 to 1926 epitomizes this aspect of regional separation in recent history. Another general characteristic of Chinese politics has been the trend toward local initiative and self-government. In this section we will briefly examine the development of regionalism in provincial politics.

The terms *provincialism, regionalism,* and *localism* have been used to describe the problems of regions versus the center, or the central authority in Beijing. These terms are used here somewhat interchangeably because they all denote the centrifugal force constantly at play in Chinese politics. Regionalism has been defined as "the phenomenon whereby distinct groups, living in discrete territorial enclaves within larger political communities, exert pressures for recognition of their differences."[6]

The presence of regional forces that tend to pull away from the center in Chinese politics may be accounted for, to a large extent, by China's vast size and by the various cultures represented in her different geographic areas. It is common to speak of China as divided into the north, south, central, east, west, and the Asian portions of Inner Mongolia, Xinjiang, and Xizang.[7] Each of these regions may be considered an entity dominated by features of climate, drainage systems, soil composition, or dialect variations. A visitor who enters China by train from Hong Kong will notice the subtropical climate of southern China, which permits the harvest of two rice crops each year. The rugged hills and mountains of the south tend to foster a variety of dialects among the inhabitants. A visitor arriving at Beijing in the north sees an entirely different China in terms of climate, which is temperate and thus cold in the winter, and soil formation, which is the dry powdery loess of the Huanghe (Yellow) River basin. Wheat, millet, and cotton are the main crops grown in the north and northeast. Central and east China are watered by the Changjiang (Yangtse) River, whose vast plains permit the cultivation of rice and other crops that support a large population. The mountainous west and southwest are sparsely populated, except for the fertile valley of Sichuan, one of the richest but most difficult provinces to govern because of its geographic isolation and its relative economic self-sufficiency. These geographic and topographic variations are primary factors that have contributed to the feelings of sectional independence.

New Economic Regions and Regional Conflicts.[8] As an integral part of economic reform, an effort has been made since 1984 to promote the growth of lateral, or horizontal, economic relations between geographic regions. This was advocated by the CCP decision on October 29, 1984 on economic structural reform: "We must . . . strive to develop lateral economic relations among enterprises and regions, promote appropriate exchanges of funds, equipment, technology and qualified personnel."[9] The detailed plan for promoting these lateral regional economic relations was presented to the Fourth Plenum of the Sixth NPC in March 1986.[10] The goal was to remove barriers between central departments and regions.[11]

Regional conflict discussed here focuses on inland versus coastal areas in the share of resources allocated for economic development.[12] To gain support from the peasantry and to have a more equitable economic distribution, China initiated in the 1950s a deliberate policy of avoiding concentration of industrial development in the coastal areas.

Instead, industrial plants, resources, and skilled manpower were redistributed to scattered inland provinces. Susan Shirk's study indicated that before 1978 the inland regions received a much larger share of capital investment and fiscal subsidies from the central government.[13] Then in 1978 a shift in development strategy took place. Central control over investment and allocation of resources for coastal regions was modified to accommodate the open door policy. The coastal areas with their easy access for foreigners and "good economic foundations" (availability of factories, skilled labor, and port facilities)[14] were given higher priorities to attract foreign investors. These coastal regions had a broad history of industrialization and commerce prior to 1949 and were more receptive to investment. Further, many overseas Chinese had their roots there. Thus, it was logical to designate the first special economic zones in the coastal provinces of Guangdong and Fujian (see Chapter 12).

New Coastal Development Strategy.   In February 1988 the party's Politburo approved the Coastal Development Strategy (CDS), which aimed at expanding the export capacity of the coastal regions by linking them with the inland areas adjacent to the coast.[15] Under the plan some 284 cities and counties in some fourteen coastal regions were opened for trade and foreign investment. In many respects these cities and counties became foreign trade zones where raw materials could be processed and assembled as unfinished or industrial goods for export. These coastal areas reached from the Liaodong and Shandong peninsulas in the northeast and north to the central coastal regions of the Changjiang (Yangtze) River, which included Shanghai, to Zhejiang, southern Fujian, and the Zhujiang (Pearl) River delta in Guangdong in the south (see Chapter 8).

As pointed out in a study by Fuh-wen Tzeng, one of the problems in the strategy for developing the coastal regions has been persistent conflicts between the central government and provincial and local governments over control of trade and investment.[16] To the annoyance of the central government's Ministry of Foreign Economic Relations, there has also been cutthroat competition among the provincial and local authorities in bidding on foreign capital and equipment.[17] In these instances the local authorities demanded autonomy from Beijing's control and allocation of funds for infrastructure. Take, for example, the case of Guangdong. Guangdong province is China's "Gold Coast" today, with the fastest-growing economy anywhere in the world; in 1991 its annual growth rate was 27 percent. (In conversations with some provincial officials during my 1993 visit, I was repeatedly told that Guangdong points the way for China's future; its current per capita income is about $500 per year, the highest in China.) Guangdong Investment Ltd., one of China's biggest conglomerates, is an investment arm of the provincial government and is listed on the Hong Kong stock exchange.[18] In 1992 Guangdong won the central government's approval for greater economic autonomy in launching large-scale projects—such as power plants—as well as authorization for local initiative in wage setting and loan and bond issuance. (These grants of local autonomy in economic matters were originally approved by the State Council in 1988, but implementation was blocked by the conservative hard-liners.)[19] In 1992 it was reported that the local municipalities on the Pearl River delta, close to Hong Kong and Guangzhou, had formed a consortium that had invested in a prime real estate property in central Hong Kong for U.S. $490 million.[20]

As coastal provinces gained the center's attention and received more autonomy, inland areas began to feel what Susan Shirk termed a "competitive disadvantage."[21] Soon the hinterland provinces demanded that the center reinstitute centralization to safeguard their vested economic interests.[22] Provincial officials in the inland areas mapped out strategies to "sabotage the economic reforms."[23] They intensified the 1983–84 "spiritual pollution" campaign that was aimed largely at the coastal provinces. When the "spiritual pollution" campaign failed to gain sufficient support, provincial officials began openly opposing Deng's open door policy. To mitigate opposition to Deng's reforms and the open door policy from the inland provinces, the central government embarked on a new strategy of "inter-provincial cooperation" to allow the inland regions and the coastal areas to participate in joint ventures and trade with each other.[24] Moreover, the central government even allowed a coastal enterprise to invest its retained profits in inland mines and factories.[25] In short, economic reform since 1978 has seen the rise of regional interests and of regional influence on policy making.

The rise of Guangdong as one of the leading provinces in the development of hi-tech industry is rather significant, particularly in the number of Internet users and mobile-phone subscribers which have surpassed even those in Shanghai.[26] Guangdong's strategy for hi-tech development is to encourage private companies to join foreign investors, often rivals, in developing the information industry.[27] The strategy has worked to such an extent that in 1999 the province attracted about 30 percent of overseas investment in China.

Centralization versus Decentralization

In a continuous search for an appropriate administrative formula, China has alternated between emphases on decentralization and centralization since 1949. When the communists took over in 1949, the provincial and local governments were built upon the base of the guerilla army and governments, which by their very nature operated with a great deal of autonomy in implementing government policies and programs. These new governments were staffed largely by local residents, both for convenience and to avoid accusations of a takeover by outsiders. To aid the central government's administration in Beijing and the coordination of the provinces, the six regional districts (government bureaus) were established. Each region was governed by both a military and an administrative committee. A corps of veteran party-military leaders headed these committees with considerable authority and flexibility. A good deal of local autonomy was permitted under this regional arrangement while the regime consolidated its rule. The communists had neither the administrative personnel nor the experience to mount a tight central administration over the vast population and area. Under these conditions the ever-present local tendencies exerted themselves, frequently resulting in political factions at the local level.[28] Local officials often manipulated party officials at the regional level.

The conflict between the central and regional power structures came to a head with the introduction of the First Five-Year Plan. Centralized planning—with allocated resources, production quotas, forced savings, and formation of the voluntary Agricultural Producers' Cooperatives (APCs)—required strong central control. Gao Gang, chairperson of the Northeast Military and Administrative Committee as well as the area's party chief, was purged for opposing the APCs and for disagreeing with the party over allocation of investment funds for Manchuria. Similarly, Rao Shushi, chairperson of the East China Military and Administrative Committee and party chief, was purged for demanding a slower-paced introduction of the APCs into his area. It was alleged that both powerful regional leaders had attempted to solicit support from the military stationed in their respective areas. The six regional government bureaus and the six party bureaus were abolished following these purges.[29] The 1954 constitution specifically stipulated that China was to have a single form of government, with headquarters in Beijing. Under the constitution the provincial authorities were the agents of the central government, with limited power to implement and execute the plans and directives from the center.

The years from 1953 to 1957 turned out to be a period of overcentralization, with excessive control over the provinces by the central authority in Beijing, particularly by those central functional ministries that proliferated under the First Five-Year Plan. All economic enterprises were placed under the direct control and management of the central ministries. Regulatory control devices were promulgated at the center, and all important decisions had to be made in Beijing. Even the acquisition of fixed property worth about $100 needed specific permission from the central ministry concerned.[30] This frequently resulted in delay and frustration in decision making. Even worse, the centralization of decision making resulted in ministerial autarky. A ministry became an independent economic system that tightly controlled the supply of materials and the allocation of resources under its jurisdiction. Instead of regional, independent fiefdoms, there were centralized, ministerial, independent kingdoms that interfered with provincial and local administration, drew up ill-conceived plans, and made repeated revisions of the plans. This resulted in the neglect of priorities and the waste of raw materials.[31]

At the end of the First Five-Year Plan, the Chinese leaders made an agonizing reappraisal of their experience with the Stalinist model of development. In advocating the return to decentralization, Mao spoke out openly for the extension of power in the regions. In his 1956 speech on the ten major relations or contradictions, Mao criticized the central functional ministries' habit of issuing orders directly to their counterparts at the provincial and municipal levels without even consulting the State Council and the party's Central Committee. He pointed out that local interests must be given due consideration if the central authority was to be respected and strengthened at the provincial and local levels.[32]

While Mao was genuinely concerned about the excess of centralization and the loss of local and provincial initiative, he might have been motivated also by purely political considerations. Centralism had placed tremendous power in the centralized ministries and with the members of the State Council, who, from time to time, challenged Mao's policies and who were opposed to rapid collectivization. By advocating the return of power to the provinces, Mao would receive support from the provincially based political forces, which could serve as a counterweight in a showdown with the top party-government officials at the center.[33] Mao's view on the return to decentralization was evidently accepted by the party leadership: In the fall of 1956, it met to endorse the Second Five-Year Plan, which provided for local initiative and administration that would be appropriate to local needs and interests.

The Great Leap of 1958 marked the beginning of real efforts at decentralization. Under the decentralization policy, the provincial and local authorities were granted a variety of powers in the administration and management of economic enterprises. Control of enterprises in consumer goods industries was transferred from the Ministry of Light Industry to provincial authorities. While certain basic industries of economic importance, such as oil refining and mining, were still controlled by the central ministries, the provincial authorities were given some say in their operations. In the area of finances, the provincial and local governments gained considerable power. Under the decentralization plan of 1957, provincial and local authorities were granted their own sources of revenues from profits of local enterprises and taxes, freeing them from complete dependence on central government grants for their budgets. The provincial authorities were to retain 20 percent of the profits from the enterprises transferred to the local authorities and a share of local taxes on commodities, commercial transactions, and agriculture. The provinces were even allowed to levy new taxes and to issue bonds, as long as the methods were approved by the center. Even more important for the initiative and growth of the provinces, local authorities were allowed to rearrange or adjust production targets within the framework of the targets of the overall state plan.[34] Thus, in the latter part of the 1950s, the top leaders, including Mao, recognized that the provinces had a definite role to play in the top-level decision-making process. By 1956 Mao had formulated a set of guidelines to be applied in the debates over central versus local issues. A key provision of these guidelines was Mao's insistence that the center must consult the provinces: "It is the practice of the Central Committee of the Party to consult the local authorities; it never hastily issues orders without prior consultation."[35]

A direct consequence of the 1957 decentralization under the Great Leap was the emergence of the provinces as independent entities. The provinces behaved as though they were little "underdeveloped nations"; each wanted to build its own self-sufficient industrial complex.[36] The inevitable result of the weakened centralized ministerial supervision over economic activities in the provinces was the rapid growth of localism, with provincial leaders acquiring an economic power base that challenged the center on policies and programs. In addition to being the agents of the party at the center, the provincial party secretaries also became spokespersons for the particular interests of their own provinces.

With the failure of the Great Leap in 1959, the Central Committee enacted a recentralization program to strengthen the leadership of the center over the provincial leaders. In 1961 the regional bureaus were reestablished to supervise the provinces and to control their tendencies to become "subnational administrations."[37] These regional bureaus also were mandated to supervise the rectification campaign launched by the Liu Shaoqi group to purge the radicalized provincial party leaders who supported the Great Leap program.[38] The recentralization in the early 1960s did not return the center–local relationship to the pre-1957 status of overcentralization. Many of the powers granted to the provincial and local authorities during the Great Leap remained intact. However, the crucial functions of economic planning and coordination were largely returned to the central authority.[39] Provincial politics remained a very important force during the early 1960s. During the period from the end of the Great Leap in 1961 to the eve of the Cultural Revolution in 1966, the provincial leaders were active participants at regularized central work conferences—a form of enlarged meetings of the Politburo or the Central Committee. These meetings also included selected party leaders who were not members of the highest decision-making body.

During the initial period of economic readjustment from 1979 to 1980 (to be discussed in Chapter 11), the provinces were given considerable autonomy in foreign trade matters. Provinces were encouraged to expand their foreign trade by obtaining from Beijing the right to import from or export to foreign countries directly. It was common for trading corporations to be formed at the provincial level to participate in foreign trade. A number of provinces—Guangdong and Fujian in particular—were designated as Special Economic Zones (SEZs) for foreign trade and were encouraged to enter into joint investment ventures with foreign concerns. This policy led to a scramble to export provincial products in many inland localities. Decentralization also gave rise to price cutting, bureaucratic game playing, and overlapping of responsibilities between and among provincial and local enterprises. Finally, the central authorities in Beijing had to revert to the policy of "balancing decentralization with unified planning,"[40] meaning more centralized control over provincial activities.

The 1984 urban economic reform promoted decentralized decision making at the local level.[41] Local governments under the reform had become "primary economic agents" for their own investment and production.[42] Decentralization created serious problems of "excessive and redundant investment."[43] Christine Wong gives an example from Henan province to illustrate the problem: To bolster Henan's economic development and profits, Henan officials fought to set up their own tobacco processing facilities rather than send their crop to an established processing center like Shanghai on the east coast.[44] In 1983 the central government initiated policies to reshape the local governments' pattern of profit retention and investment in order to reduce capital construction outlays. These policies, especially a 10–15 percent surtax on state-owned enterprises in the provinces imposed to help reduce construction or fixed asset accumulation, were met with some local resistance.[45] The 1984 urban reform promoted decision making at the local level; while this "enhanced local power," it "exacerbated problems of localism."[46] It became a common practice in the 1980s for provincial and local governments to band together as "lobbying groups" to protect their interests and resist changes that would restrict benefits to their localities.[47] Thus, a new center versus regional/local relationship has evolved in the ever-changing political scene in China.

In a recent study of provincial elites,[48] Xiaowei Zang points out that the average age of the then provincial elites—governors and party secretaries—was 55 years, and about 47 percent of the 274 provincial leaders included in the study had a college education. However, over 70 percent of the provincial elites devoted their careers to serving as provincial party-government workers. In that sense they tend to be advocates of localism.[49]

Tensions in Provincial-Center Relations

On the eve of the Cultural Revolution, the new center–provincial relationship showed signs of uneasiness as dissension within the top leadership deepened. Two major areas of tension were the allocation of resources and the types of economic activities to be carried on in the various provinces. For example, the party leader in the southern province of Guangdong was accused of promoting the development of a complete industrial complex for his province rather than concentrating on the development of light industries as dictated by the center.[50] On occasion, particular local conditions were used by provincial leaders as justification for resisting certain economic programs initiated by the center. Ganshu province used its backwardness as justification for not embarking on a rapid program of economic development.[51]

The degree of provincial autonomy or independence from the center varied according to the province's share of China's total industrial and agricultural resources and the stature of the provincial leaders in the hierarchy of the party and the central government. The provinces of the northeast—the massive industrial base in Manchuria—and the provinces of eastern and central China, with their commanding share of the resources, were in a better bargaining position when it came to allocation and distribution of these resources. The southwestern province of Sichuan has traditionally been known as a difficult province for the center to govern because of its rich resources and its remoteness from Beijing. Li Qingchuan, the party leader in Sichuan before the Cultural Revolution, was an old revolutionary veteran with close supporters at the center. He was also the party secretary for the southwest region before the Cultural Revolution. He enjoyed considerable autonomy and independence in governing the province of Sichuan and the southwest region.[52] Ulanhu, a powerful member of the Politburo at the beginning of the Cultural Revolution who had long governed the affairs of Inner Mongolia, could be described as an overlord for the autonomous region. Ulanhu not only identified himself with, but also banked on, local nationalism to provide local resistance to orders from the center during the Cultural Revolution.[53] Prior to their purges during the Cultural Revolution, both Li Qingchuan and Ulanhu had been brought into the decision-making process at the Central Committee level. After 1978 many provinces formed their own independent shipping services to Hong Kong, Japan, and Southeast Asia in order to avoid domestic transportation bottlenecks. One province in southwest China offered preferential tax incentives in order to attract contracts from foreign investors for exploration of the province's hydroelectric power resources and ore mines.[54] Provincial autonomy was also reflected in the language, messages, and issues articulated in political communications between the center at Beijing and the provinces.[55]

In the 1980s, tensions between the center and the provinces developed in two areas. One, as pointed out earlier, was the local resistance to those economic reform measures that aimed at curbing the increased power of the local governments in making their own economic decisions. The other was the decision made by the party to replace aged and less-educated provincial leaders with younger Deng supporters. During the first six months of 1983, according to one calculation, "some 950 of China's 1,350 top provincial leaders were retired and replaced by about 160 new officials."[56] In addition, provincial leadership bodies, such as party secretaries, governors, and members of the standing committees for provincial NPCs, were reduced by as much as 38 percent, from a total of 1,082 to only 669.[57] The average age for provincial top leaders after 1983 was about 56, and one-third of them had college educations.[58] Despite widespread press reports of deliberate obstruction of reforms by local government organizations, the center won the fight for personnel changes at the provincial leadership level through a combination of actions: moving aged veteran leaders to advisory bodies so that they could still keep their salaries and privileges; demoting leaders considered unsuitable; and retaining those who pledged support to Deng and his reform policies.[59]

CHANGING CENTER–PROVINCIAL RELATIONS IN THE POST-DENG TRANSITION

There have been two parallel developments in center–provincial relations since the Tiananmen crackdown on June 4, 1989. First, there has been a resurgence of centripetal forces as the central government has tightened its control over the allocation of credits, resources, and market-oriented reforms introduced during the reform decade. In fact, there has been some recentralization over the provincial autonomy in economic development since the launching of the austerity program in October 1988, as discussed in Chapter 11. After the 1989 Tiananmen crackdown the hard-liners imposed more measures for centralization by reducing the scale of government investment, requiring state approval of major construction projects, and checking any "excessive rise in consumer demands." One outcome of the central government's efforts in depressing retail markets, and a second development since the Tiananmen crackdown, has been an outbreak of "regional trade protectionism," or trade wars waged by provinces against each other's products.[60] Roadblocks had been erected by local authorities to prevent or curtail incoming goods desired by local consumers. This led to a decision by the central government to impose controls over production of textiles, electronics, and light industrial goods, in addition to reinstituting a state monopoly over cotton and grain distribution.[61] Regional and local authorities seem to have determined to maintain their local autonomy enjoyed under the reform decade.

As one province that most enjoyed the local autonomy in economic development, the southern province of Guangdong has become targeted for resurgence of central control.[62] In a bargaining session on the budget and finance with the center, Guangdong must turn over to the central government a fixed amount, about 1.4 to 1.7 billion yuan, from its annual earnings. The central government had also taken over many commodities in the foreign trade sector for the province and had thus restricted its provincial exports.[63] Since 1988, when the austerity strategy was launched, the province had faced many problems, which included shortage of capital, a sluggish market for both capital and consumer goods, and widespread individual business failures that have caused unemployment in the province. In addition, there were then uncertainties in foreign trade caused by the Tiananmen crackdown that affected one-fourth of the provincial income as foreign investment and earnings from tourism had declined.

Unlike Guangdong, Shanghai's economic development receives no such restrictions imposed by the center. For 1990, a list of four construction projects for urban infrastructure, including the ambitious Huangpu River bridge, have been issued, plus investment for energy, steel (at Baoshan), and modernization of textile, electric, and machine tool development projects.[64] One may read the developments in Guangdong and Shanghai as a reflection of the prevailing political climate since Tianamen: Guangdong had been considered the reformer's showcase under Zhao Ziyang, and Shanghai is the metropolis once run by Jiang Zemin, former mayor and now the party chief.

In the 1990 winter debate, the provincial leaders and the reformers seemed to have won the argument that there be no alteration in the contract system for revenue sharing between the center and the provinces. One of Zhao Ziyang's key reform measures had been permission for the provincial government and state enterprises to retain profits above and beyond the contracted amount instead of turning them over to the central authorities. The result has been a reduction of central government revenue and an increase of decision-making power in the hands of the provincial, township, and village enterprises.

The decline in central government revenue may serve as a warning of a possible disintegration of the Chinese central government, echoing the crumbling of the Yugoslavia federation after Tito's death. This was the central thesis presented in 1993 by two Chinese economists at Yale. According to their calculations, state revenue collected by the central government had dropped in 1992 to about 14 percent of China's GNP from 32 percent in 1978, at the onset of Deng's economic reform.[65] They reckoned in 1993 that the decline would continue to drop to as low as 11 percent of China's GNP by the year 2000. Their conclusion was that, in a matter of perhaps ten years, the conflicts and contests between the provincial and central authorities would eventually bring about political disintegration.[66] We will have to wait until the year 2003 to see whether this rather pessimistic prediction is going to be a reality.

While one may not have subscribed to the soothsayers' dire predictions of the early 1990s for China in the future, or do so today, one must recognize the emergence of economic regionalism in China after Deng (to be discussed more fully in Chapter 8). Already there is in existence a long-term plan for regional economic zonal arrangements. The fourth session of the Eighth NPC approved the gradual establishment of seven trans-provincial (regional and municipal) economic regions: the Yangtze River Delta, the Bohai Sea Rim, coastal areas in southeast China, provinces and autonomous regions in south and southwest China, the northeast region, five provinces in central

China, and the northwest region.[67] Since then numerous special articles have appeared in *The Beijing Review* concerning these regional economic developments. For instance, in recent issues, special reports have been published on regional economic developments for Chongqing in Sichuan in western China,[68] in Yunnan near the Vietnamese border,[69] and in Inner Mongolia.[70] In Chapter 8 our focus will be on the development of a "greater South China," now that Hong Kong has reverted to China, followed by Macao in December 1999, constituting a formidable booming Pearl River Delta region.

"Revive the West" or "The Great Western Development."   The focus of economic development in China has been in the coastal provinces and the areas adjacent to these provinces. The vast region of western China has been neglected or left out of the economic boom. First, a few key statistics may be necessary to show the state of China's western region:[71] It has 23 percent of China's total population and more than half of China's total area of more than three million square miles. However, in terms of economic growth, considering it has about 60 percent of China's natural gas reserves and other mineral deposits, China's west as a whole has only less than 15 percent of the Gross Domestic Product (GDP), and the average urban resident in the west earns only $632 compared with $1,320 for his or her counterpart in Shanghai in eastern China.[72] Most importantly, this region includes 80 percent of China's minority groups (a discussion will follow).

In 1999 the central government's decision to make appreciable investment in the region has resulted in launching of a campaign for western development. Under consideration is a proposed project to build a natural gas pipeline linking western Xinjiang (the old Chinese Turkistan, as it was then called) to Shanghai. Also under construction is a highway in Shaanxi province, a gateway to the rest of China. For these neglected western provinces of Xinjiang, Qinghai, Gansu, Ningxia, Shaanxi, Sichuan, Hunan, Yunnan, and Tibet, there is a dire need to develop the infra-structure in this vast region before a large volume of investment can come in. Investments (about $195 billion) from the central government for the five-year period, 2000–2005, have been designated for tourism, education, and hi-tech industry, in addition to infrastructure development. There is some skepticism in China's western region about the newly proposed western development: As some point out, what is needed is a change in policies, to then be followed by investment.[73]

One serious problem for China's west and its intended economic development is continued unrest among the ethnic minority groups located in the region. (See sections on discussion about Muslim unrest and the Tibetan problem in this chapter.)

LOCAL GOVERNMENTS IN CHINA

The County Government[74]

Below the province is the administrative unit called the county, or *xien*. There are approximately 2,000 counties in China; each has a population of about half a million or less. The people's government is elected by the people's congress and supervised by the standing committee at the county level, which administers a host of local government activities. First, the county government exercises control over the personnel assignments for the entire county. In this manner the party manages to keep an eye on all the cadres working for the various units of county government. It is at the county seat that a people's court hears and handles serious cases of deviance. It is at the county level that we find the procuratorate operating when serious crimes are to be prosecuted. It is also at the county level that the public security bureau maintains a station for the surveillance of the county populace and for arresting criminals and counterrevolutionaries. Militia activities and relations with the regular PLA are handled at the county level.

The Township as a Local Government Unit[75]

The lowest level of government used to be the commune. In China there were about 75,000 communes, varying in number of households and the total farm acreage under production. Each commune was organized into production brigades and teams.

A typical production team had from 100 to 200 members and was subdivided into work groups. The work groups were led by team cadres, who were seldom members of the party. The team members elected a committee to conduct the team's affairs. Frequently, group leaders were placed on the nomination slate and elected to the committee. We should note that the slate of candidates for the committee election must be approved by the party cell. The team served as the basic accounting unit on the commune. Team committee members were assigned specific jobs, such as treasurer, accountant, work-points recorder, or security officer. The most important were the accountant and work-points recorder, who must keep detailed books on expenditures and income and on team members' earned work points, respectively. The work points usually ranged from zero to ten, with an able-bodied adult earning between eight and nine points per unit of time worked. The number of work points earned by a team member for a unit of time worked was determined at the beginning of each year by a meeting of all team members. Each member made a claim to this worth. This claim was evaluated by the assembled team members and a decision was reached on the points to be earned for each member for the coming year.

An average production brigade consisted of five or six production teams—over 1,000 people. Each production brigade had an elected people's congress, whose main responsibility was to elect a brigade chief and a revolutionary committee to assist the chief in administering the brigade's daily affairs. Frequently, the brigade chief was also chairperson of the revolutionary committee as well as the party secretary. The revolutionary committee and its staff were responsible for managing economic and financial affairs, including planning, budgeting, record keeping, and accounting. The committee was also in charge of providing social welfare, and medical and educational services. Brigades using agricultural machinery also maintained repair service units. In a number of communes visited by the author, a small-scale research and development unit was attached to the brigade's revolutionary committee.

From 1958 until 1982, the commune officially served two functions: It was the grassroots government below the county level, and the collective economic management unit. This combination of government administrative and economic management functions created a number of problems.[76] Many of the problems stemmed from the overconcentration of decision-making powers in the hands of a few commune leaders. Particularly troublesome was the interference of the commune, in its role as governmental administrator, in the activities of the production teams. Zhao Ziyang's experiments with local government in three counties in Sichuan province indicated that the separation of government administration from economic management in communes improved both economic activity and "the people's democratic life."[77] Specifically, the new local structure for the rural areas permitted a greater degree of independent management of the rural economy. Formerly, the cadres at the commune centers held too many positions; it was practically impossible for them to devote much of their limited energy to economic activities. Too often these commune cadres had to spend most of their time supervising governmental affairs—such as planning, finances, and taxation for the communes—with insufficient time left to supervise production. In addition, there was a pressing need for a separate and more effective local government organization to discharge responsibilities in the areas of dispute mediation, public security maintenance, tax collection, and welfare distribution in rural areas.

The 1982 constitution reestablished the township government that existed before 1958 as the local grassroots government and limited the commune system to the status of an economic management unit. Under the new local government arrangement, the township people's congress elects the township people's government. Administration of law, education, public health, and family planning are the exclusive responsibilities of the township people's government.

With the introduction of the rural responsibility system as the first of a series of economic reforms, (see Chapter 11) the commune system was more or less dismantled. In 1983 it was replaced by the "Township-Collective-Household System" with five distinct separate entities:[78] (1) local government; (2) the party committee; (3) state owned and managed units; (4) collective economic organizations (such as brigades, teams, supply and marketing); and (5) households (both contract and specialized). The township is also responsible for military affairs, public security, and statistics-gathering.

As of 1990 there were a total of 18 million township enterprises employing about 95 million workers who constituted 24 percent of the total agricultural labor force and earned $8 billion in foreign currency.

Village Committees[79]

Article 111 of the 1982 constitution also provided a grassroots level of local self-government below the township structure in rural areas. While this unit, the village committee, initially was not recognized formally as a local government unit, it undertook a number of administrative tasks in areas such as water conservation, village welfare programs, mediation of civil disputes, public order, and rules governing villagers' conduct. At the end of 1986, there were 948,600 village committees in rural areas. From 1986 to 1987, the NPC's Standing Committee debated questions concerning the relation between the village committee and township government, as well as administrative expenses incurred by the village committees.[80] The NPC's aim was to prepare a draft organic law that would stipulate the specific responsibilities of the village committees and their relationship with the township local government. Two major issues arose: the role of the village committee to serve as "a bridge" between the villagers and local township authorities, and the question of the direct election of committee members by the villagers even though village committees were not a governmental organ but a mass organization.[81] The Fifth Plenum of the Sixth NPC, held in April 1987, did not take up the draft law on village committees, but postponed it for further study and investigation by the Standing Committee. Peng Zhen, chairman of the Standing Committee, explained that the proposed draft law on village committees was "a big issue" because it would allow peasants to "exercise autonomy over their own affairs." Peng believed that the proposed law could provide an opportunity for the 800 million peasants to learn and "practice democracy" through election of village committees.[82]

The Standing Committee of the Sixth NPC eventually approved in November 1987 the Village Committee Law for some 900,000 rural villages in China. Responsibilities of the village committees are now defined as follows: road and bridge repairs; nurseries and homes for the aged; cultural and recreational activities; public order and security; and serving as a channel between the government and the masses. Any villager over age 18 can participate in village conferences to discuss and decide village affairs. Village committees are responsible to the village conference, the highest power in the village.

It must be noted that the organic law pertaining to village committees was approved by the NPC's Standing Committee on a trial basis and was opposed by a number of its members as "premature."[83]

Direct Popular Elections in the Villages: Grassroots Democracy

The move toward popular democracy at the village level proceeded in rural China with considerable caution as evidenced by the institution of demonstration pilot projects in some 1,093 selected villages by the Ministry of Civil Affairs for the 1988–90 period. In these chosen villages the Ministry of Civil Affairs conducted special classes or workshops on the rudiments of how to manage village committee elections. After a nationwide conference on direct democracy and political work demonstration, villages were selected by the counties as models.[84] Kevin O'Brien pointed out that by mid-1992, 75 percent of China's 900,000 rural villages had held popular elections.[85] The design for introducing the democratic experiment was the "demonstration villages," which had been selected in various counties in many provinces by the Minister of Civil Affairs.[86] The "demonstration villages" experimented with the official guidelines, adopted and made public in April 1994 by the Ministry of Civil Affairs, on introducing (1) "direct-semi-competitive elections," whereby there must be more candidates than positions; (2) establishment of "village representative assemblies" to oversee the elected village committees,[87] and (3) drafting and enactment of village charters and codes of conduct for cadres and villagers by the representative village assemblies.

China's village elections have attracted considerable attention and interest from the outside world, as witnessed by the advice and financial aid extended to China by the Asia Foundation, Ford Foundation, the International Republican Institute, and the United Nations Development Program, as well as field work conducted by Western scholars in recent years.

At the September (1997) Fifteenth Party Congress, Jiang Zemin, the party chief, declared the expansion of direct elections from the village to the township level—(a township is generally said to have a population up to 100,000): "We shall extend the scope of democracy at the grassroots level;" and "The grassroots organs of power and self-governing mass organizations in both urban and rural areas should establish a sound system of democratic elections."[88]

How do we assess the new "village self-government," or "democracy Chinese style?" One could make a tentative assessment that direct village elections may be the beginning of a grassroots democracy leading to eventual direct elections in China at all political levels, as declared by Jiang Zemin at the Fifteenth Party Congress, which concluded on September 19, 1997. One critic points out that the village committee is not a "primary level of political power," but merely a rural reform measure.[89] Direct democratic elections at the village level would constitute a threat to the party's control over the primary or grassroots level political organizations.[90] On the other hand, in the view of Daniel Kelliher, there is the argument that village level elections "have nothing to do with the rights of the people to govern their own affairs."[91] Village elections represent a way by which the center is assured of its control through "key leaders," or "to reverse the crisis in authority that has eroded the state's rural presence."[92] Kelliher also argues that it is through village elections that the state can make villagers do "what the state wants."[93] The village election process has not produced the state's desire for village leadership to be in the hands of "younger, dynamic, educated cadres."[94] While it is true that in some cases "the electoral process is by-passed, faked, rigged, or just plain misunderstood" in the villages, direct popular village elections may offer some hope for future grassroots democracy to germinate in China. In the meantime, direct village election of village leaders has been a good method for releasing the rural farmers' anger over the Cultural Revolution's abuses and mistakes.[95] Direct popular elections, or democracy for China, according to Deng Xiaoping's schedule set in 1987, may not become a reality until fifty years hence. Or, as pointed out by Tyrene White, the enactment of the Organic Law of Village Committees in 1987 was to reduce the continued cadre-peasant tensions exacerbated by coercive policy implementation in the countryside.[96]

Recently, in 1999–2000, a significant new procedure has been introduced in the direct village-level election system: the introduction of a primary election in which villagers can write the names of their favored candidates on a blank ballot: Those receiving the most votes in the primary election would become the candidates for the final election. The new primary nomination procedural change at the village level has compelled local party members to meet after the primary nomination to select the party's village-level committee chief in accordance with the popular will, thus ensuring the party's control and social stability at the village level.[97] However, as argued by one observer from the Georgia-based Carter Center, if the individual voter nomination system were to be extended to the next tier, at the county level, it would produce a situation whereby the votes would be spread so thin as to make the entire election meaningless.[98]

In Western democracies the political parties serve a "filtering role" by nominating their chosen candidates for election. As pointed out by several Western observers at one village election, this is not something that the Chinese Communist Party would tolerate, for it still adheres to its party monopoly.[99] One study shows that the CCP are most likely concerned about voters at the village-level elections ousting incumbent party members. In one northeastern province of Jilin, about 40 percent of the newly elected village officials were not members of the party.[100] Thus, extending village popular elections, now involving more than 800,000 villages, to the township and county or higher levels would be a significant step toward grassroots democracy in China but might be damaging to the party's control, if not prestige.

Local Government in the Urban Areas

There are two types of municipalities in China. One type includes the important urban centers—Beijing, Shanghai, and Tianjin—administered directly by the central government. The other type includes subdivisions of the provincial governments.

The municipal government of both types of cities—for example Beijing and Guangzhou—is administered by a municipal people's government, elected by the municipal people's congress. As a municipal government, the people's government for the city must supervise a large number of functional departments or bureaus dealing with law and order, finance, trade, economic enterprises, and industries located within the city limits. We also find in these cities subdivisions of state organs, such as the people's court, the procuratorate, and the public security bureau for social control and law and order. Because of the size of some of the larger municipalities, the administration of the municipal government is subdivided into districts. The municipality of Beijing, with a total population of more than seven million, is divided into ten districts as administrative subunits. Each district has a district people's congress, which elects a district people's government as the executive organ for district affairs.

Within each district of a city are numerous neighborhood committees, which are—in the words of the 1982 constitution—"mass organizations of self-management at the grassroots level" (Article 111, Appendix A). More than 1,794 neighborhood committees in Beijing city serve as arms of district government within the city. Each neighborhood committee has a staff of trained cadres whose work is to mobilize and provide political education for the residents in the area. Generally, a neighborhood committee has 2,500 to 3,000 residents.

The neighborhood committees perform a variety of functions, including organizing workers, teachers, and students in the neighborhood for political study and work; organizing and managing small factories in the neighborhood; providing social welfare services, such as nurseries and dining halls, to supplement those provided by the cities; and administering health, educational, and cultural programs. They also perform surveillance activities in cooperation with the public security units in the area.[101]

Neighborhood committees are the self-governing units organized and staffed voluntarily by the residents. A typical neighborhood committee has about twenty families, or approximately one hundred persons. It is generally headed by an elderly or retired woman, and it can deal with any matter of concern to the residents. It is common in the cities to find that a neighborhood committee is linked to a city hospital for family planning or birth control: The neighborhood committee disseminates information about the need for family planning. Meetings of all residents decide how to allocate the allowable births and who may have them.

Since 1954 there have been nearly 100,000 neighborhood committees established in China's urban areas, thus placing a total of more than 200 million urban residents under control and surveillance. The January 1990 Organic Law of the Urban Neighborhood Committees formally entrusted the following tasks to them: publicize state law and policy; protect residents' legal rights and interests; administer public welfare; mediate civil disputes; maintain social order and security; and serve as the "transmission belt" by channeling citizens' opinions and needs to the government.

As evident in my spring 1999 visit to Beijing's *hutong* (street-alley residential complex), economic reform initiated in 1987-88 and the decline of revolutionary fervor have not caused the disappearance of neighborhood committees. Some of the basic functions, such as keeping watch over everyone who lives in the neighborhood, are still very evident. However, the committees are now managed by younger matrons and their assistants. The neighborhood committees have assumed some of the social services, such as health clinic help and the care for elderly retired workers, that were once the responsibility of the work units. As rural migrants pour into the city, it is these neighborhood committees which report to the city authorities about their presence on the streets. Committee heads are now elected by the neighborhood, residents but must still be approved by the party. Of course, with many new apartment buildings all over Beijing City, many prosperous residents have no need for the newly transformed neighborhood committees. In the neighborhood residential area that I visited in the spring of 1999 I was told that the residents are professionals or self-employed, and they prefer consultation with the trained apartment complex managerial staff for solving problems. In less affluent residential areas the neighborhood committees render assistance to the elderly in health care or assist in finding employment for those who need it. Often the committees still provide crime patrols or watch for thefts to homes. In Beijing some of the old residential areas, particularly the *hutong* or alleyways, are being torn down to make way for new apartment buildings.

Rural Migrants.   Like many other cities in China, Beijing alone has more than 3 million migrants who came from poor rural areas seeking employment and a new life. These migrants (total number for Chinese cities may reach as high as 65–100 million) are the "floating population," or *liunang*. These rural migrants often contribute to the rising rate of crime and crowded environment on the city streets.

It has been estimated that rural migrants accounted for over 70 percent of all crimes in Bejing[102] Simply because they are migrants from the countryside or the "floating population," these rural migrants are often discriminated against in terms of employment or housing or any other social services usually made available to residents. They often lack two important documents necessary for residents in cities: One is the resident identification card issued by the local public security bureau or the police, and the other is the city household registration identity, known as *baomu* or the individual household registration card in the residential population file recorded by the city. As a family household member, an individual resident is registered with the address of his or her household. It is the registered city residents who can receive government subsidies such as grain or welfare aid. Because they lack urban resident permits, the migrants must seek piece-work in sweat shops and live in crowded rooms with others.

ETHNIC POLITICS: AUTONOMOUS REGIONS AND NATIONAL MINORITIES

One of the interesting things about China is that it too has a minority problem. Like many of China's policies on major political, economic, and social matters, policies toward ethnic minorities have been subject to the periodic pendulum swings of the past two decades. This section will discuss the development of China's policies on national minorities and the reasons for policy changes, the status of autonomous regions, and minority group representation in party and government.

First, a few essential facts about China's national minorities are in order. There are about 91 million people in China who are considered to be national minorities. The largest of the fifty-six minority groups are the Zhuangs (15.4 million), Hui or Chinese Muslims (8.6 million), Uygur (7.2 million), Yi (6.5 million), Tibetans (4.5 million), Miao (7.3 million), Manchus (9.8 million), Mongols (4.8 million), Bouyei (2.1 million), and Koreans (1.9 million).[103] Although these minority groups—the non-Han people—total only 91 million, or 8 percent of China's population, they inhabit almost 60 percent of China's territory, covering sixteen different provinces. In two autonomous regions, Xizang (Tibet) and Inner Mongolia, the minority people constitute the majority. An extremely important element in understanding China's policies toward minorities is that over 90 percent of China's border areas with neighboring countries are inhabited by these minority people. When we discuss the border dispute between China and the Soviet Union, we are inevitably reminded that the disputed areas are inhabited by the Manchus, Mongolians, Uygurs, Kazakh, and Koreans. China's relations with Laos, Cambodia, and Vietnam bring to mind the minority people of Zhuang, Yi, Miao, and Bouyei in the autonomous region of Guangxi and the provinces of Yunnan and Guizhou. The border dispute between India and China involves the Tibetans living in Chinese territory in Xizang, Sichuan, and Qinghai. Changes in China's minority policies in recent years have been influenced to a large extent by concern for the security of her border areas.[104]

When the Chinese People's Republic was established in October 1949, the regime followed a policy that can best be described as one of gradualism and pluralism. Primarily for the purpose of a united front to consolidate control of the nation immediately after the civil war, minority customs and habits were tolerated in regions inhabited by minorities. Compromises were made to include as political leaders prominent minority elites of feudal origin in the newly formed autonomous areas for the minority nationalities. At the same time, modern transportation and communication networks were constructed to link the autonomous regions with the adjacent centers of political and economic power populated by the Chinese. The nomadic Mongols in pastoral areas were exempt from the application of land reform measures. The concept and practices of class struggle, so prevalent in other parts of China, were purposefully muted when applied to minority regions. However, no serious attempts were made to assimilate the national minorities into the mainstream of the revolutionary movement in other parts of China.

The period of the Great Leap ushered in a rapid change in policies toward the national minorities. From 1956 to 1968, the policy shifted from gradualism and pluralism to one of radical assimilation. For the first time, the Chinese spoken language was introduced in the minority areas. Training of minority cadres was intensified. More important, socialist reforms such as cooperatives and communization were introduced. The campaign against the rightists was also extended in the minority areas, aimed at those who advocated local nationalism. These policies of assimilation resulted in tension and violent clashes in the early 1960s between the Hans (Chinese) and the minority groups, particularly in Xizang and Xinjiang. It was precisely because of these disturbances in the minority areas that the assimilation programs were relaxed in the mid-1960s, prior to the Cultural Revolution. Radicalized communization programs in certain minority areas were disbanded. The slowdown did not last long, however. The Cultural Revolution brought back the radical line of assimilation for minority groups. Many prominent minority leaders in the border areas were subject to purges and vilification by the Red Guards, who were encouraged by the radicals. Ulanhu, of Inner Mongolia; Li Qingchuan, of Xizang; and Wang Enmao, of Xinjiang, were purged by the time the Cultural Revolution ran its full course (1966–76).[105] But the Sino–Soviet border dispute, according to Lucian Pye, made the Chinese realize the necessity of winning over the minority groups for reasons of national security.[106] The policy of assimilation was again modified to provide for diversity. In addition to having minority nationalities learn Chinese, the Chinese cadres were asked to learn the minority languages. Minority customs, dress, music, and dance were encouraged as expressions of ethnic diversity. It was within this policy of pluralism and diversity in the post–Cultural Revolution era that we began to see an increase in the representation of China's minority groups in party and government organs.

The constitutions of 1954, 1978, and 1982 provided identical detailed provisions for self-government in autonomous regions, in marked contrast to the brevity of such provisions in the 1975 constitution. This can be interpreted as a return to the policy of pluralism and gradualism. The people's congresses, as local organs of self-government for the autonomous regions, can make specific regulations in light of the special characteristics of the national minorities in these areas. This concept of diversity and pluralism was not mentioned in the 1975 constitution. In addition, the 1954, 1978, and

1982 constitutions mandated that local organs of self-government in these minority areas employ their own ethnic language in the performance of their duties. This represents a marked departure from past policies of assimilation, which urged the use of the Chinese language, both written and spoken, as the official medium of communication.

There has been increased recognition of minority groups in both the party and the government. Special efforts evidently were made to recruit new party members from the minority regions. We have figures that show that from 1964 to 1973, over 140,000 new members from the minority areas were admitted into the party.[107] There is no precise breakdown of party membership distribution over the various autonomous regions, but there appears to have been a steady increase in party membership. Three minority leaders (Wei Guoqing, a Zhuang; Seypidin, an Uygur; and Ulanhu, a Mongol) were elected to the presidium of the Eleventh Party Congress, and thirteen minority representatives were elected to the Eleventh Central Committee (seven full and six alternate members). Thirteen national minority leaders representing eight national minority groups were elected to full membership of the Twelfth Central Committee in 1982. Sixteen other minority leaders were elected to alternate membership. National minority leaders have held key government positions in various autonomous regions. For example, the chairpersons of the standing committees of the people's congresses for the autonomous regions of Xinjiang, Xizang (Tibet), Guangxi, and Ningxia were leading cadres of national minorities.[108] At the national level, Ulanhu, a Mongol, was elected to the vice-presidency of the republic in June 1983. Similarly, the Fifth National People's Congress, which promulgated the 1978 constitution, had 11 percent of its deputies drawn from the fifty-five national minority groups. At least four of the minority leaders (Wei Guoqing, Ulanhu, Seypidin, and Ngapo Ngawang-jigme) were elected as vice-chairpersons of the congress. Thus, after more than two decades of policy vacillation in search of an appropriate formula for dealing with the minority groups in the border areas, China seems to have found a solution that stresses the preservation of the cultural diversity of the 91 million national minority peoples and at the same time opens up channels for minority participation in decision making at the highest levels in the Chinese political process.

Muslim Unrest. Muslim revolt in the border area of Xinjiang resurfaced in early April 1990. The armed revolt, in the form of jihad or "holy war," organized by the Islamic Party of East Turkistan, occurred near the city of Kashgar on the ancient Silk Road. Suppression of the revolt by the Chinese army involved more than twenty-two deaths. The revolt was triggered by the issuance of new identity cards to Kirghiz and Uighurs and restrictions on building a mosque. The recent rebellion in Xinjiang is only one of the continued challenges by the Muslim population to Chinese rule.

Despite the increase in political participation and representation by national minorities in the party and government, instituted in the 1990s, tensions and conflict still exist in Tibet and the Xinjiang autonomous regions, containing East Turkistan populated by Uighurs, where Chinese Muslims constitute the majority. Using Xinjiang as an example, we find that problems for Xinjiang, which shares its border with the former Soviet Union, are mainly in four areas. First, the region has been under the strong influence of the Cultural Revolution radicals. There has been some foot-dragging by the local authorities in implementing the new party line and economic reforms launched by Deng Xiaoping and his pragmatic reformers. Several top Chinese leaders, including Deng, made inspection trips to the region in 1981. These led to the reappointment of Wang Enmao, a twenty-year party overlord for the region before the Cultural Revolution, as the party's first secretary. Wang's return to the troubled region was contrived to reestablish political stability and bolster China's defense measures designed to cope with the Russian military might across the border.

Second, there has evidently been a strong desire on the part of the ethnic groups, which constitute the vast majority of the region's population of 12 million, to be free to manage their own affairs. There are more than 7 million Muslim Uighurs, Kazakhs, Kirghiz, Uzbeks, and Tajiks compared with only 4 million Chinese in the region. At issue is the right of these central Asian Muslims to practice their religion without interference. These ethnic groups want to establish their own communities in accordance with Islamic code and beliefs under the religious leadership of the imam, who is also a political leader. Chinese efforts to integrate the Muslim groups have failed in the past, and the policy of assimilation has generated ill feelings toward the party authorities and Chinese "chauvinism." The Muslim communities have opposed the use of Latin script, introduced by the Chinese authorities in the late 1950s for writing their Uighur and Kazakh languages, instead of Arabic script. It was not until 1981 that the Latin script was officially replaced by Arabic. There have also been race and/or religious riots against the Chinese authorities. In 1962 there was a mass exodus of Kazakhs from the Ili district in Xinjiang to the then Soviet Union across the border. The Chinese have since prevented such crossings by tightly sealing the border. The presence of large contingents of Chinese soldiers tends to increase the tension in Xinjiang.

Third, the unrest of urbanized educated Chinese youth "sent down" to remote Xinjiang during the Cultural Revolution decade had been a thorn in the side of the Chinese authorities. At one time there were as many as one million Chinese youth sent from urban areas to work on state farms and reclamation projects in the region. Among the reasons for sending the city-bred youth to Xinjiang may have been a hidden policy of populating the remote region with more Chinese. Many youth settled down in Xinjiang, married local girls, and obtained responsible jobs. But a sizable portion of them were unhappy and wanted to be returned to their cities. In desperation they staged riots and demonstrations to bring attention to their plight. In recent years there has been a definite and steady migration of Han Chinese into Xinjiang, estimated at the rate of a quarter of a million per year; thus, the Han Chinese today constitute 40 percent of the region's population.[109]

There have been many reports of human rights violations against the Uighurs. There have been hundreds of executions and thousands of Uighurs detained between 1997 and 1999.[110] The dissidents from Xinjiang have been trying to form a united movement to oppose the Chinese by banding together approximately seven million Uighurs, one million Kazakhs, and about another million Kirghiz and Tungan Muslims—the latter ethnic groups are mostly nomads.

The official Chinese position has been that ethnic minorities have the right to regional autonomy in those so-called autonomous areas where organs of self-government are established for the exercise of autonomy and "for the people of ethnic minorities to become masters and manage the internal affairs of their own regions."[111] This is presumably the state policy under the 1982 state constitution. However, in a CIA-funded study by the University of Hawaii it has been suggested that conditions in the Xinjiang region might indicate a potential for "significant violence in the next three years."[112] It is highly questionable whether there is real autonomy in troubled Xinjiang, as the regional province contains large reserves (as much as a billion tons) of crude oil and mineral deposits of coal, copper, and gold. It is also the site of China's nuclear testing facilities, not to mention the location of *laogai*, the prison-labor camp system for dissidents.

TIBET: A CASE STUDY

Tibet—Xizang in Chinese—is known as the "Roof of the World." It includes Mount Everest at 29,028 feet and it has an average elevation of 16,000 feet. Lying in the southwest part of China, it is dominated by the awesome Himalayas, which ring the southern part of the Tibetan plateau. The 4.5 million Tibetans who inhabit the region are devoted to Lamaism, a branch of Mahayana Buddhism. The lamas are the monks, "teachers or masters," who once controlled some 1,300 monasteries. Traditionally the monasteries serve as the main source of political, economic, and spiritual power. The Dalai Lama (meaning the "Ocean of Wisdom") is the temporal and spiritual leader of Lamaism in Tibet. The present Dalai Lama, who has been in exile in India since 1959, is the fourteenth reincarnation of the founder of the "Yellow-Head" sect, who was proclaimed the first Dalai Lama by the Mongols in 1570–1580. The Dalai Lama is more than the Tibetans' spiritual leader, for in their traditional theocracy he is the ruler of the land and of the people for all of Tibet.

Tibet was an independent kingdom by the seventh century. But by the time of the Yuan Dynasty (1279–1368) under the Mongol conquest, Tibet was controlled nominally by Mongol rulers such as Kublai Khan, who had become a convert to Lamaism. This system of nominal control by China over Tibet, known as *suzerainty*—sovereignty in internal affairs, but control over external affairs by a stronger outside power—continued during the Qing Dynasty (1644–1911) under the Manchus.

With the eruption of the 1911 revolution, which brought down the Manchu empire, Tibet declared its independence. However, in 1886, the British in India had established trade relations with Tibet by consent of Chinese officials. In fact, the lamas had protested the signing of subsequent British trade treaties negotiated by the Chinese. Then through the influence of a converted Russian lama who came to Lhasa in 1880, Russia became interested in Tibet. Because of Russian influence on the Dalai Lama at that time, Tibet was about to obtain czarist Russia's pledge of aid to eliminate the British influence, in view of China's repeated humiliation at the hands of the European powers (see Chapter 1).

With the specific objective of bringing Tibet under exclusive British control, in 1903–1904 the British overlord in India decided to send military expeditions to Tibet from next-door Sikkim, then a British protectorate. The Tibetans mounted military opposition to the British expeditions. The British, with Chinese consent, in September 1904 were able to force Tibet to sign a treaty granting territorial and trade concessions, in addition to a Tibetan pledge to keep all other foreign powers out of Tibet.

In 1907 a treaty was concluded between the British and the Russians that recognized Chinese suzerainty over Tibet and internal territorial and administrative integrity for Tibet. In 1908 the Dalai Lama was received by the Chinese emperor, who then granted his holiness the authority to resume internal autonomous administration of Tibet. But in 1909 Chinese troops arrived to quell a rebellion by insurgent lamas; this military action forced the Dalai Lama to flee to China. In an attempt to make Tibet a buffer zone between China and India, in 1913 the British convened the Simla Conference in India to include three powers: China, Tibet, and Great Britain. The conference divided Tibet into an inner portion comprising the southwestern provinces of China, and an outer portion that was to be fully autonomous. The Chinese refused to ratify the convention.

In 1950, the Chinese communist government sent its PLA troops to Tibet for the purpose of reclaiming Tibet as an integral part of China and ending Tibet's declaration of independence, which dated back to 1911. The Tibetans initially resisted but finally capitulated, signing an agreement on May 23, 1951, under which Tibet was to have nominal autonomy but China was to exercise full control as a sovereign power. Tibet was to be governed internally by a committee headed by the Dalai Lama. This 1951 agreement raised the international legal status of Tibet. Despite the settlement, there were widespread uprisings against the Chinese garrisons, particularly by the militant Khamba tribe. In March 1959 the Chinese authorities in Tibet summoned the Dalai Lama to military garrison command headquarters in Lhasa and requested that he use his temporal power to suppress the uprisings. This precipitated uprisings all over Lhasa, but the Chinese were able to restore order in a short time by brutally crushing the rebel forces. Meanwhile secret plans were made for the fourteenth Dalai Lama to escape from Chinese oppression. On March 31, 1959 the Dalai Lama led a detachment of follow- ers in escaping from Tibet into India.[113] In Dharmsla, a hill station in North India, the Dalai Lama and his 10,000 followers established the Tibetan exile government, which has been sustained for more than thirty years. The question of Tibet was placed on the 1960 U.N. General Assembly agenda for discussion. The United Nation addressed only the human rights issue, expressing its concern in a resolution, but recognized the prevailing international stance that the Chinese maintained sovereignty over Tibet.

In recent years a great amount of world attention has been focused on Tibet as one of China's most troubled autonomous regions.[114] In 1980 Hu Yaobang, the party chief, and Wan Li, a member of the party's Central Secretariat, made an inspection tour of Tibet. Then, in the summer of 1982, the Chinese announced that 11,000 Chinese (Han) cadres would be withdrawn gradually from Tibet to permit the native Tibetans to take over and manage their own affairs. The immediate objective of this new self-government policy for Tibet was to replace more than two-thirds of Tibet's governmental functionaries with native Tibetans by 1983.[115] Ngapo Ngawang-jigme, chairman of the Tibetan Autonomous Regional Government, indicated that more than 12,000 Tibetans were being trained to take over the administration of Tibetan affairs from the Chinese cadres.[116] As of 1981 there were 29,400 Tibetan cadres in the autonomous regional government, constituting 54 percent of the total.[117] Other changes for Tibet included the abrogation of certain regulations imposed on the region that were deemed unsuitable to Tibetan conditions. In addition, farm and animal products were to be exempt from taxation for two years. More state funds were to be allocated for Tibet to improve the economy and living conditions in the region.[118]

The policy changes in Tibet must be viewed in the context of China's continu- ing attempt to persuade the Dalai Lama to return to Lhasa after more than thirty years of exile in India.[119] Since his escape to India, the Dalai Lama has been joined by over 100,000 Tibetan refugees who refused to live under Chinese rule. The Dalai Lama's exile and his continuing criticism of Chinese misrule in Tibet have been an embar- rassment for Beijing. Since 1978 the Chinese official position has been to relax its control over Tibet with the hope that the Dalai Lama might be persuaded to return. However, his holiness has shrewdly used the Chinese desire to seek reconciliation, manipulating it as a bargaining chip to obtain concessions for his people. He has remained abroad to speak out against Chinese rule in Tibet and has delivered lectures in numerous countries to arouse world opinion in favor of Tibetan causes.[120] In 1982 a three-member delegation was dispatched by the Dalai Lama to Beijing, after the 1980 visit by the Dalai Lama's sister, to negotiate possible terms of reconciliation with China's new leaders. So far no tangible progress has been made in these negotiations. The Dalai Lama was reported to have proposed (1) that Tibet should not be treated as an autonomous region but should be given a special status with complete autonomy; and

(2) that a larger Tibet should be created to include Tibetans now living in southeast China.[121] The Chinese did not accept these proposals, and the impasse continued. In the meantime, the Chinese have made further concessions by allowing pilgrimages to the lamaseries (monasteries) and the use of the Tibetan language in schools. In 1983, the Dalai Lama told Western reporters that he would like to pay a visit to Tibet by 1985.[122]

In 1985 the Chinese banned a visit to Tibet by a delegation organized by the exiled Dalai Lama. The Chinese maintain the policy that they would welcome the Dalai Lama's return to Tibet only if he abandons the idea of an "independent Tibet" and accepts Tibet as an integral part of China.[123] In his 1987 visit to the United States, the Dalai Lama not only repeated his rejection of the Chinese offer to return to Tibet but also proposed a five-point peace plan for a future Tibet[124]: (1) demilitarize Tibet as a zone of "peace and nonviolence"; (2) curb further immigration of Chinese into Tibet; (3) initiate respect for human rights of Tibetans; (4) cease nuclear weapons production in eastern Tibet; and (5) conduct negotiations with the Chinese on the future status of Tibet.

The Dalai Lama's appeal to the United States for support for Tibetan independence provided the impetus for a protest rally in late September 1987 in Lhasa, Tibet's capital, staged and led by some two dozen Tibetan monks.[125] On October 1, more than 2,000 Tibetans demonstrated against Chinese rule by stoning police vehicles.[126] Chinese authorities in Tibet responded by arresting the monks who led the protest and by calling in reinforcements to quell the riot that resulted in six people killed and a dozen officers of the People's Armed Police injured.[127] For several days, Tibetan riots continued and the Chinese arrested more than sixty Tibetan protesters.[128] By then a curfew was declared for the capital city of Lhasa and foreigners were kept from entering Tibet.

The Chinese blamed the Dalai Lama for inciting the riots in Tibet, pointing out that he had advocated an "independent Tibet" during his ten-day tour of the United States.[129] The Chinese also opposed the Dalai Lama's "political activities" in other countries and condemned his repeated call for a separate Tibet as "detrimental" to achieving unity among national minority groups in China.[130] However, the riots in Lhasa clearly showed Tibetan dissatisfaction with Chinese rule in Tibet.

In an attempt to make up for neglecting Tibet's economic development, the Chinese launched in 1985 a package of forty-three development projects costing about $140 million. These projects, designed to woo support and allegiance from rebellious Tibetans, included tax exemptions for Tibetans for fifteen years, the right to own private farm land, and a thirty-year lease on grazing land and livestock.[131] A number of these projects were for the development of infrastructure (sewer systems, transportation facilities, and two tourist hotels) for Lhasa. The Chinese also claimed that the percentage of Tibetan cadres to Chinese (Han) cadres had been significantly increased, to 70 percent Tibetans and 30 percent Chinese.[132] The fact remains, however, that no Tibetan had been appointed as the party's first secretary for the autonomous region. Worse still, a 1985 report by an economic research team from Beijing painted a rather gloomy picture of an almost bankrupt Tibetan economy.[133] The Tibetan Development Fund, a nongovernmental and nonprofit organization, was formed in July 1990 in Beijing to raise money from private and public sources to provide for more schools, homes for the aged, orphanages, and repairs of temples and monasteries.[134]

On March 8, 1989, after three days of rioting in Lhasa, the Chinese authorities imposed martial law on Tibet. The anti-Chinese riot resulted in at least thirty dead and marked the fourth time since 1987 that the 100,000 Chinese soldiers stationed in Tibet had crushed anti-Chinese uprisings. Under martial law Chinese soldiers raided lamaseries in and around the capital city of Lhasa and arrested monks suspected of being loyal to the Dalai Lama. Most monasteries in Lhasa were empty as monks fled to the countryside to hide.

The Dalai Lama has campaigned vigorously against the Chinese suppression. His worldwide influence increased considerably when the Nobel Peace Prize Committee named him the recipient of its 1989 award. In Oslo, in December 1989, as he had done in Strasbourg, France, before the Council of Europe on June 15, 1988, the Dalai Lama proposed that Tibet be recognized as an independent country, thus becoming a "self-governing democratic political entity." He argued that independence for Tibet must be the basis for negotiation with the Chinese. The latter, of course, rejected the idea of an independent Tibet by unequivocally declaring that "China's sovereignty over Tibet is undeniable" and that "independence, semi-independence in a disguised form, is unacceptable."[135]

As a gesture intended both to mitigate criticism of human rights violations and to improve China's tarnished international image, China announced, effective May 1, 1990, the end of martial law in Lhasa. In lifting martial law for Tibet, Chinese premier Li Peng declared that the capital city had become stable and order had returned to normal.[136] The Dalai Lama viewed the lifting of martial law as "a public relations exercise" by the Chinese, since suppression and intimidation against the Tibetans continued unabated. In short, Tibetan protests and demonstrations are also indicative of a failed ethnic policy toward that troubled region.

As discussed in the prior section, China's policy toward its national minorities has been to a large extent dictated by the strategic considerations vis-à-vis its relations with neighboring countries. China's policy toward Tibet must be viewed in the context of its strategic importance in China's relations with the former Soviet Union and India.[137] (In 1962 China and India engaged in an armed conflict along the southern sections of their 700-mile-long joint border in the Himalayas. A cease-fire was accepted by both sides after the armed clash, but no progress has been made to negotiate the demarcation of their boundaries in almost inaccessible mountain ranges, even though the two neighboring nations have met seven times since 1981.)

While in 1991–92 there were continued Tibetan protests in Lhasa, the capital of Tibet, the issue of human rights violations against Tibetans by the Chinese has won significant international attention. First, the Tibetan human rights issue became a part of the conditions attached to the United States' extension of the most-favored-nation trade agreement to China. The U.S. Congress had inserted tough language into the trade extension bill to the effect that if the Chinese did not stop migration of Han Chinese into Tibet within a year, China's free trade status would be terminated. Asia Watch, the human rights monitoring group, reported the continued deterioration of human rights conditions in Tibet. To the chagrin of the Beijing government, President Clinton received the Dalai Lama in the White House in the spring of 1993. This was a high point in the Dalai Lama's continuing campaign abroad to call attention to the plight of the Tibetans under Chinese rule. However, China won a victory in March 1992 when the U.N. Human Rights Commission in Geneva supported a motion, sponsored by European nations, to end debate on condemning China's human rights abuses in Tibet. The United States opposed the resolution on the grounds that the UN must uphold the human rights of all citizens under Beijing's control, not just Tibetans. The U.S. effort toward that end had failed to obtain majority support in the UN Human Rights Commission on as many as six occasions, the last of which occurred on April 23, 1996.

For over a decade there has been a dialogue and negotiation process going on between Beijing and the Dalai Lama in exile, as discussed earlier.[138] The Dalai Lama is said to be increasingly conciliatory and willing to compromise with the Chinese, as evidenced by his Strasbourg speech in 1988 recognizing China's security interest and sovereignty. The Chinese have shown no willingness to compromise on the issue of Tibetan independence, but they are under increasing pressure from abroad to resolve the Tibetan issue by at least granting Tibet a higher degree of autonomy. In July 1993 the Dalai Lama sent his first official delegation to Beijing in about ten years, led by his older brother, Gyalo Thondup, for talks with Chinese officials. These talks were probably designed to build mutual trust and confidence without getting into the contentious issue of Tibetan independence.

The Dalai Lama pointed out in his visit to the United States—he met with President Clinton in the White House, but not in the Oval Office—that he sought only self-rule for the Tibetans and that China would then have the power in foreign affairs and defense of Tibet.[139] While China reacted rather mildly to the Dalai Lama's visit to Washington, it protested the Dalai Lama's plan to set up a Tibetan office in Taiwan during the latter's visit in June 1997. Beijing pointed out that the plan confirmed its suspicions of a strategy for a separate, independent Tibet.[140] Taiwan has abandoned its long-held position that Nationalist China had sovereignty over Tibet but had never exercised effective control. Taiwan's legislature gestured to please Tibet by abolishing the Tibetan-Mongolian Affairs Commission which had been established by the Nationalists in the 1930s as a political vehicle through which Tibet and Mongolia were treated as Chinese territories with special status.

The Geneva-based International Commission of Jurists called on China in December 1997 to permit a UN-sponsored referendum in Tibet to decide whether Tibet is to remain under Chinese control. The call was rejected by the Chinese government, which has maintained that Tibet is part of China.

The Dalai Lama made it pointedly clear at his news conference in Taiwan that he only wanted China to apply Deng Xiaoping's famous "one country, two systems" to Tibet as well as to Hong Kong.[141] Before the Dalai Lama's visit to Taiwan in April 1997, Beijing had launched a campaign by publishing a series of four articles aimed at foreign consumption in the *Beijing Review* declaring that Tibet "has never been an independent state."[142] At any rate, Beijing will continue not to engage the Dalai Lama while the latter will certainly continue to influence world public opinion with his position of securing "religious freedom" for his people and recognition that Tibet be treated with special consideration from a cultural perspective.[143]

But time may not be on the side of the Dalai Lama, as he is over 60 years of age. Beijing can afford to wait, and if the current Dalai Lama passes away, China can, as it has done so historically, manipulate the reincarnation process so that the incoming Dalai Lama would be a boy born on Chinese soil. The Panchen Lama, the second highest in rank next to the Dalai Lama, has the exclusive religious power to recognize officially the reincarnation process of the Dalai Lama. The boy Panchen Lama, born as Gyaincain Norbu, had been chosen as the one recognized and blessed by Beijing when the boy's predecessor, a long-time supporter of Beijing, passed away several years ago. In the future China would most likely have on its side the support of both the current young Panchen Lama and the future reincarnated Dalai Lama.[144]

Lhasa, the capital of Tibet, has been undergoing rapid changes.[145] Modern hotels, such as Holiday Inn, have been built in Lhasa to accommodate the 70,000 tourists who visited Tibet in 1996. The Han Chinese are flocking to Lhasa to set up businesses, as Tibet enjoys preferential tax policies. There is also a building boom in the capital city. The beneficiaries of the economic boom in Tibet are the Han Chinese immigrants.[146]

As a final comment on Tibet, it is interesting to note that while visiting America in the fall of 1997 President Jiang Zemin remarked in response to questions from Harvard's academic audience that the 1959 Chinese military action in Tibet "liberated" Tibetan people from "serfdom." Evidently, Jiang Zemin, who consolidated his power at the Fifteenth Party Congress, seemed to justify the Chinese brutal action in Tibet, not as an act of suppression but rather of emancipation. Jiang Zemin's view clearly illustrates a fundamental problem of perception that has existed for some time in China's approach to Tibet. There is simply no way for China to defend its action in Tibet in terms of human rights violation. China will have to face the reality that the Tibetan issue will have to be resolved if China is to be a player in international politics and economic development. One way of resolving the Tibetan issue is to engage in a dialogue with the Dalai Lama, who has made it clear in recent years that he does not advocate independence for Tibet but wants only "genuine self-rule in the fields of education, culture and particularly religion."[147] All international efforts with respect to Tibet should be directed toward that end—the facilitation of a dialogue between the Dalai Lama and China.

CHINA'S ENVIRONMENTAL PROBLEMS

As China accelerates its pace for economic growth, 7.5 percent in the year 2000 from 7.1 percent in 1999, its environmental protection problems are also rising exponentially. Like many other developing nations, China is facing the dilemma of how to provide environmental protection without retarding its economic growth. In the sections to follow we shall discuss briefly the extent or scope of the problem, government actions in terms of laws and regulations enacted, the matter of cost for environmental problems, and the implications for China and the region.

Extent of the Problem.   Environmental pollution in China covers a wide area with conditions deteriorating at an alarming rate. All of China's major seven rivers have developed serious pollution problems caused by waste water discharge by industrial enterprises, humans, and animals. The discharge of sulfur dioxide by industries and households has been on the increase for years and remains high. The discharge of solid waste not only takes up land space but also pollutes underground water sources. In 1998 China produced a total of 800 million tons of industrial solid waste.[148] Every visitor to China's urban areas has noticed and felt the effects of smog caused by the presence of sulfur dioxide and other industrial dust. Acid rain, covering about one-third of China's land area, has been a serious problem. The pressure of pollution exerted on the fragile environment by urbanization, population increase, and the ever-increasing use of automobiles in urban areas has contributed to environmental deterioration all over China.

Most of China's rivers have been contaminated; so has the underground water for most cities.[149] China's water supply is dwindling rapidly—in 1999 some 20 million tons of grain were lost because there was not enough water for irrigation.[150] The Chinese Academy of Social Sciences estimated recently that usage of water in China will rise by 60 percent over the next half-century, and by then, as demand surpasses reserves, China will face a water shortage crisis.[151] There have been extensive problems of soil erosion, increasing desert, and weakened forest and grassland functions,[152] in addition to serious annual flooding conditions by at least two of China's major river systems, the Huanghe

(Yellow) and the Changjiang (Yangstse). By the government's own admission, it is estimated that 367 million square kilometers of land area in China suffer from water shortage and soil erosion, and over 27 percent of China has become desertlike; the proportion is increasing annually.[153]

According to World Bank estimates, in 1998 economic losses caused by air and water pollution reached an annual U.S. $54 billion. This is about 8 percent of China's Gross Domestic Product (GDP) and compares with less than 1 percent for Japan and a fraction of 1 percent for the United States.[154]

Government Action.   The Chinese government has been placing importance on environmental protection in recent years. In 1998 action was taken to reduce the central government bureaucracy by as much as 50 percent (as discussed in Chapter 4). But the State Environmental Protection Administration suffered no such reduction in staff, after having been upgraded to ministerial status as China's chief agency responsible for environmental protection under direct administration of the State Council. Laws and regulations are being drafted by a committee of the NPC. In addition, there is a maze of interministerial and local environmental agencies responsible for administering protection regulations and performing technical and monitoring tasks.[155]

The central government environmental protection organizations and the local-level units have been aided financially by international environmental groups such as the Worldwide Fund for Nature (WWF), augmented by domestic independent environmental organizations, such as Friends of Nature, China's Nongovernmental Organizations (NGOs), and the Environmental Defense Fund (EDF). Of course, all NGOs must be approved by the Ministry for Civil Affairs in order to function legally.[156] All the efforts by these organizations on behalf of China's environmental protection must constantly overcome several obstacles in their administration and management, namely interjurisdictional coordination and regional or local economic interests.[157]

Laws Enacted.   A body of laws has been enacted to protect the environment.[158] The earliest one, the 1956 Regulation of the Protection of Mineral Resources, forbids pollution of local waters in developing mineral resources. Also in 1956, the Regulations of Factory Safety were enacted regarding the disposal of dangerous gas, dust, and other hazardous waste material so as not to endanger workers and inhabitants. Then in 1962 the State Council issued a directive for active protection and preservation of wildlife and natural resources. China's 1989 Environmental Protection Law was the first of more comprehensive and coordinated legislation which declared that Article 26 of the 1982 constitution must be implemented. That article declares that

> The state protects and improves the living environment and the ecological environment, and prevents and remedies pollution and other public hazards.

The 1989 law encourages any one individual or unit to report any action that may cause pollution. And in 1997, as a way of reinforcing the 1979 Criminal Procedure Law (revised in 1996), the Chinese parliament enacted its latest legislation regarding prevention and control of noise pollution, mandating that destruction of the environment and resources are criminal offenses. The Criminal Procedure Law had already placed environmental pollution as constituting criminal liability subject to penalty with imprisonment up to seven years. Enactment of some of these regulations by the central government has been influenced to some extent by China's participation in international conferences and signing international protocols, such as the 1972 UN Conference on Environment, the Ministerial Meeting on Environment and Development in 1991, and the 1992 conference on environment held in Brazil.

Finally, even though the annual cost of environmental degradation has been estimated at about 8 to 15 percent of China's GDP, the state spends perhaps as little as 1.5 percent of the GDP for environmental protection and management.[159]

Despite some "bright prospects" in regard to China's environmental protection in terms of the legislation enacted and the increased public and governmental attention to the conditions, there are many problems. First, there is underdevelopment in promoting environmental protection among domestic industries and a lack of plans at the government level.[160] Then there is, as indicated earlier, the relatively low level of funding allocated for the purpose of protecting the deteriorating environment. As pointed out by one study, despite the recent enactment of various environmental protection regulations by the state, these laws are mainly "administrative rather than legal in nature."[161] There are also insufficient clearly stated provisions in these regulations for enforcement of environmental violations before the courts. When a violation is established, the emphasis is on punishment or on severe penalty rather than on "education, persuasion and mediation" to resolve the disputes and problems.[162] The founder of China's legal environmental nongovernmental organization has pointed out that there is a need for public education through a popular magazine about the environmental problems in China that is "scientifically correct" for ordinary people, as well as training school teachers about the dangers of environmental deterioration in China and what can be done to prevent the impending disaster.[163]

THE THREE GORGES DAM: A GIGANTIC RESERVOIR AND AN ENVIRONMENTAL PROBLEM

In the context of flooding of fertile plains by China's major river systems and the deterioration of water resources caused by pollution, we must now discuss briefly the controversial proposal for building the Three Gorges Dam on the upper reaches of the Changjiang (Yangtze) River.

One of the main purposes for building a gigantic dam would be to control flooding and save the lives of people who live on the banks of the Changjiang (Yangtze). Historically, there have been as many as more than 300,000 lives lost to these floods. In the July 1999 flood the high-water mark reached 15 feet in some forty hours and the flood crest rushing downstream reached over the 100-foot level, thus making it the worst flooding in fifty years. The idea of erecting a huge dam to control the floods has been advocated by a number of modern Chinese leaders, including Dr. Sun Yat-sen, founder of the Chinese Republic in 1919, Mao Zedong in the 1950s, and Deng Xiaoping in the 1980s. The current proposal is to build the largest dam in the world, eight times the size of the Aswan Dam. The proposed Three Gorges Dam would be 700 feet high and have a 1.2 mile-long wall with a reservoir or lake 370 miles in length, the size of Lake Superior. Cost for the project has been estimated to be perhaps $72 billion if inflation and interest on loans are included. When and if completed in 2009, it will have twenty-six generators to provide 10 to 15 percent (or 84 billion kilowatt hours) of China's electricity needs. But to complete the huge project some twenty-two counties will have to be submerged under water, along with some significant historical and archaeological sites. As many as 1.2 million residents will have to be relocated elsewhere in several phases. The first phase, completed between 1993 and 1997, involved resettlement of 103,000 people.[164]

Criticisms have been leveled against the Three Gorges Dam project. One such criticism is really environmental: The building up of sediment and silt above the dam would create a huge pollution problem. A known geologist at the University of California at Berkeley has pointed out that

> the sediment deprived waters discharged by the dam would be highly erosive, thus undermining flood control levees downstream.[165]

Thus, silting can threaten some of the basic functions of the dam as the Changjiang carries over 680 million tons of soil, silt, and sand to the sea.[166] Then, industrial and human solid waste, plastic, and petrochemicals would accumulate and flow to the East China Sea, in addition to depriving many cities of drinking water sources and creating sanitation and health problems.

Perhaps the most controversial aspect of the dam project has been the human one: the relocation or resettlement of some 1.2 million people who would have to be uprooted as 13 cities, 140 towns, 1,352 villages and some 115,000 acres of prime agricultural land would have to be submerged with the water level rising to 574 feet between Wuhan in central China and Chongqing, China's wartime capital in the west.[167] The uprooted residents on the banks of the river have complained bitterly about the loss of their homes and their fertile agricultural land. The government has promised only a little over $500 million as compensation for resettlement, but the actual financial need may be over $1 billion.[168] Financial compensation is allocated by the local government, which has been slow in disbursement. There is in fact a shortage of suitable cropland for those farmers to be resettled in; there is also a great deal of criticism about official corruption in the resettlement compensation scheme.[169] Some critics have also pointed out that it would be better to build smaller hydroelectric plants for generating needed power and to control floods along the tributaries of the river at lesser loss.[170] In short, not only the environmental factors and costs but also the human costs, in terms of people's livelihoods and the loss of homes and suffering, have become major factors in opposition to the gigantic dam project.

NOTES

1. Peng Zhen, "Explanations on the Draft of the Revised Constitution of the PRC," *Beijing Review*, 19 (May 10, 1982) 25–26.
2. Feng Wenbin, "Reforming the Political Structure," *Beijing Review*, 4 (January 26, 1981), 18.
3. Hua Guofeng, "Report on the Work of the Government," *Beijing Review*, 4 (January 26, 1981), 23–24. Also see "Amendments to the Constitution," *Beijing Review*, 28 (July 13, 1979), 10.
4. "Amendments to the Constitution," 10.
5. Peng Zhen, "Explanations on Seven Laws," *Beijing Review*, 28 (July 13, 1979), 9.
6. See Dorothy J. Solinger, *Regional Government and Political Integration in Southwest China, 1949–1954: A Case Study* (Berkeley: University of California Press, 1977), p. vii. Also see "Politics in Yunnan Province in the Decade of Disorder: Elite Factional Strategies and Central–Local Relations, 1967–1980," *China Quarterly*, 92 (December 1982), 628–62.

For a recent study of regional development see David S. G. Goodman, *China's Regional Development* (Routledge, N.Y.: Royal Institute of International Affairs, 1989). Also see Joseph W. Esherick and Mary Backus Rankin, eds., *Chinese Local Elites and Patterns of Dominance* (Berkeley: University of California Press, 1989).

7. George Cressey, *Asia's Lands and Peoples* (New York: McGraw-Hill, 1951), pp. 96–165.
8. See the following issues of *People's Daily*: March 13, 1986, p. 1; March 17, 1986, p. 1; and March 24, 1986, pp. 1 and 2. Also see *China News Analysis*, 1311 (June 1, 1986), 1–9.
9. "Decision of the Central Committee of the CCP on Reform of the Economic Structure," *Beijing Review*, 44 (October 29, 1984), xiv. Also see *People's Daily*, October 21, 1984, p. 3.
10. "Decision on Some Questions Relating to Lateral Economic Ties," *People's Daily*, March 24, 1986, pp. 1–2.
11. Ibid.
12. *People's Daily*, April 15, 1986, p. 1.
13. "The Politics of Industrial Reform," in Elizabeth J. Perry and Christine Wong, *The Political Economy of Reform in Post-Mao China*, Harvard Contemporary China Series: 2 (Cambridge, Mass.: Harvard University Press, 1985), p. 210.
14. Ibid., p. 211.
15. See Fuh-wen Tzeng, "The Political Economy of China's Coastal Development Strategy," *Asian Survey*, 31, 3 (March 1991), 270–84. Also see *Beijing Review*, 25 April, 1988, 35–37 for background of the strategy as outlined by Li Peng at the NPC session.
16. Ibid., 279.
17. Ibid., 279–80.
18. See *Wall Street Journal*, January 10, 1992, A-7A.
19. *Christian Science Monitor*, April 3, 1992, p. 6.
20. See *Asian Wall Street Journal*, March 17, 1992, p. 6. Also see Chen Zhen Xiong, "Foreign Direct Investment in Guangdong," paper presented at the 34th International Congress on Asian Studies held in Hong Kong, August 1993.
21. "Politics of Industrial Reform," p. 211.
22. Ibid.
23. Ibid.
24. Ibid.
25. Ibid.
26. See Bruce Gilley, "Southern Challenge" in *Far Eastern Economic Review*, (March 16, 2000), 50-51.
27. Ibid.
28. Franz Schurmann, *Ideology and Organization*, (Berkeley and Los Angeles, University of California Press, 1966) p. 214.
29. For an account of the purge of Gao and Rao, see Jurgen Domes, "Party Politics and the Cultural Revolution," 64–65; Edward E. Rice, *Mao's Way* (Berkeley: University of California Press, 1972), pp. 130–32; Albert Ravenholt, "Feud Among the Red Mandarins," American University Field Service, East Asia Series (February 1954); Parris Chang, *Power and Policy in China*, (University Park and London: The Pennsylvania State University Press, 1978) pp. 47–48; Jurgen Domes, *The Internal Politics of China* (New York: Holt, Rinehart & Winston, 1973), pp. 24–25.
30. Chang, *Power and Policy in China*, p. 50.
31. Chang, *Power and Policy in China*, p. 51; and Audrey Donnithorne, *China's Economic System* (London: Allen and Unwin, 1967), p. 460.
32. The text of "On the Ten Major Relations" is to be found in *Peking Review* 1 (January 1, 1977), 16, and *Selected Works of Mao Tse-tung*, vol. v (Peking: Foreign Language Press, 1977), p. 293.
33. Chang, *Power and Policy in China*, pp. 52–53.
34. For a detailed discussion on the powers granted to the provinces, see Chang, *Power and Policy in China*, pp. 55–61; and Victor C. Falkenheim, "Decentralization Revisited: A Maoist Perspective," *Current Scene*, 16, no. 1 (January 1978), 1–5.
35. "On the Ten Major Relations," in *Selected Works of Mao Tse-tung*, vol. v, p. 293.
36. Schurmann, *Ideology and Organization*, p. 210.
37. Ibid.
38. See Chang, *Power and Policy in China*, pp. 129–30.
39. Ibid., pp. 144–45.
40. *China Trade Report* (March 1981), 8.
41. See Barry Naughton, "False Starts and Second Wind; Financial Reforms in China's Industrial System" in Perry and Wong, *The Political Economy of Reforms in Post-Mao China*, (Cambridge and London: The Council on East Asian Studies, Harvard University Press, 1985) pp. 234–235 and 251–252.

42. Christine Wong, "Material Allocation and Decentralization: Impact of Local Sector on Industrial Reform," in ibid., pp. 268–278.
43. Ibid., p. 224.
44. Ibid.
45. *Far Eastern Economic Review* (June 23, 1983), 57–58.
46. Wong, "Material Allocation and Decentralization," p. 224.
47. Ibid.
48. Xiaowei Zang, "Provincial Elite in Post-Mao China," *Asian Survey*, 31, 6 (June 1991), 512–25.
49. Ibid., 524.
50. See Frederick C. Teiwes, "Provincial Politics in China: Themes and Variations," in John Lindbeck, ed., *Management of a Revolutionary Society* (Seattle: University of Washington Press, 1971), pp. 126–27.
51. Ibid.
52. See Thomas Jay Mathews, "The Cultural Revolution in Szechwan," in *The Cultural Revolution in the Provinces* (Cambridge, Mass.: Harvard University Press, 1971), pp. 94–146.
53. See Paul Hyer and William Heaton, "The Cultural Revolution in Inner Mongolia," *The China Quarterly*, 36 (October–December 1968), 114–28.
54. Vigor Keung Fang, "Chinese Region Offers Lures to Foreign Investors," *Asian Wall Street Journal Weekly,* December 21, 1981, p. 6.
55. Lewis M. Stern, "Politics Without Consensus: Center–Province Relations and Political Communication in China, January 1976–January 1977," *Asian Survey*, 19, no. 3 (March 1979), 260–80.
56. William deB. Mills, "Leadership Change in China's Provinces," *Problems of Communism*, 34, 3 (May–June 1985), 24.
57. Ibid., 27.
58. Ibid., 29.
59. Ibid., 31–40.
60. See *Christian Science Monitor,* October 18, 1990, p. 5.
61. Ibid.
62. See *China News Analysis*, 1404 (February 15, 1990), 1–9. For an in-depth treatment, see Ezra F. Vogel, *One Step Ahead in China: Guangdong under Reform* (Cambridge, Mass.: Harvard University Press, 1989). Also see *Far Eastern Economic Review* (April 4, 1991), 21–28.
63. *China News Analysis*, 1404 (February 15, 1990), 2.
64. See *China News Analysis*, 1409 (May 1, 1990), 5. Also see *Far Eastern Economic Review* (April 4, 1991), 24.
65. Wang Shaoguang and Hu Angang, *Report on the State of the Nation: Strengthening the Leading Role of the Central Government during the Transition to the Market Economy.* (New Haven, Conn.: Yale University, 1993). Also see summary in *China, Hong Kong, Taiwan, Inc.* (New York: Alfred A. Knopf, 1997), pp. 267–268.
66. See "Outline of the Ninth Five-Year Plan for National and Economic and Social Development and Long-Term Targets through the Year 2010," approved at the Fourth Session of the Eighth National People's Congress, *Beijing Review* (April 29–May 5, 1996), 20. Also see "Regional Economic Zones in National Development Programme Debated," Xinhua News Agency, March 11, 1990.
67. For a detailed breakdown of the regional areas, see the Xinhua News Agency report as summarized in van Kemenade, *China, Hong Kong, Taiwan, Inc.*, pp. 258–60. There have been a number of Canadian studies published recently on China's regional development: B. Michael Frolic, *China's Second Wave of Development: The Yangtze River Region* (Toronto: University of Toronto, York University Joint Center for Asia Pacific Studies, 1994); Linda Hershkowitz, *Regional Change in China: The Urban Dimension* (Toronto: University of Toronto, York University Joint Center for Asia Pacific Studies, 1995); Victor C. Falkenheim, *China's Regional Development: Trends and Implications* (Toronto: University of Toronto, York University Joint Center for Asia Pacific Studies, 1995).
68. Wu Wei, "Chongqing: Greater Opportunities for Development," *Beijing Review* (April 28–May 4, 1997), 13–15.
69. Da Wei, "Yunnan: Changes and Hopes," *Beijing Review* (June 2–8, 1997), 15–18; and Zheng Ling, "Opportunities Abound in Yunnan," *Beijing Review*, (February 10–16, 1997), 19–21. Yunnan seems to be poised to be "The Nexus for Trade and Investment with Southeast Asia," *Far Eastern Economic Review*, (September 11, 1997), 54–57.
70. Cui Lili, "A Model of Regional National Autonomy," *Beijing Review* (July 7–13, 1997), 12–15; and Han Baocheng, "Inner Mongolia: An Interesting Place for Investment," *Beijing Review* (July 7–13, 1997), 15–18.
71. See Karby Legett, "China's Bid to 'Revive the West' Faces Resistance," *Wall Street Journal*, April 9, 2000, p. A26.

72. Ibid.
73. Bruce Gilley, "Saving the West," *Far Eastern Economic Review*, (May 4, 2000), 23.
74. Information on the local government structure and functions is based on Doak Barnett, *Cadres, Bureaucracy, and Political Power in Communist China* (New York: Columbia University Press, 1967), Chu Li and Tien Chien-yun, *Inside a People's Commune* (Peking: Foreign Language Press, 1975); personal notes of my visits to China in 1972–73 and 1978; and "Our Neighborhood Revolutionary Committee," *China Reconstructs*, 22, no. 8 (August 1973), 2–3.
75. Barnett, *Cadres, Bureaucracy, and Political Power in Communist China*; Li and Chien-yun, *Inside a People's Commune*; personal notes of my visits to China; and "Our Neighborhood Revolutionary Committee." Also see footnotes 69, 81 and 84.
76. "Important Changes in the System of People's Communes," *Beijing Review*, 29 (April 19, 1982), 13–15.
77. Ibid.; also see *Ta Kung Pao Weekly Supplement* (Hong Kong), June 17, 1982, p. 2.
78. For township structure see Frederick W. Crook, "The Rise of the Commune-Household System," *China's Economy Looks Toward the Year 2000*, Joint Economic Committee, U.S. Congress, vol. 1: *The Four Modernizations* (Washington, D.C.: U.S. Printing Office, May 21, 1986), pp. 360–361.
79. *Beijing Review*, 16 (April 20, 1987), 6.
80. Ibid.
81. *Beijing Review*, 15 (April 13, 1987), 5.
82. *Beijing Review*, 17 (April 28, 1987), 15.
83. See Kevin J. O'Brien, "Is China's National People's Congress a Conservative Legislature?" *Asian Survey*, 30, no. 8 (August 1990), 787–88; and his "Implementating Political Reform in China's Villages," *Australian Journal of Chinese Affairs,* 32 (July 1994), 37–38.
84. O'Brien "Implementating Political Reforms in China's Villages,"42.
85. Ibid.,
86. The guidelines issued by the Ministry of Civil Affairs were adopted and publicized in an April 1994 article entitled "Nationwide Village Self-Government Demonstration Directives and Guidelines," as summarized in ibid., 42–43.
87. See Susan V. Lawrence, "Village Representative Assemblies: Democracy Chinese Style," *Australian Journal of Chinese Affairs*, 32 (July 1994), 62–68. Her study is based on a trip in October 1992 to Beiwang Village in a county in Hebei province.
88. See Jiang Zemin's speech to the Fifteenth Party Congress, "Hold High the Great Banner of Deng Xiaoping Theory," *Beijing Review*, 40, no. 40 (October 6–12, 1997), 24–25.
89. See Qu Tao, "'Cu weihui Zhi Zuan' Jioshi" (Inside Look at the Village Direct Election), *Zhengming*, (June 1997), 30–33.
90. Ibid., 30.
91. "The Chinese Debate over Village Self-Government," *China Journal*, no. 37 (January 1997), 70.
92. Ibid.
93. Ibid., 70–72.
94. Ibid., 78.
95. See Mark O'Neil, "Vote of Confidence in Village Elections," *South China Morning Post International Weekly*, 19 (April 1997), A–8.
96. See Tyrene White, "Reforming the Countryside," *Current History* (September 1992), 274.
97. See Susan V. Lawrence, "Village Democracy," *Far Eastern Economic Review* (January 27, 2000), 17. Also see *Carter Center Delegation Report: Village Elections in China* (Atlanta, Ga.: Carter Center, 1998).
98. Ibid.
99. Ibid. Also see James A. Robinson, "An Election with Chinese Characteristics," Foreign Policy Research Institute, February 14, 2000, p. 3.
100. See Tianjian Shi, "Village Committee Elections in China: Institutional Tactics for Democracy," *World Politics*, 51, no. 3 (April 1999), 386. Also see *Carter Center Delegation Report*.
101. "Our Neighborhood Revolutionary Committee," 3; "City Dwellers and the Neighborhood Committee," *Beijing Review*, 44 (November 3, 1980), 19–25; and John Roderick, "Kunming Housewife Helps Govern China," reprinted in *Honolulu Star Bulletin*, October 29, 1981, p. 8
102. For a detailed discussion of street life, see Michael Dutton, *Street Life China* (Cambridge: Cambridge University Press, 1998). The percentage figure is on p. 88 of the study.
103. Figures for minorities in China are taken from *The Far East and Australia*, 28th ed. (London: Europa Publications, 1997), p. 225.
104. Lucian W. Pye, "China: Ethnic Minorities and National Security," *Current Scene: Developments in the People's Republic of China*, 14, no. 12 (December 1976), 7–10.

105. For an account of the change of policies toward the minority groups from 1957–69, see Dorothy Dreyer, *China's Forty Millions* (Cambridge, Mass.: Harvard University Press, 1976), pp. 140–259; "China's Quest for a Socialist Solution," *Problems of Communism*, 24 (September–October 1975), 49–62; Pye, "China: Ethnic Minorities," 5–11; and Hung-mao Tien, "Sinoization of National Minorities in China," *Current Scene*, 12, no. 11 (November 1974), 1–14.
106. Pye, "China: Ethnic Minorities," 9–10.
107. "New Party Members—A Dynamic Force," *Peking Review*, 27 (July 6, 1973), 6–7.
108. "Minority Leader Cadres in Various Provinces and Autonomous Regions," *Beijing Review*, 10 (March 10, 1980), 23.
109. See Erling Hoh, "Hear Our Prayers," *Far Eastern Economic Review* (April 13, 2000), 25.
110. Ibid., 24.
111. See State Council Information Office, "China's Policy on National Minorities and Its Practice," *Beijing Review* (October 18, 1999), 21–22.
112. "China's Muslims Most Likely to Fight for Freedom, Study Finds," *Honolulu Advertiser*, November 18, 1996, p. A-5.
113. See two recent works on the Dalai Lama's exile: *Freedom in Exile: The Autobiography of the Dalai Lama* (New York: A Cornelia and Michael Bessie Book/HarperCollins, 1990); and *My Tibet: Text By His Holiness The Fourteenth Dalai Lama of Tibet* (Berkeley: Mountain Light Press and University of California Press, 1990). For related works see Melvyn C. Goldstein, *A History of Modern Tibet* (Berkeley: University of California Press, 1989); and Tom Grunfeld, *The Making of Modern Tibet* (Bombay, India: Oxford University Press, 1988).
114. For earlier discussion about Tibet, see the following issues of the *Beijing Review*: 40 (October 4, 1982), 5–7; 46 (November 15, 1982), 3–4; 47 (November 22, 1982), 15–18; 48 (November 29, 1982), 14–17; 49 (December 6, 1982), 21–24; 50 (December 13, 1982), 28–29; and 51 (December 20, 1982), 37–38.
115. "New Principles for Building up Tibet," *Beijing Review*, 24 (June 16, 1980), 3.
116. "Latest Development in Tibet," *Beijing Review*, 25 (June 21, 1982), 19.
117. "Tibet: An Inside View II," *Beijing Review*, 48 (November 29, 1982), 14.
118. "New Economic Policy for Tibet," *Beijing Review*, 27 (July 7, 1980), 4; and Ngapoi Jigme, "Great Historical Changes in Tibet," *Beijing Review*, 22 (June 1, 1981), 17–19.
119. "Situation in Tibet," *Beijing Review*, 31 (August 2, 1982), 6. Also see Harrison E. Salisbury, "Return of Dalai Lama to Tibet Is Expected Soon," *New York Times*, August 31, 1980, p. 11; Liu Heung Shing, "China Pulling Officials from Tibet," Associated Press, reprinted in *Honolulu Star-Bulletin,* August 12, 1982, p. C-5; and David Chen, "Dalai Lama Team Plans Visit to Tibet," *South China Morning Post* (Hong Kong), April 24, 1982, p. 1; Christopher S. Wren, "Chinese Trying to Undo Damage in Tibet," *New York Times,* May 31, 1983, pp. A-1, A-8.
120. This was made very clear to the author in a rare luncheon meeting with the Dalai Lama when he came to Hawaii to dedicate a Tibetan temple in Woods Valley on October 28, 1980.
121. "Policy Towards Dalai Lama," *Beijing Review*, 46 (November 15, 1982), 3.
122. See Michael Ross, "Tibet's Dalai Lama Ponders Return," United Press International, as reprinted in *Honolulu Advertiser,* August 18, 1983, p. A-19.
123. *Beijing Review*, 16 (April 21, 1986), 9, and "Questions and Answers on Tibet," *Beijing Review*, 28 (July 13, 1987), 16.
124. See Gene Kramer, "Dalai Lama Rejects Offer by China to Repatriate," Associated Press as reprinted in *Honolulu Star-Bulletin,* September 22, 1987, p. A-12.
125. *New York Times,* October 3, 1987, p. 1.
126. *New York Times,* October 4, 1987, p. 1.
127. *Christian Science Monitor,* October 5, 1987, p. 9.
128. *New York Times,* October 4, 1987, p. 1, and *Asian Wall Street Journal,* October 5, 1987, pp. 1 and 6.
129. *Beijing Review*, 41 (October 12, 1987), 4.
130. *Beijing Review*, 42 (October 19, 1987), 15.
131. *Far Eastern Economic Review* (July 1, 1985), 20.
132. *Ta Kung Pao Weekly Supplement* (Hong Kong), May 3, 1984, p. 3.
133. *Far Eastern Economic Review* (July 1, 1985), 21–22.
134. "Questions and Answers on Tibet," 14–15.
135. See *Beijing Review* (February 19–25, 1990), 22.
136. See *New York Times,* May 1, 1990, p. A-6; *Beijing Review* (April 16–22, 1990), 7; and *Hong Kong Sunday Standard,* May 20, 1990, p. 8.
137. Dawa Norbu, "Strategic Development in Tibet: Implications for Its Neighbors," *Asian Survey*, 19, no. 3 (March 1979), 245–59.

138. See Dawa Norbu, "China's Dialogue with the Dalai Lama 1978–90: Prenegotiation Stage or Dead End?" *Pacific Affairs*, 64, no. 3 (Fall 1991), 367 and 371.

139. The Dalai Lama made these statements while being interviewed by Larry King and Jim Lehrer on public television on April 22, 1997.

140. See Julia Baum and Matt Forney, "Free Associations: Beijing Looks on in Horror as Taiwan and the Dalai Lama Steal the Limelight in Mutual Admiration," *Far Eastern Economic Review* (April 10, 1997), 14–15.

141. Ibid., 15. Also see Barry Sautman and Shia-Hing Ho, *The Tibet Question and the Hong Kong Experience* (Baltimore: School of Law, University of Maryland, Occasional Papers/Reprints Series in Contemporary Asian Studies, no. 2, 1995).

142. See Xin Lai, "'Tibet Has Never Been an Independent State,' Scholars Say,"*Beijing Review* (March 3–9, 1997), 13–14; Li Songyi, "Facts Refute the Dalai's Charges," *Beijing Review* (March 3–9, 1997), 14–15; Li Songyi, "Some Anecdotes Worth Repeating," *Beijing Review* (March 3–9, 1997), 16–18.

143. "Free Associations," 15.

144. For a description of the reincarnation process and the life of the young Panchen Lama, see a special article by Wang Guozhen and Wang Yanjuan, "The 11th Panchen Lama: One Year of Buddhist Life," *Beijing Review*, (February 3–9, 1997), 12–21.

145. See Hans Vriens, "Lhasa Lost," *Far Eastern Economic Review* (May 29, 1997), 44–45.

146. Ibid., 45.

147. See John Kennedy, "Lost World of a Living Buddha: An Interview," *George Magazine,* December 1997, p. 103.

148. Figure comes from Li Wen, "China's Environmental Conditions in 1998," *Beijing Review* (July 12, 1999), 15.

149. Ibid.

150. Lorien Holland, "Running Dry," *Far Eastern Economic Review* (February 3, 2000), 18.

151. Ibid.

152. See Robert F. Ash and Richard Louis Edmonds, "China's Land Resources, Environment and Agricultural Production," *China Quarterly*, no. 156 (September 1998), 836–874.

153. See Li Rongxia, "Environment Becoming of More Concern to the Public," *Beijing Review* (May 3–9, 1999), 17 and 24.

154. Ibid., 24.

155. See Abigail R. Jahiel, "The Organizations of Environmental Protection in China," *China Quarterly*, no. 159 (December 1998), 757–787.

156. "China's First Environmental Leader Talks to EDF," *EDF Letters* (March 1995), 7.

157. See A. Jahiel, "The Organizations of Environmental Protection in China," 786–787 and A. R. Jahiel, *China Quarterly*, no. 195 (December 1998).

158. Summary of environmental protection laws and regulation is culled from Li Rongxia, "Environment Becoming More of Concern to the Public," and "Chronicle of China's Environmental Protection Work," *Beijing Review*, (May 3–9, 1999), 16–18. Also, see Michael Palmer, "Environmental Regulations in the PRC: The Face of Domestic Law," *China Quarterly*, no. 159 (December 1998), 788–808.

159. See Vaclar Smil, *Environmental Problems in China: Estimates of Economic Cost*, no. 5 (April 1996), p. 2, a special report by the East-West Center in Honolulu, Hawaii.

160. Li Rongxia, "Environmental Protection Sector Presents Bright Prospects," *Beijing Review* (January 25–31, 1999), 9.

161. Palmer "Environmental Regulation in the PRC," 808.

162. Ibid.

163. "China's First Environmental Leader Talks to the EDF."

164. "Dangerous Waters," *Far Eastern Economic Review* (April 1, 1999), 39.

165. See Patience Berkman, "The Three Gorges Dam: Energy, the Environment, and the New Emperor," *Education about Asia*, 1, no. 1 (Spring 1998), 31.

166. Ibid.

167. See Ann Zwinger, "Last Look at the Long River," *Audubon* (May-June 1997), 78; and Audrey R. Topping, "Ecological Roulette: Damming the Yangtze," *Foreign Affairs* (September-October, 1995), 144. Also see "China Wrestles with Plan to Move Residents Whose Lands Will Flood," *Christian Science Monitor*, May 11, 1994, pp. 11–12.

168. "Energy, Environment, and the New Emperor," 35.

169. "Corruption: Dangerous Rivers," *Far Eastern Economic Review* (April 1, 1999), 38–40; and Erik Eckholm, "Criticism of China's Plan for a Big Dam," *New York Times*, March 18, 1999, pp. A-1 and A-2.

170. See "China: Do Risks Outweigh the Expected Benefits of The Massive Three Gorges Dam?" *Honolulu Advertiser*, December 31, 1995, p. B-4.

SUGGESTED READINGS

Dutton, Michael. *Street-Life China* (Cambridge: Cambridge University Press, 1998).

Goldstein, Melvyn C. *The Snow Lion and the Dragon: China, Tibet and the Dalai Lama* (Berkeley: University of California Press, 1997).

Hendrischke, Hans, and Feng Chongye (eds.). *The Political Economics of China's Provinces: Comparative and Competitive Advantage* (New York: Routledge, 1999).

Hershkowitz, Linda. *Regional Change in China: The Urban Dimension* (Toronto: University of Toronto and York University, 1994).

Li, Linda Chelan. *Centre and Provinces—China 1978-1993: Power as Non-Zero Sum* (Oxford, UK: Clarendon Press, 1998).

Mackerras, Colin. *China's Minorities: Integration and Modernization in the 20th Century* (Hong Kong: Oxford University Press, 1994).

McElroy, Michael B., Chris P. Nielson, and Peter Lydon. *Energizing China: Reconciling Environmental Protection and Economic Growth* (Cambridge, Mass.: Harvard University Press, 1998).

Qing, Dai. *The River Dragon Has Gone! The Three Gorges Dam and the Fate of China's Yangtze River and People* (Armonk, N.Y.: M. E. Sharpe, 1997).

Shakya, Tsering. *The Dragon in the Land of Snows: A History of Modern Tibet since 1947* (New York: Columbia University Press, 1999).

Shi, Tianjian. *Political Participation in Beijing* (Cambridge, Mass.: Harvard University Press, 1998).

Vogel, Ezra F. *One Step Ahead in China: Guangdong under Reform* (Cambridge, Mass.: Harvard University Press, 1989).

Yang, Dali L. *Beyond Beijing: Liberalization and the Regions in China* (London and New York: Routledge, 1997).

Chapter Eight

Greater China

*Reversion of Hong Kong
and Macao, the Pearl River Delta
Regional Development,
and the Taiwan Question*

The concept of "Greater China" is complex, if not controversial. As pointed out by Harry Harding, the concept contains three major themes: "political unification," "economic integration," and "cultural interaction."[1] Frequently the concept refers to the economic integration of Hong Kong, Taiwan, and the southern coastal provinces of Guangdong and Fujian.[2] It is controversial for two main reasons. One is the potential economic power to be possessed by "Greater China" in terms of the combined gross domestic product, which could very well surpass that of the United States; and its dominant trade position in the next century, in addition to its military power.[3] Thus, for some the concept conjures up the Greater East Asia Co-Prosperity Sphere instigated by imperial Japan during the Second World War.[4] "Greater China" implies some degree of emergence of a superpower for East Asia cemented by cultural affinity. The controversial aspect of the concept is that "Greater China" does refer to a "cultural community" with identical links to the Chinese civilization, a sort of cultural expansionism apart from the rest of East Asia.

While the origin of the term "Greater China" may be traced to the Chinese empire and its dependencies outside of the Great Wall in the old imperial days, the recent use of the term, beginning in 1970–1980, seems to have focused on the economic ties and expansion of mainland China, Taiwan, or perhaps Singapore, with Hong Kong–Macao as its nexus.[5] The term, "Greater China," by linking the economic integration of Hong Kong, Taiwan, and the Peoples' Republic of China (PRC), had gained more acceptance by 1992–1993 when two scholarly conferences and a seminar were held to discuss the meaning and implications of the concept.[6] Thus, as pointed out by Harry Harding, there emerged the themes of an "Asian Chinese Common Market" or "Greater Chinese Economic Community" and "Greater South China."[7]

The focus of this chapter is on the variations of the "Greater China" theme—that is, the emergence of a Greater China in terms of the political unification of Hong Kong and Macao with mainland China and the Pearl River Delta regional economic development as a realistic possibility. In short, this chapter discusses the political development and reunification of Hong Kong and Macao with China in the context of the gradual emergence of the Pearl River Delta as a regional economic force.

HONG KONG: CHINA'S SPECIAL ADMINISTRATIVE REGION

Hong Kong had been administered by Britain as a crown colony for over 155 years. After June 30, 1997, Hong Kong consists of three parts: (1) Hong Kong Island, a rock of about 30 square miles; (2) Kowloon Peninsula, 3.5 square miles, the southern extension of the Chinese mainland below the hills of the so-called nine peaks; and (3) the New Territories, 377 square miles that extend into the Guangdong Province. These land areas, plus some 235 outlying islands, add up to the former crown colony and represents a total land area of 415 square miles. Hong Kong Island was ceded in perpetuity to Britain by the 1842 Treaty of Nanking at the end of the Opium War; the Kowloon Peninsula was ceded to Britain under the 1860 Treaty of Peking; but the New Territories were leased by China to Britain for 99 years beginning in 1898.

The total population of Hong Kong on July 1, 1997, was about 6.3 million, excluding illegal immigrants. Taking Hong Kong as a whole, it is one of the most densely populated areas in the world, with an average density of more than 5,000 persons per square mile; on Hong Kong Island, density has been measured at over 1,500 per square mile. About 98 percent of the 6.3 million total population are Chinese by ethnic origin; they speak the southern dialect, Cantonese. Since 1984 a movement has been launched to encourage Hong Kong people to learn to speak the Chinese Mandarin, or the *putonghua*. However, there were two official languages for Hong Kong—English and Chinese—before the reversion. There is, as of this writing, no change with respect to the use of English and the Chinese written language. One would expect that Chinese Mandarin would increasingly become the spoken language of Hong Kong.

HONG KONG: HISTORIC BACKGROUND

At the very beginning when the rock on which the island of Hong Kong rested was taken over by the British in 1842, it was basically considered a barren piece of real estate, subject periodically to typhoons and epidemics of disease. For the British the island was the place for supervising trade with the newly opened treaty ports from south to east China. Then it became obvious, in the vision of some of the early governors of the Crown Colony, such as Palmeston and Aberdeen, that Hong Kong could be developed as the military and commercial center for the Far East, as it was the only British possession east of Singapore. British commercial firms were persuaded to begin operating in Hong Kong by 1844.[8] Hong Kong as a new trade center was then dominated by the British pattern in India and under the influence of the British East India Company. Jan Morris points out that the three Crown Colony governors were of Anglo-Indian background. With the trading firms there came European merchants, shopkeepers, and physicians. Trading companies were dominated by Jardine and Matheson.

The colonial administration for the Crown Colony was best characterized as "minimal"[9] in that it was the London-designated governor who ran the affairs of the colony with assistance from his appointed counselors. Administrative concerns were largely those of land reclamation and management, law and order, the development of reservoirs, and improvement in sanitary conditions and public works. For the first decade taxes collected were not sufficient enough to do anything beyond paying government employees. In matters of budget and finance the merchants had a more influential voice with the governor. Hong Kong's economy prior to the end of World War II was based on *entrepot* trade, which consisted of shipping, marine insurance, banking, and warehouse facilities and services. Manufacturing was underdeveloped and insignificant.

After the Japanese surrendered and the war ended, with the return of the British administration and garrison command, Hong Kong struggled to survive and support the feeding of a population of 600,000. It recovered quickly, but remained as an *entrepot* and export center for primary commodities of bristles, feathers, goat skins, tea, seed oil, and knitted fabrics. For most of the 1950s Hong Kong was not by any means considered an industrial city.

As the PRC was established in October 1949, refugees flooded to Hong Kong and boosted its population to 1.4 million in 1950. Then the Korean War broke out in June 1950 and an embargo was imposed on China by the United Nations. Hong Kong soon went into a serious economic depression—unemployment was at a 30 percent high and the colony lacked capital for economic development. Hong Kong was a "dying city,"[10] for trade with China was at a low ebb and the *entrepot* trade as a whole was not sufficient to enable the colony to survive economically. In addition, Hong Kong's future was politically uncertain in the light of a war in the Far East involving the major powers.

A shift of strategy then took place with hardly any input from the colonial government—from the old pattern of an *entrepot* to that of an export-oriented manufacturing base. For by then refugee entrepreneurs, the Shanghai owners of industries, particularly the textile complex, brought to Hong Kong capital, know-how, and hardworking labor—factors needed for the development of light industries geared to export to the United States markets. As indicated by the Hong Kong government's 1966 annual report, by the 1960s textiles constituted 52 percent of Hong Kong's export trade, employing 41 percent of the colony's industrial force.[11] By then Hong Kong was well on its way to sustained economic growth.

From the end of the Korean War in 1953 until 1982 Hong Kong was caught in a rapid whirl of economic growth, to be discussed shortly in another section. Politically, it was a period of relative calm and apathy on the part of the population. The calm was interrupted briefly by riots—one caused by a rise in the ferryboat fares across the harbor from Kowloon to Hong Kong Island in 1956 and another by communist-instigated demonstrations in 1967 inspired by the Cultural Revolution upheaval in China.

The 1967 riot campaign waged in Hong Kong under the slogan "opposing the British, resisting brutality" was not a part of the Chinese Cultural Revolution foreign policy design to export the Chinese revolutionary model.[12] But, the disturbances—including work stoppages, terrorism, and bombings—were instigated by labor unions under the influence of Chinese communist organizations operating in the colony.[13] As Ian Scott points out, the 1967 riots forced the ruling business elites of the colony to begin thinking about how to deal with social instability and the decision-making process by utilizing partially elected representatives.[14] Political reforms were instituted: the concept of a city district officer, Chinese as an official language, the office of unofficial members of the legislative council to advise the governor, new labor legislation.[15]

Sino–British Negotiation for Hong Kong's Return to China, 1982–1984

One of the most compelling reasons on the part of the British for initiating negotiation on the future of Hong Kong was the 1898 ninety-nine-year lease of the 377 square miles (or 93 percent of total Hong Kong territory) of the New Territories, which was due to expire on June 30, 1997.[16] It has been said that this was due to pressure exerted by Hong Kong businessmen. In the late 1970s they had made it clear to the British government in Hong Kong that unless there were some assurance of New Territories lease renewal by the Chinese government, there would be no long-term investment in the new towns developed for export industries.[17] In March 1979 the then-Governor Sir Murray (now Lord) MacLehose decided to go to Beijing to sound out the Chinese about their plans for Hong Kong after June 30, 1997.[18]

Governor MacLehose had a meeting with Deng Xiaoping, the paramount leader who had opened China to the outside world. Deng obviously was not prepared to give any definitive answers to the key question about the lease renewal except to say that China must acquire sovereignty over the entire expanse of Hong Kong, but he did not know when and that Hong Kong investors need not worry.[19] (At that point in time Hong Kong had generated one-third of China's foreign exchange and two-thirds of China's investment from abroad.[20]) The Chinese leader's assurance initially ignited an "irrational exuberance" in the real estate market in Hong Kong. Bolstered by the Chinese assurance of Hong Kong's continued financial role and reflective of the British experience in the expulsion of Argentine invaders from the Falkland Islands in 1980, Prime Minister Thatcher decided to pay a visit to Beijing to explore a permanent solution to Hong Kong's status. On the eve of her arrival in China in September 1982, the Hong Kong property or real estate market took a tumble and the Hong Kong dollar fell from HK$6 to HK$9 to U.S.$1.

At the outset of the negotiation,[21] the British options were rather limited, or it had no viable alternatives on the Hong Kong sovereignty issue. The Chinese leaders, from Deng Xiaoping to Zhao Ziyang, then China's premier, insisted that the sovereignty issue was nonnegotiable since the 1842 and 1860 treaties that had been negotiated under the Qing (Manchu) dynasty were "unequal treaties," not recognized by China. China had been forced to sign them under duress and those unequal treaties had represented gross national humiliation for the Chinese people as a whole. The Chinese position was for complete sovereignty in 1997, but with an endeavor to preserve Hong Kong's economic prosperity.[22]

In July 1982 at the National People's Congress, Chinese leader Peng Zhen had drafted a new Article 30, which eventually became Article 31 of the 1982 state constitution (see Appendix A). As a response to the initial British argument for the separation of "sovereignty" and "administration" this article would authorize the central government to establish a "special administrative region"[23] when necessary. Article 31 provides a legal device to allow Taiwan or Hong Kong to be reunited with China:

> The State may establish special administrative regions when necessary. The systems to be instituted in special administrative regions shall be prescribed by law enacted by the National People's Congress in the light of the specific conditions.[24]

The two years of negotiation produced the 1984 Joint Declaration of Great Britain and the PRC on Hong Kong, which was signed by Prime Minister Thatcher and Chinese Premier Zhao Ziyang on December 19, 1984. Key provisions of the joint agreement were the following: (1) China is to resume its sovereignty over Hong Kong effective July 1, 1997; (2) in accordance with Article 31 of the PRC constitution, Hong Kong will become a special administrative region under the authority of the PRC central government but will enjoy a high degree of autonomy except in areas of foreign affairs and defense; (3) laws in force in Hong Kong will remain unchanged; (4) current social and economic systems, as well as lifestyle, in Hong Kong will also remain unchanged; and (5) as an SAR Hong Kong may establish its own economic and cultural relations and conclude agreements with other nations, regions, or relevant international organizations.

The Joint Declaration under paragraph 3(12) provided a time limit for Hong Kong's higher degree of autonomy as an SAR was based on Deng Xiaoping's repeated statement that the social and economic systems would not change for as long as fifty years, operating under Deng's concept of "one country, two systems." Until Hong Kong reverted to China in July 1997, the Joint Declaration also entrusted Great Britain to continue administering Hong Kong. During the interim the implementation of the agreement and the actual transfer of sovereignty were to be consulted upon by a Joint Liaison Group of PRC and British representatives.

"One Country, Two Systems"

The 1984 Joint British-Chinese Declaration on Hong Kong and Article 31 of the 1982 PRC constitution produced two underlying operating principles or formulas for future administration of Hong Kong once sovereignty returned to China. One such principle is the often-quoted phrase, its coinage attributed to Deng Xiaoping, "one country, two systems." In the case of Hong Kong the phrase implies the coexistence of a capitalist system under a socialist regime, or as someone said more aptly, Hong Kong would be "the capitalist pearl" in a "socialist oyster." Or, as described by one Chinese scholar, it might be called a model for "unification-led political pluralization" when it applies to the unification of Taiwan.[25] The idea of coexistence of two disparate systems in a socialist China may be viewed as a Chinese pragmatic compromise to accommodate the British basic objective. As revealed in Thatcher's press conference to the Hong Kong business community on September 27, 1982, this objective was to preserve Hong Kong's economic prosperity and political/social stability.[26]

For the Chinese, besides its main argument of not recognizing the unequal treaties of 1842 and 1860, the primary goal was also for continued "economic growth and social stability" for Hong Kong once the issue of sovereignty had been resolved.[27] And, more importantly, the very idea of "one country, two systems" would be used by the Chinese as a model to achieve Taiwan's unification with China.[28] The intent of Article 31 also applied to Taiwan, as indicated by the late Marshal Ye Jianying, the PRC's president at the time of adoption of the article. Ye was quoted as saying, "After our national unification, Taiwan shall become an SAR with a high degree of autonomy and with its own army."[29]

"Hong Kongers Rule Hong Kong"

As a corollary to the operating formula for the return of Hong Kong to China, Beijing adopted the idea that the people of Hong Kong must rule Hong Kong. The idea of "Hong Kongers rule Hong Kong" is said to have originated with Zhou Enlai, who advocated the concept as a way of preventing the American effort to make Taiwan independent. Zhou was said to have instructed CCP workers to observe the Hong Kong law and legal system.[30] This idea eventually became the "Hong Kong People Model," implying only Hong Kongers will administer, run, and manage the affairs of Hong Kong.[31] In other words, after June 30, 1997, Hong Kong would not be legally administered by Chinese officials on the mainland. During the intense Sino–British negotiations, the corollary was revealed to outsiders. However, the formula was strengthened from its earlier vagueness to a more assertive stance after lobbying and input by what Professor Alvin Y. So called the new middle-class-influential Hong Kong–business professions and intellectuals who were as a group "highly educated, skillful in articulating ideas, and had strong links with the mass media and other cultural apparatus."[32] This new Hong Kong middle class was generally nationalistic or pro-Chinese, but they were also fearful of communist rule and wanted to preserve their way of life as privileged elites who were basically in favor of democratic reform in Hong Kong. Alvin So takes the position that it was this "new middle class" in Hong Kong who influenced the outcome of the negotiation process, which had been verging on breakdown during the crucial period, 1982–1983. He offers two important factors to support the notion that the "new middle class" in Hong Kong contributed to the Sino–British negotiations:[33] One was its ability to communicate and clarify the vague concept of "Hong Kongers must rule Hong Kong" after the 1997 reversion, and the other was its ability to influence the shift in public opinion in Hong Kong from "pro-British to a pro-Chinese stance."

THE BASIC LAW OF HONG KONG AFTER 1997[34]

By decree on April 4, 1990, the PRC president promulgated the Basic Law of the Hong Kong Special Administrative Region as the post-1997 constitution for Hong Kong, prepared for approval by the Chinese National People's Congress by a fifteen-member Drafting Committee for the Basic Law. The draft was the result of four and one-half years of work. Details on the political structure of the future Hong Kong government and its power as an SAR under China will be discussed in the pertinent sections to follow.

The future political structure of Hong Kong as provided by the Basic Law of the Hong Kong Special Administrative Region (hereafter referred to as the Basic Law) approved by China's Seventh National People's Congress on April 4, 1990, consists of four institutions: the chief executive, the legislature, the judiciary, and the district organizations.[35]

The Chief Executive

The chief executive for the Hong Kong SAR is accountable to the Chinese central government. The central government here refers to the State Council, headed by a premier who is appointed by the PRC president, based on prior arrangement by the Chinese Communist Party (CCP) Politburo, of which the premier and the PRC president are members. The reading of Article 43 leaves little doubt that the Hong Kong SAR has the same status as any other Chinese province or autonomous region. If there is any difference, the Basic Law has not defined it clearly or singled out a differentiation.

Under Article 48, the powers and authorities of the chief executive include the following: to lead the government and to implement laws applicable to the Hong Kong SAR; to sign and promulgate laws enacted by the Legislative Council; to approve budgets and decide on policies; to implement directives issued by the Chinese central government; to conduct external relations on behalf of Hong Kong as authorized by the Chinese government; and, finally, to appoint and remove judges and other public office-holders. The text of the Basic Law provisions on the powers of the chief executive for the Hong Kong SAR leaves no doubt that the office is designed to be that of a strong and powerful executive, restrained in only a rather vague way by accountability to the Chinese central government and the Basic Law.

The qualifications, term of office, and method of selecting the chief executive are laid down in Articles 44, 45, and Annex I, 46 and 47. He or she is to be a Chinese citizen, not less than 40 years of age, a permanent resident, with no right of abode in any other country; must have resided continuously in Hong Kong for at least twenty years; and must be a person of integrity, dedicated to his or her duties. The term of office (Article 46) provides for a five-year term but is limited to not more than two consecutive terms.

While Article 45 states that the chief executive will ultimately be selected by universal suffrage upon nomination by a broadly representative nomination committee, in the meantime the selection of the first chief executive is governed by Annex I to the Basic Law. Annex I provides for an Election Committee, a sort of electoral college, of 800 members to represent basically the "functional constituencies" of occupational and professional groups, distributed as follows: 200 for the industrial, commercial, and financial sectors; 200 for the professions; 200 for labor, social services, and religious groups; and 200 for members of the Legislative Council and district-based organizations plus representatives from Hong Kong to the National People's Congress and to the Chinese People's Political Consultative Conference (a CCP-manipulated and controlled rubber-stamp body for the Chinese NPC). This 800-member Election Committee shall serve for a five-year term and vote by secret ballot in their individual capacities. However, the most important aspect of the selection process is the veto power over the appointment that may be exercised by the Chinese central government, in this case the State Council. Article 45 states clearly that "the Chief Executive shall be selected by election or through consultations held locally and be appointed by the Central Government."[36] As indicated by a Chinese official, the requirement that the appointment be approved by the Chinese central government is not "a mere formality" but is a rather "substantial one."[37] As argued by a Hong Kong scholar, there would be "a constitutional crisis" that would affect Hong Kong's "stability and prosperity" if an impasse developed in the future in which selection by universal suffrage was not accepted by the Chinese central government.[38]

There is also to be established under Article 54 of the Basic Law an Executive Council to assist the chief executive in policy making. Under Article 55, the chief executive appoints an unspecified number of persons to the Executive Council, which functions in much the same manner as the pre-1997 Executive Council, except that the Basic Law now stipulates that members must be Chinese citizens.

The Legislature

Legislative powers rest with the Legislative Council of sixty members, as stipulated in Annex II on the method for formation of the body for the Hong Kong SAR. Under Article 67, membership is divided into two categories: Chinese citizens with permanent residence, but with no right of abode in any foreign country; and non-Chinese permanent residents who have the right of abode in foreign countries—the total for this category must not exceed 20 percent of the total Legislative Council membership. Members are to serve for a term of four years, except those elected for the first term, which is limited to two years.

In accordance with Annex II and the decision by the Chinese National People's Congress on the first term of the first Legislative Council, there shall be a sixty-member Legislative Council distributed as follows: twenty members by geographic constituencies through direct election, ten by the Election Committee, and thirty by functional constituencies (occupational and professional groups). For the second term, membership composition for the Legislative Council will be as follows: thirty by functional constituencies, six by the Election Committee, and twenty-four by geographical constituencies through direct election. For the third term: thirty by functional constituencies and thirty by geographical constituencies through direct election.

As provided by Article 73, powers and functions of the Legislative Council include the following: to enact laws; to approve budgets and public expenditures; to debate on public issues and to raise questions on the work of the government; to appoint or remove judges on the Court of Final Appeal and the chief judge for the High Court. A bill so enacted by the Legislative Council cannot take effect unless it is signed and promulgated by the chief executive (Article 76).

Another form of check and balance is provided under Article 73(9), which grants the Legislative Council the power of impeachment of the chief executive on a motion passed by a two-thirds majority vote, or forty members of the entire body. However, impeachment of the chief executive must be based on an investigation by an independent committee headed by the chief justice of the Court of Final Appeal. This impeachment provision may be interpreted as a needed safeguard to protect Hong Kong against a chief executive who is too subservient to the officials of the central government in opposition to the expressed wishes of the people of Hong Kong. Or it may be seen as a mere facade in view of the overall power of the Chinese central government, for the action—the impeachment—must be reported to the Chinese State Council for a final decision.

Executive–legislative relations for the Hong Kong SAR are governed by Articles 49–52 in the Basic Law. If the Legislative Council passes a law that in the view of the chief executive is not compatible with Hong Kong's interests, he or she must return it to the Legislative Council for reconsideration within three months. If the original bill is passed for the second time by a two-thirds majority vote, the chief executive must sign and promulgate it within a month. If he or she refuses to sign it, then Article 50 comes into play: the Legislative Council is to be dissolved by the chief executive after consultation with the Executive Council. The Legislative Council can also be dissolved if it refuses to enact a budget or any other important bill introduced by the government. However, the chief executive may dissolve the Legislative Council only once in each term of his or her office.

As a means of resolving a possible legislative impasse or refusal to act on the budget, Article 51 allows the chief executive to apply to the Legislative Council for a provisional appropriation. If such an appropriation is not possible because the Legislative Council is already dissolved, then prior to the election of the new Legislative Council, the chief executive merely approves on his or her own the provisional short-term appropriation at the level of the previous year.

Article 52 also states that the chief executive must resign if, after having dissolved the old Legislative Council, the new Legislative Council again passes by a two-thirds majority vote the disputed original budget bill that has still been refused by the chief executive. Or the chief executive must resign if the new Legislative Council still refuses to enact the original bill in dispute.

According to one Hong Kong scholar, the above procedural provisions to resolve executive–legislative conflict over the budget or any other key bills may not even be necessary, since the chief executive "controls" the budget submission process in the first place. He or she can alter the bill to meet any objections from the Legislative Council, so as to ensure final passage and thus make it unnecessary to be forced to resign.[39] Or, after a Legislative Council has been dissolved and a new one formed, the chief executive can make concessions or seek compromises on the disputed bill to such an extent that it is guaranteed passage, and thus can avoid the necessity for resigning from the office.[40]

The Judiciary

Under Articles 8 and 18 of the Basic Law for the Hong Kong SAR, the laws previously in force in Hong Kong and the laws that may be enacted by the Legislative Council shall be applicable. Article 8 specifies the previous laws enforceable for the Hong Kong SAR as follows: the common law, rules of equity, ordinances, subordinate legislation, and customary law, except those that may contradict the Basic Law.

Under Article 81, the court structure consists of the Court of Final Appeal, the High Court (Court of Appeals and the Court of First Instance), district courts, and magistrate courts. Article 85 states that the courts must exercise independent judicial power and must be free from any interference. The principle of jury trial shall be maintained, and the principles previously applied to Hong Kong and the rights previously enjoyed by parties to criminal and civil proceedings shall also remain intact under the provision in Article 86.

Judges are appointed by the chief executive for the Hong Kong SAR based on recommendations of an independent commission made up of local judges, the legal profession, and other eminent persons. They can be removed only for inability to discharge their duties; dismissal is by the chief executive upon recommendation from a tribunal of at least three local judges appointed by the chief justice of the Court of Final Appeal (Article 89). All judges must be Chinese citizens who are permanent residents with no right of abode in any foreign country (Article 90).

A most controversial aspect in the Basic Law on the judicial system for the Hong Kong SAR has been the changes made dealing with the Court of Final Appeal. As stated in Article 82, the final adjudication power rests with the Court of Final Appeal, composed of five judges, some of them invited judges from other common law jurisdictions. This final appellate court will replace the old system of appeal to the British Privy Council sitting in London. A point of dispute or controversy has been that perhaps two out of the five sitting judges for the Court of Final Appeal should be invited judges from other common law jurisdictions. But at the September 1991 meeting in London of the Chinese–British Joint Liaison Group for Hong Kong, agreement was reached to establish such a court of final appeal in 1993, to be composed of a chief justice, three Hong Kong local judges, and a fifth invited member from two alternate panels: Panel A from retired Hong Kong judges, and Panel B from retired judges from other common law jurisdictions so as to ensure the presence of a foreign judge for only half of its sessions.[41] The post-1991 constituted Hong Kong Legislative Council by a vote of 34–11 rejected the agreement described above, but the rejection was ignored by both the British and Chinese authorities.[42]

POPULAR ELECTORAL CONTESTS: 1991 AND 1995

There were two popular elections for the people of Hong Kong before the takeover on July 1, 1997.

The 1991 Election

The first Legislative Council popular.election was held on September 15, 1991. It was the most significant election that occurred before Hong Kong's scheduled reversion to China for a number of reasons. First, this was the first time in 150 years of Hong Kong's history that a direct election for legislative seats by the eligible voters had taken place. Second, the direct election took place two years after the Chinese military crackdown at Tiananmen, which had suppressed demonstrations by students for democracy and political reform for China. Third, this was the election in which organized liberal groups participated; one leading group that supported a speedy democratic reform for Hong Kong and China won a stunning victory at the polls, a feat that embarrassed the Chinese government during the countdown toward its takeover of Hong Kong in 1997.

At stake in the September 1991 election were eighteen seats from nine multi-member districts on the sixty-member Legislative Council for the crown colony to be chosen by direct popular vote. There was a total of fifty-four candidates competing for the eighteen seats. While local issues of traffic and crime were debated by candidates, the subjects of China's control of Hong Kong affairs and the Tiananmen crackdown as a violation of human rights were some of the more emotional topics raised in the debates; two of the candidates had been labeled by Beijing as "subversive."[43] Other candidates were supportive of China or pro-Beijing.

The Hong Kong government tightly regulated the campaigning for this direct election. There was a stipulation that equal time must be made available to all candidates on radio and television, with the result that there were no election reports on evening news programs. Political advertising was strictly prohibited on radio and television. Candidates relied on posters and leaflets and door-to-door canvassing.

There were 1.9 million registered voters out of a total of 3.8 million eligible. The turnout by registered voters was a low 39.2 percent, or fewer than 800,000 who cast their ballots.[44] This was an indication that the main concern of the people of Hong Kong was still economic prosperity rather than political participation. In a public poll taken by a Chinese daily newspaper in August 1991, more than 41 percent of those polled indicated economic development as their primary concern, whereas only 11.4 percent viewed political development as more important.[45]

Political Parties and Groups. Prior to 1982 organized groups such as the Professional Teachers' Union, the Federation of Civil Service Unions, the Workers' League, or others affiliated with the Chinese Communist party organization exerted their influence and pressure on government policies in Hong Kong through protests, demonstrations, and petitions.[46] From 1982 to 1984 there appeared a number of political groups organized to lobby for Hong Kong's future in view of the British–Chinese Joint Declaration to revert Hong Kong to China. Among those were the Reform Club and Civic Association, an alliance that at first advocated moderate constitutional changes and then in 1982 lobbied in London for Hong Kong's future. After 1984 new political interest groups grew, including the Meeting Point of 350 members, who not only supported reversion of Hong Kong's sovereignty to China but also advocated democracy and nationalism. Basically it is considered a liberal group. There was also the Hong Kong Affairs Society of thirty-some members who engaged themselves in the study of government policy. In addition, there was the New Hong Kong Society, a study group concerned with influencing government policies on education and housing.

The only declared political party in Hong Kong has been the United Democrats of Hong Kong (UDHK), formed in 1990 and led by Martin Lee, a barrister, and Szets Wah, a school principal. It is a formal political party of six liberal groups. It is generally considered liberal/reform-minded, but anti-Beijing. Lee and Wah were elected to the Legislative Council in 1985 through the functional constituency system of occupational and professional groups. Once elected to the LegCo they became outspoken on issues. In June 1989 they joined other liberals in the Hong Kong Alliance in Support of Democratic Movement in China, the civic group that raised money, among its other activities, for the exiled Chinese dissenters after the June 1989 Tiananmen crackdown.

In opposition to the UDHK is the Liberal Democratic Federation (LDF) formed in November 1990, a conservative elite group of businessmen and professionals who wanted less democratic reform, but are pro-Beijing. One of the leaders of the LDF hailed from a well-known family that owned Wing On Bank, a leading financial institution in Hong Kong. The LDF's position with respect to relations with Beijing has been one of caution and moderation. By 1995 there had been some regrouping and reorganization for these political groups or parties.

Functional Constituency. A word must be said about the functional constituency of occupational and professional groups, an electoral college system introduced by the British in Hong Kong in 1985, which has been incorporated into the Basic Law for Hong Kong to constitute half of the Legislative Council in post-1997 Hong Kong. It is a system of limited representation for professional and business groups that elect twenty-one of the sixty-member LegCo. For instance, only two representatives are allocated for the 2.8 million workers in Hong Kong. A British reform group describes the functional system as: "flawed in principle and unfair in practice."[47] For the September 1991 election, Table 8.1 shows how the various functional groups participated.

It will be recalled from the discussion of the post-1997 legislature for Hong Kong that, as stipulated by the Basic Law, for both the first and second terms, half of its membership of sixty will be composed of functional constituencies whose representatives on the whole have not been really interested in political issues. For most of them, as the *Far Eastern Economic Review* points out, "the main attraction of standing for a functional constituency is to gain both prestige and business contacts rather than answering the needs of constituents."[48] Collectively, these functional constituencies are oriented toward the status quo and there have been "abuses and drawbacks" in the system's selection process of candidates for election.[49]

The 1995 Election

This was the first election before Hong Kong became a part of China. The September 17, 1995, election was for the entire sixty-member Legislative Council. It was denounced by Beijing as "illegal"; Beijing objected to the election before the takeover in 1997. It argued that the old Legislative council, known as LegCo, ceased to exist until a new election was called after July 1, 1997. Beijing made it clear to the Hong Kong government under Governor Christopher Patten that the pre-1997 LegCo and all other district boards were to be abolished and discarded after July 1, 1997.

Nevertheless, the election took place on September 17. However, 36 percent (or about one million) of the registered voters participated. Five major political groups, plus the independents, fielded a total of 138 candidates for the sixty-seat Legislative Council. The result was a defeat for the pro-China group, led by the Democratic Alliance

TABLE 8.1 Hong Kong's Functional Constituencies

Constituency	Eligible Voters	Number Registered	Percent Registered	Candidates
Commercial (HKGCC)	2,380	1,609	67.6	2
Commercial (CGCC)	5,658	2,348	41.5	1
Industrial (HKFI)	744	460	61.8	1
Industrial (CMA)	2,090	1,366	65.4	2
Finance (banking)	398	234	59.1	1
Financial services	1,200	694	57.8	6
Labour (2 reps)	455	378	83.1	2
Social services	207	181	87.4	1
Tourism	1,204	847	70.4	3
Real estate and construction	579	373	64.4	1
Medical	6,518	4,031	61.8	1
Health care	17,073	10,636	62.3	1
Teaching	53,243	38,678	72.6	3
Legal	2,544	1,240	48.7	2
Engineering	3,205	2,848	88.9	2
Architectural, surveying, and planning	2,238	1,438	64.3	4
Accountancy	4,660	2,276	48.8	1
Urban council	40	40	100.0	4
Regional council	36	36	100.0	4
Rural	139	112	80.6	1
Total	104,609	69,825	66.8	40

Source: Far Eastern Economic Review (August 29, 1991), 17. By permission of the publisher.

for Betterment of Hong Kong (DAB), with sixteen seats; the pro-democracy group (or faction) led by Martin Lee's Democratic Party, won nineteen seats, and the smaller independent groups, seven seats, for a total of twenty-six seats, a majority. Between the two groups was the pro-business Liberal Party, ten seats, and the moderates with eight seats.[50]

HONG KONG AFTER THE REVERSION

The Provisional Legislature

It will be recalled that the Basic Law for Hong Kong provides for a legislative council of sixty members to enact laws and ordinances and to appropriate funds for Hong Kong's SAR budget. Governor Christopher Patten assumed that the nineteen popularly elected legislative council, the first such popular election ever held during Britain's 155 years of colonial rule, would serve as the "through train" after the July 1 Chinese takeover. It turned out that Beijing did not want the 1995 elected legislative council to be the "through train," for the simple reason that that popularly elected legislative council was dominated by a majority led by outspoken democracy-movement supporters such as Martin Lee and Emily Lau. Instead, in a move that appeared illegal to some, Beijing instituted a provisional legislative council of its own choosing to serve until an election, as mandated by Articles 67-68 and Annex II of the Basic Law, held sometime after the reversion. (The date for this election was set for May 1998, see discussion below.) It is this controversial provisional legislative council that was installed after midnight on July 1. Both Tony Blair, the British prime minister, and Madeleine Albright, the U.S. Secretary of State, boycotted this installation ceremony.

The provisional legislature was criticized by a formerly elected legislator as a violation of the "Hong Kongers rule Hong Kong" principle, as well as the pledge in the Sino–British joint declaration for a "higher degree of autonomy."[51] Yan Jinqi, exiled former advisor to deposed Premier Zhao Ziyang, argued that the provisional legislature was not only a violation of the organizational rule by the National People's Congress, but also a "non-governmental organization."[52] It is interesting to note that the new provisional legislature met in a closed-door session in Shenzhen near Hong Kong on January 26, 1997, six months prior to the handover, and elected Rita Fan, a former legislator and advisor to British governors, as its presiding officer.

The provisional legislature was sworn in after midnight on July 1, 1997, in Hong Kong. In less than a month the question of the legality of the provisional legislature was raised in a court hearing at the Hong Kong Court of Appeals. Hong Kong's solicitor general, Daniel Fung, presented the argument at the hearing that the court should have accepted the provisional legislature as legal and proper.[53] In addition, Hong Kong's Labor Advisory Board, consisting of government, labor unions, and employers, had decided to review an ordinance on labor matters that has been suspended by the provisional legislature.[54] At any rate, on July 29, 1997, the Hong Kong Court of Appeals ruled that the provisional legislature was a legal body. These and other court challenges on the legal status of the provisional legislature most likely would continue and would have to be resolved by the Court of Final Appeal of fifteen retired or serving judges (four of whom are from the Australian and New Zealand judicial systems).

In retrospect, as pointed out by Frank Ching, the controversy over the legality of the provisional legislature could have been solved before the reversion if Britain had not rejected the option of the Chinese proposal to hold legislative elections immediately after July 1, 1997.[55]

The first election after the reversion for the legislative council took place on May 24, 1998, as decreed by Tung Cheehwa soon after he was sworn in as Hong Kong's chief executive on July 1, 1997. The election not only replaced the provisional legislative council set up by the Chinese authorities on the eve of the reversion with an elected first legislative council, it also proved that voters in Hong Kong were keenly interested in political participation by an unprecedented voter turnout at the polls. About 53.2 percent of the 2.7 million registered voters cast their ballots on May 24. In accordance with the provisions in the Basic Law (in Annex II) the sixty-member legislative council is to be chosen in the following manner: twenty members by direct popular election from geographic districts; ten members by the 800-member Election Council, and the remaining thirty by the functional constituencies, discussed earlier in Table 8.1. The election results showed that in the direct popular election from the geographic districts, the most significant aspect of the election system gave the four pro-democracy parties, led by Martin Lee's Democratic Party, over 67 percent of the popular votes, which yielded fourteen seats out of a total twenty in the legislative council. Although those elected by the indirect methods constituted the majority in the legislature, they only represented less than 150,000 individual voters selected from the pro-Beijing election council and the twenty-eight occupational, professional, or business groups. Thus, while the pro-democracy groups were the minority in the legislative council, they collectively issued a clear signal to Beijing that Hong Kong people wanted indeed a freely elected representative democracy.

Tung Cheehwa: The Chief Executive Officer and Political Leadership

Under the Basic Law, the key government position is that of the chief executive for Hong Kong SAR. Under Articles 43, and 45–46 of the Basic Law, the chief executive is to be selected by a committee of 400 members from Hong Kong business and professional groups who are either pro-Beijing or who have established connections with mainland Chinese government and/or businesses.

On December 11, 1996 the selection committee picked Tung Cheehwa, who was born in Shanghai in 1937. He is the son of a Hong Kong shipping tycoon and was raised in and is a long-time resident of Hong Kong. Before his selection Tung was the chief executive officer for Orient Overseas, a family-owned giant Hong Kong shipping concern. Tung was educated in Britain and spent many years in the United States. Under the Basic Law, Tung's selection and appointment required approval from Beijing, which was granted almost immediately after his selection. Tung's responsibility and power are comparable to those of Chris Patten, the last governor under the British. Unlike Patten, Tung enjoys confidence and support from leaders in Beijing. (He has Jiang Zemin's private telephone number and was told that he can call whenever the need arises.) In fact, as pointed out by one commentator, Tung was selected because he is someone who is acceptable to Beijing, Britain, and the Hong Kong people, and he has the respect of the international business community.[56]

Tung has said that he was selected not by Beijing, but by the 400 Selection Committee members whose constituencies represent the people of Hong Kong.[57] He has made it clear to interviewers that he is not a member of the Chinese Communist Party and said he has no intention of becoming one.[58] Tung has chosen Paul Yip as his special advisor, a man of liberal and pro-China connections. Paul Yip has been a member of the Preparatory Committee for the Hong Kong handover and founder of the Hong Kong Policy Research Institute, a think tank. He also has business contacts in Shanghai, and through these associations he became acquainted with the Shanghai political leaders who are now the CCP's top decision makers (Jiang Zemin, Zhu Rongji, and Wu Bangguo).

Tung's critics say that Hong Kong's chief executive officer has two main weaknesses. One is his lack of political sensitivity, since his life experience has been in private business—which carries with it a management style quite different from that of government. Tung is also known as a behind-the-scenes operator and more at ease doing things in a "murky cocktail of money and politics."[59]

One of the legacies of British colonial rule in Hong Kong was that there were established a set of "legitimate institutional structures, but with no trusted leaders," a conclusion drawn by Hong Kong scholar Lau Siu-Kai.[60] His argument was that Hong Kong must have trusted leaders who could "perpetuate the institutional structure left behind by the colonial government."[61] The popular elections introduced by the British before the reversion served as "a channel of political recruitment" that would establish "linkages" between the leaders and the public.[62]

Amending Public Order and Societies' Ordinances

In the spring of 1997, it was revealed that revisions to the civil liberties ordinances would be made after the reversion. The public order ordinance would be changed to require a prior police permit seven days in advance instead of by simply notifying the authorities. There was some discussion by the Preparatory Committee for the reversion pertaining to prohibiting protests in support of independence for Tibet and Taiwan.[63] Another controversial proposal was to amend the societies' ordinance to allow police to cancel registration of groups and societies believed to be a risk to "national security."[64] Hong Kong's attorney general challenged the wording "national security" as grounds for banning organizations wishing to be registered by maintaining there was no "comprehensive" definition in common law explaining what is or what was not "national security."[65] One critic from the University of Hong Kong termed the attempt to revise the societies' ordinance as "a threat to freedom of expression."[66]

The controversial aspects of these proposed changes to Hong Kong's civil liberties had been not only whether the provisional legislature was legal after the reversion, but also whether the legality of that body's enacted ordinances on civil liberties could be challenged in Hong Kong courts. Chief Justice Patrick Chan has declared that not only was the provisional legislature legal, but the acts of that body could not be challenged in Hong Kong courts.[67] However, Hong Kong's attorney general, J. F. Mathew, argued that "whether an act is or is not an act of state is a question of law, which the courts must decide," as he read from Article 158 of the Basic Law.[68] These issues remained unresolved.

The "Independent" Civil Service

Another important post-colonial government institution on which all eyes have been focused is Hong Kong's civil service, about 50,000 in strength, known for its efficiency and being free from corruption. The civil service has been headed by Mrs. Anson Chan, whose grandfather was a Nationalist general from Anhui, and who is known for her "independent spirit." Many knowledgeable observers believe that the Hong Kong government might collapse if the civil service is not permitted to function properly.

Tung Cheehwa, as Hong Kong's chief executive officer, will have to work well with the civil service, the career bureaucrats, through its long-time senior officers—many of whom (over 150) retired and returned to the United Kingdom on the eve of July 1, 1997. It has been reported that at one time Chinese officials responsible for Hong Kong–Macao affairs preferred a top official in the civil service as chief executive after 1997 for the simple reason that "they know how to run the government."[69] The person they had in mind then was Anson Chan, the chief administrator of Hong Kong's civil service. Unfortunately, Anson Chan was Chris Patten's deputy and loyal to the colonial government, as it had been the tradition for the civil service to be trained and molded by the British. Thus, there is considerable argument on the part of Chinese officials to treat the Hong Kong civil service with respect and kindness. The top officials of the civil service did not have to vacate their jobs after the reversion. As a demonstration of good will, Chinese officials on the mainland permitted development by the Hong Kong Civil Servants Union of a housing estate project, across the border in Shenzhen, for sale primarily to Hong Kong civil servants.[70]

The traditional independent stance exhibited from time to time by the Hong Kong civil service—career bureaucrats and their top officers—had been undergoing some change in recent years, particularly since Chris Patten's reform of the popularly elected legislative council.[71] As explained by Hong Kong public administration scholars, under colonial rule the civil service was accountable to the Queen in London; the popular election reforms and the Basic Law have altered that relationship. Article 64 of the Basic

Law now decrees that the executive must be accountable to the elected legislative council.[72] In addition, Article 98 in the Basic Law mandates the civil servants to be responsible to the Hong Kong SAR government. (There have been reports that there is tension between Tung Cheehwa, the chief executive, and Anson Chan, the top bureaucrat in the civil service.[73]) Using the data they collected for their study on the perception of career bureaucrats over the policy issues for Hong Kong after 1977, Joseph Cheng and Jane Lee point out that the bureaucrats were unwilling to accept PRC influence as the elected legislators.[74] This meant that there could be tensions in the "bureaucrat politician relationship."[75] While the senior and career bureaucrats in Hong Kong's civil service desired autonomy and respect in their relationship with China, after the reversion, they "will resist any attempt by China to dictate its policies to Hong Kong."[76] Thus, it would not be unlikely to see tension and competition for power by the political blocks or actors in Hong Kong after 1997 but the tension might be harmful to Hong Kong's political stability in the long run. It would be very "devastating" to Hong Kong's stability if China were to exert pressure or interfere with Hong Kong's government. In the future will China attempt to force out those senior bureaucrats who are Hong Kongers, but who may still be "pro-British?" Will there be a review of the dossiers of senior bureaucrats, and will the review documentation be forwarded to China if so requested? (This was suggested by the liaison group in the early stages of the Sino–British negotiations.)[77] Again, these issues raised here remained unresolved at time of writing.

The 1998 Election for the Legislative Council. The 1998 election for the twenty directly elected seats in Hong Kong's Legislative Council (legislature) was contested by no less than seven political parties. About three-fourths of the twenty directly elected seats, out of a total of sixty, were won by pro-democracy candidates. Among the winning democratic parties was Martin Lee's Democratic Party, which received 43 percent of the popular votes and captured 13 seats. The pro-Beijing Democratic Alliance for a Better Hong Kong (DAB) received 25 percent of the popular votes and nine seats in the legislature. One needs to be reminded that even though the democratic groups held more than 55 percent of the total popular votes, they held only eighteen of the Legislative Council's sixty seats; the remaining forty seats were chosen indirectly by business and professional organization or special election committees under Hong Kong's functional constituencies system for special interest groups.

Total voter turnout was 53 percent of the eligible voters, up from 35 percent in 1993 and 39 percent in 1991.

Hong Kong's election in September 2000 is significant simply because about half of the sixty-seat Legislative Council were elected by popular vote. Election results showed that of thirty seats to the Legislative Council, the pro-democracy candidates won a total of nineteen seats and the pro-Beijing candidates won eleven seats. Voter turnout decreased to 43 percent for a total of 1.3 million registered voters for the Septmeber 2000 election.

HONG KONG'S "MIRACLE" ECONOMY

Hong Kong is one of Asia's Newly Industrialized Countries (NICs) which has a record of a creditable rate of economic growth. Its Gross Domestic Product (GDP) ranged from 6 to 8 percent in the 1950s. Then the GDP soared to 9 to 10 percent in the 1960s as Hong Kong shifted from *entrepot* to manufacturing exports. From 1950 to 1984 the average annual GDP was about 8.3 percent, followed by a rate of record growth in 1987, which chalked up almost 14 percent, and in 1988, which recorded a 7.9 percent rate. However, by 1989 and 1990 Hong Kong's growth rate was 2.3 and 2.4 percent, respectively. Its GDP for 1991 was estimated at 3.5 percent. A number of reasons serve to explain the rather modest economic performance beginning in 1989. First, the double-digit growth for 1986–88 had created "the capacity and the manpower constraints" as the labor force became static and aged.[78] Then the Tiananmen massacre in June 1989 generated fear and uncertainty for Hong Kong's future. And a worldwide slowdown in the developing nations has had some bearing on Hong Kong's economic performance. But despite the modern growth rate, Hong Kong's per capita income is still one of the highest in Asia: For 1990 it was over $10,000, next only to Singapore and Japan.

Hong Kong economist Y. C. Yao has attributed Hong Kong's "economic miracle" to at least three major factors.[79] First, Hong Kong enjoyed political stability under British colonial rule for four decades. There was a high degree of "rule by consent" practiced by "a paternalistic and enlightened colonial civil service."[80] Second, while there has been frequent reference to Hong Kong as a model of Adam Smith's laissez-faire economy or free capitalism at its best, Hong Kong does enjoy economic freedom to a considerable extent. However, the government does play a leading role in public housing, the bus and mass transit system (including ferry services), rent control, social welfare and labor legislation, and inflation control in recent years, as when the rate reached almost 14 percent in the spring of 1991.

Third, under British colonial rule Hong Kong had a well-established legal system which protects individual rights as well as property and contract rights. Y. C. Yao points out that it has been the enjoyment of these economic freedoms and rights—for instance, the guaranteed "flow of funds across national boundaries in the Asian-Pacific area"—that has enabled the development of Hong Kong as a financial center for the region.[81] The political stability, economic freedom, and enjoyment of individual and property rights have created an atmosphere conducive to doing business and for investment opportunity.

One other factor needs to be added to the list: the industrious character of the people, a large percentage of them refugees from the PRC. To a large measure it has been the willingness of the Hong Kong people to work hard, to develop the necessary skills to do their jobs, and the desire to take risks if given the opportunities that has made Hong Kong what it is today.

Thus, with the combination of the above characteristics of Hong Kong, added to the infrastructure conscientiously developed through the years—the world's busiest free container port, airport (a new one opened in 1998), and the automated mass transit system—therein lies their economic success.

The Trade Pattern

Roughly 90 percent of Hong Kong's industries are geared for an export trade that was dominated by textiles and footwear, watches and electronics. Hong Kong's major trade partners in 1990 were the United States (35 percent), China (21 percent), and Japan (5 percent). Most of the export industries in Hong Kong were skill-intensive light-manufacturing industries, or so-called Small Manufacturing Establishments (SMEs) with fewer than fifty employees.[82] In the past decade Hong Kong has reemerged as an important re-exporter, particularly in trade with China in the areas of processing and packaging. In 1990 the value of re-exports reached more than $52 billion (27 percent went to China and 58 percent imported from China) in textiles, clothing, and electronics.[83]

It must also be pointed out that 70 percent of China's $12 billion export to the United States in 1989 passed through Hong Kong—a point that the Bush administration emphasized to show that Hong Kong would actually be hurt more if the United States revoked the most-favored-nation status with China.[84]

Changing Nature of Hong Kong's Economy

The character of Hong Kong's economy has changed considerably since China's economic reform in the 1980s. It is now basically a service-dominated economy—more than 80 percent of Hong Kong's output comes from the service sector, not from manufacturing.[85] Factories have migrated to nearby Shenzhen or to the Pearl River Delta area where labor costs are low and land is plentiful. Today's Hong Kong service economy is highly skilled, sophisticated, and high-tech-oriented. Hong Kong investors entered into garment manufacturing contracts all over the developing world and the products are shipped to the United States. Government information services statistics indicate that service employment in Hong Kong ranges from import-export trade, to finance, to business services, and to retailing.[86]

Economic prosperity and political-social stability are the twin guarantees in the Sino–British Joint Declaration, as well as in the Basic Law. These guarantees have recently been reiterated by Lu Ping, China's chief negotiator with the British and the man in charge of the central government's Hong Kong–Macao affairs. He has affirmed that it is the Chinese intention to keep strong in Hong Kong the free market operation and that

> the central government will neither make financial claims on the region, nor will it levy taxes. The SAR government will use local financial revenues for its own purposes.[87]

This statement, together with the agreement reached in November 1996 by Britain and Beijing that the Hong Kong SAR government will keep control of Hong Kong's $62 billion foreign reserves is the basis of these guarantees.[88]

Another aspect of Hong Kong's economy that needs to be outlined is the Chinese investment in Hong Kong, which in 1993 reached to about U.S.$20 billion; it may provide a base of influence in Hong Kong's economy. One study advances the "hostage theory," which states that the Chinese investment in Hong Kong would serve as a "hostage" if Beijing fails to honor its pledges for Hong Kong.[89] The "hostage" theory has been questioned on several grounds.[90] One is that Beijing has relied on Hong Kong for the purpose of not only investing, but also for raising capital in Hong Kong as well; and the size of Hong Kong investment in China, which represents over 65 percent of all overseas investment in China, has contributed to China's economic development. However, there is the concern that some of the Chinese investments in Hong Kong, which have their sources in government-owned and monopolized companies, are connected with offsprings of top party officials, with the sole objective of making quick returns.[91]

In short, there are strong reasons not to cast doubts about Hong Kong's future economy. There are signs of close integration between China and Hong Kong in terms of investment and trade, which in the long run would benefit both economies.

In terms of continued economic prosperity for the territory, there was a brief euphoria soon after the British handed over Hong Kong to China. But then East Asian economies went into a dive which affected Hong Kong for a short period thereafter. According to a Hong Kong economics and trade official in San Francisco, unemployment rose to almost 5 percent, real estate values dropped by 40 percent and the stock market tumbled.[92] As a result, the territory's economy declined by 4 percent for 1998.[93] Through a combination of the business sector's own efforts and most importantly, government action, the island's economy perked up by the end of 1998. Government actions included extending credits of $265 million to small and medium-sized businesses, tax incentives to corporations to lure back foreign deposits, and tax rebates to citizens to stimulate consumer spending. However, the most significant government action was its massive intervention in the Hong Kong stock market. Acting for the government, firms spent about $7-9 billion buying blue-chip stocks designed to stem the sale of stocks on the Hong Kong Exchange. What is most significant about the government intervention in the stock market is that the image of Hong Kong as a model for the free enterprise system in the world is no longer valid, provoking its foremost admirer, Milton Friedman, to condemn it as "insane."[94]

By the fall of 1999 Hong Kong's economy rebounded to about 4 percent GDP, contributed to by Asian regional economic improvement, tourism revival, and strong private consumption for the territory as a whole, plus positive government actions as discussed earlier.[95]

Future Prospects

It is certain that Hong Kong will continue to be one of the world's financial centers. Beijing knows, as well as does Washington, that 60 percent of China's exports to the United States go through Hong Kong as do 42 percent of American exports to China. Notwithstanding the familiar refrain from the American press expressing fear for Hong Kong's future under Chinese rule, considerable confidence has been expressed by American businessmen stationed in Hong Kong. A poll taken recently by an affiliate of the Dow Jones company showed that, of the 533 members of the American Chamber of Commerce in Hong Kong, more than 91 percent said they were rather optimistic about Hong Kong's future. Many of the American business representatives polled in the survey have established trade headquarters in Hong Kong. In the first Hong Kong SAR survey taken after the reversion, conducted by the *South China Morning Post*, the political confidence index for Hong Kongers polled remained at 95 points, and the economic confidence index went up to 98 points.[96]

Of course there is really no way for anyone to predict what will happen to Hong Kong in the future. The worst possible scenario would be if Hong Kong authorities could not handle massive public demonstrations involving perhaps hundreds of thousands of Hong Kong citizens in the streets.[97] Under these conditions the Chinese troops of the People's Liberation Army, stationed in Hong Kong and in nearby Guangdong province, could be called in to suppress the protesters. This might appear to be another Tiananmen crackdown in the making. That is why one of the first restrictions issued by Tung Cheehwa, the chief executive for the Hong Kong SAR, was to require police permission prior to any public demonstration. This restriction was widely criticized as a curtailment, if not violation, of Hong Kong's civil liberties.

It is expected that China will keep its pledge to make Hong Kong the "capitalist pearl" in a "socialist oyster," which is another way of saying what Deng Xiaoping's "one country, two systems" is all about. The fulfillment of that pledge is dependent on China's political stability, which, in turn, rests on how well its economy is managed. Hong Kong has played an important role in China's economic development. It is inconceivable for China to do anything to upset Hong Kong's unique status as a valuable participant in the international economic system, particularly in the Asian-Pacific region. Furthermore, there is reason to believe that Chinese leaders want to make Hong Kong a shining example for other "lost territories" to follow: Macao in 1999 and perhaps Taiwan in the future. Singapore's Lee Kuan Yew believes that Hong Kong may become "a catalyst" not only for China's economic growth, but also as "the most prosperous city in Greater China."[98]

THE ISSUE OF HONG KONG'S JUDICIAL INDEPENDENCE

Several cases have occurred recently to heighten the important question of Hong Kong's judicial independence as China's special autonomous administrative region under the slogan, "One country, two systems."

***Execution of Hong Kong Crime Boss in China.*[99]** This case concerns the members of a crime syndicate engaged in arms smuggling and kidnapping of business tycoons in Hong Kong. The crime boss was arrested and tried in China's Guangdong provincial capital. Since the crime boss was a resident of Hong Kong and committed most of the crimes, including the kidnapping, in Hong Kong, it was argued by his lawyers that he should be moved to Hong Kong for trial. However, Hong Kong officials maintained that the crime boss also committed crimes, such as purchasing explosives, in China. The Chinese across the border from Hong Kong also had jurisdiction in the case. But, as argued by the Hong Kong lawyers, the Chinese criminal law does not apply to Hong Kong in accordance with the Basic Law.[100] If the crime boss had been tried and the convicted in Hong Kong, the sentence would have been a life sentence instead of death by execution. This case points to the possibility of an arrest being made in China for a crime committed in Hong Kong but tried in China. If that is so, then where is the judicial independence of the Hong Kong courts?

***Defacing the Chinese Flag Case.*[101]** Another case brings up the legal question of whether mainland Chinese laws apply to Hong Kong as a special autonomous administrative region under the formula of "one country, two systems."

Two Hong Kong residents were found guilty of desecrating both the Chinese national flag and Hong Kong's own flag in violation of the territory's flag ordinance provisions. Defense lawyers for the two men argued that the defacing of both flags was a form of freedom of expression protected by Article 19 of the International Covenant on Civil and Political Rights which applies to Hong Kong under the Basic Law or the constitution of Hong Kong. The case ended up in Hong Kong's Court of Final Appeals, after appeal by the government on a lower court ruling. The five judges on the Court of Final Appeals ruled unanimously that, in the first place, freedom of expression is not "absolute" and that legislative acts enacted as ordinances to protect the flag are constitutional. The ruling angered many lawyers but pointed clearly to the key question of Hong Kong's judicial independence.

To a large extent, who has the first say on the interpretation of Hong Kong's Basic Law? For an answer to this question, we must now turn to the residency or "the right of abode" case.

***The Residency Ruling Controversy.*[102]** On the surface this ruling by Hong Kong's highest court was its interpretation of the Basic Law, Hong Kong's constitution, on whether some 1.6 million mainland-born children have the right to move to Hong Kong if one or both of their parents are Hong Kong residents, even though the children were born before the parents arrived in Hong Kong.

When Hong Kong reverted to China in 1997, the territory of high wages and higher living standards was placed by both sides under very strict limitations to mainland Chinese who wished to enter into the territory—the daily quota for legal entry to Hong Kong was then about 150. The territory is overcrowded with a population of 6.8 million and limited housing and available social services—the reality in the entire situation which is of primary concern for the Hong Kong government.[103]

Then in 1997 an exception was made in Hong Kong's Basic Law to allow children of Hong Kong residents who were born in the mainland the right to live in the territory— the rule known as the "right of abode." Under that provision some 40,000 of them entered as residents.

As discussed in an earlier section, a provisional legislature for Hong Kong was instituted by Beijing immediately after the reversion in 1997 until a new election could take place in 1998. This provisional legislature changed the law to require children of Hong Kong residents to apply for permission for entry into the territory. The revision was challenged and the case ended up in the Final Court of Appeals, which ruled on January 29, 1999 that children born in China to Hong Kong parents must be allowed to apply to Hong Kong courts for the right of entry to the territory. Hong Kong's highest court decision was hailed in Hong Kong but caused displeasure and anger in Beijing for Beijing evidently disliked the idea that Hong Kong courts could make such a ruling, instead of its being made by courts in China. Then in May 1999, the Hong Kong government issued a seventeen-page report calling attention to the situation in which schools and welfare rolls would be swamped, in addition to possible rising unemployment— most likely causing an "unbearable burden to Hong Kong," in the words of a Hong Kong government official.[104]

With backing by the Hong Kong government, the Final Appeals Court ruling permitting mainland children of Hong Kong parents to enter the territory was referred to the PRC's National People's Congress through its Standing Committee for reinterpretation and, if possible, the overturn of the Final Court of Appeals ruling. This move, though supported by Hong Kong's people, would in essence do damage to the concept of "one country, two systems" or "Hong Kongers rule Hong Kong." Nevertheless, the issue was referred to the Chinese parliament's Standing Committee, which reinterpreted the Hong Kong Final Court of Appeals' ruling. The reinterpretation in effect reversed, or invalidated, the Hong Kong court's earlier ruling to permit some 1.6 million Chinese mainland children born to parents of Hong Kong residents the right of abode or to apply for entry into the territory.

The Chinese parliament ruled that the Hong Kong Court of Final Appeals committed two basic errors: One was its failure to consult China's National People's Congress, since in the final analysis, Hong Kong's Basic Law was enacted by the Chinese parliament; second, the Hong Kong court misinterpreted Hong Kong's constitution, and thus its action had "infringed" upon China's sovereign rights.[105] However, as pointed out by Gordon G. Chang, "judicial invalidation of legislation" has been a long established common law practice.[106] But in this case it is the Chinese legislature which has the final say on the meaning of legislation or power to interpret or reinterpret it. For Hong Kong the case may usher in the end of "one country, two systems" and "Hong Kongers rule Hong Kong."

MACAO: THE SECOND SPECIAL ADMINISTRATIVE REGION

Macao, which reverted to Chinese control on December 20, 1999, had been a Portuguese enclave for more than 440 years, dating to the first landing on the peninsula by the Portuguese in 1553 near the Magog Temple—thus, the Portuguese named it Macau, or Macao (hereafter used in this book). It had been Europe's oldest colony in Asia, even though there has never been a treaty giving the Portuguese sovereignty over Macao. It is plausible that the Chinese tolerated the presence of the Portuguese in Macao in 1553 simply because the latter were helpful in ejecting the pirates who infested the coastal waters of the area. Then came Portuguese settlers and other Europeans seeking trade with China, Japan, and India. Macao quickly became the trading post, since Chinese ports were closed to all foreigners.

Macao consists of a peninsula and two small islands (Taipa and Coloane) totaling 7.6 square miles, or about 17.5 square kilometers. In comparison, Hong Kong is more than sixty-one times larger in size than Macao. Whereas Hong Kong has a population of 6.3 million, there are only half a million in Macao. About 98 percent of the populations of both Hong Kong and Macao are ethnic Chinese. A majority of the people in Macao live on the peninsula.

Brief History of Macao[107]

In its first eighty-three years, from 1557 to 1640, Macao served as a fortified trading center and a gateway to China, primarily because of its proximity by land and sea to other parts of the Guangdong province. As a part of Portuguese colonization there came the settlers and the Jesuits who built churches, one of which, St. Paul's Cathedral, is now a tourist attraction—a 400-year-old ruin consisting only of the empty towering gate frame. For the next hundred years (from the mid-eighteenth to the mid-nineteenth centuries), Macao was on the decline as a Portuguese trading post. The Dutch challenged and contested the Portuguese maritime power in Asia; in addition, Portugal's revolt from Spain (1640) brought disaster and neglect to the enclave. Then came the Opium War (1842) between China and Britain, which resulted in China's capitulation under the "unequal treaties," opening China to European trade and missionary activities. Unlike the situation in Hong Kong, the Chinese empire at the time of the Opium War did not surrender its sovereignty of Macao to Portugal; the Portuguese nevertheless took advantage of the Qing Dynasty's weakness by removing Chinese officials from the peninsula. In December 1887 the Portuguese forced China to sign the Sino–Portuguese Treaty at Peking under which Portugal would "permanently" administer Macao. And, under Chinese protest, Portugal unilaterally established the border demarcation between the Macao peninsula and Xiangshan county of Guangdong province. With the demise of the Qing Dynasty and ushering in of the new, but ineffective, Chinese republic, followed by incessant fighting between the warlords in a disintegrated China, Macao became a place for refugees from China. The Chinese migration influx into the Portuguese enclave provided economic development opportunities for the "cheap industries" of matches and fireworks, plus the introduction of casino gambling.

When the Chinese Communist Revolution became victorious in 1949–50, Macao's status was not challenged by the new regime. Thus, like Hong Kong, it remained undisturbed as a colony except for a continuous influx of refugees into the enclave, largely forgotten by the rest of the world. Nevertheless, Macao survived economically by the growth of light industries which produced, for much of the 1960s and 1970s, matches, joss sticks, and handicrafts for export. By then gambling had become, as it is now, a flourishing business attracting the more affluent people from Hong Kong, in addition to tourism, which stimulated the growth of the building industries.

By the 1970s and 1980s a growing export trade in clothing, toys, electronics, and artificial flowers had developed in Macao, distributing to more than one hundred countries worldwide. In the mid-1980s there were more than one thousand small factories employing 70,000 workers in Macao. The total output was valued at U.S.$1 billion, and its per capita income rose to U.S.$2,000.[108] Visitors to Macao in the mid-1980s saw construction of office buildings, hotels, casinos, and apartments on the peninsula. (This author first visited Macao in 1984 and again in 1986 and 1993.) By 1995 Macao's per capita had reached U.S.$17,300, compared with booming Hong Kong's per capita of U.S.$24,000. Like Hong Kong, the Portuguese enclave has been a free port and there is free entry from Hong Kong and elsewhere without a visa requirement. The total number of visitors to Macao reached over two million in 1996. Much of the investment in Macao has come from Hong Kong and abroad.

Gambling in Macao has become one of the key industries—it has been estimated that 60 percent of the government's revenue has been from taxes on casino gambling.[109] Along with the increase in gambling activity there has developed an increase in gang murders—a disturbing factor in Macao.[110] Organized gangs have been contesting each other's power and control over gambling business by engaging in murder and assassination on the streets. Macao's authorities have been criticized for their inability to control the gang wars.[111] A Chinese foreign ministry spokesman is reported to have urged Portugal to take steps to stamp out gang wars in Macao for the sake of restoring social order to Macao.[112]

Localization of the Macao Civil Service

The total population of Macao is about 500,000, by latest count. Of these, 97 percent are Chinese, with a majority of them speaking Cantonese, as do the people in Hong Kong. The next population groups is the Macanese—that is, anyone who was born in Macao of Chinese-Portuguese parents, as Eurasians. They number not more than 11,000 in all, or less than 3 percent of the total and speak Portuguese. The remainder are those born or raised in Portugal. While the Macanese identify themselves with neither China nor Portugal, but with Macao only, they often do claim that they are Portuguese nationals and hold Portuguese passports, which gives them the right to enter, leave, or work in Portugal. The total number of Portuguese passport holders is about 100,000, including some members of the Chinese community.

While the Macanese constitute the minority in population makeup in Macao, they are the majority ethnic group in Macao's civil service. In 1990 there was a total of 14,644 civil servants in the Macao government. The ethnic distribution was as follows:[113] 1,811 (12.4 percent) were Portuguese; 10,467 (71.4 percent) were Macanese or Portuguese passport holders; and 3,700 (25 percent) were Chinese. The Portuguese, of course, were the top-ranking administrators, judges, prosecutors, and lawyers; but the middle- and some upper-level members of the civil service were Macanese.[114]

Beijing has made its view known that Macao's civil service must be localized at the time of reversion to China in late 1999. The government in Macao announced in December 1989 that it would gradually localize the civil service: 80 percent by 1997 and 100 percent by 1999.[115] But localization of civil service, particularly at the higher levels, does create some serious problems.[116] One problem is the retention, after reversion in 1999, of those civil servants who were Portuguese passport holders. How many will be retained if there is no expressed assurance from China regarding their continued stay in Macao? This would be a concern to the Macanese who hold Portuguese passports. Another problem is the matter of language. Bills in Macao legislative assembly have been drafted in Portuguese, and Chinese-language translation has been used as "reference only." In addition, as pointed out by Herbert Yee and Sonny Lo, many Chinese in the civil service would have difficulty obtaining promotions, since many of them do not read or write Portuguese.[117] These and other related problems of language would need to be addressed in 1999 and in the years after reversion.

MACAO UNDER THE 1987 SINO–PORTUGUESE JOINT DECLARATION AND THE 1993 BASIC LAW

The Sino–Portuguese Joint Declaration on Macao, 1987

Beijing and Portugal entered into a secret agreement in 1979 that China possesses sovereignty over Macao—the secret agreement was not disclosed until 1987.[118] Negotiations in the early 1980s between Beijing and London concerning Hong Kong's future definitely had some impact on the future status for Macao.[119] In April 1987, three years after the signing of the Sino–British Joint Declaration on Hong Kong, the Sino–Portuguese Joint Declaration on Macao was signed. First, it affirmed China's sovereignty over Macao on December 20, 1999.[120] Second, the joint declaration for Macao declared a set of fundamental policies which, similar to the Basic Law of Hong Kong, were based on or were "in line with the principle of one country, two systems." Thus, this was the second time Deng Xiaoping's general, but undefined, pragmatic formula had been incorporated in an international treaty or protocol.

Similar to that of Hong Kong, Macao's status after 1999 would be as a Special Administrative Region enjoying a higher degree of autonomy except in defense and foreign affairs. As in the case of Hong Kong, the Macao government after reversion will be composed of local inhabitants. As in the case of Hong Kong, public servants of Chinese nationality and Portuguese previously serving in Macao "may remain in employment." In identical language, both joint declarations state that "the current social and economic systems will remain unchanged, and so will the life-style." In both joint declarations the identical wording is present with respect to the guarantee of law currently in force, as well as all rights and freedoms of the inhabitants.

In Annex I to the 1987 Sino–Portuguese Joint Declaration there is an elaboration of the executive, legislative, and judicial powers for the Macao SAR—these powers were subsequently spelled out in the Basic Law for Macao.

The Basic Law for Macao, 1993

The constitution (Basic Law) for Macao after December 20, 1999, was adopted by the Eighth NPC at its first session on March 31, 1993. There is a great deal of not only similar arrangements but also identical language in both constitutions for the future Hong Kong and Macao. It is quite evident that the draft of Hong Kong's Basic Law (1988) was used as a model for Macao. As in the Basic Law for Hong Kong, interpretation and amendment of the Macao Basic Law is vested in the Standing Committee of the National People's Congress in Beijing. The power to propose amendments to the Basic Law for both Hong Kong and Macao rests with the National People's Congress. The following is a brief summary of the Basic Law for Macao.

The Chief Executive.   As in the case of Hong Kong, the chief executive for Macao must be a permanent resident no less than 40 years of age who has resided continuously in Macao for at least twenty years. As outlined in Annex I of the Basic Law for Macao, the person is to be selected by an election committee of 300 members representing the various sectors of the Macao community: business, cultural, labor, and so on. Candidates for the office are to be nominated by the election committee members and voted upon by secret ballot. The term of office is five years, and the person so selected may not serve more than ten years consecutively. Duties of the chief executive include implementation of law and order, signing bills (such as budget) enacted by the legislative body, and appointing and removing judges.

Under Article 51 of the Basic Law for Macao, the chief executive can return bills for reconsideration within ninety days of passage by the legislative body, which can override the chief executive by a two-thirds majority within thirty days. Under Article 52 the chief executive can dissolve the legislature if he or she refuses to sign a bill passed the second time. Or, the legislature can be dissolved if it refuses to enact the government bill on the budget. In this circumstance, the chief executive may approve a provisional short-term appropriation at the level of the previous fiscal year. The chief executive must resign if the new legislature again passes the original bill by a two-thirds majority and the chief executive still refuses to sign it within thirty days (Article 54).

Thus, the executive-legislative relationship prescribed under Articles 51–54 as outlined above would be an entirely new experience for Macao. Under the 1976 Organic Law for Macao it is the president of Portugal in Lisbon who has the ultimate responsibility for managing Macao. A 1988 case of an alleged financial misappropriation by a television company involving the governor was decided by the Portuguese president in Lisbon.[121]

The Legislative Council.   The first Legislative Council for Macao after 1999 was the last Macao legislative body established before December 20, 1999, if it is confirmed by the fifty-member preparatory committee for the transition. The last Macao legislature before December 20, 1999, consists of twenty-three members: eight by direct election by eligible voters; eight by indirect election through constituency groups representing the various segments of the Macao society such as business, labor, and cultural or religious groups; and seven to be appointed by the new chief executive designate. The first Legislative Council will serve until October 15, 2001.

Under Annex II of the Basic Law for Macao, the second term for the second Legislative Council will have a membership of twenty-seven: ten by direct election, ten by indirect election through the constituency groups, and seven appointed. For subsequent legislative councils total membership will increase to twenty-nine: twelve directly elected, ten indirectly by constituency groups, and seven appointed. The term of office, beginning with the second Legislative Council after October 15, 2001, will be four years (Article 69).

Under Article 71 of the Basic Law for Macao, the Legislative Council is empowered to enact, amend, or repeal laws, to approve budgets and taxation, and to debate on policies or issues of public interest. An interesting provision is contained in Article 71(7): In a motion initiated by one-third of the members, the Legislative Council may file charges against the chief executive for "serious breach of law or dereliction of duty." If the chief executive refuses to resign, the Legislative Council may, by a resolution, "give a mandate" to the Court of Final Appeal to appoint an independent committee to investigate the charges. If there is sufficient evidence to substantiate the charges as found by the independent investigation, then the Legislative Council may institute impeachment proceedings by a two-thirds vote. (A similar provision is contained in the Basic Law for Hong Kong.)

The Judiciary. Under Article 84, three levels of courts have been defined for the Macao SAR: the primary, intermediate and the Court of Final Appeal. Also, there is, under Article 86, an administrative court presiding over administrative and tax cases. Decisions of the administrative court may be appealed to the intermediate court. Judges for all levels of the judiciary shall be appointed by the chief executive upon recommendation of an independent commission of three local judges, lawyers and other eminent persons (Article 87). Judges can be removed by the chief executive for failure to discharge their responsibilities; such removal must be recommended by a review committee made up of legislative council members. All of the above provisions were originally outlined in the Sino–Portuguese Joint Declaration (Part IV).

Public Civil Service. Under Articles 98 and 99 all previous public or civil service personnel, including police and supporting staff for the judiciary, may remain in employment and continue their service after December 20, 1999, with the same pension entitlements and benefits as before. Portuguese and other foreign nations previously serving in the Macao public service may remain as advisers and/or to fill professional and technical manpower needs. This provision is also granted to holders of Permanent Identity Cards. In Part IX, the Sino–Portuguese Joint Declaration specifies that these categories of people are holders of Permanent Identity Cards: Chinese nationals who were born or who have resided in Macao for a continuous period of seven or more years before or after December 20, 1999; Portuguese who were born or have resided in Macao before or after December 20, 1999 (this is the category for the Macanese); and those persons who have resided in Macao and who have taken Macao as their place of permanent residence.[122] It should be noted that, while the Hong Kong Basic Law contains similar provisions as the Macao Basic Law with reference to foreign nationals with Permanent Identity Cards, the Hong Kong Basic Law requires that only Chinese nationals among permanent residents of the SAR may fill positions as secretaries and deputy secretaries of executive departments, commissioners and deputy commissioners for police, director for audit, civil service, and immigration.

Citizenship. Finally, there is the matter of Macao residents who hold dual Chinese and Portuguese citizenship. Dual nationality or citizenship is not permitted under Chinese nationality law. However, some 80,000 to 100,000 Chinese residents are holders of Portuguese passports. In one memorandum attached to the Sino–Portuguese Joint Declaration, an exception or concession has been made to allow Macao residents who are citizens—and therefore holders of Portuguese passports—to continue to use them after December 20, 1999. This means that these holders of Portuguese passports are entitled to the right of abode or residence in Portugal.[123] Children born in China with one parent with permanent residence in Macao would be permitted to remain in Macao. In contrast, evidently it has not been the case in Hong Kong, as discussed earlier.

Macao after December 1999. Macao's return to China on December 20, 1999 created very little stir in Macao city, except for the handover ceremony the evening before the Portuguese departure after 442 years of colonial rule. When the 500 Chinese troops entered Macao an hour after the handover, the citizens of Macao gave them a large and warm welcome on the streets. There was some expectation that the Chinese troops now stationed in the enclave would be able to restore law and order against the violent triad gang which has terrorized the former colony with street killing over the control of the casinos.

     Edmund Ho, a 44-year-old banker, became the chief executive under Article 51 of the Basic Law for Macao, discussed previously. He was chosen by the Election Committee of 300. Ho is considered to be loyal to Beijing, but tactful and reliable. He has been a strong supporter of continued stationing of Chinese troops for law and order enforcement in Macao after the handover. Only time will tell whether the chief executive will be able to provide law and order during his first five-year term, or until 2004. At any rate, what is important is the fact that the return of Macao to China is perhaps another precursor to the eventual unification of Taiwan under the "one country, two systems" formula.

GREATER CHINA: PEARL RIVER DELTA REGIONAL DEVELOPMENT

The Pearl River, or Zhujiang, (China's fifth-longest river) flows southeast from Guangzhou (Canton) to the South China Sea. The Pearl River Delta, also known as the Canton Delta, covers an area of more than 3,000 square miles stretching from Guangzhou in the north to the lower Pearl River estuary between Hong Kong and Macao in the south. The delta is formed by three other streams that drain in the low-lying area to converge on a common delta before they reach the sea: The Tung (East) River, Pei (North) River, and Si (West) River. The Pearl River is rather shallow, but about 9 to 10 miles down it deepens. In his classical text on the geography of Asia, George B. Cressey discusses the three major cities of the Pearl River Delta: Guangzhou, Hong Kong, and Macao.[124]

     Generally speaking, the Pearl River Delta (hereafter referred to as PRD) area consists of three distinct types of political-economic-social entities: Hong Kong and Macao as SARs; their neighboring Special Economic Zones (SEZs); and the once simple rural towns, soon to emerge as vibrant new industrial cities.

     We have discussed so far Hong Kong and Macao as SARs; we now focus the discussion on the two Special Economic Zones of Shenzhen, next door to Hong Kong, and Zhuhai, next door to Macao.

Shenzhen and Zhuhai SEZs: The Success Stories for Greater South China

     One of the more important reasons why both Shenzhen and Zhuhai have been designated as SEZs is the availability of inexpensive land. Industrial property is not only scarce in Hong Kong, but also very expensive. For instance, in 1981 the land rent in

Hong Kong was U.S.$57 per square meter, but only U.S.$5–15 in neighboring Shenzhen. Generally the Chinese partner in a joint venture contributes the land to the enterprise to be established and provides much of the infrastructure. Land may be leased by a foreign investor for a maximum of thirty years for industrial use and a longer period for educational, scientific, and medical use.

The largest SEZ, Shenzhen, comprising 327.6 square kilometers (126 square miles), is located on the eastern shore of the Pearl River estuary, 150 kilometers southeast of Guangzhou (Canton). It shares the northern boundary with Hong Kong and is only about 40 kilometers from the old Kowloon Railway Station on the peninsula. Shenzhen can now be reached by automated subway from Hong Kong in less than half an hour.

The most striking scene in Shenzhen SEZ was its rapid transformation from a bleak border town north of Hong Kong's New Territory to a bustling metropolis in a short period of less than four years from its inception in 1980. Chinese figures show that the city built or widened more than fifty-five urban streets, totaling 80 kilometers in length. Less visible is the development of other elements in the infrastructure, including water, gas, sewage disposal, electricity, and communication systems. By the end of June 1984, the Chinese claimed to have invested a total of 2.5 billion yuan in construction projects for the zone that provided more than 4 million square meters of floor space for industrial buildings, factories, residential high-rise buildings (many of them are more than twenty stories high), department stores, modern hotels, and restaurants. Foreign enterprises in the zone, it has been reported, invested approximately U.S.$800 million in capital construction in Shenzhen during the four-year period from 1984 to 1988.

Because of Shenzhen's proximity to Hong Kong, special emphasis was placed in the development of housing and residential property in the zone. Apartment buildings for overseas Chinese have been much in demand and consequently more high-rise buildings are being built in the zone. The *China Business Review* reported that the housing program in Shenzhen SEZ was rather successful in that the average living space per person in 1982 was 6.5 square meters, compared with 2.7 in 1978.[125]

Transportation facilities linking the Shenzhen SEZ with Hong Kong and Guangzhou (Canton) were expanded rapidly. In addition to sea routes to Hong Kong and the rail to both Guangzhou and Hong Kong, an expressway of 240 kilometers linking Shenzhen-Guangzhou-Zhuhai, which also links with a six-lane, 30-kilometer expressway with Hong Kong in a joint venture between the Shenzhen SEZ and Hopewell China Development Company of Hong Kong was constructed. The project cost was estimated at HK$450 million and was completed in 1987. There is an international airport in Shenzhen SEZ that serves the offshore oil drilling companies in the South China Sea.

The Zhuhai SEZ, adjacent to Macao, is much smaller in area. Originally established with only 6.8 square kilometers, recently Zhuhai was authorized to expand to 14 square kilometers. Zhuhai SEZ can be reached from Hong Kong by hydrofoil in less than 75 minutes. It lies in the estuary of the Pearl River Delta. It has a population of approximately 175,000.

Much of the Zhuhai SEZ is still underdeveloped or awaiting large injection of foreign and/or overseas Chinese investment funds. Before any large-scale industrial development can take place in Zhuhai, it needs basic infrastructure construction such as roads and port facilities. Sources available show that Zhuhai SEZ spent about U.S.$50 million in infrastructure, mainly on roads, water, and electricity for housing development. Another U.S.$100 million was earmarked for more infrastructure beginning in 1984.[126] Since then there have been more funds made available by the provincial government for economic development for Zhuhai. In addition, a heliport has been completed for the zone to link

Zhuhai with Guangzhou, the provincial capital, with six flights per week and with Hong Kong. The heliport serves mainly to aid offshore oil exploration in the South China Sea; it also provides telecommunication facilities for Zhuhai SEZ as a whole. The zone now includes a tourist center, the Zhuhai Hotel complex, and a woolen mill in the Gonbei custom district on the border with Macao. Two growth industries for Zhuhai have been the development of a service center for offshore oil drilling in the South China Sea and tourism, which can take advantage of the subtropical climate and the pastoral beauty in nearby Zhongshan county, the birthplace of Dr. Sun Yatsen, founder of the Chinese republic. In fact, tourists from Hong Kong and Macao can now make a one-day visit to Zhongshan from Zhuhai with Dr. Sun's memorial hall as the highlight for the short trip.

Preferential Tax Policies

One of the most important incentives to attract foreign capital investment into the SEZs is, for instance, preferential tax treatment. There is the income tax rate of 15 percent applied to enterprises in both Shenzhen and Zhuhai with no other local surcharges. This compares rather favorably with neighboring Hong Kong, which is 18 percent, or with inland cities elsewhere in China where the income tax may go as high as 20 to 30 percent or more.[127] However, if an enterprise has an investment of more than U.S.$5 million or is using advanced technology, it can have a reduction of income tax by a further 20 to 50 percent or an exemption from such taxation for from one to three years.[128] There is a 100 percent tax holiday in the first two profit-making years and 50 percent reduction in the following three years.

In addition, machinery, spare parts, and raw materials for production needed by the enterprise in the zones are exempted from custom duties and import tax, as well as items for daily use (except cigarettes and liquor). Products produced by the enterprise in the zone for export are also exempt from custom duties. These rates and exemptions apply to all enterprises in the zones, be it joint venture or wholly owned by foreign investor or overseas Chinese. Goods shipped from the zones to elsewhere in China are subject to import duties since the SEZs produce goods mainly for export—a sore point with foreign investors. Profits from the enterprise in the SEZs are exempt from taxation if they are reinvested into enterprises. Profits for foreign investors can be remitted in the hard currencies outside of China. Personal income is subject to a tax that ranges from 3 percent to no more than 30 percent.

By the end of 1992, Special Economic Zones in coastal southern China had helped to boost the regional growth rate to China's highest: 19.5 percent for Guangdong. The per capita income for Guangdong in 1992 was over U.S.$3,000. The economic boom in Guangdong has been helped by investment capital from Hong Kong, particularly in the Shenzhen Special Economic Zone.

Pearl River Delta (PRD) Township Enterprises

Next to the Shenzhen and Zhuhai SEZs are some two dozen or so districts and townships under the confines and jurisdiction of the Guangdong provincial administration.[129] In November 1994 the Pearl River Delta Economic Region was established for the purpose of stimulating a higher economic growth rate by as much as 16 percent annually with the goal of making the PRD region the most prosperous region in China. With availability of land and labor, the region has concentrated its economic activities on manufacturing by attracting investments from Hong Kong and overseas in areas such as processing and reprocessing imported materials with samples supplied by Hong Kong and foreign business concerns.

As an example, in Dongguan, about a two-hour drive from Hong Kong, labor-intensive township enterprises have grown steadily in a rural setting. Raw material from Hong Kong can be trucked to Dongguan in the morning and the finished products returned to Hong Kong in the afternoon. The manufacturing boom has in turn stimulated a building or real estate expansion in rural Dongguan. It has been reported that by the end of 1995 foreign investment capital totaling U.S.$5.2 billion had been pumped into the township economy, which was able to support some 13,000 enterprises.[130] As a result Dongguan's exports in 1995 were valued at U.S.$6.3 billion, about 10 percent of the province's total export value.[131] Today Dongguan's industrial base is revolving around these industries: electronics, electrical appliances, textiles, clothing, food processing, pharmaceutical and building materials.[132]

Another Pearl River Delta township that serves as an example of rural township transformation into a manufacturing city is the Shunde township, where electric fans are now manufactured in Asia. Other Shunde township enterprises manufacture refrigerators and air conditioning units, employing advanced technology from the leading industrial powers of the United States, Germany, and Japan. It has been reported that the Guangdong Kiln Electrical Holding Co., now listed on the Hong Kong Stock Exchange, can produce one refrigerator every eighteen minutes.[133]

The pattern of enterprise development for most of these Pearl River Delta township's has been that they began with processing and assembling imported materials and parts. As most foreign investment came in from Hong Kong, processing or reprocessing enterprises were able to apply advanced technology to direct manufacturing of light industrial goods for export (textiles, plastics, chemicals, and toys).

A major concern for the Pearl River region's economic development has been an increased rate of environmental pollution. One study showed that there has been a significant increase in gaseous pollutants, as well as an increase in the occurrence of acid rain produced by industrial contaminants.[134] Additionally, there seems to be a serious problem with the discharge of untreated wastewater and the dumping of human waste into waterways. The environmental deterioration has been quite noticeable in the delta area even by casual visitors. (The author has visited the PRD region three times in recent years.)

The Rise of "Greater China": A New Region-State?

The idea of a "Greater China," a term this author prefers to use, is an expansion of the original concept proposed by a 1920 political thinker, Ou Qujia: Only in a "federated" China was it possible for the province to become independent, competitive, and strong—thus the birth of a "New Guangdong" (*Xin Guangdong*).[135]

The Pearl River Delta, as defined here, covers less than 3,000 square miles (or about 47,000 square kilometers) and contain a population of 21.3 million, excluding the itinerant population of 8.5 million. In 1995 the per capita Gross Domestic Product (GDP) for the entire delta was about U.S.$2,250—it is the most affluent region of China except for Hong Kong or Shenzhen. The Pearl River Delta region not only has a thriving agricultural economy, which produces two or three harvests each year because of its subtropical climate, but the area also features advanced industries, fueled by investment from Hong Kong and from abroad. Eighty percent of some 60,000 foreign-related enterprises in Guangdong province are supported by Hong Kong investors.[136]

The PRD region was the first to introduce economic reform and was the site of the birth of China's first Special Economic Zones in Shenzhen and Zhuhai, as discussed earlier. If we look at the Pearl River as a development region from today's perspective we see the larger triangular formation of Guangzhou (Canton) in the north at the top of the triangle with Hong Kong and Macau as the SARs at the base, plus the economic growth of the Special Economic Zones of Shenzhen and Zhuhai. Eventually, these industrially booming cities will be linked by the Guangzhou (Canton)-Shenzhen-Zhuhai superhighway and the planned 40-mile (38-kilometer) roadway across the Pearl River Delta that will link Hong Kong and Macao.[137] One can normally travel by sea from Hong Kong to Macao by hydrofoil in less than one hour. The Beijing-Zhuhai highway, linking Macao SAR, is expected to be built by 1999.[138] By then there will be a network of smaller, but growing, cities to be linked to constitute a greater Pearl River Delta region. There are already several airports in the delta area, excluding the new Hong Kong International Airport.

All of these economic and infrastructure developments in the Pearl River Delta indicate a strong possible emergence of what David G. Goodman has described as "economic regionalism," centered around Guangdong and Hong Kong—more "independent" from the hub at Beijing in areas of economic development. But this is not necessarily "separatism" or "warlordism."[139] The new regionalism, as it seems to be the case for "Greater China" in the Pearl River Delta, is basically influenced and shaped more by "international economic involvement" than anything else.[140]

ECONOMIC REGIONALISM, OR "FEDERALISM, CHINESE STYLE"

Guangdong, because of its geographic makeup, its distance from Beijing, the center, and the tendency to advocate its "deep-rooted regional particularisms,"[141] now reinforced by the phenomenal economic growth in the Pearl River Delta region, will more than ever before exert its local autonomy, but not necessarily the desire to break away from the center. In 1990, Guangdong and the Pearl River Delta region, plus Hong Kong and Macao, contained 6 percent of China's total population and produced 10 percent of the nation's GNP.[142] In 1991 the region commanded 32 percent of China's exports (74 percent of which came from the Pearl River Delta) and about 40 to 50 percent of China's total foreign investment.[143] As pointed out by Helen F. Siu, the region is attempting to "redefine" itself politically and economically.[144]

At the same time, Beijing has made attempts to compel Guangdong's political leaders to adhere to the center's wishes. Typically, the center attempted to dislodge the entrenched power base in the province led by Ye Xuanping, son of the late PLA marshal Ye Jianyin, by "promoting" him and several other provincial top party officials to the center. Ye Xuanping, the "boss of Guangdong," was promoted to the vice-chairmanship for the National People's Political Consultative Conference (NPPCC), an advisory group to the NPC.

Ye has been known for his unhappiness and desire to return to Guangdong. In June 1995 he submitted his resignation for the fourth time to the central authorities and requested permission to return to his native province. Then in July of that year the Guangdong provincial governor and party's secretary also submitted their resignations for the third time. These actions openly highlighted the center-provincial conflict in Guangdong. In 1994, Guangdong provincial leaders were criticized by central leaders in Beijing for promoting "localism" and "mountain-topism" (factionalism).[145] They were also being criticized for making Guangdong more "capitalistic" than Hong Kong or Macao.[146] The central authorities in Beijing faced an intractable dilemma in that Guangdong's political stability could be adversely affected if the center insists on its unpopular demands. The confrontation between the center and the province over the appointment of a mayor for Guangzhou in 1996, the provincial capital, which was in the end resolved by a compromise, is another case in point. Since then Beijing has made the decision to place some sixteen cities under its direct control, thus emasculating provincial authority.

Former Premier Li Peng was said to have complained about local leaders making constant demands on the center and issuing threats to "retire" if they did not get what they wanted.[147] Qiao Shi, then the NPC Standing Committee chairman, was quoted as having accused provincial and local leaders of having the habit of placing their importance above the center's, simply because they have been economically successful.[148] In short, it is obvious that the central government's lack of control over provincial and local leadership remains a serious unresolved problem in the post-Deng transition period. Beijing seems to have adopted a two-pronged approach toward Guangdong: continued preoccupation with provincial concerns as evidenced by the appointment of a new provincial governor, Lu Ruihua, a "local boy," former mayor of Guangzhou and Foshan; and the dispatch to Guangdong of senior party cadres to watch over the leaders.[149]

The dramatic change in the center-local power relationship, brought on by Deng's economic reform, has been the subject of a recent study by China scholars at Stanford University.[150] They have analyzed the rise of a new political system as "federalism, Chinese style," which is driven by the need for market preservation, under which "political decentralization" has not only "altered" the center-local relationship, but also "enhanced the power of local government."[151] The study concludes by listing a number of factors that have contributed to the lasting effect of the economic reform in which the central government's discretion has been limited.[152] These factors are the emergence of new rival power centers in China in fast-growing areas which now possess a "substantial independent source of revenue, authority and political support"; the decline of personal authority of leaders at the center, which has weakened the party's control since local leaders now owe loyalty to localities; and the ability of the central government to control local economic behavior has been weakened as the private market economy has expanded.[153]

The analysis seems to support Susan Shirk's 1994 study, in which she pointed out that success in economic reform has given rise to decentralization, local government control over the economy, and a local system of patronage and loyalty.[154] Other studies in recent years have also made the same point about the changing center-local relationship which has resulted from decentralization.[155] From another perspective, the center at Beijing probably was relieved by the lessening of interregional rivalry or disparities as the center no longer promoted its "one-sided pro-coastal policy," a point made by Victor C. Falkenheim in his examination of China's regional development.[156]

THE TAIWAN QUESTION: SUGGESTION FOR A POSSIBLE SOLUTION

Historic Legacies. Part of the tourist attraction to Taiwan is the exhibits of the aborigines of Taiwan. Most anthropologists adhere to the theory that the original people of Taiwan migrated from Malay tribes to these islands, for there are linguistic similarities between the two cultural groups. Some, however, propose that the aborigines in Taiwan were related to the Miao people from southern China.[157] At any rate, Chinese migration to Taiwan occurred during the Tang dynasty in the seventh and eighth centuries. and the first Chinese settlement did not take place until the fourteenth century under the Yuan, or the Mongol rule. It was during the seventeenth century that Western contact with Taiwan began.

First, around 1517 Portuguese sailors sighted and named the islands *Formosa*, the "beautiful islands." In 1624 the Dutch arrived in southern China and used it as a base for harassing the Portuguese, and in 1626 the Spanish arrived at the northern portion of the island. In 1642 the Dutch drove out the Spanish, and by 1661 Chinese Ming loyalists under Cheng Chi Lung, a pirate in the Taiwan Strait who married a Japanese or Okinawan, had driven out the Dutch and passed rule over the islands to his legendary son, Koxinga. For years before Koxinga's rule and thereafter he raided the coast of Fujian province on the mainland for the purpose of harassing the Manchu empire, which had conquered China. The Manchu authorities evacuated the coastal areas in fear of Koxinga's marauding pirates. During this evacuation the Fujian people migrated to the Taiwan islands. In 1663 Manchu troops finally prevailed and the islands became a part of the vast Manchu empire. For the period from 1663 to 1895 Taiwan was administered as a part of the Fujian province. The Manchu empire had no interest in providing effective and efficient rule for the islands, which were beset with uprisings and rebellions to the extent that China was reluctant to even claim its sovereignty over Taiwan. This indicated to the Western powers, including the United States, that China was not really interested in possessing the islands, even though more than 200,000 mainland Chinese had sought refuge there before its war with Japan in 1895.

Japanese rule, 1895–1945.   In 1886 Taiwan became a province of the Chinese empire. Three years later the Sino–Japanese War was fought over the control of Korea. By the Treaty of Shimonoseki, signed on April 17, 1895, China ceded to Japan the island of Taiwan and the Pescadore Islands, in addition to suzerainty over Korea and the Liaodong Peninsula. For the next fifty years, Japan fully exploited Taiwan's agricultural resources in rice and sugar, as well as vegetables, meat and fruit, which were exported to Japan to meet the people's food needs. The Japanese also built roads, railroads, a communication system, modern banking facilities, and hydroelectric projects. There were also improvements in health and education. Taiwan was for all intents and purposes a colony that served the needs of the Japanese nation. The Japanese also established in Taiwan a regimented political control system that divided the population into households with the head of each 100 households responsible for law and order.[158] Political stability, except for occasional aborigine uprisings in the mountainous areas, and economic improvements enabled the doubling of Taiwan's population on the eve of Japan's war in the Pacific. By the 1940's Taiwan had already become a formidable Japanese military base in the Pacific.

Chinese Nationalist Rule, 1947–Present.   At the Potsdam Conference held from July 17 to August 1, 1945, the leaders of the Allied powers—Harry Truman, Clement Attlee, and Joseph Stalin—dictated the terms of Japanese surrender to include implementation of the Cairo Declaration: Namely, Japan was to be confined to its home islands and Taiwan was to be returned to China. The Japanese forces and the colonial administration departed Taiwan in the fall of 1945. By October Nationalist Chinese authorities had taken military and political control of Taiwan, and Taiwan became a province of China. Chiang Kai Shek appointed General Chen Yi the military governor. Immediately, ill feelings developed under the military government between the Taiwanese and the Nationalists.

Some of the ill feelings or distrust exhibited by both were caused by the inability to communicate in their own languages, for the Taiwanese spoke the language akin to the southern Fujian dialect, which was not understood by most of the Mandarin-speaking Nationalists. the Nationalists maintained the feeling that the Taiwanese were collaborators for the Japanese. The Nationalists were preoccupied with civil war on the mainland and paid little attention to Taiwanese problems.[159]

The accumulated ill will and distrust came to a head on February 28, 1947, when an initial disagreement over black marketeering in cigarettes escalated into a full-blown uprising against the Nationalists, who were obsessed by fears of communist infiltration among the Taiwanese. A crackdown on the populace was ordered by the military governor; it resulted in the killing of as many as 28,000—some private estimates placed the slain in the range of 100,000.[160] The 1947 massacre was not openly revealed until 1992, when an official investigation report of twelve volumes was made public by leaders of the ruling Kuomintang (KMT). While there were no official apologies as demanded by some, except expression of regrets by President Lee Teng Hui, there have been discussions about possible compensation for the victims' families and the designation of February 28 as a memorial day.[161]

Taiwan's Legal Status Disputed. As Mao Zedong's forces gained victories on the battlefields in China's raging civil war, preparation was made by the Nationalists to retreat to Taiwan. By late September 1949 some two million Nationalist government officials and soldiers, plus their dependents, were evacuated to the island of Taiwan in wholesale retreat from the mainland which Mao proclaimed on October 1, 1949, as the Peoples' Republic of China. In the meantime, the Nationalists under Chiang Kai Shek, vowed to reconquer the mainland in the name of the Republic of China, now exiled to Taiwan. A state of civil war continued, but only to be quarantined or restrained by the U.S. 7th Fleet in the Strait of Formosa.

Nationalist security in Taiwan was guaranteed by the 1954 Mutual Security Treaty, signed between the United States and the Nationalist government in Taiwan, which still claimed to be the lawful government of all China. Soon a diplomatic battle began at the United Nations over the question as to which side should lawfully represent the people of China—the Nationalists were seated at the headquarters of the United Nations as the Chinese representatives. This contest was finally terminated in 1971, when the Nationalist representatives were unseated and replaced by the People's Republic of China as the United States and the PRC moved closer to rapprochement. When the United States recognized the PRC as the only legitimate government for China, the 1954 Mutual Security Treaty was also terminated and replaced by the 1979 Taiwan Relations Act, under which the United States maintained economic and cultural contacts with Taiwan.[162] In addition, the Taiwan Relations Act also permitted the United States to provide defensive arms for Taiwan. U.S. arms sales to Taiwan aroused controversy in U.S.-PRC relations in the 1980s.[163] By 1991 Taiwan's isolation had been eased as more than twenty nations had established diplomatic relations with it, excluding the expanding commercial and trade relations, including that with the Soviet Union before its disintegration.

Unofficial contacts with the PRC began in the mid-1980s with travel permitted to the people of Taiwan to visit relatives on the mainland. There has been a flourishing bilateral trade across the Taiwan Straits. In 1987 the ruling KMT made a significant decision to end the martial law, which had been enforced for almost four decades in Taiwan. As Taiwan became more prosperous economically and old-guard political leaders aged, the desire for democratic political reform was more evident.

"One China" Formula.   Because the United States' eager desire to seek rapprochement in its relationship with China, a breakthrough was made on February 28, 1972, when visiting President Richard Nixon and Chinese Premier Zhou Enlai signed the Shanghai Communiqué, which addressed the question of Taiwan. The communiqué declared that "There is but one China and Taiwan is a part of China."[164] Thus, the long debate over the status of Taiwan seems to have ended. Having made a major pledge to the Chinese that Taiwan is a part of China, the United States then expressed its desire that the Taiwan question be settled peacefully by the Chinese themselves.

For the past three decades since the 1972 Shanghai Communiqué there has been no unification of Taiwan with China. The problem has been complicated by the increasing voices in Taiwan and elsewhere for a separate status, or even an independent Taiwan, or the "Two China" thesis. The Democratic Progressive Party in Taiwan has won elections in recent years, including the year 2000 election for the presidency of Taiwan has advocated independence for Taiwan.[165]. Mainland China has reacted very strongly to the movement for an independent Taiwan or the "Two China" concept to such an extent that, in addition to its constant verbal attacks, it launched missiles as a threat to Taiwan on the eve of the presidential elections. It has recently stepped up its vehement opposition to the "Two China" thesis and mounted a rhetorical barrage against Taiwan politicians who advocate an independence path for Taiwan.

On and off, there have been official talks across the Taiwan Strait in the hope of finding a peaceful method for solving the thorny problem. Taiwan's newly elected President Chen Shui-bian made a proposal in June 2000 for a summit talk. On the other hand, Beijing's message seems to be that if Taiwan refuses to accept the "One China" formula, sooner or later military action cannot be ruled out.[166] The United States position has been to keep both China and Taiwan talking, as evidenced by Secretary of State Madeleine Albright's June 2000 visit with Chinese President Jiang Zemin.[167] However, a statement by former Taiwan President Lee Tunghui increased tension when he proposed that the "One China" formula should be rejected and that the two sides should resume negotiations on the basis of two separate states. Fortunately, in March 2000 the newly elected Taiwan president pledged that Taiwan would not declare independence if China abandoned its military threat.

Recently a clear, but blunt, message from a friend of both China and Taiwan has emerged out of all these semantic debates over the meaning of "One China" or "Two Chinas." The former prime minister and now the senior minister of Singapore, Lee Kuan Yew, said in an interview in May 2000 that the Taiwan people must accept the inevitability of unification with China as the only path to a peaceful future for all concerned in the region.[168] Lee warned, in the first place, that no Chinese leader would ever survive if Taiwan were to separate from China; and, Lee argued, that it would be a "cruel game" to cause Taiwan people to believe that it is possible to have "a separate and different identity" from mainland China indefinitely.[169]

The Possible Solution: A Federal Union of One China.   Thus, we must look for a possible solution to the Taiwan problem beyond the narrow semantic confines of "One China" or "Two Chinas." Yan Jiaqi, the exited former political adviser to former Premier Zhao Ziyang before the 1989 Tiananmen student demonstration, argued in accord with Singapore's Lee Kuan Yew that Taiwan must accept the inevitable fact that it is a part of China, as this has been accepted by all major powers in the world, particularly by all Asian nations in the region.

Yan then proposed that a Chinese federal system (*lianbang zhidu*) could be the solution to the "One China" puzzle in that Taiwan would not be a "local government" or a province within a unified China.[170] Under the proposed arrangement, Yan argued that Taiwan would have self-rule because it would not be a province or a local political entity. Taiwan under such an arrangement would be represented or recognized internationally, not as part of a mainland government entity, nor as a Taiwan government, but as a cross-strait united federal government of one China.[171] In other words, it would then be "one China with equal status across the strait, interchanging peacefully, and building together a federal government."[172]

Yan's proposal for a united federal China is different from other federal forms of government, such as the United States, Canada, Australia or the Federal Republic of Germany, in that defense and foreign policy would not be "unified as one." Taiwan's armed forces would not be commanded by the mainland, and conversely Taiwan would have no say with regard to the People's Liberation Army (PLA) on the mainland—Yan labels such an arrangement a "cooperative (*xietong*) diplomacy or defense."[173]

In conclusion, it may be that the solution to the Taiwan question lies in the inevitable acceptance of "One China" in a form or arrangement that would provide self-rule or self-government for Taiwan not as a separate province, an arrangement in which there would be no overwhelming control and dominance by Beijing. Yan Jiaqi's proposal has one other added advantage: It provides a possible solution to China's other separatist problems, such as Tibet, Xinjiang, and Inner Mongolia where ethnic tension has been intense and needs solution, as discussed in chapter 7. A proposed federated union of China would consist of possibly six self-governing Special Administrative Regions (SARs) of Hong Kong, Macao, Taiwan, Tibet, Xinjiang, and Inner Mongolia.

In my view, in order to accomplish the proposal it requires at least two possible actions by the National People's Congress—these actions must have the endorsement and support of the Chinese Communist Party. The first action may not be difficult—involving a constitutional amendment to Article 31 of the 1982 state constitution (see Appendix A). Article 31 now declares that "the state may establish special administrative regions when necessary"; and that these arrangements "shall be prescribed by law enacted by the National People's Congress in the light of special conditions." Both Hong Kong and Macao have been returned to China and established as special administrative regions with their own autonomy, as discussed in this chapter. However, it may be very difficult, but not necessarily impossible or unthinkable, to amend China's 1982 constitution with an added provision preceding the present Article 2 for the establishment of a federal union of special administrative regions, as prescribed in Article 31. These special administrative regions would possess autonomy and equal status with the People's Republic of China but would not be regarded as provincial or local governments. The equal and autonomous status for these special administrative regions would be guaranteed by a special "basic law" or constitution to be enacted as has been done in the cases of Hong Kong and Macao.

Also difficult will be convincing Taiwan that such an arrangement for a federal union of a greater China with political and economic autonomy would perhaps be a way of achieving unification under the inevitable "One China" formula in order to preserve and perpetuate Taiwan's own economic and democratic status without opting for an independent stance.

NOTES

1. Harry Harding, "The Concept of 'Greater China:' Themes, Variations and Reservations," *China Quarterly*, no. 136 (December 1993), 661 and 684.
2. Maria Hsia Chang. "Greater China and the Chinese 'Global Tide,'" *Asian Survey*, 35, 10 (October 1995), 958–61; and James T. Myers and Donald J. Puchula, "'Greater China:' Some American Reflections," *Asian Affairs: An American Review*, 21, no. 1 (Spring 1994), 3–4.
3. David Shambaugh, "Introduction: The Emergence of 'Greater China.'" *China Quarterly*, no. 136 (December 1993), 653.
4. Harding, "Concept of 'Greater China:' Themes, Variations and Reservations," 661.
5. See *Far Eastern Economic Review* (July 20, 1979), 24.
6. The first conference on Greater China was held in Hong Kong in January 1992; the second at Stanford, Calif. in June 1993; and a regional seminar at Berkeley, Calif. in February 1993.
7. Harding "Concept of 'Greater China:' Themes, Variations and Reservations," 665. In footnotes 17–19 Harding lists literature published in Chinese journals that refers to the concept and its variations.
8. For a detailed discussion of colonial rule in Hong Kong, consult the following works: Morris, *Hong Kong*, 68–89, 136–54, and pp. 198–216; Rafferty, *City on the Rocks*, pp. 51–145; and Ian Scott, *Political Change and Crisis of Legitimacy in Hong Kong* (Honolulu: University of Hawaii Press, 1989), pp. 39–65.
9. Scott, *Political Change and Crisis of Legitimacy in Hong Kong*, p. 40.
10. Quote from G. B. Endacott, *A History of Hong Kong*, 2d ed. (Hong Kong: Oxford University Press, 1964), p. 316.
11. Scott, *Political Change and Crisis of Legitimacy*, p. 72.
12. See James C. F. Wang, *Contemporary Chinese Politics: An Introduction*, 4th ed. (Upper Saddle River, NJ: Prentice Hall, 1991), p. 317.
13. See a full discussion in Scott, *Political Change and the Crisis of Legitimacy in Hong Kong*, pp. 96–106.
14. Ibid., p. 79.
15. Ibid., pp. 107–26.
16. For discussion on the initiative for negotiation on Hong Kong, see Willem Van Kemenade, *China, Hong Kong, Taiwan, Inc.* (New York: Alfred A. Knopf, 1997), pp. 61–72; Alvin Y. So, "Hong Kong People Ruling Hong Kong! The Rise of the New Middle Class in Negotiation Politics, 1982–1984," *Asian Affairs: An American Review*, 20, no. 2 (Summer 1993), 67–84; Michael Yahuda, "Dilemmas and Problems in the Sino–British Negotiations over Hong Kong," *Pacific Review*, 6, no. 4 (1993), 375–80; and William H. Overholt, "China and British Hong Kong," *Current History* (September 1991), 270–74.
17. Margaret Thatcher, "No Regrets," in *Wall Street Journal*, June 27, 1997, p. A-14. Also see So, "Hong Kong People Ruling Hong Kong!" 67.
18. Ibid., and Van Kemenade, *China, Hong Kong, and Taiwan, Inc.*, p. 61.
19. Van Kemenade, *China, Hong Kong, and Taiwan, Inc.*, p. 61; and So, "Hong Kong People Ruling Hong Kong!" 67.
20. Overholt, "China and British Hong Kong," 270.
21. For Thatcher's statements regarding Britain's position on Hong Kong in the initial 1982 negotiations, and other statements, see Joseph Y. S. Cheng, *Hong Kong: In Search of a Future* (Hong Kong, Oxford, and New York: Oxford University Press, 1984), pp. 28–44. And for the Chinese government position, ibid., pp. 45–74. Also see So, "Hong Kong People Ruling Hong Kong!" 72–74.
22. So, "Hong Kong People Ruling Hong Kong!" 74.
23. Cheng, *Hong Kong in Search of a Future*, p. 51.
24. For text of the 1982 constitution see James C. F. Wang, *Contemporary Chinese Politics: An Introduction*, 5th ed. (Upper Saddle River, N.J.: Prentice Hall, 1995), p. 327.
25. John Quan Zhao, "'One Country, Two Systems' and 'One Country, Two Parties:' PRC-Taiwan Unification and Its Political Implications," *Pacific Review*, 2, no. 4 (February 4, 1989), 312–19. Also see Van Kemenade, *China, Hong Kong, and Taiwan, Inc.*, pp. 150–51.
26. So, *Hong Kong: In Search of a Future*, pp. 37 and 55.
27. Ibid., pp. 48–49. Also see Lu Ping, "Hong Kong to Maintain Prosperity and Stability," *Beijing Review* (February 17–March 3, 1997), 18.
28. Van Kemenade, *China, Hong Kong, Taiwan, Inc.*, pp. 151–54; and Zhao, "'One Country, Two Systems' and 'One Country, Two Parties.'" Also see So, *Hong Kong: In Search of a Future*, pp. 46–47.
29. Ye Jianying's speech was revealed in a commentary by the *Ta Kung Pao* on November 28, 1982; see So, *Hong Kong: In Search of a Future*, pp. 222–23.
30. Chang Wei-guo, "Hong Kongers Rule Hong Kong (Gangren Zhegang) Must Be the Basis for Federalism," *Zhengming* (Hong Kong) (January 1, 1994), 71.

31. See So, "Hong Kong People Ruling Hong Kong!" 74–75.
32. Ibid., p. 83.
33. Ibid.
34. In addition to the text of the Basic Law as approved by the Chinese National People's Congress on April 4, 1990, the following contain discussion, analysis and criticism of the Basic Law, both in draft form and in the approved version: Ian Scott, *Political Change and the Crisis of Legitimacy in Hong Kong* (Honolulu: University of Hawaii Press, 1989); Jungen Domes and Yu-Ming Shaw, *Hong Kong: A Chinese and International Concern*, (Boulder, Colo., and London: Westview Press, 1988), particularly the chapter by George L. Hicks, "Hong Kong after the Sino–British Agreement: The Illusion of Stability," pp. 231–45; Joseph Y. S. Cheng, "The Post-1997 Government of Hong Kong: Toward a Stronger Legislature," *Asian Survey*, 29, no. 8 (August 1989), 731–48; "The Basic Law and Hong Kong's Future," *Asian Wall Street Journal,* 5 April 1990, p. A-8; *New York Times,* February 17, 1990, p. A-3; Daniel R. Fung, "The Basic Law of the Hong Kong Special Administrative Region of the People's Republic of China: Problems of Interpretation," *International and Comparative Law Quarterly*, 37 (July 1988), 701–14; and Hungdah Chiu, ed., *The Draft Basic Law of Hong Kong: Analysis and Documents*, occasional papers/reprint series in *Contemporary Asian Studies*, no. 5, 1988, School of Law, University of Maryland; and *Ming Pao Daily* (Hong Kong), December 14, 1987, p. 2.
35. Text is found in *Beijing Review* (April 30–May 6, 1990), entitled "The Basic Law of the Hong Kong Special Administrative Region of the People's Republic of China," ii–xxiv, as approved by the Chinese Seventh National People's Congress at its Third Session on April 4, 1990 and put into effect as of July 1, 1997.
36. Ibid., vii.
37. As reported by Cheng, "The Post–1997 Government of Hong Kong," 734.
38. Ibid.
39. Ibid.,737
40. Ibid.
41. *Far Eastern Economic Review* (October 11, 1991), 12.
42. *Far Eastern Economic Review* (September 19, 1991), 10.
43. *New York Times,* September 8. 1991, p. A-6.
44. See *New York Times,* September 17, 1991, p. A-4; and *Christian Science Monitor,* September 17, 1991, p. 4.
45. *Ming Pao Daily* (Hong Kong), August 26, 1991, 4.
46. See two informative articles about Hong Kong group activities: "Decolonization and Political Development in Hong Kong;" and John L. Burns, "The Structure of Communist Party Control in Hong Kong," *Asian Survey,* vol. 30, no. 8 (August 1990), 614–20.
47. *Far Eastern Economic Review*, (August 30, 1991), 18.
48. Ibid., 19.
49. Ibid., 20.
50. See Louise do Rosario, "Stand Up and Be Counted," *Far Eastern Economic Review*, (September 28, 1995), 16–17; and Kuo Fei-shan, "Xiang gang Da Xuan; Gong Dang Dzai Bai," *Zhengming* (Hong Kong), (October 1995), 33–34.
51. See Liang Yaozhong, "Wei ming zhu huiquei di Kangxi," *Trend* (Hong Kong), (July 1996), 50–51.
52. See Yan Jiaqi, "Linshi Lifahui Iz NGO," *Trend* (Hong Kong), (April 1996), 49–51.
53. See Charlotte Parsons, "'Legal Vacuum' Chaos Warning," *South China Morning Post International Weekly*, July 26, 1997, p. 1.
54. Sharon Cheuing, "Labor Body Halts SAR Bid to Stop Pre-Handover Bill," *South China Morning Post International Weekly*, July 26, 1997.
55. See Frank Ching, "Missed Hong Kong Opportunity," *Far Eastern Economic Review* (July 3, 1997), 32.
56. See Frank Ching, "Tung, a Reluctant Candidate," *Far Eastern Economic Review* (July 25, 1996), 40.
57. Linda Choy and Chris Yeung, "Tung Tries to Show He Is His Own Man," *South China Morning Post International Weekly*, May 20, 1997, p. 3. However, Tung had been China's choice many years prior to his formal selection; see Bruce Gilley, "Balancing Act," *Far Eastern Economic Review*, (March 3, 1997), 25.
58. Bruce Gilley, "Balancing Act," Ibid.
59. See Bruce Gilley, "Henry . . . Who?" *Far Eastern Economic Review* (January 9, 1997), 82.
60. Lau Siu-Kai, "Institutions without Leaders: The Hong Kong Chinese View of Political Leadership," *Pacific Affairs*, 63, no. 2 (Summer 1990), 208.
61. Ibid.
62. Lau Siu-Kai, "Social Irrelevance of Politics: Hong Kong Chinese Attitudes toward Political Leadership," *Pacific Affairs*, 65, no. 2, (Summer 1992), 245.

63. See "Tung Softens Line on Civil Liberties Curb," *South China Morning Post International Weekly*, April 26, 1997, p. 3.
64. Ibid.
65. See Stella Lee and Angela Li, "Security Ban on Protests," *South China Morning Post International Weekly*, July 26, 1997, p. 2.
66. Ibid.
67. See editorial in *Wall Street Journal*, August 1, 1997, p. 10.
68. J. F. Mathews, Attorney-General, Letter to the Editor, in *South China Morning Post International Weekly*, April 26, 1997, p. 10.
69. See Frank Ching, "Chan: An Independent Spirit," *Far Eastern Economic Review*, (August 8, 1996), 34.
70. Bruce Gilley, "Perks for Patriots," *Far Eastern Economic Review* (March 13, 1997), 27.
71. See Joseph Y. S. Cheng and Jane C. Y. Lee, "The Changing Political Attitudes of the Senior Bureaucrats in Hong Kong's Transition," *China Quarterly*, no. 147 (September 1996), 913 and 931. Also see Kathleen Cheek-Milby, "The Changing Political Role of the Hong Kong Civil Servant," *Pacific Affairs*, 62, no. 2 (Summer 1989), 221 and 223–28.
72. Cheng and Lee, "Changing Political Attitudes of the Senior Bureaucrats in Hong Kong's Transition," 931.
73. See Fanny Wong, "Air of Disquiet in Tung's Camp," *South China Morning Post International Weekly*, May 17, 1997, p. 11.
74. Cheng and Lee "Changing Political Attitudes of the Senior Bureaucrats in Hong Kong's Transition," 933.
75. Ibid., 932.
76. See Benjamin T. M. Lam, "Administrative Culture and Democracy in Hong Kong," *Asian Affairs: An American Review* (Fall 1994), 177–78.
77. See article in *Trend* (Hong Kong) (February 1995), 54–56.
78. *Far Eastern Economic Review* (March 21, 1991), 62.
79. "Hong Kong's Future as a Free Market Economy," in Domes and Shaw, *Hong Kong: A Chinese and International Concern*, pp. 205–207.
80. Ibid., p. 206.
81. "The Rise of Hong Kong as a Financial Center," *Asian Survey*, 19, no. 7 (July 1979), 675.
82. See Victor F. S. Sit, "Dynamism in Small Industries—The Case of Hong Kong," *Asian Survey*, 22, no. 4 (April 1982), 399–408.
83. *The Far East and Australia, 1991*, 23d ed. (London: Europa Publications, 1992), p. 265.
84. See Wang, *Contemporary Chinese Politics*, 4th ed., p. 363.
85. Craig S. Smith, "Hong Kong Fears for Vital Service Sector," *Wall Street Journal*, May 15, 1997, p. A-18.
86. Ibid.
87. Ping, "Hong Kong to Maintain Prosperity and Stability," 19.
88. See Marcus Eliason, "Hong Kong's Economy Belies Dire Predictions," Associated Press as reprinted in *Honolulu Advertiser*, December 6, 1996, p. B-5.
89. See B. Baches, O. Lorz, and L. Schuknecht, "Chinese Investments 'Hostages' for Hong Kong?" *Journal of International and Theoretical Economics*, no. 123, 645–54.
90 Hing Lin Chan, "Chinese Investment in Hong Kong: Issues and Problems," *Asian Survey*, vol. 35, no. 10 (October 1995), 947.
91. Ibid., 949 and 951.
92. See Susan Kreifels, "Hong Kong Official Says There Are Opportunities There," *Honolulu Star Bulletin*, September 22, 1998, p. A-4.
93. See Bruce Knecht, "Hong Kong Buys Stock as GDP Falls Again," *Wall Street Journal*, August 31, 1998, p. A-8.
94. See Erik Guyot, "Hong Kong's Stock Purchases Harms Currency, Friedman Says," *Wall Street Journal*, September 3, 1998, p. A-19.
95. See Jeffrey Timmermans and Eric Van Zant, "Hong Kong Economics Exhibits Surprising, Inexplicable Strengthening," *Wall Street Journal*, August 20, 1999, p. A-23. Also see "Back to Basics," Far Eastern Economic Review (December 10, 1999), 11–12.
96. See Alex Lo, "First SAR Survey Finds Public in Buoyant Mood," *South China Morning Post International Weekly*, August 2, 1997, p. 1.
97. David Grossman, "Teaching about the Hong Kong Transition," *Education about Asia*, 2, no. 1 (Spring 1997), 53.
98. Lee Kuan Yew, "A Place for Business, Not Politics," *Far Eastern Economic Review* (July 3, 1997), 29.
99. See Mark Landler, "Trial Raises Fear on Hong Kong Autonomy," *New York Times*, November 13, 1999, p. A-8.

100. Ibid.
101. Information on the case is culled from Frank Ching, "Fault Line: Legal Cases Test 'One Country' formula," *Far Eastern Economic Review* (April 8, 1999), 21; "Flag Damage," *Far Eastern Economic Review* (December 23, 1999), 18; and Mark Landler, "Hong Kong Court Upholds Protection of China Flag," *New York Times*, December 16, 1999, p. A-9.
102. Information is culled from Todd Crowell, "In Hong Kong, Challenge to 'One Country, Two Systems'" *Christian Science Monitor*, February 18, 1999, p. 8; Mark Landler, "Beijing Resists Hong Kong Immigration," *New York Times*, February 24, 1999, p. A-6 and "Hong Kong May Clarify Ruling Beijing Disliked," February 25, 1999, p. A-15; Kevin Platt, "Hong Kong's Rule, for Now," *Christian Science Monitor*, March 12, 1999, p. 6; Frank Ching, "Scare Tactics," *Far Eastern Economic Review*, May 13, 1999, pp. 18–19; and Gordon G. Chang, "Civil and Common Law Collide," *Far Eastern Economic Review* (June 10, 1999), 32.
103. See Mark Landler, "Study Depicts Mainlanders in Hong Kong as Nightmare," *New York Times*, May 7, 1999, p. A-7; and Frank Ching, "Scare Tactics," *Far Eastern Economic Review* (May 13, 1999), 18–19.
104. Ching, "Scare Tactics."
105. See Associated Press release as reprinted in *Honolulu Advertiser*, June 26, 1999, p. A-3.
106. Chang, "Civil and Common Law Collide."
107. See Austin Coates, *A Macao Narrative* (Hong Kong: Heinemann, 1978); and Jonathan Porter, "The Transformation of Macau," *Pacific Affairs*, 66, no. 1 (Spring 1993), 8–10.
108. See *Beijing Review*, no. 14 (April 6, 1987), xii.
109. See Peter Stein, "Tiny Macao, Besieged by Gang Violence," *Wall Street Journal*, May 6, 1997, p. A-19.
110. Fraser, "Murders That Have Shaken Macau."
111. See Niall Fraser, "The Murders That Have Shaken Macau," *South China Morning Post International Weekly*, May 17. 1997, p. 6. Also see Edward A. Gurgan, "Close to Hong Kong, Yet Worlds Apart," *New York Times*, September 2, 1997, p. A-9; and his earlier article "Eclipsed and Fraying Macao Limps toward Chinese Rule," *New York Times*, August 24, 1997, pp. A-1 and A-6.
112. Information on Macao's politics before 1999 is culled from the following works: Richard Louis Edmonds, "Macau and Greater China," *China Quarterly*, no. 136 (December 1993), 878–84; Jonathan Porter, "The Transformation of Macau," *Pacific Affairs*, 66, no. 1 (Spring 1993), 16–20; Herbert S. Yee and Sonny S. H. Ho, "Macau in Transition: The Politics of Decolonization," *Asian Survey*, 31, no. 10 (October 1991), 905–19; Lo Shiu-hing, "Aspects of Political Development in Macao," *China Quarterly*, no. 120 (December 1989), 837–51.
113. Ho, "Macau in Transition," 906.
114. Porter, "The Transformation of Macau," 16.
115. Ho, "Macau in Transition," 913.
116. Ibid., 913–17.
117. Ibid., 914.
118. See Shiu-hing, "Aspects of Political Development in Macau," 837; and Edmonds, "Macau and Greater China," 878.
119. Shiu-hing "Aspects of Political Development in Macau," 848–49.
120. For the initial text of the Sino–Portuguese Joint Declaration on the Question of Macao, see *Beijing Review* (April 6, 1987), i–xii.
121. See Shiu-hing, "Aspects of Political Development in Macau," 840.
122. See text of the joint declaration, Part IX, *Beijing Review* (April 6, 1987), viii.
123. Ibid., xi.
124. George B. Cressey, *Asia's Lands and People* (New York and London: McGraw-Hill, 1951), pp. 140–44.
125. *China Business Review*, (March–April 1984), 12.
126. *Asian Wall Street Journal*, March 27, 1984, p. 11.
127. See Zhimin Tang and Ding Lu, "China's Region-Oriented Preferential Policies At the Crossroad," *Asia-Pacific Development Journal,* 3, no. 2 (December 1996), 120–21.
128. See *Beijing Review,* no. 4, (January 23, 1984), 26.
129. Researchers present a slightly different number of districts and townships in the Pearl River Delta region, ranging from 28 to 31. See C. K. Leung, J. Onodera, and L. Zhang, "Employment Growth in Pearl River Delta: A Spatial Analysis," paper delivered at the 34th International Congress of African and Asian Studies, Hong Kong, August 1993, p. 10; and Zhang Zjin, *"Xiangjan Yu Zhujiang San jiaozhou de jingji guanxi,"* paper delivered at the 34th International Congress of African and Asian studies, Hong Kong, August 1993, pp. 1–2.
130. See Li Ning, "Pearl River Delta Heading toward Modernization," *Beijing Review* (January 27–February 2, 1997), 14. Also see George C. S. Lin, "Transformation of a Rural Economy in the Zhujiang Delta," *China Quarterly,* no. 149 (March 1997), 58–80.

131. Ibid.
132. Ibid.
133. Ning, "Pearl River Delta Heading toward Modernization," 15.
134. C. Y. Jim, "Major Environmental Problems and Their Prospects Associated with Recent Developments in the Pearl River Delta," paper presented at the 34th International Congress of African and Asian Studies, August 1993, Hong Kong.
135. Ou Qujia's "New Guangdong" was brought to the attention of other scholars in Prasenjit Duara, "De-Construct the Chinese Nation," *Australian Journal of Chinese Affairs*, no. 30 (July 1993), 18. Then the above idea by Ou Qujia was brought to my attention by Willem Van Kemenade's valuable work *China, Hong Kong, Taiwan, Inc.*, p. 280. Ou Qujia's original essay *"Xin Guangdong"* was to be found in a book edited by Zhang Yufa, *Wan qing geming wenxue* (Taipei: Xinzhi Zazhishe, 1971), pp. 2–3,(as provided in footnote 45 in Prasenjit Duara's article cited above).
136. *South China Morning Post International Weekly*, July 19, 1997, p. 9.
137. *South China Morning Post International Weekly*, May 10, 1997, p. 3.
138. Ibid.
139. "The PLA and Regionalism in Guangdong," *Pacific Review*, 7, no. 1 (1994), 31–33.
140. Ibid., p. 38. For a discussion about regional economics, also see Kenichi Ohmae, *The End of Nation-State; The Rise of Regional Economics: How Engines of Prosperity Are Reshaping Global Markets*.
141. See Helen F. Siu, "Cultural Identity and the Politics of Difference in South China," in Tu Wei-ming, ed., *China in Transition* (Cambridge and London: Harvard University Press, 1994), pp. 19–20.
142. Ibid., p. 36.
143. Ibid.
144. Ibid., p. 37.
145. See Yueh Shan, "Guangdong San ju tou qing ci," (Guangdong Three Bosses Submit Resignation), *Zhengming* (Hong Kong) (August 1995), 18–19.
146. Ibid., 19.
147. Ni Zijing, *"Difang lingdao da Zhengdun"* (Local Leadership Needs Rectification), *Zhengming* (Hong Kong) (December 1996), 17–18.
148. Ibid., 18.
149. See Bruce Gilley, "Local Talent: New Guangdong Governor Treads the Middle Way," *Far Eastern Economic Review* (February 22, 1996), 20.
150. Gabriella Montinola, Ying yi Qian, and Barry R. Weingast, "Federalism, Chinese Style: The Political Basis for Economic Success in China," *World Politics*, 48, no. 1 (October 1995), 50–81.
151. Ibid., 52–53.
152. Ibid., 72.
153. Ibid.
154. Susan Shirk, *How China Opened Its Door* (Washington, D.C.: Brookings Institution, 1994).
155. See Jae Ho Chung, "Studies of Central-Provincial Relations in the People's Republic of China: A Mid-Term Appraisal," *China Quarterly* (June 1995), 487–508; Dai Yang, "Patterns of China's Regional Development Strategy," *China Quarterly*, no. 122 (June 1990), 230–57; and Michel Oksenberg and James Tong, "The Evolution of Center-Provincial Fiscal Relations in China, 1971–1984: The Formal System," *China Quarterly*, no. 125 (March 1991), 1–32.
156. Victor C. Falkenheim, *China's Regional Development: Trends and Implications* (Toronto: University of Toronto; York University Joint Center for Asia Pacific Studies, 1995), pp. 20–21.
157. John F. Cooper, Taiwan: *Nation-State or Province?* (Boulder, Colo.: Westview Press, 1990), p. 17.
158. Ibid., p. 24.
159. Ibid., pp.26–27.
160. *Far Eastern Economic Review*, (March 19, 1992), 30; and (February 27, 1992), 48–49, on how historians rediscover the story of the massacre. In a different account of the February 28 tragedy, which seemed to absolve the KMT of responsibility, see Lai Tse-lian, Raymon H. Myers, and Wei Wou, *The Tragic Beginning: The Taiwann Uprising of February 28, 1947* (Stanford, Calif.: Stanford University Press, 1992).
161. *Far Eastern Economic Review* (March 19, 1992), 30.
162. For details, see Wang, *Contemporary Chinese Politics*, 4th ed., pp. 338–43.
163. Ibid., pp. 334–46.
164. Ibid., pp. 339–343.
165. See Yu-Shan Wu, "Taiwanese Elections and Cross-Strait Relations," *Asian Survey*, 34, no. 4 (July–August 1999), 565–587.
166. Susan V. Lawrence, "Cross-Strait Relations: Breathing Space," *Far Eastern Economic Review* (June 1, 2000), 16–17.

167. See "Albright Appeals to China to Begin Talks with Taiwan," *Washington Post*, as reprinted in *Honolulu Advertiser*, June 23, 2000, p.A-2.
168. See "Lee: The Cruel Game," *Far Eastern Economic Review* (June 8, 2000), 17.
169. Ibid.
170. Yan Jiaqi has published three articles on the proposal in the following three issues of *Zhengming Magazine* (Hong Kong): no. 264 (October 1999), 58–61; no. 270 (April 1, 2000), 39–40; and no. 272 (June 1, 2000), 25–26.
171. See *Zhengming Magazine* (April 1, 2000), 40.
172. Ibid.
173. See *Zhengming Magazine* (June 1, 2000), 26.

SUGGESTED READINGS

Copper, John F. *Taiwan: Nation-State or Province?*, 2d ed. (Boulder, Colo.: Westview Press, 1996).

Ghai, Yashi. *Hong Kong's New Constitutional Order: The Resumption of Chinese Sovereignty and the Basic Law* (Hong Kong: Hong Kong University Press, 1998).

Gunn, Geoffrey C. *Encountering Macau: A Portuguese City—State on the Periphery of China, 1557-1999* (Boulder, Colo.: Westview Press, 1996).

Lo, Shui Hing. *Political Development in Macau* (Hong Kong: The Chinese University of Hong Kong, 1995).

Mole, David (ed.). *Managing the New Hong Kong Economy* (Hong Kong: Oxford University Press, 1996).

Rubinstein, Murray A. *Taiwan: A New History* (New York and London: M. E. Sharpe, 1999).

Tien, Hung-Mao. *Taiwan's Electoral Politics and Democratic Transition: Riding the Third Wave* (Armonk, N.Y.: M. E. Sharpe, 1996).

Van Kemenade, Willem. *China, Hong Kong, Taiwan, Inc.* (New York: Alfred A. Knopf, 1997).

Wang, Enbao. *Hong Kong, 1997: The Politics of Transition* (Boulder, Colo.: Lynne Rienner Publishers, 1997).

Yahuda, Michael. *Hong Kong: China's Challenge* (London and New York: Routledge, 1996).

Chapter Nine

The Military's Role in Chinese Politics

Chinese politics has been complicated by participation of the military establishment at both the central and provincial levels. In fact, following the Cultural Revolution, the military assumed the dominant political role at all levels of government and the party. The death of Deng Xiaoping, China's paramount leader for the past two decades, has once again elevated the question of the military's future role in the forefront of Chinese politics during the transitional period.

In this chapter we shall first examine the ongoing debate among scholars as to what should be the appropriate approach in explaining the military's role in Chinese politics: the traditional dichotomous civil-military relations approach, the generally accepted party-army symbiosis approach, or the legitimate right to participation approach? The chapter will then discuss military reform of the two decades under Deng: procurement of advanced weaponry, elevation of the educational level for the officer corps, demobilization, and the controversy over defense expenditures. Jiang Zemin's relationship with the PLA officer corps will also be discussed, as well as the Chinese military's "realpolitik world view" in terms of arms sales abroad and the development of limited nuclear deterrence strategy. Finally, a discussion is provided about the formation, role, or mission of the People's Armed Police force as an instrument for law enforcement and suppression.

HOW TO EXPLAIN THE MILITARY'S ROLE IN CHINESE POLITICS

Analysis of the military role in politics falls in general into two main categories or themes. First is the traditional concept of "military separateness," which is based on the European and American experience commonly known as civil-military relations.[1] Second is the popular theme for explaining military coups in the postwar era in most developing nations of the Third World. This theme depicts the professional military as "agents for change," or "modernizing agents," led by young officers who claimed to be the agents for change in the slow process of nation building;[2] they were impatient or frustrated enough to seize the opportunity to intervene in politics by staging military coups. However, the military role in Chinese politics has often been explained in terms of China's modern history—that is, the presence of militarism must be viewed as an integral part of the development of China's social and political organizations and as a driving force in the transformation in Chinese society.

Martin Wilbur defined militarism in Chinese political development as a "system of organizing political power in which force is the normal arbiter in the distribution of power and in the establishment of policy."[3] Modern Chinese political development is, to a large extent, influenced by the power of armies, on one hand, and by the techniques involved in the use of armies and in military organization, on the other.

For decades prior to the unification effort undertaken by the Chinese Nationalists in 1926, a system of regional military separatism dominated the political scene in China. Under the system, independent military-political groupings, each occupying one or more provinces, functioned as separate political entities and engaged in internecine warfare in order to preserve their own separate regions and to prevent their rivals from establishing a unified and centralized political system. To say that contemporary China has been plagued by the problem of control by armies is really an understatement. It is largely by military means and through military organization and technique that the Chinese Nationalists tried, and the Chinese communists succeeded, in reestablishing a "unified hierarchical and centralized political system."[4] The military thus constitutes a dominant group in society, and the military institution has played a dominant role in political development.[5] The military has always occupied a special position in Chinese communist society. As mentioned in Chapter 4, the Chinese Communist Party, for a long time, was the army. Party membership grew from the 40,000 Long March survivors in 1935 to over 1.2 million members in 1945. Over 1 million of the total membership in 1945 constituted the military supply system.[6] These people were regular members of either the army or the party, working without salary and under a military type of discipline. Robert Tucker has labeled this unique system of militarizing the party as military communism, to distinguish it from all other forms of communism.[7] It became evident in recent years that party leadership has depended upon party members in the army to carry on political work, to restore order, and to use the army as a coercive instrument in the contest for political power and succession.

However, Martin Wilbur's definition of "militarism" in the Chinese historic context serves only as a partial explanation for the role of the military in Chinese politics. In fact, there is really no general agreement among China scholars about the PLA's role in Chinese politics, a topic which has generated a cascade of literature in recent decades. (Many of these studies have been cited in the footnotes to this chapter.) Some analysts adhere to what Harlan Jencks has called "the factionalism school," which argues that many key military officers embrace Mao's ideological approach and would enter into a power struggle in due time to depose the reformers.[8] The PLA has been viewed as "the repository of Mao's Thought" and as "the generator and legitimizer of the Chinese communist ideology."[9] For some time the military was the model of ideological purity and revolutionary character for the nation as a whole. Then there is the "professional school," which believes that the Chinese military strives for professionalism and accepts civilian (party) supremacy.[10] Falling somewhere between these two opposing schools is an array of views, from the continued dominance of party-army personalities to influence of the field army lineage on party politics.[11] The dominance of the party-army personalities has now become the more acceptable analytical framework known as "party-army symbiosis,"[12] or "party-in-uniform."

PARTY-ARMY SYMBIOSIS APPROACH[13]

The conceptual framework of party-army symbiosis focuses on the close relationship established between top party leaders and the guerrilla forces. Thus, it has been pointed out that Deng Xiaoping, who passed away at age 92 in February 1997, and Mao Zedong were both political commissars for the guerrilla armies. Deng, perhaps more than any other top leader, was known as "a political-soldier and military-politician." Deng's rise to the pinnacle of power was attributable to his political acumen and organizational skill as political commissar in the guerrilla and civil war days. Deng was a disciple of Mao, who had insisted that the party must command the gun at all times. Mao formulated the principle of the party's political control and education, or indoctrination, of the guerrilla forces in his 1929 Gutian resolution, which placed emphasis on improving the fighting guerrilla's solidarity and discipline. From the 1930s to this day, the heart of the political control system has been the party committee for a given military unit, usually at the company level, which is composed of the military commander, the political commissar, and other principal staff officers. The political branch, known as *zhengzhibu*, established at all levels of the military, implements the decisions of the party (political) committee. This practice of party control over the military has eventually evolved into a system of "interlocking directorates" under which military commanders serve as party leaders at provincial, regional and national levels. This relationship is often cemented by personal and individual networks. Because of Mao's and Deng's position as supreme political commissars for the military, they were able to use the army as a power base in elite politics. This salient characteristic of party-army relationship has been termed a "symbiotic institutional marriage," whereby military leaders sit as members of the party's central committee (or Politburo), the apex of the party decision-making body, and top party leaders serve as political commissars and/or as chairman and vice-chairman of the party's military affairs committee. It was no surprise that each time Deng returned to power from the purge he was promptly given the pivotal position as the army's chief-of-staff. For the simple reason that Deng had established a long and close relationship with the military as political commissar and as the party's general secretary, who not only recommended, but approved, the military officers' promotion, there was really no one else at the party's top echelon who could command the respect of the military.

Party-Army Interlocking Directorate at the Top, 1968–1997

An important aspect of the party-army symbiosis theme is the "interlocking" relationship at the top level. Ellis Joffe writes in one of his more recent articles that the most important pattern in Chinese civil-military relations, dating back to the guerrilla and civil war days, has been "the close integration of political and military leaders at the uppermost level of decision-making."[14] While the military's role during the Cultural Revolution may be viewed as an aberration, it nevertheless is illustrative not only of the extent of its dominance in politics, but also of the pronounced integration with the party at the top decision-making level.

The rapid expansion of military power in the provinces, and the continued dominance of the PLA in Chinese politics in general (following the conclusion of the Ninth Party Congress) became a major factor in the Lin Biao affair, which came to a head in September 1971.[15] The key question raised in the Lin Biao affair was who should have control of the political system in China: a civilian party under Mao, or the military under Lin Biao. The purge of Lin was a direct consequence of the tensions that developed between the civilian party and the military as it expanded its power, and the tensions that had developed between the central military command and the regional military power base in the provinces. In the end, the powerful regional commanders who opposed Lin had contributed significantly to his purge.[16] The Lin Biao affair was an important benchmark in party–army relations. It also meant that the rapid expansion of the military's role under Lin had constituted a threat to the power and authority of Mao and Zhou Enlai. Events of the post–Lin Biao period from 1971 to 1974 largely centered on restoring the party's control over the military under Mao's 1929 dictum that "the party must command the gun." These events can be summarized as follows.

First, a massive purge was undertaken at the central command structure level, which had been the main base of Lin's support. In addition to the disappearance of some nine senior military leaders—including the chief of staff and the commanders of general logistics, the air force, and the navy—more than forty other ranking officers associated with the Lin group were purged.

Second, a movement was launched to reduce the involvement and role of the military in politics. A January 4, 1973, announcement issued by the State Council, headed by Zhou Enlai, and by the party's Military Affairs Committee, headed by Zhou's close ally Marshal Ye Jianying, directed PLA units in all regions and provinces to observe strictly the policies of the party. They stressed that the PLA's role was primarily military, rather than political. Public media stressed the need to observe military discipline and to concentrate on military affairs. Visitors to China now found fewer military representatives on school and university campuses and in factories. Coincident with the campaign to play down the role of the military in Chinese society was the reappearance of many party veterans who had been vilified during the Cultural Revolution.

Third, some analysts of Chinese politics suggest that there was also a deliberate attempt by Mao and Zhou Enlai to reduce the influence of the military in the decision-making process at both the national level and the regional and provincial levels.[17] Members of the military serving as party secretaries in the provinces declined in numbers from ninety-five (60 percent) in the period from 1970 to 1971 to seventy-four (47 percent) in the period from 1974 to 1975. The most dramatic decline in military participation in the political process came at the powerful Politburo level. In 1969 the twenty-five-member Politburo included thirteen PLA senior officers, or 52 percent of the membership. In 1973 the twenty-one-member Politburo included only seven PLA senior officers, or 33 percent of the membership. Military representation on the Central Committee declined less drastically, from 43 percent of the full members on the Ninth Central Committee in 1969 to approximately 32 percent on the Tenth and Eleventh Central Committees. Interestingly, while PLA regional or provincial commanders holding concurrently the post of provincial party secretary decreased from fourteen to eight during the post-Lin period, their representation on the Central Committee remained fairly stable. The continued high participation rate in the Central Committee by the military commanders and political commissars for the regional and provincial commands apparently reflects their continuing importance in the Chinese political power structure.

The Fifteenth Party Congress, convened September 12–18, 1997, elected a total of 193 full members for the new Central Committee. Of the total, about 42, or 21.8 percent, represented the military ranks—about the same as the Fourteenth Central Committee elected in 1992.[18] For the 151 alternate members of the Central Committee elected in 1997, the military representation was 20 from the PLA ranks, or about 13 percent, slightly less than its representation of the 1992 alternate members on that Central Committee.[19] However, when it came to the election of the Politburo, the Fifteenth Central Committee elected two military representatives to that important party organ: Zhang Wannian and Chi Haotian, the two vice-chairmen for the Military Affairs Committee. With the retirement of Liu Huaqing, no military officer has been elected to the all-powerful seven-member Standing Committee of the Politburo. In addition, Zhang Wannian now sits on the Central Committee's Secretariat.

In summary, the party-army interlocking directorate at the top decision-making level is still the established pattern. It was the dominant and important pattern from the late 1960s to the late 1970s. The party-army interlocking pattern showed less dominance by the 1980s but its presence has by no means disappeared as Jiang Zemin assumed his consolidated control at the Fifteenth Party Congress in the fall of 1997.

The Military Participation in the Tiananmen Crackdown, 1989: Dissent and Effect on PLA Role

The military was said to have played an important role in the political struggle over Hu Yaobang's forced resignation as party chief. It was reported that in December 1986, at the time of the student demonstrations, Deng presided over a large gathering of PLA leaders who pressured him to take action.[20] A week after that meeting, Deng met with other top party leaders and then ordered the crackdown on the students and intellectuals, who seemed to have supported the student demonstrations.[21] While the PLA continued its support for Deng,[22] it steadfastly refused even to entertain the thought of naming Hu Yaobang concurrently as chairman of the party and of the MAC, a tradition long held by Mao. In the view of Parris Chang, the military questioned Hu's ability to oversee the military apparatus and personnel even though Hu had been Deng's protégé for some time. The officer corps of the PLA was "antagonistic" toward Hu for his "excessive indictment of Mao's errors."[23] Rural economic prosperity brought on by the reforms deterred rural youth from joining the army; China's open door to "bourgeois tendencies;" and the forced retirement of many aged military officers—all these reform measures had brought on criticism within the PLA. One must point out that these were the very measures initiated and supported by Deng himself, including the indictment of Mao's mistakes (see Chapter 3). It is possible that the PLA ground forces leaders, the so-called "military traditionalists," formed a temporary alliance with the orthodox, hard-liners to block Hu's ascendancy.

The massive deployment of units of the PLA, estimated at more than 150,000, was unprecedented and unnecessary for the purpose of suppressing student demonstrators at Tiananmen in 1989. (See Chapter 10 for a full discussion on the Tiananmen Massacre on June 4, 1989.) The armed units dispatched to Tiananmen came from six military regions: the Beijing Military Region (including the 38th Army from the Beijing Garrison Command, as well as the 24th, 27th, 28th, 63rd, 64th, and 65th Armies); the Nanjing-Fuzhou Military Region (the 12th Army); the Lanzhou-Inner Mongolian Military Region (the 20th Army); the Shenyang Military Region (the 39th Army); the

Jinan-Wuhan Military Region (the 54th Army); and the Guangzhou Military Region (the 12th Army and the 15th Air Force).

Initially the task of suppressing the students fell to the 38th Army of the Beijing Garrison Command. But two days after the imposition of martial law, the 38th Army had failed to implement orders from the central government to move on the students. There were at least two basic reasons why the 38th Army failed to move with deliberate speed on Tiananmen. One is thought to have been the professional younger officers' reluctance to be involved in using force to quell the student demonstration.[24] Another reason, as revealed by a former member of the 38th Army who was a doctoral candidate in political science at Stanford University in 1989, was that the 38th Army, stationed on the southern outskirts of Beijing, had enjoyed a close association with the people of the capital city, particularly the students who spent summers at the military camp and were recruited into the 38th Army as conscripts.[25] Unlike its intervention in the Cultural Revolution, the PLA now had serious dissent in its ranks.

Dissension within the PLA. The reluctance of the 38th Army to move against the students of Tiananmen was a symptom of a larger problem within the PLA concerning the use of force against civilians in a domestic disturbance. On May 22, 1989, seven senior military officers circulated a memorandum protesting the use of troops to put down the demonstration at Tiananmen. The letter urged that the PLA troops refrain from the use of force and that they not enter Beijing City.[26] The signers of the appeal included a former defense minister, a former deputy defense minister, a former army chief of staff when Deng came to power, a former commander of a military region, and one from the Chinese navy; the rest were senior officers of the military academy. Senior Army General Qin Jiwei, then the defense minister and a member of the Politburo, was also opposed to the use of troops to quell the disturbance. Two of China's most respected retired marshals, Nie Rongzhen and Xu Xiangqian, tried to negotiate with the student leaders at Tiananmen. The two senior PLA marshals were said to have telephoned the martial law administrators, advising them against the use of force.[27]

Perhaps sensing the dissent and disagreement with the PLA over carrying out the martial law decree, or merely following past practice of using his personal prestige to win the support of the military regions, Deng Xiaoping convened an emergency meeting of the seven regional military commanders at Wuhan. The meeting was said to be stormy, and three regional military commanders expressed their opposition to the use of force.[28]

In the end, Deng's persuasion seemed to have prevailed, for by May 25 six of the seven regional military commanders pledged their support to the martial law decree—the one holdout was the pivotal Beijing Military Region. Soon after the agreement, troops began to be deployed from other parts of China, ostensibly for the purpose of enforcing martial law; but in reality they were intended to prevent a possible military rebellion by the 38th Army, or possibly by other military units.[29] The size of the military deployment, estimated at 150,000 troops, and the equipment employed (including tanks, heavy artillery, antiaircraft weapons, paratroopers, and missiles)[30] certainly indicated that they were not intended merely for suppression of the unarmed student demonstrators and the Beijing City residents who erected barriers to block the soldiers marching into Tiananmen. The troops that finally entered the square and opened fire on the students and residents near or on the square were the 27th Army from Hepei countryside, commanded by a relative of Yang Shangkun, then permanent general secretary for the MAC and a leader of the hard-liners. Recruits for the 27th Army were not urban youth, but mainly of peasant background.

The Purge and Continued Discontent within the PLA.   The upshot of military dissent over the use of force at Tiananmen was a reorganization and a change of personnel—thus a purge—within the PLA command structure.

In the aftermath of Tiananmen, one of the most significant personnel changes for the PLA was Deng's resignation of his long-held chairmanship of the powerful MAC. His successor in that post, tantamount to commander-in-chief for the entire armed forces, was not Yang Shangkun, who reportedly coveted the position, but the new party general secretary, Jiang Zemin, who up until then had had hardly any experience with the military. However, the real power of the PLA rested with Yang Shangkun, who became the first vice chairman of the MAC. In addition, Yang's brother, Yang Baibing, became permanent general secretary of the MAC. There have been some complaints inside and outside the PLA that the Yangs have made the military their "family enterprise."[31]

By the spring of 1990 a major reshuffle of regional military commands had been completed by transfer of military commanders from one region to another as a way of preventing their becoming entrenched within their local power bases. While there were no officially publicized dismissals of officers in the aftermath of Tiananmen, one Western source indicated that discharges or purges of 400 officers and 1,600 soldiers might have taken place within the PLA, either for refusal or inability to carry out the martial law decree to crack down on the students.[32] On the whole, there was no purge at the highest military levels, mainly because the hard-liners wanted to avoid the upheaval that might result from provoking the military officer corps.[33] Contrary to the claim that the military had enhanced its political role,[34] the PLA did not secure any new influential position in the reshuffle of the party's Politburo Standing Committee after having ousted Zhao Ziyang and Hu Qili, the two reformers. However, there was a rise in the defense budget for 1990 to 28.97 billion yuan, as compared with the 1989 budget of 24.5 billion yuan (U.S.$15 billion).

Promotion in the military in the aftermath of Tiananmen seems to have been based on individuals' willingness to use force against the students under martial law, and on personal loyalty to the Yang brothers, who were in control of the MAC and its high command structure until 1992.[35]

In spite of purges within the military, younger officers who were promoted and selected on the basis of professionalism and competence have been unhappy with the present state of affairs in the PLA. Their chief complaints were nepotism and the reemphasis on political study or "redness" at the expense of military professional competence. While nepotism has been endemic within the party and the military, the progress under Deng's military reform and modernization, which stressed professionalism and competence, has been deemphasized. In its stead, the traditional Maoist political and ideological study has become the order of the day—six out of every ten hours must be spent on political sessions. The PLA's General Political Department has ordered all officers to spend time attending political sessions studying Mao's thought and Marxism-Leninism. It was pointed out that bourgeois liberalization included ideas of "separation of army from politics." Party-controlled mass media and the PLA's own *Liberation Army Daily* had waged a campaign to urge military officers to study a special circular that presented the threefold tasks of "ensuring the absolute leadership of the party, ensuring a high degree of stability and unity, and ensuring an everlasting political quality" for the military.[36] The rationale for urging the need to engage in political study was the infiltration of "antagonistic forces" from outside to subvert the PLA's quality.[37] Mao's old dictum that the guns must be in the party was revived and stressed as a priority for study by the younger officers, who seem to have been the opposition in recanting the ideological lines of yesteryear.

For the soldiers as well as the officers in the military, there is also the crisis of the decline in the respect and prestige which the PLA had enjoyed before the Tiananmen crackdown. The traditional refrain that "the people love the PLA" was no longer a cherished thought, after what happened to the students and the Beijing residents on the early morning of June 4. The soldiers, in addition to losing public respect, also faced the reality of economic hardship brought on by inflation. Their low pay could no longer purchase needed provisions. They must, as always, labor hard on the military rice farms and in factories to produce goods to be sold on the market for supplementing the military budget[38]—about 80 percent of defense industries produce consumer goods.[39]

Continued discontent within the PLA motivated some officers from Shenyang, Beijing, and Nanjing Military Regions to produce a secret anti-Yang Shangkun circular. They accused Yang of refusing to support Jiang Zemin as party chief and of nepotism by appointing his brother as general secretary of the MAC, while concurrently serving as director of the PLA's General Political Department.[40] The resentment against increasing domination and control of the PLA by the Yang brothers reached its height when some twenty senior retired PLA generals confronted Jiang Zemin, the party chief, on the eve of the August 1, 1990, Army Day to register their complaints and concerns.[41]

Presumably, the removal of the Yang brothers from positions of power at the 1992 Party Congress assuaged the resentment against them within the PLA command. This was followed by a massive purge of nearly half the generals who were considered to be followers of the Yang brothers. This move was considered essential to ensure Deng's hand-picked successors' survival in case of a possible military coup in future power contests. As mentioned earlier, Jiang Zemin, the party head, was actively cultivating support from the PLA senior officers toward that end.

However, General Yang Baibing, who no longer held membership in the Military Affairs Commission and the Politburo, did not remain silent on party affairs. In November 1996, as "an ordinary party member," he submitted a "letter of opinion" to the Central Committee in which he pointed out the decline of party prestige, the continued corruption within the party ranks, and generally criticized the party leadership.[42] Yang Baibing even offered the suggestion that there should be a maximum age limit, 68 to 70, beyond which no one should be permitted to hold any top-level position as party general secretary or prime minister. Evidently the suggestion of an age limit for top leadership positions was aimed at Jiang Zemin who was then 71 years of age. Then in January 1997 nine PLA top level officers, who served as members of the Central Committee, were "disciplinarily reprimanded" by the Military Affairs Committee for circulating Yang Baibing's "letter of opinion."[43]

In the aftermath of Tiananmen the Chinese military establishment was faced with internal dissension and discontent, not only for its role in the crackdown on the students, but over its ultimate place in society. Having lost its traditional prestige, the PLA is confronted with growing resentment and criticism, if not a risk of violence, from the populace. It will take more than political study or the emulation of Lei Feng to restore the PLA's relationship with the people. The Chinese military is now trying to resolve its political and professional identity. Ultimately, it must answer the basic questions of civil-military relations: Is it always the instrument of the party, and what must it do when there are contending factions within the party? How do the PLA officers and men reconcile the inevitable contradiction between "party reliability" and military professionalism?

MILITARY REFORM AND MODERNIZATION

Nothing has really changed with regard to Mao's old dictum: Political power grows out of the gun barrel, and the party must command the gun. After Mao's death, the man in the party in command of the gun was Deng Xiaoping. In 1974, when Deng was reinstated after being purged during the Cultural Revolution, one of the pivotal positions he held was that of chief of staff for the PLA. Because of Deng's many years of close association with the military—both as political commissar and as the party's general secretary—he was the only person in the top hierarchy after Mao's death who could command respect and support from most PLA officers.

Deng Xiaoping's Initial Moves to Reform the PLA

When Deng returned for the second time in 1977, he was not only the PLA's chief of staff but also the vice-chairperson of the MAC—the de facto political supervisor of the armed forces.

One of Deng's first goals was to consolidate his control over the central command structure of the armed forces. He accomplished the task in two carefully planned moves. One was to reshuffle the commanders and commissars for the military regions so as to ensure the retention of only those who supported his policies. By the spring of 1980, Deng was able to appoint ten of the eleven commanders for the eleven military regions. The only regional military commander who retained his appointment (uninterrupted since 1969) was Li Desheng of the Shengyang Military Region for the northeast provinces facing the Soviet border. Li was finally removed from that position in 1985, and subsequently was retired from the Politburo in the 1985 reshuffle, which installed a number of new Politburo members.[44] Li was reported to have been forced to retire because of his political views, which were considered contrary to Deng's.[45] (But that interpretation may not be correct because in 1985 Li was appointed vice-president of a newly established PLA University for Defense, a prestigious institution comparable to West Point. Li was said to have refused the PLA University presidency because of his advanced age.)[46] An extensive reshuffling and purge were also carried out in the provincial military districts. As a part of the ongoing PLA reorganization, the eleven military regional commands, as mentioned earlier, were reduced to seven through merger.

Deng's second move was to staff key military positions at the central command headquarters with his trusted associates. On the eve of the Twelfth Party Congress in September 1982, it was clear that Deng had established firm control over the central command structure. Deng was elected chairman of the MAC, a position comparable to supreme commander-in-chief for the armed forces. Yang Shangkun, his associate and a Politburo member, was made the permanent vice-chairman and general secretary for the MAC. Deng packed the standing committee of the MAC with his supporters. He promoted Yang Dezhi, the commander of the Chinese forces in the 1979 border war with Vietnam, to the position of chief of staff for the PLA. By 1981 all senior officers for the general logistics, rear services, and all commanders of the Chinese air force and navy were considered Deng's supporters.

Deng's next objective was to implement reforms in the command structure and in personnel. He recommended the following three reforms: (1) streamline the military command structure below the MAC level; (2) modernize officer training; (3) upgrade the competence of military officers. The PLA organizational structure was fragmented in such a way that there were separate commands for the air force, navy, artillery, armored units (tank corps), antichemical units, railway corps, engineering corps, and regional and provincial military districts. The thirty-eight army corps stationed in the military regions generally received their operational orders from the PLA general headquarters at the center.[47] Similarly, the air force, the navy, and the artillery in the military regions received their orders directly from their own headquarters in Beijing. Deng felt that it would be more efficient to have the forces and services all placed under the direct command of the military regions. For instance, the artillery corps would not be placed under the "dual command" of the military regions and the artillery's own headquarters.[48]

Deng also thought that reform was needed in PLA military officer corps training. Deng and his senior military associates believed that modern warfare requires knowledge and understanding about science and technology, and that special skills in modern warfare must be developed among the military officer corps through curriculum improvement in the military academies. The course content at the military academies seemed outdated in terms of tactics and strategies, and a large portion of the curriculum remained devoted to Mao's guerrilla strategy of a people's war.[49]

Since 1983 some actions have been taken to improve armed forces officers' training. A joint MAC and State Council decision was made to recruit university graduates below the age of 24 for PLA officers' training.[50] A military science degree was also established by the State Council as a forward step to encourage development in military science and modernization.[51] Special PLA cadre schools were set up in many provincial military districts to offer a year-long course in leadership training. After the year's training, graduates would be sent to the various military academies for further studies.[52] In the effort to upgrade the educational level of the officer corps, the air force seems to have taken the lead.[53] In December 1985 the new PLA University of Defense was established by merging the three separate military academies.[54] As of 1986 there were over one hundred technical military academies and specialized training schools, with "an enrollment of over 100,000 cadets, designed to produce a new generation of officers."[55]

Deng also felt the need to replace the large number of aging officers who clung to their posts but who had limited education and outdated concepts. These officers had little knowledge or understanding of modern military science and tactics. While they remained in their positions, artificial barriers had been erected between the armed forces and the service academies, preventing able young academy officers from receiving actual command posts.[56] Deng proposed a concerted campaign to elevate younger service academy officers with knowledge of modern science and with the needed stamina to command posts.[57]

By the summer of 1983, some measures had been introduced to support Deng's proposed reforms. One guaranteed aged officers a retirement pension equivalent to their full salary. In addition, a special bonus would be granted to every retired officer for each year of service. This meant that a military officer who served fifty years would receive an additional fifty yuan per month.[58] A housing allowance and a car would be added as special inducements for early retirement of high-ranking officers. For example, a political commissar could receive as much as 120,000 yuan in housing allowance and retirement.[59] Simultaneously, age limits were imposed on the commanders at various levels. The following age limits were reported: corps commanders, 55; divisional commanders, 45; regimental commanders, 35; battalion commanders, 30; and company commanders, 25.[60] Finally, a system of rapid promotion for younger officers in the military was instituted to provide youthfulness and competence.

By 1986, PLA commanders and political commissars for the newly merged seven military regions were younger in age and better educated. One report stated that 91 percent of all newly appointed officers in the military regions had studied in the military academies and about 60 percent had completed their junior middle school education (or the equivalent of U.S. junior high education).[61] About 25 percent of the officers on the active list had a college education in 1986. The PLA as a whole has become a relatively young military force, with a vast majority of the recruits within the age range of 18 to 39; only 2.5 percent were 50 and over.[62] Han Huaizhi, deputy chief for the PLA general staff, stated that more than half the aged officers in the seven military regions had been retired.[63]

But some of the policies for military reform have aroused strong dissent within the military. Since the military has traditionally stood for Mao's ideological purity, the reassessment of Mao's role in party history generated some resentment within PLA ranks. The assessment of Mao as a man who made mistakes in his later years might be regarded as a political compromise to placate old guard military leaders who still view Mao as infallible. Deng's lengthy lecture at the 1978 All-Army Political Conference praising Mao and his three rules of discipline and eight points of attention, formulated in the guerrilla days during the 1930s, might also be viewed as a concession to the PLA old guard.

The campaign for "socialist spiritual civilization," articulated by Deng and Hu Yaobang, also caused controversy among the military.[64] This campaign reemphasized moral standards, education, culture, science, literature and arts, and a general knowledge of humankind.[65] Deng was reported to have summarized the "socialist spiritual civilization" campaign by coining the phrase: "To possess ideals, moral standards, civilization, and discipline."[66] When Deng instructed the military to emphasize culture and general knowledge as well as politics, some of the old guard military leaders protested. It was said that Wei Guoqing, then the director of the PLA general political department in charge of education and propaganda, did not share Deng's view on the importance of cultural emphasis in military training.[67] Yang Shangkun, then the MAC's general secretary, rebuked Wei by pointing out that both science and culture were equally important in military training.[68] Subsequently, Wei was replaced by Yu Qiuli, also a Politburo member. The removal of Wei indicated the continued presence of dissent in the military.

Military Professionalism and Modernization

There has always been a demand for military professionalism and modernization. China's decision to develop a nuclear bomb in the early 1960s, the purge of Peng Dehuai, and the debate over Mao's military strategy all revolved around the question of military modernization and professionalism. This demand most likely became more urgent after 1969, as Sino–Soviet relations deteriorated and border incidents increased. After almost twenty years of debate and neglect, the new Chinese leadership has come out squarely on the side of military modernization.

The theme of military modernization has been stressed continuously by Deng Xiaoping and his successors to this day. At the 1996 reception commemorating the sixty-ninth anniversary of the founding of the PLA, the defense minister, General Chi Haotian, pledged that China would

> . . . build up a powerful army by relying on the advancement of science and technology, making greater progress in defense related science and technology, improving weaponry and equipment, and strengthening research in military science.[69]

He added further that "the army should upgrade its defense ability to cope with the possibility of high tech wars."[70] General Chi seemed to have echoed what Jiang Zemin had said a year earlier on September 28, 1995, at the closing meeting of the Fifth Plenary Session of the CCP's Fourteenth Central Committee. Jiang had called for "upgrading" the combat capacity of the armed forces under conditions of modern high technology by "strengthening scientific research in national defense and upgrading the modern defense" and through "modernization" of Chinese armed forces equipment.[71]

For some time in the recent past, this emphasis on military modernization had been a perennial theme for high-ranking Chinese military officers. For instance, Yang Shangkun, a professional military leader who was one of Deng's most valued supporters in the party's MAC, said in 1982 that it was essential for the military to acquire modern "scientific, cultural and technical knowledge." He made it abundantly clear that strength in war was more than a matter of the army's size—it must be seen "in the degree of modernization of equipment and the people's ability to use such equipment."[72] Yang Dezhi, the PLA chief of staff in 1982, also spoke of the urgent need to upgrade the technical level of military personnel through advanced training and education.[73] One Western military expert indicated that the Chinese military probably was then fifteen years behind the U.S. military in technological training.[74]

Early Procurement Strategy: Shopping Abroad for High-Tech Weaponry. When Deng Xiaoping came back to power in 1977-78, the Chinese realized that the basic requirement for military modernization was the rapid development of heavy industries, as well as research in science and technology, which would take time. To fill the large deficiencies that existed in their technology, the Chinese at first thought they could embark on a program of weapons purchase from abroad. Chinese military missions, headed by senior military officers, most of whom were vilified for advocating military professionalism during the Cultural Revolution, shopped around in England, France, and West Germany with an eye toward the possible purchase of the latest weapons: tanks, anti-tank missiles, fighter planes, and helicopters. While the United States remained opposed to sales of sophisticated modern weapons to the Chinese, it had tacitly given approval to its allies in Western Europe to sell such weapons to China.[75] In 1978 an agreement was signed between China and West Germany, under which China was reportedly to have purchased 600 antitank missiles.[76] Then China and Italy reached an agreement for a missile guidance system and helicopters.[77] China's interest in the purchase of modern arms was also encouraged by a change in United States policy under the Carter administration. In January 1980 former Secretary of Defense Harold Brown paid a visit to China. He indicated to the Chinese that the United States was willing to sell, on a case-by-case basis, certain kinds of equipment, including trucks, communication gear, and possibly early warning radar systems. In 1980 the Pentagon also approved sales of battlefield radar and computers, helicopters, and transport planes.[78] In July 1980 the Chinese signed an agreement with France to purchase fifty helicopters costing about $57 million.[79] There were reports that the Chinese were interested in purchasing French Mirage F-1 fighter planes and heavy-duty helicopters.[80] In 1981 Canada offered to sell the Chinese certain defensive weapons, mostly aircraft and radar equipment.[81] Chinese agents also concluded an agreement with Great Britain for the purchase of Rolls-Royce supersonic jet engines.[82] The Chinese strategy involved studying the mechanisms of the sophisticated modern weaponry purchased in limited quantities from the West, as a means of acquiring the needed weapon-making technology. This would be more beneficial for military modernization from a long-term point of view, and it would be less costly than massive purchases of the available modern weapons.

After many years of window shopping, the Chinese finally signed a letter of intent in November 1986 for the purchase from the U.S. of $550 million worth of radar, computer, and avionics equipment for jet fighters. It was a six-year agreement under which bids could be submitted by American firms to supply the sophisticated equipment by early 1987.[83] There was some expectation that these initial purchases would pave the way for subsequent U.S. sales of modern weaponry in areas where the Chinese defense needs were the greatest: artillery, anti-submarine warfare, and battlefield equipment.[84] The sale of sophisticated arms to China raised a number of policy questions for the United States.[85] For instance, would China be more cooperative with the United States? Would a militarily strong China make Asia more secure? In addition, it must be kept in mind that while China attempted to upgrade her defense capability by purchasing sophisticated weapons from the United States, she also embarked on an accelerated program of arms sales abroad. China was said to have sold Iran more than $1 billion worth of jet fighters, tanks, and small arms.[86] In 1986, China held an international arms exhibition to display its military hardware, mostly a decade old in design, to buyers in the Third World nations.[87] China's active engagement in arms sales abroad may have been motivated more by the need to earn foreign exchange than by the desire to export revolution to other parts of the world. (See the discussion later in this chapter on China's arms sales abroad.)

Economic Development or Modernization: The Ongoing Debate

When we discuss the complex issue of Chinese military modernization, we need to keep in mind that there is a running debate among Chinese leaders on the priority of this issue—a conflict between the need to develop and modernize basic industries and the need to develop the military. The conflict has usually been resolved by placing military modernization second to the need for economic development.[88] In fact, the Chinese have always stressed the importance of economic development as basic to all progress. One of the reasons for the late Marshal Peng Dehuai's criticism of Mao's 1958 Great Leap policy was Peng's concern over the delay in modernizing China's military—a criticism that brought on Mao's wrath and led to Peng's eventual purge. Peng's concern stemmed from his experience in commanding Chinese forces in Korea during the early 1950s. Peng argued that a strong industrial base was the foundation for military modernization. Mao's view prevailed, and the concept of a revolutionary army with stress on the human element, not on sophisticated weapons, remained a basic military doctrine. After that the "people's war" concept dominated Chinese military thinking. Not until 1975, when the late premier Zhou Enlai proposed a ten-year modernization plan, was the issue of military modernization placed on a par with modernization of agriculture, industry, and science and technology. In fact, modernization of defense was not openly discussed by the Chinese leaders until 1977, when Mao had passed away and the Gang of Four had been arrested. Even in 1977 Marshal Ye insisted that modernization of China's basic industries was essential and necessary for its national defense.[89] (This view was not shared by one special interest group, the National Defense Industry Office within the Chinese defense establishment, which argued that modernization of defense industries would stimulate the growth of other industries and thus motivate the progress of the economy as a whole.)[90] In a frank speech to the Royal Institute of International Affairs in London in

June 1986, six months before he was ousted, former party chief Hu Yaobang revealed that Chinese leaders had debated the question of priority between national economic development and defense modernization. He said the conclusion of the debate was "to concentrate on economic development vis-à-vis the national defense."[91]

As discussed earlier, although in his closing remarks to the party Central Committee in the fall of 1995, Jiang Zemin pledged his continued support to upgrading defense and the combat capacity of the armed forces, he nevertheless interjected the ongoing debate about the need for developing the national economy:

> . . . only when the national economy is developed can it provide the necessary material and technical basis for national defense construction.[92]

Then Jiang seemed to have issued both a caveat and a gesture of appeasement to the PLA by saying in the same breath that

> the country should support and enhance national defense construction in accordance with the need and possibility.[93]

He elaborated the statement with the suggestion for

> simultaneous military and civilian production and the ability to inter-shift the two kinds of production.[94]

By 1990–91 the size of China's military force was about 3.9 to 3.03 million. In 1994 the International Institute of Strategic Studies in London had reported the PLA strength at 2.93 million.[95] By 1998–99 the Chinese armed forces had been reduced to about 2.5 million.

An indirect cause of friction between the pragmatic leaders and the military was generated by the new agricultural policies for the rural areas. Peasant families have always provided the major source of recruitment for the PLA. The new liberal agricultural policies of fixing output quota at the household level and of permitting sideline production have brought general prosperity to rural peasants—so much so that those who stay on the farm are earning more than military recruits.[96] This has led to low morale in the military. Many soldiers are thinking of getting out of military service and returning to the rural communes. Aware of the morale problem within the military, Deng sought ways to boost spirits. One measure he suggested was to restore the rank and insignia that had been abolished in 1965 by Mao in his desire to make the army more egalitarian. The reinstitution of military rank for the officers and soldiers would mean more prestige, if not more pay.

For the officers, demobilization was more difficult to accomplish. Only 40 percent of the officers had opted for retirement at the end of 1986.[97] As a general rule, few soldiers and officers wanted to reenter civilian life even if prior arrangements had been made in terms of jobs available for them and their spouses. In many cases retraining had to be provided for the demobilized soldiers to help them find suitable employment in industries.[98]

Available statistics now show that of about half a million demobilized soldiers—approximately 80,000, or less than 30 percent—were transferred to civilian jobs in industries, commerce, and other government departments; as many as 22 percent, or 100,000, were recruited for public security work.[99] But from 1986–1992 a sizable number of demobilized soldiers, about one million in all, were transferred to the People's Armed Police (PAP).[100] Yitzak Shichor writes that China's demobilization of its armed forces not only has not "eroded its military capabilities" but has also improved upon it, as it has assumed the status of a great power.[101]

There has been a large, if not complete, turnover in the PLA high commands from membership in the powerful Military Affairs Commission to commanders and political commissars for the seven regional commands. There is now more emphasis being placed on training and education at the military academies and battlefield experience for high military positions.[102]

CHINA'S DEFENSE SPENDING

The simultaneous evolution of military modernization and economic development is understandable, at least from the standpoint of cost factor. In the early 1980s the Rand Corporation estimated that China would have to spend between $41 billion and $63 billion in order to completely modernize her conventional fighting forces.[103] This estimate was for 3,000 to 8,000 new medium tanks, 6,000 air-to-air missiles, and 200 to 300 fighter-bombers.[104] Closely linked to this enormous price tag of $41 billion to $63 billion was the lack of available foreign exchange needed to pay for the weapons. Western analysts speculated that one means of paying for the arms modernization would be to step up, as has already been done, exports from China of strategic metals, such as titanium, tantalum, and vanadium—all lightweight and heat-resistant metals used in aircraft.[105]

With economic development as the top priority, from 1978 to 1985 there had been reductions in defense spending. China's defense outlay was 22.2 billion yuan ($14.3 billion). It was reduced to 19.2 billion yuan ($13.0 billion) in 1980 and was further reduced in 1981 to 16.8 billion yuan ($9.9 billion).[106] Thus, the 1981 defense expenditure was down 5.4 billion yuan, or almost 25 percent, from the 1979 level. This reduction in military spending aroused the PLA's concern and criticism. The level of defense expenditure was held at about 17.8 billion yuan ($9.5 billion) for 1983 and 1984.[107] There was a further reduction in China's military expenditures for 1985 to about 10.5 percent from 14 percent in 1983, but the 1991–92 budget called for military spending at about U.S.$16.25 billion, an increase of 12 percent from the 1990 U.S.$14.5 billion.[108] In terms of China's total national expenditures, defense spending represented only about 15 percent in 1982 and 14 percent in 1983.

However, China's defense budget, as approved by the Eighth NPC in April 1993, was set at U.S.$17.5 billion, an almost 13 percent increase over the previous year. The increase was justified on the grounds that there would continue to be regional conflicts and wars, and China must be combat-ready to meet changing international situations.

It must be pointed out that these defense figures, as reported by the Chinese, represented only a portion of the actual defense spending. If we use methodology employed by the U.S. Defense Department that includes all portions of defense expenditure such as research and development and rocket space industries,[109] the 1983 figure of 17.8 billion yuan would have been increased to about 40 billion yuan, or 30 percent, of China's total state budget.[110] This is what Arthur A. Ding has described as "vagueness and intentional obfuscation."[111] For instance, nuclear, space programs, aeronautics, and research and development as well as allocations for defense industries or corporations are excluded from the overall defense expenditure. One recent study has shown that spending for

Research and Development (R&D), or purchase of foreign military hardware, including imports of major weapon systems from Russia (SU-27 fighter jets or kilo-class submarines), and arms sales abroad are not included in the official defense outlay.[112] Another recent study showed that the "real" military expenditure for 1993—that is to include items listed above—would have been over 66.5 billion yuan, or about U.S.$12 billion,[113] definitely a considerable increase, not decrease as officially reported. As pointed out by David Shambaugh, the 75 billion yuan, or U.S.$8.3 billion for the defense outlay in 1996–97 was at least 10 percent, but certainly not 1.5 percent of China's gross national product.[114] China's total defense spending in the mid-1990s was somewhere between U.S.$28 to $36 billion, or about five times the officially reported figure.[115]

A recent study (1999–2000) by the International Institute for Strategic Studies put China's total defense budget for 1998 at about U.S.$37 to $38 billion, comparable to that of Japan or Britain.[116]

JIANG ZEMIN AND THE PROFESSIONAL OFFICER CORPS

Before discussing the professional officer corps of the PLA, a few brief remarks must be made with regard to the overall military organization, particularly the Central Military Commission (CMC).[117] It is the most important, if not most powerful, central organ of the entire PLA (as pointed out in Chapter 4), as one of the principal organs of the party. It is responsible and accountable to the party's Politburo. Thus it is, in fact, under the party's control, even though a similarly named central military commission is provided under the National People's Congress, or the State Council.

When the overall supervisory and policy-setting body on military affairs is in the hands of the party, it thus produces two main consequences: a lack of "civilian coordination" via a state agency, such as the State Council, in political or foreign policy areas, and a lack of a military which is not "politically neutral" or "nonpartisan."[118] As discussed earlier, one of the key moves made by Deng Xiaoping when he returned to power in 1977–78 was to head the party's powerful MAC and staff key military positions in the central PLA command headquarters with his trusted associates. As concluded in a recent study by Nan Li, it is only under recent reform that MAC membership has been transformed from a political-partisan orientation to a membership no longer dominated by "political-military and nonmilitary" members to yield more coherent policies with "a higher level of consensus."[119]

As defined by June T. Dryer, the PLA officer corps consists of those officers with the rank of second lieutenant and upward,[120] numbering at least 700,000 in a total armed forces of 2.9 million. Among the officer corps, those with the rank of colonel to general are considered most influential in terms of providing direction for the PLA in the post-Deng era. In 1994 the National People's Congress enacted a law requiring senior officers, such as those who occupied the position of regional military commanders, to retire at age 65. However, there were a few exceptions to the rule; prior to September 1997 the two vice-chairs for the Military Affairs Commission remained in office: Liu Huaqing, 80, and Zhang Zhen, 82. According to one study, commanders at the platoon-to-regiment levels range from 30 to 45.[121]

An element of Deng's late 1970s reform of the military was to upgrade the educational level of the officers by mandating that all military officers must be graduates of military academies. In the meantime, part-time, short-term special schools were established to provide training for those who were already in the service but had only less than junior high schooling and who grew up in the communes.[122] As revealed by Dreyer, by the mid-1980s there were as many as over one hundred military academies and schools with a total enrollment of about three million armed forces students.[123] At the top of officer's training is the National Defense University, established in 1985. The duration of education and training at the National Defense Academy ranges from a two-year course for divisional commanders to a one-year course for army commanders slated to be generals. Beginning in 1993 senior commanders and personnel could enroll in a short-term program (about 100 days in duration) on national security.

On the whole, as reported by Dreyer, Western intelligence rating of the PLA's efforts in raising the educational level of the officer corps has been generally high. However these Western experts also point out that unless the PLA can develop the "strategic and doctrinal concepts" it will most likely take time for it to become truly modernized.[124]

Recently, however, some concern has been expressed by the vice-chair of the MAC that military cadres have engaged in corruption or undesirable behavior, such as using public funds for travel abroad, acquiring fancy apartments, and sending offspring abroad for study and/or travel.[125]

Can the Party Control the Gun?

Questions have been raised with respect to the ultimate loyalty of a more professionalized officer corps. Or, to put the question in more familiar terms: Can the party after Deng control the gun?

Jiang Zemin, the key leader for the "third generation" of successors, hand-picked by Deng in 1992, does not command the esteem that Deng enjoyed with the People's Liberation Army. Jiang came from a background that had little or nothing at all to do with the military. He is a Soviet-trained technocrat whose base of support has been mainly the Shanghai party and technocratic elite, the so-called "Shanghai mafia." Deng made sure that Jiang was placed in pivotal positions, not only as party chief, but as the head of the party's powerful Military Affairs Committee, traditionally occupied by leaders with stature such as Mao and Deng.

Deng's efforts to introduce modernization and professionalism into the military during the 1980s resulted in the emergence of two significant developments: (1) the rise of a better-educated and professionally oriented officer corps whose major concerns have been those of modern weaponry acquisition and tactical-doctrinal changes; and (2) an attempt to "disengage" or "downgrade" the military's role in politics. There was evidence indicating that both Deng and the officer corps intended the military to be professional, provided that the PLA obediently accept the party leadership at all times. Some question whether the military acted professionally during the Cultural Revolution and the 1989 Tiananmen crackdown on the students.

However, it must be pointed out that, as discussed earlier, the military did not intervene on its own initiative at the height of the Cultural Revolution in 1967–68; it was directed by Mao to restore order under conditions of utter chaos. The PLA intervention at Tiananmen was to suppress the demonstration under martial law. It did not intervene in order to arbitrate the party leadership's factional struggle or to engineer a coup; the PLA intervened reluctantly or grudgingly. When martial law was declared, the 38th Army of the Beijing Garrison was ordered, but failed, to move in on the students in the square. Evidently, the 38th Army's professional (younger) officers were reluctant to be drawn into the messy political entanglement. As a result, Deng had to dispatch armies from the outlying provinces to carry out the crackdown. The episode of the 38th Army's failure to act when ordered, and the criticism made by some of the aged revolutionary marshals against the military's involvement, created some grave concern at the top party-military commands. This was revealed in the Central Committee circular (Central Document No. 4, 1990), which pointedly asked the military officers then attending an all-army work conference to ensure *dangde jueduilingdao*, or "absolute leadership of the party over the army."[126] There is no doubt that, in the aftermath of Tiananmen, Deng and some of his political commissars in the military wanted to reaffirm and reassert traditional absolute party control over the army as a check against military professionalism.

Jiang Zemin's control of the military has been rather tenuous. Despite Deng Xiaoping's insistence that the military establishment pledge allegiance to the party chief, important reports from the military were routinely routed to Generals Zhang Zhen and Liu Huaqing as former vice-chairmen of the powerful military affairs committee—a conscious move to bypass Jiang Zemin's office. In March 1995, perhaps at the urging of the Politburo, a special meeting was arranged at Deng's residence so that the paramount leader could personally appeal to the army leaders. The meeting lasted for about thirty minutes, with Deng fervently pleading with the military top officers for their acceptance of the revolutionary tradition of the party's control over the military. Deng also urged them to pledge their loyal support to Jiang Zemin as the head of the party's collective leadership.[127] In subsequent reports, it was revealed that Deng had warned the military officers of problems, or even chaos, that might result from the military's failure to accept the party's command from Jiang Zemin as the party head.[128]

One obvious strategy for obtaining support for his leadership core is rather obvious: that is, promotion of leading military officers to full general status. A most significant move was made on July 25, 1993. Jiang made the announcement at the joint working conference of the Politburo, State Council, and Military Affairs Commission that the six senior PLA officers were promoted to full generalship, thus making a total of ten senior generals, counting the four already holding the top-most rank in the PLA. All of these ten top-ranked senior officers were permitted to attend the Politburo meetings. Then in January 1996 Jiang promoted an additional four senior officers to full generalship, including two from the air force.

PLA Interference in Foreign Policy

As Deng was near death there were already signs of the military's predilection toward interference in politics. For instance, the military officers have criticized Jiang Zemin and the foreign minister for "weakness" in confronting interference by the United States in Chinese domestic affairs and over Taiwan. Then, a faction of "hawks" was identified among the PLA officer corps, mostly those in senior high command positions. They seem to have gained the upper hand in the decision concerning firing missiles over the strait on the eve of the Taiwan presidential election in March 1996. However, their interference in foreign policy had surfaced in April 1993 when 160 PLA generals had petitioned Deng Xiaoping and Jiang Zemin for a change in China–U.S. policy.[129] This was followed by a second letter in May by sixty-three senior generals pleading with Deng Xiaoping to modify China's policy toward the United States.[130] The thrust of the appeal from the senior PLA generals was that China's policy toward the United States had been too "lenient (*kuanrong*), conciliatory (*renrang*), and compromising (*tuoxie*)."[131] Jiang Zemin's response to the "hawkish" appeal was that it had been the basic policy of the Politburo to seek cooperation, not confrontation; but this did not mean compromising with American hegemony.[132] Deng Xiaoping's response was reportedly transmitted at a meeting of the Politburo Standing Committee, which, on the one hand, admitted the need for "self-criticism." Then he emphatically told the "Long March" generals that his American policy was basically correct.[133] The episode illustrated the existence of a "hawkish" or hard line faction within the ranks of the PLA senior officers insofar as policy toward the United States was concerned.

The "hawkish" stance exhibited by the PLA high command, led by General Zhang Wannian, chief of staff for the PLA, and General Chi Haotian, the defense minister, was even more evident in March 1996 when the United States dispatched two aircraft carriers to the Taiwan Strait on the eve of the firing of missiles over the waterway for the purpose of intimidating the popular presidential election in Taiwan. The letter was signed by no less than 500 high-ranking PLA officers and requested mobilization in opposition to the United States move in support of Taiwan. General Zhang Wannian, also vice-chair of the powerful Military Affairs Committee, even boasted of sinking the American aircraft carriers and the recall of China's ambassador to Washington.[134] By all indications, Jiang may have acquiesced by giving final approval for the firing of missiles over Taiwan Strait—Jiang is said to have been a "prey to the whims of competing interest groups," which included the hard-line military officers and the "neo-conservatives" within the party.[135]

It has been reported that Jiang Zemin received appeals from thirty-eight retired and forty-eight active PLA generals urging him not to seek rapprochement with the United States through top-level visits to each other's capitals. Jiang then met with some of the generals at Zougnanhai and indicated his willingness to entertain the generals' ideas and concerns with respect to China–U.S. relations.[136] But he reaffirmed that no change had been made in China's policy of opposing any United States interference in China's internal affairs.[137]

CHINA'S NUCLEAR WEAPON DEVELOPMENT: "LIMITED DETERRENCE" CONCEPT

From the mid-1980s to the end of 1992 there were a total of thirty-four nuclear tests, and China probably had stockpiled "from 300 up to 600–900 warheads."[138] The size of China's nuclear arsenal would most likely increase in the next decade, as projected by Alastair Johnston in 1996.[139]

China's official position with respect to the nuclear force development has been, at least at the initial stage, that the nuclear monopoly by the superpowers must be broken. As argued by some, by acquiring nuclear capability China could compete with other powers in the international arena.[140] We know that in 1957–58 Mao was urging Nikita Khrushchev to extend to China the Soviet nuclear umbrella to deter the United States' determination to help Taiwan defend the islands 12 miles offshore from the Chinese coast. Deng Xiaoping had been quoted to have verbalized in 1983 about developing the nuclear force for retaliation against superpower hegemony.[141]

John W. Lewis and Xue Litai of Stanford University have provided the thesis that China's nuclear development was motivated by technology rather than by strategic doctrine.[142] However, Alastair I. Johnston has pointed out that the Chinese "doctrinal ambiguity" might have been designed to keep potential enemies "guessing" on timing and targeting in the event of nuclear retaliation, or it might simply have been a case of lack of "coherent publicly articulated nuclear doctrine."[143] Johnston then pointed to the change which has occurred in the past decades up to 2000 with emergence of the concept of "limited deterrence" (*youxian weixie*)—the ability "to deter conventional, theatre and strategic war" and/or "to suppress escalation during a nuclear war."[144] China's reluctance to participate or engage in multilateral arms control talks may be an indication of its fear of doing anything that may introduce "constraining" elements in its nuclear capabilities for limited deterrence.[145]

According to one analyst, it is most likely that China is augmenting its nuclear arsenal after "a major strategic policy review" undertaken in the aftermath of the mistaken bombing of the Chinese Embassy in Belgrade during the 1996 Kosovo conflict. According to Robert A. Manning of the Council on Foreign Relations in Washington, China may now have already developed "miniaturized designs" for more accurate and longer-range multiple independent reentry vehicles to be deployed by 2010.[146]

The New China News Agency reported recently that a new long-range missile had been tested; experts believe it to be the Dong-Feng-31 missile which could carry a 1500-pound nuclear warhead with a range of about 5,000 miles.[147] China is expected to build between ten and twenty such long-range missiles on mobile launchers by 2000, as reported by *Jane's Defense Weekly*.[148] Also, China has purchased from Russia a guided missile destroyer for the China East Sea Fleet, which must be viewed as a threat to American aircraft carriers in the Taiwan Strait. They have also purchased four quiet kilo-class submarines designed to detonate torpedoes beneath a ship's keel.[149]

CHINESE ARMS SALES ABROAD AND THE MISSILE PROLIFERATION

In recent years there has been considerable concern over China's arms sales abroad. That concern led to a probe of China's defense industries and China's military machine.[150] At a time when international superpower conflicts have been reduced after the collapse of the former Soviet Union, China's arms sales abroad have created apprehension, if not a feeling of instability and insecurity, in Asia. In this section we will discuss some aspects of the problem.

China's Arms Sales

For more than a decade China has been identified by international experts as one of the major suppliers not only of conventional weapons, but of ballistic missiles and nuclear technology as well, to the Islamic world and to North Korea. China's arms sales abroad began in the early 1970s, when it supplied Egypt with military weapons that included jet fighters and anti-submarine ships. During the eight-year war between Iran and Iraq in the 1980s, China exported arms to both belligerents in the Persian Gulf. In 1986 the world discovered that China had also provided Iran with the short-range anti-ship ballistic missile known as the "Silk Worm." The missiles have a 50-mile range and are packed with 1,000 pounds of warheads, three times as powerful as Exocet, the French-made missile that hit the United States naval vessel *Stark* in the Gulf in 1987.[151]

In the early 1980s China concluded a missile sales agreement with Saudi Arabia. It became known in 1985, through United States intelligence sources, that China had exported between 25 and 50 CSS-2 ballistic missiles with a range of 2,650 kilometers, capable of reaching most targets in the Middle East.[152] Soon China was ready to supply Syria with the M-9 short-range ballistic missile, but delivery was postponed after the United States protested. After the Soviet Union invaded Afghanistan, China delivered to Pakistan, its long-time ally and friendly neighbor, not only conventional weapons, but also M-11 short-range ballistic missiles, believed to have a range of 650 miles and capable of carrying nuclear warheads. With Chinese assistance, Pakistan has been developing nuclear bombs. Solid fuel surface-to-surface M-11 missiles have also been delivered by China to Syria, Iran, and Libya.

Wendy Frieman provides a picture which shows that China has made arms transfers to eight Islamic nations (Bangladesh, Egypt, Indonesia, Iran, Iraq, Pakistan, Saudi Arabia, and Syria) of a variety of ballistic missiles including short-range, intermediate-range, surface-to-air and anti-ship missiles.[153]

Under international pressure, particularly from the United States, China pledged to be bound by the 1987 Missile Technology Control Regime (MTCR), an international agreement signed by major Western powers but not by China, that sets guidelines intended to restrict the export and transfer of medium-range missiles and missile technology. China pledged to adhere to the MTCR guidelines and parameters in February 1992. The MTCR guidelines of 1987 was an international instrument designed to restrict the transfer of missile technology between states and thus reduce the deployment of such weapons of mass destruction. Nations parties to the agreement pledge to bar sales of missiles that weigh 500 kilograms to a minimum range of 300 kilometers.

While it has been denied repeatedly by Chinese officials, U.S. intelligence sources have clear evidence that China continues to export M-11 missiles and technology to Pakistan. This was revealed in an intelligence briefing for members of the Senate Foreign Relations Committee in May 1993.[154] The United States was concerned about the M-11 missile transfers to Pakistan for possible nuclear bomb delivery systems, and it was applying leverage through a set of conditions attached to the 1993 extension of the "most-favored-nation" trade agreement with China. One such condition stipulated that China must show evidence of its adherence to the MTCR guidelines by 1994. Earlier, the United States had imposed sanctions on the export of certain U.S.–missile-related technology to China. In response, China had threatened in late August 1993 that it might not abide by the MTCR guidelines. In late 1993, the United States lifted the sanctions, presumably in order to obtain concessions from China on human rights and trade issues.

Then in October 1994 China and the United States entered into an agreement to "halt" the sales of guidance and propulsion components as listed in Category II of the MTCR. However, there were reports that despite its pledge China continued to provide Pakistan with M-11 missile systems[155] and land-based C-802s, a new generation of cruise missiles, to Iran. In 1993 the Clinton administration banned the export of high-technology systems to Beijing. The ban was lifted in 1994 after the Chinese gave assurances that it would not transfer missile components abroad. Then, in May 1997 the Clinton administration issued trade sanctions against two Chinese firms for providing Iran with chemical weapons technology.

According to a report submitted in July 1997 to the United States Congress by the CIA's Nonproliferation Center, China, along with Russia, is the major source for the spread of weapons of mass destruction—both nuclear and chemical—for the world.[156]

Motives behind China's Arms Sales.   There may be as many as four possible motives for China's continued sale of missiles and missile technology abroad. One is the profit motive. Arms exports translate into foreign currency accumulation and a favorable balance of trade for China. In the 1980s when China was engaged in economic reform by stimulating export trade, arms sales abroad earned an estimated U.S.$1.3 to $2 billion.[157] Eric Hyer estimated that during the Iran-Iraq war in the 1980s, arms sales to Iraq by China were worth about U.S.$5 billion and sales to Iran were worth about U.S.$3 billion.[158] Total arms sales by China to Saudi Arabia were valued at least U.S.$2 billion in the 1980s.[159] The military dictatorship in Myanmar (Burma) purchased as much as U.S.$1.2 billion worth of jet fighters and other conventional weapons from China.[160] It has been reported that between 1989 and 1991 the Chinese also exported about two million guns to the United States.[161]

Another motive behind Chinese arms sales abroad may be political, or even ideological. Major arms transfers abroad to Third World nations that are China's friends or allies have the potential of altering the delicate regional balance in the Middle East and South Asia. A Chinese policy supporting the Third World allows China to develop a broad coalition all over the world. A united front of Third World nations implies a realignment in existing international relations.

Robert E. Mullins points out that the Gulf War in 1991 had some impact on the need for the Chinese military to step up their weapons modernization in preparation for a possible future conflict that surely would require high-tech or electronic weaponry in the battlefield a third possible motive.[162] Adherence to the MTCR guidelines would only enhance the United States domination, if not control, in weaponry development.

Still another motive for China's arms sales to major Mideast countries could be China's need for oil to fuel its expanding economy. Estimates have shown that at their current rate of economic growth, China needs nearly 1 million barrels of oil per day, increasing to 3 million by 2010 .[163]

CHINA'S DEFENSE INDUSTRIES: THE MILITARY-INDUSTRIAL COMPLEX, CHINESE STYLE[164]

China's defense industries are under the command of the PLA and those agencies controlled by the central government through several ministries in the State Council. The PLA command at the central level—that is, through the party's powerful Military Affairs Committee—controls the Commission of Science, Technology, and Industry for National Defense (COSTIND), which, in turn, controls and operates some 50,000 factories for manufacturing weapons and civilian goods for consumption under economic reform. COSTIND is said to be responsible for defense research and development, nuclear weapons test sites, satellite launches and monitoring, and administration of two academic institutions for defense science and technology.[165] Most importantly, COSTIND engages in the on-going process of "defense conversion"—the merging of civilian and military organizational and technical facilities and personnel for military modernization in accordance with Deng Xiaoping's rather vague instructions in 1978.[166]

The State Council's two ministries for advanced technology development—the Ministry of Machine Building and Electronics Industry, and the Ministry of Aeronautics and Astronautics—also maintain research and development facilities, as well as factories for manufacturing consumer goods and weapons. In addition, Frieman identifies the

China State Shipbuilding Corporation as responsible to both the military and the central government for operating hundreds of factories and research and development activities.[167] The PLA's general staff controls the Equipment Bureau, which provides weapons specifications to weapons factories, whereas COSTIND is responsible for weapons research production and development. Both COSTIND and the State Council ministries mentioned here negotiate with certain export trading corporations for arms sales abroad. For instance, the New Era Corporation and Poly Technologies serve as regulating firms under the command or control of COSTIND for a host of weapons export trading companies that have indirect relationships with the two State Council ministries (Machine Building and Aeronautics).

This is in addition to the PLA's tradition for self-sufficiency in providing needed provisions—from food to equipment to transport—for the troops. By the end of the 1980s, the PLA operated more than 100,000 enterprises with 700,000 employees, excluding the numerous "collecting enterprises" or businesses run by families of the PLA officers and servicemen. In the case of the PLA's most successful enterprise, Poly Technologies, its main exporter, powerful family ties to China's top leaders have been crucial in its operations. Information based on Thomas Bickford's study reveals that, as of 1993, the total number of business enterprises either directly controlled or coordinated by the PLA spread to over twenty-five transnational corporations engaged in trade abroad and investment in export enterprises. How much money have these military enterprises generated? One estimate indicated that in 1993 these PLA business groups earned over U.S.$6 billion a year in revenues.[168]

The Chinese policy on arms and missile sales abroad is generally a puzzle to the West.[169] That is, China's pledge to observe the Missile Technology Control Regime's guidelines and restrictions, on the one hand, and the mounting intelligence evidence indicating otherwise, on the other hand, illustrate the autonomous or separate relationship that has existed between the PLA high command and the State Council of the central government over the arms and missile sales issue.[170] Also, the PLA-controlled arms trading corporation negotiated the sale of 650-mile intermediate-range ballistic missiles to Saudi Arabia in spite of the foreign ministry's protest.[171] In addition, as pointed out by Peter Grier, one of the PLA-controlled arms export trading companies, Poly Technologies, has been headed by Deng Xiaoping's son-in-law since 1991.[172]

The Chinese defense industry bureaucracy maintains close ties with the powerful policy makers at the State Council level. There is a clear move by the defense industries to convert their factories into civilian uses.[173] It is therefore likely that Chinese defense industries may have acted independently, and that their bureaucracy is powerful enough to disregard the views of other central government agencies, including the Ministry of Foreign Affairs.

In a recent study of the five largest defense enterprises—two in the southwest and three in northeast China—it was revealed that they employ an aggregate of about 187,000 workers and produce civilian goods ranging from auto parts and aero-engines to cigarette-making machines to minicars and light trucks to refrigerators and television sets.[174] One favorite location for setting up defense enterprises to produce civilian goods seems to be the Shenzhen special economic zone next door to Hong Kong. Speculation is that Hong Kong will soon attract some of these defense industries.[175]

On July 22, 1998, Chinese President Jiang Zemin ordered the PLA to divest itself of business enterprises. By the summer of 1999 the military had surrendered some of its business enterprises through an arrangement under which the government made a one-time only payment to sell the businesses, plus a promise by the government for a significant budget increase to more than the 12.7 percent for 1997–98. (American visitors to Beijing are impressed by the five-star Palace Hotel within walking distance of Tiananmen Square, of which the PLA owned about 60 percent as a joint venture with Hong Kong's famed Peninsular group.) However, the military owned at least several conglomerates—the Poly Group and the Xinxing Corporation with many diversified subsidiaries—which had not been completely divested as of the summer of 1999. The problem seemed to be that as many as 15,000 military-owned companies were in debt and thus it was hard to find new owners to take over.[176]

In short, despite the military's attempts to circumvent the divestiture order, one estimate indicated that about one-third of the military's some 15,000 business enterprises had transferred their assets to the State Economic and Trade Commission as ordered by the central government.[177]

THE PEOPLE'S ARMED POLICE: A COUNTERVAILING FORCE TO THE PLA?

The national armed police force of China had its origin as a public security unit during 1949–50. It was not until 1961 that the title was changed to people's police army, under the supervision and control of the PLA and its regional commands in the provinces. Then by 1972 the people's armed police was placed under the Ministry for Public Security.

A decisive organizational change for the national armed police came in 1982 when it was named officially the People's Armed Police (PAP), under the supervision of the party's Central Military Commission and the State Council, with operational responsibility in the hands of the Ministry of Public Security.

As a semi-independent armed police force, the PAP drew its recruitment from the various local police units of the PLA, augmented by transfers to its command from the internal guard troops, border patrol units and fire fighting contingents, to make up a total strength of about 600,000 in 1985.[178] When student demonstrations in Tiananmen escalated from May to June 1989, it was apparent the PAP was not able to carry out its primary mission—that is, suppression of the unrest and restoration of stability. As the party leadership's dissatisfaction mounted in the aftermath of the student crackdown in June 1989, also reflecting the failure on the part of the Ministry of Public Security, a reorganization of the PAP was effected in 1995. A key feature of the reform was to place the PAP under the command of the PLA's General Staff Office, the Central Military Commission, which, along with the State Council under then-Premier Li Peng, would set policies for the newly organized PAP.[179] By 1995 the PAP had not only received a larger state funding (about U.S.\$1.8 billion) but had increased its strength to 700,000.[180]

PAP's Mission

Peng Zhen, then the chairman of the Standing Committee of the National People's Congress, was said to have played a major role in the initial formation of the PAP in 1982.[181] Its then-political commissar said that although the PAP lacked legal education in law enforcement work, it nevertheless was "an armed force of the party and the State."[182] The implication then seemed to be, as it does now, that the newly formed national police force might play an influential role in competition with the regular PLA as the drama for political succession unfolds in the foreseeable future.

For the moment, as evidenced by the increased funding and recruitment in the PAP's size, it seems that the party leadership's overall concern is social stability and order in the transitional period after Deng's death,[183] even though the PAP's performance at the 1989 Tiananmen protest movement was unsatisfactory—its units in Beijing had to be taken over by regular PLA forces. The PAP has now been organized to undertake such tasks as drawing up contingency plans for dealing with social unrest and violent social disorder, particularly in urban areas, as incidents of violence and crime have been on the increase. Ethnic unrest and disturbances of public order in the border regions in southwest China, Tibet, and Xinjiang Uygar have also been the PAP's concern. An enlarged PAP party commissar meeting, held in July 1996, indicated that the PAP must serve as the key element in maintaining internal social and political stability in support of the PLA, whose main responsibility is to defend the nation against external threat.[184] Thus, the PAP may have become the main armed instrument for suppressing those elements which disturb social and political stability.

While Jiang Zemin, the party chief and Deng's compromise choice, may not have complete control over the PLA establishment, he has been cultivating his support from the PAP. As pointed out by one China scholar, Jiang has shared the same views as the PAP commanders and commissars that social stability must be the top priority.[185] Jiang's appointment of General Yang Guoping, a former Shanghai garrison commander at the time Jiang was Shanghai party chief and mayor, might imply that Jiang could rely on the PAP as a countervailing force should a succession struggle occur during the transition period after Deng's death. The PAP may gain influence politically if social instability and unrest become rampant.[186]

However, the PAP's performance in maintaining law and order has been under criticism by top party leaders in recent years. In April 1996 there were repeated orders from the State Council and the Central Military Commission demanding the various law enforcement agencies, particularly public security and the PAP, to rectify and strengthen their work.[187] These documents reveal that in 1995 there were some four thousand PAP members dismissed for failure to perform their duties; and, there were over 1,500 cases of illegal actions by the PAP that resulted in armed conflicts with other law enforcement units and with the populace.[188] Qiao Shi, then a Politburo member and National People's Congress Standing Committee chairman, complained about the increasing deterioration in law enforcement and advanced the reason that the problem was a result of corruption within the law enforcement units.[189] This raises the question of the PAP's reliability in law and order enforcement.

NOTES

1. Gabriel A. Almond and G. Bingham Powell, Jr., eds., *Comparative Politics Today: A World View* (Boston and Toronto: Little, Brown, 1980), p. 67.
2. Samuel Huntington, *Political Order in Changing Societies* (New Haven, Conn.: Yale University Press, 1968), pp. 194–96. Also see David Rapoport, "Comparative Theory of Military and Political Types," in Huntington, ed., *Changing Pattern of Military Politics* (New York: The Free Press of Glencoe, 1962), pp. 71–89.
3. Martin Wilbur, "Military Separatism and the Process of Reunification under the Nationalist Regime, 1922–1937," in *China in Crisis*, 1 no. 1, ed. Ho Pi-ting and Tang Tsou (Chicago: University of Chicago, 1968), p. 203.
4. Ibid.
5. Ibid.
6. Theodore Treadgold, *Soviet and Chinese Communism: Similarities and Differences* (Seattle: University of Washington Press, 1967), p. 25.

7. Robert C. Tucker, "On the Contemporary Study of Communism," *World Politics*, 19, no. 2 (January 1967), 242–57.
8. Harlan W. Jencks, *From Muskets to Missiles: Politics and Professionalism in the Chinese Army, 1945–1984* (Boulder, Colo.: Westview Press, 1982); and his "Party and Military in China: Professionalism in Command?" *Problems of Communism*, 32 (September–October 1983), 48–63. Also see Alastair Johnston, "Changing Party-Army Relations in China, 1979–1984," *Asian Survey*, 24, no. 10 (October 1984), 1012–39.
9. Johnston, "Changing Party-Army Relations in China, 1979–1984," 1015.
10. Shu-Shin Wang, "Revamping China's Military," *Problems of Communism* (March–April 1985), 111–17.
11. For more recent studies on the subject of Chinese civil-military relations, see David Shambaugh, "China's Military in Transition: Politics, Professionalism, Procurement and Power Projection," *China Quarterly*, no. 146 (June 1996) 265–98; Ellis Joffe, "Party-Army Relations in China: Retrospect and Prospect," *China Quarterly*, no. 146 (June 1996), 299–314; Jeremy T. Paltiel, "PLA Allegiance on Parade: Civil-Military Relations in Transition," *China Quarterly*, no. 143 (September 1995), 784–800; Li Cheng and Lynn White, "The Army in the Succession to Deng Xiaoping; Familiar Fealties and Technocratic Trends," *Asian Survey*, 33, no. 8 (August 1993), 757–86; Michael D. Swaine, *The Military and Political Succession in China: Leadership, Institutions, Beliefs* (Santa Monica, Calif.: The Rand Corporation, 1992). Also see two earlier articles published in 1991: David Shambaugh, "The Political Work System in the People's Liberation Army," *China Quarterly*, no. 127 (September 1991), 527–68; and Harlan W. Jencks, "Civil-Military Relations in China: Tiananmen and After," *Problems of Communism*, 40, no. 3 (May–June 1991), 14–29.
12. Shambaugh, "China's Military in Transition," 269.
13. In addition to David Shambaugh's article, also see Joffe, "Party-Army Relations in China" 300–14; and Jencks, "Civil-Military Relations in China," 14–29.
14. Ellis Joffe, "Party-Army Relations in China," 300.
15. Ellis Joffe, "The Chinese Army after the Cultural Revolution," 450–77. For the account of Biao's crash, see Cheng Huan, "The Killing of Comrade Lin Biao," *Far Eastern Economic Review* (July 22, 1972); *New York Times*, July 23, 1972, pp. 1, 16. For the official version, see Chou En-lai, "Report to the Tenth National Congress of the Communist Party of China," *Peking Review*, 35–36 (September 7, 1973), 18. Also see Philip Bridgham, "The Fall of Lin Biao," in *China Quarterly*, 55 (July–September 1973), 427–49; Yingmao Kau and Pierre M. Perrolle, "The Politics of Lin Biao's Abortive Military Coup," *Asian Survey*, 14, no. 6 (June 1974), 558–77; and Y. M. Kau, *The Lin Biao Affair*, pp. xix–li.
16. See Parris Chang, "China Military," *Current History*, 67, no. 397 (September 1974), 101–5; Ellis Joffe, "The PLA in Internal Politics," *Problems of Communism*, 24, no. 6 (November–December 1975), 1–12.
17. Joffe, "PLA in Internal Politics," 12.
18. "The Fifteenth Party Congress," *China Analysis,* October 1, 1997, p. 4.
19. Ibid.
20. See *Zhengming* (Hong Kong), 111 (January 1987), 10.
21. Ibid.
22. See statement made by Xu Xin, PLA deputy chief-of-staff as printed in *Ming Pao Daily* (Hong Kong), July 26, 1987, p. 1. Also see Jim Mann, "China's Army Backs Deng, Official Says," Los Angeles Times Service as reprinted in *Sunday Honolulu Star-Bulletin and Advertiser,* April 5, 1987, p. A-14.
23. See Johnston, "Changing Party-Army Relations in China," 1012–39.
24. *New York Times,* May 23, 1989, p. A-5.
25. Article by Yu Bin distributed by the Pacific News Service, as reprinted in *Honolulu Star-Bulletin,* June 9, 1989, p. A-20.
26. *New York Times,* May 23, 1989, p. A-1.
27. See June Teufel Dreyer, "The People's Liberation Army and the Power Struggle of 1989," *Problems of Communism*, 38, no. 5 (September–October 1989), 42; and *Zhengming* (Hong Kong), 143 (September 1989), 6.
28. Dreyer, "People's Liberation Army," 42.
29. *Zhengming* (Hong Kong), 140 (June 1989), 10–11. Also see *Christian Science Monitor,* May 14, 1990, p. 4.
30. *Zhengming* (Hong Kong), 140 (June 1989), 8 and 43.
31. See *Zhengming* (Hong Kong), 143 (September 1989), 6–7.
32. Ann S. Tyson's figure was based on PLA and Chinese sources in her article, which appeared in *Christian Science Monitor,* May 14, 1990, p. 4.
33. See Dreyer, "People's Liberation Army," 47.
34. See *Far Eastern Economic Review* (July 6, 1989), 12.

35. Ibid.
36. See *People's Daily,* February 28, 1990, p. 1; and *Liberation Army Daily,* February 28, 1990, p. 1.
37. *People's Daily,* March 1, 1990, p. 1.
38. *Christian Science Monitor,* May 14, 1990, p. 5.
39. *China Daily,* January 23, 1990, p. 1.
40. *Zhengming* (Hong Kong), 149 (March 1990), 6–8; and 147 (January 1990), 10.
41. *Zhengming* (Hong Kong), 155 (September 1990), 6–7.
42. Lo Bing, "Yang Baibing Challenges Jiang Zemin," *Zhengming* (Hong Kong), (February 1997), 10.
43. Ibid., 11.
44. *Ming Pao Daily* (Hong Kong), September 27, 1985, p. 8.
45. *Wall Street Journal,* September 17, 1985, p. 3.
46. "A New Army for a New Society," *China News Analysis,* 1303 (February 1, 1986), 4.
47. Harvey W. Nelsen, *The Chinese Military System: An Organizational Study of the PLA* (Boulder,Colo.: Westview Press, 1977), p. 10.
48. See Lo Bing, "Inside Story about PLA Reform," *Zhengming* (Hong Kong), 66 (April 1983), 8.
49. William R. Heaton, Jr., "Professional Military Education in China: A Visit to the Military Academy of the PLA," *China Quarterly,* 81 (March 1980), 122–28.
50. *Ming Pao Daily* (Hong Kong), May 27, 1983, p. 1; and *Ta Kung Pao Weekly* (Hong Kong), May 26, 1983, p. 1.
51. *Ming Pao Daily* (Hong Kong), December 8, 1983, p. 1.
52. *Ming Pao Daily* (Hong Kong), September 18, 1983, p. 1.
53. *Ming Pao Daily* (Hong Kong), April 4, 1983, p. 1, and May 25, 1983, p. 1.
54. *People's Daily,* October 28, 1985, p. 1.
55. See Paul H. B. Godwin, "Overview: China's Defense Modernization" in *China's Economy Looks toward the Year 2000,* vol. 2, Joint Economic Committee, Congress of the United States (Washington, D.C.: U.S. Government Printing Office, May 21, 1986), p. 143. Also see "For Peace and National Security," *Beijing Review,* 31 (August 3, 1987), 4.
56. *Ming Pao Daily* (Hong Kong), March 6, 1983, p. 1.
57. See *Beijing Review,* 31 (August 4, 1978), 3–4. Also see *Ming Pao Daily* (Hong Kong), March 6, 1983, p. 1.
58. *Ming Pao Daily* (Hong Kong), March 24, 1982, p. 1.
59. Ibid.
60. *Zhengming* (Hong Kong), 66 (April 1983), 9.
61. "New Army for a New Society," 3. Also see "For Peace and National Security," 4.
62. Ibid.
63. *Beijing Review,* 15 (April 14, 1986), 5.
64. On socialist spiritual civilization, see the following: *Beijing Review,* 45 (November 8, 1982), 13; *Beijing Review,* 37 (September 13, 1982), 21–26; *Beijing Review,* 47 (November 22, 1982), 3. Also see *Hongqi,* 15 (August 1, 1982); *Zhengming* (Hong Kong), 61 (November 1982), 8–9.
65. *Zhengming* (Hong Kong), 61 (November 1982), 8–9.
66. Ibid.
67. Ibid.
68. *Hongqi,* 15 (August 1, 1982), 8–9. Also see *Zhengming* (Hong Kong), 61 (November 1982), 9.
69. See *Beijing Review,* (August 19–25, 1996), 7.
70. Ibid.
71. Jiang Zemin, "Principles on Modernization Drive," summary of a speech on September 28, 1995 in *Beijing Review,* (November 6–12, 1995), 7.
72. "August 1 Army Day," *Beijing Review,* 32 (August 9, 1982), 6.
73. *Ta Kung Pao Weekly Supplement,* August 5, 1982, p. 3.
74. See Drew Middleton, "Supplying Weapons to China," New York Times Service, as reprinted in the *Honolulu Star-Bulletin,* April 16, 1981, p. A-14. For articles on China's military modernization, see Christopher M. Clark, "Defense Modernization: How China Plans to Rebuild Its Crumbling Great Wall," *China Business Review* (July–August, 1984), 40–44; Jonathan Pollack, "The Men but Not the Guns," in *Far Eastern Economic Review* (December 18, 1981), 26–29; Robert S. Wong, "China's Evolving Strategic Doctrine," in *Asian Survey,* 24, no. 10 (October 1984), 1040–55; Paul H. B. Godwin, "Overview: China's Defense Modernization," 133–47; and Harlan Jencks, "Watching China's Military: A Personal View," 74–76. Also see the following: Charles D. Lovejoy, Jr., and Bruce W. Watson, eds., *China's Military Reforms: International and Domestic Implications* (Boulder, Colo.: Westview Press, 1986); Ellis Joffe, *The Chinese Army after Mao* (Cambridge, Mass.: Harvard University Press, 1987); Monte R. Bullard, *China's*

Political-Military Evolution: The Party and the Military in the PRC, 1960–1984 (Boulder, Colo.: Westview Press, 1985); and June Teufel Dreyer, "The Modernization of China's Military," *Problems of Communism*, 39, no. 3 (May–June 1990), 104–121. Also see Ngok Lee, *China's Defence Modernization and Military Leadership* (Canberra: Australian National University Press, 1991).

75. *New York Times,* May 18, 1978, p. A-6.
76. See Leo Y. Y. Liu, "The Modernization of the Chinese Military," *Current History* (September 1980), 11.
77. *Far Eastern Economic Review* (November 16, 1979), 21–22; and "Premier Hua Visits Italy: Building a Bridge of Friendship," *Beijing Review*, 45 (November 9, 1979), 13–14.
78. See *New York Times,* May 30, 1980, p. 1; *Honolulu Advertiser,* May 30, 1980, p. A-1. Also see Christopher F. Chuba, "U.S. Military Support Equipment Sales to PRC," *Asian Survey*, 21, no. 4 (April 1981), 469–84. Also see Michael Gelter, "U.S. Willing to Sell Military Equipment to the Chinese," Washington Post Service, as reprinted in *Honolulu Advertiser,* January 25, 1981, p. A-20.
79. *Ming Pao Daily* (Hong Kong), August 28, 1982, p. 1.
80. Ibid.
81. *Honolulu Advertiser,* August 21, 1981 p., B-1.
82. See Jonathan Pollack, *Defense Modernization in the PRC* (The Rand Corporation, N-1214-1-AP, 1979).
83. *Asian Wall Street Journal,* May 5, 1986, p. 1; *Business Week,* October 27, 1985, p. 63. Also see Roger W. Sullivan, "U.S. Military Sales to China: How Long Will the Window-Shopping Last?" *China Business Review* (March–April 1985), 6–9; and *Christian Science Monitor,* October 27, 1983, p. 4, and June 11, 1984, p. 3.
84. *Ming Pao Daily* (Hong Kong), May 9, 1986, p. 2.
85. *Asian Wall Street Journal,* May 5, 1986, pp. 1 and 7. Also see *Business Week,* October 27, 1985, p. 63.
86. *Far Eastern Economic Review* (December 18, 1986), 23.
87. Ibid.
88. See Chuba, "U.S. Military Support Equipment Sales to PRC," 483; Francis J. Romance, "Modernization of China's Armed Forces," *Asian Survey,* 20, no. 3 (March 1980), 304–5; and Harlan W. Jencks, "Defending China in 1982," *Current History*, 476 (September 1982), 249.
89. *Peking Review*, 21 (May 10, 1977), 18.
90. *Guangming Daily,* January 20, 1977, p. 5.
91. *Ta Kung Pao Weekly Supplement* (Hong Kong), June 12, 1985, p. 1.
92. "Principles on Modernization Dive," *Beijing Review*, (November 6–12, 1995), 14.
93. Ibid.
94. Ibid.
95. See Yitzhak Shichor, "Demobilization: The Dialectics of PLA Troop Reduction," *China Quarterly*, 146 (June 1996), 340 (Table 1).
96. *Far Eastern Economic Review* (September 25, 1981), 55. Also see Lo Bin, "Candid View of a PLA Divisional Cadre," *Zhengming* (Hong Kong), 65 (March 1983), 17.
97. *Zhengming* (Hong Kong), 108 (October 1986), 8.
98. *People's Daily,* November 1985, p. 4.
99. Shichor, "Demobilization: Dialectics of PLA Troop Reduction," 347.
100. Ibid., 354.
101. Ibid., 358–59.
102. See David Shambaugh, "The People's Liberation Army and the People's Republic at 50: Reform at Last," *Chinese Quarterly*, no. 159 (September 1999), 666.
103. *New York Times,* January 4, 1980, p. A-3.
104. Middleton, "Supplying Weapons to China;" and Pollack, *Defense Modernization in the PRC.* Also see Angus M. Fraser, "Military Modernization in China," *Problems of Communism* (September–December 1979), 34–49. For an earlier estimate, see Edward N. Lutwak, "Problems of Military Modernization for Mainland China," *Issues and Studies*, 14, no. 7 (July 1978), 58.
105. Drew Middleton, "Sales of Rare Metals May Pay for China's Armed Buildup," New York Times Service, as reprinted in *Honolulu Star-Bulletin,* December 31, 1981, p. A-34. Also see Chuba, "U.S. Military Support Equipment Sales to the PRC," 460–84; and Douglas T. Stuart and William T. Tow, "Chinese Military Modernization: The Western Arms Connection," *China Quarterly*, 90 (June 1982), 262.
106. Wang Bingqian, "Report on Financial Work," *Beijing Review*, 39 (September 29, 1980), 17; "Report on the Final State Account for 1980 and Implementation of the Financial Estimates for 1981," *Beijing Review*, 2 (January 11, 1982), 16; and "Report on the Implementation of the State Budget for 1982 and the Draft Budget for 1983," *Beijing Review*, 3 (January 13, 1983), 16.
107. *Beijing Review* (October 27, 1986), 3.
108. Ibid.; and Kathy Wilheim, "China Budget Hefty Increase for the Militia," Associated Press as reprinted in *Honolulu Star-Bulletin,* March 26, 1991, p. A-11.

109. See Edward Parris, "Chinese Defense Expenditures, 1967–83" in *China's Economy Looks Toward the Year 2000*, pp. 149–50.

110. Ibid. For a discussion on the relationship between economic development and defense needs, see Tai Ming Cheung, "Disarmament and Development in China: The Relationship between National Defense and Economic Development," *Asian Survey*, 28, no. 7 (July 1988), 757–74.

111. Arthur A. Ding, "China's Defence Finance: Content, Process and Administration," *China Quarterly*, 146 (June 1996), 429; and Shambaugh, "China's Military in Transition," 288.

112. See Amitar Achanya and Paul M. Evans, *China's Defense Expenditures and Implications* (Toronto: University of Toronto-York University, Joint Center for Asian Pacific Studies, 1994).

113. Ibid., pp. 910–11.

114. Shambaugh, "China's Military in Transition" 287.

115. Ibid., 288.

116. See "Military Must Change for the 21st Century—But How?" *Wall Street Journal*, November 12, 1999, p. A-8.

117. Information on military organization is culled mostly from Nan Li, "Organizational Changes of the PLA, 1985–1997," *China Quarterly*, no. 158 (June 1999), 314–349.

118. Ibid., 322.

119. Ibid., 347.

120. See "The New Officer Corps: Implications for the Future," *China Quarterly*, 146 (June 1996), 316.

121. Ibid., 317.

122. Ibid., 319.

123. Ibid., 321.

124. Ibid., 323.

125. See "The Case of Shanxi Military Region Corruptive Practices," *Zhengming Magazine* (Hong Kong), no. 262 (August 1, 1999), 20–21.

126. Text is to be found in "Quarterly Chronicle and Documentation," *China Quarterly*, 131 (September 1992), 877–78.

127. See Nee Zijing, "Deng Xiaoping Rebukes Top Military Leaders," *Dongxiang* (Hong Kong), (January 1995), 9–10.

128. Lo Bing, "Deng's Meeting with Top PLA Heads with Four Messages," *Dongxiang* (Hong Kong), (April 1995), 8–9.

129. Lo Bing, "Hundred Generals' Letter of Appeal to Deng Xiaoping," *Zhengming* (Hong Kong), (June 1993), 14–16.

130. Ibid., 15.

131. Ibid., 14.

132. Ibid., 16. Also see Nayan Chanda and Lincoln Kaye, "Circling Hawks," *Far Eastern Economic Review*, (October 1, 1993), 13.

133. Bing, "Hundred Generals' Letter of Appeal," 6.

134. Lo Bing, "PLA Generals Demanding War—Hawk Faction Criticize Jiang as Rightest," *Zhengming* (Hong Kong), (April 1996), 6–7. Also see Nee Zijing, "Zhang Wannien Boasting of Capability for Sinking U.S. Carriers," *Zhengming* (Hong Kong), (April 1996), 14–15.

135. See Matt Forney, "Signs of Struggle," *Far Eastern Economic Review* (February 1, 1996), 14.

136. Lo Bing, "Military Opposition to Jiang Zemin's Visit to the United States," *Dongxiang* (Hong Kong), (May 1997), 6–8.

137. Ibid., 7.

138. See Alastair I. Johnston, "Prospects for Chinese Nuclear Force Modernization: Limited Deterrence Versus Multilateral Arms Control," *China Quarterly*, 146 (September 1996), 562. Figure was based on interview with Chinese officials in July 1995. Also see Robert G. Sutter, *Chinese Nuclear Weapons and Arms Control Policy: Implications and Options for the United States* (Washington, D.C.: Congressional Research Service, CRS Report for Congress, no. 94-422S, March 25, 1994).

139. Johnston, "Prospects for Chinese Nuclear Force Modernization," 551 and 554.

140. Ibid.

141. Ibid., 553.

142. See John W. Lewis and Xue Lital, *China Builds the Bomb* (Palo Alto, Calif.: Stanford University Press, 1988).

143. Johnston, "Prospects for Chinese Nuclear Force Modernization," 562. Also see Robert E. Mullins, "The Dynamics of Chinese Missile Proliferation," *Pacific Review*, 8, no. 1, (1995), 140–46.

144. Johnston, "Prospects for Chinese Nuclear Force Modernization," 562.

153. Ibid.

146. See Robert A. Manning, "China's New Nuclear Doctrine," reprinted in *Honolulu Advertiser*, June 25, 1999, p. A-18.
147. See Seth Faison, "In Unusual Announcement, China Tells of a Missile Test," *New York Times*, August 1, 1999, p. A-6.
148. Ibid.
149. See Craig S. Smith, "Purchase of Guided-Missile Ship by China Heightens Tension," *New York Times*, February 9, 2000, pp. A-1 and A-3.
150. See Eric Hyer, "China's Arms Merchants: Profits in Command," *China Quarterly*, 132 (December 1992), 1101–18; Dennis Van V. Kickey, "New Directions in China's Arms for Export Policy: An Analysis of China's Military Ties with Iran," *Asian Affairs: An American Review*, vol. 17, no. 1 (1990), 15–29; John Pomfret, "Reform Fuels China's Military Machines," *Asian Wall Street Journal,* June 30, 1992, p. 8; and Wendy Frieman, "China's Defence Industries," *Pacific Review*, 6, no. 1 (1993), 51–62.
151. *New York Times*, June 7, 1987, p. 1.
152. Hyer, "China's Arms Merchants: Profits in Command," 1104.
153. Frieman, " China's Defence Industries," 52.
154. Ann Devroy, "New Evidence of Chinese Arms Sales," *Washington Post*, reprinted in *Honolulu Advertiser,* May 18, 1993, p. A-6.
155. See Mullins, "Dynamics of Chinese Missile Proliferation," 138. Also see Jeffrey Smith and Thomas W. Lippman, "Pakistan M-11 Funding Is Reported," *Washington Post*, September 8, 1994, p. A-32.
156. See Associated Press release as reprinted in *Honolulu Advertiser*, July 3, 1999, p. A-16.
157. Hyer, "China's Arms Merchants: Profits in Command," 1101.
158. Ibid., 1103.
159. Ibid.
160. Ibid.. 1105.
161. A *Washington Post* story from the Associated Press as reprinted in summary form in *Honolulu Advertiser,* March 4, 1993, p. A-12.
162. Mullins, "Dynamics of Chinese Missile Proliferation," 148–149.
163. See Mark Yost, "China's Deadly Trade in the Mideast," *Wall Street Journal*, December 4, 1996, p. A-18.
164. Frieman, "China's Defence Industries," 51–62. Also see Pomfret, "Reform Fuels China's Military Machine," 8; and *Far Eastern Economic Review* (October 14, 1993), 64–66. Also see John Frankenstein and Bates Gill, "Current and Future Challenges Facing Chinese Defense Industries," *China Quarterly*, 146 (June 1996), 394–426; Thomas J. Bickford, "The Chinese Military and Its Business Operations: The PLA as Entrepreneur," *Asian Survey*, 34, no. 5 (May 1994), 460–73; Tai Ming Cheung, "Serving the People," *Far Eastern Economic Review*, (October 14, 1993), 64–66; Mel Gurtov, "Swords into Market Shares: China's Conversion of Military Industry to Civilian Production," *China Quarterly*, 134 (June 1993).
165. Frankenstein and Gill, "Current and Future Challenges Facing China's Defense Industries," 404 and 406.
166. Ibid., 417.
167. Frieman, "China's Defence Industries," 53. Also see a more recent article by Bickford, "Chinese Military and Its Business Operations: PLA as Entrepreneur," 461.
168. Ibid., Frieman, 467. The estimate was from *Economist* (February 26, 1993), 30.
169. Peter Grier, "China Arms Policy Puzzles West," *Christian Science Monitor*, (July 3, 1992), p. 2.
170. See John L. Lewis, Hua Di, and Xue-Letaè, "Beijing's Defense Establishment: Solving the Arms Export Enigma," *International Security*, 15, no. 4 (Spring 1991).
171. Grier, "China Arms Policy Puzzles West."
172. Ibid. Also see *Far Eastern Economic Review* (October 14, 1993), 64.
173. See *Far Eastern Economic Review* (February 6, 1992), 40–43; and (October 14, 1993), 68.
174. Tai Ming Cheung, "Serving the People," p. 65.
175. Ibid., 66.
176. See Susan V. Lawrence and Bruce Gilley, "Bitter Harvest: The Handover of the Military's Business Empire Has Stirred up a Hornet's Nest," *Far Eastern Economic Review* (April 29, 1999), 22–26.
177. See David Shambaugh, "The People's Liberation Army and The People's Republic at 50: Reform at Last," *China Quarterly*, no. 159 (September 1999), 663.
178. See Tai Ming Cheung, "Guarding China's Domestic Front Line: The People's Armed Police and China's Stability," *China Quarterly*, 146 (June 1996), 527.
179. Ibid.
180. Ibid., 533.
181. *People's Daily*, October 28, 1985, p. 1.
182. "For Peace and National Security," *Beijing Review*, 31 (August 3,1997), 4.

183. Cheung, "Guarding China's Domestic Front Line," 535 and 538. Also see Wu Shang, "Public Security and Armed Police Expansion: Plan Revealed," *Zhengming* (Hong Kong), (February 1996), 22.
184. Wu Shang, "A Million Men Increase for the People's Armed Police," *Dongxiang* (Hong Kong), (August 1996), 19.
185. Cheung, "Guarding China's Domestic Front Line," 545. Also see "Jiang Calls on Party to Boost Law and Order," *China Daily*, December 25, 1993, p. 1.
186. Cheung, "Guarding China's Domestic Front Line," p. 547.
187. See Nee Zijing, "People's Armed Force Corruption as Seen from Party's Internal Documents," *Dongxiang* (Hong Kong), (May 1996), 16–18.
188. Ibid., 18.
189. Ibid.

SUGGESTED READINGS

Jencks, Harlan W. *From Muskets to Missiles: Politics and Professionalism in the Chinese Military System, 1945–1981* (Boulder, Colo.: Westview Press, 1982).
Joffe, Ellis. *The Chinese Army after Mao* (Cambridge, Mass.: Harvard University Press, 1987).
Lilley, James, and David Shambaugh (eds.). *China's Military Faces the Future* (Armonk, N.Y.: M. E. Sharpe, 1999).
Mulvenon, James C., and Richard H. Yang (eds.). *The PLA in the Information Age* (Santa Monica, Calif.: Rand, 1999).
Nelsen, Harvey W. *The Chinese Military System* (Boulder, Colo.: Westview Press, 1997).
Shambaugh, David, and Richard H. Yang (eds.). *China's Military in Transition* (Oxford, UK: Clarendon Press, 1997).
Sutter, Robert G. *Chinese Nuclear Weapons and Arms Control Policy: Implications and Options for the United States* (Washington, D.C.: Congressional Research Service; Report for Congress, no. 94–4225; March 25, 1994).
Yu, Peter Kien-hong. *The Chinese PLA's Perception of an Invasion of Taiwan* (New York: Contemporary US–Asia Research Institute, 1996).
Zhu, Fang. *Gun Barrel Politics: Party-Army Relations in Mao's China* (Boulder, Colo.: Westview Press, 1998).

Chapter Ten

Democracy, Dissent, and the Tiananmen Mass Movement

Before we discuss Chinese student dissent and the Tiananmen mass movement for democracy, we need to place these events in some conceptual framework. We may begin by describing a type of event that occurred frequently, in developing as well as developed nations, during the modern era, particularly during the turbulent times of the 1960s and 1970s—events that have been defined by Gabriel Almond and Bingham Powell as *anomic activities.* They often have erupted spontaneously in response to pent-up frustrations and the inability of governments to provide solutions to problems that beset societies.[1] Anomic behaviors, episodic and often violent, represent unconventional political action to address grievances and injustices and to demand action for change or reform. For American university students in the 1960s and 1970s, this meant street demonstrations for civil rights, anti-Vietnam War protests, and participatory democracy on campuses. From our American perspective and in view of the success of the civil rights movement and the anti-war demonstrations, Kenneth Prewitt and Sidney Verba, political scientists who have studied citizen participation in American politics, postulate that demonstrations, marches, and violence may be the "new political style."[2] However, direct political action has always been part of America's political process. The Boston Tea Party was a protest against British rule. In the First Amendment, the United States Constitution guarantees citizens the right to petition and to demonstrate peacefully. Some political scientists hold the view that exertion of public pressure on the decision makers through the use of demonstrations or protests may be essential to political change.[3] Protests, of course, are often employed "to resist change as well as to initiate it."[4] While protest politics is not new, it has become more frequent and more important in American politics since the 1960s. Whenever a large segment of the population takes part in a demonstration or protest, it can be considered an effective form of political participation. Finally, as pointed out by Almond and Powell, anomic political behavior can be the result of planning rather than spontaneity, or it may be the result of prolonged frustration and indignation.[5]

Now back to student protests in China. There has been a tradition in modern Chinese history to view protests and demonstrations by high school and college students as necessary anomic political behavior in the republican eras, beginning with the May Fourth Movement in 1919, to force change on the government, be it against warlords or the Nationalists. It will be recalled that the 1919 May Fourth Movement was a reaction by Chinese intellectuals to the encroachment of the West and Japan on Chinese political independence and territorial integrity. It also represented China's desperate search for ways to modernize the nation. Since then, student demonstrations have been the harbinger of change. Many leading members of the Chinese Communist Party made their debut in politics as participants in student demonstrations in the 1930s. The pages of modern Chinese history are colored with student demonstrations or similar anomic political behavior that too often ended in tragedy and bloodshed.

DEMOCRACY AND DISSENT IN CHINA: PROBLEMS IN EXERCISING POLITICAL RIGHTS

It is ironic to note that every constitution promulgated in China since 1954 has guaranteed certain basic political rights to citizens, but in practice these rights have on the whole been ignored by the party and government. The 1982 constitution is no exception. Article 35 of the 1982 constitution states that citizens of China "enjoy freedom of speech, of the press, of assembly, of association, of procession and of demonstration." On the surface, these words sound like the civil liberties guaranteed by the First Amendment in the American Constitution. In reality, the exercise of these "fundamental rights" by the citizens of China has always been restrained and restricted within the confines of the "Four Basic Principles," interpreted by Deng Xiaoping in 1978–79 to mean that the exercise of these political rights is guaranteed as long as they are not in conflict with "the socialist road, people's democratic dictatorship, leadership of the party, and essence of Marxism-Leninism-Mao's Thought." The following are case studies that illustrate the problem.

The Democracy Wall Movement Since 1978–1979[6]

For more than a year, between November 1978 and December 1979, worldwide attention was focused on the daily posting of handwritten messages on a brick wall, 12 feet in height and about 120 feet long, located at Changan Avenue near the Xidan crossing in the western district of downtown Beijing. Later, this wall came to be known as the Democracy Wall. Initially the appearance of the wall posters at the Xidan crossing may have had the blessing of the leadership faction, following the practice established during the early days of the Cultural Revolution. Some of the contents may have been leaked deliberately to the activists, who then aired them in the posters.

In March 1978 the first series of wall posters, in the form of poems, appeared on the Xidan Democracy Wall. Wu De, then the mayor of Beijing, and the Politburo members who had read the riot act to the 1976 demonstrators at Tiananmen, were attacked by name in the wall posters by some of the participants in the 1976 demonstration. This seemed to have signaled the events to come. The first officially approved act was the publication of a demand for a reversal of the verdict on the 1976 Tiananmen demonstration in the CYL periodical. By October 11, 1978, Wu was forced to resign as mayor of Beijing, and shortly thereafter hundreds of participants arrested in the 1976 Tiananmen riot were released and exonerated. During late October and early November, a sudden release of pent-up feelings increased the output of posters dramatically. This seemingly spontaneous outpouring of wall posters on the Democracy Wall might have coincided with the convening of the party's central work conference, which was planning the Third Plenum of the Eleventh Central Committee. During this period the leaders under Deng had locked horns with the "Whatever" faction on issues such as the new ideological line of "seeking truth from fact," the reversal of the 1976 Tiananmen demonstration verdict, the rehabilitation and exoneration of purged leaders of the Cultural Revolution, and, most important of all, the assessment of Mao and his role in the Cultural Revolution.

A study of the wall posters for that period revealed three main trends: the condemnation of political persecution authorized by Mao; petitions for the redress of personal grievances inflicted upon those who were persecuted during the Cultural Revolution; and the advocacy of democracy, justice, and human rights.[7] The proliferation of wall posters provided Deng Xiaoping with public support in his contest for power against the "Whatever" faction at the party's Third Plenum. As if by coincidence, decisions adopted by the party were identical to the concerns expressed by the posters on the Democracy Wall. For instance, the Third Plenum corrected the "erroneous conclusions" on veteran party leaders such as Peng Dehuai, Bo Yibo, and Yang Shangkun by exonerating and rehabilitating them.[8] The plenum also declared that the Tiananmen events of 1976 were "revolutionary actions."[9] It adopted the ideological line that "practice is the sole criterion for testing truth."[10] It was also decided to establish a discipline inspection commission within the party to enforce and investigate violation of party rules and regulations. While the plenum did not yet make an assessment of Mao's role in the Cultural Revolution, it hinted strongly that Mao, as a Marxist revolutionary leader, could not possibly be free of "shortcomings and errors."[11] It became evident that Deng Xiaoping had encouraged the wall posters when he told both a group of Japanese visitors and then Robert Novak, an American syndicated newspaper columnist, that the wall posters were officially tolerated.[12]

The Democracy Wall movement entered its second phase early in December 1978. In addition to candid expressions in support of sexual freedom and human rights, some criticisms of Deng Xiaoping now appeared. Deng then shifted his earlier stand and now expressed disapproval of the posters' criticism of the socialist system. There may have been other reasons for Deng's change of mind. It is possible that Deng had been subjected to criticism within the party for not having taken a stronger stand to curb the expressions of dissent at the Democracy Wall—members of the "Whatever" faction still sat on the Politburo even though they were criticized for their past role in the Cultural Revolution. Perhaps genuine concern about restoring stability and unity led to curbing the freewheeling activities at the wall. It was also very possible that Deng and his intimate colleagues were really apprehensive about the close contacts established by the participants with the foreign reporters who had been invited into the dissenters' homes to talk about democracy and human rights.[13]

During December 1978 activists associated with the Democracy Wall movement became dissatisfied with the success of their poster campaign and looked for ways to expand the campaign. They formed dissident organizations and study groups with names such as Enlightenment Society, China Human Rights Alliance, and the Thaw Society.

Each published its own underground journals and offered them for sale at the Democracy Wall. Most publications were poorly produced with primitive mimeograph machines. Nevertheless, some of the underground publications soon attracted worldwide attention as American, British, Canadian, and French reporters were given copies for overseas consumption. Excerpts from underground journals, such as *Beijing Spring*, obviously inspired by the 1968 "Prague Spring" of the Soviet invasion of Czechoslovakia; *April Fifth Forum*, derived from the demonstration at Tiananmen on April 5, 1976; and *Tansuo (Exploration)*[14] were translated and published in foreign newspapers all over the world. The appearance of these underground journals, and the topics they discussed (freedom of speech, democracy, law and justice, human rights, and modernization of science and technology) were reminiscent of the May Fourth Movement sixty years earlier. The new movement spread to many provinces and cities in China. It also tried to forge an alliance with the many protest groups formed by demobilized soldiers and peasants who came to Beijing in increasing numbers. Then China launched its border war with Vietnam. Pressures now mounted on Deng Xiaoping to curb the dissident movement.

It was reported on March 16, 1979 that Deng informed the senior cadres of central government departments that a ban would be imposed on activities at the Democracy Wall.[15] When news of Deng's decision leaked out, Wei Jingsheng, an articulate editor, published an attack on Deng in a special issue of his underground journal, *Tansuo (Exploration)*. Deng did not at first place an immediate ban on dissident activities at the Democracy Wall. Instead, he outlined the "Four Basic Principles," which held that officials could accept wall poster dissent if it upheld the socialist road, the dictatorship of the proletariat, the leadership of the party, and Marxism-Leninism and Mao's Thought.[16] Wei's editorials had slandered Marxism-Leninism and Mao's Thought and had advocated the abandonment of the socialist system. Wei was arrested on March 29 along with thirty other dissidents. Simultaneously, the government-controlled mass media strongly criticized activities at the Democracy Wall. While the dissidents were under arrest, wall posters were allowed on the Democracy Wall, including ones that accused two leaders of the "Whatever" faction (Wang Dongxing and Chen Xilian) of alleged financial irregularities and misconduct. These wall posters were believed to have been sanctioned by the Deng group in its move to oust Politburo members who were key figures in the "Whatever" faction.[17]

Wei was not brought to trial until October 16; in a one-day trial he was sentenced to fifteen years' imprisonment for having supplied military intelligence to Western reporters (including names of commanders and troop numbers in China's war with Vietnam), for slandering Marxism-Leninism, and for encouraging the overthrow of the socialist system.[18] Wei subsequently appealed to the Beijing Municipal Higher Court, but his plea was rejected.[19] Meanwhile, on the recommendation of the Standing Committee of the National People's Congress, the Beijing Municipal Revolutionary Committee issued an order on December 6, 1979, which (1) prohibited wall posters on the Democracy Wall at Xidan but allowed such activities to take place at the Moon Altar Park, an area removed from downtown Beijing; (2) required registration of all those who wanted to display wall posters at the new site; (3) declared unlawful any disclosure of "state secrets" and false information; and (4) imposed punishments on those who created disturbances or riots at the new site.[20] On the night of December 7, a cleaning crew whitewashed the remaining posters still glued to the Democracy Wall at Xidan and thus ended the second phase of a movement that had attracted worldwide attention. (Wei was finally released from prison on September 13, 1993.)

The final phase of the Democracy Wall movement came in February 1980, when the Fifth Plenum of the Eleventh Central Committee decided to rehabilitate Liu Shaoqi, to remove the "Whatever" faction leaders from the Politburo, and to install Deng's close supporters Hu Yaobang and Zhao Ziyang to membership in the Politburo's Standing Committee.[21] With the removal of the "Whatever" faction from the Politburo, Deng proceeded to remove the last vestige of the Cultural Revolution: Article 45 of the 1978 state constitution, known as the "Sida" or the "four big rights"—*daming* ("speak out freely"), *dafang* ("air views fully"), *dabianlun* ("hold great debate"), and *dazibao* ("put up big-character posters"). In Deng's view the four big rights "had never played a positive role in safeguarding the people's democratic rights."[22] Instead, Deng argued that they had become weapons and tools employed by ultra-leftists like Lin Biao and the Gang of Four to advance their aims.[23] It was now the party's view that the very use of these rights had caused chaos during the Cultural Revolution decade. The wall posters, it was now charged, tended to incite "anarchism" and "factionalism."[24] Thus, Article 45 needed to be stricken from the 1978 constitution if political unity and stability were to be preserved.[25] The National People's Congress in its third session endorsed the party's stand, amending the 1978 constitution by deleting the "Sida" rights.[26] The removal of Article 45 ended China's youthful dissenters' brief flirtation with democracy and human rights. Having been encouraged initially by the forces under Deng to exercise the "Sida" rights, particularly the use of wall posters, to discredit Deng's opponents on the Politburo, the young dissenters were then "betrayed" by Deng as he gained power and control in the party and government. However, it might also be argued that to Deng and his colleagues, victims of the Cultural Revolution, any appearance of anarchy and chaos, reinforced by the pent-up energy and frustration of the young, constituted a serious threat to China's political stability. Deng and his supporters believed that the energy of the people must be directed toward modernization, not toward dissent. It could also be true, as many Western reporters and diplomats believe, that Deng had to crack down on the movement as a "trade-off" for support from other leaders in his maneuvers to consolidate his power.[27]

STUDENT DEMONSTRATIONS FOR DEMOCRACY AND POLITICAL REFORM, 1986–1987

While 1985 was marked by the successful reshuffle of the Politburo, achieved by promoting a number of Deng's younger supporters, 1986 was marred by criticism and challenge mounted by the orthodox hard-liners that culminated by year's end with a massive student protest movement and the ouster of the party chief, Hu Yaobang. The main cause of the student protests seemed to be the lack of democratic procedures in local direct elections and the slow pace of political reform. Once again Chinese university students dared to jeopardize their future careers by expressing dissent and criticism over the fundamental question in Chinese politics: the legitimacy of CCP rule.

On December 9, 1986, the anniversary of the 1935 nationwide protest against Japan's attack on China, students at the Anhui provincial capital's China University of Science and Technology, known as "Keda," in Hefei and those in the city of Wuhan in Hubei province took to the streets, simultaneously chanting slogans for democracy and political reform. In the beginning the size of these protests was small. But, by December 12, the Hefei demonstration was estimated at 17,000. That same day the first of a series of big-character wall posters appeared on the campus of Beida in Beijing, the nation's capital, but without any street demonstration by the students. However, student demonstrations appeared on university campuses in six different provinces following the December 9 protests in Hefei and Wuhan.[28] On December 18, some 2,000 students marched on the streets of Kunming in the southwest. This demonstration was followed by a much larger student gathering in Shanghai. The number of protesters there was estimated from an official low count of 10,000 to more than 35,000 by Western observers.[29] On December 23, several thousand students from Qinghua University in Beijing took to the streets in freezing weather.[30] But much of the world's attention was drawn to the Shanghai protests, which involved students from fifty campuses in and around the largest city in China. The December 21 student demonstration in Shanghai was joined by industrial workers—a significant new development feared by the authorities.[31] At this point, student protests had spread to cities in eleven provinces.[32] On December 20, Beijing municipal authorities issued a set of regulations that made demonstrations and parades illegal unless permits were obtained five days before the event. Protest activities were also prohibited in areas that housed party and government offices.[33] Despite the ban, 3,000 students from Beida and some 5,000 more students from the People's University in Beijing staged their protests on Tiananmen Square on New Year's Day, 1987. The parade signaled a direct challenge to the authorities who had banned such activity in the capital. The next day, student protesters burned copies of the *Beijing Daily* for its inaccurate and distorted reporting on student demonstrations. At least twenty-four students were arrested on the square by the public security personnel but were released shortly thereafter.[34] Through a variety of means—including appeals from families of students, official warnings, propaganda in the media, rebukes from workers and peasants on television and radio, and deliberate isolation of students from the press—the wave of student protests was finally terminated.[35] Chinese officials attempted to minimize the magnitude of university student involvement in these protests by claiming that not more than a total of 40,000 had participated in the demonstrations, about 2 percent of the two million university students in China.[36]

By analyzing slogans, wall posters, and interviews with the protesters, it appears that student demands fell into four main categories: (1) democratization of local NPC election procedure; (2) the question of the party's legitimacy to rule; (3) exercise of basic freedoms; and (4) accelerating the tempo of political reform. In addition, the slogans and wall posters also revealed concerns about making decisions on their own careers, reform in higher education, and the rising consumer prices in urban areas.

The spark that initially ignited the student protests in Hefei and Wuhan was the undemocratic procedures superimposed on the nomination of candidates for local direct election to district NPC delegateship. What started out as a local issue soon spread like wildfire and expanded to the whole range of related issues of political rights and democracy. The issue of Hefei's Keda demonstration was the students' protest against the manner by which six candidates were nominated to represent the university district at the local NPC election. The issue was soon taken up by the protesters in Wuhan and Shanghai. The students wanted the right to nominate their own candidates and to campaign for nominated candidates before an election. Keda Vice-President Fang Lizhi later complained that students did not know anything about the six candidates proposed for the basic level, thus depriving the students of freedom of choice.[37] Another student protester offered the view that "people should be able to choose some of their representatives."[38]

On the issue of the party's legitimacy, student dissenters from 1986 to 1987 were quite blunt when they questioned the party's monopolizing power. In a dramatic encounter with the students in Shanghai, the city's party secretary was booed and was asked who, in fact, elected him in the first place.[39] A Beida student protester pointed out the need for more than one party and his preference for a multiparty system as in Japan.[40] Wall posters on display on the campus of Beida contained expressions such as: "Must we always obey the party?" "By party leadership, does it mean we cannot criticize the party?" "Party dictatorship that monopolizes everything will in the end bring despotism," "Party power must be checked and balanced," and "There must be separation of party and government."[41] In short, these expressions served as direct challenges to Deng's Four Basic Principles, which placed the party leadership at the center.

Students' demand for fundamental political freedoms, as seen from the wall posters, focused on the lack of free speech and a free press. They argued that it was necessary to put up the posters because it was "the only way to express opinions," and the wall posters became "the tool of speech and expression."[42] On many campuses it was a common practice to hold "bedroom conferences" in student dormitories to discuss issues of concern freely.[43] One issue that seemed to have been shared by all protesting university students was the lack of freedom and independence to choose their own careers. Wall posters demanded "self-determination" for their own lives.[44] With personal frustration came cynicism toward their own university educations, which did not even allow them to choose their own course work. The frustration and cynicism easily extended to doubts about socialism and the party's tight grip that monopolized power. Student dissenters in one Shanghai university issued a "manifesto" demanding the propagation of democratic ideals, opposition to bureaucratism, and greater freedom.[45] In defiance of Deng's Four Basic Principles, a Beida student told a Western reporter that he wanted "Western-style democracy and multi-party system."[46] An eight-page poster on the Beida campus stated bluntly that Western democracy was a better alternative for China.[47]

Student protesters' demand for democracy was also influenced by the extensive discussion on political reform in the summer of 1986, when mass media generated numerous articles and reports about the debate by party leaders on the issue. (See Chapter 4.) Student discussion of political reform at Hefei's Keda was singled out as a model in the early fall of 1986. The *People's Daily* ran a series of five articles in October and November, evidently with the backing of the reform leaders.[48] Fang Lizhi, the vice-president from Keda, was the most frequently quoted speaker on political reform by the mass media as he lectured at many universities in eastern China. Fang's ideas about the university as a marketplace of ideas freely exchanged, his criticism of the failure of socialism for thirty years in China, his advocacy of "complete Westernization," his criticism of Deng's Four Basic Principles as dogmatic, and, finally, his charge that democracy could only come from below and from individuals but not from above— all of these statements were well publicized when the students took to the streets in early December in Hefei. Fang had told the university students that the power of the government came from the people, not from the party in control. He said that the NPC must not always be in unanimous agreement or be a perennial "rubber-stamp" to the party. Obviously referring to the short-lived spiritual pollution campaign from 1983 to 1984, Fang urged China to compete with the "assaults of Western culture, ideas, and goods" in order to yield better "ideological results."[49] He even jokingly wrote that "China not only should import new technology, but what is more important, China should also import a prime minister."[50] Vividly displayed on Tiananmen Square was the slogan: "Support Reform."[51] To the student dissenters, protests and demonstrations "would serve as catalysts for further political reform."[52]

What were the consequences of the protests? One thing seems certain: There would be more time spent on ideological studies by the students. When Deng came to power in 1978, he vowed to reduce the time spent on political and ideological education in factories and schools. He wanted everyone to work hard and engage less in "empty talk." Now that approach might have to be modified in the light of the students' protests. A typical official response to the unrest was that more ideological work for students was necessary.[53] But if more ideological study were to be reimposed on university campuses, the party could be on the horns of a dilemma. To insist that more time be spent on ideological study could increase discontent and frustration among students. As pointed out in Chapter 3, few students today want to study Marxist ideology and economics on university campuses.[54] Past records show that the experience of students who spent time and effort on ideological studies was mostly negative.[55] To revive ideological studies in the universities might only build up more resentment and cynicism, sowing the seeds of future discontent and unrest among China's youth.

Another possible consequence to students, beyond additional ideological study, was the threat of being sent to do manual labor in factories and on farms in the countryside. He Dongchang, vice-minister for education, urged the revival of this Cultural Revolution practice as ideologically sound. An editorial comment was published later which stated that

> Correcting the mistakes of the Cultural Revolution does not mean negating the correct approaches such as integrating theory with practice, intellectuals with workers and farmers, and education with productive labor.[56]

The editorial comment added that manual labor for intellectuals was different from the "leftist mistakes" of the Cultural Revolution by rationalizing that "these activities will not affect normal teaching or lowering the colleges' theoretical requirement."[57] (He seemed to have forgotten the excessive application of Marxist theories during the Cultural Revolution.) A call was issued by CYL officials for students to offer themselves for work in "construction teams or battalions" or be sent down to poor areas to acquire practical experience.[58] The most immediate consequence to be felt personally by the student protesters was the fear that the party and government would institute punishment by assigning them to "undesirable jobs" upon graduation. The fear was intensified when the vice-minister for education indicated that "the employing organizations had the right to make their own choices," even if the party and government forgave them.[59]

Finally, there were signs of retrenchment in the push for more thorough political reform, even though Deng had indicated the speedup on the eve of the Thirteenth Party Congress. Control would have to be reimposed on debates about political reform after a six-month freedom allowing lively discussion in the media and at the university campuses. The reformers' call for a revival of Mao's 1957 "let a hundred flowers bloom" concept had been muted since the January 1987 crackdown on the student protests, despite official insistence that it had not yet been abandoned. More importantly, Chinese intellectuals were once again silenced under the renewed campaign against "bourgeois liberalization." Officially, student protests were said to have been influenced by the intellectuals' call for "complete Westernization." Editorials from the *People's Daily* repeatedly called for party members to oppose "bourgeois liberalization," which now was defined as the "denial of the socialist system and the advocacy of the capitalist system."[60] The message was quite clear that the exploration of new ideas for political reform, which Fang Lizhi and others pushed for briefly in 1986, had to be stopped, and that there definitely were limits to criticizing and challenging the basic tenets of socialism. Thus, ironically, while the student protests and dissent in the winter of 1986–87 were motivated by the desire of the university students—the cream of China's future—to "quicken the pace" of political reform, these very disturbances in the end only made the CCP leadership on both ends of the opinion spectrum cautious about reform. In the final analysis, they dimmed the prospects for genuine political reform in China.

THE TIANANMEN MASS MOVEMENT: APRIL–JUNE 1989[61]

Reform in China entered a critical period from the summer of 1988 to the spring of 1989. The reformers' retail price reform, initiated by party chief Zhao Ziyang, had generated seemingly uncontrolled inflation of more than 30 percent. The government was experiencing a severe financial deficit and a host of other problems. The crime rate was rising rapidly and the nagging problem of widespread official corruption, brought on by economic reforms and the relaxation of control, became a source of major popular complaint. Leaders of the old generation expressed fear of the gradual erosion of socialist moral values such as selflessness and concern for the collective welfare.

Even more alarming to the old revolutionary veterans was the rising criticism by the intellectuals and concerned party members of the party's continued authoritarian rule and monopoly of power. Writers and scholars, many of them members of the party, demanded the release of political prisoners and observance of human rights. They not only expressed opposition to the mass campaigns of spiritual pollution and anti-bourgeois liberalization but also demanded political reform that would include proposals for a multiparty system and the speedup of the privatization of enterprises. Zhao was already under attack by the hard-liners, made up mostly of old party conservative veterans, for not implementing fully the anti-bourgeois campaign, despite Zhao's attempt to appease the hard-liners by criticizing the intellectuals. The reform-minded intellectuals, protégés of the deposed Hu Yaobang and supporters of Zhao, needed a voice in the party's inner circle. Hu rose to the occasion, for he was still a member of the Politburo. Speaking at the April 8 enlarged meeting of the Politburo, he stated the case for the intellectuals and reformers in an emotional speech that was highly critical of the party for the poor state of education and the lack of improvement in the lives of the intellectuals. Additionally, Hu cited grain production problems.[62] Evidently under great emotional strain, Hu collapsed without completing his statement.[63] He was hospitalized and then went home to recuperate from a known heart problem.

However, the seeds of the 1989 Tiananmen protest were actually planted in the student demonstrations during 1986 and 1987. While those were terminated without bloodshed, the events that culminated in the removal of Hu Yaobang set the stage for an ongoing debate over the nature of Chinese socialism and the pace of economic and political reform. For much of 1988 and the early months of 1989, Chinese students abroad and intellectuals at home, many of them party members, petitioned the party in open letters for radical solutions to China's problems. There was a rising wave of intellectual discontent and criticism of the regime. It was against this background of dissent, coupled with the rising inflation and official corruption, that the spontaneous, student-led mass movement emerged in April 1989.

Genesis of the Protest[64]

University students at Beida, in cooperation with students from the People's University and the Central Institute for National Minorities, met secretly in the spring of 1988 to plan a national signature drive that would bring to the attention of CCP leaders—particularly Deng Xiaoping, Zhao Ziyang, Li Peng, and Wan Li—the problems of inflation, neglect of workers' living conditions, and lack of improvement in education.[65] Typically, the official response to the student unrest was to impose military training on the students or traditional downward transfer of students to factories and farms for the summer months.

For the university students there were the ringing messages of Fang Lizhi, who was invited to the Beida campus as an alumnus to give a lecture in early May commemorating the ninetieth anniversary of Beida's founding. Fang, already ousted from party membership and severely criticized by Deng, made three points: (1) There must be freedom of thought and speech; (2) modernization and science must be accompanied by democratic development; and (3) since the realization of democracy requires hard struggle, its attainment would be a complex process.[66]

The simmering student yearning for democracy and freedom of the press found expression a year later. A demonstration was planned for the seventieth anniversary of the 1919 May Fourth Movement. But the death on April 15 of Hu Yaobang, the deposed party chief, made it necessary for the student leaders to move up the date of the demonstration. For the second time in recent history, the death of a leader became the occasion for massive spontaneous demonstrations at Tiananmen. (The first time was April 1976 on the death of Zhou Enlai.) On the evening of Hu's death, poetry and commemorative mourning material appeared on the Beida campus. On April 16, the next day, students from five universities in Beijing—Beida, Qinghua, Beijing Normal, Beijing Institute of Politics and Law, and the People's University—used the memorial for Hu as an occasion for criticism of the party. On April 17, Wang Dan, the student leader at Beida, made a speech in praise of the deceased Hu at a campus gathering. About one hundred students were in attendance. On the spot they decided to march on campus. Soon the modest gathering had swelled to about 5,000 students and it was decided to march for a distance of about 25 miles from the campus on the eastern side of the city to Tiananmen Square, at the heart of Beijing. Amidst shouting of slogans such as "Long Live Democracy" and "Down with Party Bureaucracy," there erupted, like a slow but steadily active volcano, the 1989 Tiananmen student demonstration that rocked China and captivated the world's attention for almost two months via live television coverage.

On April 18 there were approximately 100,000 student demonstrators at Tiananmen. They presented a list of demands:[67] the reevaluation of Hu Yaobang's career before his dismissal; the rehabilitation of three leading intellectuals—Fang Lizhi, Wang Ruowang, and Liu Binyan; public disclosure of party leaders' and their children's finances; freedom of the press; an increase in funding for education and the proper treatment of intellectuals; cancellation of the city's regulations against demonstrators; and reevaluation of the 1986 student protest movement. On April 19 these student demands on petitions were carried by 5,000 marchers to Zhongnanhai, the compound that houses the party and its leaders. The student marchers demanded a dialogue with the leaders, but they were met by police, who dispersed them.[68] At 10 o'clock that evening another demand for dialogue was made, with students shouting for Li Peng, the premier, to come out and receive them instead of sending three members of the National People's Congress. This was unavailing. On the morning of April 20, a contingent of

5,000 students marched again to Zhongnanhai to demand a dialogue with party leaders. This time, not only was there no dialogue, but they were attacked and beaten by the police. The marchers retreated to the square. The beating of the students prompted a group of 140 university professors to issue an open letter to the National People's Congress to force the leaders to have a dialogue with the students. The brutal treatment by the police also aroused concern and sympathy from many Beijing residents, who provided aid to the injured and now-hungry students.

While the official memorial service for Hu Yaobang was being held inside the Great Hall of the People on April 22, attended by all the top leaders, including Deng Xiaoping and Li Peng, some 80,000 students were conducting their own memorial ceremonies on the square despite the city's last-minute curfew for the area. As the leaders were departing through the north gate of the Great Hall without confronting the demonstrating students, three student representatives went up the steps and knelt there for about forty minutes, appealing without avail for a dialogue with Premier Li. Meanwhile, the funeral cortege left the Great Hall on the square by a different route. The funeral procession was viewed in silence by over a million Beijing residents; some mourners wept.

By April 21–22 there were about 200,000 student marchers on the square, augmented by contingents from institutions of higher learning from Shanghai and nearby Tianjin, in addition to the students from some 30 universities in the Beijing area. They were coordinated by an interim student alliance or association formed under the leadership of Wuer Kaixi, Wang Dan, and a few others. Elsewhere in China there were riots: in Xian in the northwest, and in Changsha and Wuhan in central China. The student marchers at Tiananmen called for a national strike on April 24 by sending their representatives to fifteen major cities to inform the people what had happened at Tiananmen and to solicit popular support for their cause. The students had no access to mass media; what had been reported in the press, in the students' view, were officially approved distortions.

On the evening of April 22, the Politburo decided not to be pressured by student protests to relax the campaign against bourgeois liberalization. The next day, April 23, Zhao Ziyang, the party chief left for North Korea as scheduled. On April 24 the students declared a class boycott of indefinite duration. However, in Zhao's absence, the Standing Committee of the Politburo met on April 24 and decided that the party must take action over the Tiananmen situation. But their decision had to be approved ultimately by Deng Xiaoping. So Premier Li and Yang Sungkun, then president of the PRC, went to see Deng, the paramount leader, now in semiretirement. Deng wanted to call in the military to crack down on the students, regardless of bloodshed and international repercussions.[69] But first, as a means of frightening the student marchers, a strongly worded statement was authorized to appear in the *People's Daily* on April 26. In the statement, entitled "Resolutely Oppose Rebellion," the Chinese authorities officially characterized the student protest as *dung luan* ("turmoil" or "rebellion") and as "counterrevolutionary insurrection" by a handful of people against the party and the socialist system.[70] To the students and the Chinese people the statement was an unmistakable warning of an impending military crackdown if the students did not disperse from Tiananmen. What followed on April 27 was a peaceful demonstration of 200,000, joined now by about one million Beijing residents, workers, and intellectuals who swarmed around the police. At major intersections people blocked the passage of armed vehicles headed for the square. What Deng feared most, a Poland-type opposition to communist control,[71] was now in the making.

The Escalation of the Demonstration

Undaunted by the provocative and strongly worded newspaper warning, the April 27 demonstration—peaceful, massive, but disciplined, involving 100,000 students and supported by the residents, sympathetic intellectuals, and workers—caused the authorities to hesitate, seeking some form of mediation. This time, at the invitation of the government-approved student associations, the State Council dispatched its spokesman, Yuan Mu, to meet with student representatives of the universities in the Beijing area. The government spokesman tried to tone down the official charge against the students, as contained in the April 26 statement, by implying that only a small minority would be considered instigators.

On May 2, student leaders from Beijing universities handed an appeal to the State Council and the National People's Congress for a dialogue. The appeal was refused by Yuan as the premier's representative. Meanwhile, Zhao Ziyang, after his return from North Korea, had received a vague instruction from Deng to adopt a more conciliatory approach to the student demonstrators.[72] He was said to have sought "democratic and legal means with reason and discipline" to solve the problem.[73] Zhao even went so far as to suggest an official reaffirmation of the need for political reform and the retirement of party veterans above 75 years of age.[74] But even if this softening of the government position were true and understood by the demonstrating students, the protest at Tiananmen persisted without any slackening.

The May Fourth anniversary demonstration and parade at Tiananmen by some 100,000 students went on as scheduled, but it was more subdued. Some students were planning to return to classes. The government's reaction was restrained, as the meetings of the Asian Development Bank were being convened for the first time in China. However, the movement gathered new momentum and inspiration with the historic visit of former Soviet President Mikhail Gorbachev to China, an event that Deng Xiaoping considered to be a signal of normalization of Sino–Soviet relations and the crowning success in his stewardship since he assumed power in 1978. An escalation of the demonstration was underway as a final effort to induce the government to engage in a true dialogue to resolve the impasse.

The chief vehicle the students selected for the escalation was a hunger strike. On May 13 an initial group of 200 Beida students gathered on their campus to declare their pledge to fast until death if the government refused to meet their demands. The group marched to the Beijing Normal University campus; by then the number of students pledged to a hunger strike had reached 800. In the afternoon when they reached Tiananmen over 1,000 had joined their ranks seeking to force a dialogue with the government on the eve of the historic Sino–Soviet summit. Soon the total number of hunger strikers reached 3,000. The fasting students wore red and white headbands emblazoned with their college names and the Chinese characters for "hunger strike," a familiar device used by student demonstrators in Japan and South Korea.

Residents of Beijing poured into the square to show their support for the hunger-striking students, who endured hot sun during the day and chilling wind at night. Many fainted or suffered from stomach difficulties and had to be taken to hospitals in ambulances. By the third day of fasting, many felt dizzy and numb. Others, in a spirit of sacrifice, stopped taking water in addition to food. By May 17 a total of over 1,000 hunger-striking students had been hospitalized. And their demands had been reduced to two items: rescind the April 26 statement by recognizing the student demonstration as patriotic, and schedule a dialogue. They had expected the government to cave in and they were surprised when it did not budge.

On May 16, Gorbachev arrived and was officially received by Deng inside the Great Hall, out of sight and sound of the demonstrating students at Tiananmen, who now were joined by a throng of some 200 journalists and thousands of workers. A day before Gorbachev's arrival, Zhao proposed to the Politburo Standing Committee a four-point plan to resolve the conflict: (1) repudiation of the April 26 provocative editorial that officially labeled the student protest as rebellious; (2) investigation into corruption by high-level officials and their relatives; (3) public disclosure of finances of high-level party cadres; (4) elimination of special privileges for party officials.[75] But Zhao was outvoted 4 to 1 in the Politburo Standing Committee.

Popular pressure mounted the next day, May 17, in support of the students and for democratic reform as more than a million people took to the streets of Beijing and demanded the ouster of Deng and other leaders.[76] It seemed that the government had lost control and was paralyzed by the popular protests, not only at Tiananmen, but in many of the other cities as well. As more hunger-striking students became unconscious and were rushed to hospitals by ambulance, Zhao reportedly moved again on May 17 at top-level Politburo meetings to rescind the April 26 charges against the students; again his appeal was turned down by Li Peng and presumably by Deng. On May 19, Zhao, having offered his resignation, which was rejected by Deng, made a last effort at mediation after a heated exchange with Deng. (Zhao was nevertheless voted out of office between May 19 and 20.)

Meantime, Premier Li issued a warning on Thursday, May 18, for restraint; this was ignored by another million protesters, who poured out of their homes, offices, and factories to show support for the students. However, Li, in a gesture of conciliation, did agree to hold a nationally televised meeting with the student leaders on May 18.[77] The televised meeting represented a faint effort by Li to get the students to call off the protest at the square for, as will be seen in next the section, by then a decision had been made at the top to use force on the protesters. The student leaders, such as Wuer Kaixi and Wang Dan, exhibited their impatience and frustration at the meeting by being discourteous to the premier.

At this point, the seventh day of the hunger strike, the month-old movement had reached a critical point: Should they accede to the government ultimatum for a cessation of the strike, or persist on to the inevitable bloody crackdown? On the early morning of May 19, Zhao came to Tiananmen Square and begged the students to cease their hunger strike. That evening, after heated debate, the student leaders announced cessation of the hunger strike as 3,000 fasting students were on the verge of collapse and exhaustion. At 10:00 P.M. martial law was declared for the center of Beijing and the suburbs. The martial law order was broadcast six times each hour. The government sent troops into Beijing on Saturday, May 20 to restore order. Now an astounding event occurred and was viewed on worldwide television: As military vehicles and tanks moved to the outskirts of Beijing City, students and sympathetic residents climbed on army trucks to stop their advance. Residents along the major pathways also erected barricades to block the passage of the army vehicles. Millions of Beijing citizens held the PLA at bay in defiance of martial law. While the hunger strike had been called off, a student sit-in had begun at Tiananmen as barricades went up in Beijing City.

The Massacre on June 4, 1989

By June 2–3, it was estimated that there were at least 150,000 PLA soldiers, backed by armored vehicles and tanks, taking positions in various parts of the city and waiting to move into the square occupied by the students. The decision to order the PLA into the square was made on the afternoon of June 2 by Deng and Yang Shangkun, the three members of the Politburo's Standing Committee (Li Peng, Qiao Shi, and Yao Yilin), plus Wang Zhen and Bo Yibo, representing the retired hard-line party veterans. The die was cast. A last-minute telephone appeal by Zhao was futile.

On the morning of Saturday, June 3, in front of the Xinhua Gate leading to the compound of Zhongnanhai, the central government and CCP headquarters, 300 soldiers made a surprise move on the sit-in students from the Beijing Institute of Politics and Law. The students were beaten severely with hardened clubs. Meanwhile, thousands of soldiers and armed police came out of the west gate of Zhongnanhai and showered the civilians on Fuyou Street and Xidan with tear gas, blinding many. In the afternoon, thousands of police and soldiers were dispatched from the western end of the Great Hall on the edge of the square, but they were immobilized and mobbed by hundreds of residents, who overturned army vehicles and traffic control towers.

At 6:00 P.M., radio and television broadcast the government's emergency warnings to the residents to stay home. Instead, thousands of them defiantly rushed to the square. Three hours later great numbers of troops moved from the eastern suburbs, a heavily populated district of Beijing, where they encountered blockades erected by the residents. The students on the square were conducting classes beside the temporarily erected Goddess of Democracy statue, now a prominent site on the square. However, on the west of Tiananmen, facing Changan Avenue, peasant soldiers of the 27th Division from Hepei had opened fire with automatic weapons aimed indiscriminately at buildings and people.

As a long column of armored vehicles and tanks moved into the Xidan intersection, residents and workers tried desperately to erect barriers to stop the advancing vehicles. A dead silence followed; then the soldiers jumped out of their vehicles and opened fire on residents and students. On the east of the square two army tanks sped on Changan Avenue leading to Tiananmen and collided with each other. In the accident, one tank ran over four bystanders. The crowd went wild, forced the tank to stop, and set fire to it.

Around midnight, troops moved into the center of the square from the east and west. By 1:00 A.M. on June 4, an estimated 600 soldiers had taken control of the Great Hall. An hour later the students retreated to the Monument to the People's Heroes, ready to meet their death. They sang the Communist "Internationale" as they were surrounded by the advancing soldiers. In an attempt to avoid bloodshed, Hou Dejian, the famous Taiwan rock singer, and Liu Xiaobo, the young literary critic, who had been participating in the hunger strike, went to the PLA commanders to negotiate a peaceful retreat for the students on the square.

At 4:30 A.M., with the lights still turned off on the square, Hou Dejian, having won army consent to a peaceful retreat, appealed to the students to leave. But nine or ten minutes later, the lights came on and the soldiers rushed in, firing at the public address system, the banners, and the tents. At 4:55 A.M., students began to leave the square, moving westward to exit from Xidan. Tanks rolled in at 5:00 A.M. and overran the Goddess of Democracy statue and the tents. The soldiers were chasing and shooting randomly at the retreating students, who linked arms while singing the "Internationale." The shooting and carnage went on until sunrise; the casualties mounted.

There have been various estimates of the number of students killed on the early morning of June 4. The Chinese official figure, dubious at best, put the number at 23 students and 300 soldiers killed. The Beijing Red Cross put the figure at 2,600. Hong Kong newspapers gave much higher estimates, ranging from 3,500 to over 8,000. The best unofficial estimate of the number of students killed by the government troops puts the figure at between 1,000 and 1,500. Add to this the number of residents and bystanders killed on the street and the total fatalities could have reached 3,000.[78] The brunt of the army's assault at Tiananmen was borne by the students from the provinces, because a majority of the marchers from Beijing campuses voted to withdraw from the square while those students who came from the provinces, constituting a minority of the total, remained.

Why the Tiananmen Movement?

By reviewing post-Tiananmen analyses offered by China scholars, it is possible to discern a number of themes that serve to explain why the students demonstrated and why the movement ended in mass tragedy. First, there is the political culture thesis, which points out that the student demonstration escalated from "playfulness to moralizing, to shaming the government, to acting as a more righteous government." This caused not only great pain for the aged leaders, but also anger to the extent that the "children" must be punished, in that they drove their father figure, Deng Xiaopeng, "into a fit of rage."[79]

Then there is the thesis of "leadership cleavages" along generational and ideological lines, starting with the emergence in 1988 of an influential group of older, conservative (leftist), and anti-reform party leaders; they were challenged by a corps of younger, pragmatic, but pro-reform intellectuals, many of them party members, who advocated more attention to human rights, privatization, and a multiparty political system for democratizing China.[80] Thus it was fundamentally an issue of "legitimacy" and "authoritarianism."[81] As a consequence of China's democracy movement, the 1989 Tiananmen protest sharpened the conflict between the intellectuals and the regime over "the nature of socialist democracy" and the appropriate speed with which to attain that goal.[82]

A third explanation for the Tiananmen massacre is that of "popular rebellion," which argues that the student demonstration at Tiananmen cannot be explained solely by student dissatisfaction with the regime in the reform decade. Rather, it was a "popular rebellion" that the regime was not able to control. The regime's ability to control demonstrations of this magnitude had been weakened by a divided top leadership.[83] The protest at Tiananmen became a "popular rebellion" only after the students had gained the support and sympathy of one of the contending factions, the reformers within the government and party under the leadership of Zhao Ziyang.[84]

Still another explanation is that the weakening of party control over the economic work units and the emergence, or reemergence, of a degree of "independent social identity" in associations and institutions in cities in the reformist 1980s "facilitated the development of a pro-democracy movement and open dissent." These institutions included universities, newspapers, and factories. In this view they provided both an impetus and a rationale for dissent and protest.[85] This thesis is explained in terms of two dimensions of political life that "underpin democratic theory and practice: the 'civil society' or the 'autonomy of individuals and groups' in their relation to the state, and 'public sphere' or the presence of a critical public which holds the government responsible for its actions."[86] Unlike the previous protests from 1978 to 1979 and from 1986 to 1987, the 1989 demonstration at Tiananmen "represented a dramatic enlargement of the scope of dissent" by support from the residents of the capital city. However, the reemergence of a "civil society" and a "public sphere" does not mean a movement of "society" against the "state" as in the case of the Solidarity struggle in Poland.[87] Rather, the 1989 Tiananmen protest resembled the 1956 Hungarian uprising in that it was a result of "growing restiveness among students and intellectuals exacerbated by existing divisions within the regime" that drew support and participation from the general population.[88] More importantly, the thesis of "civil society" points to the "potential for independent authority over politics"—that is, state-controlled institutions, such as the universities, newspapers, and factories, developed an independent social identity by forming "the social basis of protest against the regime itself," as had happened in Eastern Europe.[89]

David Strand's "civil society" thesis as an explanation for the eruption of the Tiananmen mass movement for democracy is expanded on by Barrett L. McCormick and his associates as "the expression of a fundamental conflict between a state with totalitarian intentions and an emerging civil society."[90] McCormick and his associates argue that an autonomous civil society has been growing in China for over a century, and that it has reemerged under Deng's reforms to come into conflict with "an increasingly uncertain and fragmented state." What happened in 1989 was the reemergence in China of "autonomous organizations" permitted by the party and the state—for example, private institutions such as the Beijing Social and Economic Science Research Institute, whose founders were arrested by the authorities after the Tiananmen massacre. Such research institutes and a host of entrepreneurial economic organizations provided inspiration and impetus for debate and discourse on government action or lack of action on societal problems. McCormick and associates present the thesis that the Tiananmen mass movement was a "civil disobedience movement" that had its roots in modern Chinese history (the 1919 May Fourth Movement), fostered and nurtured by the Hundred Flowers Bloom movement launched by Mao in the 1950s. The Tiananmen mass movement in 1989 was part of a continuing process for "democratic activism" and change.

Could the Tiananmen Massacre Have Been Averted?

The haunting questions raised by the 1989 student demonstrations are these: First, why was there no peaceful resolution to the student demands, so that bloodshed could have been avoided? Second, was there an opportunity for the reformers within the party to forge a coalition with the pro-democracy and pro-reform forces manifested in the student demonstration at Tiananmen for a united challenge to the hard-liners led by Deng?

In providing reasonable answers to these questions, one needs to consider the generational differences between the aging hard-liners led by Deng and Yang Shangkun and the young, mostly first- and second-year university students. As noted by Liu Binyan, the investigative reporter for the *People's Daily* who was expelled from party membership in 1987 for dissent, these university students valued highly their individuality and freedom, and were "contemptuous of all authority."[91] The movement produced a few leaders—Wang Dan, Wuer Kaixi (who was born a Uygur in Xinjiang but grew up in Beijing), and Chai Ling—who developed skills in organizing and coordinating massive student protest activities. Unlike the young students who took to the streets during the Cultural Revolution, the 1989 university protesters were fiercely independent and exercised great caution not to be used politically. They did not really care about ideology or loyalty to any political leader. They desired changes, political reform, the government's recognition of political rights as embodied in the 1982 constitution, and the end of the party's monopoly of power, even though initially they did not call for the removal of the party or its leaders. On the other hand, the hard-liners stood for loyalty and sacrifice for the socialist society for which they had fought hard as guerrillas in the 1930s and 1940s. The core of the hard-liner group, the so-called seven old party veterans, acting as an extralegal "inner cabinet"—Chen Yun, Deng Liqun, Hu Qiaomu, Peng Zhen, Wang Zhen, Yang Shangkun, and Bo Yibo—had been the victims of the Cultural Revolution. They were not so much opposed to reforms launched by Deng Xiaoping as they were obsessed by the need for stability and party control of the government. Because they had been victims of Red Guard abuse during the Cultural Revolution, they developed an aversion to student demonstrations for fear of chaos or "luan." Deng's main concern, as expressed in the April 26 editorial condemning the Tiananmen demonstration as "dongluan" or "turmoil," represented the typical mental outlook shared by the "gang of old men." For by 1987, when they forced Deng to dismiss his protégé Hu Yaobang from the party chief position, the hard-liners had gained in influence. Furthermore, these old party veterans were true believers in military solutions to political crises—a symptom of the guerrilla mentality that was the only experience they understood. Thus, from this perspective, the young and the old were on an irreversible collision course.

The students have been criticized for being too independent and uncompromising. The movement as a whole lacked "guidance in theory and in strategy."[92] It became a spontaneous movement with the naive expectation that the students could achieve "complete success at one stroke." For journalist Liu Binyan this attitude was reminiscent of "left tendencies" that prevented them from making concessions.[93] Wuer Kaixi, the exiled student leader, admitted later in Paris that at the time of the hunger strike he had urged the students to leave Tiananmen as a "tactical move" to provide the reformers within the party with a chance to get organized.[94] But Wuer was overruled by the students who wanted to stay and force the government to capitulate to their demands by lifting the martial law, removing the troops, guaranteeing no reprisals, and permitting a free press.

The independence exhibited by the students at Tiananmen in refusing to be used by any political bloc is illustrated by the failed negotiation with Yan Mingfu, who represented the State Council. Some of Zhao's supporters appealed to the students to end their hunger strike for the sake of long-term victory for the reform movement. Yan (a respected intellectual whose father was a close aide to the late Zhou Enlai), who speaks fluent Russian and has served as interpreter for former President Yang Shangkun, was dispatched to talk with the student leaders. The negotiation went well but in the end failed to produce an agreement because of the student leaders' insistence on television coverage of the entire negotiation proceedings. Yan appealed to the students to cool down the protest and to call off the hunger strike, so as not to provide the conservative hard-liners with the pretext to get tough and not to give them an excuse to blame or destroy the reform leaders for the disturbance. Yan was said to have argued in the inner council of the party for avoiding bloodshed by confrontation,[95] but there was no compromise or concession on the part of the students; instead they seemed to have relied on the public relations opportunities provided by worldwide television coverage to exact concessions from the government under Li Peng. (Singapore Prime Minister Lee Kuan Yew blamed television coverage for encouraging students to pursue the protest that led to the tragedy.)[96] This strategy on the part of the protesters may have played right into the hands of the conservative hard-liners. As worldwide TV coverage of the activities of the protesters intensified, the hard-liners' position toughened.

During the weeks preceding the June 4 crackdown, the student protesters' stance became increasingly intransigent. Wuer Kaixi, Wang Dan, and Shen Tong had gradually lost their leadership influence. Wuer lost his leadership position partly because he proposed withdrawal from Tiananmen to avert the impending slaughter by the army, and partly because of the power struggle among rival factions among the student protesters at Tiananmen. In retrospect, China's dissident intellectual, Fang Lizhi, remarked recently that "the movement was completely out of control" in the last weeks of the protest.[97]

To one observer, the only chance of defeating the hard-liners and their anti-reform influence was the alliance of the student democracy movement with the "pro-reform forces" in the party.[98] The failure of the 1989 democracy movement in China was laid squarely on the reform element in the Communist Party for its lack of initiative and its indecisiveness in failing to forge a strong alliance with the students at Tiananmen.[99] Liu Binyan pointed out in retrospect that three "mistakes" were made by the reformers in the party and by Zhao Ziyang during these crucial weeks prior to the June 4 crackdown. First, the reformers within the party did not seize the initiative to make Li Peng conduct a genuine dialogue with the students. Zhao was blamed for his failure in early May to organize "a prestigious and influential group of leaders" to negotiate with the students.[100] Zhao had hesitated and had gone to the students on his own too late to alter the situation. Second, Zhao and his reformers within the party failed to maneuver, by available legal means, either a general conference of the party or the convening of the Standing Committee of the National People's Congress to rally support to oust Li Peng and avoid martial law. These moves were not attempted, even though for the period May 16 to 23 at least six senior military leaders had disagreed on the deployment of the PLA for internal political purposes,[101] and some party reformers had considered convening the NPC's Standing Committee as a method of opening debate over the martial law.[102] Thus, the chance was lost to legally outmaneuver the hard-liners; the seven members of the "gang of old men" and the four members on the Politburo's Standing Committee, with Deng's consent, were able to vote for the removal of Zhao as party chief.

The third mistake made by Zhao's reformers was their failure to use the news media, then sympathetic to the democracy movement, to generate public support by publicizing the urgent need for convening the Central Committee and the NPC to avert the impending disaster and to checkmate the hard-liners' next move. (In fact, many of the news media personnel had been actively participating in the protest at Tiananmen.) Liu Binyan later observed sorrowfully that because the reformers were not organized or united and because of Zhao's hesitancy and weak personality, the 1989 democracy movement was, in the end, crushed despite the military's own divided view about using force on the students.[103] The opportunity for forging an alliance between the party reformers and the forces for democracy was there, but it was lost for lack of initiative on the part of the reformers, so lamented by Liu Binyan.

However, Liu Binyan's criticism of Zhao's supporters within the party for failing to seize the legal initiative to oust Li Peng may not be entirely accurate. For on May 19, on the eve of martial law, Zhao's supporters, party officials and intellectuals, issued a six-point statement that contained a demand for a special meeting of the NPC Standing Committee to review Li's actions and a special session of the party to restore Zhao to power.[104] Liu's criticism of the intellectuals' failure to join the protesting students may be too harsh. For during the demonstrations in May, large numbers of intellectuals— "professors, lecturers, research fellows, doctors, masters and staff members from research institutes and the Chinese Academy of Social Sciences, Beijing University,

Qinghua University and 60 other units marched behind the banner of 'Chinese Intellectual Circles,'" and particularly notable were the journalists.[105]

THE STATE OF DISSENT AND POSSIBLE FUTURE PROTESTS

Twelve years after Tiananmen the mood concerning the historic event in China has been a mixed one. In the first place, for the general populace outside the capital city of Beijing, memories of the event are fading rapidly and generate very little anger and resentment toward the army crackdown on the student protestors. While twelve years ago student demonstrators demanded political reform and were against party-government corruption and nepotism, the major concerns today for the people in general are rising inflation and corruption, in that order.

In March 1993 the government, under pressure from the United States and European governments, and as a gesture to gain international support for China's application for GATT (General Agreement on Tariffs and Trade) membership and its bid to host the Olympics in the year 2000, released three leading student dissidents from jail. Among them was Wang Dan, 23, the most wanted of the student leaders at Tiananmen. Wang then reported that he had decided to seek readmission to Beijing University, but he remained dedicated to continuing his work for a democratic China.[106] (However, Wang Dan was rearrested on flimsy, if not baseless, charges in November 1996 and sentenced again to eleven years prison.)

The Chinese government has taken some other conciliatory steps. For example, a noted intellectual and the grandfather of the dissident movement, Wang Raowang, was permitted to be a visiting scholar at Columbia University in New York after he was imprisoned for more than a year for leading a protest march in Shanghai in 1989. Other long-time dissidents, one who organized an independent trade union in China and one who was a democracy movement activist, were allowed to leave China to go abroad. (The trade union organizer, Han Dongfang, was denied reentry after authorities expelled him at the border of Hong Kong in late August 1993 by confiscating his Chinese passport; thus he became stateless.) Wei Jingsheng, the dissident imprisoned longest for his role at the Democracy Wall in 1978–79, was released, on Deng's orders, almost fifteen years after his arrest. Wei's early release may have been influenced by China's failure to win the bid for the Olympics in the year 2000. Wei was jailed again in 1995. He was finally released and exiled to the United States in November 1997 soon after Jiang Zemin returned to Beijing after a week's official visit to the United States, a gesture to placate America's concern over China's human rights violations.

On the other hand, there are still as many as 4,000 political prisoners, those who committed "crimes of counterrevolution," languishing in the Chinese *gulags* (prison labor camps). Many of them must endure a daily regimen of torture (chaining, whipping, shocking with electric batons, and overdosing with pills).[107] As late as 1992, dissidents, some of them ex-government officials who took part at Tiananmen or lent support to the protesting students, were sentenced to jail for terms as long as seven years.[108] A number of the dissidents who were put on trial by the people's courts were given five-year prison terms (a gesture of leniency) for counterrevolutionary activities related to the Tiananmen democracy movement.[109]

Shen Tong, who escaped and was exiled in the United States in the fall of 1992 became the first student leader on the most-wanted list to return to China. Shen Tong, who wrote his own personal account of the Tiananmen demonstration,[110] was a Boston University graduate when he decided to return home. He was arrested by public security officers at his family home. He was charged with violating the law by opening a branch of the Democracy for China Fund in Newton, Massachusetts.[111] However, he was subsequently released to permit his return to the United States.

On the tenth anniversary of the Tiananmen protest, a group of now-exiled former dissident student leaders who took part in the democracy movement and the demonstration on the square had a reunion at the Harvard University campus. Among those who attended were Wei Jingsheng, best known for his poster on the Democracy Wall; Wang Dan, organizer of student discussion groups on the Beijing University campus and protest organizer at the time of the Tiananmen demonstration, who was jailed for seven years before his release and exile to the United States; Wuer Kaixi, then a student at Beijing Normal University and a leader at the square who scolded Premier Li Peng for the latter's tardiness to an arranged meeting with the demonstrating students—Wuer Kaixi now lives in Taiwan; and Chai Ling, then a leader and spokesman for the students on the square and now head of her Internet company in the United States.[112] They, however, offered no plans for political reform and democracy for China. Nor have they offered any idea as to how they, as exiled dissidents, might help to reignite the flame for political reform and democracy in China.

As a final postscript on the 1989 Tiananmen demonstration: Some twenty people—mothers of those men killed by the military who opened fire at the square and the athlete who lost his legs when run over by a tank when the crackdown was ordered in the early hours on June 4, 1989—sent a petition to the then condemning National People's Congress in Beijing for a reversal of the verdict that the student demonstration and protest were "counterrevolutionary," investigation of the armed suppression of the student protest, and compensation for the victims. The petition was never answered.

Former Dissidents as Entrepreneurs

Perhaps the most interesting development in China's booming market economy reform is the phenomenon of formerly imprisoned Tiananmen dissidents engaging in entrepreneurial activities under the collective description of "going to the sea" or *xiahai*.[113] They represent the new breed of entrepreneurs known as the "turmoil elite" who have pooled their skills and resources to go into business under Deng's economic reforms. Most of the "turmoil elites," or "activists-turned-businessmen," have selected the economically booming southern Chinese provinces to conduct their business. What they have in mind is the development of a middle class, like those in Taiwan and South Korea that provided the impetus for the emergence of democratic reform in those countries.[114] This new role for the Chinese democracy movement activists resembles that of the 1960s American anti-Vietnam War activists who later became Wall Street stockbrokers and business entrepreneurs.

As the Beijing government increasingly becomes overrun by "corrupt bureaucrat-capitalist cliques," exiled dissidents like Liu Binyan, now at Princeton University, expect more Tiananmen incidents in the future with a different format in the continuing strife for "a future free society."[115]

A final comment may be in order: Despite some of the formidable obstacles in the way of democratization for China—the lack of historical experience with democracy and legal traditions, the monopoly of the CCP, the low level of education for the vast majority of the population, and poverty—there are, according to Martin King Whyte, a number of forces that favor democracy in China.[116] Of those discussed by Whyte, two major forces may eventually foster democracy in China: (1) The decade-long economic reforms have weakened central party-government control over society; and (2) the rapid changes in Asia, particularly in the former authoritarian regimes of Taiwan and South Korea, have produced economic growth and have thereby encouraged the rise of an educated middle class. In turn this middle class has demanded and obtained democratic reforms.[117]

DEMOCRACY FOR CHINA: DIVERGENT VIEWS FROM EXILED DISSIDENTS*

The meaning of democracy in China from the days of the 1978–1979 Democracy Wall movement to the Tiananmen crackdown in 1989 has been a complex and sometimes contradictory problem for anyone concerned about China and its future—and especially for its dissident intellectuals. There are questions that need to be answered by dissidents inside and outside of China. How committed are they to democracy? How have they defined democracy in a Chinese context, and how divergent are their views? What ideas can exiled dissidents offer for the possible liberalization and democratization of China? The 1995 direct popular election of the president of Taiwan raises the question: Do dissidents in exile support the thesis that economic reform will in time lead to political reform or democracy in China, as it has in Taiwan?

As pointed out previously, Wei Jingsheng was released from prison in September 1993, but in December 1995 Wei was again arrested, tried, and sentenced to fourteen more years for "sedition" and for writing for newspapers abroad provocative articles that were critical of the government. (He was exiled to the United States in 1997.) Wei is known, particularly in the West, for writing "The Fifth Modernization: Democracy," which advocates that China must have democracy first and then modernization. This famous essay discusses why democracy is better than autocracy. There are three themes: (1) Why democracy? (2) what kind of democracy? and (3) democracy should come first, before implementing the modernization of agriculture, education, science, technology, industry and defense.[118] To Wei, the "dictatorship of the proletariat" is nothing more than a "Chinese socialist autocracy" that does not guarantee any of the basic human rights; the "dictatorship of the proletariat" is seen as a "feudal socialism" that would enslave and impoverish people. Thus, democracy is seen as the only viable choice of government for the people, and "if we want modernized economics, science, military science and so forth, then there must be modernization of the people and of the social system."[119] Wei argues that true democracy means that political power belongs to the "laboring masses" and that it can come about only if the people have the power to choose and replace their representatives at any time, because these are fundamental rights: "We want to be masters of the world and not instruments used by the autocrats

*This section is produced from the review article I wrote for *China Review International,* 4, no. 1, 1997, pp. 153–58. The article is a review of the book by Tom Hart and Torbjörn Loden, ed., *Wei Jingshen and the Prospects for Democracy in China* (Stockholm, Sweden: The Center for Pacific Asia Studies, Stockholm University, 1995). Permission from publisher.

to carry out their wild ambitions."[120] Wei advocates democratic socialism as a prerequisite for all modernization.

It must be noted here that Wei's concept of democracy as the right of the people to elect their representatives, or "electoral politics," was only a minor plank in the agenda for the majority of the students who demonstrated at Tiananmen in 1989. Craig Calhoun's study of the demonstrators at the square reveals that, in one student's view, "electoral politics" was not as important as limiting the power of leaders, who must permit the voices of the intellectuals to be heard. Whereas in his essay Wei Jingsheng argues that true democracy means that the working class holds political power, the students at the 1989 Tiananmen demonstration saw themselves as "the voice of the people." Like the students, Wei in his essay does not mention law or the need for an independent judiciary as integral to what democracy means in China, although the students did point out the importance of a free press.

In a more recent article, written by Wei during the period between his release in 1993 and his rearrest in December 1995, published by a Hong Kong newspaper and translated by Reuters, he disagrees with some China scholars from the West that the forces of economic reform could foster democracy in China. Wei warns

> The potential of China's vast market is very seductive. But if investors fail to invest in helping the rational forces of democratic reform and instead leave China's fate in the hands of reactionary autocrats or other unpredictable elements, then this is not merely harmful to the interests of the Chinese people. It is also harmful to the interests of businessmen who have invested in the China market themselves.[121]

In the debate over the extension of most-favored-nation status to China, this is certainly a strong protest against the prevailing view that human rights must be severed from trade. It is interesting to note that in Wei's closing argument at his December 1995 trial, he defended his views on democracy and challenged the authorities to produce evidence against him. It seems clear that Wei has not changed his original position on democracy in China, and that he has refuted the popular Western assumption that China's impressive economic growth may have laid the foundation for the possible democratization of China in the years ahead.

In one of the first articles Wei wrote after his release in 1993, published in *Open Magazine* in Hong Kong, he cautioned against looking for a "savior" to free the Chinese people:

> Only when we are determined to rescue ourselves will others be willing or able to help us. . . . But when people dare to insist on their rights and become good at this insistence, rulers have no choice but to back off. This is a profound lesson, stained with blood, that the Chinese people cannot afford to forget.[122]

It is also interesting to note that not all exiled dissidents were overly concerned about Wei's rearrest. Some hoped that Washington would punish Beijing by restricting U.S. trade with China. But Xue Haipei, a participant in the 1989 Tiananmen hunger strike, and now the director of the Council on U.S.–China Affairs based in Washington, D.C., argues that the Chinese economy has been the "driving force" behind the recent sweeping changes in Chinese society, including great improvements in the production of food, the supply of housing, and the development of infrastructure. As pointed out by Xue, the beneficiaries of these changes are not limited to urban elites but include peasants as well.

With the information superhighway spreading to China via television and computers, Xue sees China moving into the twenty-first century despite the continuing problem of human rights,[123] evidenced by Wei Jingsheng's rearrest and the continued imprisonment of many other dissidents.

On the other hand, Liu Qing, another dissenter, insists that the struggle for human rights and democracy must continue both inside and outside China; struggle is essential to helping the Chinese people "find the door" through which they may achieve both of these objectives.[124] Liu was imprisoned for eight years for making public the transcript of Wei's trial in 1979; Liu Qing is now the head of a New York–based group that is concerned with China's human rights situation. He is somewhat more specific than Wei on how to achieve democracy and human rights in his country. He refutes the prevailing argument advanced by the Chinese government that democracy and human rights are ideals emanating from Western culture and therefore unsuitable for China. Liu believes that this argument merely serves as a justification for the government's continued autocratic and authoritarian rule.[125] Liu Qing argues that an observance of democracy and human rights would help to solve the problems of people's livelihood.[126] He also refutes the Chinese government's outdated argument that the persistent cry for China to improve its human rights policy is an interference in China's internal affairs; he points out that the Chinese government condemned apartheid in South Africa and racial discrimination in the United States before and during the civil rights movement.[127]

Liu Qing offers several suggestions for promoting human rights and democracy in China. He believes that the democracy movement should be directed toward change of the political system rather than economic power; and he emphasizes the need to "uphold the principles of openness, reliance on the law, and reason." Liu Qing also argues that achieving freedom of speech is a first stage in the struggle; then the actual struggle must be waged one step at a time, with the expectation that results will not be achieved all in one gigantic step; and finally, support must be sought from abroad.[128]

Liu Binyan, former investigative reporter for the *People's Daily*, now an exiled dissident at Princeton, foresees additional turmoil for China because the legitimacy of the Communist Party has deteriorated, and peasants and workers are on the verge of a new uprising. But he is worried that the next rebellion against party rule will result only in a repeat of the tragedy of 1989, because there is a lack of unity among Chinese intellectuals; he also believes that people as a whole do not know what they want.[129] In a collection of essays Liu Binyan equates the commonly used term *liberation* with freedom and happiness: "Liberation is letting everyone have freedom." He continues that it is abnormal to be afraid of any discussion about freedom in general, freedom of speech, and even happiness. Liu Binyan once remarked that the eras of both Mao and Deng were the only periods in the twentieth century when Chinese people were denied any freedom of expression, when there was no trace of civil society, and when not even the slightest amount of freedom of assembly or association was permitted.[130] Liu Binyan questions whether "the most important rights of the Chinese are the right to exist and the right to economic development," an argument currently endorsed by Chinese authorities.

Still another prominent exiled dissident, Yan Jiaqi, an advisor to former Premier Zhao Ziyang at the time of the 1989 Tiananmen demonstration, advocates constitutional reform and the development of "democratic constitutionalism" with a parliament elected by the people. He proposes a three-stage evolution of his democratic constitutionalism:

a fair election system, constitutional revision, and a "unified constituent assembly" based on a federal system of provinces and regions. This government would constitute the "Third Chinese Republic," which would include a confederation with Taiwan and Hong Kong.[131] In his recent suggestion for "A Plan for a Federated China" (Lianbang Zhongguo Gouxiang), there would be guarantees of human rights and individual liberties, in contrast to his earlier writings in the 1970s and 1980s, which showed little understanding of democracy as a political process.

Until the 1989 Tiananmen tragedy, Yan Jiaqi was the voice within the party advocating political reform and structural change. Only recently has he begun to develop his ideas to include democracy and human rights. Only very recently has Yan argued for the elimination of the autocratic and personal politics so characteristic of the Mao and Deng regimes. He has published two articles in a Hong Kong magazine in which he stressed that an independent legal system is fundamental to the guarantee of individual human rights.[132]

Fang Lizhi, a prominent intellectual now in exile, was one of the first Chinese intellectuals to petition Deng Xiaoping in the mid-1980s to release Wei from prison. One well-known lecture of Fang's, given in November 1986 to students at Tongji University in Shanghai, stressed that a key to understanding democracy was recognition of the rights of individuals. Fang pointed out that democracy includes these basic rights: to live, to think, and to get an education. He emphasized that democracy must be built from the bottom up.[133]

The foregoing summary of the divergent views of China's exiled and imprisoned dissidents points to two possible paths for democracy for China. One is Wei Jingsheng's long-held position that democracy, or the right for the people to rule, must come first before modernization. Wei's original position is strengthened by the argument that China's democracy movement must be aimed at changing the political system and ensuring human rights as espoused by Liu Qing and Yan Jiaqi. Their views are further reinforced by the suggestions of Liu Binyan and Liu Qing for "liberating" the people with freedom of speech and happiness, and the essential requirement for an independent legal system in order to guarantee individual human rights.[134]

The other path for achieving democracy in China is through economic growth and development, as argued by Xue Haipei and also by Liu Binyan. One might add that this has been the position taken by the "turmoil elites"—former dissidents who have gone into business, and who have benefited from the economic boom as business entrepreneurs in southern coastal cities. It is now popular in the West to assume that China may go the route of today's South Korea or Taiwan, in that economic growth and prosperity could create the necessary demand for democratization of the authoritarian system. But, in the final analysis, will China be able to control and manage the undesirable features of corruption, crime, and inequality that can accompany a transition to democracy and that would endanger democracy at its very inception? This is a question that was raised by Marina Svensson of Sweden in her illuminating lecture on the occasion of awarding the Olof Palme prize in 1994 to Wei Jingsheng.[135]

While the exiled dissidents are offering varied paths for democracy in China, three brave intellectuals inside China openly attempted formation of an alternative political party to challenge the communist monopoly. They were arrested and tried as "criminals" for engaging in illegal activities, and for threatening national security. They were given prison terms of eleven to thirteen years. Thus, the China Democratic Party died by government suppression.

FALUN GONG BAN ("THE WHEEL OF LAW"):
WHY CRACKDOWN MYSTICISM?

Before we proceed with a discussion of the official suppression of a quasi-religious meditation sect, known as the Falun Gong ("The Wheel of Law"), it is perhaps necessary to paint briefly a historic backdrop in order to place the matter in perspective.

Chinese history has recorded numerous instances of religious sects transformed into political movements once they became politicized. In the twelfth century there were the White Lily and White Clouds Societies, founded by Buddhist monks, which were responsible for some serious uprisings. The Triad Society of Heaven and Earth was implicated in rebellion against Mongol rule. Then in the 1850s, the Taiping, or "Great Peace," a religious movement based on rather superficial knowledge of Christianity through the missionaries by its founder, became such a powerful political movement waging battles against Manchu rule that in 1853–54 the Taiping armies conquered almost one-half of China by establishing a new, but short-lived, dynasty in Nanjing. In 1900, in a desperate attempt to fend off foreign incursion into China by Europeans and Japanese, the Manchu rulers relied on the "magic power" of the Boxers, or "the Righteous Harmony Fists," to "protect the country and expel foreigners," resulting in the killing of Western Christian missionaries in China. The Boxer Rebellion was put down by an expeditionary force of European powers, including American marines, which marked the expansion of dismembering of the Chinese empire.

The Appearance of the Falun Gong.   Since the 1989 student demonstration at Tiananmen, Chinese authorities have been fearful of and vigilant against formation of large numbers of people in public places. On April 25, 1999, a sizable crowd of more than 10,000 strong marched silently and peacefully in front of the government and party headquarters in Beijing to protest publication by a government-controlled magazine of an article critical of Falun Gong, a spiritual meditation group. This sudden appearance of a large-sized, but well-organized crowd gathering to make an appeal to the government constituted a reminder to the officials that the sect could pose a militant threat for the future or it might be another Tiananmen protest demonstration in the making, even though the group members were not militant students, but nonsmoking and nondrinking housewives and retirees who merely wanted to practice their breathing exercises or meditation in public parks. Upon subsequent investigation, perhaps even more shocking to the party and government was the size of the group's total membership, estimated at between 60 to 100 million, equal to or even larger than the total Chinese Communist Party membership of 59–60 million. Upon further investigation, the authorities discovered that the group's membership included not only party members, some of them holding high positions in the party-government hierarchy, but military members as well. The central party document also revealed later that 200,000 party members had joined the said religious group, or about one-tenth of the sect's total number of adherents.[136]

What are the practices and preachings of the sect that made the authorities fearful in the first place?

Falun Gong, the Law of Wheel Breathing Exercise, is a Tai-Chi type of exercise which stresses meditation along with slow, gentle motion and breathing, a way of getting out the vital energy known as *qi* from one's body. In traditional Chinese folk medicine, *qi* can enable the practitioner to balance physical and mental health. Teachings by the founder, who now lives in the United States, include not only the slow-motion meditative breathing exercise, but no smoking or drinking, or even sex; it also urges members to be good citizens and good neighbors to each other. The cultivation of *qi*, the energy, comes from Buddhism's and Daoism's tradition and practice for quiet meditation.

In order to understand the increasing popularity among urban residents of the traditional meditative breathing exercises, one needs to consider the effects of China's recent economic reform measures which include the phasing out or merger of nonprofitable state-owned enterprises on which Chinese workers depend, for not only steady employment, but also benefits such as medical clinics at the factories and pension benefits after retirement. Economic reforms have created not only an unemployment problem, but also the loss of social welfare service deliveries once provided to workers by the state-owned enterprises. For many urban workers today there is no longer a guaranteed job, nor are the medical-social welfare services available. The desire for inner peace and tranquility, as well as health care, must come from somewhere. Thus, Falun Gong, the Law of Wheel Breathing Exercise, seems to be an answer or substitute to their plight or spiritual need. It has nothing to do with revolt or opposition to the party rule, as pointed out by their overseas leaders.

Since April 1999 thousands of Falun Gong members have been arrested; the crackdown continues unabated and has been intensified as the state Supreme Court and the National People's Congress, through its Standing Committee, have made the official decision to ban the Falun Gong as a "cult organization." First, on October 8–9, China's Supreme People's Court invoked Article 300 of the Criminal Law, charging Falun Gong as a "heretical cult organization," illegally formed under the guise of religion for the purpose of "spreading superstitious fallacies, recruiting and controlling their members and endangering the society."[137] The court decision followed the decision made by the Standing Committee of the National People's Congress to ban Falun Gong activities. Specific charges in the Court's decision included "illegal" organs; holding assemblies, parades, and demonstrations; and publishing, printing and distributing publications of cult fallacies.[138]

Now let us return for a moment to the Chinese history with which we opened the discussion on this topic. Chinese history has provided the evidence, as discussed earlier, to point out that religious movements, such as the Taiping Rebellion in the 1850s or the 1900 Boxer Rebellion, became implicated with a political movement to produce serious uprisings against the established order. It is in this historic perspective that we may say that the Chinese official reaction to Falun Gong is somewhat paranoid or an "overreaction" to such an extent that it has already "politicized" an otherwise folksy meditative movement or exercise group into something that its founder and adherents never intended it to be, that is, political.

It is interesting to note that despite the official crackdown on the Falun Gong religious movement, its adherents continue to appear in public parks such as Beijing's Tiananmen Square and subject themselves to arrest and jail. Evidently the authorities have not been able to prevent the sect members from communicating with each other. As far as can be determined the sect members employ personal contacts by using public phones in a random fashion in order to avoid detection by police. When taveling they use, typically in the city of Beijing, the many unregistered cabs to get around.[139]

POSSIBLE PROTESTS FOR THE FUTURE

In the years to come there could be surfacing on the chinese political landscape several possible or potential protest movements, in addition to the Falun Gong supporters just discussed. First, there is always the potential for student protests in the future about democracy and political reform in China. Then, in 1999 there were rising violent peasant protests against numerous arbitrary taxes levied by local officials and the peasants' resentment over extravagant lifestyles, or corruption, of local party and government officials, even though the central government has decreed that taxes on farmers must not exceed 5 percent of the previous year's income.[140] Also, government officials have expressed fear of frequent protests by unemployed workers in cities. The unemployment rate has been estimated to be more than twenty million, or 15 percent of the nation's total work force.[141]

Religious persecution of Christian church leaders and Buddhist monks and nuns has been reported in the Western press in recent years. The Chinese permit worship in those Protestant and Roman Catholic churches which accept the Chinese government leadership in regulating church affairs. There may be tens of millions of Chinese worshipers in these churches all over China today.[142] Thus, unauthorized worship activities in these so-called "house churches" or underground churches would be considered "illegal" and their leaders placed under detention or in jail.[143] This, along with the students, and farmers, and the urban unemployed may be the source of future discontent and protests.

NOTES

1. Gabriel A. Almond and G. Bingham Powell, Jr., *Comparative Politics Today: A World View*, 2d ed. (Boston and Toronto: Little, Brown, 1980), p. 72.
2. Kenneth Prewitt and Sidney Verba, *Principles of American Government*, 3d ed. (New York: Harper & Row, 1977), pp. 71–72.
3. James M. Burns, J.W. Peltason, and Thomas E. Cronin, eds., *Government by the People*, 14th ed. (Upper Saddle River, N.J.: Prentice Hall, 1990), pp. 227–28.
4. Raymond Wolfinger, Martin Shapiro, and Fred Greenstein, eds., *Dynamics of American Politics* (Upper Saddle River, N.J.: Prentice Hall, 1976), p. 259.
5. Almond and Powell, *Comparative Politics Today*, p. 73.
6. For an excellent book on the subject see Andrew Nathan, *Chinese Democracy* (New York: Alfred A. Knopf, 1985). For the coverage of the Democracy Wall movement by Western reporters stationed in China, see Roger Garside, *Coming Alive: China After Mao* (New York: McGraw-Hill, 1981), pp. 212–39; Fox Butterfield, *China Alive in the Bitter Sea* (New York: Times Books, 1982) pp. 406–34; Richard Bernstein, *From the Center of the Earth* (Boston: Little, Brown, 1982), pp. 215–42, 246–56; and John Fraser, *The Chinese: Portrait of a People* (New York: Summit Books, 1980), pp. 203–71. Also see Jay Matthews, "Dissident's Sentence Stirs Sharp Criticism," Washington Post Service, as reprinted in *Honolulu Advertiser,* October 26, 1979, and *Newsweek,* December 11, 1978, pp. 41–43. For an analysis of the movement as a whole, see Kjeld Erik Brodsguard, "The Democracy Movement in China, 1978–1979: Opposition Movements, Wall Posters Campaign, and Underground Journals," *Asian Survey,* 20. no. 7 (July 1981), 747–74. For Chinese coverage in the *Beijing Review,* see the following issues: 8 (February 23, 1979), 6; 49 (December 7, 1979), 3–4; 50 (December 14, 1979), 6–7; 10 (March 10, 1980), 10; 17 (April 28, 1980), 3–5; 40 (October 6, 1980), 22–28; 45 (November 9, 1979), 17–20. For a collection of translations of writings by the Chinese on human rights, see James D. Seymour, ed. *The Fifth Modernization: China's Human Rights Movement, 1978–1979* (Stanfordville, N.Y.: Earl McColemen Enterprises, Inc. 1980). Also see Philip Short, *The Dragon and the Bear: China and Russia in the Eighties* (New York: William Morrow, 1982), pp. 252–64.
7. See Brodsguard, "The Democracy Movement in China, 1978–1979," 759–61; and Garside, *Coming Alive: China After Mao,* pp. 213–22.
8. "Communiqué of the Third Plenary Session of the Eleventh Central Committee of the CCP," *Beijing Review,* 52 (December 29, 1978), 6.
9. Ibid., 13.
10. Ibid., 15.
11. Ibid.

12. Garside, *Coming Alive: China After Mao*, pp. 223–26. Also see John Fraser: *Portrait of a People The Chinese*, p. 245.
13. Garside, *Coming Alive: China After Mao*, pp. 264–98.
14. See Brodsguard, "Democracy Movement in China: 1978–1979," 747–74. Also see "China's Dissidents," Washington Post Service, as reprinted in *Honolulu Advertiser* (September 15, 1979), p. A-17; and Melinda Liu, "Wei and the Fifth Modernization," *Far Eastern Economic Review* (November 27, 1979), 22–23.
15. Garside, *Coming Alive: China After Mao*, p. 256.
16. See *Hongqi*, 5 (May 4, 1979), 11–15. Also see David Bonavia, "The Flight from Freedom," *Far Eastern Economic Review* (October 26, 1979), 9–10.
17. *New York Times,* July 1, 1979, p. 6.
18. "Wei Jingsheng Sentenced," *Beijing Review*, 43 (October 26, 1979), 6–7.
19. "The People's Verdict," *Beijing Review*, 46 (November 6, 1979), 15–16.
20. See *Beijing Review*, 50 (December 14, 1979), 6; *New York Times,* December 9, 1979, p. 3; *Christian Science Monitor,* December 11, 1979, p. 7; and *Ming Pao* (Hong Kong), December 9, 1979, p. 1.
21. "Communiqué of the Fifth Plenary Session of the Eleventh Central Committee of the CCP," *Beijing Review*, 10 (March 10, 1980), 8–9.
22. Ibid., 10.
23. "The 'Dazibao': Its Rise and Fall," *Beijing Review*, 40 (October 6, 1980), 23–24.
24. "Big Character Posters Not Equivalent to Democracy," *Beijing Review*, 17 (April 28, 1980), 4.
25. "Communiqué of the Fifth Plenary Session," 10.
26. "National People's Congress Ends Session," *Beijing Review*, 37 (September 15, 1980), 3.
27. See *Far Eastern Economic Review* (October 26, 1979), 9, and (October 19, 1979), 38–40.
28. *Christian Science Monitor,* December 18, 1979, p. 1.
29. Washington Post Service as reprinted in *Honolulu Advertiser and Star-Bulletin*, Sunday Edition, December 21, 1986, p. A-34.
30. *New York Times,* December 24, 1986, p. 3.
31. *Honolulu Advertiser,* December 22, 1986, p. D-4.
32. *Far Eastern Economic Review* (January 8, 1987), 9.
33. *New York Times,* December 27, 1986, p. 1. Also see *Beijing Review*, 8 (February 8, 1987), 20.
34. *Asian Wall Street Journal,* January 1–2, 1987, p. 1.
35. Los Angeles Times Service as reprinted in *Honolulu Star-Bulletin,* (January 1, 1987), p. A-21.
36. *Beijing Review*, 1 (January 5, 1987), 5. Also see *Time,* January 2, 1987, p. 38.
37. *Asian Wall Street Journal,* January 8, 1987, p. 7.
38. *Business Week,* January 19, 1987, p. 49.
39. *China News Analysis*, 1328 (February 1, 1987), 7.
40. *Asian Wall Street Journal,* January 8, 1987, p. 1.
41. *Far Eastern Economic Review* (January 15, 1987), 8–9.
42. Ibid., 9.
43. *China News Analysis*, 1328 (February 1, 1987), 3.
44. See *Christian Science Monitor,* January 22, 1987, p. 14.
45. Ibid.
46. *Asian Wall Street Journal,* January 1–2, 1987, p. 1.
47. Ibid.
48. *Ming Pao Daily* (Hong Kong), December 19, 1986, p. 2; and *China News Analysis*, 1328, 5.
49. See *Beijing Review*, 8 (February 23, 1987), 17–18. Also see *China News Analysis*, 1328, 4–5; and *Renmin Ribao*, September 21, 1986, pp. 3, 5–6.
50. See Jim Mann, "Dissident Shapes Up as China's Sakharov," Los Angeles Times Service as reprinted in *Honolulu Advertiser,* June 28, 1987, p. A-21. Also see Ge Sheng, "Fang Lizhi—A Model of Chinese Intellectuals," *China Spring Digest*, 2, no. 1 (March–April 1987), 2–11.
51. Ibid.
52. *Far Eastern Economic Review* (January 15, 1987), 8; and *Business Week,* January 19, 1987, p. 49.
53. *Beijing Review*, 1 (January 5, 1987), 5.
54. Stanley Rosen, "Prosperity, Privatization, and China's Youth," *Problems of Communism*, 34, 2 (April–May 1985), 26.
55. *Beijing Review*, 15 (April 13, 1987), 1.
56. Ibid., 5.
57. *Los Angeles Times,* January 18, 1987, p. A-21.
58. *Beijing Review*, 8 (February 23, 1987), 15; and *Asian Wall Street Journal,* January 8, 1987, p. 1.
59. *People's Daily,* January 5 and 6, 1987, p. 1. Also see *Far Eastern Economic Review* (January 15, 1987), 9.
60. Ibid.

61. There is voluminous published material about the student protest and demonstration at Tiananmen. Reports and statements on the Tiananmen tragedy referenced in this chapter are culled from the following: Harrison Salisbury, *Tiananmen Diary: Thirteen Days in June* (Boston: Little, Brown, 1989); *Massacre in Beijing: China's Struggle for Democracy* (New York: Warner, 1989); Melinda Liu, Orville Schell, and Howard Chapnick, *Beijing Spring* (New York: Stewart, Tabori & Chang, 1989); Yi Mu, *Crisis at Tiananmen* (San Francisco: China Books Publishers, 1989); Scott Simmie and Bob Nixon, *Tiananmen Square* (Seattle: University of Washington Press, 1989); Michael Fathers and Andrew Higgins, *Tiananmen: The Rape of Peking* (Toronto and London: Doubleday, 1989); Liu Binyan, *"Tell the World": What Happened in China and Why* (New York: Pantheon, 1990); Andrew Nathan, *China's Crisis: Dilemmas of Reform and Prospects for Democracy* (New York: Columbia University Press, 1990); Han Minzhou (comp.), *A Book of Writings and Speeches from the Democracy Movement* (Princeton, N.J.: Princeton Press, 1990); John Roderice, ed., *China: From the Long March to Tiananmen Square* (New York: Henry Holt, 1990); Michael Oksenberg, ed., *Orthodoxy and Dissent in China, Spring 1989* (Armonk, N.Y.: M.E. Sharpe, 1990); Suzanne Ogden, ed., *China's Search for Democracy: The Student and Mass Movement of 1989* (Armonk, N.Y.: M.E. Sharpe, 1990); *Gate of Heavenly Peace: The Struggle for Democracy in China* (Toronto: Macmillan, 1990); *A Day in the Life of China* (San Francisco: Collins, and Hong Kong: Weldon Owen Publishing, 1990); Geremie Barmei and John Minford, *Seeds of Fire: Chinese Voices of Conscience* (New York: Hill & Wang, 1990); *Flames of Freedom: Chinese Voices of Protest* (New York: Hill & Wang, 1990); Yan Jiaqi, *History of the Chinese Cultural Revolution*, rev. ed. (Honolulu: University of Hawaii Press, 1990); Steven M. Mosher, *China Misperceived* (New York: Basic Books, 1990); and Jonathan Spence, *Modern China* (New York: Norton, 1990).

Also, the following articles: James C. Hsuing, "From the Vantage of Beijing Hotel: Peering into the 1989 Student Unrest in China"; John C.H. Fei, "A Cultural Approach to the Beijing Crisis, 1989"; and William T. Liu, "A Social Study of the 1989 Beijing Crisis." All the above appeared in *Asian Affairs: An American Review*, 16, no. 2 (Summer 1989).

For more recent books on the Tiananmen mass movement and examination of the aftermath, see Geremie Barme and Linda Jaivin, *New Ghosts, Old Dreams: Chinese Rebel Voices* (New York: Times Books, 1992); Ann F. Thurston, *A Chinese Odyssey: The Life and Times of a Chinese Dissident* (New York: Scribner's, 1992); Shen Tong, *Almost a Revolution* (New York: Houghton-Mifflin, 1990); Chu Yuan Cheng, *Behind the Tiananmen Massacre: Social and Economic Ferment in China* (Boulder, Colo.: Westview Press, 1990); Lee Feigon, *China Rising: The Meaning of Tiananmen* (Chicago: Ivan R. Dee, 1990); and Mu Yi and Mark V. Thompson, *Crisis at Tiananmen: Reform and Reality in Modern China* (San Francisco: China Books and Periodicals, 1989).

62. See *Zhengming* (Hong Kong), 139, (May 1989), 8–9.

63. Ibid., 9.

64. In addition to the extensive daily news coverage of events at Tiananmen from April to June 1989 by major national newspapers such as the *New York Times, Washington Post, Los Angeles Times*, and *Christian Science Monitor*, the following entries represent a collection of reporting and analyses of the Tiananmen protests: Lucian W. Pye, "Tiananmen and Chinese Political Culture," *Asian Survey*, 30, no. 4 (April 1990), 331–47; Alan P.L. Liu, "Aspects of Beijing's Crisis Management: The Tiananmen Square Demonstration," *Asian Survey*, 30, no. 5 (May 1990), 505–21; Corinna-Barbara Francis, "The Progress of Protest in China: The Spring of 1989," *Asian Survey*, 30, no. 9 (September 1989), 898–918; Lowell Dittmer, "The Tiananmen Massacre," *Problems of Communism*, 38, no. 5, (September–October 1989), 2–15; Andrew J. Nathan, "Chinese Democracy in 1989: Continuity and Change," *Problems of Communism*, 39, no. 5 (September–October 1989), 16–29; Andrew G. Walder, "The Political Sociology of the Beijing Upheaval of 1989," *Problems of Communism*, 38, no. 5 (September–October 1989), 30–40; and David Strand, "Protest in Beijing: Civil Society and Public Sphere in China," *Problems of Communism*, 39 no. 3, (May–June 1990), 1–19.

Also see Li Lu, *Moving the Mountain: My Life in China* (London: Macmillan, 1990); and George Hicks, ed., *The Broken Mirror: China after Tiananmen* (London: Longman, 1990). For a good general introduction, accompanied by a collection of documents, see Michael Oksenberg and Marc Lambert, eds., *Beijing Spring, 1989—Confrontation and Conflict: The Basic Documents* (Armonk, N.Y.: M.E. Sharpe, 1990); and Francis, "Progress of Protest in China: Spring of 1989." Also see Julia Kwong, "The 1986 Student Demonstrations in China: A Democratic Movement?" *Asian Survey*, 38, no. 9 (September 1988), 970–1017.

65. See *Zhengming* (Hong Kong), 128, (June 1988), 8–9.

66. Ibid., 7.

67. See Binyan, *"Tell the World"* p. 9; Julia Ching, *Probing China's Soul* (San Francisco: Harper & Row, 1990), pp. 17–18; and Dittmer, "Tiananmen Massacre," 6.

68. *New York Times,* April 19, 1989, p. A-1.

69. See Nicholas D. Kristof, "How the Hardliners Won," pp. 40–41; and Binyan, *"Tell the World,"* p. 15.
70. *People's Daily,* overseas edition, April 26, 1989, p. 1.
71. Dittmer, "Tiananmen Massacre," 7.
72. *Ming Pao Daily* (Hong Kong), May 16, 1989, p. 1; and Dittmer, "Tiananmen Massacre," 7.
73. See *Zhengming* (Hong Kong), 140 (June 1989), 1.
74. *Ming Pao Daily* (Hong Kong), June 1, 1989, p. 1.
75. Ibid., May 21, 1989, p. 1.
76. *New York Times,* May 18, 1989, p. A-1; and *Asian Wall Street Journal,* May 18, 1989, p. 1.
77. *New York Times,* May 19, 1989, pp. A-1 and A-4. Also see *China Daily,* May 19, 1989, p. 1.
78. For some breakdown on the Tiananmen casualties see *The Massacre of June 1989 and Its Aftermath* (New York: Amnesty International, USA, April 1990), p. 31; and *Preliminary Findings on Killings of Unarmed Civilians, Arbitrary Arrests and Summary Executions since June 3, 1989* (New York: Amnesty International, USA, August 1989), p. 23. Also see Ching, *Probing China's Soul,* p. 32.
79. Pye, "Tiananmen and Chinese Political Culture," 331–43. Also see Peter R. Moody, Jr., "The Political Culture of Chinese Students and Intellectuals: A Historical Examination," *Asian Survey,* 28, no. 11 (November 1988), 1140–60.
80. Dittmer, "Tiananmen Massacre," 2–15.
81. Ibid., p. 2; and Pye, "Tiananmen and Chinese Political Culture," pp. 331–33.
82. See Nathan, "Chinese Democracy in 1989: Continuity and Change," 16–27; and his *China's Crisis* (New York: Columbia University Press, 1990).
83. Walder, "Political Sociology of the Beijing Upheaval of 1989," 30–40.
84. Ibid. 38.
85. Strand, "Protest in Beijing: Civil Society and Public Sphere," 1–19.
86. Ibid., 2. Also see Barrett L. McCormick, Su Shaozhi, and Xiao Xiaoming, "The 1989 Democracy Movement: A Review of the Prospects for Civil Society in China," *Pacific Affairs,* 65, no. 2 (Summer 1992), 182.
87. Strand, "Protest in Beijing," 11.
88. Ibid., 12.
89. Ibid., 18. Also see Michael D. Swaine, "China Faces the 1990s: A System in Crisis," *Problems of Communism.* 39, no. 3 (May–June 1990), 20–35.
90. See McCormick, Shaozhin, and Xiaming, "1989 Democracy Movement: Review of the Prospects for Civil Society in China."
91. Binyan, *"Tell the World,"* p. 34.
92. Ibid., p. 27.
93. Ibid., p. 54.
94. For text of interview with Wuer Kaixi, see *Zhengming* (Hong Kong), 143 (September 1989), 28.
95. Nicholas D. Kristof, "How the Hardliners Won," *New York Times Magazine,* November 12, 1989, pp. 66–67. Also see Dittmer, "The Tiananmen Massacre," 11. Transcript of Li Peng's speech about the failure of dialogues with the students can be found in the *New York Times,* May 20, 1989, p. A-4.
96. See Lee Kuan Yew's remarks in Hong Kong as reported in the *New York Times,* October 17, 1990, p. A-4.
97. See Lu, *Moving the Mountain: My Life in China*; and David Aikman, "Interview: The Science of Human Rights," *Time,* August 20, 1990, p. 12.
98. Binyan, *"Tell the World,"* p. 104.
99. Ibid.
100. Ibid., p. 105.
101. Ibid.; also see *New York Times,* May 20, 1989, p. A-4.
102. Binyan, *"Tell the World,"* p. 107; and Kristof, "How the Hardliners Won," 67.
103. *New York Times,* May 23, 1989, p. A-1.
104. Nathan, "Chinese Democracy in 1989: Continuity and Change," 16 and 19.
105. Strand, "Protest in Beijing: Civil Society and Public Sphere," 16, as quoted from *People's Daily,* May 16, 1989. Also see Frank Tan, "The *People's Daily*: Politics and Popular Will—Journalist Defiance in China during the Spring of 1989," *Pacific Affairs,* 63, no. 2 (Summer 1990), 151–169.
106. See *Far Eastern Economic Review* (3 March 1993), 13.
107. *New York Times,* September 1, 1992, pp. A-4 and 5.
108. *New York Times,* July 22, 1992, p. A-3.
109. *New York Times,* February 19, 1992, p. 3; and February 26, 1992, p. A-5.
110. Shen Tong, *Almost a Revolution* (New York: Houghton-Mifflin, 1990).
111. See Bob Hohler, "Arrest of Dissident on Return Is Cause Celebre," *Boston Globe* as reprinted in *Honolulu Sunday Star-Bulletin and Advertiser,* September 6, 1992, p. A-36. Also see *Far Eastern Economic Review* (September 10, 1992), 13.

112. For an interesting, but critical, article about her life in the United States, see Ian Buruma, "Tiananmen, Inc.," *The New Yorker Magazine*, May 31, 1999, pp. 45–52.
113. See *Christian Science Monitor,* March 9, 1993, p. 6.
114. Ibid.
115. *China Focus* (a publication of the Princeton China Initiative), 1, no. 4 (May 30, 1993), 3.
116. See Martin King Whyte, "Prospects for Democratization in China," *Problems of Communism*, 41, no. 3 (May–June 1992), 59–62.
117. See James C.F. Wang, *Comparative Asian Politics: Power, Policy, and Change, 5th ed.,* (Upper Saddle River, N.J.: Prentice Hall, 1995), ch. 2, pp. 129–33 and 137–43.
118. See Tom Hart and Torbjörn Loden, eds., *Wei Jingsheng and the Prospects for Democracy in China* (Stockholm, Sweden: The Center for Pacific Asia Studies, Stockholm University, 1995), pp. 38–48.
119. The text of Wei's essay, "The Fifth Modernization" in *Wei Jingsheng and the Prospects for Democracy in China*, p. 42.
120. Ibid., p. 45.
121. See David Schlesinger, "Wei Case Shows China Will Abide No Dissent," Reuters as reprinted in *Honolulu Star-Bulletin*, April 5, 1994, p. A-9.
122. Wei Jingsheng, "Who Should Take the Responsibility?" Translation into English is provided by *China Focus* (a publication of the Princeton China Initiative), 1, no. 10, (November 30, 1993), p. 1.
123. See Xue Haipei, "Wei Jingsheng and China's Future," *Wall Street Journal*, January 6, 1996, p. A-14.
124. Liu Qing, "Human Rights, Democracy and China," in *Wei Jingsheng and the Prospects for Democracy in China*, p. 14.
125. Ibid., p. 16.
126. Ibid., p. 17.
127. Ibid., p. 18.
128. Ibid., p. 26.
129. Liu Binyan, "China: A Country Politically Rich but Also Poor," in *Wei Jingsheng and the Prospects for Democracy in China,* p. 31.
130. Liu Binyan, *China Focus*, September 30, 1993, p. 4.
131. See Yan Jiaqi, "China's Path to Democratic Constitutionalism," in *Wei Jingsheng and the Prospects for Democracy in China*," p. 37.
132. See his essay, "Xin Xianzheng Yundong (New Constitutional Movement)" in *Zhengming* (Hong Kong), (December 1994), 85–89, and (January 1995), 84–93.
133. Fang Lizhi, *Bringing Down the Great Wall* (New York: W. W. Norton, 1992), p. 166.
134. See Marina Svensson, "Historic Perspectives on Chinese Debate on Democracy," in *Wei Jingsheng and the Prospects for Democracy in China*, p. 11.
135. Ibid., pp. 3–13.
136. See Lo Bing, "The Inside Story for Oppressing the Falun Gong," *Zhengming Magazine* (Hong Kong), no. 262 (August 1999), 8.
137. See "Explanations of the Supreme People's Court and Supreme People's Procuratorate Concerning Laws Applicable to Handling Cases of Organizing and Employing Heretical Cult Organizations to Commit Crimes," *Beijing Review* (November 8, 1999), 8–9.
138. Ibid., 8.
139. For a report, see Jan Johnson, "In China, the survival of Falun Rests on Beepers and Faith," *Wall Street Journal,* August 25, 2000, pp. A-1 and A-6.
140. See *New York Times*, February 1, 1999, p. A-12. Also see the January 16, 1999 issue, p. A-3.
141. See John Templeman, "Rice Bowl Protests Have Beijing Quaking," *Business Week*, February 1, 1999, p. 60.
142. See *New York Times*, November 26, 1999, p. A-9.
143. See an article by Amy L. Sherman, "China's Christians Are Witnesses to Persecution," *Wall Street Journal*, August 9, 1990, p. A-8.

SUGGESTED READINGS

Barne, Geremine and Linda Jaivin. *New Ghosts, Old Dreams: Chinese Rebel Voices* (New York: Times Books, 1992).

Brook, Timothy. *Quelling the People: The Military Suppression of the Beijing Democracy Movement* (Stanford, Calif.: Stanford University Press, 1998).

Calhoun, Craig. *Neither Gods Nor Emperors: Students and the Struggle for Democracy in China* (Berkeley: University of California Press, 1995).

Hinton, William. *Hundred Day War: The Cultural Revolution at Tsinghua University* (New York and London: Monthly Review Press, 1972).

Kent, Ann. *China, the United Nations and Human Rights: The Limits of Compliance* (Philadelphia: University of Pennsylvania Press, 1999).

Liu, Binyan. *"Tell the World:" What Happened in China and Why* (New York: Pantheon, 1990).

Nathan, Andrew J. *China's Crisis: Dilemmas of Reform and Prospects for Democracy* (New York: Columbia University Press, 1992).

Salisbury, Harrison. *Tiananmen Diary: Thirteen Days in June* (Boston, Mass.: Little, Brown, 1989).

Seymour, James D. and Richard Anderson. *New Ghosts, Old Ghosts: Prisons and Labor Camps in China* (Armonk, N.Y.: M. E. Sharpe, 1998).

Thurston, Ann F. *A Chinese Odyssey: The Life and Times of a Chinese Dissident* (New York: Scribners, 1992).

Unger, Jonathan (ed.). *The Pro-Democracy Protests in China* (Armonk, N.Y.: M. E. Sharpe, 1992).

Yan, Jiaqi. *Toward a Democratic China* (Honolulu: University of Hawai Press, 1992).

Zhang, Xudong. *Intellectual Politics in Post-Tiananmen China* (Durham, N.C.: Duke University Press, 1998).

Chapter Eleven

The Politics
of Modernization

Rural and Urban
Economic Reforms

MODERNIZATION AS A CONCEPT

Modernization, in the social sciences, usually refers to a general approach that focuses on the dual process of improving and modifying traditional political institutions, typically of Third World nations, for the purpose of achieving industrialization or economic development. As discussed in Chapter 1, China began undergoing periods of political modernization in the 1860s and 1870s, advocating the need to acquire Western scientific and technological expertise, particularly in areas relating to military science. This was followed in 1895 by the "self-strengthening" movement for the study of Western ideas and methods, including railroad building and military reform. Certainly the 1919 May Fourth Movement was an important step in China's political modernization. As discussed in Chapter 1, this was basically an intellectual enlightenment movement that revolved around the themes of nationalism and a "New Society" that would advance "democracy and science." During the republican period of the Nationalists, earnest attempts were made to build modern political institutions in the areas of military organization, state bureaucracy, and education. Lastly, fundamental political modernization or changes have taken place in China since 1949, as discussed in previous chapters. Now, in this chapter, the focus will be on China's efforts at economic modernization in order to attain the goal of industrialization.

. . . So the main task of socialism is to develop the productive forces, steadily improve the life of the people and keep increasing the material wealth of society. Therefore, there can be no communism with pauperism, or socialism with pauperism. So to get rich is no sin. . .[1]

Deng Xiaoping
September 2, 1986

Give full play to the role of market mechanism and improve the macro-economic control system. We should accelerate the process of building a complete market system in the national economy.[2]

Jiang Zemin
September 12, 1997

The quotations above are from statements by China's two most powerful leaders at the height of the economic reform period from 1980 to 1997: Deng Xiaoping, the paramount leader who passed away in early 1997, and Jiang Zemin, the CCP general secretary. In a nutshell, the goal of China's modernization program is to improve the living standards of the people and the material wealth of the society. Deng made it clear that one cannot build socialism with pauperism or "blanket poverty," as Mao was fond of saying. Jiang defended the use of market forces and macroeconomic tools to invigorate the economy as the correct policy. Jiang vowed not to go back to a highly centralized, planned economy.

What then was the centralized planned economy?

Up to 1978 when Deng Xiaoping introduced his economic reform, China had adhered to the Stalinist, or Soviet, model of centralized planning for economic development. In discussing the Soviet model of centralized planning in China, one must keep in mind that it was the economic planners who had control over all factors of production from land, buildings, labor, resources to all capital goods. All productive facilities from farms and enterprises owned by the state were placed at the disposal and under the control of economic planners who assigned targets and quotas for every factory and farm. As the authorities over economic control the economic planners also decided the prices and the amounts to be purchased by the central purchasing agent authorized by the planners. Under the central planning process, producers (farms and factories) and consumers made no decisions with respect to what was to be produced and how goods were to be distributed. Thus, for about two decades (1953–78) there developed "an irrational system" of highly centralized bureaucratic control over production and distribution by economic planners at various levels, monitored from the top.

The centralized planning system produced these fundamental defects in the Chinese economy: a command economy, a biased emphasis on heavy industries, and a highly centralized bureaucratic state monopoly. Soon there emerged a vast array of bureaucratic institutions engaged in complex decision making. At the top of the hierarchy, leaving aside the party's Politburo, the apex of policy making, stood the State Council headed by the premier. Six planning organs were under the direct supervision of the State Council: the State Planning Commission, the State Statistical Bureau, the State Economic Commission, the Commission on Restructure of the Economic

System, the Scientific and Technological Commission, and the People's Bank. No less than twenty-seven ministries were at one time involved in economic planning activities.

BRIEF OVERVIEW OF CHINA'S ECONOMIC DEVELOPMENT

The development of the Chinese economy has not been a smooth process. On the contrary, it has been erratic and volatile. In the initial years, from 1949 to 1952, the regime's priority was to seek, as rapidly as possible, economic recovery and rehabilitation in the aftermath of a long period of war and the dislocation of the country's productive capacity. In 1953 the regime embarked on long-range planning of its economic development, employing the Stalinist model of centralized planning with emphasis on development of heavy industries. As was indicated in Chapter 2, the First Five-Year Plan was followed by a shift in development strategy in 1958, which placed emphasis on mass mobilization and intensive use of human labor under the Great Leap. While rapid economic recovery followed the failure of the Great Leap, this recovery was disrupted by the Cultural Revolution in the mid-1960s. The post-Cultural Revolution period, from 1969 to 1975, witnessed mixed emphases, both on local economic self-reliance and self-sufficiency and on continued selective centralized management of a number of heavy industries, transport, banking, and foreign trade. No major new economic policy was formulated until 1975, when Zhou Enlai consolidated his political power in the aftermath of the Lin Biao affair.

Between 1953 and 1975, covered by the economic development policies discussed above, the rate of economic growth in China was approximately 6 percent. This was quite an impressive record when compared with other developing nations,[3] particularly in view of the size and density of China's population and the interruptions that occurred during the Great Leap and the Cultural Revolution.

Deng Xiaoping's Economic Reform 1978–1992

In December 1978 Deng Xiaoping had steered the party to adopt a policy of "open door" for foreign investment in China. (See Chapter 12's section on technology transfer.) Then in April 1979 a central work conference was convened to discuss corrections and readjustments in the 1978 modernization program. Simultaneously, the Chinese central government was forced to revise, postpone, or cancel many contracts signed with foreign concerns, particularly Japanese firms. The NPC at its second session in June 1979 approved a series of urgent measures to readjust the modernization program by retrenchment.[4] First, it decided to readjust the priorities. Light and consumer industries were to be given equal, if not greater, emphasis with heavy industry. The overambitious plan for 60 million metric tons of steel by 1985 was revised to 45 million metric tons. Energy and power industries were scheduled to be developed and expanded more rapidly. Capital construction projects for heavy industries were to be curtailed, so that a large amount of investment funds would be freed. Second, it reached the conclusion that the economic management structure had to be overhauled. Enterprises were to be given real decision-making power and initiative. The concept of "egalitarian tendency" was discarded; those who had demonstrated success would now be given authority and reward. Provinces and localities were to be given increased power in planning, financing, and foreign trade. Third, it decided that factory managers must be given power in the operation of the plants to spur production. Managers were permitted to set prices for their own products; and they were allowed to apply to the banks to borrow operating funds and pay interest. Fourth, it mandated that all enterprises must produce quality products.

This austere readjustment program was to span the three-year period from 1979 to 1981. Reform measures in the economy would slow down China's planned growth rate from 12 percent in 1978 to about 7 percent in 1979 and to just over 5 percent in 1980.[5] These scaled-down goals represented an admission that the country had gone ahead too fast and was forced to apply the brakes.[6]

The 1979 economic reforms were intended to correct two basic problems: the overemphasis on the investment in and accumulation of heavy industries, discussed earlier, and the need for incentives to spur production. China's leading economists and planners such as Chen Yun (a Politburo member and former director of state planning) and Xue Muqiao (an adviser for state planning), argued that the "scale of economic construction must be commensurate with the nation's capabilities": The state should make a substantial investment in capital construction in heavy industries only when the people's livelihood had made marked improvement.[7] Chen Yun was quoted as saying that the distribution of the limited supply of raw materials should be given first to those industries "that ensure the production of people's daily necessities."[8] To proceed otherwise would be "Leftist thinking." It would be a "Leftist" error if the percentage of accumulation in national income—that is, the amount of money and material resources channeled into construction of large-scale heavy industrial projects as fixed assets and inventories—was disproportionately high. The accumulation ratio of fixed assets and inventories channeled into the building of heavy industrial projects was 36 percent of the national income.[9] When this imbalance occurred, Chen Yun was the most influential voice arguing for a reduction in capital construction investment and an increase in consumer goods industries.

In terms of state investment in the two sectors, the development strategy shift from heavy to light industries was made not only because of the need to provide consumer goods for the rapidly increasing population, but also for more expedient reasons. Heavy industries consume an enormous quantity of energy resources. Light industries require less energy, and also provide more jobs. (It has been pointed out that in China a 1 percent shift in the ratio from heavy to light industries saves six million tons of coal.[10])

The Emergence of Individual (Private) Enterprises as "Market Socialism," 1979

In 1979 a familiar sight in many Chinese cities was individual vendors, hawkers, and shopkeepers selling their goods and services—activities long prohibited by the government. When urban authorities began granting licenses to private entrepreneurs in 1979 for business, Westerners were delighted to be able to purchase fresh produce from the countryside and eat a good meal in a small family restaurant without waiting in line. Some 300,000 small private enterprises were reported to be operating in cities in 1979, with over 810,000 in existence at the end of 1980, and 2.6 million in 1983.[11]

The rationale for this new policy was that "individual economy," or private enterprise, should no longer be considered "capitalistic," and that it must be allowed to play a role in supporting the socialist economy.[12] Apparently, there was some resistance to the new policy. For example, the *People's Daily* accused the state commercial agencies of hanging on to the old practice of "monopoly economy."[13] Still, before 1966 there were at least two million small individual producers providing goods and services to meet the market demands that the state-owned economy failed to deliver.[14] These individual producers disappeared during the Cultural Revolution and were not revived until 1979, when economic readjustment and reform became necessary. The leadership hoped that the incentives provided by the "individual economy" would help spur production and fill gaps in the system once again. In addition, it was realized that the "individual economy" would open up jobs for the urban unemployed.

The existence of individual enterprises alongside the socialist collective enterprises raises serious questions, since the two are seemingly incompatible. It must be remembered that within the Soviet model of a centralized planned economy, China has had a pattern of alternating policy approaches over the extent to which market forces should play a role in the economy. These policies, as pointed out in Chapter 2, became the focus of debate and dissension among the top leaders. The fiasco of the 1958 Great Leap crash program paved the way for the economic readjustment and recovery in the 1960s, when there was a relaxation in strict control over market forces. The Cultural Revolution, with its excessive emphasis on the role of ideology, destroyed the gains made during the early 1960s, and with them went the permissible free markets for peasants and the profit-and-loss principle for industrial management. Now China once again returned to the pre-1966 policy of relaxing the state's control over market forces in the midst of a planned economy.

Under the 1979 adjustment, not only were market forces allowed in the "individual economy," but they were also introduced into state enterprises as part of a series of reforms to generate growth. Many of the reforms had emerged from experiments conducted by Zhao Ziyang in enterprises selected as pilot projects in the province of Sichuan. During 1980–81 thousands of state enterprises were subjected to "market socialism" experiments through the introduction of the following reform measures:[15] (1) state-owned factories were allowed to produce for market demand as long as they fulfilled the assigned state quota; (2) state-owned enterprises were given the freedom to purchase needed raw material through the market, rather than remaining dependent on central allocation; (3) prices for the products were to be set by the supply and demand mechanism. In other words, for these enterprises microeconomic decisions on production would be governed by market forces, not by the state plan. All state-owned enterprises were to be responsible for their own profit and loss.

Austerity, Retrenchment, and Recession: China's Economy after Tiananmen, 1989–1991

High inflation and rampant corruption were some of the underlying causes of student demonstrations and unrest in the spring of 1989. (For a more detailed discussion, see Chapter 10.) Long before the Tiananmen crackdown the Chinese economy was already in serious trouble. The reform decade, from 1978 to 1988, had brought on excessive growth that contributed to an overheated economy. Industrial growth for the decade increased at an average rate of about 12 percent annually. In 1988 the total industrial growth rate was 20 to 21 percent against the official planned growth target of not more than 8 percent.[16] The "uncontrolled industrial investment hunger" was stimulated by the haphazard fixed investment initiated by provincial and local authorities without regard for conservation of resources and real market demand. As explained by Jan Prybyla:[17] This surge in economic activity placed enormous strain on scarce raw material and energy supplies and on the badly overburdened and bottlenecked transportation system. It also contributed to an already thriving black market and the concurrent corruption. At the same time, after the peak 1984 production of 407 million tons, grain production had leveled off so that rationing for many key agricultural commodities had to be instituted.[18] In the first quarter of 1988 prices for fresh vegetables rose more than 48 percent and prices for nonstaple foods rose by 24 percent. Chinese consumers spent more than half of their income on food. This high inflation rate for the three-year period from 1986 to 1988 brought down real income for urban wage earners.[19]

Austerity and Retrenchment.   After some heated and lengthy debate, Chinese leaders decided to inaugurate a price-reform policy—decontrol of prices in accordance with supply and demand and the introduction of a wage index to cost of living, insisted on by reform leader Zhao Ziyang. Decontrol in prices produced some panic in urban areas: "runs on the bank, a spending spree, stockpiling, and unauthorized price hikes."[20] The consumer panic was accompanied by deliberate increases in bonuses and subsidies to workers and staff in state enterprises, a hefty jump to 36 percent in the first seven months of 1988 as compared to the same period in 1987. At this juncture advocates of price reform, led by Zhao and his reformers, were in trouble and under criticism by the hard-liners. In fact, economic policy decision making was now taken away from the reformers and transferred to Li Peng and Yao Yilin, supporters of hard-liners on the Politburo at the CCP's Tenth Plenum in mid-August. By September and October, after more lengthy debate at party and State Council work conferences, Zhao admitted mistakes in economic policies and accepted the alternative of a new program of economic austerity and retrenchment. This policy included tightening credit for capital construction, reducing the purchasing power of various social groups, cracking down on corruption by cadres, recentralizing trade and foreign investment, reducing spending by party and government agencies, and reviving ideological indoctrination.[21]

The austerity and retrenchment policy adopted in the fall of 1988 meant a retreat in the partial market system experiment. What had been reinstituted was centralized "administrative command" and "compulsion."

Recession.   Six months after the military crackdown at Tiananmen, China was in an economic recession. Tightened and controlled credit and loan policies under the austerity program produced a slowdown in industrial output to a yearly gain of about 2.3 percent. Inflation was still estimated at 21.4 percent in 35 major cities for the first ten months of 1989.[22] As credit and loans became restricted and squeezed or not available at all, many factories ceased production. Enterprises or firms, established when credit and investment were readily obtainable and there was momentum for reform, now went bankrupt or fell deeply in debt. By the time the Tiananmen crackdown occurred, demand for durable consumer goods in urban areas had reached a saturation point and rural peasants were more interested in housing investment. The result was large inventories of durable goods and refrigerators and television sets in the warehouses.

The crackdown also brought fear and uncertainty to the flourishing rural enterprises, as now the political winds shifted to the right. By the end of 1989 many rural or village industries also stopped producing. About one million rural enterprises across China ceased production within one year of the austerity and retrenchment policy that began in the fall of 1988.[23] These small-scale but semiprivate rural industries depended on credit and loans from banks.

The industrial slowdown for both urban and rural sectors created serious unemployment problems after Tiananmen: In 1989 urban unemployment was 3.5 percent, or 5.4 million workers, out of a total labor force of more than 150 million.[24] The rural jobless rate for 1989 was estimated at 40 percent of the rural work force, or about 120 million in the countryside.[25] Urban workers bore the brunt of these stringent economic measures, for they had to endure wage cuts or unemployment. There were worker strikes in 1989 and small-scale protest marches in cities in western and central China.[26]

The overall goals for the austerity program and the tight money measures were to bring down the inflation rate to about 10 percent and the growth rate to 5 or 6 percent per year. The reinstitution of ideological studies in state-owned enterprises, a reaction to the student protests at Tiananmen, meant further loss in productivity, as workers spent time in political indoctrination instead of in production. As state-run enterprises slowed their productivity, the state was required to provide large amounts of money for resource purchasing and worker benefits, thus aggravating the state budget deficit. It has been estimated that the state would have to bail out the state-owned enterprises by as much as $12 billion, or about one-third of its revenue. To make up for the deficit, the government resorted to issuance of printed money, spurring more inflation. Furthermore, about twenty million workers, about one-fifth of the personnel in state enterprises, came to work each day and got paid even though there was no work to be done.[27]

Impact of Global Sanctions on the Chinese Economy in the Tiananmen Aftermath.
Initial world reaction to the Tiananmen massacre included a tourism boycott and the withholding of foreign loans and investment from China. For the months from July to December 1989 China expected about one million tourists, whose spending would have enriched its treasury by about $2.2 billion in foreign currency. Instead, thanks to the global tourism boycott, only 500,000 tourists visited the country in the last six months of 1989, causing a loss of at least $1 billion in foreign exchange revenue. Most new hotels built by joint ventures in the 1980s suffered a low occupancy rate. Then many Western industrial nations withheld loans and extensions of credit to China for the remainder of 1989. For a while even Japan halted its aid projects to China. The World Bank stopped action on its seven loan projects for power, transport, and industrial development. (However, in May 1990 the World Bank decided to lend $300,000 for reforestation projects.)

The cumulative effects of withholding foreign loans and credit to China were delays in developing much-needed energy projects plus the drying up of funds for Chinese banks, which in turn contributed to recession. Direct foreign investment in China declined after Tiananmen. However, the gap seemed to have been filled by cumulative investment from Taiwan—$1 billion at the end of 1989, which then doubled in 1990.[28]

Easing Austerity to Revive the Sagging Economy:
The Boom Cycle Again, 1992–1995

To relieve the deepening economic recession, Premier Li Peng announced in July 1990 a five-point plan to revive the sagging economy. A key point in the plan was to extend low-interest loans to state enterprises to reduce their debts. The beneficiaries of the new low-interest loans seemed to be those large-scale state enterprises engaged in export trade—grain procurement units and joint venture projects with foreign investment. The easing of credit and loan extension began in the spring of 1990 when the Industrial and Commercial Bank of China extended an initial amount of $510 million in new loans to industrial enterprises in major cities.[29] This was later increased to $1.06 billion.

Some of the large-scale state enterprises in the industrial northeast (including the giant Anshan Iron and Steel Works, Daqing Oil fields, Shenyang Electric Cable Plant, and other mining and chemical plants) signed contracts with the state under which it had guaranteed energy, raw material, and transportation services in return for a commitment to meet fixed quotas for finished products and to pay taxes.[30] The new guaranteed loans enabled large-scale state enterprises to resolve their debt problems and develop new products. Since 1988, when the austerity program was initiated, many state enterprises had defaulted on bank loans. These loan arrangements were made at the provincial level without specific approval from the central government when decentralization reform was in vogue. Some of these loan arrangements involved joint venture or foreign investment. With tightening of credit under the austerity program, plant managers faced mounting problems of finding available working capital to purchase raw material and supplies, in addition to meeting their long-term debt obligations.[31] A plant manager's life was further complicated by the two-tiered pricing system for raw material and supplies: the low state-subsidized price and a market price.

The easing of credit and loan extension to state enterprises was aimed at revival of the sagging economy, but it also could create a new round of boom–bust cycles if not accompanied by price reform. Inflation, at 10 percent—down from its high of 30 percent before the Tiananmen massacre—could easily increase again, in turn requiring the reinstitution of austerity measures.

The government budget presented to the 1992 March NPC session disclosed the government's plan to step up capital spending and subsidies for the military, the bureaucracy, and education by as much as 12 percent; at the same time imposing more "fiscal discipline" to reduce the deficit.[32] At any rate the 1992 economic boom came at the time when the ideological debate over the nature of socialist economy ended when Deng returned from his southern tour.

In short, Chinese leaders embarked on two basic approaches to China's economic difficulties: continued austerity which ended in 1993, and the reinstitution of centralized administrative control immediately after Tiananmen, followed by easing of the austerity restrictions and emphasis on more growth. Under the Eighth Five-Year Plan (1991–95) some reform measures were proposed in enterprise management, foreign trade, the financial system, and housing. However, the most important reform—doing away with the two-tiered price system (a fixed price on certain products and a floating or fluctuating price for the remaining goods produced) remained in controversy.

Under the Eighth Five-Year Plan for 1991–95, China expected a slower growth rate of about 6 percent a year. The overall goal was to double its gross national product to U.S.$538 billion by the year 2000.

In 1993 the growth rate was set at 8 percent, slightly higher than the 6 percent targeted under the Eighth Five-Year Plan. However, the economy in fact grew at over 12 percent for 1992—the result of credit expansion as desired by Deng Xiaoping, the "apostle of double-digit growth."[33] Zhu Rongji, the vice-premier and economic "czar" admitted that the urban inflation rate was at 20 percent, but only 12 percent for the country as a whole.[34]

For 1993–94 there were some significant economic structure reforms which included making the People's Bank a central bank with power to independently make uniform monetary policy. By 1993 it was evident that the collective and private production contribution to the total economy had grown to 36 percent. Private production contributed about 11 percent, while the state-owned enterprises produced 53 percent, instead of the 78 percent of a decade ago.[35]

The Increased Use of Macroeconomic Tools to Regulate Economic Reforms, 1995–1997

By definition, macroeconomics does not refer only to the economy as a whole. It is also concerned with the economic system's subdivisions, such as governmental-administrative policies, the productive or business sectors, and the aggregates of the economic structure—unemployment, public expenditure and revenue, and prices. In 1993–94 the most significant macroeconomic policy had been in the area of tax reform— the central government extended a value-added tax to the entire economic system accompanied by an income tax reduction, from 55 to 33 percent, on state-owned enterprises, as well as for collective and foreign enterprises.[36] At the disposal of "bureaucratic elites" central government organizations imposed industrial policies to regulate industries, such as suspension of negotiations on joint ventures for auto production with foreign firms.[37] In 1994-1995 there were as many as 100,000 industrial enterprises employing about 100 million workers. As the central government demanded that the state-owned enterprises operate efficiently on a loss-profit basis, workers were laid off; this created a serious unemployment problem in urban areas.

In the case of smaller state-owned enterprises, in 1993 the central government authorized leasing or selling them to collectives or individuals through public bidding. Monetary operations, such as stock markets, were also permitted, but under the state's macrocontrol. Efforts were also being made to allow prices to be determined by market forces within state regulations; to lift control over purchasing and selling of grains; and to establish a single-price system for basic industrial commodities such as coal, electricity and oil. The state then began to exercise "macro-control over investment, reform in management, and the full use of economic levers such as credit and interest rates to regulate investment."[38]

It seems that by relying on the increasing use of macroeconomic tools in the form of monetary and fiscal policies, China was able, for the period 1995–97, to control economic growth without creating economic contraction. For much of 1995 and 1996 China's gross domestic product (gross national product minus foreign investment) was hovering around 9.7 percent. This economic success prompted the central bank to cut interest rates and relax credit extension. China's economic success can also be observed by the reduction in inflation: 7 percent for 1996 and 15 percent for 1995, as compared to 25 percent for 1994. However, as reported by Avery Goldstein, the economic success also yielded some shortcomings: Increases in food, rent and utility, costs became a burden for most lowincome urban residents; heavy tax burdens were imposed on rural residents by local officials, and millions of migrants roamed the cities looking for jobs.[39]

The Institute of Economy of the State Planning Commission predicted that in 1997 China's economy would grow at the rate of 10.5 percent with inflation being kept at 6 percent.[40] By 1997 China's growth rate had been kept at about 7 percent.

By the end of 1999 China's growth rate was estimated to be 7.5 percent, a slight improvement over the previous two years. According to the Chinese Academy of Social Sciences, factors contributing to the progress included the following:[41] fading deflation and slightly increased consumer consumption; increased export volume as the Asian economy recovered; reform in state-owned industries (see discussion to follow); and large-scale development in western China (as discussed in Chapter 7).

Also contributing to the improvement in China's growth rate has been the rise in direct foreign investment which was estimated to total about $40 billion for 1998. As the Asian economies have recovered, foreign investments in China from Hong Kong, Taiwan, and South Korea have shown some increase, contributing to China's total growth pattern by their investment in the manufacturing sectors in textiles, garments, footwear and sporting equipment for China's export.[42]

AGRICULTURAL (RURAL) REFORM: THE RESPONSIBILITY SYSTEM

The single most important change in recent years for the rural areas has been the introduction of the responsibility system for the peasants. It is, in essence, an incentive system. The system—introduced in 1978 but put into effect in 1980—is a modification of Liu Shaoqi's "Three Freedoms and One Contract," which was introduced in the early 1960s as a part of the economic recovery program after the failure of the Great Leap. Both Liu and his policy were attacked by the radicals during the Cultural Revolution as "revisionist" and "capitalist." Liu's policy included (1) free markets, (2) private plots, and (3) peasant responsibility for managing their own farms on the basis of contracts for fixed output quotas for each household. In 1978, at the Third Plenum of the Eleventh Central Committee, the party under the leadership of Deng Xiaoping revived the main features of the old Liu policy as a way to step up agricultural production.

The 1978 party resolution on agricultural reform urged that remuneration for work in the communes be based on the principle of "to each according to his work" by stressing quality of work. In addition, the party resolution directed that private plots and sideline production were now "necessary adjuncts of the socialist economy and must not be interfered with."[43] Central Committee Document No. 75, issued in November 1980, outlined a number of approved methods for use of the "responsibility system."[44] These methods were all based on contracts issued by the production teams to the peasants for specific quotas of output or work accomplished. Under all methods, pay was to be based on the level of production or work accomplished. The contracts, depending on local conditions and tradition, could be issued to individuals, to households, or to work teams. One type, "Baochan Daohu" ("to fix farm output quota for each household"), permitted a township to make land available to each household, usually a family, in accordance with its labor capacity. The production team and the household signed a contract fixing the quota the household was obligated to fulfill. This quota included a portion for the team's quota for the state and a portion to meet township expenses.

Another type of rural responsibility system was the concept of full responsibility to the household. Under this method the household signed a contract with the village to assume all responsibility for work on the land and to bear the entire responsibility for its own profit and loss.

Under this arrangement, land was contracted to the household on a per capita basis by the village. In addition, farm implements and draft animals were permanently assigned to the household under contract. The household not only had to meet the state procurement requirements, but it also had to assume full responsibility for managing the land and fulfilling all its obligations to the collective—in this case, the village. After deduction of the various cost items for the state and the collective, the remainder of the earnings went to the household.

Unique advantages of the job responsibility system described above were (1) encouraging peasants to work harder in order to receive more income; (2) allowing the peasants to manage their own production under the most favorable local conditions, rather than under the "commandism" of rural cadres—thus permitting the peasants to have more initiative and autonomy; and (3) avoiding the problem of constant complaints by peasants about unfair distribution of earnings. The advantages of the responsibility system, combined with the policy of private plots and free markets, gave a tremendous boost to peasant morale and resulted in increased output and work enthusiasm.

By 1981 the rural responsibility system had been adopted in all the provinces. By mid-1982, official figures reported that 90 percent of the villages in the townships had adopted some form of the responsibility system.[45] While there were differences in the methods or arrangements adopted, depending on type of produce and locale, on the whole the income of the peasants increased significantly under the incentive system.[46]

The introduction of the incentive system for agricultural production was not without criticism. Some felt that China was about to abolish the collective commune system, which in short time did just that. Others cried out that the new agricultural policy was a "bourgeois policy."[47] Defenders of the new policy countered that under it, peasants could expect increased income and general prosperity. Premier Zhao pointed out, when he introduced the agricultural reform experiment in Sichuan, that any innovation must be considered socialist as long as the means of production are publicly owned and as long as the Marxist principle of "to each according to his work" is observed.[48] One Western scholar noted: "In Guangdong, at least, it seems not to have weakened the commitment to a collective economy."[49] As a final note, the new reform in agricultural productivity eventually may remove some of the glaring shortcomings of the collective commune system in China; Premier Zhao pointedly told the NPC in December 1982:

> Many places report that, with the introduction of the responsibility system, production has gone up, the relationship between cadres and peasants has markedly improved and bureaucraticism, arbitrary orders, corruption, waste, and other obnoxious practices have declined sharply.[50]

Extension of Leased Land Under Contract

The success of the responsibility system in the countryside enabled the reformers to move a step further, to "legitimize" and "institutionalize" the widely accepted "Baogan Daohu," or simply "Da Baogan" system of leasing land owned collectively by the township under contract. This step had been termed the "second land reform" or the "decollectivization" of the communes in the countryside.[51] Party Document No. 1 of 1984 extended the duration of household contracts from a period of three to five years to fifteen years. The fifteen-year extension of land contracted not only signified to peasants the legitimacy of the responsibility system but also gave them a sense of permanence and stability in their contracts,[52] and alleviated the fear that the leased land contracts, the "Da Baogan," might be subject to shifting political winds. In addition, the longer period for leased land provided the peasants with "a greater incentive to invest in the land" and to make other improvements needed to enable the land to be continuously productive.[53] Inducing the peasants to invest capital and labor on the land also lightened the state's burden of providing subsidies to agricultural production.[54]

Another significant change endorsed by the party was the gradual abolition of the state monopoly to buy farm products. In its place, a new price system based on market demand was introduced. In other words, the state would gradually relinquish its position as the sole and exclusive purchasing agent for agricultural products at a fixed price. Instead of selling grain to the state grain bureau, the peasants now could enter into contracts with a variety of buyers and purchasing agents on the basis of 70 percent at above-quota price and 30 percent at the state quota price, depending on the quality of the product. Premier Zhao argued that the new rural reform not only would result in better quality but also would entice the peasants to produce the needed marketable goods. In the past, the monopolistic price system tended to force the peasants to produce only grains and cotton, regardless of the market demands for other products, such as silk, jute, tea, and tobacco.[55]

Diversification and Specialization by Households

New rural policies contained in Document No. 1 (1984) also encouraged the rapid development of a new rural institution, the "special households" and "key-point households."[56] As of 1985–86, more than 25 million households in the countryside, or about 14 percent of the total rural population, were classified as "special" and "key point" households.[57] These households engaged not only in agricultural production, but also in services, such as transport and commerce. Wan Li, a Politburo member and a vice-premier who was considered one of the key architects of rural reform, revealed that many peasants had become prosperous because of their expanded activities as "special households."[58] Based on the study of a county in Shanxi province, Wan Li distinguished several types of peasants involved in the specialized households: production and team leaders with managerial skills, demobilized soldiers, peasants with skills in specific grain or cash crop cultivation (such as silk, tobacco, livestock, poultry breeding, fishery cultivation, or forestry), and individuals providing services.[59]

Typically a specialized household signs a contract with the collective village for a piece of cultivatable land, forest, fruit orchard, fish pond, or grazing pasture. Under the contract, the specialized household is obligated to turn over a part of the income derived from the production to the collective but is allowed to keep the rest. The specialized household must operate and manage its projects without any help from the township. It is the sole responsibility of the specialized household to make its own arrangements with other economic organizations based on market demand and supply. The state and the township come into the picture only when loans and credit are needed. While peasants engaged in specialized production must assume their own risks, they also keep profits.

The introduction of specialized households in rural China has provided a distinct shift in China's agriculture from basically subsistence farming—providing enough grain to feed the families—to commercial commodity production.[60]Peasants operating under the specialized household contracts enter into service trades, commodity production, manufacturing, and transportation of locally produced goods to distant locations. Thomas Bernstein sees this development not only as a major shift to commodity production, but also as a way of "unleashing the entrepreneurial talents of China's peasants."[61] The development of specialized households has enabled the peasants to diversify. Under this arrangement, peasants now grow any type of high-yield commercial commodity crop suitable to the land and able to be produced efficiently— as long as the grain quota imposed by the state is met. Diversification is not limited to farming, but extends to cottage industries as well.[62] The new system also allows more mobility for the peasants. During the off-season peasants may leave their villages for more lucrative jobs at construction sites in nearby towns or cities rather than remaining idle.[63] In interviewing Chinese immigrants in Hong Kong, Jonathan Ungar found that hired field hands had been allowed to move from poor farming areas to rich areas, thus opening for peasant families the alternative of mobility instead of being hopelessly bound to the poor villages as destitutes.

The need to encourage peasants to specialize and diversify led to another important change in rural China. Land contracted from the collective can now be transferred from one household to another, allowing for the more efficient households to replace the less efficient. Specialized households may also form partnerships and companies, either by themselves or in joint ventures with the state or the marketing cooperatives. They can even hire workers as "helpers" under "labor exchange."

Some of the specialized households have prospered and reportedly earned as much as 10,000 yuan (about U.S. $3,500) per year. On the other hand, the rate of failures and bankruptcy cases multiplied. In one county in Henan province, a survey showed that a total of 819 specialized households, about 3 percent of the total specialized households for the county, ended in bankruptcy. Reasons for failure included lack of technological know-how and managerial skills, inability to understand the need for financial skills, and the peasants' lack of the necessary skills and ties.[64]

It seems safe to say that what has taken place in rural reform under the term "responsibility system" is what Martin K. Whyte has depicted as "the rural family reemerged as a 'primary' unit of agricultural production."[65] Although land still belongs to the collective, the rural family has been assured of land use security tantamount to "private ownership" in terms of "inheritance, rent and transfer."[66] Whyte argues that the family farm contributes in large part to the overall success of China's rural economic reform.[67] However, a 1977–82 study of rural reform in Sichuan pointed out that the rural responsibility system was not a decisive factor in that province's rural growth.[68]

Rural Surplus Labor and Rural Industries: "A Factory in Every Village"

As specialized households multiplied and agricultural production became more efficient, there arose a problem of rural surplus labor. In 1985 Xinhua news agency reported that as many as one-third of China's total rural labor force had been idled, or "freed" from farming.[69] In the eastern coastal province of Zhejiang, half of the rural labor force was reported to have gone into nonagricultural pursuits. From 1975 to 1985, some nine million peasants left their farms.[70] One expert on rural China has reported that 30 to 40 percent of China's rural labor force, about 370 million, most likely will be engaged in industries and sideline occupations in the future, thus creating "a class of landless land-lords" in the future.[71] Instead of allowing the idled peasants to roam around or migrate to the already overpopulated cities, authorities permitted them to engage in nonagricultural activities in small towns created for them. Surplus rural workers and those unemployed seasonally could work in animal husbandry, fish farming, forestry, and other sideline production, or in the service trades.[72]

During the mid-1980s China began a program of rural industrialization using the slogan "A factory for every village."[73] The program was designed to utilize rural surplus labor in industries to process agricultural products. A number of small rural towns, par-ticularly those with flourishing markets, developed rapidly. The rural cottage industries were owned by townships (formerly the entire commune), villages (formerly the pro-duction brigade), individual peasants, and rural cadres. From 1984 to 1985 the rural cot-tage industries employed 52 million, or 14 percent of the surplus rural labor force, and contributed about 40 percent of rural output.[74] In 1985, rural industries had absorbed 60 million surplus workers. Jean C. Oi has provided statistics showing that by 1996 there were a total of 23 million rural enterprises with over 135 million workers, or about one-third of China's total rural labor force.[75] The cottage industries operated outside of the cen-tralized planning system and were independent of state-owned enterprises. Many were free-wheeling private business enterprises that contributed in some measure to the "overheating" of China's economy. The central authorities have tried to curb the rapid growth of rural industries by limiting lending and investment credits to village cottage industries.[76] Many observers doubt that these efforts will succeed, because rural industries can continue to expand by retaining profits and by issuing stock to workers in order to raise more invest-ment capital.

Rural Reform: Cadres' Opposition and Accommodation

When the responsibility system was first introduced in 1978, rural cadres reacted with resentment and opposition to the change. Rural and "grassroot" party cadres were in many ways "earth emperors" over the peasants because of their power and authority to make decisions affecting life in the countryside. Under the collectivized commune sys-tem, rural party cadres could order what, when, and how to plant; they often mobilized the peasants for work on collective projects, such as water conservation and roads. Under the responsibility system, individual households could contract for collectively owned land and manage production by themselves. The responsibility system reduced the admin-istrative cost at the brigade and team levels by the elimination of administrative staff in the collective.[77] Under the commune system the tasks such as record keeping, work assignment, and accounting were normal responsibilities of the cadres and the commune staff under their direction.[78] With the household contract system, these managerial tasks gradually decreased.[79] Moreover, rural party cadres soon discovered they no longer had the power to allocate funds for nonproductive party activities.[80] In the past, collective income had been appropriated by the rural party cadres to cover these overhead costs. As the rural cadres' managerial and supervisory tasks decreased, their income also declined. Provincial media reported many instances of rural cadres abandoning their posts as production team leaders and leaving these positions vacant.[81] However, many of the rural cadres who remained and accepted the responsibility system as a needed reform took the initiative by becoming "the middlemen brokering business deals and acting as entrepreneurs."[82]

With the declining functions of the commune, the 1982 state constitution, as discussed in Chapter 4, mandated the transfer of basic local governmental functions from the commune to the township people's government (see Article 95 in Appendix A).

In short, rural reform has created a new breed of local cadres: skilled, better educated, more technologically inclined, younger, and with the necessary "connections" to make things happen. Many former local cadres—brigade and team leaders—have abandoned their leadership positions to become prosperous holders of specialized household contracts.[83] To a large extent the local cadres have been the beneficiaries of the success of the rural reforms. It should be noted that a close relationship existed between the local cadres and the prosperous specialized households in the countryside, and the latter have often received "preferential treatment" in the contracting of land and distribution of sales contracts.[84]

Rural Privately Owned Enterprises.   An interesting outcome in the rapid growth of rural industries has been the new role of village-township-county governments as the "local corporate state" or "corporate headquarters"[85] for rural enterprises: "Each level is an approximate equivalent to what is termed a 'profit center' in decentralized management schemes used in business firms,"[86] operating in similar fashion to a "multinational corporation" in many of the Newly Industrialized Nations (NICs) of South Korea, Taiwan, and Singapore. Jean Oi even ventures the thought that the successful model in China's rural enterprise experience may be offered as an alternative to privatization for economic development.[87] There are as many as 18.5 million privately owned "small, market-driven factories" in rural villages throughout China, except in some of the remote regions. It is in a sense a sort of "grassroots industrialization."[88] Ann and James Tyson referred to the 1992 World Bank report which had forecast 150 million rural jobs and half, instead of a quarter, of China's gross national product.[89] While these rural enterprises are privately owned, a target of attack by conservative party leaders as being "capitalistic," they are also "enterprises of rural cadres" who have transformed themselves into the new rural elites.

Rural Reforms: Problems and Crisis

While the success of rural reform has provided unprecedented prosperity for the peasants as a whole, it has also created a number of problems for China's agrarian society.

One problem was the rise in rural violence from social tension generated by the reforms.[90] Household contracts created disputes over land and water rights.[91] A contributing factor to violence was the gradual erosion of local authority. Clashes among feuding peasants over ancestral temples and shrines became frequent.[92] Under the collective command structure, the local cadres had exercised a great deal of control over the lives of the peasantry. Now, under rural reform, that authority had been eroded to such an extent that local cadres could no longer restrain the feuding peasants from violence. Moreover, in many cases the restive local cadres served as instigators of violence. Large-scale looting led by local party cadres was reported frequently in China's local press.

Along with the rise of rural violence was the revival of feudalistic and superstitious practices. Feudal superstition, such as the use of Daoist priests to select tombs for the deceased and to conduct religious rituals, resurfaced in rural China.[93] There were even cases where work points were granted by party cadres for participating in these religious practices.[94] Gradually, kinship ties became more important than community interests.

Thomas Bernstein points out other side effects, or "unanticipated outcomes," of rural reform. Among these was a continuing reduction in arable land and forestry resources brought on by a steady housing construction boom in the countryside. Expansion in rural economic activities also siphoned off investment needed for irrigation projects.[95] Those familiar with China's farming have noted an increase in strip farming—the division of land into tiny strips. William Hinton was alarmed by the neglect of rural education as the young were drawn into work for the households under household contracts.[96] Rural education was not only inferior in quality as compared with urban areas, but also in terms of the number of children attending schools. There seemed to be a general neglect of rural education as attention focused on those reform measures that would increase peasants' prosperity. Many of the collectives' tangible assets, including schools and machinery, were divided among contracting households. Other collective services also were neglected as the individual household contract system took root: social welfare for the aged, irrigation projects, and insecticide spraying. Finally, the differences between the poor and more prosperous peasants in the countryside became increasingly evident—a point that alarmed some China observers.[97]

The Chinese grain harvest for 1990 reached a targeted record high of 422 million tons. But China's rural economy has been in crisis for several years due to a number of difficulties. Despite the grain increase, the total tonnage needed to feed the population, which is increasing by at least 15–20 million people annually, exceeds 422 million tons. China needs an additional 40–80 million tons of grain production per year before the year 2000 in order to adequately feed its people. One needs to bear in mind that in recent years a larger share of consumer spending, as much as 60 percent in 1988, has been for food.[98]

Then, there has been an increase in the consumption of meat and liquor, which require additional increases in grain production of about 20–40 million tons. Grain production can be increased in only three ways: an increase in land acreage for cultivation; improvement in existing land utilization; or the importation of grain from abroad. Arable acreage for agricultural production is shrinking rapidly in China. The reasons for this include the population increase, which places additional demands on land; peasants shifting production to more lucrative crops other than basic grain production; declining soil fertility; excessive use of chemical fertilizers; and soil erosion. Official estimates put the decline of arable land acreage for 1985 and 1986 at from 600,000 to one million hectares.[99]

The 1986 Land Administration Law and Village Leaders. The central government's concern over declining arable land led to passage of the 1986 land administration and management law.[100] The law was aimed at developing land management policies and plans for protecting arable land, punishing misuse or illegal use of land for construction purchases as rural industries expanded, and for conserving the scarce natural resources. However, the law issued by the central government has been hampered by local governments at the village-township-county levels, whose parochial interests are often at variance with directives from the center. As viewed by George P. Brown's study, the land management plan can be complied with only if local level leaders can be persuaded that it is in "the fundamental national interest" to preserve arable land.[101]

Improvement of existing arable land means that, for an additional increase of 50 million tons of grain, there must be 15 million more tons of chemical fertilizers, 10 billion more kilowatt-hours of electricity, and 1.3 million more tons of diesel oil.[102] But agricultural investment credits have been on the decline, amounting to about 3 percent of total state spending for 1986–90, a 50 percent decrease as compared to 6 percent for 1981–85.[103] In 1979 total investment in agriculture was 5.8 billion yuan; but in 1986 it declined to about 3.5 billion yuan.[104] Realizing the difficulties in boosting grain production, the State Planning Commission revealed, in its draft 1990 plan to the NPC, a decision to invest an additional 1 billion yuan ($212 million) in agriculture, with most of the investment funds earmarked for irrigation facilities and grain and cotton production.[105] Agricultural investment loans and credit have been one of the hardest hit sectors since June 1989 due to the fact that overseas lending to Chinese agriculture had been suspended and delayed as a result of economic sanctions in reaction to the Tiananmen crackdown.

Importation of needed grain from abroad involves at least one major problem: China's foreign indebtedness and government deficit. In 1989, a good harvest year, grain imports reached almost 15 million tons. For 1990 the government tried to reduce grain imports—principally from Australia, Canada, the European Economic Community (EEC) group, and the United States.

Even if these difficulties in China's rural economy could be solved, either wholly or partially, grain production would still lag behind unless there is price reform in the government purchasing system. Grain purchasing by the government is operating on the old system of low administering price, currently at the 1989 level, rather than the market price for what is produced under state quotas. This policy provides little incentive for the peasants to grow grain, since other production costs such as fertilizer and pesticides have gone up many times. On top of the state-administered low price for grain are the unpaid debts local purchasing authorities owe to the peasants for "contracted purchases." The local authorities' inability to honor debts for purchases from the peasants is a direct result of the center-imposed austerity program over state funds that are made available to local authorities. The consequence is more discontent in the countryside.

After initial gains in the reform decade, since 1989 the gap in income between coastal urban areas and the hinterland has widened considerably. In 1984, as reported in one study, the rural-urban income ratio was 1 to 1.85, but in recent years the ratio has reached the prereform level of 1 to 2.[106] Average annual income for peasants was $137 in 1992 as compared with an average annual urban income of $313. A farm hand in 1995 could be expected to earn annually $106 on the land, $262 in a village enterprise or factory, or he could opt for a city job for $419.[107]

A recent study has shown that rural reform and industrialization (as described earlier) have improved the livelihood of the countryside. Production by rural factories or industries now account for one-third of China's total gross domestic product. Jean C.

Oi has labeled this recent rural development "local state corporatism," an "institutional foundation" for rural reform, with local officials in rural areas playing a leading role.[108]

The 1992 IOU Crisis. The peasants have been burdened by local taxes and fees and have faced the constant problem of the local governments' inability to pay cash—they have been paid with government IOUs which are honored slowly. Reports of peasant uprisings have become more frequent—a matter of concern for a party which came into power through the support of peasants. The issuance of promissory notes, the IOUs, came as a result of the change from uniform procurement for peasants' produce to a system of fixed procurement contracts with the peasants, a significant aspect of rural reform in the 1980s.[109] As a means of payment for contracted purchases, procurement agencies issued these promissory notes to supplement their working capital by borrowing. In a sense, this issuance of IOUs to peasants for contracted purchases by the purchasing agencies and wholesalers has been described as a form of "institutional corruption."

A central party-government decision was made in April 1997 to reduce the burden on peasants by demanding no new taxes be levied on them and by prohibiting "rampant unlawful charges" by local authorities. Under this central directive peasants now have the right to turn down illegal charges and take their cases to local courts.

It seems clear that unless the government can lighten the burden on peasants, unrest in the countryside, which has become increasingly recurrent, may trouble the regime in the years to come. Ironically, it was with the support of the peasantry that the CCP came to power a half-century ago.

URBAN REFORM: MEANING AND PROBLEMS

The average annual rate of growth for industrial production from 1953 to 1974 has been estimated at a very respectable rate of about 11 percent. The performance from 1975 to 1977 was placed at a slightly lower rate, between 9 and 10 percent per year.[110] The official Chinese estimate put the annual growth rate from 1966 to 1977 at 12 percent.[111] In his presentation of the Sixth Five-Year Plan (from 1981 to 1985) to the NPC, Premier Zhao proposed a lower growth rate for industrial production than had existed during the previous twenty-eight years.[112] He pointed out candidly that although the growth rate for industrial output was not low in the past, the economic results—meaning quality, variety, and design of industrial products—had been "very poor." In the Sixth Five-Year Plan, he demanded better economic results. Before we discuss recent attempts to introduce reforms into the industrial system, it will be necessary to review very briefly some of the features of China's industrial system that made it possible for the nation to achieve a 10 to 11 percent average annual increase.

What were the key features of the Chinese industrial system? One obvious factor was the nationalization of basic industries. State ownership of all large enterprises since 1956 had enabled the state not only to establish a centralized budget process but also to reinvest a sizable share of earnings in new plants and equipment for increases in production. One specialist on the Chinese economy pointed out that by the end of the First Five-Year Plan, 75 percent of state revenues came from the earnings of state-owned enterprises, and that state revenues constituted one-third of China's national income.[113] Closely related to the capacity for reinvestment was the policy of keeping industrial wages at low levels; income not distributed to the workers could be reinvested.

Another key factor was the initial strategy of placing emphasis on the development of heavy industries, particularly machine tool factories and iron and steel plants. Iron and steel production remains the key to the future growth of China's industries.[114] Steel plants are located strategically in eight major centers, with the largest at Anshan in the northeast, producing about 25 percent of the total national output. During the 1980s a new steel plant, the Baoshan complex, was added to the Shanghai industrial region (with loans from Japan); there is also the Wuhan steel complex in central China. The nation now needs new mines for both coal and iron to feed the steel furnaces. In addition, efficient coal- and iron-mining equipment will have to be imported from abroad in order to boost production. Modern large-scale blast furnaces are needed. Most of the furnaces in use in 1978 were built by the Soviets in the 1950s.

Finally, emphasis on the development of a large number of medium-and small-scale, labor-intensive industries has been a major factor in the rapid gains in industrial production. These decentralized, relatively small enterprises take advantage of the abundance of labor in rural areas, using a minimum of capital goods, and thus freeing investment for heavy industry. The policy of "walking on two legs" therefore develops simultaneously heavy industry, which is capital-intensive and centralized, and medium to small industry, which is labor-intensive and decentralized. The small industries, with employment ranging from 15 to 600, were owned by either the state, the county, or the communes.[115] Many of the small- and medium-sized industries, such as cement, brick, fertilizer, and farm machinery plants, are linked to agricultural production. The importance of small-scale industries in rural communes can be illustrated by the following cycle of development: Annual rainfall must be caught by dams and reservoirs, which are constructed with cement; with the availability of water for irrigation of the fields, more chemical fertilizer is needed to produce a higher yield of crops; with the prospect of a higher yield, agricultural machinery, such as tractors, harvesters, and water pumps, is needed. In one year, 54 percent of China's synthetic ammonia was produced by about 1,000 small fertilizer plants.[116] The United States delegation on small-scale industry, which visited China in 1975, pointed out that these small-scale industries save time in construction, solve the problem of limited transport facilities for rural areas, and allow for the exploitation of available local resources.[117] These small-scale industries in rural areas also have the ideological justification of removing the urban–rural dichotomy.

"Socialism with Chinese Characteristics"

Following on the heels of the emerging success in rural reform, the party authorized in the fall of 1984 a comprehensive set of directives for reform in the economic structure, known as urban reform.[118] The document on urban reform has been described as "socialism with Chinese characteristics."[119]

We may begin the discussion on urban reform by asking the following questions. Why urban reform? What were areas of concern for the party in October 1984? What problems were created as a result of urban reform? And finally, what are the political and economic implications of urban reform?

The party's 1984 document on urban reform called for a major overhaul of China's state-owned enterprises in urban areas. The reform was deemed necessary because of inherent defects in state-owned urban enterprises: the lack of distinction between governmental functions and enterprise management, and the rigid bureaucratic control exercised by the state over these enterprises. Further, market forces were seen as a means to stimulate worker initiative and enthusiasm. As a first step leading toward enterprise autonomy, the number of products regulated by centralized planning was reduced from 120 to 30. In other words, mandatory planning was retained for certain key products and resources. "Guided planning" still applied to other products and economic activities. Under "guided planning," market forces are permitted to operate for the production of minor industrial and consumer goods. Similarly, lesser industrial raw material and producer goods of local importance are permitted to be exchanged on the market.

Urban Reform—What Does It Mean?

A priority item for reform, according to the 1984 party document, was to invigorate the state-owned enterprises (numbering about 400,000 with a total labor force of more than 100 million) by separating the ownership from the operational functions. Instead of exercising "excessive and rigid control," the party document said, a state-owned enterprise "should be truly made a relatively independent economic entity." This meant that such enterprises must operate and manage their own affairs, assume responsibility for their own profits and losses, and develop themselves as "legal persons with certain rights and duties."[120] The party decision called for the factory managers to assume "full responsibility" and the party leaders in factories and service enterprises to "provide active support," without interference, to managers so as to establish unified direction in production and operation.[121] This meant that factory managers must have the right to determine matters such as job description and performance for workers as well as the right to set wages and bonuses. Full responsibility also implied that managers must be responsible for profit and loss. As a departure from previous reforms, the October 1984 urban reform advocated the practice of profit retention. In the past, profits from state-owned enterprises had to be returned to the state treasury. The state, then, reallocated these funds as supplies and resources needed for production according to the state plan.

Closely related to the reform in managerial autonomy was the introduction of the industrial contract responsibility system. Under the factory responsibility system, the workers and the factory director sign a contract with the state obligating them to turn over "a certain amount of taxes and profits to the state" and allowing them to keep for their own use "any or almost any amount above the set quota." However, they must make up any amount below the quota.[122] By 1986, 9,270 larger state-owned industrial enterprises, or about 75 percent of a total of 12,380, had introduced the contract system. Under the system, the most qualified directors for the enterprises are selected competitively through public bidding. The ultimate objective of the industrial contract system is to enable each state-owned large enterprise to "either turn out cheap commodities of good quality or lag behind and be eliminated."[123] The 1984 party document recommended, based on selective experiments over the previous few years, the formation of "diverse economic forms" in the cities and "other diverse and flexible forms of cooperative management and economic associations among the state, collective and individual sectors of the economy." The party document then suggested that the state have collectives of individuals learn or run them on a contract basis, by relying on "voluntary participation and mutual benefit."[124] In a sense this was nothing new, because the mixture of public and private enterprises had been in operation since the early 1950s.[125] What was new was the scope of enterprise ownership reform. Between 1985 and 1987, all small-sized state-owned enterprises with fixed assets of less than 1.5 million yuan (about $400,000)—mostly retail service, repair, and catering businesses—were to be leased out under contract to individuals or cooperatives for a period of five years. These arrangements were to be managed independently without state supervision, provided rent and taxes were paid to the state treasury. These new arrangements, according to one estimate, accounted for more than half of the value of total gross industrial output in China in 1985.[126]

Existing large-scale state-owned enterprises not engaged in vital productive activities could voluntarily become joint stock companies with limited liability.[127] New companies thus formed became shareholding enterprises "with stocks purchased by workers and individuals outside the enterprises."[128] In the place of the heavy-handed government-party management style, a board of directors was to assume the overall management policies for the new shareholding enterprises. (It should be noted that the government retained 51 percent of the stock, or the controlling shares, for these large-scale enterprises.) The arrangement also applied to joint ventures with participation from foreign investors. Members of the boards of directors could be shareholding or nonshareholding, with the latter elected by and representing the interests of the workers and small individual shareholders.

Urban enterprise reform, in effect, created a "two-tier ownership" structure: large and key enterprises with their controlled subsidiaries as industrial combines engaged in high-tech development; and numerous small enterprises, cooperatives, and individual enterprises with mixed ownership devoted to the processing of farm and sideline production and improvement of services in both urban and rural areas. One immediate and tangible result of workers owning shares in the enterprises was increased initiative and productivity resulting from the pride of ownership and an incentive to be efficient.[129]

Urban Reform: Problems

One immediate result of urban reform was a rapid increase in output: a 23 percent growth rate for the first quarter of 1985 marked China as one of the world's overheated economies. Local authorities accumulated fixed assets by investing in plants, machinery, and other capital goods. This led to the reinstitution of administrative controls over credits and the money supply. By July 1986 the central government had to issue a new set of regulations to monitor fixed asset investment and placed all capital construction plans under state supervision.

Urban households immediately experienced the effect of price decontrol: Food prices rose by as much as 37 percent in 1985. The official inflation rate was put at 6 percent in 1985, but the actual inflation rate was at least 20 percent for retail goods in urban areas. The authorities had not been able to devise a workable mechanism to prevent inflation for decontrolled prices, and soon it became necessary to reinstitute price controls for vegetables by placing a ceiling on their market prices. Then by January 1988 price ceilings were set for oil, gas, electricity, steel, timber, coal, and other raw materials.

Decentralization and decontrol under urban reform did not curb the growth of bureaucratic power and prerogatives. For more than thirty years, China had operated under a rigid system of centralized control. The party cadres, who held the decision-making power, had become a special privileged class. Reform in the urban areas yielded two conflicting trends. One was resistance, or foot-dragging, by the cadres against introduction of the market mechanism called for by the urban reform. Jan Prybyla has pointed out that "marketization," in fact, threatened the bureaucracy's role as planners and supervisors.[130] At the same time, bureaucrats in the cadre system were the ultimate survivors. They had access to both information and power. Therefore, they were in a position to exploit the new circumstances to enrich themselves. Soon they had transformed their position and seized the unique opportunities made available to form instant "briefcase companies" (these were bureaucratic entities organized overnight by the cadres who became the new owners of enterprises). Many of these bureaucrat-entrepreneurs now behaved "like capitalists" and committed economic crimes, such as black-marketeering, embezzling public funds or resources, and "lining their own pockets."[131]

While the 1984 party document mandated the party secretaries to gradually turn over managerial authority in the factories to plant managers (or directors), in reality party secretaries were unable to "break their habit" of making decisions in the plant. Often a factory director was not sure of his power vis-à-vis the party secretary's prerogatives.[132] Party committees in factories could still institute proceedings to overrule a factory manager's decisions by appealing to a higher party organization.[133] Then the turmoil caused by the 1986–87 student demonstrations provided the occasion for the orthodox hard-liners to launch an attack against the pragmatic reformers. A set of new regulations on the factory responsibility system was announced.[134] The decision-making power in the factory was to be in the hands of the workers' congresses under the overall control of the All-China Federation of Trade Unions. Now it was the workers' congress, not the factory manager or party secretary, who had the right to adjust plans and wages, and to provide incentives and punishment leading up to dismissal, including the right to dismiss the factory manager. Factory managers could be appointed, elected by the workers, or recruited through open advertisement. In August 1987, it was reported that the manager responsibility system had been instituted in more than 30,000, or over 7.5 percent, of the 400,000 state-owned industrial enterprises.[135] Then, finally, in January 1988, after nine years of delay, the enterprise reform law was approved by the Standing Committee of the NPC for ratification. The new law would, in theory, grant power to the factory manager.

This change meant there must be a separation of party from managerial function—in other words, party cadres would no longer be in the dominant position in factory management. For a while the new arrangement permitted close "consultation" between the plant's professional managerial staff and the party cadres, with the former responsible for day-to-day management. However, as pointed out by Andrew G. Walder, in most cases the professional managerial staff were members of the party; and too often the enterprise directors served concurrently as party deputy secretaries in the plant.[136] Thus, Andrew Walder maintained that unless there were some "fundamental changes" in the structure of party organizations, the social-political community which existed within the enterprise, there would not be any "decisive change" in managerial behavior.[137]

Reform in the Management System[138]

Managerial reform calls for the development of effective intermediate and lower-level leadership to implement the plans for modernization. This factor will be influenced or shaped to a large extent by the unity and cohesiveness at the top levels of leadership. Closely related to the development of effective leadership is the urgent need to acquire managerial skills in the industrial and agricultural sectors. While the American business community is beginning to unlock the secrets of Japanese management success,[139] the Chinese economy is characterized by inefficiency, waste, and poor management. We have mentioned earlier that corrective measures were introduced in order to make the Chinese economic system more efficient and productive, but a great deal still needs to be done to improve management techniques at the enterprise level.

Several years ago Sir Yue-Kong Pao, a Hong Kong-based shipping tycoon, complained that when he cabled Beijing on business matters, it usually took three to five days to get someone to reply. When he made a long-distance telephone call to Beijing, he found that no one seemed to be responsible for making any decisions. The problem here is that the Chinese management executive does not behave as a businessperson normally behaves elsewhere in the world. A Chinese management executive typically acts like a bureaucrat. Management decisions are made vertically. Clearance is required in the bureaucratic hierarchy before a decision can be made. There is also a tendency in Chinese bureaucratic management to place a high value on conformity.[140] The end result has been that no one wants to take a different approach or be innovative. Thus, the prevailing climate in Chinese organizations is one of "indifference or irrelevance."[141] Worse still, Chinese management executives make no decisions, nor do they take any risks at all.

A further problem is that workers in a Chinese factory are typically inexperienced and lack the skill required to do their jobs adequately.[142] This general lack of skill and experience extends to managers as well.[143] The concept of an unbroken "iron rice bowl" (job security) is so deeply implanted in the minds of Chinese workers that it is difficult to introduce any system of evaluation of job performance. The Chinese economist Xue Muqiao urged that the state institute "a system of examination, appraisal and promotion and transfer" for industrial workers as a basic management reform.[144] He also asked that incompetent workers be dismissed, a management right that most Chinese enterprises are very reluctant to exercise.

In 1980 the State Council issued a set of guidelines to allow enterprises to experiment with self-management. The guidelines, among other things, specified (1) that the type of merchandise produced must meet market demands; (2) that certain levels of profits must be retained for expansion and/or improvement of plant facilities; and (3) that enterprises must recruit their own workers.[145] Effective implementation of these reform measures, however, depended on the adoption of modern management techniques and some fundamental changes in the existing personnel system. (Some provinces, such as Guangdong, had formed business management associations to study management skills, with a view toward improving provincial enterprise management.)[146] In short, managerial training for cadres in industry was urgently needed. In addition, China's pragmatic leaders must now find ways to improve work efficiency by solving such problems as overstaffing, bureaucratic red tape, and endless meetings.

The need for managerial training is best demonstrated by the fact that about two-thirds of China's industrial managers have a very low level of educational attainment, not more than the equivalent of a secondary school education in America.[147] Only very recently have the Chinese begun to send cadres abroad for training in modern managerial skills. Management training under the State Economic Commission has involved only a small fraction of some nine million state cadres.[148] A German managerial consultant to

China has suggested that a center for technical training and professional ethics education be established by every factory to upgrade quality control and reduce the waste of resources by factory workers.[149] The German consultant found it intolerable that a deputy factory director received only half of the wage paid to a factory storehouse keeper because the latter had longer service.[150]

STATE-OWNED ENTERPRISES: REFORM OR PRIVATIZATION?

In 1999 there were approximately over 100,000 large and medium-sized State-Owned Enterprises, known as SOEs, such as the giant Capital Iron and Steel Mill or the Shanghai No. 2 Cotton Mill, employing a total of 108 million, or about three of every four urban workers. They dominate basic industries in China which engage in the production of energy, electricity, heavy machinery, iron, steel, chemicals, high technology, and transportation. Roughly 60 percent of the state's revenue comes from these state-owned enterprises. Many of these enterprises were originally built with Soviet aid in the 1950s and their machinery has become obsolete. For decades they operated under tight state controls and with generous government subsidies. These large-scale state-owned enterprises in China are going through a difficult time. Some state-owned firms are in deep financial trouble because they no longer produce goods that people want, or "they make too much of what people don't want."[151] Their goods are stockpiled in warehouses, and about 40 percent of these state-owned enterprises are in debt—estimated at U.S.$30–50 billion. As the market economy grew under Deng's reform, state-owned enterprises simply failed to keep up or operate competitively. In recent years some small state-owned enterprises have been leased, merged, or sold since 1994—a sort of limited privatization in the view of one analyst.[152] Others thought of selling out to foreign investors.[153] But as of 1995, about 50 percent of these state-owned enterprises were operating under loss, while their total share of China's gross domestic product were just short of 60 percent.[154]

The problems of the state-owned enterprises have been a serious concern for China's top leaders for some years. On July 24, 1992, the State Council enacted a set of management regulations for the "transformation" of state-owned enterprises which included the power and right (1) to become independent producers and managers, and the power to sign contracts with customers; (2) to set prices on what they produce; (3) to use their reserve funds for investment purposes; (4) to hire and fire workers under the personnel contract system; and (5) to set wages and bonus distribution.[155] The overall purpose of the 1992 management regulation for state-owned enterprises was to make it possible for them to compete in the market economy. The new management regulation was also intended to help solve the problems of "overstaffing, low efficiency and poor economic performance."[156] In many respects large state-owned enterprises represent "one of the most important Communist symbols left" in China, or simply "a cancer in the economy."[157]

As pointed out by former Premier Li Peng in his March 1997 report on the work of the government to the Fifth Session of the Eighth NPC, the plight of China's state-owned enterprises continued to occupy the attention of the top leaders. Li Peng cited in his report that Jiang Zemin, the party's chief, viewed the survival of the state-owned enterprises not only as "a major economic issue," but also "a major political issue" for the "destiny of the socialist system."[158] Li Peng offered six instructional guides for reorganizing and upgrading the management of state-owned enterprises. First, as many as 511 large state-owned enterprises, half of some one thousand considered the backbone of China's national economy, were to receive bank credits or financial support with close supervision by the bank on the use of these credits. Thus, what has been done by the central government is to continue the financial bailout for these failed large-scale state-owned enterprises. Second, the central government wanted to step up the process of autonomy for small state-owned enterprises, now managed by local governments, by allowing these firms to reorganize through merger, joint stock partnerships with employees, or sell-off. The new joint stock companies would have, as has been experimented with in some areas in recent years, limited liability.[159] New companies thus formed became shareholding enterprises "with stocks purchased by workers and individuals outside the enterprises."[160] In place of the heavy-handed government-party management style, a board of directors was to assume the overall management policies for the new shareholding enterprises. (It should be noted that the government retained 51 percent of the stock, or the controlling shares, for these "privatized" large-scale enterprises.) The arrangement also applied to joint ventures with participation from foreign investors. Members of the boards of directors could be shareholding or non-shareholding, the latter elected by and representing the interests of the workers and small individual shareholders.

Third, there are attempts now being made not only to encourage the merger of state-owned enterprises in some 110 cities, but also to restructure these firms through bankruptcy proceedings which would make proper arrangements for repaying debts and for workers. Former Vice-Premier, now Premier Zhu Rongji disclosed in March 1997 to the Qinghai delegates to the NPC that the State Council had decided to set aside 30 billion yuan in 1997 to establish a reserve fund for mergers and bankruptcies of state-owned enterprises.[161] Fourth, permission would be extended for some large state-owned enterprises or groups to raise funds by issuing stocks and convertible bonds. Fifth, more emphasis would be placed on "scientific management" of the enterprises in production, technology, product quality, and marketing. And, finally, former Premier Li Peng called on the central and local governments to make efforts toward eliminating losses in state-owned enterprises which had experienced "big losses" in the textile, coal, machinery, forestry, and military industries.

For many of these large state-owned enterprises management reform has produced some side effects—for example, the spawning of multitier subsidiaries whose managers either have mismanaged or engaged in corruptive practices. Too often there has been "overconcentration of power" in the hands of the managers in state-owned enterprises and their subsidiaries which has produced managerial "theft" on a large scale because of the "lack of internal control" or audit.[162] To correct this mismanagement the state has reinstituted political control by setting up the "party committee" made up of the managers, workers and experts in each of these state enterprises for the purpose of major managerial decision making.[163] (In the reform decade from 1982–92, the state lost U.S.$87 billion in assets caused by mismanagement and "managerial theft" in state-owned enterprises.)[164] The restoration of the "party presence" in these enterprises demonstrates the severity of the managerial problems.

Soon after Deng's death party chief Jiang Zemin and his close advisers were discussing the possibility of reforming the ailing state-owned enterprises by privatization, a word or concept hitherto not openly used by top leaders. The idea of reorganizing the state-owned enterprises as private enterprises became official at the party's Fifteenth Congress held in the fall of 1997. President Jiang Zemin told the delegates to the Fifteenth Party Congress that the state must convert large and medium-sized state-owned enterprises into "standard corporations" with clearly defined ownership, power, and separation of enterprise from administration so that they would become "corporate entities and competitors" to the market.[165]

The target has been set for 1999–2002 for real progress in terms of reform in the troubled State-Owned Enterprises (SOEs)—a target period set by the State Economic and Trade Commission as reported to the 1999 Spring Session of the National People's Congress.[166] As described by the state agency overseeing SOE reform, about half of the 6,000 large and medium-sized enterprises had made some progress in 1998–1999 by decreasing monetary losses in their operations.[167] Reforms undertaken include: reducing the number of state-owned firms in terms of size and number to only 512 large ones through bankruptcy and merger; imposing the practices of modern managerial techniques so that their performance would be up to standard; and reducing or eliminating the social welfare burden of these firms.

Then the 1999 Fall Session of the party's Central Committee plenum adopted several basic objectives or principles for SOE reform:[168] develop many forms of ownership alongside public or state ownership; devote efforts to improving overall quality of these firms in order to meet the demands of a market economy; stress enterprise management efficiency; and encourage mergers and downsizing staff. An interesting point was made in the party Central Committee decision about SOEs: the recommendation for development of "a unified national accounting system," which would provide "timely compiled charts of assets and debts, losses and profits, and cash flow" in order to reveal the true state of these enterprises.[169] In other words, there may be more than one-third (2,346) of some 7,600 large and medium-sized state-owned firms in China reported to have been operating at a loss.

Privatizing SOEs as a Key to Enterprise Reform.   The 1997 Fifteenth Party Congress endorsed a program for reform of SOEs, which are often called the shareholding enterprises or *gufenzhi*, in which private individuals can purchase shares as part owners of the state enterprises. Their origin came in 1983–84 when rural peasants were allowed to invest in joint-stock township and village enterprises. In 1994 the National People's Congress enacted the Company Law for uniform regulation of shareholder enterprises, for by then the growth of such entities had risen from 2,580 to 7,760.[170] In 1997 shareholder enterprises became the government's mainstream reform program. Note that the Chinese government does not feel comfortable describing these growing shareholding enterprises as privatization, as seen from the leadership's debate that touches on the central thesis in Marxian ideology.[171]

CHINA'S ECONOMIC REFORM AND MODERNIZATION: DENG'S LEGACY

Deng Xiaoping's ideas and policies on economic reform during 1978–97 have been collectively named the "Theory of Deng" or "Dengism." Basically, this is a collection of Deng's remarks concerning the building of socialism with Chinese characteristics that include market-style reforms and an open door to foreign investment. At the Fourteenth Party Congress, held in October 1992, Deng's ideas and policies on reform were elevated to the status of a theory: "Comrade Deng Xiaoping is the chief architect of our socialist reform, of the open door policy and of the modernization program."[172] Deng's theory is now regarded as "the product of the integration of the universal principle of Marxism-Leninism with the practice of the Chinese Second Revolution—economic construction, reform and opening to the outside world."[173] Reminiscent of the adulation for Mao, Deng was cited no fewer than thirteen times in Jiang Zemin's report to the party congress in 1992; an annotated dictionary, the *Thought of Deng Xiaoping*, has been published containing some 2,000 of Deng's speeches.

Finally, Deng's theory was enshrined by the Eighth NPC, held March 15–31, 1993, which amended Article 15 of the 1982 state constitution by deleting the requirement for state enterprises to fulfill their obligations under the state plan. Words in the constitution that referred to a planned economy have been replaced by the words "socialist market economy." In short, Deng's market reform for China's economy has won the final battle over the hard-liners. Thus, as Deng Xiaoping approached his final years, he saw to it that market reform was firmly established as China's road to modernization.

China in 1992–93 was in the midst of a booming economy. In 1992 its domestic growth product (minus foreign investment) was over 12 percent. By 1993 it had become evident that China must once again apply the brakes to its fast-growing economy as banks began to face shortages of cash and inflation soared to more than 20–30 percent in most urban areas. Drastic measures had to be taken such as raising interest rates, reducing government operations by 20 percent, curbing bank lending for speculative investments, cutting down infrastructure spending, and calling a temporary halt to price decontrol. Some of these measures were recommended by the World Bank in its August 1993 report on China. The International Monetary Fund reported in the spring of 1993 that the Chinese economy had become the third largest in the world, next only to the United States and Japan, based on a new method of comparing a country's goods and services in terms of purchasing power instead of as compared with some other nation's currency.[174] By this new measure, China in 1992 produced $1.7 trillion in goods and services instead of $400 billion.[175] At any rate, China experienced continued economic growth with the gross domestic product expected to increase to close to 10 percent for 1996.[176] (However, China's continued economic growth rate may be affected by the economic turmoil that has occurred in several parts of Asia in 1997–1998. As some of the Asian economies required International Monetary Fund's rescue and their currencies devalued, it may be only a matter of time for China too to make the necessary currency adjustment by devaluation in order to compete with other Asian countries in the export trade.) In this chapter we have tried to present a picture of China's efforts to modernize after 1949, with emphasis on the post-Mao era. Modernization means industrialization and economic growth, supported and strengthened by a formula of universal education that emphasizes the learning of modern science and technology. The politics of modernization in China since 1949 has focused primarily, although not exclusively, on how China can be transformed into an industrialized nation, equal to other nations that are in the forefront of technological development. Because of the lack of unity among the leaders in answering this question, policies and programs for modernization have vacillated between the revolutionary mass mobilization model and the professional and orderly development model. The continuous conflict and ambivalence toward these strategies for modernization dominated the flow of Chinese politics during the past several decades. Beneath the struggle, however, is the pervasive feeling in Chinese society and among peoples of all developing nations that they want a better way of life in terms of both moral and material well-being and that this can come about only through the continuous acquisition of knowledge in science and technology.

Will China be able to achieve its goal of modernization? The answer rests on a number of factors. One is the ability of the leaders to maintain unity and some degree of cohesiveness so as to provide the needed political stability and climate for orderly development. This is extremely crucial as the paramount leader, Deng, has gone and his successor Jiang Zemin must be able to repel his attackers and challengers within the party and keep up the momentum for economic reform. As Joseph Tewsmith has pointed out, the "economic debate in China must be understood in the context of power struggle and political debate or conflict."[177] Jiang's tenancy as the undisputed leader rests to a large measure on his ability to manage the economy well and keep the economic reform from faltering. China's political stability is attainable in the years after Deng's death if there is continued economic growth, which in turn is dependent on China's willingness to keep her doors open to trade with other nations of the world.

Political stability also means control and prevention of corruption in the officialdom. In fact, the party image has declined in recent years to the extent that some questions have been raised about the party's survival and legitimacy to rule.

To some observers China's continued economic growth and future prosperity may rest squarely on its ability to control its population growth in the decades to come. It is perhaps useful to devote some space in this concluding section about China's modernization to the trend and prospects of population control.

Population Control.[178]   As expected by many demographers, the July 1982 national census showed that China's total population was over one billion, with an annual growth rate of 1.5 percent. Of the total, 51.5 percent were male, and 48.5 percent were female. The far-ranging implication of this huge population for China's economic development is quite obvious. Premier Zhao told the 1982 NPC that "the execution of our national economic plan and the improvement of the people's living standards will be adversely affected" if population growth is not controlled.[179] This was certainly a most candid admission by a top Chinese leader that the Malthusian theory of population was valid—a theory that Mao Zedong never accepted as applicable to a socialist China. Premier Zhao directed that population growth be kept below 1.3 percent per annum, so that China's total population would not exceed 1.06 billion by 1985.[180]

How can China's population explosion be controlled? During the 1970s the much-publicized measure for population control was delayed marriage for the young. In addition, clinics were permitted to provide abortion services. Some birth control devices were disseminated in factories. Then, in 1977, the target became one child per family. As the 1982 census demonstrated, these measures were not able to check the enormous population growth. A major factor was the persistence of the traditional preference among the rural population for male offspring. While female infanticide was still an accepted practice in some rural areas, Premier Zhao condemned the practice.[181] The difficulty in controlling population growth was aggravated by the fact that 62 percent of the population in 1982 was under 35 years of age. As young people reach the age of marriage and childbearing, the total number of births can be expected to rise dramatically—unless strict control measures are imposed. So far, the one-child-per-couple policy has been observed widely only in the urban areas. Under this policy the state imposes punitive measures, such as a 2 percent reduction in salary, if a couple refuses abortion of their second child. Following the birth of the second child, a flat 15 percent salary reduction is imposed on the parents until the child has reached the age of seven. In urban areas couples have been encouraged to sign contracts pledging a one-child family in order to receive better and more spacious housing.[182] Obtaining general acceptance of the one-child-per-family policy among the peasants in rural China remains a Herculean task involving education, persuasion, and strong pressure from the state. Such efforts must be made, however, if China is to defuse its population bomb.

Unfortunately, resistance to the one-child family policy has been particularly prevalent in rural areas. There also have been "exceptions" granted in response either to "local conditions" or "hardships."[183] Exemptions from the policy usually have been granted to sparsely populated areas or in cases where the first child was a girl. The most common complaint in rural areas against the harshness of the one-child family policy is the desire for a son. Under rural reform, a one-child family pledge has been incorporated into household contracts.[184] But the desire for a son is as strong as ever.

Some final comments about the single-child policy are in order. The one-child family policy is not national. Two obvious reasons serve to explain why no national law has been enacted to restrict family size to only one child: its controversial nature, and the possible effect on recruitment for the military, which traditionally exempted one-child families.[185] The single-child family policy is a temporary measure and is to remain in effect until the year 2000, when the Chinese population is expected to be 1.2 billion.[186] China was able to hold total population for the first half of the 1980s to a relatively stable level,[187] but by 1987 projections of demographic figures indicated a rising rate of growth. And if the birth rate is maintained at more than 1.5 or up to 2.0 percent, China will have a population of two billion by the year 2030.[188]

A national door-to-door census was taken in 1990; the result showed China's total population to be 1.13 billion. If the present trend of increasing population continues, there will be a growth of about 17 million more people each year, or close to two billion by the year 2035. Of more significance, a large component of China's population will be 65 and over, possibly 16 to 19 percent of the total by the year 2035.[189] This would mean further financial burden on families in providing support for their aging parents. The 12.45 percent increase in population since 1982 also raised doubt about the effectiveness of the one-child family policy.

A Chinese statistical report in 1993 indicated a drop in the birth rate from 21.1 per 1,000 population in 1987 to 18.2 in 1992.[190] Now Chinese women are estimated to have an average of 1.8 or 1.9 children in a lifetime, the same as in the United States.[191] A new population policy calls for compulsory sterilization in the villages for those childbearing women who have already borne children. Chinese public health officials have also prepared new legislation—the Draft Law on Eugenics and Health Protection—for the NPC to ratify in 1994. Though denied by officials, the proposed law advocates forced abortion and sterilization to prevent "inferior quality" births.[192]

However, the government's policy on one-child per family has not been working in rural areas. There have been ways by which peasant households have evaded the registration system.[193] Peasants choose to leave their homes by becoming members of the "floating" or migrant population (estimated to be over 100 million) roaming in the cities;

or, for the purpose of evasion, peasants simply smuggle their children to relatives living elsewhere. As the number of fertile women increased to 350 million by year 2000, it is expected that there would be 23 million newborns each year for the next decade, total population may reach to 1.6 billion by 2010.

Unintended Consequences of Reform

Finally, economic reform in China has produced some unintended consequences. One is the development of a large number of "nongovernmental associations" which serve, as "bridges," or as "intermediaries between the state and diverse constituencies" representing various civil groups in private businesses, social-cultural organizations and sports.[194] As reported by *China Daily,* as of 1993 there were some 1,400 registered with the central government; 19,600 registered at the provincial level; and a massive 160,000 registered at the county level.[195] At the invitation of the government these "civil associations" made input into or helped with implementation of government policies.[196] As interpreted by Ungar's case study, the existence of these civic associations was the result of a gradual "relaxation" of party control as economic reform intensified in the mid-1980s. The growth of these "civic associations" as examples of "state corporatist mechanisms" may impact the state-society relations in the years to come.

As discussed in our section on rural reform, the second unintended consequence of economic reform has been the development of multiple claims of ownership rights in the township-village enterprises by the local governments, the enterprise managers, and the rural workers in these industries, not to mention the state's ideological symbol of collective ownership of the land. This indicates that there is a need for clarification about the question of private ownership within the framework of collective (community) ownership.[197]

As the rural privately owned enterprises have expanded and grown, the power of control has shifted increasingly to local authorities—the village-township-county levels of government, instead of the central or provincial government as in the days of preeconomic reform. In 1978, state-owned enterprises produced about 78 percent of China's industrial production; as discussed earlier, as of 1993 their total share of production had decreased to 43 percent.[198] The privately owned enterprises and the collectives, plus others, have already produced a larger share of China's total industrial output to a combined total of 57 percent. What this means is that the central government has a declining influence over these privately owned enterprises.[199] This is not to say, as argued by David S. G. Goodman, that state control will disappear and that an "independent capitalism" will surface as private sectors in urban and rural areas expand.[200] What has taken place is the development of a new relationship in the urban areas between the party-state and private entrepreneurs is that the latter "cultivate good relationships with cadres in the state system" so as to allow "experimentation" to take place without interference from the former.[201]

NOTES

1. See *Beijing Review*, 38 (September 22, 1986), 5.
2. See *Beijing Review* (October 6–12, 1997), 21.
3. See Arthur G. Ashbrook, "China: Economic Overview, 1975," in *China: A Reassessment of the Economy*, Joint Economic Committee, U.S. Congress (Washington, D.C.: Government Printing Office, July 10, 1975), p. 24; and Jan S. Prybyla, "Some Economic Strengths and Weaknesses of the People's Republic of China," *Asian Survey*, 10, no. 12 (December 1977), 1122.
4. "Report on the Work of the Government," *Beijing Review*, 27 (July 6, 1979), 12–20; and *Far Eastern Economic Review* (October 5, 1979), 78–80.
5. See Lowell Dittmer, "China in 1981: Reform, Readjustment, Rectification," *Asian Survey*, 22, no. 2 (January 1982), 35.
6. These were the words used by Huang Hua, then minister for foreign affairs, in an interview in Ottawa, Canada. See Peter Stursberg, "Restructuring China Policy in the Wake of Chairman Mao," *Canadian Journal of World Affairs* (May–June 1981), 5.
7. "Further Economic Readjustment: A Break with 'Leftist' Thinking," *Beijing Review*, 12 (March 23, 1981), 27. Also see Xue Muqiao, *Current Problems of the Chinese Economy* (Beijing: The People's Publishers, 1980).
8. "Further Economic Readjustment," 28.
9. See Nai-Ruenn Chen, "China's Capital Construction: Current Retrenchment and Prospects for Foreign Participation," *China Under the Four Modernizations*, Part 2, pp. 50–52; and Richard Y.C. Yin, "China's Socialist Economy in Action: An Insider's View," *Journal of Northeast Asian Studies*, 1, no. 2 (June 1982), 97–98.
10. *Asiaweek,* February 20, 1981, p. 33.
11. Sidney Lens, "Private Enterprises in China," reprinted in *Honolulu Star-Bulletin,* October 1, 1981, p. A-19. Also see Takashi Oda, "Private Enterprise in China Fills the Gap," *Christian Science Monitor,* February 2, 1983, p. 6; and Bradley K. Martin, "Capitalism with a Chinese Flavor," *Baltimore Sun*, as reprinted in *Honolulu Sunday Star-Bulletin and Advertiser,* December 21, 1980, C-19. For 1983 figure see Robert Delfs, "Private Enterprise Without Capitalism Is China's Goal: An Incentive Socialism," *Far Eastern Economic Review* (April 28, 1983), 40. Also see *The New Yorker,* January 23, 1984, pp. 43–85.
12. *People's Daily,* January 9, 1983, p. 1. Also see *Takung Pao* (Hong Kong), June 2, 1983, p. 1.
13. *People's Daily,* January 9, 1983.
14. *Ming Pao Daily* (Hong Kong), August 17, 1980, p. 1.
15. See David Bonavia, "Peking Watch," in *China Trade Report* (August 1982), 2, and (February 1, 1981), 10; Zhu Minzhi and Zou Siguo, "Chen Yun on Planned Economy," *Beijing Review*, 12 (March 12, 1982), 12.
16. *China News Analysis*, vol. 1385, no.3; and Jan S. Prybyla, "China's Economic Experiment: Back from the Market," *Problems of Communism*, 38, no. 1 (January–February 1989), 3–4.
17. Prybyla, "China's Economic Experiment," 4. Also see his "Why China's Economic Reform," *Asian Survey*, 29, no. 11 (November 1989), 1017–32.
18. Prybyla, "China's Economic Experiment," 3. And also see Joseph Fewsmith, "Agricultural Crisis in the PRC," *Problems of Communism*, 37 no. 6 (November–December 1988), 78–93.
19. See Lowell Dittmer, "China in 1988: The Continued Dilemma of Socialist Reform," *Asian Survey*, 29, no. 1 (January 1989), 21.
20. Dittmer, "China in 1988," 22. Also see Li Peng's report on the work of the government in *Beijing Review* (April 16–22, 1990), ix.
21. Dittmer, "China in 1988," 24–25.
22. *Christian Science Monitor,* November 29, 1989, p. 8.
23. Ibid., p. 3.
24. *Far Eastern Economic Review* (July 9, 1990), 49.
25. Ibid.
26. *Wall Street Journal,* July 27, 1990; *Far Eastern Economic Review* (January 25, 1990), 46; and *New York Times,* October 28, 1989, p. 2.

27. *Wall Street Journal,* February 20, 1990, p. A-10.

28. *Wall Street Journal,* August 17, 1990, p. A-7B.

29. *Wall Street Journal,* March 15, 1990, p. A-11.

30. *Far Eastern Economic Review* (March 22, 1990), 51; and (April 5, 1990), 38.

31. *Wall Street Journal,* April 13, 1990, p. A-1.

32. Lincoln Kage, "Business as Usual," *Far Eastern Economic Review* (April 2, 1992), 63–64.

33. Lincoln Kage, "Bold Blueprint: Premier Stresses Economic Reform and Political Caution," *Far Eastern Economic Review* (March 25, 1993), 13.

34. "Head for Heights: Vice Premier Zhu Rongji Says Economic Reform Will Continue," interview with Dow Jones reporter in *Far Eastern Economic Review* (December 23, 1993), 28.

35. See Elizabeth J. Perry, "China in 1992: An Experiment in Neo-Authoritarianism," *Asian Survey* (January 1993), 15.

36. See Tsang Shu-ki and Cheng Yuk-shing, "China's Tax Reforms of 1994: Breakthrough or Compromise?" *Asian Survey* (September 1994), 769-788.

37. See David Bachman, "China in 1994: Making Time, Making Money," *Asian Survey* (January 1995), 41.

38. Li Peng, "Report on the Work of the Government," to the First Session of the Eighth NPC on March 15, 1993. See *Beijing Review* (April 12–18, 1993), x.

39. "China in 1996: Achievements, Assertiveness, Anxiety," *Asian Survey* (January 1997), 30–31.

40. *Beijing Review* (January 20–26, 1997), 4.

41. See *Beijing Review (January 17, 2000),* 5.

42. See Sumner J. LaCroix, Michael Plummer, Keun Lee, ed. *Emerging Patterns of East Asian Investment in China* (Armonk, N.Y.: M. E. Sharpe, 1995).

43. "Communiqué of the Third Plenary Session of the Eleventh Central Committee," *Beijing Review,* 10 (March 10, 1978), 12.

44. For the text of the document, see "Several Questions in Strengthening and Perfecting the Job-Responsibility System for Agricultural Production," *Issues and Studies,* 17, no. 5 (May 1981), 77–82. Also see "Rural Contract," *Beijing Review,* 45 (November 10, 1980) 5–6.

45. "A Programme for Current Agricultural Work," *Beijing Review,* 24 (June 14, 1982), 21.

46. See Graham E. Johnson, "The Production Responsibility System in Chinese Agriculture: Some Examples from Guangdong," *Pacific Affairs,* 55, no. 3 (Fall 1982), 430–51.

47. "Let Some Localities and Peasants Prosper First," *Beijing Review,* 3 (January 19, 1981), 19–22; "System of Responsibility in Agricultural Production," *Beijing Review,* 11 (March 16, 1981), 3–4; and "Small Plots for Private Use," *Beijing Review,* 26 (June 29, 1981), 3–4.

48. "System of Responsibility in Agricultural Production," 4.

49. Johnson, "Production Responsibility System," 451.

50. "Report on the Sixth Five-Year Plan," 33.

51. Y.Y. Kulh, "The Economies of the 'Second Land Reform' in China," *China Quarterly,* 101 (March 1985), 122–31. Also see Jonathan Unger, "The Decollectivization of the Chinese Countryside: A Survey of Twenty-Eight Villages," *Pacific Affairs,* 58, no. 4 (Winter 1985–86), 585–606.

52. For the text of the document see "Circular of the Central Committee of the CCP on Rural Work During 1984" see *China Quarterly,* 101 (March 1985), 132–42. Also see N. Lardy, "Agricultural Reform in China," *Journal of International Affairs,* 39 (Winter 1986), 97 and 99–100.

53. See Joseph Fewsmith, "Rural Reform in China: Stage Two," *Problems of Communism* (July–August 1985), 52–53 and *China Daily,* July 4, 1984, p. 1.

54. Fewsmith, "Rural Reform in China: Stage Two," 52. Also see Lardy, "Agricultural Reform in China," 99.

55. Ibid., 49.

56. See Kathleen Hartford, "Socialist Agriculture Is Dead; Long Live Socialist Agriculture; Organizational Transformations in Rural China," *China Quarterly,* No. 101 (March 1995), 45–46; and *Beijing Review,* 9 (February 27, 1984), 4.

57. Fewsmith, "Rural Reform in China: Stage Two," 52–53.

58. *Beijing Review,* 9 (February 27, 1984), 18.

59. Ibid.

60. See T. Bernstein, "Reforming Chinese Agriculture: The Consequences of Unanticipated Consequences," in *China Business Review,* May–April 1985, p. 46. Also see Fewsmith, "Rural Reform in China: Stage Two," 50.

61. Bernstein, "Reforming Chinese Agriculture" 52.
62. Unger, "Decollectivization of the Chinese Countryside," 594.
63. Ibid., 599.
64. Ibid., 600–601.
65. See "The Social Roots of China's Economic Development," *China Quarterly*, 144 (December 1995), 1013.
66. Ibid.
67. Ibid, 1019.
68. Chris Bramall, "Origins of the 'Agricultural Miracle:' Some Evidence from Sichuan," *China Quarterly*, 143 (September 1995), 731–55.
69. Xinhua news release, January 8, 1985, p. 1.
70. See Patrice de Beer, "A Factory in Every Village," in *The Guardian,* July 14, 1985, p. 13.
71. *Beijing Review*, 18 (April 30, 1984), 18. Lardy also provided the percentage figure of 30% shift of surplus labor to nonagricultural activities. See Lardy, "Agricultural Reform in China," *Journal of International Affairs*, 100.
72. *Beijing Review*, 47 (November 24, 1986), 16–18.
73. de Beer, "Factory in Every Village," 13; and *Beijing Review*, 47 (November 24, 1986), 18–19.
74. *Beijing Review* (January 6, 1986), 4.
75. Jean C. Oi, *Rural China Takes Off: Institutional Foundations of Economic Reform* (Berkeley: University of California Press, 1999).
76. Ibid., and *Far Eastern Economic Review* (December 5, 1985), 65.
77. See *Far Eastern Economic Review* (July 11, 1985), 57, and *Ta Kung Pao Weekly Supplement,* May 1, 1986, p. 6. Also see *Beijing Review*, 26 (June 30, 1986), 14–17.
78. Richard J. Latham, "The Implications of Rural Reforms for Grass-Roots Cadres," *The Political Economy of Reform in Post-Mao China*, 165. Also see John P. Burns, "Local Cadre Accommodation to the 'Responsibility System' in Rural China," *Pacific Affairs,* 58, no. 4 (Winter 1985–86), 607. Also see *China Daily,* January 16, 1986, p. 1.
79. Latham, "Implications of Rural Reforms for Grass-Roots Cadres," 168; and Burns, "Local Cadre Accommodation," 613.
80. *People's Daily,* April 22, 1982, p. 2.
81. Burns, "Local Cadre Accommodation," 614 and 617.
82. Jean C. Oi, "Commercializing China's Rural Cadres," *Problems of Communism* (September–October, 1986), 2.
83. Ibid., 10.
84. Ibid., 13.
85. See Jean C. Oi, "The Role of the Local State in China's Transitional Economy," *China Quarterly*, 144 (December 1995), 1138–39.
86. Ibid., 1138.
87. Ibid., 1148.
88. See Ann Scott Tyson and James L. Tyson, "Rural Engine Powers Market Reform," *Christian Science Monitor,* July 29, 1992, p. 9.
89. Ibid. Also see Christopher Findlay, Andrew Watson and Harry X. Wu, eds., *Rural Enterprises in China* (New York: St. Martin's Press, 1994).
90. See Elizabeth J. Perry, "Rural Collective Violence: The Fruits of Recent Reform," *The Political Economy of Reform in Post-Mao China*, pp. 175–92.
91. Ibid., p. 180.
92. Ibid.
93. Ibid., p. 183.
94. Ibid.
95. Bernstein, "Reforming Chinese Agriculture," 46–47.
96. "Transformation in the Countryside, Part I," *Beijing Review*, 9 (February 27, 1984), 9.
97. Ibid., 11. Also see Lardy, "Agricultural Reform in China," 101. For an overview of rural changes, see Kathleen Hartford and Steven M. Goldstein, eds., *Single Sparks: China's Rural Revolutions* (Armonk, N.Y.: M. E. Sharpe, 1989).
98. Chu-yuan Cheng, "China's Economy in Retrenchment," *Current History* (September 1990), 253.

99. *People's Daily,* May 18, 1987; and Vaclar Smil, "Feeding China's People," *Current History* (September 1998), 276–77.

100. See George P. Brown, "Arable Land Loss in Rural China," *Asian Survey* (October 1995), 924–27.

101. Ibid., 940. For a discussion of village leaders' decision-making role see Scott Rozelle, "Decision-making in China's Rural Economy: The Linkages between Village Leaders and Farm Households," *The China Quarterly*, no. 137 (March 1994), pp. 99–124.

102. *Far Eastern Economic Review* (August 30, 1990), 54.

103. Ibid., 55.

104. *China News Analysis*, 1401 (January 1, 1990), 5.

105. *Beijing Review* (April 2–8, 1990), 7.

106. See Zheng Yi, "The Perils Faced by Chinese Peasants," *China Focus*, 1, no. 3 (April 30, 1993), 1.

107. Figures are from "Down on China's Farms," editorial in *Wall Street Journal,* February 3, 1995, p. A-10.

108. Jean C. Oi, "Two Decades of Rural Reform in China: An Overview and Assessment," *China Quarterly*, no. 159 (September 1999), 630.

109. For a discussion on this topic see the unpublished article by Andrew Wedeman, delivered at the annual meeting of the Association for Asian Studies held in Honolulu, Hawaii, April 12, 1996, entitled "Stealing from the Farmers: Institutional Corruption and the 1992 IOU Crisis."

110. See "PRC Economic Performance in 1975," *Current Scene*, 14, no. 6 (June 1976), 1–14; and "The PRC Economy in 1976," *Current Scene*, 15, nos. 4 and 5 (April–May 1977), 1–10.

111. Kuo-feng, "Report on the Work of Government," 20.

112. "Report on the Sixth Five-Year Plan," 12.

113. Robert F. Dernberger, "Past Performance and Present State of China's Economy," in *China's Future: Foreign Policy and Economic Development in the Post-Mao Era*, ed. Allen S. Whiting and Robert F. Dernberger (New York: McGraw-Hill, 1977), pp. 95, 140.

114. For information on China's steel production, see Alfred H. Usack, Jr., and James D. Egan, "China's Iron and Steel Industry," in *China: Reassessment of the Economy*, pp. 264–88.

115. American Rural Small-Scale Industry Delegation, *Rural Small-Scale Industry in the People's Republic of China* (Berkeley: University of California Press, 1977), p. 1. Also, for an article on the evolution of China's policy toward the development of small industries, see Carl Riskin, "Small Industry and the Chinese Model of Development," *China Quarterly*, 46 (April–June 1971), 245–73; and Carl Riskin, "China's Rural Industries: Self-Reliant System or Independent Kingdom?" *China Quarterly*, 73 (March 1978), 77–98.

116. Chaing Hung, "Small and Medium-sized Industries Play Big Role," *Peking Review*, 45 (November 7, 1975), 23–25.

117. See *Rural Small-Scale Industries in the People's Republic of China*; and "Small Enterprises," *Peking Review*, 46 (November 15, 1974), 22.

118. See *Beijing Review*, 44 (October 29, 1984), i–xvi.

119. *Far Eastern Economic Review* (November 1, 1984), 24.

120. *Beijing Review*, 44 (October 29, 1984), vi.

121. Prybyla, "China's Economic Experiment," 34.

122. *Beijing Review*, 34 (August 24, 1987), 4. Also see *Beijing Review*, 29 (February 10, 1984), xi.

123. *Beijing Review*, 34 (August 24, 1987), 5.

124. *Beijing Review*, 44 (October 29, 1984), xiii.

125. Prybyla, "China's Economic Experiment," 34.

126. Ibid. For a discussion of China's industrial policy, see Yu-Shan Wa, "Reforming the Revolution: Industrial Policy in China," *Pacific Review*, 3, no. 3 (1990), 243–56.

127. *Beijing Review*, 52 (December 29, 1986), 18.

128. Ibid.

129. See *Asian Wall Street Journal,* January 20, 1987, p. 1, and *Wall Street Journal,* February 2, 1987, p. 22.

130. Prybyla, "China's Economic Experiment," 38.

131. Ibid., 37.

132. See *Wall Street Journal,* February 6, 1985, p. 31.

133. See *Far Eastern Economic Review* (January 29, 1987), 14.

134. Ibid.

135. See *China Daily,* August 16, 1987, p. 1.

136. See Andrew G. Walder, "Factory and Manager in the Era of Reform," *China Quarterly,* 118 (June 1989),

246. Also for a comprehensive scholarly treatment on China's state-owned enterprises, see Donald Hay, Derek Morris, Guy Liu, and Shujie Yao, *Economic Reform and State-Owned Enterprises, 1979–1987* (Oxford: Clarendon Press, 1994).

137. Walder, "Factory and Manager in the Era of Reform," 264.

138. See the following article for a discussion of China's management problems: Xue Muqiao, "On Reforming the Economic Management System, I, II, III," *Beijing Review*, 5 (February 4, 1980), 16–21; 12 (March 24, 1980), 21–25; and 14 (April 7, 1980), 20–26; Richard Y.C. Yin, "China's Socialist Economy in Action," *Journal of Northeast Asian Studies*, 1, no. 2 (June 1982), 105–9; and James O'Toole, "The Good Managers of Sichuan," *Harvard Business Review*, 59, no. 3 (May–June 1981), 28–40.

139. See at least two of the more popular books on Japanese management theories: William Ouchi, *Theory Z: How American Business Can Meet the Japanese Challenge* (New York: Addison-Wesley, 1980); and Richard T. Pascale and Anthony G. Athos, *The Art of Japanese Management: Applications for American Executives* (New York: Warner Books, 1982).

140. David A. Hayden. "The Art of Managing Chinese Ventures," *Asian Wall Street Journal Weekly,* July 6, 1981, p. 12.

141. Ibid., p. 12.

142. Frank Ching, "Poor Management and Irresponsible Workers Frustrate Foreign Partners in Chinese Factory," *Asian Wall Street Journal Weekly,* December 15, 1980, p. 2.

143. O'Toole, "Good Managers of Sichuan," 38. Also see *Ta Kung Pao Weekly Supplement,* December 2, 1982, p. 11.

144. Muqiao, "On Reforming the Economic Management System (I)," 24.

145. Muquio, "On Reforming the Economic Management System (I)," 25.

146. *Ta Kung Pao Weekly Supplement,* December 22, 1980, p. 6.

147. Malcolm Warner, "The 'Long March' of Chinese Management Education, 1979–84," *China Quarterly*, 106 (June 1986), 326.

148. Ibid., 340–341.

149. *Ta Kung Pao Weekly Supplement* (Hong Kong), January 23, 1986, p. 10.

150 Ibid.

151. *Christian Science Monitor*, December 5, 1991, p. 8.

152. See Woo Wing Thye, "What China Must Do," *Far Eastern Economic Review* (May 29, 1997). 34. (Woo is a professor of economics at the University of California, Davis, and a special adviser to the United States Treasury.)

153. *Christian Science Monitor,* December 5, 1991, p. 8.

154. See Nayan Chanda, "Withering State: The End Is Near," *Far Eastern Economic Review* (February 23, 1995), 49.

155. Wu Naitao, "State-Owned Enterprises No Longer State Run," *Beijing Review* (November 16–22, 1992), 17–21.

156. Ibid., 20. Also see Sheryl Wu Dunn, "China's Economy Thrives While Public Sector Flounders," *New York Times,* April 18, 1991, pp. A-1 and A-6.

157. Li Peng, "Report on the Work of the Government," *Beijing Review* (March 31–April 6, 1997), viii–x.

158. "Leaders on Reform of State-Owned Firms," *Beijing Review* (March 24–30, 1997), 5.

159. *Beijing Review,* 52 (December 29, 1986), 18.

160. Ibid.

161. "Leaders on Reform of State-Owned Firms," 5.

162. Pamela Yatsko, "Party's over: Authorities Try to Clean up State Enterprises," *Far Eastern Economic Review* (June 5, 1997), 59.

163. Ibid. Also see *People's Daily,* March 12, 1997, p. 1, for publication of the party announcement.

164. *People's Daily*, March 12, 1997, p. 1.

165. Jiang Zemin, "Hold High the Great Banner of Deng Xiaoping Theory," report to the Fifteenth Party Congress on September 12, 1997. See *Beijing Review* (October 6–12, 1997), 19–20.

166. See "SOE Reform on Healthy Track," *Beijing Review* (April 3, 2000), 9–13.

167. Ibid.

168. For text of "The Decisions of the Central Committee on Major Issues Concerning the Reform and Development of State-Owned Enterprises," adopted at the Fourth Plenum of the Fifteenth CCP Central Committee on September 22, 1999, see *Beijing Review* (October 11, 1999), 18–33.

169. Ibid., 26.

170. See Shu Y. Ma, "The Chinese Route to Privatization," *Asian Survey*, 38, no. 4 (April 1998), 387.

171. Ibid., 393–395.

172. Jiang Zemin, "Accelerating Reform and Opening up," *Beijing Review* (October 26–November 1, 1992), 16.

173. Li Haibo, "The Man Who Makes History," *Beijing Review* (October 12–18, 1992), 17.

174. New York Times Service as reprinted in the *Honolulu Star-Bulletin,* May 20, 1992, p. A-12.

175. Ibid.

176. See Zong Yan, "Retrospective on 1996 Economic Reform, *Beijing Review* (January 6–12, 1997), 25; and Zhou Jin, "China's Economy Realizes a 'Soft Landing,'" *Beijing Review* (January 6–12, 1997), 4.

177. See his "Dilemmas of Reform in China," *Political Conflict and Economic Debate* (Armonk, N.Y. and London: M. E. Sharpe, 1994).

178. For China's 1982 population census, see "The World's Biggest Census," *Beijing Review*, 32 (August 9, 1982), 16; "The 1982 Census Results," *Beijing Review*, 45 (November 8, 1982), 20–21; and "Report on the Sixth Five-Year Plan," 18.

179. "1982 Census Results," 20; and "Report on the Sixth Five-Year Plan," 181.

180. "Report on The Sixth Five-Year Plan," 18.

181. Ibid.

182. See Michele Vink, "China's Draconian Birth Control Program Weighs Heavily on Its Women," *Asian Wall Street Journal Weekly,* November 23, 1981, pp. 1, 21.

183. See Jeffrey Wasserstrom, "Resistance to One Child Family," *Modern China*, 10, no. 3 (July 1984), 345–72.

184. See Joyce K. Kallgren, "Politics, Welfare, and Change: The Single Child Family in China," in *Political Economy of Reform in Post-Mao China*, p. 151.

185. Ibid.

186. Wang Wee's statement in an interview in *Honolulu Star-Bulletin,* August 17, 1984, p. A-4.

187. See *Christian Science Monitor*, February 18, 1987, p. 8.

188. See *Honolulu Advertiser,* July 31, 1987, p. A-21.

189. For results of 1990 census, see *Beijing Review* (December 17–23, 1990), 27.

190. See Nicholas D. Kristoff, "China's Crackdown on Births: A Stunning and Harsh Success," *New York Times,* 25 April 1993, p. 6.

191. Ibid.

192. See *Honolulu Star Bulletin*, December 20, 1993, p. A-1. And a comment from an editorial in *New York Times*, December 27, 1993, p. A-14.

193. For a story on population control evasion, see Patrick E. Tyler, "Population Control in China Falls to Coercion and Evasion," *New York Times,* June 25, 1995, pp. A-1 and A-6.

194. See Jonathan Ungar, "'Bridges': Private Business, the Chinese Government and the Rise of New Associations," *China Quarterly,* 43 (September 1995), 795 and 814. Also see Gordon White, "Prospects for Civil Society in China: A Case Study of Xioshan City," *Australian Journal of Chinese Affairs,* 29 (January 1993), 63–87.

195. *China Daily,* May 7, 1993, p. 3.

196. Ungar, "'Bridges': Private Business, Chinese Government and Rise of New Associations," 795, 815–16.

197. This question has been raised by Professor Woo Wing Thye, University of California at Davis, in his article "What China Must Do," *Far Eastern Economic Review* (May 29, 1997), 34.

198. Figures are from China's Statistical Bureau. See Patrick E. Tyler, "As Deng Wanes, a Backlash Stalls His Big Reform," *New York Times,* June 25, 1995, pp. A-1 and A-7.

199. See Mitsuru Kitano, "The New China: Dynamism and Vulnerability," *Pacific Review*, 7, no. 3 (1994), 158–59.

200. David S. G. Goodman, "China: The State and Capitalist Revolution," *Pacific Review*, 5, no. 4 (1992), 358.

201. Ibid., 355.

SUGGESTED READINGS

Fewsmith, Joseph. *Dilemmas of Reform in China: Political Conflict and Economic Debate* (Armonk, N.Y.: M. E. Sharpe, 1994).

Harding, Harry. *China's Second Revolution: Reform after Mao* (Washington, D.C.: Brookings Institution, 1987).

Lardy, Nicholas R. *China's Unfinished Economic Revolution* (Washington, D.C.: Brookings Institution, 1998).

Milwertz, Cecilia Nathanser. *Accepting Population Control: Urban Chinese Women and the One-Child Policy* (Richard: Curzon Press, 1997).

Naughton, Barry. *Growing out of the Plan: Chinese Economic Reform, 1978-1993* (Cambridge: Cambridge University Press, 1995).

Oi, Jean C. *Rural China Takes Off: Institutional Foundations of Economic Reform* (Berkeley: University of California Press, 1999).

Solinger, Dorothy. *Contesting Citizenship in Urban China: Peasants, Migrants, the State and the Logic of Market* (Berkeley: University of California Press, 1999).

Chapter Twelve

The Politics
of Modernization

Education,
Science and Technology,
the Open Door Policy,
and the Intellectuals

Two important factors have influenced, if not dominated, Chinese educational policies since 1949. First, education has been used as an instrument for the inculcation of new values and beliefs to build a new socialist revolutionary society. Second, changes in the content and form of education invariably have been intertwined with the shifting policies and strategies of economic development. Although the basic goal of the regime has been to construct a socialist state, the implementation of this basic goal has involved periodic shifts in emphasis between "red" (politics) and "expert" (technology).

DEVASTATING EFFECTS OF THE CULTURAL REVOLUTION ON CHINA'S EDUCATIONAL SYSTEM

It must be kept in mind that for at least two years, from 1966 to 1968, all schools and universities were closed because of the disruption caused by the students' participation in the Cultural Revolution. When the central government ordered the schools to reopen and students to return to their classes in late 1967 and early 1968, the normal combined length of attendance for both primary and middle schools was shortened from twelve years to nine years.[1] Most rural areas shortened the combined length of attendance in both primary and middle schools to a bare seven years. It was reasoned that by the time the young-sters completed their middle school educations, they would be 15 or 16, "a suitable age to begin taking part in farm work." Those who finished the shortened secondary educa-tion in urban areas were expected to work in factories to gain practical experience. Upon reaching the age of 15 or 16, all youths who had completed secondary education were required to render at least three years of practical work or service before considering entrance to higher education. This requirement for three years of practical work experience relieved some of the pressure for entrance to colleges and universities. University education, particularly at technical colleges, was shortened to three years or less.

The Cultural Revolution severely condemned the system of evaluating student performance by examination. Entrance examinations and the practice of holding students back a year for failure to pass the examinations were labeled as the "revisionist line of education." Entrance examinations for universities were abolished when these institutions were reopened in 1970. In their place a system of nominations and recommendations was adopted for all institutions of higher learning. The new system called for the following methods of nomination: (1) self-nomination by individual students; (2) nomination by the masses; and (3) recommendation by the party leadership. High school graduates thus nominated then had to be approved by the institutions. The purpose of the new system was to enable youngsters from a "revolutionary social background"—workers, poor and lower-middle peasants, members of the army, and youths who had gone down to live with the peasants—to have the opportunity to enter universities. Clearly, the system was designed to meet complaints at the time that the universities, the road to one's future station in life, had become the preserve of the elite and tended to exclude those political activists who were endowed with revolutionary fervor. The new admissions policy was aimed not only at greatly increasing recruitment of youths from the proper "revolutionary social background," but it also limited admissions to those who had acquired practical experience, either as workers in factories or in communes. In 1970 most universities required two or three years of practical experience prior to entrance. Thus, under the new system—with its lack of entrance examinations—150,000 workers, peasants, and PLA members were admitted to universities from 1970 to 1973. With the admission of large numbers of students who did not have adequate preparation, academic standards had to be lowered and remedial classes organized.

The administration and management of education during the Cultural Revolution was taken out of the hands of the professional educators. Local revolutionary committees began taking control of the schools in October 1968 through the dispatch of worker and peasant "Mao's Thought Propaganda Teams," with the active participation of PLA soldiers.[2] These teams ended strife among the students[3] and worked with the students and teachers to reorganize educational content, placing more emphasis on the study of Mao's thought and relating education to productive labor. In addition to the revolutionary committees that administered the schools and universities, there was a "Revolution in Education Committee" on campuses to provide daily guidance in carrying out the reform measures in these institutions, particularly in higher education.[4] Members of these educational committees were cadres and teachers. At Fudan University in Shanghai, where the author visited in 1973, cadres who were workers in the revolutionary committee dominated the university's administration; the leading cadre who directed Fudan University was a skilled worker in a textile factory in Shanghai.

In rural areas primary schools were run by the production brigades, and secondary schools by the communes. This meant that the revolutionary committees on the communes were in full charge of education. Two reasons were generally given for the reform. One was purely ideological: "Since the fundamental question of revolution is political power" and the "fundamental question of revolution in education is also the question of power," proletarian education must be in the hands of the people in order to prevent the growth of the revisionist educational line. The second was more practical: "We (lower-middle peasants) can decide the teaching contents and, in a way we see fit, plan when classes take place."[5] Another important fact was that in brigade-run schools, teachers were members of the same commune, "eating the same kind of food and living in the same kind of housing as the poor and lower-middle peasants."[6] In urban areas primary schools were generally run by neighborhood revolutionary committees or street committees; secondary schools were run by neighborhood revolutionary committees and factories located in the area. The new revolutionary management of schools by local units reflected the Cultural Revolution's emphasis on decentralization. It also relieved the state from spending enormous amounts of money for primary and secondary education.

EDUCATIONAL REFORM, 1985–1989

The buzzword in China in 1984 and 1985 was reform. Not only were there major decisions on rural and urban reform, but on educational reform as well. The party's decision on educational reform was made public on May 28, 1985, following a national educational conference in Beijing.[7] The conference, the first since 1978, listened to appeals and pep talks by China's reform leaders, such as Deng Xiaoping and Wan Li, on the need to place educational reform on a par with economic reform.[8] The conference identified some of the urgent problems in China's educational system. The party's subsequent educational reform was aimed at providing remedies.

Top on the agenda for major educational reform was the party's decision to call for nine years of compulsory education for all school-age children. The decision was followed by a national law on compulsory education, enacted by the NPC in the spring of 1986.[9] The new law called for a step-by-step implementation of compulsory nine-year elementary education, beginning with urban areas by 1990, most rural areas by 1995, and for all backward areas by the end of this century. Under the law, school-age children in all rural areas would be guaranteed a nine-year compulsory education by the year 2000. The Seventh Five-Year Plan (1986–90) increased educational outlays by 72 percent to 116.6 billion yuan (about $40 billion). Under the national compulsory education law, local governments were permitted to collect "educational funds." The new law mandated that parents send their children to schools and, thus, made illegal the traditional practice of sending children into the field to work. The law prohibited recruitment of school-age children for employment. It also prohibited local government officials from engaging in the practice of diverting (or misappropriating) funds earmarked for education, and local government was prohibited from seizing educational buildings for noneducational use.

Another weakness in China's educational system was the low social status of teachers. Added to the persistent problem of low teachers' morale was the widespread practice of recruiting teachers into lucrative employment in noneducational areas. Vice-premier Wan Li told the national educational conference in May 1985 that luring teachers away from schools with higher pay was analogous to "killing the goose that lays the golden egg."[10] The average monthly wage for a teacher was about 50 to 60 yuan, the equivalent of U.S.$20, one of the lowest wages paid in China. It was no wonder that many teachers had left that profession. Wan Li emphasized at the 1985 national conference that teachers must receive an annual increase in salary in order to reduce the rate of attrition.[11] Primary and middle school teachers did receive raises as well as special seniority pay in 1985. The fact remains, however, that few secondary school graduates have opted for teacher training, and the shortage of qualified schoolteachers has deepened as a result.[12]

In a report on rural education, the local government for the ancient city of Luoyang in north China showed that only 20 percent of its 50,000 primary school teachers had graduated from teacher-training school and were considered qualified.[13] To implement the nine-year compulsory education law by the end of this century, an additional 30,000 trained teachers will be required for primary and junior middle schools in Luoyang alone.[14] The problem of a teacher shortage is probably found in most parts of the nation. China faces an enormous task if the nine-year compulsory education program is to be successfully implemented.

Reform in Higher Education

In higher education, the main problem has been the limited number of students who can be admitted into the universities. In 1985 about 1.7 million secondary school graduates took the grueling, three-day nationwide entrance examination in the hot and humid month of July, but only 560,000, or about one out three, were admitted to the universities. China expects to increase total university enrollment to 7 million by the year 2000, as compared to 1.7 million in 1985–86 and 1.9 million in 1987. By the year 2000 only about 8 to 9 percent of those who take the national entrance examinations will be admitted to the universities. This leaves a large number of disappointed, if not psychologically damaged, youth to be absorbed into gainful employment. It also creates the prospect of discontent and unrest among a significant number of talented young people.

A possible solution lies in the expansion of vocational education and training—a neglected area that needs to be emphasized. It is estimated that by the turn of the century China will need as many as 17 million polytechnic school graduates.[15] One estimate made during the reform period of the mid-1980s put the number of junior and middle-level technicians and managers required for 1990 at eight million—an enormous increase that could only be fulfilled by expanded vocational education and training. The 1985 party decision on educational reform made it very clear that vocational and technical school graduates must be given preference in job assignments.[16] In 1984 there were only 3.7 million students enrolled in technical vocational schools, compared to over 45.5 million students enrolled in general middle schools.[17] The dire need for skilled technicians in all fields resulted in an upsurge in part-time education for workers and staff members in state-owned enterprises. Special courses were designed in areas such as computers, drafting, and accounting. Government departments, factories, and trade union congresses set up schools to promote vocational education. Special courses were offered over radio and television or through correspondence arrangements. Television and radio universities graduated 160,000 students in 1984.[18] These electronic universities, "Dianda" as they are known in Chinese, enrolled over one million students in the mid-1980s.[19] It seems obvious that only through expanded funding by the central and local governments for vocational education could the unemployed youth become skilled workers in a rapidly expanding but increasingly technically oriented economy.[20] In response to the urgent need for trained skilled workers, a number of short-term vocational courses were offered by many institutes of higher learning, leading up to degrees comparable to two-year vocational degrees in American community colleges.[21] Thus the emphasis was less on theoretical instruction in mathematics and hard sciences and more on the acquisition of practical knowledge and skills. Other structural reform measures for higher education included the extension of well-known universities from developed coastal areas to the hinterland and border regions, with increased funding and establishment of facilities for postgraduate study, as part of an ongoing effort to encourage scientific research at the universities.

The single most important reform in higher education in the mid-1980s was the recognition by the state and party of the need to grant more autonomy to the universities by dismantling centralized control.[22] There had been too much rigid control over schools and universities by the party. In June 1986 the State Council announced a set of regulations dealing with the management, or decision making, power of the universities. As a part of the ongoing decentralization in the economic system, the university presidents were granted autonomous power to make decisions regarding university governance and management, finances (including the right to allocate funds and collect fees from students), construction of buildings, and personnel matters involving job and teaching assignments.[23] Under the regulations, a university president presumably could appoint and dismiss other university officials, teachers, and staff. Faculty also could determine their own academic curricula, as well as having the right to select their own teaching material. On paper at least, these reform measures seemed to provide university administrators and faculty with the instruments to fend off control and constant political interference from the party bureaucrats. These reform measures have not been entirely successful. The vice president for Hefei's Science and Technology University was dismissed by Deng Xiaoping and expelled from party membership in January 1987 after student protests erupted in many cities. This occurred two and a half years before the 1989 mass protest.

Another important reform decision made in the mid-1980s was that the state would no longer be "responsible for all cash outlays for universities and colleges."[24] Students were to help pay for part of their education or participate in part-work, part-study programs. A new scholarship and loan program was established to reward students who (1) had excellent scholastic standing (350 yuan a year); (2) wanted to specialize in teacher training or other high-demand fields such as agriculture or forestry (400 yuan a year); and (3) opted to work in the poor and border areas (500 yuan a year).[25] A student loan program was established to enable needy students to borrow a maximum of 300 yuan a year without interest. In 1987, the scholarship and loans were made available at 85 selected institutions under experimental pilot programs.

EDUCATION IN CHINA AFTER TIANANMEN

China's educational system was beset with persistent problems that have been aggravated by the effects of the 1989 Tiananmen upheaval. These problems include the declining school attendance of school-age children caused by the rural reform or the responsibility incentive system; the intense competition and pressure between lower schools to promote their better students, thus placing undue stress on passing examinations rather than on learning; the continued problem of illiteracy affecting over 230 million among China's rural population; and the "brain drain," or loss, of some of China's best minds to advanced industrialized nations. Out of a total of more than 64,000 Chinese students who have been sent abroad to study since 1978, only about 22,000 had returned by 1990.[26] Complicating these educational problems are the shortage of qualified teachers and the low pay for the profession. In 1988 about 40 percent of primary school teachers and 47 percent of secondary school teachers were not qualified or trained.[27]

The austerity program, which was launched in the fall of 1988, and the policy changes since the Tiananmen upheaval in June 1989, have made the situation worse in rural areas, in particular in terms of availability of local financial resources for basic education. Since local taxes paid by rural enterprises and local individual entrepreneurs finance rural basic educational institutions, the austerity program (see Chapter 11) has caused a sharp reduction in local tax revenues. Many such tax-producing rural enterprises suffered losses or went bankrupt, a familiar occurrence in the latter part of 1989. As a result, the much-heralded goal of compulsory education has not been achieved. In short, the educational level of the Chinese has moved backward. The nation ranked sixtieth among 122 nations in the proportion of people over 25 years of age who have received higher or secondary education, and eightieth among 139 nations for the entrance rate of secondary school children.[28]

Certainly the most significant development that has taken place in the early 1990s has been in the area of vocational education. In October 1991 the State Council decided to expand and strengthen vocational education for the purpose of meeting growing national needs for manpower training, which have resulted from continued economic reform. Vocational education in the early 1990s focused on the development of polytechnic, skilled-worker, and secondary vocational schools. As mentioned earlier, China will need about 17 million polytechnic school graduates by the turn of the century. Government figures now show that in 1990 China had about 4,000 polytechnic schools, with 2.2 million students; this has been augmented by over 4,000 skilled-worker schools, with 1.3 million students, and over 9,000 secondary vocational schools, with almost 3 million students. Many state-owned enterprises, such as the Anshan Iron and Steel Company and some of the automobile factories, have participated in the vocational education program. Local governments at the county level are expected to operate at least one vocational school devoted to agricultural skills.

Another development in the 1990s addressed the need for university education to place some emphasis on its mission, not only in arts and sciences, but in manufacturing and trade as well. The prestigious Beijing University (Beida) established on campus the Beida Fangzheng Company, which specializes in electronic typesetting with Chinese characters for domestic and foreign markets. The academic department of biology ran the Beida Weimin Bioengineering Company in cooperation with some eighteen high-tech-oriented enterprises formed and managed by the university. In addition, Beida expanded its graduate programs by offering advanced degrees.

During my 1995 visit to Guangzhou in south China, it was common to see private school newspaper advertisements offering training in skills in order to meet industry's demands under economic reform and the economic boom. In Guangzhou alone there were hundreds of these private schools, with an annual student enrollment of 60,000.

CAMPUS DOCILITY AND STATE SURVEILLANCE

Students on Chinese university campuses nowadays (1999–2000) are best described as politically tractable, if not obedient to authorities. Rarely do students discuss or get fired up by fighting words like democracy or freedom. Campus life today involves, besides studying hard and getting good marks, dancing and money making if possible. Students are unlike those in the olden days when their forebears were young, or in the 1980s, when college students often took to the streets to protest or demonstrate against the authorities for they were then the harbingers of change. Today, college students are submissive to the state's insistence and requirement that they must show devotion to communist ideology before admission or study abroad upon graduation. In fact one finds, as this author did in his 1999 visit, that Public Security Bureau substations are present on university campuses for surveillance and enforcing discipline. Nowadays, college students are more worried about getting good jobs, preferably in cities. They may feel discontentment, but only in silence. To do otherwise would mean jeopardizing their futures.

Perhaps it would be useful to review briefly the state of Chinese youth some two decades ago and the changes that have taken place during these two decades.

About 160 million young people who were between the ages of 8 and 18 at the time of the Cultural Revolution have been termed the "lost generation." These youths, who were in their mid-twenties to mid-thirties in 1980, had their educations interrupted by the great upheaval. Among this group, at least twenty million secondary school graduates were sent down to the countryside under the xiafang movement, or "the downward transfer."

The bulk of the "lost generation" suffered widespread discontent and disillusionment.[29] Many of these young people faced a "crisis of confidence" in attitudes toward the CCP and China's socialist system. Those dissenters who formed the core of the 1978–1979 Democracy Wall movement, discussed in Chapter 10, were drawn largely from this age group. Having wasted their time in the Cultural Revolution, many of them possessed neither the education nor the necessary skills to be gainfully employed. Rural youth fared much better, in that they always knew there would be little opportunity for them if they migrated to the cities to find jobs in the factories. Today, with the new incentive system in the countryside, more rural youngsters prefer to remain on the farm.

As a group, Chinese youth and students want more or less the same things that their counterparts in other countries want—good jobs, material goods, and a secure future as they grow up and mature. Having learned what happened to the youth during the Cultural Revolution decade, Chinese youth and students of today are more skeptical about marching behind any ideological banner. In fact, a chief characteristic of China's youth and students of today is their disillusionment about communism as preached by Marx, Lenin, and Mao Zedong. In the later 1970s the discontent and unrest of youth was expressed via demonstrations, wall posters, and disruption of city traffic. Although these feelings of discontent have been suppressed by the authorities since the Democracy Wall movement, the underlying problems of this group remain. One problem facing youth is unemployment within their ranks. It is common to find thousands upon thousands of young people between the ages of 22 and 35 jobless in the cities. Some years ago, approximately 75 percent of the secondary school graduates in the city of Shanghai could not find jobs. While it is true that the relaxed policy of permitting individual enterprises to operate in the urban areas has relieved some of the pressure of joblessness for the young, unemployed urban youth are still a source of dissent in China today. The youth of China have entered the period of "awakening" after having gone through periods of "blind faith" and "skepticism." It is in the awakening state that the young are seeking answers to their practical problems for which China's socialism does not seem to have the answers.

In the mid-1980s, the total youth population in China, age 15–18, was about 250 million. Although they may be less cynical than their elders—the "Lost Generation" described earlier—nevertheless, these youngsters are more individualistic in their orientation and outlook. Their hero is not the party's national folk hero Lei Feng, the embodiment of selflessness and a "serve-the-people" attitude toward life. Instead their national hero, as portrayed in popular cinema, is that of a "smoking, drinking, snappy dresser" who has his or her own opinion about things and who despises "rigid bureaucratic thinking."[30] While their elders accepted state-assigned jobs, today's 15- to 18-year-old youths want some freedom of choice. In the past, their elders opted for membership in the Communist Youth League (CYL); the teenagers nowadays shy away from it. The total CYL membership was about 52 million in 1985—a bare 20 percent of China's 250 million youth in the mid-1980s.[31] Teenagers are extremely interested in the outside world, particularly the West. They tend to flock to foreign visitors and are eager to practice their foreign languages, knowing that for most of them travel abroad is only a dream. With the latest campaign against "bourgeois liberalization," youth in China have become more cautious in contacting foreigners. Of course, most of them have impressions of an affluent West that may be superficial or even naïve, gleaned from an occasional movie, TV, or imported magazines. But these superficial impressions of a superior material Western civilization compel them to reflect upon their own society under socialism. They ask disturbing questions about the socialist state and the validity of Marxism. Forums sponsored by the CYL revealed that a majority of the youth were "unclear" about the "superiority of socialism" and expressed a lack of confidence in the modernization goals, Marxism, and Mao's Thought.[32] Thus, the future outlook for China's youth might be bleak. If their pent-up energy is not channeled toward useful ends, if their disillusionment about the system is not alleviated, and if they are not made a useful part of the march toward modernization, then they will remain a potential source of unrest in the future. (See Chapter 10 for a discussion of student demonstrations and dissent.)

1993-2000: TARGETS FOR RENEWED EDUCATIONAL REFORM

The year 1993 marked a new beginning in China's effort at educational reform. What motivated these renewed efforts was the impetus under accelerated economic-market reform. In his report to the first session of the Eighth NPC on March 15, 1993, former Premier Li Peng pointed out that educational reform should be "a strategic priority;" and he made no bones about the long-held principle of making education "serve socialist modernization."[33]

In fact, preparation was underway in 1989 for developing an overall program of educational reform and development; this was made public by the State Council in March 1993.[34] The overall educational reform plan for 1993–2000 was said to be the result of some twenty drafts and at times former Premier Li Peng personally presided over the meetings. The final program was issued after approval by the party's Politburo. The urgency for embarking on overall educational reform and development for this seven-year period was called for by the state of "low economic efficiency and the lack of product competitiveness of China's enterprises," as well as "the low quality of workers."[35] The driving force which has been the power behind the latest round of reform springs from the need for development of human resources in the equation for economic modernization:

> Whichever country attains higher standards of education, geared to the 21st century, will occupy an advantageous strategic position in international competition in the new age.[36]

A discussion about the new strategy and goals in China's educational development program, 1993–2000, will reveal some of the weaknesses and problems typical in Chinese education since 1978.

Nine-Year Compulsory Education

As discussed earlier, the 1986 law concerning nine-year compulsory education called for phase-by-phase implementation for elementary education in urban areas by 1990 and in most rural areas by 1995. As evidenced by former Premier Li Peng's report to the first session of the NPC in March 1993 in which he called for enforcement of the pledge for achieving the nine-year compulsory education, it became obvious that implementation had not been carried out.[37] The new seven-year (1993–2000) educational development program emphasized universal nationwide implementation of nine-year compulsory education, including vocational and technical training at the junior high level.[38] For large cities and the developed coastal areas there would be universal senior middle school education. Preschool education for large and medium-sized cities would also be provided, and one-year preschool education in rural areas.

At the second National Education Work Conference, held in 1994, the renewed pledge was to make compulsory education the "cornerstone of the development process," and it was agreed that rural areas would have it by the end of this century.[39] Of course, providing a nine-year compulsory education for 85 percent of China's 1.2 billion population is a lofty and difficult task indeed, for, most important of all, it takes adequate funding. (A later discussion will focus on this topic.) Adequate funding for compulsory education is extremely crucial, considering the size of the school-age population. As of 1993 there were 124 million students in primary schools. Another 40.8 million were enrolled in junior high schools. On the average most people received only 5.4 years of primary education.

There are two problems connected with implementing compulsory education in China. One is the high dropout rate: About one million school children drop out of school each year in rural areas of China. The problem is illustrated in the Chinese film "Not One Less," now showing in America in which a teenage substitute teacher in a rural school is contracted by a teacher who must take a leave of absence to care for his ailing parent, with the understanding that the number of students in the class must not be one less when he returns. The film's story demonstrates how the poor substitute teacher goes to a nearby city to look for and bring back a pupil who has to seek a job to help out his family. Chinese law states that no school child should be gainfully employed while schools are in session, but in rural areas this law is rarely enforced by local authorities. The other obstacle to compulsory education is that many rural girls are often not in school because their families cannot afford to pay the tuition.

Vocational Education

The demand for meeting manpower needs for the industrial and agricultural development spurred by economic reform made it necessary for China to promote and enlarge enrollment in secondary vocational education in the form of polytechnic schools. In various parts of China by 1990 some 3,982 polytechnic schools had been established, with a total enrollment of 2.2 million students.[40] During the same period there were 9,164 secondary vocational schools with a total enrollment of almost three million students.[41]

Many state enterprises, such as the giant Anshan Iron and Steel Co., had been participating in on-the-job vocational technical training for new recruits, averaging 3,000 or more each year. Many rural counties provided at least one vocational school; and agricultural middle schools also emphasized practical agricultural production techniques. As rural township enterprises grew there developed the need for extensive vocational education in many nonagricultural areas, such as service trades, commerce, and finance. As a result, the traditional rural middle schools have transformed themselves nowadays into secondary vocational schools which emphasize special training related to service trades. In many cities China's booming tourist industry is hard-pressed for vocationally trained staff and workers to serve at the hotels and restaurants catering to foreign tourists. Thus, there is a need for more graduates from secondary vocational schools to meet the increasing demand for better service for foreign tourists.[42] The trend now is to encourage students from junior and senior middle schools to enter vocational education institutions for practical training. Former Premier Li Peng told the NPC delegates in 1993 and 1997 that it is necessary to provide "vocational training for people before they are employed;" and that "vocational education is an important pillar of economic development."[43]

Adult Education

Efforts in adult education since reform have been focused on upgrading of technical skills and work qualifications for mature-aged workers in the industry and service trades. Since the advent of economic reform, there has been a "diploma-seeking spree" or "craze" among mature adults; this "craze" has gained unprecedented momentum since 1993 with expansion of the market economy coupled with wage reform. The "free labor circulation of talent," "or job-hopping" has enabled mature adults to seek additional skills and upgrade their job qualifications by enrollment in specialized institutions which have been established in many urban areas.[44] In Beijing alone there have been over 170 institutions established in recent years to accommodate the rising demand for adult education in special skills. Some 100,000 middle-aged adults enrolled in these skills-oriented institutions in the capitol city: community colleges at night, or correspondence schools. From 1979–94 the state has provided tuition scholarships for over 310,000 mature-aged adults.[45]

It is interesting to note that under conditions of market economy the concept of continuing education has gained recognition in many urban areas. The stress on continuing education is perhaps more appropriately stated by former Premier Li Peng in his 1997 report on the work of government:

> Adult education should be combined with vocational education so that people can meet the requirements for employment and the need of on-the-job training.[46]

As of 1993 there were about 1.8 million enrolled in a variety of adult education schools.

Elimination of Illiteracy

Officially, Chinese leaders speak only about the reduction of illiteracy, not elimination. For example, former Premier Li Peng spoke in March 1997 about the government's effort to reduce illiteracy by "four million"[47] without revealing China's total illiteracy rate at the moment. Vilma Seeburg, an author on the subject of literacy in China, has pointed out that for the thirty-year period from 1949–79, there was "very little improvement" in the literacy rate of school-aged and mature-aged adults; it remained unchanged and stood at 32 percent.[48] This means that over 65 percent of the 1.2 billion population remained illiterate before the 1980s. What is even more alarming is the fact that in rural areas about 70 percent of the illiterate are women. Having pointed out the slow progress in raising the literacy rate in China, one should also reveal that some achievements have been made in the combat against illiteracy: Some 143 million adults became literate between 1949 and 1982.[49]

The State Statistical Bureau revealed that the total illiteracy rate for those over 15 years of age had decreased from 182 million to 145 million[50] One also needs to bear in mind the sheer size of China's rural population, about 850 million, and the lack of resources which makes the task almost Herculean, to say the least.

Higher Education

In 1995 there were a total of 2.5 million students enrolled in some 1,065 institutions in higher and/or in specialized education. The growth figure of 2.5 million students in tertiary education reflected an increase in enrollment in skill-oriented specialized institutions or in vocational education, but not in terms of comprehensive university education. Only about 4 percent of some 2.8–3 million high school graduates can pass the rigorous university entrance examination held in the summer of each year. (High school enrollment is about 15 million for the nation as a whole, which means that only one in eight Chinese can possess a general high school education.) University education in China is certainly elitist, to say the least.

College Entrance Examination. The month of July has been considered by high school graduates as the month in "hell" or "Black July," for the college entrance examination is an extremely grueling test, a single test in their young lives which determines what the future will be. It is actually one single comprehensive examination which consists of five parts: Chinese, English langauge, mathematics, chemistry and physics, and history/politics.

In 1999 a new feature was introduced in college entrance examinations for the purpose of relieving the tremendous pressure on high school students each July; there is now a January, or winter, session for the nationwide grueling college entrance examination.

The cost for college education per year is about 10,000 yuan (U.S. $1,200) at key universities which have made available a variety of loans, grants, scholarships and work-study schemes.

The new target for higher education, as formulated in 1993, was to focus on some one hundred key universities by improving on the subject areas or majors. The new target stated that,

> by early next century, a score of advanced institutes will reach top world levels in terms of disciplines, majors, educational standards, scientific research and management.[51]

Specifically, the new targets for reform in higher education would be for strengthening small and medium-sized enterprises, township enterprises, and postgraduate work expansion in order to meet the demands of "the new global technological revolution."[52]

Of the 2.5 million college students close to 30 percent of them experienced financial difficulties and about 10 percent were living in poverty while studying at the universities.[53] In the words of Li Peng, the state has been planning for reform in the tuition system and in improving stipends and loans to the needy students.[54] As revealed in a recent survey, many college students in the Beijing area endured living standards below the poverty line for the city's residents or below 150 rmb for their living expenses.[55] The management of student grants at the universities has been such that funds often were being "siphoned off by middle bureaucrats charged with administering the programs."[56] Students and their families could apply for loans amounting to not more than 1,000 rmb per year. As implied by Li Peng's report to the NPC delegates in March 1997, there have been proposals for tuition waivers or reduction and for work-study programs. There is also an emphasis on providing more financial aid to one million poor students enrolled in some of the more prestigious academic institutions located in the Beijing area. That "unbalanced" allocation for student financial aid has resulted in a situation under which a large proportion of students in some universities receive more stipends or grants or loans. For instance, some 70 percent or more needy students at Beida or Qinghua or Chinese People's University receive scholarships or grants.[57]

Some universities can now charge tuition for those who can afford it—the average charges range from $117 to $170 per year.[58] In fact, the long-term plan is that for the next seven years (1993–2000) a tuition charging system will replace the traditional free college education in noncompulsory higher education. There would be loans and scholarships for the needy students. But the institution of tuition would impose a heavier burden on the peasant families in the countryside.

The most significant change in higher education had been the gradual abandonment of the state's monopoly in assigning or placing university graduates to jobs without considering the preference or desires of the students. There has been now free selection of job assignments. Most college graduates did not end up working for the state or party. Of course, under the market economy there were more job opportunities for college graduates in fields in which they are interested or more suited.

Postgraduate studies have also been on the increase: 280,000 have earned master's degrees and 20,000 have won doctoral degrees from thirty-three graduate schools since 1978.

Educational Funding

Despite the dialogue about the importance of education and the state's plan, pledges and targets for educational reform, the startling fact remains that China's expenditures for education are not only woefully inadequate, but also below the world average for developing countries. In 1992 the world average educational disbursement for developing nations was 3.6 percent of the gross national product; China's educational outlay was only 2.5–3.0 percent.[59] In the draft central and local budgets for 1997 it was 119 billion yuan, or a mere 1.3 percent, for educational expenditures out of a total state budget of 896 billion yuan.[60] In other words, China ranked 149th of 151 nations in the proportion of allocations for education! Instead of making demands on the government to improve educational funding, considering China's economy has grown at the rate of 10 percent per year for years, conferees at the July 1994 Second National Education Work Conference, while admitting the problem of a "shortage of educational funds," had the temerity to suggest that "society as a whole will be encouraged to raise funds for operating schools."[61] The target for educational reform, published in 1993, had the courage,

however, to argue for a 4 percent national educational expenditure by the end of this century and an average of 15 percent local government expenditure by local governments. In addition, the proposed target for educational reform suggested value-added and business taxes of 2 to 3 percent in urban areas to supplement educational fees.[62]

Related to the problem of educational refunding is the deplorable situation of delaying payment since 1992 for teacher's salaries by all local governments except Beijing and the Tibet autonomous region. By the end of 1993, it had been reported that a total of over 300 million yuan was owed to teachers in most rural areas.[63] The 1993 target for educational reform recognized the need for teachers' wage reform, so as to make teachers' salaries comparable to those of workers and staff in state owned enterprises.[64] In addition, the 1993 educational reform asked for an adjustment and increase in a teacher's wages in accordance with his or her contribution and teaching quality—a sort of merit-pay concept.

Zhu Kaixuan, the State Education Commission minister, indicated a plan for setting up an education trust and foundation for the purpose of raising funds to improve primary and secondary schools, in addition to educational taxes from social services and school tuition fees. For poverty stricken areas, the central government had in 1996 allocated some 300 million yuan to promote compulsory education.[65]

Interestingly enough, the Education Law, the result of a decade of preparation and drafting which culminated in its passage by the Third session of the Eighth NPC in September 1995, not only recognized that inadequate educational funding was a serious problem in China's educational development for the future but also placed the liability on governments at all levels responsible for educational funding. And, the law seems to provide a legal basis for raising educational funds through various channels other than government, as well as prohibiting illegal tax collection from the students.[66]

THE THREE-PRONGED APPROACH TO SCIENTIFIC AND TECHNOLOGICAL MODERNIZATION, 1978–1997

A historic milestone was reached in the spring of 1978 when some 6,000 scientists and technicians gathered in Beijing to discuss and endorse the plans for China's development of modern science and technology. In his keynote address to the conference, Deng Xiaoping, then vice-premier of the State Council, criticized the party for not providing adequate services, supplies, and working conditions for scientists.[67] This was certainly a far cry from the days when the intellectuals, scientists, and technicians were labeled, by Yao Wenyuan, "an exploiting class" with strong bourgeois prejudices,[68] and when Deng himself was charged by the radicals with advocating the "poisonous weed" of advanced scientific development.

Since 1949 science policy had vacillated between professional orientation and mass mobilization, depending on China's development policies.[69] William Whitson has noted that during each alternation the leadership embraced a different set of approaches toward the identifiable issues of planning, the role of self-sufficiency, and the place of technology transfers from abroad.[70] During the First Five-Year Plan, professionals and technical bureaucrats held a position of dominance. Consequently, they emphasized centralized planning and control over the allocation of resources, importation of some 300 complete industrial plants from the Soviet Union, and scientific and technical training of Chinese in the Soviet Union. Following the withdrawal of Soviet aid in 1960, the

Great Leap altered the basic approach from professionalism—with heavy reliance on technological transfers from abroad—to Mao's approach of self-reliance and "disdain" for foreign technology. The alternating pattern reappeared with some variations during the periods of economic recovery following the Great Leap and the Cultural Revolution.

The Cultural Revolution disrupted the scientific community in a number of ways. Scientists and technicians were criticized for their professional sins: their aloofness from and disinterest in politics; their privileged status and high salaries; and their theoretical research, unrelated to practical problems. Established in 1958 under the supervision of the State Council, the State Scientific and Technological Commission was supposed to provide direction for scientific research, administer scientific and technological programs, and approve funds for research. The organization's leading members, however, were subjected to Red Guard criticism and harassment for their "elitist" orientation. Many of the scientific cadres associated with the commission were sent to the countryside for rehabilitation through physical labor, and the commission disappeared as an organization.

The Chinese Academy of Sciences, which conducts research in the various physical and social sciences, both directly and through affiliate members, was subjected to criticism and purges. At the height of the upheaval, it was reported that thousands of its members had been sent to the factories and communes for physical labor.[71] The president of the academy, the late Guo Moruo, a noted historian, managed to survive by making self-criticism in which he repudiated all his previous writings. Typically, the academy's affairs were taken over by a revolutionary committee, with the PLA and the masses participating in decision making. Members were forced to spend long hours in political reeducation and ideological remolding.

Some members of the academy were sent to factories and communes to engage in applied research. Many of the research institutes of the academy decentralized their operations during the Cultural Revolution by establishing provincial and local branches, which proliferated and duplicated activities. Although the Cultural Revolution strategy did not contribute to basic scientific research, some observers in the West viewed some of the reforms in science and technology as innovative from a developmental perspective. Genevieve Dean has argued that China's urgent need was for the application of innovative native technology to solve immediate problems of development, and that high-level research was too sophisticated to be of any use to the ordinary peasants and workers.[72] C. H. G. Oldham and Rennselaer Lee saw the prospect of mass participation in developing native technology, based on local initiative and resources, as enriching the economic life of the Chinese.[73] Oldham noted that mass training of ordinary workers as "amateur technicians" might be viewed as a beginning step toward the eventual formation of a "highly specialized corps of technicians."[74]

In contrast to Mao and the radicals, who questioned both the practicality and the ideological impact of modern science, Deng Xiaoping and his pragmatic colleagues saw the "mastery of modern science and technology" as the key to modernization. They admitted frankly that China lagged behind some of the advanced countries, such as the United States, by as much as fifteen to twenty years in food production.[75] To catch up with the ever-expanding body of world knowledge, China planned to learn from the advanced nations and to develop her own scientific capabilities. Modernization, or "the mastery of modern science and technology," as Deng would phrase it, had involved at least a three-pronged approach since 1978: the recruitment of a "mammoth force" of scientific and technical personnel, the strengthening of China's scientific and technological institutions, and the acquisition of advanced technology from abroad.

Recruitment of Scientific and Technological Personnel

In 1978 Politburo member Kang Yi, then a vice-premier in the State Council, presented an outline of the national plan for science and technological development, in which he called for the recruitment of a force of 800,000 "professional scientific researchers" between 1978 and 1985.[76] It was obvious that there was a serious shortage of trained technical personnel. The government pointed out that in 1979 only 300,000 Scientific and Technological (S & T) personnel were working in the 2,400 national research organizations and 600 universities.[77] Richard Suttmeier estimated that almost 41 percent of the 1.3 million university graduates from 1978 to 1985 (or 553,500 to be exact) would need to be in science and engineering, and all would need to be engaged in research in order to meet the targeted personnel needs set by the national plan.[78] What was even more urgent was the need to provide a professional corps of what Suttmeier called "research S & T personnel capable of exercising scientific leadership and of conducting independent research."[79] S & T personnel would be much more highly trained than the present vast number of "scientific and technology workers" in state enterprises and organizations. It was estimated that a total of more than 5.7 million "scientific and technological workers" were employed by state enterprises in 1981.[80]

As urged by Politburo member Chen Yun, China must still recruit scientific and technological specialists as advisors in policymaking.[81] According to Suttmeier, there were ways that China could possibly overcome the huge gap in scientific leadership needs. One was to reinstitute postgraduate work for mid-career training.[82] In August 1981 the Chinese Academy of Sciences, the Academy of Social Sciences, and the Ministry of Education authorized 11,000 postgraduate students to sit for master's degree examinations, and 420 to sit for the doctoral degree.[83] Another way was to send postgraduate students abroad for advanced training in science and technology. There were about 40,000 Chinese students and scholars in the United States, a majority of them doing advanced studies in the sciences. Scientific training could also be obtained through exchanges with foreign countries. For instance, since the normalization of relations in January 1979, China's scientific contacts with the United States have expanded considerably. Under the Science and Technology Agreement, signed on January 31, 1979, during Deng's visit to the United States, numerous accords were concluded for cooperative exchanges. These included such subject areas as agriculture, space science, higher-energy physics, information science, meteorology, atmospheric science, marine and fishery science, medicine, hydroelectric power, earthquake science, and environmental protection.[84] In May 1982 more agreements were reached on cooperative programs on transportation, nuclear research, and aeronautics. These were set up under the auspices of a U.S.–China Joint Commission on Cooperation in Science and Technology.[85] A typical pattern under these agreements was to bring Chinese scientists to the United States and send American scientists to China as advisors.

A related problem in expanding recruitment of scientific personnel was how to use their talent to the fullest, a point stressed clearly by Deng at a meeting with the leaders of the State Planning Commission.[86] Generally, since the scientists were also intellectuals, they were often despised by many. Deng hit hard on this point in 1978 when he talked to the first national science conference. He publicly rejected the radicals' assertion that scientists were not part of the productive forces and instead contended that "brain workers who serve socialism" were part of the working people. At the conference Deng clearly repudiated the treatment of intellectuals and technicians over the past decade and went on to ask that the party stop interfering in the work of scientific and research institutions and restore the decision-making authority on technical matters to the directors and deputy directors of these agencies. The party committee's work in a scientific institution should be judged by the scientific results and the training of competent scientific personnel, Deng demanded.[87]

Strengthening Chinese Scientific and Technological Institutions

To supervise the development program in science, the Fifth National People's Congress reinstated the State Scientific and Technological Commission and elevated it to ministerial status under the State Council. This commission is, in essence, an overall policymaking body. The commission and its counterparts in the provinces act as scientific advisors to the party committees and government on economic development projects. The commission also has sponsored a series of national conferences on science and technology. Together with the State Planning Commission and the State Economic Commission, they plan, coordinate, and implement scientific research. A key role in scientific research was given to the prestigious Chinese Academy of Sciences. The academy provided funds and direction for 117 research institutes with a combined staff totaling 75,000.[88] Until 1981 the leadership of the academy was in the hands of party committees within each of the research institutes; since then party committees in these institutes were told that they must confine their work to political and ideological matters.[89]

Under the Sixth Five-Year Plan, allocations for education, science, culture, and public health accounted for almost 16 percent of all state expenditures. Funds allocated for science and technology were earmarked for expanding both basic and applied research to meet economic development needs.[90] To what extent Marxist ideology would continue to play a role in research on social and natural sciences remained to be seen.[91] However, in a subsequent policy outline, the State Scientific and Technological Commission stated that it was important to establish "an atmosphere of seriousness and truth seeking," and that research conclusions should be based on facts and "objective law." The commission declared that the time had come "to put a stop to the evil trends of opportunism and falsification."[92] A problem that remains in Chinese politics is the bureaucratic maze that sooner or later may disrupt scientific and technological policies. Despite the institutional reforms, the formulation of major scientific policies was done jointly by no less than six state agencies under the State Council: the state Planning Commission, the Economic Commission, the Capital Construction Commission, the Agriculture Commission, the Energy Commission, and the Machine Building Industry Commission.[93] This bureaucratic decision making will inevitably hamper China's progress in scientific and technological programs.

Reform in Science and Technology in the 1980s

From 1978 to 1981 the goal for the development of science and technology was to catch up with the world's advanced industrial powers, such as Japan and the United States, by the year 2000. But that goal was unrealistic and unattainable because the strategy was predicated on the construction of large-scale projects under a "crash program," as we discussed in Chapter 11. Research in science and technology emphasized basic research that had little to do with the improvement of China's economy. By 1981, as China was pursuing economic adjustment and reform, the emphasis on science and technology began to shift. Deng Xiaoping urged establishment of a linkage between science and technology as tools for economic development.[94] It was felt that economic growth was dependent upon steady progress in developing new technologies. In other words, "technological transformation" became a basic strategy in economic development. This meant an overall revamping in the structural, organizational, and managerial aspects for science and technology.

One of the first major decisions made was to shift emphasis from basic to applied research. Scientific and technological research was to be "integrated" with economic production. Some Chinese leaders hoped that China could reach the 1960–70 technical level of the West and Japan by the year 2000.[95] In order to achieve the revised goal, a number of reforms were introduced in 1985. "Horizontal links" were established between scientific research institutes and industries and between enterprises and local governments. Failure to link science research institutes to industries meant that many industries' problems remained unsolved or that research findings were not utilized by industries.[96] Formerly there was no coordination between various sectors doing research: "The military and civilian sectors, the various governmental departments and administrative regions of the country were also severely cut off from each other."[97] Under the reform, scientific research institutes were now responsible for disseminating applied research findings on technological development to industries and enterprises.

Another reform was the commercialization of technological development. Hundreds of large-scale "technological transaction fairs" were held to enable research institutes to exhibit and sell their technological innovations to industries. These fairs were held in key industrial cities, such as Shanghai, Wuhan, and Tianjin. By 1986 some 1,400 technological centers had been formed to handle these exhibits and fairs. Even more significant was the introduction of a contract system by some 600 research institutes. An institute engaged in applied research projects could contract for its projects with local governments and enterprises for a fee for services, a percentage of profits earned, or simply a bonus award.[98] The income derived from these contracts was to be retained by the institutes as an alternate or additional source of funding. These project contracts were awarded on the basis of bidding for costs by competing research institutes.[99] The contract system for technological research reportedly was borrowed from the Romanian system.[100] However, research institutes still could receive funding from two other sources: "by undertaking major state scientific research projects through which state funds are made available and by applying for funds from science foundations controlled by the academy and the state."[101] The contract system presumably would provide more autonomy for the research institutes in managing their activities and would perhaps lessen to some extent the rigid control exercised by the government.

A third area of reform in science and technology concerned efficient use of the talents of scientific and technological personnel. One commentator complained that "researchers in China were not fully appreciated" and were poorly understood by the bureaucrats in government and the party.[102] A majority of China's researchers associated with the Academy of Sciences were aged senior and middle-level cadres. They might be eager to conduct independent research, but they received only about $300 per person for research, a level of investment inconsequential by Western standards. Too often researchers were assigned to other jobs for lack of research funds. The system stifled initiative and made inefficient use of talent. Only recently has any effort been made to retrain factory managers and research and development personnel with the aim of eventually placing them in positions of authority or where they could use their expertise productively. A final comment: It is obvious that reform in science and technology depends on freedom from political interference and the right amount of independent inquiry and academic discussion in scientific research. Ideological labels such as "rightists" have been used in the past against scientists and researchers whose task was to discover knowledge and truth. The stirrings of political winds in January 1987 and the renewed campaign against "bourgeois liberalization" after the 1989 Tiananmen crackdown revived bitter memories of a political climate that had stifled research in science and technology and had restricted development for more than two decades.

ACCELERATING ADVANCEMENT IN SCIENCE AND TECHNOLOGY, 1995–2010

For the second time since 1978 the party's Central Committee and State Council convened the National Science and Technological Conference in May 1995 to address the need for accelerating scientific and technological advancement. The focus of the gathering, as pointed out by President Jiang Zemin, was to develop strategies for the "integration" of science and technology with the progress made in market economy. Jiang later amplified the point by stating that,"We must concentrate our strength on the economy, by giving full play to the role of science and technology."[103] The following is a brief summary of China's renewed efforts toward accelerating science and technology for 1995–2010, along with appropriate analysis or comments.

Integration of High Technology with Industry and Agriculture

An important plan or strategy endorsed by the 1995 conference has been the desire to improve China's domestic agricultural technology as well as the selective introduction of advanced agricultural technology and managerial expertise from abroad. The conference decided that the scientific and technological contribution to agricultural development should be increased by 50 percent by the end of the century in terms of production goals for grain, cotton, oil crops, as well as nonstaple foods such as meat, eggs, and vegetables.[104] In general outline, the new plan is rather extensive and ambitious, for it emphasizes a host of critical areas which require "significant" technological "breakthroughs:"[105] new animal and plant varieties, control of plant diseases, pests, processing of agricultural products, aquatic breeding, fertilizer application, irrigation, environmental protection, and forestry development.

For high-technology industrial development, the conference singled out the critical need for solutions to technical problems associated with the electronic information industry, energy saving, and environmental production. It called for priority of support policies for high-tech industries' ability to compete internationally by strengthening appropriate government policies in finance, taxation, and credit.[106] Similarly, former Premier Li Peng also stressed the need for basic scientific research in high technology and new technologies, as well as applied technology, particularly in agriculture. He advocated the need to "quicken the research and development" in these areas: electronic information, biology, energy, the ocean, astronautics, and aeronautics.[107]

Research and Development (R&D) and Role of Education

In 1994–95 China's ratio in research and development (R&D) was only 0.5 percent of the nation's Gross Domestic Product (GDP). Richard P. Suttmeier of the University of Oregon points out that even as small as it has been in terms of R&D, Chinese enterprises in the past spent "very little on R&D" because of their state ownership and lack of "market competition."[108] The 1995 conference on science and technology specified that R&D expenditure should be targeted for 1.5 percent of the GDP by the year 2000; one-tenth of that would be for basic research. It also encouraged enterprises to increase their input into science and technology.[109] In his report to the NPC delegates in March 1997, former Premier Li Peng recommended accelerated research efforts in applied technology and in high and new technologies.[110] In the 1997 budget, there has been about a 14 percent increase above 1996, or 12.5 billion yuan, a little over one billion dollars, for science undertakings.[111] However, as pointed out by Suttmeier, there has been a lack of incentive for state-owned enterprises to innovate, and that innovation has been "largely isolated from production."[112] Thus, a priority lies in reform in the structure and management of the Chinese industrial system.

Restructuring the Science and Technology System

The May 1995 conference touched on reform in the system which would be more appropriate to allowing science and technology to serve "the socialist market economy."[113] However, this view has been criticized by Zhou Guang-zhao, president of the Chinese Academy of Sciences. In Zhou's speech to the 1995 conference he was quoted as saying:

> It is incorrect to make economic returns the sole criterion for determining the level of scientific research and regard scientific research only as a part of economic activities. Such a practice would both weaken long-term basic research and damage the very foundation of sustained social development. . . ."[114]

This view is most likely to be shared by most Western scientists. Specifically, the conference was groping for a mechanism by which the disparate entities—state enterprises and their technological institutes, research centers, key universities, rural technology services, and various technological enterprises under private management—could be coordinated. In other words, the conference was searching for a structural reform in science and technology that would be in a position to better utilize government investment and research grants.

The structural reform would allow the introduction of competition in the operation and management of science and technology. It would also make it possible to competitively attract and promote qualified science and technology research personnel. The conference report also expressed interest in new legislation for the purpose of protecting "intellectual property and property rights" and interests of research institutes, personnel and inventors.[115]

The task for coordinating structural reform in science and technology has been relegated to the newly strengthened State Science and Technology Commission (SSTC), now headed by Song Jian, a space specialist and state counselor. Its main responsibility lies in the "macro management and comprehensive coordination of the national network of science and technology."[116] An SSTC research-coordination has been formed to increase grain output (wheat, rice, maize, and soybean) by 50 percent by the year 2000, using high technology in breeding, pest control, harvesting, and processing in selected regions.[117] In addition, the SSTC would also focus on the application of high technologies in the manufacturing (aviation, automobiles, and shipping) information science for trade and commerce through computer aided designs.[118]

High-Tech Industrial Belts (Zones)

Development in high technology began with the 1986 March (thus, the "863") formation of the High Technology Program for new industries in automation, biotechnology, electronic information, energy sources, lasers, new materials and space. As of 1995, there had been established some fifty-two high-tech industrial development zones, beginning with the one in Beijing in 1988, in a number of selected provinces (Jiangsu, Guangdong, Shandong, Shanxi, Hunan, and Fujian). These zones or industrial development belts receive funding first from the central government with additional money coming from provincial sources for the specific purpose of applying high-tech techniques to the industrial development of these designated belts. That is, by using advanced technology the industries would produce better products for sale under international competitive conditions. For instance, the funds and the accompanying technology would be used to modernize (transform) older factories and upgrade production techniques. Eventually, these high-tech zones would evolve into four industrial development regions strategically located around Bohai Bay, southeast China coastal areas, and the Yangtze River basin.[119] These zonal-regional industrial developments would pool 70 percent of the local technological know-how and resources from some twenty provinces to enable the traditional industries and agriculture in these areas to become highly productive, modern, and high-tech industries. Richard Suttmeier wrote about Guangdong in the south, Liaoning in the northeast, and Shanghai in the east as emerging "models" or "networks" of industrial development application with high technology and the existing local science and technology assets.[120]

Recruitment of Science and Technology Personnel

The current status for training and recruitment of science and technology personnel is that China has trained more than ten million S & T workers over the past decade.[121] It must be pointed out that this vast number of S & T workers were not really highly trained with university degrees in engineering. When interviewed by Arthur Fisher, Song Jian, state counselor and head of the State Commission on Science and Technology, alleged that, as of 1995–96, there were some 1.35 million scientists and technicians in China and more than half of them were engaged in basic research.[122] However, there are some 100,000 postgraduate students now enrolled in institutions of higher learning working for master's or doctoral degrees in related and science and technology disciplines.[123]

Unfortunately, institutions of higher learning in China have not been able to receive state funding for advanced scientific research. As candidly admitted by the vice minister for the State Education Commission, only 5 percent of the total state funding from various sources has gone to advanced scientific and technological training and research at universities.[124] State funding for advanced research seems to be going in many directions. For instance, there is the State Natural Science Funding Committee, formed in 1986, which now receives an aggregate of 500 million yuan per year in support of basic research projects, as well as in support of applied science research. This committee also established a Youth Science Fund in 1987 and the State Outstanding Young Scientists Fund. There may be as many as fifty science funds established by the State Natural Science Funding Committee alone.[125] Some of these funding programs were designed to reward S & T workers under age 35 with advanced university degrees; some were established in 1992 to support outstanding middle-aged scientists; or then there is the Outstanding Young Scientists Fund, initiated in 1994 for exceptional young scientists.

Yet another funding program has been launched—this one from the State Education Commission. It is designed for training a talented new crop of young university leaders in advanced levels. As many as over one thousand such young talented personnel with engineering degrees and research experience would constitute the core for some four hundred "key discipline centers" and research laboratories.

Probably it would make more sense to place or channel these disparate funding programs into one source—a national science foundation, for example—rather than scattering limited state research grants into three large, but complicated, bureaucracies overseeing some 860 research and applied institutions.

In short, the problems associated with China's efforts in science and technology reform still ring true over a decade later:

> Limited resources, poor organization, an underdeveloped infrastructure, and inefficient use of qualified personnel are all persistent problems.[126]

THE OPEN DOOR POLICY: ACQUISITION AND TRANSFER OF SCIENCE AND TECHNOLOGY

China's main strategy for technological transfer in the 1970s was purchase from abroad—frequently acquiring complete industrial plants. This strategy was called "turnkey," because the complete facility required only the keys to open it for operation. Between 1972 and 1975, China imported some 170 complete industrial plants, valued at $2.6 billion, from eight European nations, Japan, the United States, and the Soviet Union.[127] Most of these plants were for basic industries, such as steel, electricity, petroleum, and chemical fertilizer. The Chinese could expand capital formation by copying a complete imported plant, which was a "carrier of new technology."[128] Former vice-premier Fang Yi made it very clear in 1978 that "an important way to develop science and technology at high speed is to utilize fully the latest achievements in the world of science and technology and absorb their quintessence." He said, "We should introduce selected techniques that play a key and pace-setting role."[129] During a brief spell of euphoria from 1977 to 1978, proposed contracts for purchasing technology from abroad proliferated; however, financial realities forced a readjustment of priorities in 1979. The government then made efforts to address the questions of how to digest and absorb foreign technology and how to deal with the problem of financing. The purchase of complete sets of equipment was not always satisfactory. At times imported equipment was found to be unsuitable for the intended localities. In other cases there was too much equipment imported, or the technology imported was inappropriate. There was a failure generally "to study the equipment, and master and spread knowledge of its use."[130]

The policy for scientific and technological purchases from abroad consists of the following guidelines:[131] (1) purchases must be selective—"We should start by considering our national economic requirements, our technical base, etc., not just go after the newest and most advanced"; (2) foreign technology "must be integrated with China's own research projects, otherwise there can be no true digestion and absorption"; and (3) scientists must study foreign scientific techniques through published journals, conferences, and exchanges. The policy in science and technology calls for "buying techniques, software and samples of machinery." The Chinese are trying to restrict purchases of equipment to what will be the most useful for their technological development, or as the Chinese say, "To buy hens for them to lay eggs." Hu Yaobang told the 1982 Party Congress: "We must refrain from indiscriminate import of equipment, and particularly of consumer goods that can be manufactured and supplied at home."[132] It is interesting to note that the Reagan administration granted China a "friendly but non-allied" status to permit it to purchase higher-level electronics and computers under some restrictive guidelines. The Chinese have also discovered three effective ways to acquire advanced foreign technology rapidly: joint ventures with foreign business concerns, countertrade factors, and special economic zones for trade and foreign investment. These strategies are key components of the new open door policy.

The Open Door Policy

Of the reforms instituted by China's pragmatic leaders under Deng Xiaoping, the policy of opening China's doors to foreign investment has been one of the most significant departures from decades of largely self-imposed ideological rigidity under Mao. The purpose of the "open door"—*kaifang zhenze*—was stated in the communiqué of the third session of the Eleventh Central Committee in December 1978:

> We are now . . . adopting a number of major new economic measures, on conscientiously transforming the system and methods on terms of equality and mutual benefit with other countries on the basis of self-reliance, striving to adopt the world's advanced technologies and equipment and greatly strengthening scientific and educational work to meet the needs of modernization.[133]

The party's 1978 decision to open up China to the outside world was included in the 1982 state constitution adopted by the Sixth National People's Congress.[134] The open door policy involved, in addition to the acquisition of advanced equipment, the acquisition of what is known as "codified technology," such as blueprints and drawings, and "undocumented technology," or technical information and skills.[135]

Let us review briefly the various methods China has employed to acquire advanced technology.

Joint Venture.[136]   The idea of cooperative business ventures between a communist nation and a capitalist one was pioneered by the Yugoslavs in 1967. In July 1979 the Fifth NPC at its second session adopted a joint venture law governing both Chinese and foreign investments.[137] The law contains three basic provisions:[138] (1) protection by the Chinese government of investment by a foreign concern in a joint venture; (2) a pledge by the foreign concern that the technology or equipment contributed from abroad "shall be truly advanced and appropriate to Chinese needs"; and (3) a guarantee of the retention by the foreign concern in the joint venture of the net profits after appropriate Chinese income taxes are paid.[139] The joint venture law also serves as a framework allowing foreign investors to negotiate and enter into contracts with the

Chinese government. While the law defines the role of foreign investment on Chinese soil, its emphasis is on the advanced technology a foreign investor or firm can share with the Chinese. A usual format in such arrangements is the 51–49 percent joint ownership agreement between the Chinese government and foreign firms. The Chinese provide land, labor, and the necessary infrastructure, and the foreign investor provides the investment capital and equipment.

Since 1979 there have been more than 2,000 joint venture agreements concluded, totaling about $16 billion. Many of these agreements, however, were merely pledges, and actual operations remained unfulfilled. The actual amount contracted and spent for joint ventures amounted to only about $4.8 to $5.0 billion by 1986.[140] Most investments came from Japan, the United States, France, West Germany, Australia, and Switzerland. A model of this type of investment was the China–Schindler joint venture, involving a Swiss manufacturer in partnership with Jardine Matheson of Hong Kong.[141] They formed a partnership to set up factories in China to produce lifts, or elevators. In its first year of operation (from 1980 to 1981), this joint venture yielded about $3.5 million in profits. Another such arrangement was the joint $51 million deal between China and American Motors Corporation (AMC) to produce Jeeps and Jeep engines at Beijing Auto Works. According to the contract, AMC was to invest $8 million initially, with another $8 million in advanced technology, to assist in the modernization of Beijing Auto Works. For AMC the advantage lay in cheap labor costs, enabling AMC's Chinese-made Jeeps to compete favorably in the Southeast Asian market.[142]

The original expectation was that the newly modernized Beijing auto plant would be able to produce 20,000 Cherokee Jeeps a year by 1990, using mostly locally made components and material.[143] However, the AMC–China joint venture ran into a number of problems from 1985 to 1986, and its Jeep production was interrupted for about seven weeks in 1986. One problem in the venture was the Chinese regulation that prohibited the company from obtaining foreign exchange needed to pay for imported components. The original joint venture agreement called for Beijing Auto Works to follow the new design for the Cherokee Jeep by using Chinese components, but the vehicles assembled with Chinese components were defective. AMC wanted to import about 90 percent of the Cherokee Jeep components as an alternative. As a partner in the joint venture, AMC had expected to pay for the imports with the United States dollar earnings from the sale of the Jeeps. But the second problem was that the Chinese foreign exchange regulation reduced the amount of foreign exchange allotted to the joint venture and added a 60 percent duty on imported parts.[144] After seven weeks of negotiation (during which the case received worldwide publicity threatening China's reputation as a country that welcomed foreign investment), Chinese authorities made changes in the foreign exchange regulation to permit buyers of Cherokee Jeeps to pay in United States dollars to enable the joint venture to import the needed spare parts.

The AMC joint venture episode illustrates some of the frustrations experienced by foreign investors in joint ventures with China. A major problem was converting Chinese currency earnings into United States dollars. The 1986 currency exchange regulations seem to have eased the problem. In February 1986 the new regulations permitted joint ventures that were short of hard currency to sell their products in China for needed hard currency or to reinvest their earnings in Chinese currency (renmimbi) in Chinese enterprises that earn hard currencies.[145] But the new regulations on joint ventures also discriminate against small foreign investors by allowing no debt on paid-up capital—a rule designed to prevent financially unsound foreign investors from entering the Chinese market.[146]

The new regulations may discourage formation of more joint ventures. In any event, by the late 1980s the Chinese were beginning to take a tougher stance in approving joint ventures.[147]

THE TREATMENT OF CHINESE INTELLECTUALS[148]

As of 1982 there were about 20 million intellectuals in China—defined as anyone who has had more than secondary education. Thus, a teacher, a university professor, a technician, a writer, or an engineer is defined as an intellectual. It is believed that the vast majority of them are not CCP members. In most societies this category of educated person is treated with respect and valued as a precious human resource. In China this was not the case between 1957 and 1978. In 1957 Chinese intellectuals were labeled "rightists"; they were suspected, put down, and despised. From 1957 through the decade of the Cultural Revolution (from 1966 to 1976), Chinese intellectuals were not only labeled as "rightist" but also as "the stinking ninth category" by the radicals. They were despised and persecuted merely because they possessed education, knowledge, and skills. The Cultural Revolution radicals did not consider them productive members of the socialist society. To the radical ideologues, it was better to be a peasant or a worker than a "stinking" intellectual.

When the pragmatic reformers came back to power in 1977, they set out to correct this negative attitude toward the intellectuals. The new leaders realized that China's modernization could not possibly proceed without the people who possessed the "brain power." In 1978 Deng quoted Marx and Lenin to prove that scientists and technological personnel were integral parts of the productive force. "Intellectuals," Deng cited Lenin as saying, "engage in scientific and technical work who themselves are not capitalists but scholars."[149] Deng went on to say that "brain workers who serve socialism are a part of the working people."[150] He argued further that as long as intellectuals were not opposed to the party or socialism, "we should, in line with the party's policy of uniting with, educating and remolding the intellectuals, bring out their specialized abilities, respect their labor and take interest in their progress, giving them a warm helping hand."[151]

However, "Leftist" attitudes toward intellectuals lingered on into the era of the Sixth Five-Year Plan. The truth of the matter is that many intellectuals were still not given full opportunities to apply their specialized knowledge and skill. In an article in *Hongqi (Red Flag)*, Politburo member Nie Rongzhen made it clear that the middle-aged intellectuals—about five million men and women in their forties and fifties, serving as the backbone of China's modernization program—continued to receive low wages and to face many difficulties.[152] Marshal Nie, in the winter of 1982, urged that provisions be made to take good care of the middle-aged intellectuals, who could provide enormous contributions to China's modernization. Nie indicated that in many government units, the intellectuals were still not being treated well and were not trusted.[153] There were frequent stories in the mass media about how some intellectuals were mistreated, demoted, and castigated by jealous local people. While most workers had received two wage increases since 1977, middle-aged intellectuals with twenty years of service received only one raise, a mere 7 yuan, or the equivalent of $3.50. They were also given cramped housing arrangements. During the author's 1995 visit to China, some middle-aged intellectuals spoke about "three heavies and two neglects"; namely, heavy family burden, heavy responsibility, and heavy pressure at work; and inadequate remuneration and meager living conditions.[154] Discrimination against the intellectuals continued mainly because of the lingering fear among the people of the "bourgeois academic authority." For many intellectuals the memory of their persecution after 1957 was too vivid for them to be optimistic about the future. Unless the pragmatic leaders successfully reversed the anti-intellectual climate, China's success in modernization will be in jeopardy.

Some developments concerning China's intellectuals need to be discussed here. One is the decision by the national conference in January 1986 to have a system of professional titles for those engaged in intellectual endeavors.[155] The new system was designed to provide better monetary rewards and promotional advancement for individuals working in science, technology, and higher education. Under this system, salary is based on professional title rather than on educational background or seniority in length of service. Under the old system a young scientist could not attain a position commensurate with his or her ability and competence. Now workers in professional fields may be given a professional title, such as engineer, researcher, economist, or editor. Hiring, salary, and promotion are in accordance with their professional title, which, in turn, is based on ability and competence. The system was instituted as an experiment in July 1985 in the Academies of Sciences and Social Sciences, the State Education Commission, and the ministries of agriculture, health, and mineral resources.

While Chinese intellectuals welcomed the "new deal" accorded to them in status, compensation, and career advancement, they also realized that their fate is still subject to the constantly shifting political winds. It has always been hard for intellectuals to know for sure how far they can go in expressing their thoughts. Their confidence in the party's willingness to provide an environment of relaxation and liberalization was jolted when the crusade against "spiritual pollution" was launched by the ideologues in 1983. Although the spiritual pollution campaign was abruptly terminated, it deeply shocked the intellectuals. Then, at the end of 1984, authors, artists, and writers were given an enormous boost on the issue of artistic free expression. In a speech to the Fourth Congress of the Writers' Association, Politburo member Hu Qili said: "Writers must have the freedom to choose material, themes and artistic methods and to express their own feeling and thoughts so that they could produce touching and inspiring works."[156] Hu's speech was interrupted thirty-three times by applause from the 12,500 members present. This speech, along with demands from intellectuals for freedom to think, ushered in a period of "freedom of creation." Professor Fang Lizhi made speeches stating that the "emergence and development of new theories necessitates creating an atmosphere of democracy and freedom in the universities, an atmosphere of intellectual ideology."[157] The "freedom of creation" and thought was cut short by the 1987 crackdown on student protest and demonstration as the campaign against "bourgeois liberalization" intensified. Fang Lizhi and other outspoken intellectuals were dismissed from their posts and expelled from party membership. This was followed by more expulsions and dismissals of authors, writers, and journalists. Once again Chinese intellectuals had to exercise caution, despite the official position that intellectuals were not the target in the fight against "bourgeois liberalization."[158] Former Premier Li Peng reemphasized that the party "will not change its policy on intellectuals, whose skills and knowledge are indispensable to China's drive for modernization." But for many Chinese intellectuals there is a crisis of confidence in the party. That pledge by Li has not been fulfilled, and a widespread feeling of fear and oppression has developed among Chinese intellectuals since the June 4 killings at Tiananmen.

CHINESE INTELLECTUALS AFTER TIANANMEN

In his report to the Seventh NPC Standing Committee on June 30, 1989, Chen Xitong, then mayor of Beijing and recently expelled from the CCP for embezzlement of public funds for personal uses, charged that a handful of China's intellectuals, inside and outside the CCP, had engineered the Tiananmen "conspiracy" to "overthrow" the party's leadership.[159] He then presented a list of allegedly incriminating political assemblies, seminars, big-character posters, and joint petitions organized by Chinese intellectuals, who had used their positions in various institutions to criticize the party for its failure to act on inflation, corruption, and the slowdown in reform. One of these petitions was Fang Lizhi's open letter to Deng Xiaoping, co-signed by forty-two scientists and thirty-two other intellectuals, urging the release of political prisoners.[160]

Mayor Chen's report on this situation was, however, only a culmination of a long-standing antagonism between the government and China's intellectual vanguard—an antagonism that was destined to reach a breaking point in June 1989 at Tiananmen Square. By January 1989 the government's relationship with the intellectuals had reached the point of confrontation. In fact, the party leaders' relationship with Chinese intellectuals had already gone sour during the December 1986–87 student demonstration, when the party's response was to expel from party membership those intellectuals—Fang Lizhi, Wang Ruowang, and Liu Binyan—who were openly critical of the campaign against "bourgeois liberalization." This was the beginning of the "desertion of the intellectuals," as scientists, writers, and some journalists—many of them party veterans—protested and withdrew from party membership.[161]

Provocative new ideas being advanced by young social science researchers in 1988 and 1989 also generated official wrath. One such idea was the concept of "New Authoritarianism" that surfaced just prior to Hu Yaobang's death on April 15, 1989. Researcher Wu Jianliang, working in the Party's general office, advocated that the government be entrusted to a leader who is committed to modern economic views; protection of individual freedom; and opening the country to foreign capital, culture, and technology.[162] Another idea advocated by the now-exiled political scientist Yan Jiaqi and many other intellectuals was direct popular election of delegates to the NPC.

The Tiananmen crackdown not only silenced the intellectuals, but also forced a number of them into exile. Moreover, scholars, researchers, and thinkers in the prestigious Chinese Academy of Social Sciences—the bastion of new ideas for solving China's social and economic problems—were subjected to indoctrination and intimidation by the regime. They were forced to attend periodic political study sessions. When not forced into political indoctrination, Chinese intellectuals have merely kept silent, waiting quietly for a leadership change.[163] Immediately after Tiananmen their research institutions were placed under military control, and directors for these institutions were interrogated. Dissidents were dismissed and expelled from the party after investigation.

A year after the Tiananmen crackdown, the new party chief, Jiang Zemin, made overtures to appease the alienated Chinese intellectuals, who as of 1989 numbered more than 22 million. He praised them as "an excellent contingent" supporting Deng's "Four Basic Principles": the leadership of the party, and the socialist road, the dictatorship of the proletariat, and Marxism-Leninism and Mao's Thought. However, Jiang warned that China's young intellectuals, almost half of the total 22 million, have some "shortcomings and deficiencies" as a result of their lack of experience in life. He reiterated the traditional national attitudes toward intellectuals, such as "inadequate attention" to and lack of appreciation for their work. He pointed out that their living and working conditions still need improvement.[164] He paid lip service to academic freedom and literary creativeness. He assured them that "academic disputes on scientific and cultural issues must not be subject to official sanction." What this presages for the future in terms of an improvement in official status is hard to predict. Meanwhile, the bulk of China's intellectuals are anything but pessimistic; they wait silently, but hopefully, for a change.

Some encouraging signs have emerged as China has decided to continue full speed ahead with economic reform. One such sign is monetary reward for scientific intellectuals in order to encourage applied or practical research to enhance production.[165] One engineer in the Zhuhai SEZ received a cash reward of $200,000, a car, and an apartment for designing a method of extracting a clotting agent from animal blood and helping to open a factory to produce it. A biologist in Beijing was granted a cash reward of about $4,000 for breeding better pigs. Finally, in its decision to move forward in establishing a socialist market economy, the CCP's Central Committee laid stress on the need for trained skilled workers and professionals in all fields.[166] Thus for the 1990s scientific and technological workers have been given their due recognition and respect.

However, expansion in China's economic reform has also prompted party officials to take recent actions against intellectuals; these actions are aimed at placing restrictions on some vocal liberal intellectuals who publish their ideas or criticisms or advocate human rights or multiple parties in academic circles and in newspapers. For instance, there is a case involving the firing of a political scientist from the Chinese Academy of Social Sciences for urging the need for political reform, and the deportation of an American citizen because he worked in the United States on human rights issues.[167] In July 2000 party chair Jiang Zemin stepped up a campaign of intellectual suppression by forming a small group of top leaders for the purpose of providing monitoring mechanisms and directions to the media so that the party's policies and directives will be strictly observed.[168] All this has been done in the name of stability which, in essence, means the party's monopoly of political power.

NOTES

1. "It Is Essential to Rely on the Poor and Lower-Middle Peasants in the Educational Revolution in the Countryside," *Peking Review*, 39 (September 27, 1968), 21.
2. See Ellen K. Ong, "Education in China since the Cultural Revolution," *Studies in Comparative Communism*, 3, nos. 3 and 4 (July–August 1970), 158–75.
3. See William Hinton, *Hundred Day War: The Cultural Revolution at Tsinghua University* (New York and London: Monthly Review Press, 1972).
4. Robert McCormick, "Revolution in Education Committees," *China Quarterly*, 57 (January–March 1974), 134–39.
5. "Power Is the Fundamental Question of Revolution in Education," *Peking Review*, 51 (December 21, 1968), 8.
6. Ibid., p. 8.
7. *Beijing Review*, 2 (May 27, 1985), 3; and 3 (June 6, 1985), 16.
8. *Ta Kung Pao Weekly Supplement* (Hong Kong), May 23, 1985, p. 1. Also see *Beijing Review*, 21 (May 27, 1985), 6; 23 (June 10, 1985), 15; and 24 (June 17, 1985), 19.
9. *Beijing Review* (May 12, 1986), 4–5.
10. *Beijing Review*, 21 (May 27, 1985), 6.
11. *Ta Kung Pao Weekly Supplement* (Hong Kong), May 23, 1985, p. 1.
12. *Beijing Review*, 19 (May 13, 1985), 4.
13. *Beijing Review*, 33 (August 18, 1986), 22.

14. Ibid.
15. *Beijing Review*, 29 (July 21, 1986), 4.
16. *Beijing Review*, 23 (June 10, 1985), 16.
17. Ibid. Also see Austin Swanson and Zhang Zhian, "Education Reform in China," *Phi Delta Kappan* (January 1987), 373–378.
18. *Beijing Review*, 7–8 (February 18, 1985), 30.
19. Ibid. And also see Robert McCormick, "The Radio and Television Universities and the Development of Higher Education in China," *China Quarterly*, 105 (March 1986), 74–94.
20. McCormick, "Radio and Television Universities," 93–94.
21. *Beijing Review*, 47 (November 24, 1986), 15.
22. *Beijing Review*, 24 (June 16, 1986), 5. Also see Swanson and Zhian, "Education Reform in China," 373–78.
23. Ibid. Also see Swanson and Zhian, "Education Reform in China," 371.
24. *Beijing Review*, 34 (August 24, 1987), 6.
25. Ibid.
26. *China News Analysis*, 1377 (January 15, 1989), 1–9, and 1414 (July 15, 1990), 1–3.
27. *China News Analysis*, 1414 (July 15, 1990), 5.
28. *Beijing Review* (July 17–23, 1989), 25.
29. Thomas B. Gold, "Alienated Youth Cloud China's Future," *Asian Wall Street Journal Weekly,* May 18, 1981, p. 13; John Roderick, "China's Youth Problem," Associated Press, as reprinted in *Honolulu Star-Bulletin*, September 15, 1980, p. A-21; and Richard Critchfield, "Youth Turn out Dogma, Turn on Radios," *Christian Science Monitor,* August 1, 1980, p. 13. Also see Mary-Louise O'Callaghan, "A Streak of Individualism in China's Youth," *Christian Science Monitor,* July 22, 1983, p. 3.
30. *Christian Science Monitor,* July 22, 1983, p. 3.
31. Stanley Rosen, "Prosperity, Privatization, and China's Youth," *Problems of Communism*, 34, no. 2 (March–April, 1985), 3.
32. Ibid., 13.
33. Li Peng, "Report on the Work of the Government," *Beijing Review,* (April 12–18, 1993), vii.
34. See Cui Lili, "New Target for Educational Reform," *Beijing Review,* (May 31–June 6, 1993), 13–18.
35. Ibid., 14.
36. Ibid.
37. Peng, "Report on the Work of the Government," vii.
38. Lili, "New Target for Educational Reform," 14.
39. See Dai Yannian, "New Focus on Education," *Beijing Review.* (July 11–17, 1994), 4.
40. See Liu Junfang, "Progress in Vocational Education," *Beijing Review,* (March 23–29, 1992), 32.
41. Ibid.
42. Ibid., 35.
43. Peng, "Report on the Work of the Government," March 1993, vii; and "Report on the Work of the Government," March 1997, x.
44. See *Beijing Qingnian Bao* (Beijing Youth Daily), April 21, 1994, p. 8.
45. See "Adult Education in Beijing," *Beijing Review,* (May 30–June 5, 1994), 24.
46. Peng, "Report on the Work of the Government," March 1997, x.
47. See Cui Lili, "Invigorating China through Science and Education," *Beijing Review,* (July 17–27, 1995), 12.
48. Vilma Seeburg, *Literacy in China: The Effects of the National Development Context and Policy on Literacy Levels, 1949–1979* (Bochum: Brockmeyer, 1990), p. 268.
49. Glen Peterson, "State Literacy Ideologies and the Transformation of Rural China," *Australian Journal of Chinese Affairs*, Issue 32 (July 1994), 120.
50. See *Beijing Review* (October 19-25, 1998), 30.
51. Lili, "New Target for Educational Reform," 14.
52. Ibid., 15. Also see Cui Lili, "The Metamorphosis of Beijing University," *Beijing Review,* (March 29–April 4, 1993), 19–22; and Sheila Tefft, "China Universities Learn Capitalism," *Christian Science Monitor,* June 3, 1993, pp. 8–9.
53. Zhang Chao and Ying Xing, "The Third World in Universities," *China Focus* (September 1, 1996), 6.
54. Peng, "Report on the Work of the Government, March 1, 1997," xi.
55. Chao and Xing, "Third World in Universities," 6.
56. Ibid.
57. Ibid.
58. See Marcus W. Brauchli, "Wary of Education, but Needing Brains, China Faces a Dilemma," *Wall Street Journal,* November 15, 1994, p. A-1.

59. See Ibid., p. A-5; and Yan Ji, "Chinese Education and the Crisis of the Nation," *China Focus* (July 1, 1995), 4.

60. See Liu Zhongli, Minister of Finance, "Report on the Implementation of the Central and Local Budgets for 1996 and on the Draft Central and Local Budgets for 1997," *Beijing Review* (March 10-16, 1997), 31.

61. See Yannian, "New Focus on Education," 4.

62. "New Target for Educational Reform," 15.

63. *Beijing Review,* (January 24–30, 1994), 6.

64. Lili, "New Target for Educational Reform," 17.

65. *Beijing Review,* (May 6–10, 1996), 6.

66. See Huang Wei, "Authoritative Comments on China's Education Law," *Beijing Review,* (May 22–28, 1995), 14.

67. Teng Hsiao-p'ing, "Speech at Opening Ceremony of National Science Conference (March 18, 1978)," *Peking Review*, 12 (March 24, 1978), 17.

68. Theoretical Group of the Chinese Academy of Sciences, "A Serious Struggle in Scientific and Technical Circles," *Peking Review*, 16 (April 15, 1977), 24–27.

69. Richard Suttmeier, "Science Policy Shifts, Organizational Change and China's Development," *China Quarterly*, 62 (June 1975), 207–41. Also see William W. Whitson, "China's Quest for Technology," *Problems of Communism*, 12 (July–August 1973), 16–30.

70. Whitson, "China's Quest for Technology," 17–18.

71. Bruce J. Esposito, "The Cultural Revolution and China's Scientific Establishment," *Current Scene*, 12, no. 4 (April 1974), 2–3.

72. Genevieve Dean, "China's Technological Development," *New Scientist* (May 18, 1972), 371–73.

73. C. H. G. Oldham, "Technology in China: Science for the Masses?" *Far Eastern Economic Review* (May 16, 1968), 353–55; and Rennselaer W. Lee III, "The Politics of Technology in Communist China," in *Ideology and Politics in Contemporary China*, ed. Chalmers Johnson (Seattle, Wash. and London: University of Washington Press, 1973), pp. 301–25; Jonathan Unger, "Mao's Million Amateur Technicians," *Far Eastern Economic Review* (April 3, 1971), 115–18.

74. C.H.G. Oldham, "Science and Technological Policies," in *China's Developmental Experience*, ed. Michael Oksenberg (New York, Washington, and London: Praeger Publications, 1973), pp. 80–94.

75. Teng Hsiao-p'ing, "Speech at Opening Ceremony of National Science Conference," 10; and Hua Kuo-feng, "Raise the Scientific and Cultural Level of the Entire Chinese Nation," *Peking Review*, 31 (March 13, 1978), 6–14.

76. "Outline National Plan for Development of Science and Technology, Relevant Policies and Measures," *Beijing Review*, 14 (April 7, 1978), 7.

77. "30th Anniversary of Chinese Academy of Sciences," *Beijing Review*, 46 (November 16, 1979), 3.

78. Richard Suttmeier, "Politics, Modernization, and Science," *Problems of Communism*, 30, no. 1 (January–February 1981), 30.

79. Ibid., 30.

80. "Updating Science and Technology," *Beijing Review*, 7 (February 14, 1983), 16.

81. See "Outline Report on Policy Governing the Development of Our National Science and Technology the State Science and Technology Commission (February 23, 1981)," in *Issues and Studies*, 18, no. 5 (May 1982), 88–101.

82. Suttmeier, "Politics, Modernization, and Science," 31.

83. See *Ming Pai Dail* (Hong Kong), February 20, 1982, p. 1; and *Ta Kung Pao Weekly Supplement*, August 6, 1981, p. 4.

84. See *GIST*, Bureau of Public Affairs, Department of State, March, 1981.

85. *Honolulu Advertiser,* May 11, 1983, p. H-1.

86. *Ta Kung Pao Weekly Supplement*, December 2, 1982, p. 1.

87. Hsiao-p'ing, "Speech at Opening Ceremony of National Science Conference," 15 and 17.

88. *Ta Kung Pao Weekly Supplement* (Hong Kong), May 14, 1981, p. 1.

89. Ibid., p.1; and issue of May 21, 1981, p.3.

90. "Report on the Sixth Five Year Plan," 16.

91. See James Reardon-Anderson, "Science and Technology in Post-Mao China," *Contemporary China*, 2, no. 4 (Winter 1978), 42–4.

92. "Outline Report on Policy Governing the Development of Our National Science and Technology," 99.

93. Ibid., 94.

94. *Beijing Review*, 11 (March 18, 1985), 6.

95. See Richard Conrou, "Technological Change and Industrial Development" in Graham Young, ed., *China's Dilemma of Modernization* (London: Croom Helm, 1985), pp. 118–23.

96. *Beijing Review*, 24 (June 16, 1984), 22. Also see Dennis Fred Simon, "S & T Reforms," *China Business Review* (March–April 1985), 31.
97. *Beijing Review*, 24 (June 16, 1984), 22.
98. Simon, "S & T Reforms," 32.
99. Ibid.
100. *Beijing Review*, 24 (June 16, 1984), 22.
101. Ibid. For an overview of science and reform, see Richard P. Suttmeier, "Reform, Modernization, and the Changing Constitution of Science in China," *Asian Survey*, 29, no. 10 (October 1989), 999–1015.
102. Ibid., 27.
103. Speech to the Fifth National Congress of the Chinese Association for Science and Technology held in Beijing May 27–31, 1996. *Beijing Review,* (June 17–23, 1996), 5.
104. See "Accelerating the Advance of Science and Technology," *Beijing Review,* (July 17–23, 1995), 8. For information about grain production increase through the application of high technology, see "Role of Technology Stressed," *Beijing Review,* (March 11–17, 1996), 5.
105. "Accelerating the Advance of Science and Technology," 8.
106. Ibid.
107. Ibid.
108. Richard P. Suttmeier, "Emerging Innovation Networks and Changing Strategies for Industrial Technology in China: Some Observations." Paper given at the 1996 annual meeting of the Association for Asian Studies, Honolulu, Hawaii., April 1996, p. 2. This author is grateful for Prof. Suttmeier's courtesy in providing me with the text of his paper.
109. "Accelerating the Advance of Science and Technology," 10.
110. "Report on the Work of the Government," on March 1997, x and xi.
111. Liu Zhongli, Minister of Finance, "Report on the Draft Central and Local Budgets for 1977," *Beijing Review,* (April 4–13, 1997), 31.
112. Suttmeier, "Emerging Innovation Networks and Changing Strategies for Industrial Technology in China," p. 2.
113. "Accelerating the Advance of Science and Technology," 8–9.
114. See Cui Lili, "Invigorating China through Science and Education," *Beijing Review,* (July 17–27, 1995), 12.
115. Ibid., 13.
116. Ibid., 11.
117. See "Role of Technology Stressed," *Beijing Review,* (March 11–17, 1996), 5.
118. Ibid.
119. Lili, See "Invigorating China through Science and Education," 12–13.
120. Suttmeier, "Emerging Innovation Networks and Changing Strategies," p. 2.
121. Figures came from Wei Yu, Vice Minister for the State Education Commission, in his talk to the May 1995 National Science and Technology Conference in Beijing. See Lili's report on "Invigorating China through Science and Education," 14.
122. See Arthur Fisher, "A Long Haul for Chinese Science," *Popular Science,* August 1996, p. 39.
123. Ibid.
124. Ibid., p. 13.
125. Ibid., p. 15.
126. Denis Fred Simon, "The Challenge of Modernizing Industrial Technology in China," *Asian Survey*, 26, no. 4 (April 1986), 432.
127. See Dave L. Denny, "International Finance in the People's Republic of China," in *China: A Reassessment of the Economy*, pp. 701–2. Also see Kent Morrison, "Domestic Politics and Industrialization in China: The Foreign Trade Factor," *Asian Survey*, 18, no.7 (July 1978) 690–98.
128. Shannon Brown, "Foreign Technology and Economic Growth," *Problems of Communism*, 26, (July–August 1977), 30–32.
129. "Outline Report on Policy Governing the Development of Our National Science and Technology," 93.
130. "On China's Economic Relations with Foreign Countries," *Beijing Review*, 22 (May 31, 1982), 15.
131. "Outline Report on Policy Governing the Development of Our National Science and Technology," 93.
132. "Creating a New Situation in All Fields of Socialist Modernization," *Beijing Review*, 51 (December 20, 1985), 20.
133. "Communiqué of the Third Plenary Session of the Eleventh Central Committee of the Communist Party of China," *Peking Review*, 52 (December 29, 1978), 11.
134. See Appendix A, p. 371.
135. *China's Open Door Policy: The Quest for Foreign Technology and Capital* (Vancouver, Canada: University of British Columbia Press, 1984), p. 23.

136. For joint venture projects and laws, see Peter Nehemkis and Alexis Nehemkis, "China's Law on Joint Ventures," *California Management Review*, 22, no. 4 (Summer 1980), 37–46; *Law of the PRC on Joint Ventures Using Chinese & Foreign Investment*, Wen Wei Po (Hong Kong), July 1979; James Roselle, "Local Lenders May Aid China Venture," *Asian Wall Street Journal Weekly*, September 7, 1981, p. 12; Frank Ching, "China Is Adopting Cautious Approach to Joint Ventures," *Asian Wall Street Journal Weekly*, July 27, 1981, p. 4; Phijit Chong, "More Clues to a Taxing Puzzle," *Far Eastern Economic Review* (March 21, 1980), 99; *Joint Venture Agreements in the People's Republic of China*, U.S. Department of Commerce, 1982; and David C. Brown, "Sino-Foreign Joint Ventures: Contemporary Developments and Historical Perspective," *Journal of Northeast Asian Studies*, 1, no. 4 (December 1982), 25–55. Also for a study on doing business in China, see Graeme Browning, *If Everybody Bought One Shoe: American Capitalism in Communist China* (New York: Hill and Wang, 1989).

137. Nehemkis and Nehemkis, "China's Law on Joint Ventures," 37–46. Also see Lev P. Deliusin, "Reforms in China: Problems and Prospects," *Asian Survey*, 27, no. 11 (November 1988), 1101–16. For a thorough treatment of the origin, direction, content and the future of reform, see Harry Harding's *China's Second Revolution: Reform after Mao* (Washington, D.C.: The Brookings Institution, 1987).

138. "The Law of PRC on Joint Ventures Using Chinese and Foreign Investment," *Beijing Review*, 29 (July 20, 1979), 24–26.

139. Ibid., 24.

140. *Asian Wall Street Journal*, July 19, 1986, p. 4.

141. *China Trade Report* (October 1981), 8.

142. *Newsweek*, May 16, 1983, pp. 75–76. For a discussion on the history and the partnership of AMC in China, see Jim Mann, *Beijing Jeep: The Short, Unhappy Romance of American Business in China* (New York: Simon & Schuster, 1989).

143. *China Daily*, September 17, 1986, p. 4.

144. *China Business Review* (July–August, 1986), 34.

145. *China Trade Report* (March 1986), 1.

146. *Ta Kung Pao Weekly Supplement* (Hong Kong), January 30, 1986, p. 4.

147. See *China Trade Report* (March 1986), 1; and *Asian Wall Street Journal*, January 15, 1986, p. 3.

148. For more discussion about the Chinese intellectuals, see Jerome B. Grieder, *Intellectuals and the State in Modern China: A Narrative History* (New York: Free Press, 1981); Merle Goldman, *China's Intellectuals: Advise and Dissent* (Cambridge, Mass.: Harvard University Press, 1981); Richard C. Kraus, "Intellectuals and the State in China," *Problems of Communism*, 31, no. 6 (November–December 1982), 81–84; Takashi Oka, "China Tries to Use Once-Scorned Intellectuals for Modernizing," *Christian Science Monitor*, February 4, 1983, pp. 1, 6; Fox Butterfield, "China's Persecution of Intellectuals," *New York Times* Service, reprinted in *Honolulu Star-Bulletin*, December 10, 1981, p. A-2, and *China: Alive in the Bitter Sea*, pp. 416–19; *Hongqi*, 24 (December 16, 1982), 4–12; and Gerald Chen, "The Middle-aged Intellectuals," *Ta Kung Pao Weekly Supplement*, September 23, 1982, p. 14.

149. Hsiao-p'ing, "Speech at Opening Ceremony of National Science Conference," 11.

150. Ibid., 12.

151. Ibid., 15.

152. *Hongqi*, 24 (December 16, 1982), 10.

153. Ibid.

154. Notes taken on author's visits in 1978 and 1979. Also see *Ming Pao Daily* (Hong Kong), March 6, 1983, p. 1; and *Beijing Review*, 49 (December 6, 1982), 3–4.

155. *Ta Kung Pao Weekly Supplement* (Hong Kong), January 16, 1986, p. 7.

156. *New York Times*, January 1, 1985, p. 4.

157. *Beijing Review*, 50 (December 15, 1986), 17.

158. *Beijing Review*, 4 (January 26, 1987), 9. For recent cases of expulsion from the party membership, see *Ming Pao Daily* (Hong Kong), August 25, 1987, p. 1.

159. *Beijing Review* (July 17–23, 1989), i–iv.

160. See "Chinese Democracy in 1989: Continuity and Change," *Problems of Communism* (May 30, 1972), 24.

161. Ibid., 24; and Liu Binyan, *A Higher Kind of Loyalty*, (New York: Pantheon Books, 1990), pp. 265–268.

162. *China News Analysis*, 1387 (June 15, 1989), 6.

163. Washington Post Service as reprinted in *Honolulu Advertiser*, July 23, 1990, p. A-5.

164. *Beijing Review*, (May 14–20, 1990), 9.

165. See *Hawaii Tribune Herald* (Hilo), October 18, 1992, p. 7.

166. See *Beijing Review*, (November 22–28, 1993), 27–28.

167. See Elisabeth Rosenthal, "China Trying to Crack Down on Vocal Liberal Intellectuals," *New York Times*, May 8, 2000, pp. A-1 and A-8.

168. See Lo Bin, "Jiang Turned Left Swiftly for Cleansing the Media," *Zhengming Magazine* (Hong Kong), no. 274 (August 2000), 7–9.

SUGGESTED READINGS

Agelasto, Michael, and Bob Adamson (eds.) *Higher Education in Post-Mao China* (Hong Kong: Hong Kong University Press, 1998).

Browning, Graeme. *If Everybody Bought One Shoe: American Capitalism in Communist China* (New York: Hill and Wang, 1989).

Du, Ruiqing. *Chinese Higher Education: A Decade of Reform and Development (1978-1988)* (London: Macmillan, 1992).

Goldman, Merle. *China's Intellectuals: Advise and Dissent* Cambridge, Mass.: Harvard University Press, 1981).

Ross, Heidi, and Judith Liu. *Education in the People's Republic of China* (New York: Garland Press, 1999).

Appendix A

The Constitution of the People's Republic of China (1982)

TABLE OF CONTENTS*

PREAMBLE

China is one of the countries with the longest histories in the world. The people of all nationalities in China have jointly created a splendid culture and have a glorious revolutionary tradition.

Feudal China was gradually reduced after 1840 to a semi-colonial and semi-feudal country. The Chinese people waged wave upon wave of heroic struggles for national independence and liberation and for democracy and freedom.

Great and earth-shaking historical changes have taken place in China in the 20th century.

The Revolution of 1911, led by Dr. Sun Yat-sen, abolished the feudal monarchy and gave birth to the Republic of China. But the Chinese people had yet to fulfill their historical task of overthrowing imperialism and feudalism.

After waging hard, protracted and tortuous struggles, armed and otherwise, the Chinese people of all nationalities led by the Communist Party of China with Chairman Mao Zedong as its leader ultimately, in 1949, overthrew the rule of imperialism, feudalism and bureaucrat-capitalism, won the great victory of the new-democratic revolution and founded the People's Republic of China. Thereupon the Chinese people took state power into their own hands and became masters of the country.

After the founding of the People's Republic, the transition of Chinese society from a new-democratic to a socialist society was effected step by step. The socialist transformation of the private ownership of the means of production was completed, the system of exploitation of man by man eliminated and the socialist system established. The people's democratic dictatorship led by the working class and based on the alliance

---

Beijing Review, 52 (December 27, 1982), 10–52. (Adopted on December 4, 1982, by the Fifth National People's Congress of the People's Republic of China at its fifth session.)

of workers and peasants, which is in essence the dictatorship of the proletariat, has been consolidated and developed. The Chinese people and the Chinese People's Liberation Army have thwarted aggression, sabotage and armed provocations by imperialists and hegemonists, safeguarded China's national independence and security and strengthened its national defence. Major successes have been achieved in economic development. An independent and fairly comprehensive socialist system of industry has in the main been established. There has been a marked increase in agricultural production. Significant progress has been made in educational, scientific, cultural and other undertakings, and socialist ideological education has yielded noteworthy results. The living standards of the people have improved considerably.

Both the victory of China's new-democratic revolution and the successes of its socialist cause have been achieved by the Chinese people of all nationalities under the leadership of the Communist Party of China and the guidance of Marxism-Leninism and Mao Zedong Thought, and by upholding truth, correcting errors and overcoming numerous difficulties and hardships. The basic task of the nation in the years to come is to concentrate its effort on socialist modernization. Under the leadership of the Communist Party of China and the guidance of Marxism-Leninism and Mao Zedong Thought, the Chinese people of all nationalities will continue to adhere to the people's democratic dictatorship and follow the socialist road, steadily improve socialist institutions, develop socialist democracy, improve the socialist legal system and work hard and self-reliantly to modernize industry, agriculture, national defence and science and technology step by step to turn China into a socialist country with a high level of culture and democracy.

The exploiting classes as such have been eliminated in our country. However, class struggle will continue to exist within certain limits for a long time to come. The Chinese people must fight against those forces and elements, both at home and abroad, that are hostile to China's socialist system and try to undermine it.

Taiwan is part of the sacred territory of the People's Republic of China. It is the lofty duty of the entire Chinese people, including our compatriots in Taiwan, to accomplish the great task of reunifying the motherland.

In building socialism it is imperative to rely on the workers, peasants and intellectuals and unite with all the forces that can be united. In the long years of revolution and construction, there has been formed under the leadership of the Communist Party of China a broad patriotic united front that is composed of democratic parties and people's organizations and embraces all socialist working people, all patriots who support socialism and all patriots who stand for reunification of the motherland. This united front will continue to be consolidated and developed. The Chinese People's Political Consultative Conference is a broadly representative organization of the united front, which has played a significant historical role and will continue to do so in the political and social life of the country, in promoting friendship with the people of other countries and in the struggle for socialist modernization and for the reunification and unity of the country.

The People's Republic of China is a unitary multinational state built up jointly by the people of all its nationalities. Socialist relations of equality, unity and mutual assistance have been established among them and will continue to be strengthened. In the struggle to safeguard the unity of the nationalities, it is necessary to combat big-nation chauvinism, mainly Han chauvinism, and also necessary to combat local-national chauvinism. The state does its utmost to promote the common prosperity of all nationalities in the country.

China's achievements in revolution and construction are inseparable from support by the people of the world. The future of China is closely linked with that of the whole world. China adheres to an independent foreign policy as well as to the five principles of mutual respect for sovereignty and territorial integrity, mutual non-aggression, non-interference in each other's internal affairs, equality and mutual benefit, and peaceful coexistence in developing diplomatic relations and economic and cultural exchanges with other countries; China consistently opposes imperialism, hegemonism and colonialism, works to strengthen unity with the people of other countries, supports the oppressed nations and the developing countries in their just struggle to win and preserve national independence and develop their national economies, and strives to safeguard world peace and promote the cause of human progress.

This Constitution affirms the achievements of the struggles of the Chinese people of all nationalities and defines the basic system and basic tasks of the state in legal form; it is the fundamental law of the state and has supreme legal authority. The people of all nationalities, all state organs, the armed forces, all political parties and public organizations and all enterprises and undertakings in the country must take the Constitution as the basic norm of conduct, and they have the duty to uphold the dignity of the Constitution and ensure its implementation.

CHAPTER ONE
GENERAL PRINCIPLES

Article 1　The People's Republic of China is a socialist state under the people's democratic dictatorship led by the working class and based on the alliance of workers and peasants.

The socialist system is the basic system of the People's Republic of China. Sabotage of the socialist system by any organization or individual is prohibited.

Article 2　All power in the People's Republic of China belongs to the people.

The organs through which the people exercise state power are the National People's Congress and the local people's congresses at different levels.

The people administer state affairs and manage economic, cultural and social affairs through various channels and in various ways in accordance with the law.

Article 3　The state organs of the People's Republic of China apply the principle of democratic centralism.

The National People's Congress and the local people's congresses at different levels are instituted through democratic election. They are responsible to the people and subject to their supervision.

All administrative, judicial and procuratorial organs of the state are created by the people's congresses to which they are responsible and under whose supervision they operate.

The division of functions and powers between the central and local state organs is guided by the principle of giving full play to the initiative and enthusiasm of the local authorities under the unified leadership of the central authorities.

Article 4 All nationalities in the People's Republic of China are equal. The state protects the lawful rights and interests of the minority nationalities and upholds and develops the relationship of equality, unity and mutual assistance among all of China's nationalities. Discrimination against and oppression of any nationality are prohibited; any acts that undermine the unity of the nationalities or instigate their secession are prohibited.

The state helps the areas inhabited by minority nationalities speed up their economic and cultural development in accordance with the peculiarities and needs of the different minority nationalities.

Regional autonomy is practised in areas where people of minority nationalities live in compact communities; in these areas organs of self-government are established for the exercise of the right of autonomy. All the national autonomous areas are inalienable parts of the People's Republic of China.

The people of all nationalities have the freedom to use and develop their own spoken and written languages, and to preserve or reform their own ways and customs.

Article 5 The state upholds the uniformity and dignity of the socialist legal system. No law or administrative or local rules and regulations shall contravene the Constitution.

All state organs, the armed forces, all political parties and public organizations and all enterprises and undertakings must abide by the Constitution and the law. All acts in violation of the Constitution and the law must be looked into.

No organization or individual may enjoy the privilege of being above the Constitution and the law.

Article 6 The basis of the socialist economic system of the People's Republic of China is socialist public ownership of the means of production, namely, ownership by the whole people and collective ownership by the working people.

The system of socialist public ownership supersedes the system of exploitation of man by man; it applies the principle of "from each according to his ability, to each according to his work."

Article 7 The state economy is the sector of socialist economy under ownership by the whole people; it is the leading force in the national economy. The state ensures the consolidation and growth of the state economy.

Article 8 Rural people's communes, agricultural producers' co-operatives, and other forms of co-operative economy such as producers', supply and marketing, credit and consumers' co-operatives, belong to the sector of socialist economy under collective ownership by the working people. Working people who are members of rural economic collectives have the right, within the limits prescribed by law, to farm private plots of cropland and hilly land, engage in household sideline production and raise privately owned livestock.

The various forms of co-operative economy in the cities and towns, such as those in the handicraft, industrial, building, transport, commercial and service trades, all belong to the sector of socialist economy under collective ownership by the working people.

The state protects the lawful rights and interests of the urban and rural economic collectives and encourages, guides and helps the growth of the collective economy.

Article 9   Mineral resources, waters, forests, mountains, grassland, unreclaimed land, beaches and other natural resources are owned by the state, that is, by the whole people, with the exception of the forests, mountains, grassland, unreclaimed land and beaches that are owned by collectives in accordance with the law.

The state ensures the rational use of natural resources and protects rare animals and plants. The appropriation or damage of natural resources by any organization or individual by whatever means is prohibited.

Article 10   Land in the cities is owned by the state.

Land in the rural and suburban areas is owned by collectives except for those portions which belong to the state in accordance with the law; house sites and private plots of cropland and hilly land are also owned by collectives.

The state may in the public interest take over land for its use in accordance with the law.

No organization or individual may appropriate, buy, sell or lease land, or unlawfully transfer land in other ways.

All organizations and individuals who use land must make rational use of the land.

Article 11   The individual economy of urban and rural working people, operated within the limits prescribed by law, is a complement to the socialist public economy. The state protects the lawful rights and interests of the individual economy.

The state guides, helps and supervises the individual economy by exercising administrative control.

Article 12   Socialist public property is sacred and inviolable.

The state protects socialist public property. Appropriation or damage of state or collective property by any organization or individual by whatever means is prohibited.

Article 13   The state protects the right of citizens to own lawfully earned income, savings, houses and other lawful property.

The state protects by law the right of citizens to inherit private property.

Article 14   The state continuously raises labour productivity, improves economic results and develops the productive forces by enhancing the enthusiasm of the working people, raising the level of their technical skill, disseminating advanced science and technology, improving the systems of economic administration and enterprise operation and management, instituting the socialist system of responsibility in various forms and improving organization of work.

The state practises strict economy and combats waste.

The state properly apportions accumulation and consumption, pays attention to the interests of the collective and the individual as well as of the state and, on the basis of expanded production, gradually improves the material and cultural life of the people.

Article 15   The state practises economic planning on the basis of socialist public ownership. It ensures the proportionate and co-ordinated growth of the national economy through overall balancing by economic planning and the supplementary role of regulation by the market.

Disturbance of the orderly functioning of the social economy or disruption of the state economic plan by any organization or individual is prohibited.

Article 16   State enterprises have decision-making power in operation and management within the limits prescribed by law, on condition that they submit to unified leadership by the state and fulfil all their obligations under the state plan.

State enterprises practise democratic management through congresses of workers and staff and in other ways in accordance with the law.

Article 17   Collective economic organizations have decision-making power in conducting independent economic activities, on condition that they accept the guidance of the state plan and abide by the relevant laws.

Collective economic organizations practise democratic management in accordance with the law, with the entire body of their workers electing or removing their managerial personnel and deciding on major issues concerning operation and management.

Article 18   The People's Republic of China permits foreign enterprises, other foreign economic organizations and individual foreigners to invest in China and to enter into various forms of economic co-operation with Chinese enterprises and other economic organizations in accordance with the law of the People's Republic of China.

All foreign enterprises and other foreign economic organizations in China, as well as joint ventures with Chinese and foreign investment located in China, shall abide by the law of the People's Republic of China. Their lawful rights and interests are protected by the law of the People's Republic of China.

Article 19   The state develops socialist educational undertakings and works to raise the scientific and cultural level of the whole nation.

The state runs schools of various types, makes primary education compulsory and universal, develops secondary, vocational and higher education and promotes preschool education.

The state develops educational facilities of various types in order to wipe out illiteracy and provide political, cultural, scientific, technical and professional education for workers, peasants, state functionaries and other working people. It encourages people to become educated through self-study.

The state encourages the collective economic organizations, state enterprises and undertakings and other social forces to set up educational institutions of various types in accordance with the law.

The state promotes the nationwide use of *Putonghua* (Common Speech based on Beijing pronunciation).

Article 20   The state promotes the development of the natural and social sciences, disseminates scientific and technical knowledge, and commends and rewards achievements in scientific research as well as technological discoveries and inventions.

Article 21   The state develops medical and health services, promotes modern medicine and traditional Chinese medicine, encourages and supports the setting up of various medical and health facilities by the rural economic collectives, state enterprises and undertakings and neighbourhood organizations, and promotes sanitation activities of a mass character, all to protect the people's health.

The state develops physical culture and promotes mass sports activities to build up the people's physique.

Article 22   The state promotes the development of literature and art, the press, broadcasting and television undertakings, publishing and distribution services, libraries, museums, cultural centres and other cultural undertakings, that serve the people and socialism, and sponsors mass cultural activities.

The state protects places of scenic and historical interest, valuable cultural monuments and relics and other important items of China's historical and cultural heritage.

Article 23   The state trains specialized personnel in all fields who serve socialism, increases the number of intellectuals and creates conditions to give full scope to their role in socialist modernization.

Article 24   The state strengthens the building of socialist spiritual civilization through spreading education in high ideals and morality, general education and education in discipline and the legal system, and through promoting the formulation and observance of rules of conduct and common pledges by different sections of the people in urban and rural areas.

The state advocates the civic virtues of love for the motherland, for the people, for labour, for science and for socialism; it educates the people in patriotism, collectivism, internationalism and communism and in dialectical and historical materialism; it combats capitalist, feudalist and other decadent ideas.

Article 25   The state promotes family planning so that population growth may fit the plans for economic and social development.

Article 26   The state protects and improves the living environment and the ecological environment, and prevents and remedies pollution and other public hazards.

The state organizes and encourages afforestation and the protection of forests.

Article 27   All state organs carry out the principle of simple and efficient administration, the system of responsibility for work and the system of training functionaries and appraising their work in order to constantly improve quality of work and efficiency and combat bureaucratism.

All state organs and functionaries must rely on the support of the people, keep in close touch with them, heed their opinions and suggestions, accept their supervision and work hard to serve them.

Article 28   The state maintains public order and suppresses treasonable and other counter-revolutionary activities; it penalizes actions that endanger public security and disrupt the socialist economy and other criminal activities, and punishes and reforms criminals.

Article 29   The armed forces of the People's Republic of China belong to the people. Their tasks are to strengthen national defence, resist aggression, defend the motherland, safeguard the people's peaceful labour, participate in national reconstruction, and work hard to serve the people.

The state strengthens the revolutionization, modernization and regularization of the armed forces in order to increase the national defence capability.

Article 30   The administrative division of the People's Republic of China is as follows:

(1) The country is divided into provinces, autonomous regions and municipalities directly under the Central Government;

(2) Provinces and autonomous regions are divided into autonomous prefectures, counties, autonomous counties and cities;

(3) Counties and autonomous counties are divided into townships, nationality townships and towns.

Municipalities directly under the Central Government and other large cities are divided into districts and counties. Autonomous prefectures are divided into counties, autonomous counties, and cities.

All autonomous regions, autonomous prefectures and autonomous counties are national autonomous areas.

Article 31   The state may establish special administrative regions when necessary. The systems to be instituted in special administrative regions shall be prescribed by law enacted by the National People's Congress in the light of the specific conditions.

Article 32   The People's Republic of China protects the lawful rights and interests of foreigners within Chinese territory, and while on Chinese territory foreigners must abide by the law of the People's Republic of China.

The People's Republic of China may grant asylum to foreigners who request it for political reasons.

CHAPTER TWO
THE FUNDAMENTAL RIGHTS AND DUTIES
OF CITIZENS

Article 33   All persons holding the nationality of the People's Republic of China are citizens of the People's Republic of China.

All citizens of the People's Republic of China are equal before the law.

Every citizen enjoys the rights and at the same time must perform the duties prescribed by the Constitution and the law.

Article 34   All citizens of the People's Republic of China who have reached the age of 18 have the right to vote and stand for election, regardless of nationality, race, sex, occupation, family background, religious belief, education, property status, or length of residence, except persons deprived of political rights according to law.

Article 35   Citizens of the People's Republic of China enjoy freedom of speech, of the press, of assembly, of association, of procession and of demonstration.

Article 36   Citizens of the People's Republic of China enjoy freedom of religious belief.

No state organ, public organization or individual may compel citizens to believe in, or not to believe in, any religion; nor may they discriminate against citizens who believe in, or do not believe in, any religion.

The state protects normal religious activities. No one may make use of religion to engage in activities that disrupt public order, impair the health of citizens or interfere with the educational system of the state.

Religious bodies and religious affairs are not subject to any foreign domination.

Article 37   The freedom of person or citizens of the People's Republic of China is inviolable.

No citizen may be arrested except with the approval or by decision of a people's procuratorate or by decision of a people's court, and arrests must be made by a public security organ.

Unlawful deprivation or restriction of citizens' freedom of person by detention or other means is prohibited; and unlawful search of the person or citizens is prohibited.

Article 38   The personal dignity of citizens of the People's Republic of China is inviolable. Insult, libel, false charge or frame-up directed against citizens by any means is prohibited.

Article 39   The home of citizens of the People's Republic of China is inviolable. Unlawful search of, or intrusion into, a citizen's home is prohibited.

Article 40   The freedom and privacy of correspondence of citizens of the People's Republic of China are protected by law. No organization or individual may, on any ground, infringe upon the freedom and privacy of citizens' correspondence except in cases where, to meet the needs of state security or of investigation into criminal offences, public security or procuratorial organs are permitted to censor correspondence in accordance with procedures prescribed by law.

Article 41   Citizens of the People's Republic of China have the right to criticize and make suggestions to any state organ or functionary. Citizens have the right to make to relevant state organs complaints and charges against, or exposures of, violation of the law or dereliction of duty by any state organ or functionary; but fabrication or distortion of facts with the intention of libel or frame-up is prohibited.

In case of complaints, charges or exposures made by citizens, the state organ concerned must deal with them in a responsible manner after ascertaining the facts. No one may suppress such complaints, charges and exposures, or retaliate against the citizens making them.

Citizens who have suffered losses through infringement of their civic rights by any state organ or functionary have the right to compensation in accordance with the law.

Article 42   Citizens of the People's Republic of China have the right as well as the duty to work.

Using various channels, the state creates conditions for employment, strengthens labour protection, improves working conditions and, on the basis of expanded production, increases remuneration for work and social benefits.

Work is the glorious duty of every able-bodied citizen. All working people in state enterprises and in urban and rural economic collectives should perform their tasks with an attitude consonant with their status as masters of the country. The state promotes socialist labour emulation, and commends and rewards model and advanced workers. The state encourages citizens to take part in voluntary labour.

The state provides necessary vocational training to citizens before they are employed.

Article 43   Working people in the People's Republic of China have the right to rest. The state expands facilities for rest and recuperation of working people, and prescribes working hours and vacations for workers and staff.

Article 44   The state prescribes by law the system of retirement for workers and staff in enterprises and undertakings and for functionaries of organs of state. The livelihood of retired personnel is ensured by the state and society.

Article 45   Citizens of the People's Republic of China have the right to material assistance from the state and society when they are old, ill or disabled. The state develops the social insurance, social relief and medical and health services that are required to enable citizens to enjoy this right.

The state and society ensure the livelihood of disabled members of the armed forces, provide pensions to the families of martyrs and give preferential treatment to the families of military personnel.

The state and society help make arrangements for the work, livelihood and education of the blind, deaf-mute and other handicapped citizens.

Article 46   Citizens of the People's Republic of China have the duty as well as the right to receive education.

The state promotes the all-round moral, intellectual and physical development of children and young people.

Article 47   Citizens of the People's Republic of China have the freedom to engage in scientific research, literary and artistic creation and other cultural pursuits. The state encourages and assists creative endeavours conducive to the interests of the people that are made by citizens engaged in education, science, technology, literature, art and other cultural work.

Article 48   Women in the People's Republic of China enjoy equal rights with men in all spheres of life, political, economic, cultural and social, including family life.

The state protects the rights and interests of women, applies the principle of equal pay for equal work for men and women alike and trains and selects cadres from among women.

Article 49   Marriage, the family and mother and child are protected by the state.

Both husband and wife have the duty to practise family planning.

Parents have the duty to rear and educate their minor children, and children who have come of age have the duty to support and assist their parents.

Violation of the freedom of marriage is prohibited. Maltreatment of old people, women and children is prohibited.

Article 50   The People's Republic of China protects the legitimate rights and interests of Chinese nationals residing abroad and protects the lawful rights and interests of returned overseas Chinese and of the family members of Chinese nationals residing abroad.

Article 51   The exercise by citizens of the People's Republic of China of their freedoms and rights may not infringe upon the interests of the state, of society and of the collective, or upon the lawful freedoms and rights of other citizens.

Article 52   It is the duty of citizens of the People's Republic of China to safeguard the unity of the country and the unity of all its nationalities.

Article 53   Citizens of the People's Republic of China must abide by the Constitution and the law, keep state secrets, protect public property and observe labour discipline and public order and respect social ethics.

Article 54   It is the duty of citizens of the People's Republic of China to safeguard the security, honour and interests of the motherland; they must not commit acts detrimental to the security, honour and interests of the motherland.

Article 55   It is the sacred obligation of every citizen of the People's Republic of China to defend the motherland and resist aggression.

It is the honourable duty of citizens of the People's Republic of China to perform military service and join the militia in accordance with the law.

Article 56   It is the duty of citizens of the People's Republic of China to pay taxes in accordance with the law.

CHAPTER THREE
THE STRUCTURE OF THE STATE

Section I
The National People's Congress

Article 57   The National People's Congress of the People's Republic of China is the highest organ of state power. Its permanent body is the Standing Committee of the National People's Congress.

Article 58   The National People's Congress and its Standing Committee exercise the legislative power of the state.

Article 59   The National People's Congress is composed of deputies elected by the provinces, autonomous regions and municipalities directly under the Central Government, and by the armed forces. All the minority nationalities are entitled to appropriate representation.

Election of deputies to the National People's Congress is conducted by the Standing Committee of the National People's Congress.

The number of deputies to the National People's Congress and the manner of their election are prescribed by law.

Article 60   The National People's Congress is elected for a term of five years.

Two months before the expiration of the term of office of a National People's Congress, its Standing Committee must ensure that the election of deputies to the succeeding National People's Congress is completed. Should exceptional circumstances prevent such an election, it may be postponed by decision of a majority vote of more than two-thirds of all those on the Standing Committee of the incumbent National People's Congress, and the term of office of the incumbent National People's Congress may be extended. The election of deputies to the succeeding National People's Congress must be completed within one year after the termination of such exceptional circumstances.

Article 61   The National People's Congress meets in session once a year and is convened by its Standing Committee. A session of the National People's Congress may be convened at any time the Standing Committee deems this necessary, or when more than one-fifth of the deputies to the National People's Congress so propose.

When the National People's Congress meets, it elects a presidium to conduct its session.

Article 62   The National People's Congress exercises the following functions and powers:

(1)   to amend the Constitution;

(2)   to supervise the enforcement of the Constitution;

(3)   to enact and amend basic statutes concerning criminal offences, civil affairs, the state organs and other matters;

(4)   to elect the President and the Vice-President of the People's Republic of China;*

(5)   to decide on the choice of the Premier of the State Council upon nomination by the President of the People's Republic of China, and to decide on the choice of the Vice-Premiers, State Councillors, Ministers in charge of ministries or commissions and the Auditor-General and the Secretary-General of the State Council upon nomination by the Premier;

(6)   to elect the Chairman of the Central Military Commission and, upon his nomination, to decide on the choice of all the others on the Central Military Commission;

(7)   to elect the President of the Supreme People's Court;

(8)   to elect the Procurator-General of the Supreme People's Procuratorate;

(9)   to examine and approve the plan for national economic and social development and the reports on its implementation;

---

*Previously translated as Chairman and Vice-Chairman of the People's Republic of China.—*Trans.*

(10) to examine and approve the state budget and the report on its implementation;

(11) to alter or annul inappropriate decisions of the Standing Committee of the National People's Congress;

(12) to approve the establishment of provinces, autonomous regions, and municipalities directly under the Central Government;

(13) to decide on the establishment of special administrative regions and the systems to be instituted there;

(14) to decide on questions of war and peace; and

(15) to exercise such other functions and powers as the highest organ of state power should exercise.

Article 63 The National People's Congress has the power to recall or remove from office the following persons:

(1) the President and the Vice-President of the People's Republic of China;

(2) the Premier, Vice-Premiers, State Councillors, Ministers in charge of ministries or commissions and the Auditor-General and the Secretary-General of the State Council;

(3) the Chairman of the Central Military Commission; and others on the Commission;

(4) the President of the Supreme People's Court; and

(5) the Procurator-General of the Supreme People's Procuratorate.

Article 64 Amendments to the Constitution are to be proposed by the Standing Committee of the National People's Congress or by more than one-fifth of the deputies to the National People's Congress and adopted by a majority vote of more than two-thirds of all the deputies to the Congress.

Statutes and resolutions are adopted by a majority vote of more than one half of all the deputies to the National People's Congress.

Article 65 The Standing Committee of the National People's Congress is composed of the following:

the Chairman;

the Vice-Chairmen;

the Secretary-General; and

members.

Minority nationalities are entitled to appropriate representation on the Standing Committee of the National People's Congress.

The National People's Congress elects, and has the power to recall, all those on its Standing Committee.

No one on the Standing Committee of the National People's Congress shall hold any post in any of the administrative, judicial or procuratorial organs of the state.

Article 66 The Standing Committee of the National People's Congress is elected for the same term as the National People's Congress; it exercises its functions and powers until a new Standing Committee is elected by the succeeding National People's Congress.

The Chairman and Vice-Chairmen of the Standing Committee shall serve no more than two consecutive terms.

Article 67   The Standing Committee of the National People's Congress exercises the following functions and powers:

(1)   to interpret the Constitution and supervise its enforcement;

(2)   to enact and amend statutes with the exception of those which should be enacted by the National People's Congress;

(3)   to enact, when the National People's Congress is not in session, partial supplements and amendments to statutes enacted by the National People's Congress provided that they do not contravene the basic principles of these statutes;

(4)   to interpret statutes;

(5)   to examine and approve, when the National People's Congress is not in session, partial adjustments to the plan for national economic and social development and to the state budget that prove necessary in the course of their implementation;

(6)   to supervise the work of the State Council, the Central Military Commission, the Supreme People's Court and the Supreme People's Procuratorate;

(7)   to annul those administrative rules and regulations, decisions or orders of the State Council that contravene the Constitution or the statutes;

(8)   to annul those local regulations or decisions of the organs of state power of provinces, autonomous regions and municipalities directly under the Central Government that contravene the Constitution, the statutes or the administrative rules and regulations;

(9)   to decide, when the National People's Congress is not in session, on the choice of Ministers in charge of ministries or commissions or the Auditor-General and the Secretary-General of the State Council upon nomination by the Premier of the State Council;

(10)   to decide, upon nomination by the Chairman of the Central Military Commission, on the choice of others on the Commission, when the National People's Congress is not in session.

(11)   to appoint and remove the Vice-Presidents and judges of the Supreme People's Court, members of its Judicial Committee and the President of the Military Court at the suggestion of the President of the Supreme People's Court;

(12)   to appoint and remove the Deputy Procurators-General and procurators of the Supreme People's Procuratorate, members of its Procuratorial Committee and the Chief Procurator of the Military Procuratorate at the request of the Procurator-General of the Supreme People's Procuratorate, and to approve the appointment and removal of the chief procurators of the people's procuratorates of provinces, autonomous regions and municipalities directly under the Central Government;

(13)   to decide on the appointment and recall of plenipotentiary representatives abroad;

(14)   to decide on the ratification and abrogation of treaties and important agreements concluded with foreign states;

(15)   to institute systems of titles and ranks for military and diplomatic personnel and of other specific titles and ranks;

(16)   to institute state medals and titles of honour and decide on their conferment;

(17)   to decide on the granting of special pardons;

(18)   to decide, when the National People's Congress is not in session, on the proclamation of a state of war in the event of an armed attack on the country or in fulfillment of international treaty obligations concerning common defence against aggression;

(19)   to decide on general mobilization or partial mobilization;

(20)   to decide on the enforcement of martial law throughout the country or in particular provinces, autonomous regions or municipalities directly under the Central Government; and

(21)   to exercise such other functions and powers as the National People's Congress may assign to it.

Article 68   The Chairman of the Standing Committee of the National People's Congress presides over the work of the Standing Committee and convenes its meetings. The Vice-Chairmen and the Secretary-General assist the Chairman in his work.

Chairmanship meetings with the participation of the Chairman, Vice-Chairmen and Secretary-General handle the important day-to-day work of the Standing Committee of the National People's Congress.

Article 69   The Standing Committee of the National People's Congress is responsible to the National People's Congress and reports on its work to the Congress.

Article 70   The National People's Congress establishes a Nationalities Committee, a Law Committee, a Finance and Economic Committee, an Education, Science, Culture and Public Health Committee, a Foreign Affairs Committee, an Overseas Chinese Committee and such other special committees as are necessary. These special committees work under the direction of the Standing Committee of the National People's Congress when the Congress is not in session.

The special committees examine, discuss and draw up relevant bills and draft resolutions under the direction of the National People's Congress and its Standing Committee.

Article 71   The National People's Congress and its Standing Committee may, when they deem it necessary, appoint committees of inquiry into specific questions and adopt relevant resolutions in the light of their reports.

All organs of state, public organizations and citizens concerned are obliged to supply the necessary information to those committees of inquiry when they conduct investigations.

Article 72   Deputies to the National People's Congress and all those on its Standing Committee have the right, in accordance with procedures prescribed by law, to submit bills and proposals within the scope of the respective functions and powers of the National People's Congress and its Standing Committee.

Article 73   Deputies to the National People's Congress during its sessions, and all those on its Standing Committee during its meetings, have the right to address questions, in accordance with procedures prescribed by law, to the State Council or the ministries and commissions under the State Council, which must answer the questions in a responsible manner.

Article 74   No deputy to the National People's Congress may be arrested or placed on criminal trial without the consent of the Presidium of the current session of the National People's Congress or, when the National People's Congress is not in session, without the consent of its Standing Committee.

Article 75   Deputies to the National People's Congress may not be called to legal account for their speeches or votes at its meetings.

Article 76   Deputies to the National People's Congress must play an exemplary role in abiding by the Constitution and the law and keeping state secrets and, in production and other work and their public activities, assist in the enforcement of the Constitution and the law.

Deputies to the National People's Congress should maintain close contact with the units which elected them and with the people, listen to and convey the opinions and demands of the people and work hard to serve them.

Article 77   Deputies to the National People's Congress are subject to the supervision of the units which elected them. The electoral units have the power, through procedures prescribed by law, to recall the deputies whom they elected.

Article 78   The organization and working procedures of the National People's Congress and its Standing Committee are prescribed by law.

Section II
The President of the People's Republic of China

Article 79   The President and Vice-President of the People's Republic of China are elected by the National People's Congress.

Citizens of the People's Republic of China who have the right to vote and to stand for election and who have reached the age of 45 are eligible for election as President or Vice-President of the People's Republic of China. The term of office of the President and Vice-President of the People's Republic of China is the same as that of the National People's Congress, and they shall serve no more than two consecutive terms.

Article 80   The President of the People's Republic of China, in pursuance of decisions of the National People's Congress and its Standing Committee, promulgates statutes; appoints and removes the Premier, Vice-Premiers, State Councillors, Ministers in charge of ministries or commissions, and the Auditor-General and the Secretary-General of the State Council; confers state medals and titles of honour; issues orders of special pardons; proclaims martial law; proclaims a state of war; and issues mobilization orders.

Article 81   The President of the People's Republic of China receives foreign diplomatic representatives on behalf of the People's Republic of China and, in pursuance of decisions of the Standing Committee of the National People's Congress, appoints and recalls plenipotentiary representatives abroad, and ratifies and abrogates treaties and important agreements concluded with foreign states.

Article 82   The Vice-President of the People's Republic of China assists the President in his work.

The Vice-President of the People's Republic of China may exercise such parts of the functions and powers of the President as the President may entrust to him.

Article 83   The President and Vice-President of the People's Republic of China exercise their functions and powers until the new President and Vice-President elected by the succeeding National People's Congress assume office.

Article 84   In case the office of the President of the People's Republic of China falls vacant, the Vice-President succeeds to the office of President.

In case the office of the Vice-President of the People's Republic of China falls vacant, the National People's Congress shall elect a new Vice-President to fill the vacancy.

In the event that the offices of both the President and the Vice-President of the People's Republic of China fall vacant, the National People's Congress shall elect a new President and a new Vice-President. Prior to such election, the Chairman of the Standing Committee of the National People's Congress shall temporarily act as the President of the People's Republic of China.

Section III
The State Council

Article 85   The State Council, that is, the Central People's Government, of the People's Republic of China is the executive body of the highest organ of state power; it is the highest organ of state administration.

Article 86   The State Council is composed of the following:
the Premier;
the Vice-Premiers;
the State Councillors;
the Ministers in charge of ministries;
the Ministers in charge of commissions;
the Auditor-General; and
the Secretary-General.

The Premier has overall responsibility for the State Council. The ministers have overall responsibility for the respective ministries or commissions under their charge.

The organization of the State Council is prescribed by law.

Article 87   The term of office of the State Council is the same as that of the National People's Congress.

The Premier, Vice-Premiers and State Councillors shall serve no more than two consecutive terms.

Article 88   The Premier directs the work of the State Council. The Vice-Premiers and State Councillors assist the Premier in his work.

Executive meetings of the State Council are composed of the Premier, the Vice-Premiers, the State Councillors and the Secretary-General of the State Council.

The Premier convenes and presides over the executive meetings and plenary meetings of the State Council.

Article 89   The State Council exercises the following functions and powers:
(1)   to adopt administrative measures, enact administrative rules and regulations and issue decisions and orders in accordance with the Constitution and the statutes;

(2)   to submit proposals to the National People's Congress or its Standing Committee;

(3)   to lay down the tasks and responsibilities of the ministries and commissions of the State Council, to exercise unified leadership over the work of the ministries and commissions and to direct all other administrative work of a national character that does not fall within the jurisdiction of the ministries and commissions;

(4)   to exercise unified leadership over the work of local organs of state administration at different levels throughout the country, and to lay down the detailed division of functions and powers between the Central Government and the organs of state administration of provinces, autonomous regions and municipalities directly under the Central Government;

(5)   to draw up and implement the plan for national economic and social development and the state budget;

(6)   to direct and administer economic work and urban and rural development;

(7)   to direct and administer the work concerning education, science, culture, public health, physical culture and family planning;

(8)   to direct and administer the work concerning civil affairs, public security, judicial administration, supervision and other related matters;

(9)   to conduct foreign affairs and conclude treaties and agreements with foreign states;

(10)   to direct and administer the building of national defence;

(11)   to direct and administer affairs concerning the nationalities, and to safeguard the equal rights of minority nationalities and the right of autonomy of the national autonomous areas;

(12)   to protect the legitimate rights and interests of Chinese nationals residing abroad and protect the lawful rights and interests of returned overseas Chinese and of the family members of Chinese nationals residing abroad;

(13)   to alter or annul inappropriate orders, directives and regulations issued by the ministries or commissions;

(14)   to alter or annul inappropriate decisions and orders issued by local organs of state administration at different levels;

(15)   to approve the geographic division of provinces, autonomous regions and municipalities directly under the Central Government, and to approve the establishment and geographic division of autonomous prefectures, counties, autonomous counties and cities;

(16)   to decide on the enforcement of martial law in parts of provinces, autonomous regions and municipalities directly under the Central Government;

(17)   to examine and decide on the size of administrative organs and, in accordance with the law, to appoint, remove and train administrative officers, appraise their work and reward or punish them; and

(18)   to exercise such other functions and powers as the National People's Congress or its Standing Committee may assign it.

Article 90   The Ministers in charge of ministries or commissions of the State Council are responsible for the work of their respective departments and convene and preside over their ministerial meetings or commission meetings that discuss and decide on major issues in the work of their respective departments.

The ministries and commissions issue orders, directives and regulations within the jurisdiction of their respective departments and in accordance with the statutes and the administrative rules and regulations, decisions and orders issued by the State Council.

Article 91   The State Council establishes an auditing body to supervise through auditing the revenue and expenditure of all departments under the State Council and of the local governments at different levels, and those of the state financial and monetary organizations and of enterprises and undertakings.

Under the direction of the Premier of the State Council, the auditing body independently exercises its power to supervise through auditing in accordance with the law, subject to no interference by any other administrative organ or any public organization or individual.

Article 92   The State Council is responsible, and reports on its work, to the National People's Congress or, when the National People's Congress is not in session, to its Standing Committee.

Section IV
The Central Military Commission

Article 93   The Central Military Commission of the People's Republic of China directs the armed forces of the country.

The Central Military Commission, is composed of the following:

the Chairman;

the Vice-Chairmen; and

members.

The Chairman of the Central Military Commission has overall responsibility for the Commission.

The term of office of the Central Military Commission is the same as that of the National People's Congress.

Article 94   The Chairman of the Central Military Commission is responsible to the National People's Congress and its Standing Committee.

Section V
The Local People's Congresses and the Local People's Governments at Different Levels

Article 95   People's congresses and people's governments are established in provinces, municipalities directly under the Central Government, counties, cities, municipal districts, townships, nationality townships and towns.

The organization of local people's congresses and local people's governments at different levels is prescribed by law.

Organs of self-government are established in autonomous regions, autonomous prefectures and autonomous counties. The organization and working procedures of organs of self-government are prescribed by law in accordance with the basic principles laid down in Sections V and VI of Chapter Three of the Constitution.

Article 96   Local people's congresses at different levels are local organs of state power.

Local people's congresses at and above the county level establish standing committees.

Article 97   Deputies to the people's congresses of provinces, municipalities directly under the Central Government, and cities divided into districts are elected by the people's congresses at the next lower level; deputies to the people's congresses of counties, cities not divided into districts, municipal districts, townships, nationality townships and towns are elected directly by their constituencies.

The number of deputies to local people's congresses at different levels and the manner of their election are prescribed by law.

Article 98   The term of office of the people's congresses of provinces, municipalities directly under the Central Government and cities divided into districts is five years. The term of office of the people's congresses of counties, cities not divided into districts, municipal districts, townships, nationality townships and towns is three years.

Article 99   Local people's congresses at different levels ensure the observance and implementation of the Constitution, the statutes and the administrative rules and regulations in their respective administrative areas. Within the limits of their authority as prescribed by law, they adopt and issue resolutions and examine and decide on plans for local economic and cultural development and for the development of public services.

Local people's congresses at and above the county level examine and approve the plans for economic and social development and the budgets of their respective administrative areas, and examine and approve reports on their implementation. They have the power to alter or annul inappropriate decisions of their own standing committees.

The people's congresses of nationality townships may, within the limits of their authority as prescribed by law, take specific measures suited to the peculiarities of the nationalities concerned.

Article 100   The people's congresses of provinces and municipalities directly under the Central Government, and their standing committees, may adopt local regulations, which must not contravene the Constitution, the statutes and the administrative rules and regulations, and they shall report such local regulations to the Standing Committee of the National People's Congress for the record.

Article 101   At their respective levels, local people's congresses elect, and have the power to recall, governors and deputy governors, or mayors and deputy mayors, or heads and deputy heads of counties, districts, townships and towns.

Local people's congresses at and above the county level elect, and have the power to recall, presidents of people's courts and chief procurators of people's procuratorates at the corresponding level. The election or recall of chief procurators of people's procuratorates shall be reported to the chief procurators of the people's procuratorates at the next higher level for submission to the standing committees of the people's congresses at the corresponding level for approval.

Article 102   Deputies to the people's congresses of provinces, municipalities directly under the Central Government and cities divided into districts are subject to supervision by the units which elected them; deputies to the people's congresses of counties, cities not divided into districts, municipal districts, townships, nationality townships and towns are subject to supervision by their constituencies.

The electoral units and constituencies which elect deputies to local people's congresses at different levels have the power, according to procedures prescribed by law, to recall deputies whom they elected.

Article 103   The standing committee of a local people's congress at and above the county level is composed of a chairman, vice-chairmen and members, and is responsible, and reports on its work, to the people's congress at the corresponding level.

The local people's congress at and above the county level elects, and has the power to recall, anyone on the standing committee of the people's congress at the corresponding level.

No one on the standing committee of a local people's congress at and above the county level shall hold any post in state administrative, judicial and procuratorial organs.

Article 104   The standing committee of a local people's congress at and above the county level discusses and decides on major issues in all fields of work in its administrative area; supervises the work of the people's government, people's court and people's procuratorate at the corresponding level; annuls inappropriate decisions and orders of the people's government at the corresponding level; annuls inappropriate resolutions of the people's congress at the next lower level; decides on the appointment and removal of functionaries of state organs within its jurisdiction as prescribed by law; and, when the people's congress at the corresponding level is not in session, recalls individual deputies to the people's congress at the next higher level and elects individual deputies to fill vacancies in that people's congress.

Article 105   Local people's governments at different levels are the executive bodies of local organs of state power as well as the local organs of state administration at the corresponding level.

Local people's governments at different levels practise the system of overall responsibility by governors, mayors, county heads, district heads, township heads and town heads.

Article 106   The term of office of local people's governments at different levels is the same as that of the people's congresses at the corresponding level.

Article 107   Local people's governments at and above the county level, within the limits of their authority as prescribed by law, conduct the administrative work concerning the economy, education, science, culture, public health, physical culture, urban and rural development, finance, civil affairs, public security, nationalities affairs, judicial administration, supervision and family planning in their respective administrative areas; issue decisions and orders; appoint, remove and train administrative functionaries, appraise their work and reward or punish them.

People's governments of townships, nationality townships and towns carry out the resolutions of the people's congress at the corresponding level as well as the decisions and orders of the state administrative organs at the next higher level and conduct administrative work in their respective administrative areas.

People's governments of provinces and municipalities directly under the Central Government decide on the establishment and geographic division of townships, nationality townships and towns.

Article 108 Local people's governments at and above the county level direct the work of their subordinate departments and of people's governments at lower levels, and have the power to alter or annul inappropriate decisions of their subordinate departments and people's governments at lower levels.

Article 109 Auditing bodies are established by local people's governments at and above the county level. Local auditing bodies at different levels independently exercise their power to supervise through auditing in accordance with the law and are responsible to the people's government at the corresponding level and to the auditing body at the next higher level.

Article 110 Local people's governments at different levels are responsible, and report on their work, to people's congresses at the corresponding level. Local people's governments at and above the county level are responsible, and report on their work, to the standing committee of the people's congress at the corresponding level when the congress is not in session.

Local people's governments at different levels are responsible, and report on their work, to the state administrative organs at the next higher level. Local people's governments at different levels throughout the country are state administrative organs under the unified leadership of the State Council and are subordinate to it.

Article 111 The residents' committees and villagers' committees established among urban and rural residents on the basis of their place of residence are mass organizations of self-management at the grass-roots level. The chairman, vice-chairmen and members of each residents' or villagers' committee are elected by the residents. The relationship between the residents' and villagers' committees and the grass-roots organs of state power is prescribed by law.

The residents' and villagers' committees establish committees for people's mediation, public security, public health and other matters in order to manage public affairs and social services in their areas, mediate civil disputes, help maintain public order and convey residents' opinions and demands and make suggestions to the people's government:

Section VI
The Organs of Self-Government of National Autonomous Areas

Article 112 The organs of self-government of national autonomous areas are the people's congresses and people's governments of autonomous regions, autonomous prefectures and autonomous counties.

Article 113 In the people's congress of an autonomous region, prefecture or county, in addition to the deputies of the nationality or nationalities exercising regional autonomy in the administrative area, the other nationalities inhabiting the area are also entitled to appropriate representation.

The chairmanship and vice-chairmanships of the standing committee of the people's congress of an autonomous region, prefecture or county shall include a citizen or citizens of the nationality or nationalities exercising regional autonomy in the area concerned.

Article 114   The administrative head of an autonomous region, prefecture or county shall be a citizen of the nationality, or of one of the nationalities, exercising regional autonomy in the area concerned.

Article 115   The organs of self-government of autonomous regions, prefectures and counties exercise the functions and powers of local organs of state as specified in Section V of Chapter Three of the Constitution. At the same time, they exercise the right of autonomy within the limits of their authority as prescribed by the Constitution, the law of regional national autonomy and other laws, and implement the laws and policies of the state in the light of the existing local situation.

Article 116   People's congresses of national autonomous areas have the power to enact autonomy regulations and specific regulations in the light of the political, economic and cultural characteristics of the nationality or nationalities in the areas concerned. The autonomy regulations and specific regulations of autonomous regions shall be submitted to the Standing Committee of the National People's Congress for approval before they go into effect. Those of autonomous prefectures and counties shall be submitted to the standing committees of the people's congresses of provinces or autonomous regions for approval before they go into effect, and they shall be reported to the Standing Committee of the National People's Congress for the record.

Article 117   The organs of self-government of the national autonomous areas have the power of autonomy in administering the finances of their areas. All revenues accruing to the national autonomous areas under the financial system of the state shall be managed and used by the organs of self-government of those areas on their own.

Article 118   The organs of self-government of the national autonomous areas independently arrange for and administer local economic development under the guidance of state plans.

In exploiting natural resources and building enterprises in the national autonomous areas, the state shall give due consideration to the interests of those areas.

Article 119   The organs of self-government of the national autonomous areas independently administer educational, scientific, cultural, public health and physical culture affairs in their respective areas, protect and cull through the cultural heritage of the nationalities and work for the development and prosperity of their cultures.

Article 120   The organs of self-government of the national autonomous areas may, in accordance with the military system of the state and concrete local needs and with the approval of the State Council, organize local public security forces for the maintenance of public order.

Article 121   In performing their functions, the organs of self-government of the national autonomous areas, in accordance with the autonomy regulations of the respective areas, employ the spoken and written language or languages in common use in the locality.

Article 122   The state gives financial, material and technical assistance to the minority nationalities to accelerate their economic and cultural development.

The state helps the national autonomous areas train large numbers of cadres at different levels and specialized personnel and skilled workers of different professions and trades from among the nationality or nationalities in those areas.

Section VII
The People's Courts and the People's Procuratorates

Article 123   The people's courts in the People's Republic of China are the judicial organs of the state.

Article 124   The People's Republic of China establishes the Supreme People's Court and the local people's courts at different levels, military courts and other special people's courts.

The term of office of the President of the Supreme People's Court is the same as that of the National People's Congress; he shall serve no more than two consecutive terms.

The organization of people's courts is prescribed by law.

Article 125   All cases handled by the people's courts, except for those involving special circumstances as specified by law, shall be heard in public. The accused has the right of defence.

Article 126   The people's courts shall, in accordance with the law, exercise judicial power independently and are not subject to interference by administrative organs, public organizations or individuals.

Article 127   The Supreme People's Court is the highest judicial organ.

The Supreme People's Court supervises the administration of justice by the local people's courts at different levels and by the special people's courts; people's courts at higher levels supervise the administration of justice by those at lower levels.

Article 128   The Supreme People's Court is responsible to the National People's Congress and its Standing Committee. Local people's courts at different levels are responsible to the organs of state power which created them.

Article 129   The people's procuratorates of the People's Republic of China are state organs for legal supervision.

Article 130   The People's Republic of China establishes the Supreme People's Procuratorate and the local people's procuratorates at different levels, military procuratorates and other special people's procuratorates.

The term of office of the Procurator-General of the Supreme People's Procuratorate is the same as that of the National People's Congress; he shall serve no more than two consecutive terms.

The organization of people's procuratorates is prescribed by law.

Article 131   People's procuratorates shall, in accordance with the law, exercise procuratorial power independently and are not subject to interference by administrative organs, public organizations or individuals.

Article 132   The Supreme People's Procuratorate is the highest procuratorial organ.

The Supreme People's Procuratorate directs the work of the local people's procuratorates at different levels and of the special people's procuratorates; people's procuratorates at higher levels direct the work of those at lower levels.

Article 133   The Supreme People's Procuratorate is responsible to the National People's Congress and its Standing Committee. Local people's procuratorates at different levels are responsible to the organs of state power at the corresponding levels which created them and to the people's procuratorates at the higher level.

Article 134   Citizens of all nationalities have the right to use the spoken and written languages of their own nationalities in court proceedings. The people's courts and people's procuratorates should provide translation for any party to the court proceedings who is not familiar with the spoken or written languages in common use in the locality.

In an area where people of a minority nationality live in a compact community or where a number of nationalities live together, hearings should be conducted in the language or languages in common use in the locality; indictments, judgments, notices and other documents should be written, according to actual needs, in the language or languages in common use in the locality.

Article 135   The people's courts, people's procuratorates and public security organs shall, in handling criminal cases, divide their functions, each taking responsibility for its own work, and they shall co-ordinate their efforts and check each other to ensure correct and effective enforcement of law.

CHAPTER FOUR
THE NATIONAL FLAG, THE NATIONAL EMBLEM, AND THE CAPITAL

Article 136   The national flag of the People's Republic of China is a red flag with five stars.

Article 137   The national emblem of the People's Republic of China is Tian An Men in the centre illuminated by five stars and encircled by ears of grain and a cogwheel.

Article 138   The capital of the People's Republic of China is Beijing.

Appendix B

The Constitution
of the Communist Party
# of China (1982)

General Programme*

The Communist Party of China is the vanguard of the Chinese working class, the faithful representative of the interests of the people of all nationalities in China, and the force at the core leading China's cause of socialism. The Party's ultimate goal is the creation of a communist social system.

The Communist Party of China takes Marxism-Leninism and Mao Zedong Thought as its guide to action.

Applying dialectical materialism and historical materialism, Marx and Engels analysed the laws of development of capitalist society and founded the theory of scientific socialism. According to this theory, with the victory of the proletariat in its revolutionary struggle, the dictatorship of the bourgeoisie is inevitably replaced by the dictatorship of the proletariat, and capitalist society is inevitably transformed into socialist society in which the means of production are publicly owned, exploitation is abolished and the principle "from each according to his ability and to each according to his work" is applied; with tremendous growth of the productive forces and tremendous progress in the ideological, political and cultural fields, socialist society ultimately and inevitably advances into communist society in which the principle "from each according to his ability and to each according to his needs" is applied. Early in the 20th century, Lenin pointed out that capitalism had developed to the stage of imperialism, that the liberation struggle of the proletariat was bound to unite with that of the oppressed nations of the world, and that it was possible for socialist revolution to win victory first in countries that were the weak links of imperialist rule. The course of world history during the past half century and more, and especially the establishment and development of the socialist system in a number of countries, has borne out the correctness of the theory of scientific socialism.

The development and improvement of the socialist system is a long historical process. Fundamentally speaking, the socialist system is incomparably superior to the capitalist system, having eliminated the contradictions inherent in the capitalist system, which the latter itself is incapable of overcoming. Socialism enables the people truly to become masters of the country, gradually to shed the old ideas and ways formed under the system of exploitation and private ownership of the means of production, and steadily to raise their communist consciousness and foster common ideals, common ethics and a common discipline in their own ranks. Socialism can give full scope to the initiative and creativeness of the people, develop the productive forces rapidly, proportionately and in a planned way, and meet the growing material and cultural needs of the members of society. The cause of socialism is advancing and is bound gradually to triumph throughout the world along paths that are suited to the specific conditions of each country and are chosen by its people of their own free will.

The Chinese Communists, with Comrade Mao Zedong as their chief representative, created Mao Zedong Thought by integrating the universal principles of Marxism-Leninism with the concrete practice of the Chinese revolution. Mao Zedong Thought is Marxism-Leninism applied and developed in China; it consists of a body of theoretical principles concerning the revolution and construction in China and a summary of experience therein, both of which have been proved correct by practice; it represents the crystallized, collective wisdom of the Communist Party of China.

Beijing Review, 38 (September 20, 1982), 8–21. (Adopted by the Twelfth National Congress of the Communist Party of China on September 6, 1982.)

The Communist Party of China led the people of all nationalities in waging their prolonged revolutionary struggle against imperialism, feudalism and bureaucrat-capitalism, winning victory in the new-democratic revolution and establishing the People's Republic of China—a people's democratic dictatorship. After the founding of the People's Republic, it led them in smoothly carrying out socialist transformation, completing the transition from New Democracy to socialism, establishing the socialist system, and developing socialism in its economic, political and cultural aspects.

After the elimination of the exploiting classes as such, most of the contradictions in Chinese society do not have the nature of class struggle, and class struggle is no longer the principal contradiction. However, owing to domestic circumstances and foreign influences, class struggle will continue to exist within certain limits for a long time, and may even sharpen under certain conditions. The principal contradiction in Chinese society is that between the people's growing material and cultural needs and the backward level of our social production. The other contradictions should be resolved in the course of resolving this principal one. It is essential to strictly distinguish and correctly handle the two different types of contradictions—the contradictions between the enemy and ourselves and those among the people.

The general task of the Communist Party of China at the present stage is to unite the people of all nationalities in working hard and self-reliantly to achieve, step by step, the modernization of our industry, agriculture, national defence and science and technology and make China a culturally advanced and highly democratic socialist country.

The focus of the work of the Communist Party of China is to lead the people of all nationalities in accomplishing the socialist modernization of our economy. It is necessary vigorously to expand the productive forces and gradually perfect socialist relations of production, in keeping with the actual level of the productive forces and as required for their expansion. It is necessary to strive for the gradual improvement of the standards of material and cultural life of the urban and rural population, based on the growth of production and social wealth.

The Communist Party of China leads the people, as they work for a high level of material civilization, in building a high level of socialist spiritual civilization. Major efforts should be made to promote education, science and culture, imbue the Party members and the masses of the people with communist ideology, combat and overcome decadent bourgeois ideas, remnant feudal ideas and other non-proletarian ideas, and encourage the Chinese people to have lofty ideals, moral integrity, education and a sense of discipline.

The Communist Party of China leads the people in promoting socialist democracy, perfecting the socialist legal system, and consolidating the people's democratic dictatorship. Effective measures should be taken to protect the people's right to run the affairs of the state and of society, and to manage economic and cultural undertakings; and to strike firmly at hostile elements who deliberately sabotage the socialist system, and those who seriously breach or jeopardize public security. Great efforts should be made to strengthen the People's Liberation Army and national defence so that the country is prepared at all times to resist and wipe out any invaders.

The Communist Party of China upholds and promotes relations of equality, unity and mutual assistance among all nationalities in the country, persists in the policy of regional autonomy of minority nationalities, aids the areas inhabited by minority nationalities in their economic and cultural development, and actively trains and promotes cadres from among the minority nationalities.

The Communist Party of China unites with all workers, peasants and intellectuals, and with all the democratic parties, non-party democrats and the patriotic forces of all the nationalities in China in further expanding and fortifying the broadest possible patriotic united front embracing all socialist working people and all patriots who support socialism or who support the reunification of the motherland. We should work together with the people throughout the country, including our compatriots in Taiwan, Xianggang (Hongkong) and Aomen (Macao) and Chinese nationals residing abroad, to accomplish the great task of reunifying the motherland.

In international affairs, the Communist Party of China takes the following basic stand: It adheres to proletarian internationalism and firmly unites with the workers of all lands, with the oppressed nations and oppressed peoples and with all peace-loving and justice-upholding organizations and personages in the common struggle against imperialism, hegemonism and colonialism and for the defence of world peace and promotion of human progress. It stands for the development of state relations between China and other countries on the basis of the five principles of mutual respect for sovereignty and territorial integrity, mutual non-aggression, non-interference in each other's internal affairs, equality and mutual benefit, and peaceful co-existence. It develops relations with Communist Parties and working-class parties in other countries on the basis of Marxism and the principles of independence, complete equality, mutual respect and non-interference in each other's internal affairs.

In order to lead China's people of all nationalities in attaining the great goal of socialist modernization, the Communist Party of China must strengthen itself, carry forward its fine traditions, enhance its fighting capacity and resolutely achieve the following three essential requirements:

First, a high degree of ideological and political unity. The Communist Party of China makes the realization of communism its maximum programme, to which all its members must devote their entire lives. At the present stage, the political basis for the solidarity and unity of the whole Party consists in adherence to the socialist road, to the people's democratic dictatorship, to the leadership of the Party, and to Marxism-Leninism and Mao Zedong Thought and in the concentration of our efforts on socialist modernization. The Party's ideological line is to proceed from reality in all things, to integrate theory with practice, to seek truth from facts, and to verify and develop the truth through practice. In accordance with this ideological line, the whole Party must scientifically sum up historical experience, investigate and study actual conditions, solve new problems in domestic and international affairs, and oppose all erroneous deviations, whether "Left" or Right.

Second, wholehearted service to the people. The Party has no special interests of its own apart from the interests of the working class and the broadest masses of the people. The programme and policies of the Party are precisely the scientific expressions of the fundamental interests of the working class and the broadest masses of the people. Throughout the process of leading the masses in struggle to realize the ideal of communism, the Party always shares weal and woe with the people, keeps in closest contact with them, and does not allow any member to become divorced from the masses or place himself above them. The Party persists in educating the masses in communist ideas and follows the mass line in its work, doing everything for the masses, relying on them in every task, and turning its correct views into conscious action by the masses.

Third, adherence to democratic centralism. Within the Party, democracy is given full play, a high degree of centralism is practised on the basis of democracy and a sense of organization and discipline is strengthened, so as to ensure unity of action throughout its ranks and the prompt and effective implementation of its decisions. In its internal political life, the Party conducts criticism and self-criticism in the correct way, waging ideological struggles over matters of principle, upholding truth and rectifying mistakes. Applying the principle that all members are equally subject to Party discipline, the Party duly criticizes or punishes those members who violate it and expels those who persist in opposing and harming the Party.

Party leadership consists mainly in political, ideological and organizational leadership. The Party must formulate and implement correct lines, principles and policies, do its organizational, propaganda and educational work well and make sure that all Party members play their exemplary vanguard role in every sphere of work and every aspect of social life. The Party must conduct its activities within the limits permitted by the Constitution and the laws of the state. It must see to it that the legislative, judicial and administrative organs of the state and the economic, cultural and people's organizations work actively and with initiative, independently, responsibly and in harmony. The Party must strengthen its leadership over the trade unions, the Communist Youth League, the Women's Federation and other mass organizations, and give full scope to their roles. The Party members are a minority in the whole population, and they must work in close co-operation with the masses of non-Party people in the common effort to make our socialist motherland ever stronger and more prosperous, until the ultimate realization of communism.

CHAPTER I
MEMBERSHIP

Article 1 Any Chinese worker, peasant, member of the armed forces, intellectual or any other revolutionary who has reached the age of 18 and who accepts the Party's programme and Constitution and is willing to join and work actively in one of the Party organizations, carry out the Party's decisions and pay membership dues regularly may apply for membership of the Communist Party of China.

Article 2 Members of the Communist Party of China are vanguard fighters of the Chinese working class imbued with communist consciousness.

Members of the Communist Party of China must serve the people wholeheartedly, dedicate their whole lives to the realization of communism, and be ready to make any personal sacrifices.

Members of the Communist Party of China are at all times ordinary members of the working people. Communist Party members must not seek personal gain or privileges, although they are allowed personal benefits and job functions and powers as provided for by the relevant regulations and policies.

Article 3 Party members must fulfill the following duties:

(1) To conscientiously study Marxism-Leninism and Mao Zedong Thought, essential knowledge concerning the Party, and the Party's line, principles, policies and decisions; and acquire general, scientific and professional knowledge.

(2) To adhere to the principle that the interests of the Party and the people stand above everything, subordinate their personal interests to the interests of the Party and the people, be the first to bear hardships and the last to enjoy comforts, work selflessly for

the public interest, and absolutely never use public office for personal gain or benefit themselves at the expense of the public.

(3)   To execute the Party's decisions perseveringly, accept any job and fulfill actively any task assigned them by the Party, conscientiously observe Party discipline and the laws of the state, rigorously guard Party and state secrets and staunchly defend the interests of the Party and the state.

(4)   To uphold the Party's solidarity and unity, to firmly oppose factionalism and all factional organizations and small-group activities, and to oppose double-dealing and scheming of any kind.

(5)   To be loyal to and honest with the Party, to match words with deeds and not to conceal their political views or distort facts; to earnestly practise criticism and self-criticism, to be bold in exposing and correcting shortcomings and mistakes in work, backing good people and good deeds and fighting against bad people and bad deeds.

(6)   To maintain close ties with the masses, propagate the Party's views among them, consult with them when problems arise, listen to their views and demands with an open mind and keep the Party informed of these in good time, help them raise their political consciousness, and defend their legitimate rights and interests.

(7)   To play an exemplary vanguard role in production and other work, study and social activities, take the lead in maintaining public order, promote new socialist ways and customs and advocate communist ethics.

(8)   As required by the defence of the motherland and the interests of the people, to step forward and fight bravely in times of difficulty and danger, fearing neither hardship nor death.

Article 4   Party members enjoy the following rights:

(1)   To attend pertinent Party meetings and read pertinent Party documents, and to benefit from the Party's education and training.

(2)   To participate in the discussion, at Party meetings and in Party newspapers and journals, of questions concerning the Party's policies.

(3)   To make suggestions and proposals regarding the work of the Party.

(4)   To make well-grounded criticism of any Party organization or member at Party meetings; to present information or charges against any Party organization or member concerning violations of discipline and of the law to the Party in a responsible way, and to demand disciplinary measures against such a member, or to demand the dismissal or replacement of any cadre who is incompetent.

(5)   To vote, elect and stand for election.

(6)   To attend, with the right of self-defence, discussions held by Party organizations to decide on disciplinary measures to be taken against themselves or to appraise their work and behaviour, while other Party members may also bear witness or argue on their behalf.

(7)   In case of disagreement with a Party decision or policy, to make reservations and present their views to Party organizations at higher levels up to and including the Central Committee, provided that they resolutely carry out the decision or policy while it is in force.

(8)   To put forward any request, appeal or complaint to higher Party organizations up to and including the Central Committee and ask the organizations concerned for a responsible reply.

No Party organization, up to and including the Central Committee, has the right to deprive any Party member of the above-mentioned rights.

Article 5 New Party members must be admitted through a Party branch, and the principle of individual admission must be adhered to. It is impermissible to drag into the Party by any means those who are not qualified for membership, or to exclude those who are qualified.

An applicant for Party membership must fill in an application form and must be recommended by two full Party members. The application must be accepted by a general membership meeting of the Party branch concerned and approved by the next higher Party organization, and the applicant should undergo observation for a probationary period before being transferred to full membership.

Party members who recommend an applicant must make genuine efforts to acquaint themselves with the latter's ideology, character and personal history, to explain to each applicant the Party's programme and Constitution, qualifications for membership and the duties and rights of members, and must make a responsible report to the Party organization on the matter.

The Party branch committee must canvass the opinions of persons concerned, inside and outside the Party, about an applicant for Party membership and, after establishing the latter's qualifications following a rigorous examination, submit the application to a general membership meeting for discussion.

Before approving the admission of applicants for Party membership, the next higher Party organization concerned must appoint people to talk with them, so as to get to know them better and help deepen their understanding of the Party.

In special circumstances, the Central Committee of the Party or the Party committee of a province, an autonomous region or a municipality directly under the Central Government has the power to admit new Party members directly.

Article 6 A probationary Party member must take an admission oath in front of the Party flag. The oath reads: "It is my will to join the Communist Party of China, uphold the Party's programme, observe the provisions of the Party Constitution, fulfill a Party member's duties, carry out the Party's decisions, strictly observe Party discipline, guard Party secrets, be loyal to the Party, work hard, fight for communism throughout my life, be ready at all times to sacrifice my all for the Party and the people, and never betray the Party."

Article 7 The probationary period of a probationary member is one year. The Party organization should make serious efforts to educate and observe the probationary members.

Probationary members have the same duties as full members. They enjoy the rights of full members except those of voting, electing or standing for election.

When the probationary period of a probationary member has expired, the Party branch concerned should promptly discuss whether he is qualified to be transferred to full membership. A probationary member who conscientiously performs his duties and is qualified for membership should be transferred to full membership as scheduled; if continued observation and education are needed, the probationary period may be prolonged, but by no more than one year; if a probationary member fails to perform his duties and is found to be really unqualified for membership, his probationary membership shall be annulled. Any decision to transfer a probationary member to full membership, prolong a probationary period, or annul a probationary membership must be made through discussion by the general membership meeting of the Party branch concerned and approved by the next higher Party organization.

The probationary period of a probationary member begins from the day the general membership meeting of the Party branch admits him as a probationary member. The Party standing of a member begins from the day he is transferred to full membership on the expiration of the probationary period.

Article 8 Every Party member, irrespective of position, must be organized into a branch, cell or other specific unit of the Party to participate in the regular activities of the Party organization and accept supervision by the masses inside and outside the Party. There shall be no privileged Party members who do not participate in the regular activities of the Party organization and do not accept supervision by the masses inside and outside the Party.

Article 9 Party members are free to withdraw from the Party. When a Party member asks to withdraw, the Party branch concerned shall, after discussion by its general membership meeting, remove his name from the Party rolls, make the removal publicly known and report it to the next higher Party organization for the record.

A Party member who lacks revolutionary will, fails to fulfill the duties of a Party member, is not qualified for membership and remains incorrigible after repeated education should be persuaded to withdraw from the Party. The case shall be discussed and decided by the general membership meeting of the Party branch concerned and submitted to the next higher Party organization for approval. If the Party member being persuaded to withdraw refuses to do so, the case shall be submitted to the general membership meeting of the Party branch concerned for discussion and decision on a time limit by which the member must correct his mistakes or on the removal of his name from the Party rolls, and the decision shall be submitted to the next higher Party organization for approval.

A Party member who fails to take part in regular Party activities, pay membership dues or do work assigned by the Party for six successive months without proper reason is regarded as having given up membership. The general membership meeting of the Party branch concerned shall decide on the removal of such a person's name from the Party rolls and report the removal to the next higher Party organization for approval.

CHAPTER II
ORGANIZATIONAL SYSTEM OF THE PARTY

Article 10 The Party is an integral body organized under its programme and Constitution, on the principle of democratic centralism. It practices a high degree of centralism on the basis of a high degree of democracy. The basic principles of democratic centralism as practised by the Party are as follows:

(1) Individual Party members are subordinate to the Party organization, the minority is subordinate to the majority, the lower Party organizations are subordinate to the higher Party organizations, and all the constituent organizations and members of the Party are subordinate to the National Congress and the Central Committee of the Party.

(2) The Party's leading bodies of all levels are elected except for the representative organs dispatched by them and the leading Party members' groups in non-Party organizations.

(3) The highest leading body of the Party is the National Congress and the Central Committee elected by it. The leading bodies of local Party organizations are the Party

congresses at their respective levels and the Party committees elected by them. Party committees are responsible, and report their work, to the Party congresses at their respective levels.

(4)   Higher Party organizations shall pay constant attention to the views of the lower organizations and the rank-and-file Party members, and solve in good time the problems they raise. Lower Party organizations shall report on their work to, and request instructions from, higher Party organizations; at the same time, they shall handle, independently and in a responsible manner, matters within their jurisdiction. Higher and lower Party organizations should exchange information and support and supervise each other.

(5)   Party committees at all levels function on the principle of combining collective leadership with individual responsibility based on division of labour. All major issues shall be decided upon by the Party committees after democratic discussion.

(6)   The Party forbids all forms of personality cult. It is necessary to ensure that the activities of the Party leaders be subject to supervision by the Party and the people, while at the same time to uphold the prestige of all leaders who represent the interests of the Party and the people.

Article 11   The election of delegates to Party congresses and of members of Party committees at all levels should reflect the will of the voters. Elections shall be held by secret ballot. The lists of candidates shall be submitted to the Party organizations and voters for full deliberation and discussion. There may be a preliminary election in order to draw up a list of candidates for the formal election. Or there may be no preliminary election, in which case the number of candidates shall be greater than that of the persons to be elected. The voters have the right to inquire into the candidates, demand a change or reject one in favour of another. No organization or individual shall in any way compel voters to elect or not to elect any candidate.

If any violation of the Party Constitution occurs in the election of delegates to a local Party congress, the Party committee at the next higher level shall, after investigation and verification, decide to invalidate the election and take appropriate measures. The decision shall be reported to the Party committee at the next higher level for checking and approval before it is formally announced and implemented.

Article 12   When necessary, Party committees of and above the county level may convene conferences of delegates to discuss and decide on major problems that require timely solution. The number of delegates to such conferences and the procedure governing their election shall be determined by the Party committees convening them.

Article 13   The formation of a new Party organization or the dissolution of an existing one shall be decided upon by the higher Party organizations.

Party committees of and above the county level may send out their representative organs.

When the congress of a local Party organization at any level is not in session, the next higher Party organization may, when it deems it necessary, transfer or appoint responsible members of that organization.

Article 14   When making decisions on important questions affecting the lower organizations, the leading bodies of the Party at all levels should, in ordinary circumstances, solicit the opinions of the lower organizations. Measures should be taken to ensure that the lower organizations can exercise their functions and powers normally. Except in special circumstances, higher leading bodies should not interfere with matters that ought to be handled by lower organizations.

Article 15   Only the Central Committee of the Party has the power to make decisions on major policies of a nationwide character. Party organizations of various departments and localities may make suggestions with regard to such policies to the Central Committee, but shall not make any decisions or publicize their views outside the Party without authorization.

Lower Party organizations must firmly implement the decisions of higher Party organizations. If lower organizations consider that any decisions of higher organizations do not suit actual conditions in their localities or departments, they may request modification. If the higher organizations insist on their original decisions, the lower organizations must carry out such decisions and refrain from publicly voicing their differences, but have the right to report to the next higher Party organization.

Newspapers and journals and other means of publicity run by Party organizations at all levels must propagate the line, principles, policies and decisions of the Party.

Article 16   Party organizations must keep to the principle of subordination of the minority to the majority in discussing and making decisions on any matter. Serious consideration should be given to the differing views of a minority. In case of controversy over major issues in which supporters of the two opposing views are nearly equal in number, except in emergencies where action must be taken in accordance with the majority view, the decision should be put off to allow for further investigation, study and exchange of opinions followed by another discussion. If still no decision can be made, the controversy should be reported to the next higher Party organization for ruling.

When on behalf of the Party organization, an individual Party member is to express views on major issues beyond the scope of existing Party decisions, the content must be referred to the Party organization for prior discussion and decision, or referred to the next higher Party organization for instructions. No Party member, whatever his position, is allowed to make decisions on major issues on his own. In an emergency, when a decision by an individual is unavoidable, the matter must be reported to the Party organization immediately afterwards. No leader is allowed to decide matters arbitrarily on his own or to place himself above the Party organization.

Article 17   The central, local and primary organizations of the Party must all pay great attention to Party building. They shall regularly discuss and check up on the Party's work in propaganda education, organization and discipline inspection, its mass work and united front work. They must carefully study ideological and political developments inside and outside the Party.

CHAPTER III
CENTRAL ORGANIZATIONS OF THE PARTY

Article 18   The National Congress of the Party is held once every five years and convened by the Central Committee. It may be convened before the due date if the Central Committee deems it necessary or if more than one-third of the organizations at the provincial level so request. Except under extraordinary circumstances, the congress may not be postponed.

The number of delegates to the National Congress of the Party and the procedure governing their election shall be determined by the Central Committee.

Article 19   The functions and powers of the National Congress of the Party are as follows:

(1)   To hear and examine the reports of the Central Committee;

(2)   To hear and examine the reports of the Central Advisory Commission and the Central Commission for Discipline Inspection;

(3)   To discuss and decide on major questions concerning the Party;

(4)   To revise the Constitution of the Party;

(5)   To elect the Central Committee; and

(6)   To elect the Central Advisory Commission and the Central Commission for the Discipline Inspection.

Article 20   The Central Commission of the Party is elected for a term of five years. However, when the next National Congress is convened before or after its due date, the term shall be correspondingly shortened or extended. Members and alternate members of the Central Committee must have a Party standing of five years or more. The number of members and alternate members of the Central Committee shall be determined by the National Congress. Vacancies on the Central Committee shall be filled by its alternate members in the order of the number of votes by which they were elected.

The Central Committee of the Party meets in plenary session at least once a year, and such sessions are convened by its Political Bureau.

When the National Congress is not in session, the Central Committee carries out its decisions, directs the entire work of the Party and represents the Communist Party of China in its external relations.

Article 21   The Political Bureau, the Standing Committee of the Political Bureau, the Secretariat and the General Secretary of the Central Committee of the Party are elected by the Central Committee in plenary session. The General Secretary of the Central Committee must be a member of the Standing Committee of the Political Bureau.

When the Central Committee is not in session, the Political Bureau and its Standing Committee exercise the functions and powers of the Central Committee.

The Secretariat attends to the day-to-day work of the Central Committee under the direction of the Political Bureau and its Standing Committee.

The General Secretary of the Central Committee is responsible for convening the meetings of the Political Bureau and its Standing Committee and presides over the work of the Secretariat.

The members of the Military Commission of the Central Committee are decided on by the Central Committee. The Chairman of the Military Commission must be a member of the Standing Committee of the Political Bureau.

The central leading bodies and leaders elected by each Central Committee shall, when the next National Congress is in session, continue to preside over the Party's day-to-day work until the new central leading bodies and leaders are elected by the next Central Committee.

Article 22   The Party's Central Advisory Commission acts as political assistant and consultant to the Central Committee. Members of the Central Advisory Commission must have a Party standing of 40 years or more, have rendered considerable service to the Party, have fairly rich experience in leadership and enjoy fairly high prestige inside and outside the Party.

The Central Advisory Commission is elected for a term of the same duration as that of the Central Committee. It elects, at its plenary meeting, its Standing Committee and its Chairman and Vice-Chairmen, and reports the results to the Central Committee for approval. The Chairman of the Central Advisory Commission must be a member of the Standing Committee of the Political Bureau. Members of the Central Advisory Commission may attend plenary sessions of the Central Committee as non-voting participants. The Vice-Chairmen of the Central Advisory Commission may attend plenary meetings of the Political Bureau as non-voting participants and, when the Political Bureau deems it necessary, other members of the Standing Committee of the Central Advisory Commission may do the same.

Working under the leadership of the Central Committee of the Party, the Central Advisory Commission puts forward recommendations on the formulation and implementation of the Party's principles and policies and gives advice upon request, assists the Central Committee in investigating and handling certain important questions, propagates the Party's major principles and policies inside and outside the Party, and undertakes such other tasks as may be entrusted to it by the Central Committee.

Article 23   Party organizations in the Chinese People's Liberation Army carry on their work in accordance with the instructions of the Central Committee. The General Political Department of the Chinese People's Liberation Army is the political-work organ of the Military Commission; it directs Party and political work in the army. The organizational system and organs of the Party in the armed forces will be prescribed by the Military Commission.

CHAPTER IV
LOCAL ORGANIZATIONS OF THE PARTY

Article 24   A Party congress of a province, autonomous region, municipality directly under the Central Government, city divided into districts, or autonomous prefecture is held once every five years.

A Party congress of a county (banner), autonomous county, city not divided into districts, or municipal district is held once every three years.

Local Party congresses are convened by the Party committees at the corresponding levels. Under extraordinary circumstances, they may be held before or after their due dates upon approval by the next higher Party committees.

The number of delegates to the local Party congresses, at any level and the procedure governing their election are determined by the Party committees at the corresponding levels and should be reported to the next higher Party committees for approval.

Article 25   The functions and powers of the local Party congresses at all levels are as follows:

(1)   To hear and examine the reports of the Party committees at the corresponding levels;

(2)   To hear and examine the reports of the commissions for discipline inspection at the corresponding levels;

(3)   To discuss and decide on major issues in the given areas; and

(4)   To elect the Party committees and commissions for discipline inspection at the corresponding levels and delegates to the Party congresses at their respective next higher levels.

The Party congress of a province, autonomous region, or municipality directly under the Central Government elects the Party advisory committee at the corresponding level and hears and examines its reports.

Article 26   The Party committee of a province, autonomous region, municipality directly under the Central Government, city divided into districts, or autonomous prefecture is elected for a term of five years. The members and alternate members of such a committee must have a Party standing of five years or more.

The Party committee of a county (banner), autonomous county, city not divided into districts, or municipal district is elected for a term of three years. The members and alternate members of such a committee must have a Party standing of three years or more.

When local Party congresses at various levels are convened before or after their due dates, the terms of the committees elected by the previous congresses shall be correspondingly shortened or extended.

The number of members and alternate members of the local Party committees at various levels shall be determined by the next higher committees. Vacancies on the local Party committees at various levels shall be filled by their alternate members in the order of the number of votes by which they were elected.

The local Party committees at various levels meet in plenary session at least once a year.

Local Party committees at various levels shall, when the Party congresses of the given areas are not in session, carry out the directives of the next higher Party organizations and the decisions of the Party congresses at the corresponding levels, direct work in their own areas and report on it to the next higher Party committees at regular intervals.

Article 27   Local Party committees at various levels elect, at their plenary sessions, their standing committees, secretaries and deputy secretaries and report the results to the higher Party committees for approval. The standing committees at various levels exercise the powers and functions of local Party committees when the latter are not in session. They continue to handle the day-to-day work when the next Party congresses at their levels are in session, until the new standing committees are elected.

Article 28   The Party advisory committee of a province, autonomous region or municipality directly under the Central Government acts as political assistant and consultant to the Party committee at the corresponding level. It works under the leadership of the Party committee at the corresponding level and in the light of the relevant provisions of Article 22 of the present Constitution. The qualifications of its members shall be specified by the Party committee at the corresponding level in the light of the relevant provisions of Article 22 of the present Constitution and the actual conditions in the locality concerned. It serves a term of the same duration as the Party committee at the corresponding level.

The advisory committee of a province, autonomous region or municipality directly under the Central Government elects, at its plenary meeting, its standing committee and its chairman and vice-chairmen, and the results are subject to endorsement by the Party committee at the corresponding level and should be reported to the Central Committee for approval. Its members may attend plenary sessions of the Party committee at the corresponding level as non-voting participants, and its chairman and vice-chairmen may attend meetings of the standing committee of the Party committee at the corresponding level as non-voting participants.

Article 29   A prefectural Party committee, or an organization analogous to it, is the representative organ dispatched by a provincial or an autonomous regional Party committee to a prefecture embracing several counties, autonomous counties or cities. It exercises leadership over the work in the given region as authorized by the provincial or autonomous regional Party committee.

CHAPTER V
PRIMARY ORGANIZATIONS OF THE PARTY

Article 30   Primary Party organizations are formed in factories, shops, schools, offices, city neighbourhoods, people's communes, co-operatives, farms, townships, towns, companies of the People's Liberation Army and other basic units, where there are three or more full Party members.

In primary Party organizations, the primary Party committees, and committees of general Party branches or Party branches, are set up respectively as the work requires and according to the number of Party members, subject to approval by the higher Party organizations. A primary Party committee is elected by a general membership meeting or a delegate meeting. The committee of a general Party branch or a Party branch is elected by a general membership meeting.

Article 31   In ordinary circumstances, a primary Party organization which has set up its own committee convenes a general membership meeting or delegate meeting once a year; a general Party branch holds a general membership meeting twice a year; a Party branch holds a general membership meeting once in every three months.

A primary Party committee is elected for a term of three years, while a general Party branch committee or a Party branch committee is elected for a term of two years. Results of the election of a secretary and deputy secretaries by a primary Party committee, general branch committee or branch committee shall be reported to the higher Party organizations for approval.

Article 32   The primary Party organizations are militant bastions of the Party in the basic units of society. Their main tasks are:

(1)   To propagate and carry out the Party's line, principles and policies, the decisions of the Central Committee of the Party and other higher Party organizations, and their own decisions; to give full play to the exemplary vanguard role of Party members, and to unite and organize the cadres and the rank and file inside and outside the Party in fulfilling the tasks of their own units.

(2)   To organize Party members to conscientiously study Marxism-Leninism and Mao Zedong Thought, study essential knowledge concerning the Party, and the

Party's line, principles and policies, and acquire general, scientific and professional knowledge.

(3) To educate and supervise Party members, ensure their regular participation in the activities of the Party organization, see that Party members truly fulfill their duties and observe discipline, and protect their rights from encroachment.

(4) To maintain close ties with the masses, constantly seek their criticisms and opinions regarding Party members and the Party's work, value the knowledge and rationalization proposals of the masses and experts, safeguard the legitimate rights and interests of the masses, show concern for their material and cultural life and help them improve it, do effective ideological and political work among them, and enhance their political consciousness. They must correct, by proper methods, the erroneous ideas and unhealthy ways and customs that may exist among the masses, and properly handle the contradictions in their midst.

(5) To give full scope to the initiative and creativeness of Party members and the masses, discover advanced elements and talented people needed for the socialist cause, encourage them to improve their work and come up with innovations and inventions, and support them in these efforts.

(6) To admit new Party members, collect membership dues, examine and appraise the work and behaviour of Party members, commend exemplary deeds performed by them, and maintain and enforce Party discipline.

(7) To promote criticism and self-criticism, and expose and overcome shortcomings and mistakes in work. To educate Party and non-Party cadres; see to it that they strictly observe the law and administrative discipline and the financial and economic discipline and personnel regulations of the state; see to it that none of them infringe the interests of the state, the collective and the masses; and see to it that the financial workers including accountants and other professionals who are charged with enforcing laws and regulations in their own units do not themselves violate the laws and regulations, while at the same time ensuring and protecting their right to exercise their functions and powers independently in accordance with the law and guarding them against any reprisals for so doing.

(8) To educate Party members and the masses to raise their revolutionary vigilance and wage resolute struggles against the criminal activities of counter-revolutionaries and other saboteurs.

Article 33   In an enterprise or institution, the primary Party committee or the general branch committee or branch committee, where there is no primary Party committee, gives leadership in the work of its own unit. Such a primary Party organization discusses and decides on major questions of principle and at the same time ensures that the administrative leaders fully exercise their functions and powers, but refrains from substituting itself for, or trying to take over from, the administrative leaders. Except in special circumstances, the general branch committees and branch committees under the leadership of a primary Party committee only play a guarantory and supervisory role to see that the production targets or operational tasks assigned to their own units are properly fulfilled.

In Party or government offices at all levels, the primary Party organizations shall not lead the work of these offices. Their task here is to exercise supervision over all Party members, including the heads of these offices who are Party members, with regard to their implementation of the Party's line, principles and policies, their observance of discipline and the law, their contact with the masses, and their ideology, work style and moral character; and to assist the office heads to improve work, raise efficiency and overcome bureaucratic ways, keep them informed of the shortcomings and problems discovered in the work of these offices, or report such shortcomings and problems to the higher Party organizations.

CHAPTER VI
PARTY CADRES

Article 34   Party cadres are the backbone of the Party's cause and public servants of the people. The Party selects its cadres according to the principle that they should possess both political integrity and professional competence, persists in the practice of appointing people on their merits and opposes favouritism; it calls for genuine efforts to make the ranks of the cadres more revolutionary, younger in average age, better educated and more professionally competent.

Party cadres are obliged to accept training by the Party as well as examination and assessment of their work by the Party.

The Party should attach importance to the training and promotion of women cadres and cadres from among the minority nationalities.

Article 35   Leading Party cadres at all levels must perform in an exemplary way their duties as Party members prescribed in Article 3 of this Constitution and must meet the following basic requirements:

(1)   Have a fair grasp of the theories of Marxism-Leninism and Mao Zedong Thought and the policies based on them, and be able to adhere to the socialist road, fight against the hostile forces disrupting socialism and combat all erroneous tendencies inside and outside the Party.

(2)   In their work as leaders, conduct earnest investigations and study, persistently proceed from reality and properly carry out the line, principles and policies of the Party.

(3)   Be fervently dedicated to the revolutionary cause and imbued with a strong sense of political responsibility, and be qualified for their leading posts in organizational ability, general education and vocational knowledge.

(4)   Have a democratic work style, maintain close ties with the masses, correctly implement the Party's mass line, conscientiously accept criticism and supervision by the Party and the masses, and combat bureaucratism.

(5)   Exercise their functions and powers in the proper way, observe and uphold the rules and regulations of the Party and the state, and combat all acts of abusing power and seeking personal gain.

(6)   Be good at uniting and working with a large number of comrades, including those who hold differing opinions, while upholding the Party's principles.

Article 36   Party cadres should be able to co-operate with non-Party cadres, respect them and learn open-mindedly from their strong points.

Party organizations at all levels must be good at discovering and recommending talented and knowledgeable non-Party cadres for leading posts, and ensure that the latter enjoy authority commensurate with their posts and can play their roles to the full.

Article 37   Leading Party cadres at all levels, whether elected through democratic procedure or appointed by a leading body, are not entitled to lifelong tenure, and they can be transferred from or relieved of their posts.

Cadres no longer fit to continue working due to old age or poor health should retire according to the regulations of the state.

CHAPTER VII
PARTY DISCIPLINE

Article 38   A Communist Party member must consciously act within the bounds of Party discipline.

Party organizations shall criticize, educate or take disciplinary measures against members who violate Party discipline, depending on the nature and seriousness of their mistakes and in the spirit of "learning from past mistakes to avoid future ones, and curing the sickness to save the patient."

Party members who violate the law and administrative discipline shall be subject to administrative disciplinary action or legal action instituted by administrative or judicial organs. Those who have seriously violated criminal law shall be expelled from the Party.

Article 39   There are five measures of Party discipline: warning, serious warning, removal from Party posts and proposals for their removal from non-Party posts to the organizations concerned, placing on probation within the Party, and expulsion from the Party.

The period for which a Party member is placed on probation shall not exceed two years. During this period, the Party member concerned has no right to vote, elect or stand for election. A Party member who during this time proves to have corrected his mistake shall have his rights as a Party member restored. Party members who refuse to mend their ways shall be expelled from the Party.

Expulsion is the ultimate Party disciplinary measure. In deciding on or approving an expulsion, Party organizations at all levels should study all the relevant facts and opinions and exercise extreme caution.

It is strictly forbidden, within the Party, to take any measures against a member that contravene the Party Constitution or the laws of the state, or to retaliate against or frame up comrades. Any offending organization or individual must be dealt with according to Party discipline or the laws of the state.

Article 40   Any disciplinary measure against a Party member must be discussed and decided on at a general membership meeting of the Party branch concerned, and reported to the primary Party committee concerned for approval. If the case is relatively important or complicated, or involves the expulsion of a member, it shall be reported, on the merit of that case, to a Party commission for discipline inspection at or above the county level for examination and approval. Under special circumstances, a Party committee or a commission for discipline inspection at or above the county level has the authority to decide directly on disciplinary measures against a Party member.

Any decision to remove a member or alternate member of the Central Committee or a local committee at any level from posts within the Party, to place such a person on probation within the Party or to expel him from the Party must be taken by a two-thirds majority vote at a plenary meeting of the Party committee to which he belongs. Such a disciplinary measure against a member or alternate member of a local Party committee is subject to approval by the higher Party committees.

Members and alternate members of the Central Committee who have seriously violated criminal law shall be expelled from the Party on decision by the Political Bureau of the Central Committee; members and alternate members of local Party committees who have seriously violated criminal law shall be expelled from the Party on decision by the standing committees of the Party committees at the corresponding levels.

Article 41   When a Party organization decides on a disciplinary measure against a Party member, it should investigate and verify the facts in an objective way. The Party member in question must be informed of the decision to be made and of the facts on which it is based. He must be given a chance to account for himself and speak in his own defence. If the member does not accept the decision, he can appeal, and the Party organization concerned must promptly deal with or forward his appeal, and must not withhold or suppress it. Those who cling to erroneous views and unjustifiable demands shall be educated by criticism.

Article 42   It is an important duty of every Party organization to firmly uphold Party discipline. Failure of a Party organization to uphold Party discipline must be investigated.

In case a Party organization seriously violates Party discipline and is unable to rectify the mistake on its own, the next higher Party committee should, after verifying the facts and considering the seriousness of the case, decide on the reorganization or dissolution of the organization, report the decision to the Party committee further above for examination and approval, and then formally announce and carry out the decision.

CHAPTER VIII
PARTY ORGANS FOR DISCIPLINE INSPECTION

Article 43   The Party's Central Commission for Discipline Inspection functions under the leadership of the Central Committee of the Party. Local commissions for discipline inspection at all levels function under the dual leadership of the Party committees at the corresponding levels and the next higher commissions for discipline inspection.

The Party's central and local commissions for discipline inspection serve a term of the same duration as the Party committees at the corresponding levels.

The Central Commission for Discipline Inspection elects, in plenary session, its standing committee and secretary and deputy secretaries and reports the results to the Central Committee for approval. Local commissions for discipline inspection at all levels elect, at their plenary sessions, their respective standing committees and secretaries and deputy secretaries. The results of the elections are subject to endorsement by the Party committees at the corresponding levels and should be reported to the higher Party committees for approval. The First Secretary of the Central Commission for Discipline Inspection must be a member of the Standing Committee of the Political Bureau. The question of whether a primary Party committee should set up a commission for discipline inspection or simply appoint a discipline inspection commissioner shall be determined by the next higher Party organization in the light of the specific circumstances. The committees of general Party branches and Party branches shall have discipline inspection commissioners.

The Party's Central Commission for Discipline Inspection shall, when its work so requires, accredit discipline inspection groups or commissioners to Party or state organs at the central level. Leaders of the discipline inspection groups or discipline inspection commissioners may attend relevant meetings of the leading Party organizations in the said organs as non-voting participants. The leading Party organizations in the organs concerned must give support to their work.

Article 44 The main tasks of the central and local commissions for discipline inspection are as follows: to uphold the Constitution and the other important rules and regulations of the Party, to assist the respective Party committees in rectifying Party style, and to check up on the implementation of the line, principles, policies and decisions of the Party.

The central and local commissions for discipline inspection shall carry out constant education among Party members on their duty to observe Party discipline; they shall adopt decisions for the upholding of Party discipline, examine and deal with relatively important or complicated cases of violation of the Constitution and discipline of the party or the laws and decrees of the state by Party organizations or Party members; decide on or cancel disciplinary measures against Party members involved in such cases; and deal with complaints and appeals made by Party members.

The central and local commissions for discipline inspection should report to the Party committees at the corresponding levels on the results of their handling of cases of special importance or complexity, as well as on the problems encountered. Local commissions for discipline inspection should also present such reports to the higher commissions.

If the Central Commission for Discipline Inspection discovers any violation of Party discipline by any member of the Central Committee, it may report such an offence to the Central Committee, and the Central Committee must deal with the case promptly.

Article 45 Higher commissions for discipline inspection have the power to check up on the work of the lower commissions and to approve or modify their decisions on any case. If decisions so modified have already been ratified by the Party committee at the corresponding level, the modification must be approved by the next higher Party committee.

If a local commission for discipline inspection does not agree with a decision made by the Party committee at the corresponding level in dealing with a case, it may request the commission at the next higher level to re-examine the case; if a local commission discovers cases of violation of Party discipline or the laws and decrees of the state by the Party committee at the corresponding level or by its members, and if that Party committee fails to deal with them properly or at all, it has the right to appeal to the higher commissions for assistance in dealing with such cases.

CHAPTER IX
LEADING PARTY MEMBERS' GROUPS

Article 46 A leading Party members' group shall be formed in the leading body of a central or local state organ, people's organization, economic or cultural institution or other non-Party unit. The main tasks of such a group are: to see to it that the Party's principles and policies are implemented, to unite with the non-Party cadres and masses in fulfilling the tasks assigned by the Party and the state, and to guide the work of the Party organization of the unit.

Article 47   The members of a leading Party members' group are appointed by the Party committee that approves its establishment. The group shall have a secretary and deputy secretaries.

A leading Party members' group must accept the leadership of the Party committee that approves its establishment.

Article 48   The Central Committee of the Party shall determine specifically the functions, powers and tasks of the leading Party members' groups in those government departments which need to exercise highly centralized and unified leadership over subordinate units; it shall also determine whether such groups should be replaced by Party committees.

CHAPTER X
RELATIONSHIP BETWEEN THE PARTY AND THE COMMUNIST YOUTH LEAGUE

Article 49   The Communist Youth League of China is a mass organization of advanced young people under the leadership of the Communist Party of China; it is a school where large numbers of young people will learn about communism through practice; it is the Party's assistant and reserve force. The Central Committee of the Communist Youth League functions under the leadership of the Central Committee of the Party. The local organizations of the Communist Youth League are under the leadership of the Party committees at the corresponding levels and of the higher organizations of the League itself.

Article 50   Party committees at all levels must strengthen their leadership over the Communist Youth League organizations and pay attention to the selection anɹ training of League cadres. The Party must firmly support the Communist Youth League in the lively and creative performance of its work to suit the characteristics and needs of young people, and give full play to the League's role as a shock force and as a bridge linking the Party with the broad masses of young people.

Those secretaries of League committees, at or below the county level or in enterprises and institutions, who are Party members may attend meetings of Party committees at the corresponding levels and of their standing committees as non-voting participants.

Revision of Some Articles of the Constitution of the Communist Party of China (1987)

The 13th National Congress of the Chinese Communist Party has decided to make the following revisions* of some articles of the constitution of the Communist Party of China:

1. In the first paragraph of Article 11, the sentences, "There may be a preliminary election in order to draw up a list of candidates for the formal election. Or there may be no preliminary election, in which case the number of candidates shall be greater than that of the persons to be elected," are *replaced by* "the election procedure of nominating a larger number of candidates than the number of persons to be elected may be used directly in a formal election. Or this procedure may be used first in a preliminary election in order to draw up a list of candidates for the formal election."

2. In the first paragraph of Article 16, the sentences, "Party organizations must keep the principles of subordination of the minority to the majority in discussing and making decisions on any matter. Serious consideration should be given to the differing views of a minority. In case of controversy over major issues in which supporters of the two opposing views are nearly equal in number, except in emergencies where action must be taken in accordance with the majority view, the decision should be put off to allow for further investigation, study and exchange of opinions followed by another discussion. If still no decision can be made, the controversy should be reported to the next higher Party organization for ruling," are *replaced by* "When discussing and making decisions on any matter, Party organizations must keep to the principle of subordination of the minority to the majority. A vote must be taken when major issues are decided on. Serious consideration should be given to the differing views of a minority. In case of controversy over major issues in which supporters of the two opposing views are nearly equal in number, except in emergencies where action must be taken in accordance with the majority view, the decision should be put off to allow for further investigation, study, and exchange of opinions followed by another vote. Under special circumstances, the controversy may be reported to the next higher Party organization for ruling."

3. The following paragraph is added to the end of Article 19: "The powers and functions of the National Conference of the Party are as follows: to discuss and make decisions on major questions; to replace members and elect additional members of the Central Committee, the Central Advisory Commission, and the Central Commission for Discipline Inspection. The number of members and alternate members of the Central Committee to be replaced or newly elected shall not exceed one-fifth of the respective totals of members and alternate members of the Central Committee elected by the National Congress of the Party."

4. In the first paragraph of Article 21, the sentence, "The Political Bureau, the Standing Committee of the Political Bureau, the Secretariat and the General Secretary of the Central Committee of the Party are elected by the Central Committee in plenary session," is *replaced by* "The Political Bureau, the Standing Committee of the Political Bureau and the General Secretary of the Central Committee of the Party are elected by the Central Committee in plenary session."

Adopted at the Thirteenth CPC National Congress on November 1, 1987. Source: Beijing Review (November 16–22, 1987), 33–34.

The third paragraph of Article 21, "The Secretariat attends to the day-to-day work of the Central Committee under the direction of the Political Bureau and its Standing Committee," is *replaced by* "The Secretariat is the working body of the Political Bureau of the Central Committee and its Standing Committee. The members of the Secretariat are nominated by the Standing Committee of the Political Bureau of the Central Committee and are subject to endorsement by the Central Committee in plenary session."

The fifth paragraph of Article 21, "The members of the Military Commission of the Central Committee are decided on by the Central Committee. The Chairman of the Military Commission must be a member of the Standing Committee of the Political Bureau," is *replaced by* "The members of the Military Commission of the Central Committee are decided on by the Central Committee."

5. In the second paragraph of Article 22, the sentences, "The Central Advisory Commission is elected for a term of the same duration as that of the Central Committee. It elects, at its plenary meeting, its Standing Committee and its Chairman and Vice-Chairmen, and reports the results to the Central Committee for approval. The Chairman of the Central Advisory Commission must be a member of the Standing Committee of the Political Bureau," are *replaced by* "The Central Advisory Commission is elected for a term of the same duration as that of the Central Committee. It elects, at its plenary meeting, its Standing Committee and its Chairman and Vice-Chairmen, and reports the results to the Central Committee for approval."

6. The first paragraph of Article 30, "Primary Party organizations are formed in factories, shops, schools, offices, city neighbourhoods, people's communes, co-operatives, farms, townships, towns, companies of the People's Liberation Army and other basic units, where there are three or more full Party members," is *replaced by* "Primary Party organizations are formed in factories, shops, schools, offices, city neighbourhoods, co-operatives, farms, townships, towns, villages, companies of the People's Liberation Army and other basic units, where there are three or more full Party members."

7. The following paragraph is added before the first paragraph of Article 33: "In an enterprise or an institution where the system of administrative leader assuming full responsibility is practiced, the primary Party organization guarantees and supervises the implementation of the principles and policies of the party and the state in its own unit. Such a primary Party organization should concentrate on strengthening Party building, doing effective ideological and political work and mass work, support the administrative leaders in fully exercising their powers and functions according to regulations, and offer views and suggestions on major issues."

In the first paragraph of Article 33, the sentence, "In an enterprise or institution, the primary Party committee or the general branch committee or branch committee, where there is no primary Party committee, gives leadership in the work of its own unit," is *replaced by* "In an institution where the system of administrative leader assuming full responsibility has not yet been practiced, the primary Party committee or, where there is no primary Party committee, the general branch committee or branch committee provides leadership in the work of its own unit."

8. In the third paragraph of Article 43, the sentences, "The Central Commission for Discipline Inspection elects, in plenary session, its standing committee and secretary and deputy secretaries and reports the results to the Central Committee for approval. Local commissions for discipline inspection at all levels elect, at their plenary sessions, their respective standing committees and secretaries and deputy secretaries. The results of the elections are subject to endorsement by the party committees at the corresponding levels and should be reported to the higher Party committees for approval. The First Secretary of the Central Commission for Discipline Inspection must be a member of the Standing Committee of the Political Bureau," are *replaced by* "The Central Commission for Discipline Inspection elects, in plenary session, its standing committee and secretary and deputy secretaries and reports the results to the Central Committee for approval. Local commissions for discipline inspection at all levels elect, at their plenary sessions, their respective standing committees and secretaries and deputy secretaries. The results of the elections are subject to endorsement by the Party committees at the corresponding levels and should be reported to the next higher Party committees for approval."

9. In Article 46,   the sentence, "A leading Party members' group shall be formed in the leading body of a central or local state organ, people's organization, economic or cultural institution or other non-Party unit," is *replaced by* "A leading Party members' group may be formed within the leading body elected by the national or a local people's congress, the national or a local committee of the Chinese People's Political Consultative Conference, people's organization or other non-Party unit."

10. Article 48,   "The Central Committee of the Party shall determine specifically the functions, powers and tasks of the leading Party members' groups in those government departments which need to exercise highly centralized and unified leadership over subordinate units; it shall also determine whether such groups should be replaced by Party committees," is *replaced by* "The Central Committee of the party shall determine specifically whether Party committees should be formed in those government departments which need to exercise highly centralized and unified leadership over subordinate units; it shall also determine specifically the powers, functions and tasks of such committees."

Appendix B-2

Amendment
to the CCP Constitution
(September 1997)

Amendment adopted unanimously on September 18, 1997, by the Fifteenth Party Congress to the second paragraph under the General Programme, the following*:

The Communist Party of China takes Marxism–Leninism, Mao Zedong Thought and Deng Xiaoping Theory as its guide to action.

---

*Source: China Daily, September 19, 1997, p. 2.

INDEX